HANDBOOK OF CORPORATE COMMUNICATION AND PUBLIC RELATIONS

A comprehensive addition to existing literature, the *Handbook of Corporate Communication and Public Relations* provides an excellent overview of corporate communication, clearly positioning the field's most current debates. Synthesizing both multidisciplinary and interdisciplinary approaches, it offers readers the in-depth analysis required to truly understand corporate communication, corporate strategy and corporate affairs as well as the relevant public relations issues. Written by academics based in Europe, Asia and North America, the text is well illustrated with contemporary case studies, drawing out the most pertinent best practice outcomes and theoretically based applications.

Its four parts cover national communication; international communication; image, identity and reputation management; and the future for corporate communication theory and practice. With a refreshing new approach to this subject, the authors challenge reductionist views of corporate communication, providing persuasive evidence for the idea that without an organizational communication strategy, there is no corporate strategy.

The *Handbook of Corporate Communication and Public Relations* is an essential one-stop reference for all academics, practitioners and students seeking to understand organizational communication management and strategic public relations.

Sandra M. Oliver is a corporate communication academic at Thames Valley University, London, where she founded and also directs the MSc Corporate Communication Programme. A consultant research practitioner and former industrial PR, she is founding Editor-in-Chief of *Corporate Communication: An International Journal* and has written extensively, including *Public Relations Strategy* (2001) and *Corporate Communication: Principles, Techniques and Strategies* (1997).

3585769200

HANDBOOK OF CORPORATE COMMUNICATION AND PUBLIC RELATIONS

PURE AND APPLIED

Edited by
Sandra M. Oliver

Routledge
Taylor & Francis Group
LONDON AND NEW YORK

First published 2004
by Routledge
11 New Fetter Lane, London EC4P 4EE

Simultaneously published in the USA and Canada
by Routledge
29 West 35th Street, New York, NY 10001

Routledge is an imprint of the Taylor and Francis Group

Typeset in Chianti and Akzidenz by
Florence Production Ltd, Stoodleigh, Devon
Printed and bound in Great Britain by
Bell & Bain Ltd, Glasgow

British Library Cataloguing in Publication Data
A catalogue record for this book is available from
the British Library

Library of Congress Cataloging in Publication Data
A catalog record for this book has been requested

ISBN 0–415–33419–5

Contents

PART I: CORPORATE COMMUNICATION AT NATIONAL LEVEL

PART IV: **THE FUTURE IS NOW**

Figures

Tables

Contributors

Anthony Clive Allen is attached to the Corporate Communication Directorate at the Royal Air Force in London, UK.

Albert Atkinson is an active consultant researcher and involved in the affairs of the Library Board of Trustees and Chamber of Commerce, UK.

Deborah J. Barrett PhD lectures at Jones Graduate School of Management, Rice University, Texas, USA and directs the MBA communication programme.

Gerald Chan is Public Affairs and Education Officer at the Institute of Public Relations, London, UK and studying for a master's degree in public relations.

Colin Coulson-Thomas PhD is author of *Transforming the Company* (2002, 2nd edn), thirty other books and reports, and is Chairman of ASK Europe plc.

Krishna S. Dhir PhD is Dean of the Campbell School of Business at Berry College, Georgia, USA; formerly of CIBA-GEIGY AG in Switzerland and Borg-Warner, USA.

Richard Dolphin lectures at the Northampton Business School, UK and is author of *Fundamentals of Corporate Communication* (2000).

Gregor Eglin PhD lectures in strategic management at University of East London, UK with a particular research interest in public service communication.

Ying Fan PhD lectures and researches at Lincoln School of Management, UK.

Michael Goodman PhD lectures at Fairleigh Dickinson University, USA and is founding director of the Corporate Communication Institute at FDU.

Yvonne Harahousou, **Chris Kabitsis**, **Anna Haviara** and **Nicholas D. Theodorakis** are academics based at the University of Thrace, Greece, involved with the Organizing Committee for the Olympic Games 2004.

Owen Hargie PhD lectures at the School of Communication, University of Ulster, Ireland and is co-author of *Skilled Interpersonal Communication: Research, Theory and Practice* (2004).

Glenda Jacobs is a Research Fellow at UNITEC, Auckland, New Zealand, where she also leads computer-mediated communication courses.

Philip Kitchen PhD holds a professorial research chair and lectures at the University of Hull, UK.

Paulo Kuteev-Moreira PhD is Director of Communication for a privately managed public hospital in Portugal and a researcher for a WHO-Europe-affiliated Observatory in Health Studies.

Jacquie L'Etang PhD lectures and researches at the University of Stirling, Scotland and is an examiner for the Institute of Public Relations Membership Diploma examinations.

Wen-Ling Liu PhD lectures at Hull University, UK on integrated marketing communication.

Chris McCann is Business Consultant for an energy company in Stockholm, Sweden.

Tengku Melewar PhD lectures at the University of Warwick Business School, UK.

Kevin Moloney PhD lectures at Bournemouth University, UK and is a research specialist in government communication and pressure groups.

Michael Morley is Special Counsel for Edelman Public Relations, New York, USA and author of *How to Manage Your Reputation* (1998).

Sandra M. Oliver PhD, General Editor, is founding Editor-in-Chief of *Corporate Communication: An International Journal*; author of *Public Relations Strategy* (2001) and *Corporate Communication: Principles, Techniques and Strategies* (1997); and founding director of the international MSc in Corporate Communication programme at Thames Valley University, London, UK.

Liam Ó Móráin MSc is founder chairman of Moran Communication, Ireland with eighteen years consultancy experience of communication and PR management.

David Phillips chaired the UK PR industry Joint Internet Commission and is author of numerous papers including 'Online Public Relations' and 'Managing Reputation in Cyberspace'.

David Pickton lectures and researches at De Montfort University, UK and is co-author of *Integrated Marketing Communication* (2001).

Stephen A. Roberts PhD lectures at Thames Valley University, London, UK and directs the MSc Information Management Programme.

Martin Sims lectures at St Mary's College, London, UK and is a former BBC journalist who edits *Intermedia*, the journal of the International Institute of Communication.

Don Swanson PhD is Chair of the Communication Department at Monmouth University, USA and former President of the New Jersey Communication Association.

Dennis Tourish PhD is Professor of Communication at Aberdeen Business School, Scotland with over 50 publications in communication management.

Richard Varey PhD is a Marketing Professor at the Waikato Management School, New Zealand, who currently researches in managed communication for sustainable business.

Reginald Watts PhD is a consultant and author of four books; formerly CEO of Burson Marstellar and President of the Institute of Public Relations, London, UK.

Donald Wright PhD is President of the International Public Relations Association and an academic at the University of South Alabama, USA.

Foreword

Excellent corporate communication lies at the heart of industry, commerce and governments' abilities to build a democratic society, but this critical strategic role in organizational theory and practice rarely receives the due commitment required for quality assurance in organization life today.

A previous handbook published in 1997[1] assembled the cutting edge views and experiences of leading practitioners of the day with some solid opinion pieces that have been helpful to a wide range of audiences and readers including public relations practitioners, opinion formers, media managers, advertising executives and others. It was a source of information and advice on a vast array of topics brought together to represent the interdisciplinary and multidisciplinary nature of corporate communication as a core business discipline for senior executives in large multinational companies, small-to-medium size enterprises (SMEs) and not-for-profit organizations alike.

Now in what philosophers like to call the post-modern era, we see more clearly how the new information technologies have restructured the whole industry sector. Its impact leads us to challenge what John Milton calls 'conventional economic thinking, redefining how business is done and impacting to varying degrees every worker in the global market place . . . in a combination of interconnected phenomena embracing inter alia, globalization, the transformative impact of technology on organizational life (indeed on the very nature of organizations), successful e-business models and the changing nature of working life'. The new economy, he argues, is 'far too recent a phenomenon for any consensus to have emerged yet about what constitutes best practice' but for corporate communicators and public relations consultants and practitioners worldwide, there is a belief that there is a set of best practices and that adopting them leads to superior organizational performance and competitiveness.

The concept of good practice has to be addressed in accordance with contingency theory. No single best practice is universally applicable to all organizations because of differences in strategy, culture, management style, technology and markets. The challenge for operators is the inconsistency between the belief in best practice and the notion of corporate communication as an intangible asset limiting resource. It is crucial to match corporate strategy with corporate communication policy and practice, but given that corporate communication is as the Institute of Public Relations states the ears, eyes and voice of the organization, the in-house practitioner has a special responsibility for the overview of the organization as a whole beyond that of the chief executive officer. He or she is required to advise, counsel, monitor and measure operations in a reliable and consistent manner beyond the reductionist, functional approaches of corporate accounting or integrated marketing. Indeed he or she also accepts the role of boundary spanner in monitoring not just relations between organizations and their stakeholders but beyond to the value-added implications of policies and practices within a wider democratic society.

In 1999, Purcell[2] suggested that the concept of best practice and best fit is limited by 'the impossibility of modelling all the contingent variables, the difficulty of showing their interconnection and the way in which changes in one variable have impact on others'. Many management consultants have taken up this view and been less concerned with best practice and best fit to address more sensitive processes of organization change so that they can 'avoid being trapped in the logic of rational choice'. So what we have tried to do with this book is to adopt the concept of bundling whereby the chapters are interrelated, complement and support one another through the medium of quality research rather than mere opinion. Sometimes referred to as a configurational mode[3] or complementarity, MacDuffie[4] states that 'implicit in the notion of a bundle is the idea that practices within bundles are interrelated and internally consistent and that more is better with respect to the impact on performance, because of the overlapping and mutually reinforcing effect of multiple practices'.

It is generally accepted that to overcome these barriers to the implementation of corporate communication strategy a number of activities are essential. Michael Armstrong[5] argues that essential activities include: the conducting of a rigorous initial analysis, formulation strategy, the gaining of influential

support, assessment of barriers, preparation of action plans, project manage implementation and follow up evaluation. All these activities are basic and familiar to middle and project managers, management research students and PR campaign practitioners. The corporate communication industry which includes public relations agencies and blue chip management consultancies have relied heavily on developing the skills and techniques to carry out such activities in an essentially practical but research-based manner.

Now, with the recognition of the growth of the global knowledge economy 'the traditional factors of production – land, labour and capital – pale into insignificance alongside knowledge', as Philip Sadler says.[6] The corporate communicator is at the helm of this development. It is the corporate communicator who has to be fully aware of changing environments, major trends, opportunities or threats to the development or survival of an organization. The management of intellectual capital has to be understood but is also has to be applied through corporate communication operational strategies for it to be of added value to an organization. The pure and applied aspects of corporate communication as educational and training areas of knowledge and skill are inextricably linked. The future of corporate communication will continue to depend on its tactical skills base but it is beginning to redesign itself as a strong professional vocation based on sound research methods. In spite of the different names by which practitioners are labelled or defined whether in-house or as external consultants, ignorance is not bliss. Corporate communication has moved away from the secular public relations approaches of the 1970s and 1980s and moved into new areas of political roles and relationships between peoples and their economic environments.

Although this book is a generalist one it therefore brings together the pure and the applied to further develop the profession and those in it and all who endeavour to be a part of it in the future. Most vocational programmes provided by today's university sector have learned to balance the demands of further and higher education, training and practice albeit with some difficulty due to the demands of the university research assessment exercise in Britain and increasing governmental control of universities worldwide. The contributors to this book believe that the underpinning of specialist areas will lead to a greater self-confidence in the face of prevailing cynicism and pessimism about strategic corporate communication at local and global levels. This book supports the multifaceted roles that any corporate communicator plays, whether he or she be mentor, facilitator, monitor, co-ordinator, director, producer, broker or innovator.[7] These eight roles represent a competing values framework which together establish competency in any management field especially in corporate communication, public relations and public affairs. Whether the practitioner/consultant is at expert, proficient, competent, advanced beginner or novice stage of a career, the competing values framework is 'grounded in paradoxical thinking – it forces one to think about the competing tensions and demands that are placed on [*corporate communication*] managers in new ways'.

The research presented in this book supports what Quinn *et al.* calls 'the need to use paradoxical thinking to create both approaches to the management of opposites'. The corporate communicator is always at the cutting edge of 'informing and transforming our future leaders', even though 'every area is under siege' because of the 'crisis of confidence in accounting practices and corporate fiduciary principles. In the twenty-first century, leaders are being challenged like never before to resolve dilemmas around organisational effectiveness, economic viability and political and military security'. These chapters are based on real research. They are neither descriptive nor prescriptive but challenge reductionist views of corporate communication and provide persuasive evidence for the notion that no organizational communication strategy equals no corporate strategy at all in a postmodern, mediated internet era.

Sandra M. Oliver
General Editor

NOTES

1   Foster, T. R. V. and Jolly, A. (1997) *Corporate Communication Handbook*, London: Kogan Page.

2   Purcell, J. (1999) 'Best practice or best fit: chimera or cul-de-sac', *Human Resource Management Journal*, 9(3), 26–41.

3   Delery, J. E. and Doty, H. D. (1996) 'Modes of theorising in strategic human resource management: tests of universality, contingency and configurational performance predictions', *International Journal of Human Resource Management*, 6, 656–70.

4   MacDuffie, J. P. (1995) 'Human resource bundles and manufacturing performance', *Industrial Relations Review*, 48(2), 199–221.

5   Armstrong, M. (2001) *A Handbook of Human Resource Management Practice*, 8th edn, London: Kogan Page, 2, pp. 32–52.

6   Sadler, P. (2001) *Management Consultancy: A Handbook for Best Practice*, 2nd edn, London: Kogan Page, 1, pp. 3–16.

7   Quinn, R. E., Faerman, S. R., Thompson, M. P. and McGrath, M. R. (2003) *Becoming a Master Manager: A Competency Framework*, 3rd edn, Chichester: Wiley.

Preface

In its 250th anniversary year, the Royal Society of Arts continues its mission to encourage arts, manufactures and commerce. During the next six years, the RSA will focus on five key challenges framed within a new Manifesto: to encourage enterprise, move towards a zero waste society, foster resilient communities, develop a capable population, and advance global citizenship. These themes are going to tax the best hearts and minds in boardrooms worldwide, as well as the communication and public relations profession itself, demanding a higher degree of specialist knowledge and skill than ever before.

The publication of this book offers a powerful contribution to the range of projects we have implemented to support the Manifesto, including Visions of a Capable Society, Intellectual Property, Shared Mental Modes, Sustainable Design and Global Citizenship. Principles, techniques and strategies come together in this book from lead international researchers, academics and practitioners to help us and the international business community to meet its obligations with the help of the authors' proven expertise and wise counsel.

Sir Paul Judge
Chairman, The Royal Society for the
Encouragement of Arts, Manufacture and Commerce (RSA)

Acknowledgements

The General Editor is indebted to the following: Rachel Crookes and Francesca Poynter at Routledge; Anna Leatham, Giuliana Taborelli, Mireille Jones, Jenny Johns, Khalda Ahmed and Kay Ahluwalia for their skilled IT support throughout numerous drafts; and those friends, colleagues and organizations who have willingly participated in putting together this scholarly contribution to the corporate communication and PR discipline.

PART I CORPORATE COMMUNICATION AT NATIONAL LEVEL

CHAPTER 1

Diversity programmes in the contemporary corporate environment

Don R. Swanson

Diversity programmes have become an essential element of the modern corporation because of the varied demographics of organization members, stakeholders and potential clients. But what are the attitudes toward, and the focus of, contemporary corporate diversity programmes? The discussion of this question is addressed through the observations of diversity personnel, middle managers and corporate communication managers who carry responsibility for monitoring diversity programmes.

This chapter examines diversity programmes from a number of direct research resources developed and conducted by the author. From focus groups made up of diversity personnel, interviews with middle managers and executive management personnel, observations of interviews with corporate diversity directors, through to observations from interviews with human resource managers and corporate communicators. The study, and the essence of this chapter, shows the emergence from the observations of corporate personnel of some major corporate communication issues. These issues include the lack of dialogue regarding diversity, the nature of diversity training and performance evaluation, the complexity of diversity issues, the managers' role, and the move to integration and learning as the perspective to bring about effectiveness in corporate diversity programming.

A glance around corporate America quickly reveals new and diverse faces and the fact that successful corporate entities cross many cultural and international boundaries in the conduct of their business. Most estimates of future employment indicate that 75 per cent of new workers will be other than white males and that in 2010 white males will represent less than 40 per cent of the American workforce (Arai, Wanca-Thibault, and Shockley-Zalabak, 2001). Corporate diversity programmes and attitudes toward workplace diversity have evolved since the 1990s. Although this seems to be an age of increasing enlightenment regarding cross-cultural realities, there are numerous instances of concern.

In the later part of the decade of the 1990s it became clear that diversity is not a buzzword. Those corporate managers, in the 1980s and early 1990s, who believed diversity management was just another human resources management fad were sadly mistaken. Diversity management as a concept and an aspiration for management has 'become deeply rooted in the US federal government and has received bipartisan support from both political parties' (Ivancevich and Gilbert, 2000: 75). The economic statistics and demographic profile of the potential customers and the new additions to the workforce mandate corporate awareness of the realities of diversity. *Workplace 2000*, published by the Hudson Institute in 1987, was widely quoted in the 1990s to predict the shifts. But a powerful sense of presumption for the status quo workforce still persisted in the subconscious of many middle-aged executives. It took the reality of market shifts, and an increasingly diverse set of job applicants to force awareness of the 'demographic imperative' that required corrective action in the form of diversity management programming (Cox, 1991). Many corporations have found it difficult to maintain a diversity friendly image in the wake of harsh criticism of past abuses. By 1995 *The Economist* reported that 75 per cent of the fifty largest US companies had diversity directors or managers. Consequently a macro view of diversity programming indicates it has become an inherent part of corporate environs.

This discussion examines attitudes toward, and the focus of, contemporary corporate diversity programmes. Managers and their influence on diversity programming are at the nucleus of this discussion. It develops from a number of direct research resources developed and conducted by the author. Those resources include: six focus groups, made up of ten diversity personnel in each group, conducted in a business financial services unit of an investment bank; interviews conducted with twenty-six middle managers and eight executive management level personnel in one of the largest and most successful international investment banks; observations from interviews with corporate diversity directors who have a responsibility to keep diversity firmly on the agenda of corporate policy; and observations from interviews with human resource managers and corporate communication managers who carry the responsibility for monitoring diversity programmes.

Study of diversity personnel

At a micro level a focus group study of diversity personnel and an interview based study of mid-level managers, from two different units of a large investment banking firm, provide a snapshot of the attitudes and perceptions of personnel in a white-collar industry that espouses a commitment to diversity programming. The units in these studies are a part of one of the oldest American investment banking institutions, and it has historically been a leader that defined the nature of that business. As such, the firm conveys and maintains an image that has developed over a rich history. The image of being a leader in the investment banking industry has been exceptionally important to the firm. It defines itself as a world-class company operating in the fast-moving, highly competitive financial services marketplace, and realizes that it must attract, keep and develop the very best people. The CEO explains that: 'We are building for the next generation, not the next transaction. To do this we must be an undisputed employer of choice.' The firm appears to be committed to developing and maintaining diversity at every level of the company.

The data in this study was gathered over a period of three months with the conduct of six one-half-day focus groups. Each focus group was composed of a group of approximately ten members of the banking group that provides financial services to businesses. The focus group participants were selected because they fit into a protected category, i.e. historically minority status. Consequently this sample included the minority personnel and a cross-section of female personnel and represented approximately 10 per cent of the employees in this nationwide unit of the bank. This sample was intended to be inclusive of diversity personnel in order to focus on airing all the major issues that concerned these protected groups. Personnel were brought to the focus group location from across the United States. Two focus groups were conducted in Princeton, New Jersey, and four groups were conducted in Chicago.

The executive in charge of the financial services business unit that the focus groups were drawn from made a point of coming to each group and expressed his support for the diversity management project and this fact-finding research. Participants were impressed with his support. This was a key element to making the focus groups successful. It is clear that visible executive support is an essential element for success.

The participants in the diversity focus groups seemed to appreciate the cathartic experience of talking about a subject that they had some uncertainty about. Many lacked even a basic knowledge of the diversity mission of their corporation. They were both interested and generally pleased to discuss this topic. Several said they 'never expected to have an opportunity to discuss these sensitive issues'.

There were no major complaints that could be labelled as unique to this corporate unit. Some participants, who had worked in other units of the firm reported that this unit was much more diversity friendly than their previous group. Although this was a long-standing unit of more than six hundred members, there have been no catalytic events in recent memory in the unit that would serve as a flash point for concern over diversity. The incidents reported by the participants were generally not egregious nor widely discussed by coworkers. The negative incidents seemed to be considered as isolated incidents and not representative of the attitudes and behaviour of the majority of unit personnel.

Most of the persons in the focus groups were quite ignorant of what their company had done or not done with diversity initiatives. They had queries for information and in a sense the focus groups became a form of action research because the participants' questions were answered and they received new information on what was happening. Eden and Huxham (1999) point out why action research has become 'increasingly prominent' in the study of organizations when they indicate it is: 'research which broadly, results from an involvement by the researcher with members of an organisation over a matter which is of genuine concern to them and in which there is an intent by the organisation members to take action based on the intervention' (p. 272).

Developing and conducting the focus groups was a prelude to further action research. It should be noted that this focus group process was a catalyst for an evolving diversity initiative that included the establishment of a 'diversity council' to suggest and monitor future actions. In this way the participants had a sense of outcome from the focus group project.

Affirmative action was a frequent, but not particularly comfortable subject in these groups. They appreciate the goals of affirmative action but it can produce a somewhat uncomfortable paradox. All of the participants believe that the firm hired them because of their skill and experience. To these personnel endorsing affirmative action might connote that their hiring may have been the result of some preference. Most of these people indicate that if in a pool of equally qualified candidates there is a minority, at this point in the history of firm, the minority person should be selected. Focus group participants emphatically express the position that 'no one should ever be hired who cannot do the job'.

Discussants often mentioned the fact that traditional methods of recruiting may not reach many persons who could be in a qualified minority pool. It was frequently noted that investment banking is dominated and staffed almost completely by white males.

The dynamic in the groups was stimulating because participants were eager to make constructive action proposals. The following is a list of major suggestions made by the focus group participants. They are included in no particular order, but represent the major reactions of the sixty participants:

1   Work to maintain respect, regardless of gender, ethnicity, or race.
2   Maintain commitment to diversity and work to increase heterogeneity.
3   To assume that the whole group has a problem is not fair. Don't try to fix what is not broken. Get in with the workforce and fix the real problems that are there.
4   Provide meaningful diversity training. This should be a part of the orientation process for new employees. Continually reinforce the principles and behaviours taught in the training.
5   Managers must be well and extensively trained in diversity management.
6   The managers' performance review should include how well they manage diversity. This task of reinforcement and maintenance of effective diversity management falls upon the managers and the respective styles that they model for everyone else in the group.
7   The firm needs to do a better job of performance reviews. Managers need to do a better job of letting you know what to do to get promoted. Help us with what we need to learn and accomplish so that we perform more effectively.
8   In the interest of trying to promote diverse people, don't just promote people because of their diversity status, forgetting their qualifications. Don't put someone somewhere just to have a minority in that position.
9   Career planning is important to everyone. Career counselling and advising is important and it should be done. This could solve some of the problem we have with a high turnover rate. The people we tend to lose will be minorities who have excellent opportunities elsewhere. What are their opportunities here? They need to know.
10 As this unit grows we need to do more mentoring. It is essential to have more training and mentoring for those who want to move up to management.
11 This unit must deal more effectively with the problem of attrition. If we lowered the attrition rate there would be fewer personnel problems.
12 As a matter of course do exit interviews and listen to them. Learn from the reasons people leave.

13 Improve recruiting – go beyond putting advertisements in the paper. Be more visible at career fairs. Go to a wider range of universities to recruit.

14 Take time while hiring. Don't do it too quickly. 'Emergency hires' can't be done carefully. Go slow and get somebody really good for the job. Go past the typical criteria for hiring. Only using referrals won't accomplish the diversity goals. Instead of looking at educational background, look at their talent. Look creatively at the past history of candidates' work. Even though I am at a lower level let me do some hiring or at least be more involved in the hiring process.

15 Maintain, embrace and apply more of the quality of work–life policies that the firm brags about. Don't offer policies, if managers don't intend to use them. Walk the talk.

16 Establish a diversity council and define what it will do. It's not going to work to just talk about diversity. This group should be very active.

17 Get individual groups of particular minority categories together for sessions like this. Blacks, Asians, women, etc. See if they have more ideas to share when they are only with persons with the same category. If you want to get to the truth, do this to get a definite sense of the peer groups.

18 Do a quarterly newsletter that highlights diversity features, and initiatives. If it is put online attach it in an easy to find and read manner. Overall we are in a growth mode and we need to be able to get to know the new people.

19 Report to us. We want to hear the results of what the groups said in these focus groups.

Study of mid-level managers

The second study that provides a view of the attitudes and perceptions of personnel in a white-collar industry of investment banking is based upon a focused set of ninety-minute interviews with twenty-five mid-level managers in the mutual funds division of the firm. The sessions focused both on information gathering and coaching the managers. This again was a form of action research because the interview provided an opportunity to conduct a constructive dialogue on some of the issues of concern to the interviewees. The focus of the interviews was on both the process of evaluation and the impact of dealing with a diverse workforce. Topics included discovery of diversity sensitivity, coaching people through difficult performance evaluation sessions, working for candour, honesty, openness in performance management sessions, maintaining a climate that is non-defensive, and the general problems the supervisors faced in dealing with those who reported to them.

The performance evaluation issues reported by the managers were as follows:

1 Adapting performance appraisals to different types of people is a challenging process. Many are not sure of how their perceptions fit within the context of the cultural background of those who come from very different cultures.

2 It would be beneficial to receive more feedback regarding the nature of my leadership style. I'm not sure how it fits a range of different people.

3 Dealing with someone who used to be a peer and now I am her/his boss.

4 Discussing issues that are team issues with individuals.

5   Working to define clear and measurable critical objectives.
6   How to continue to motivate someone who is evaluated as an exceptional performer. Helping them to see how they can add value.
7   How to motivate people who are in a dead-end job.
8   Understanding the motivation, or lack thereof, of the new generation of staff.
9   How to sincerely communicate a positive sense of morale to persons who have low morale.

In this sample group the managers also had concerns about their personal performance for which they sought discussion and advice:

1   Finding ways to get better feedback from my boss.
2   Giving my boss feedback about how he/she provides feedback to me.
3   Working on personal impression management and knowing how to 'build your skills and your personal franchise'.
4   Communication/leadership aspects of forming a new team.
5   How to reinforce and maintain the communication things I am doing that are effective with my team.
6   How to encourage the culture to open up the conversations? Can we motivate by other than fear?
7   How to approach further personal development as a supervisor.
8   Dealing with cross-cultural communication differences.
9   Managing meetings.

This set of interviews demonstrates that in addition to concerns about personal and team performance, equity and accuracy in the conduct of performance evaluation is a significant issue for managers. To mid-level managers performance evaluation is where they are challenged to 'overlook differences' and treat everyone the same.

Directors of diversity programmes

Diversity directors from six organizations were interviewed for their impressions of the status of diversity management programming today. It was interesting to note that half of this group were 'professionals' in the sense that they had worked with diversity management in more than two corporations or government entities. The others were moved to this position in their corporation because of their understanding and sensitivity to the issues. In all cases they were African American female or Hispanic, or a combination of these features. Although never directly queried, there seemed to be an implicit question: 'Does it require a person who is of minority status to be in this position?' All would probably assert it as an advantage because they talked about how they could relate from personal experience to the subtle difficulties that diversity personnel in their organization were facing.

There was a feeling among the diversity directors that legality provided the genesis of the department they worked in: 'We saw a problem, noted the increase in litigation over issues of equity and fairness and responded with this unit. As the tendency increases for employees to sue when they believe they are wronged, our unit is considered as a part of the remedy.' They observe however that that reality is both reassuring, for the continued existence of their unit, and troublesome because the legal perspective is only a portion of the rationale for their programming. One director said that: 'We are trying to do the right things for the wrong reasons.' He goes on to explain that legal issues and court orders need to be addressed; however the real impetus for his unit is the economic reality the corporation must face: 'There is an entire segment of the population who are potential clients that we are not reaching. Suddenly management has realized that to ensure the future of the corporation we need to get interested in diverse customers and employ people who look like the new customers.' Others noted that the pool of qualified employees was becoming increasingly diverse and that that demographic pattern will continue to increase. They agreed that diversity management is an inescapable issue in the twenty-first-century corporate environment.

The diversity directors who were interviewed in this study often tend to speak in metaphors to describe the true nature of the challenges they see their organizations facing today in the American workplace. They believe that persons not from the dominant culture, usually referred to as diversity personnel, 'experience a longer runway to success'. This connotes the reality for most of these persons: that they must adapt to the dominant culture that is thoroughly ingrained in the corporate culture. Often learning 'the way we do business around here' is a necessary component for success. Paradoxically the diverse background, along with a divergent perspective, that encouraged the hiring of a minority category member, may be a disadvantage to that new member in functioning with the existing set of dominant culture co-workers.

Odious overt expressions of bias are rare and are the easiest situations to handle because most organizations currently practise a zero-tolerance policy for such issues. Most individual problems that employees have in the workplace are not considered as issues related to diversity. They are considered to be performance issues. In the pressured environment of the new decade 'everyone must be a producer'. It is the multiple outcomes of a person's labour that become the prime focus of evaluation. Rarely is a performance issue ever discussed in terms of its root cause, which could be cultural; rather, it is treated as a measurement issue. It is the 'bottom line' that counts. As one diversity official said: 'They have effectively removed the humanity from the equation of performance evaluation and decisions on rifts.'

Women still substantially feel there is a glass ceiling. In one large corporation the diversity director reports that: 'When we did a study of the most successful people we noted that the most successful women over the age of forty do not have children. On the other hand it is interesting to note that the most successful men over forty do have children.' Female executive interviewees repeatedly indicate that they have to adapt to the corporate leadership style in order to be successful. They need to 'be as hard-nosed as a comparable man'. Lower-level women in the organizations resent this tendency and point out that 'the most macho executives are the women who have had to be ruthless' to get to the top. 'She is tougher in her expectations of me then she is of any of the men under her.' Typically when a female executive is confronted with this impression the response is incredulity: 'Of course I've been tough and enforced high standards. It is the only way to make a mark as a leader in this corporate culture. I don't see a distinction between male and female leaders in that regard.' However the same female executives will admit in private coaching sessions that over the years they learned to modify their interaction patterns to fit those of the males in the boardroom. In the environment of pressured decision making, female executives will admit that their interaction patterns must fit 'playing the game' according to the men's rules, while being vigilant 'not to be seen as shrill or overly emotional'.

Are diversity units as proactive as they need to be? The diversity directors would respond with a resounding 'no way'. Do they know how to approach the entrenched issues? Some might say they are making progress. One feature that is required of persons in a diversity management position is that they must have patience. They recognize they are working for cultural change and it is going to occur over a significant period of time. They relate the fable of the tortoise and the hare. Small improvements will lead to eventual cultural change within the corporation. They believe in diversity training, but are guarded regarding its quality and impact. As one said: 'I haven't met a soul in the firm who liked the diversity training we have.' They doubt that the short segment of time devoted to diversity training enables the opportunity to make a lasting impact. They would rather do very limited training than poor training that only creates and reinforces stereotypes. They recognize that the most important component of the diversity training process is the mid-level managers' support and reinforcement of it. 'The persons who need real hard core coaching on diversity management are the middle managers who either don't recognize the need, or because of business pressures, won't take the time for it. They think sending new employees to a day-long diversity orientation will solve the problem.' However as the focus groups testified, and reported previously, the managers are on the precipice regarding diversity fairness perceptions and have the greatest need to be informed, sensitized, and coached. None of the diversity directors feel that their diversity programmes are approaching adequate cultural change programming with mid-level managers.

The directors, who have been in the minority position themselves, are aware that 'minorities are often in less political positions'. This provocative observation implies that in some cases diverse executives are isolated to 'safe havens' where they are impacted less by the shifting winds of corporate change. A case in point is the diversity executive who feels he is safe from rifts because he is a high-profile minority within the diversity management programme.

Some diversity managers believe that 'informal networks work in adverse ways for the minority population'. The familiar example is: 'If I don't play or talk golf, I'm at a real disadvantage.' There is a strong sense that the quality and nature of organizational members' relationships is a hidden element that bears a great deal of weight during performance evaluation and decisions on rifts and promotions. The questions can be as basic as: does the minority person have enough understanding of the majority person's value set and interests to carry on a satisfying conversation; does the majority person have enough sensitivity to recognize that not everyone shares his/her value set and interests?

Diversity directors realize that because they are expected to be cultural change agents they should be accountable for objectives that are long term and very difficult to measure. However corporate leadership prefers consistent quantification of results. Diversity managers dislike quotas just as much as the ideological critic of affirmative action. They recognize that the quality of work life and satisfaction with peer relationships may be measured by retention rates, but its impact on productivity and quality decision making is very difficult to measure. Diversity directors suffer from the corporate headquarters habit of measuring results over a brief time span yet they toil to make systemic changes that will take years. As a result, several of these directors indicate that, for the health of their career, they have to think of this as a short-term one-to-three-year position: 'Getting back to an operational role where I can demonstrate my ability to get results will be crucial to my career.'

The goal of all of the diversity directors was, as one indicated: 'weave diversity into the everyday operation of the firm'. They had no illusions about the difficulty of this task. They knew they had to come up with tactical methods of accomplishing their mission of inclusiveness. This is a term that is embraced more forcefully than previous terms such as tolerance and diversity, which can carry negative connotations. The new reality is that since the workplace will be more inclusive of a wider variety of employees and customers an 'inclusive growth strategy' is appropriate.

Dimensions of difference

It is important to note at this point in the discussion that the persons in the studies rarely placed any theoretic frame on the diversity issues they discuss. In interviews they can quickly embrace the interviewer's conceptual frames to explain what they perceive and have experienced, but there is an obvious dearth of their own application of such frames to their daily activities.

Previous work by the author has focused on employing programme objectives labelled 'dimensions of difference' (Swanson, 2001). In the main, these can be construed as communication variables. These provide a baseline for the action research discussed here. The dimensions provide a general way to bring new concepts into interviews with the goal

of organizing and focusing some of the participants' consideration of diversity. In brief they are the following:

A starting point is to employ one of the most widely applied value dimensions that explains cultural distinctions: *individualism–collectivism* (Fiske, 1991; Gudykunst and Ting-Toomey, 1988; Hofstede, 1980, 1991; Schwartz and Bilsky, 1990; Triandis, 1995). In the instance of many managers, this value dimension is highly applicable. It enables a general view of how and why the subordinates the leader supervises may hold a different worldview and mindset from that of the dominant culture manager. Ting-Toomey's (1999) discussion of the distinction between individualism and collectivism encapsulates the sort of concepts that can be applied:

Basically, *individualism* refers to the broad value tendencies of a culture in emphasising the importance of individual identity over group identity, individual rights over group rights, and individual needs over group needs. Individualism promotes self-efficiency, individual responsibilities, and personal autonomy. In contrast, *collectivism* refers to the broad value tendencies of a culture in emphasising the importance of the 'we' identity oriented needs over individual wants and desires. Collectivism promotes relational interdependence, in-group harmony, and in-group collaborative spirit.

(p 67)

Applying three basic concepts, as awareness objectives, produces a framework for productive discussion. The concepts are *worldview*, *mindset* and *intercultural communication competence*. Those concepts can be faulted for being expansive, yet they are valuable because they broadly encompass elements that assist the leader in perceiving why and how significant differences exist.

The first objective is to examine and understand that a person's *worldview* is a strong determinant of their communication patterns. Worldview is a broad concept that generalises how a cultural group orients to the world (Aldefer and Smith, 1982). 'Worldview refers to the philosophical ideas of being' (Jandt, 1995: 214). Typically those orienting factors may be most of the following: How human nature is viewed as either good or evil. Are humans considered to be in control of their destiny, or do the forces of nature determine destiny? How do humans differ from animals and what role does spiritual belief play in life? Managers are not surprised by the Sapir–Whorf hypothesis that indicates the worldview of a particular speech community is reflected in the linguistic patterns they employ. They have repeatedly been told that learning another language is vitally important. But the sense that different language groups have different cultural patterns is only a starting point for an initial awareness. As Jay (1968) argues: 'Bilingualism is not in itself the answer to cultural understanding among people. An indispensable asset, it must be fortified by the strongest possible sensitivity education. With knowledge of the language must exist a similar knowledge of the social, religious and economic attitudes of a people' (pp. 85–6). The context of an individual's life is provided by a rich array of cultural factors that shape the individual perception of the world. 'Context is a powerful organizer of experience' (Seelye, 1993: 8).

The second objective is to examine the managers' *mindset*. Although the term 'mindset' does not seem to be very precise from a social science perspective, it does have a common sense understanding typified by Webster's (1988) definition: 'a fixed mental attitude formed by experience, education, prejudice, etc.' (p. 862). Fisher (1988) selected this term to headline his approach to improving cross-cultural relations because: 'Diagnosing mindsets as they relate to immediate problems is a more manageable objective' (p. 2). People are predisposed to perceive an issue that is at hand in a particular way because of a pattern of attitudes that has developed from their experience and development of social reality. That powerful attitude set may emanate from personal history that is influenced by culture. For example assuming that a person values and employs highly rational decision making over personal relationships and loyalty, may not be an appropriate assumption. Many managers are unaware of the mindsets of their subordinates nor of their own personal mindset as it relates to other cultures.

The third objective is to consider skills of *intercultural communication competence*. This multifaceted concept conveys a pragmatic sense that an individual's personal communication characteristics will be assessed by those they interact with in diverse settings. Interpersonal communication scholars (Lustig and Koester, 1999; Wiseman and Koester, 1993; Spitzburg and Cupach, 1984) agree and focus on the concept that competent persons must practise effective interaction skills, but they must also interact appropriately with the people and the cultural environment, while striving to attain the goals of the communication. The injection of the concept of competence into the awareness of the learner seems to indicate that some behavioural elements of appropriate adaptation can be learned along with effective behaviours.

The skill of appropriate interpersonal and intercultural sensitivity and adaptation is what all managers should be expected to do. One of the key elements that some managers reported was 'knowing when to talk and when to listen'. In his discussion of constructing life through language, Shotter recognizes this reality: 'In some contexts – in offices, businesses, bureaucracies, educational establishments, etc. – knowing the order of talk required is a part of one's social competence as an adult' (1993: 4). Kikoski and Kikoski (1999) designate the 'order of talk' as a shared common necessity for colleagues in a workplace to have 'social competence'.

Discussion with this research sample of managers, perhaps typical of any discussion of intercultural communication competence, seems to be enhanced with greater clarity by the awareness that worldview and mindset are powerful synonymous determinants of communication behaviour. Thus these two concepts coupled with the aspiration of intercultural communication competence are valuable organizing concepts for training. They also function as a useful organizing tool for research interviews.

Discussion

Most managers lack familiarity with terminology that enables in-depth *dialogue regarding diversity*. Managers interviewed in this study indicated that corporate organization members rarely approach a quality of discussion of diversity issues that can be labelled as dialogue. Theorists and practitioners working to help groups accomplish dialogue indicate that it is quite difficult to achieve (Issacs, 1999; Bohm, 1992; Senge, 1991). To illustrate that difficulty it is necessary to examine how the process of dialogue may be defined and operationalized. The capacity for conducting dialogue includes three levels of interaction (Isaacs, 1999). First, in order to 'build capacity for new behaviour' members of a work group need to focus on the skills of listening carefully and 'listening together', rather than individually. If members can 'suspend certainty' and begin to externalize thought, even to the point of saying the unusual or unpopular, they have helped to open the dialogue. Second, in order to mobilise members' 'predictive intuition' the action patterns within the group must be considered. Can they balance advocacy and inquiry? Can the group 'map the systems' of their interaction, i.e., develop a coherent representation of the overall system of issues that are faced? Third, the 'architecture of the invisible' needs to be examined. This requires some boundary setting for the group's interaction and a sense of the field or process environment of the discourse. When the nature of the dialogue field is understood, then convening dialogue is based on the nature of the process environment and sensitivity to the ecology of the group. Other members of the group implicitly realize that 'the way we talk impacts the way we think', so there is a consistent concern with how each individual talks. The ultimate result will be 'ignorance management'. Those things that are not known, that participants are unaware of in specific terms, or deliberately withheld from the group, can become important input into the synergy of the group. It is when the third phase of dialogue occurs, that includes getting beyond not knowing what is not known about each others' perspectives, that the type of interaction and understanding occur that can lead to building an inclusive culture. 'Dialogue is about evoking insight, which is a way of reordering our knowledge – particularly the taken for granted assumptions that people bring to the table' (Issacs, 1999: 45). Diversity directors in particular believe that important progress can be made when members of their organizations are able to have dialogue on diversity issues. Values and interaction patterns are slow to evolve as D'Amica and D'Amica (1997) suggest in their futurist anticipation of work attitudes in the twenty-first century: 'Breaking through the inertia of entrenched patterns in both individual behaviour and organisational systems has shown itself to be much more difficult and long-term than expected' (p. 6).

Diversity training has evolved through some rough waters. In 1988 diversity was not one of the top forty training topics reported by companies in a Society for Human Resource Management study (Rynes and Rosen, 1994). By 1998 a study by the same organization reported that 75 per cent of the Fortune 500 firms and 36 per cent of companies of all sizes had some sort of diversity programme in process (Allen and Montgomery, 2001). In the 1990s diversity became a hot topic and Loden (1996) reported:

> Today, the myriad training programmes, planning councils, diversity audits, consultants, and organisation initiatives that purport to be changing corporate cultures often seem to be focused more on generating activity than results. While awareness and understanding have become a staple of every organisation's diversity strategy, many programmes to increase awareness appear to be generating more heat but not more light.
>
> (p. viii)

The heat often comes in the form of a white male backlash by those who react to training programmes as ineffective. For example one respondent in this study indicated that: 'White men are blamed for all the problems. I resent white male bashing. We built and maintain this company.' This is a major obstacle that diversity programmes must overcome. 'In effect, positioning diversity so one group must

take blame for the past makes the ultimate goal – greater unity – impossible' (Rasmussen, 1996: 5). Typical training approaches, such as those applied in most organizations considered in this study, are very brief. A half-day or full-day training session raises some awareness and provides some rationale for change, but rarely begins to work with the broader issues of diverse worldviews from diverse cultures and the resultant mindsets that guide key elements of workplace behaviour. Thomas and Ely (1996) encapsulate this sort of awareness:

> Numerous and varied initiatives to increase diversity in corporate America have been under way for more than two decades. Rarely however, have those efforts spurred leaps in organizational effectiveness. Instead, many attempts to increase diversity in the workplace have backfired, sometimes even heightening tensions among employees and hindering a company's performance. It is our belief that there is a distinct way to unleash the powerful benefits of a diverse workforce. Although these benefits include increased profitability, they go beyond financial measures to encompass learning, creativity, flexibility, organizational and individual growth, and the ability of a company to adjust rapidly and successfully to market changes. The desired transformation however, requires a fundamental change in the attitudes and behaviors of an organization's leadership.
>
> (pp. 79–80)

Performance evaluation is a focus point for diversity management programmes. Most performance appraisal systems strive to make legally defensible appraisals and this means that issues objectively covered by law become the focus (Smither, 1998). However, the perception of the process by those who are affected by it is key.

Uncertainty regarding the impact of diversity policy on evaluation of personnel takes various forms. Minority personnel consistently are alert to any cues that they are not being evaluated fairly in a manner consistent with the evaluation of personnel from the dominant culture. The majority culture personnel sometimes feel that they are being evaluated more harshly or 'held to a higher standard' than those protected by affirmative action programmes. This is particularly true of white male middle-level managers. This focuses attention upon the review process.

Supervisors, who conduct periodic reviews, are uncomfortable with the review process when it applies to someone from another culture. It is particularly true of white male supervisors who say they must strive to be 'politically correct' in all of their statements. Some indicate that in the effort to 'bend over backwards to be fair, I am probably sugar coating what I say'. 'I know I have to document any problems; my expert reaction to an employee's sub-par performance is not enough in this environment. I am sometimes uncertain of precisely how to proceed.'

Diversity personnel and mid-level managers desire greater certainty regarding how others are monitoring them. Most of the literature on performance appraisal recognizes the essential element of reducing uncertainty in the process. However, that recognition is in the context of legality and observable behaviour and does not generally include the impact of various cultures on mindsets, perceptions, and its consequent behaviour. Specific issues of cultural differences are usually neglected. The US legal requirements drive the process so that recommendations for legally sound appraisals generally set appraisal criteria. They tend to include the recommendation that appraisals be specifically job related, based on behaviour rather than individual traits, relate to specific features not holistic assessments, and should be something over which the subject of the evaluation has control (Barrett and Kernan, 1987; Beck-Dudley and McEnvoy, 1991; Bernardine, Kane, Ross, Spina and Johnson, 1995; Martin and Bartol, 1991; Veglahn, 1993). The literature also includes the ubiquitous communication expectation that the appraisal should be stated in descriptive/objective terms as opposed to subjective/evaluative terms and that the appraisal must be communicated clearly to the person being rated. Theoretically uncertainty reduction focuses on self-awareness and knowledge of others (Berger and Bradac, 1982). When the members are from divergent cultures the relationship strategies to reduce uncertainty may be quite different (Gudykunst, 1988).

Diversity is more complex than the often unspoken, but underlying, assumption about diversity that it breeds conflict which can impede work performance and reduce productivity. This common perception is at odds with group theory, and the concept of democratic decision making, that promotes the clash of expressed ideas as an effective method to work for answers to problems. The underlying worldview and mindset of many workers from collectivist cultures, is alien to the concept of expressed clash being valued in task relationships. The cultural values of an individual may well override the influence of their education and organizational environment. For example if a team member places a high value on harmony, even if she possesses informational and worldview diversity, she may not readily contribute to the group debate.

Diversity is more complex than the easily observable distinctions of race, gender, age and physical ability. As the concept of diversity evolves to fit the contemporary workplace where organizations have flattened structures and moved to new team and workgroup forms designed to increase synchronous communication, more complex categories of diversity are the focus of research. For example Jehn, Northcraft and Neale (1999) did a field study of ninety-two workgroups applying three types of workplace diversity (social category diversity, value diversity and informational diversity). They found it appropriate to question the typical hypothesis, taught as a basic concept on group dynamics, that heterogeneity in groups leads to better group performance, while homogeneity leads to better group process. However, the reality is more complex. Their field study discovered that social category diversity could be mediated by task type and task interdependence and that value diversity could be the most frequent impediment to group performance. Consequently, being alert to the impact of diverse value sets, reflected by worldview and mindset, is a key challenge to those who wish to mobilize all of the human assets in a given decision-making setting.

Contemporary theorists have described strategic stages of the development of diversity programmes. Allen and Montgomery (2001) define the stages simply as: 'unfreezing' the forces resisting change; 'moving' to cultural change; 'refreezing', or institutionalizing the change; and the 'competitive advantage' that results. In 1996 Thomas and Ely defined three paradigms to explain the evolution of a diversity programme. Initially, the 'discrimination and fairness paradigm' must be satisfied. Second, the 'access and legitimacy paradigm' must be put in place, and reinforced. Third, the programme must strive for 'the emerging paradigm' that connects diversity to work perspectives. Subsequently

the third perspective has been further defined as the 'integration-and-learning' perspective that enables dialogue on diversity issues to occur (Ely and Thomas, 2001).

From the manager's vantage point, is the goal of the diversity programme to enforce law and expectations and support incremental improvements? Or is the goal to develop and maintain a systemic programme that has a dramatic impact on the corporate culture? It is evident from the reactions of interviewees in this study that these are neither dichotomous nor mutually exclusive goals. Whatever the mission of the diversity unit is, high-level executives must be involved and champion the programme. 'Top management support for diversity is certainly critical. Management needs to begin the process of unfreezing the current culture by changing the system within which it operates' (Allen and Montgomery, 2001: 154).

Implications

This review of corporate members' perceptions raises a variety of concepts that in their application must be context dependent. 'Organizational leaders also need to examine their internal and external environments to adopt an approach to implementation that matches their particular context or with a context they believe will emerge' (Dass and Parker, 1999: 78). There is no single best set of concepts or way of dealing with diversity management. Each organization inheres its own unique demographic features.

In any effort to understand the attitude toward diversity programmes that exists in the contemporary corporate environment it seems that the appropriate focus is upon executives and their influence on the sort of diversity programming selected to fit their organization. Effective approaches to diversity management are strategic and focused on goals that are achievable.

The key to the evolution of a diversity programme to an 'integration and learning' perspective, which produces cultural change, is the ability to effectively talk through the dimensions of difference in the organization. An organization that develops the ability to discuss diversity in a manner that approaches dialogue, will also accomplish better diversity training and performance evaluation.

From the perspective of the corporate communication professional the existence of a valued and effective diversity programme is a significant element to be communicated to corporate stakeholders. In order to reduce uncertainty for organizational stakeholders, the programme rationale must be clearly explained and reinforced. A cohesive plan and programme is essential to anticipate and answer the objections that arise from internal backlash, stockholder alarm, and internal resistance to the allocation of resources to diversity programming. In both the planning and the operationalization of the diversity programme a sense of high aspirations and transparency should be evident.

Summary

Diversity programmes have become an expected element in the modern corporation because of the reality of the varied demographics of organization members, stakeholders and potential clients. However, most corporate diversity directors are not satisfied with the progress made by their own diversity programme. Diversity personnel feel that managers must develop greater sensitivity to how their diversity personnel are evaluated and led. Many organization members are ignorant of both the nature of the programme in their corporation and the dimensions of difference that have an impact on members' behaviour. Consequently, there is a challenge to find ways of developing a mature understanding of diversity within the corporate setting. Concepts such as individualism–collectivism, worldview, and mindset can be employed to provide a basic conceptualization of difference in the attempt to improve intercultural communication competence in the organization. The promotion of true dialogue regarding diversity differences, the existence of substantive diversity training, and application of diversity concepts in the conduct of performance evaluation are essential elements of an effective diversity programme. Corporations have made progress in addressing the basic programme role of working to eliminate discrimination and promote fairness. The second role of ensuring 'access and legitimacy' is also largely in place. But there is a need to move to integration and learning perspectives that will enable meaningful dialogue on diversity issues to occur.

REFERENCES

Aldefer, C. and Smith, K. (1982) 'Studying intergroup relations embedded in organizations', *Administrative Science Quarterly* 27, 35–65.

Allen, R. and Montgomery, K. (2001) 'Applying an organizational development approach to creat-ing diversity', *Organisational Dynamics*, 30, 149–61.

Arai, M., Wanca-Thibault, M. and Schockley-Zalabak, P. (2001) 'Communication theory and training approaches for multiculturally diverse organizations: have academics and the practitioners missed the connection?', *Public Personnel Management*, 30, 445–56.

Barrett, B. and Kernan, M. (1987) 'Performance appraisal and terminations: a review of court decisions since *Brito v. Zia* with implications for personnel practices', *Personnel Psychology*, 40, 489–503.

Beck-Dudley, C. and McEnvoy, G. (1991) 'Performance appraisals and discrimination suits: do courts pay attention to validity?', *Employee Responsibilities and Rights Journal*, 4, 149–63.

Berger, C. and Bradac, J. (1982) *Language and Social Knowledge: Uncertainty in Interpersonal Relations*, London: Arnold.

Bernadine, H., Kane, J., Ross, S., Spina, D. and Johnson, D. (1995) 'Performance appraisal design, development and implementation', in G. Ferris, S. Rosen, and D. Barnum (eds), *Handbook of Human Resource Management*, Cambridge, MA: Blackwell, pp. 462–93.

Bohm, D. (1992) *Thought As a System*, London: Routledge.

Cox, T. (1991) 'The multicultural organisation', *Academy of Management Executive*, 5, 34–48.

D'Amica, J. and D'Amica, C. (1997) *Workplace 2020: Work and Workers in the 21st Century*. Indianapolis, IN: Hudson Institute.

Dass, P. and Parker, B. (1999) 'Strategies for managing human resource diversity: from resistance to learning', *Academy of Management Executive*, 13, 68–80.

Economist (1995) 'Affirmative action: a strong prejudice', 17 June, 69–70.

Eden, C. and Huxham C. (1999) 'Action research for the study of organisations', in S. R. Clegg and C. Hardy (eds), *Studying Organisation: Theory & Method*, London: Sage, pp. 272–88.

Ely, R. and Thomas, D. (2001) 'Cultural diversity at work: the effects of diversity perspectives on work group processes and outcomes', *Administrative Science Quarterly*, 46, 299–73.

Fisher, G. (1988) *Mindsets*, Yarmouth, ME: Intercultural Press.

Fiske, A. (1991) *Structures of Social Life: The Four Elementary Forms of Human Relations*, New York: Free Press.

Gudykunst W. and Ting-Toomey, S., with Chua, E. (1988) *Culture and Interpersonal Communication*, Newbury Park, CA: Sage.

Gudykunst, W. (1988) 'Uncertainty and anxiety', in Y. Kim and W. Gudykunst (eds), *Theories in Intercultural Communication*, Newbury Park, CA: Sage, pp. 123–56.

Hofstede, G. (1980). *Culture's Consequences: International Differences in Work Related Values*, Beverly Hills, CA: Sage.

Hofstede, G. (1991). *Cultures and Organisations: Software of the Mind*, London: McGraw-Hill.

Issacs, W. (1999) *Dialogue: and the Art of Thinking Together*, New York: Currency.

Ivancevich, J. and Gilbert, J. (2000) 'Diversity management: time for a new approach', *Public Personnel Management*, 29, 75–92.

Jandt, F. E. (1995) *Intercultural Communication: An Introduction*, Thousand Oaks, CA: Sage.

Jay, C. (1968) 'Study of culture: relevance of foreign languages in world affairs education', in P. Castle and C. Jay (eds), *Toward Excellence in Foreign Language Education*, Springfield, IL: Office of Public Instruction.

Jehn, K., Northcraft, G. and Neal, M. (1999) 'Why difference makes a difference: a field study of diversity conflict and performance', *Administrative Science Quarterly*, 44, 741–63.

Kikoski, J. and Kikoski, C. (1999). *Reflexive Communication in the Culturally Diverse Workplace*, Westport, CT: Praeger.

Loden, M. (1996) *Implementing Diversity*, Boston: McGraw Hill.

Lustig, M. W. and Koester, J. (1999) *Intercultural Competence: Interpersonal Communication across Cultures*, New York: Longman.

Martin, D. and Bartol, K. (1991) 'The legal ramifications of performance appraisal: an update', *Employee Relations Law Journal*, 17, 257–86.

Rasmussen, T. (1996) *The ASTD Trainer's Sourcebook: Diversity*, New York: McGraw Hill.

Rynes, S. and Rosen, B. (1994) 'What makes diversity programmes work?', *HRM Magazine*, October, 67–73.

Schwartz, S., and Bilsky, W. (1990) 'Toward a theory of the universal content and structure of values', *Journal of Personality and Social Psychology*, 58, 878–91.

Seelye, H. N. (1993) *Teaching Culture: Strategies for intercultural Communication*, Lincolnwood, IL: National Textbook Company.

Senge, P. (1990) *The Fifth Discipline: The Art and*

Practice of the Learning Organisation, New York: Currency.

Shotter, J. (1993) *Conversational Realities: Constructing Life through Language*, London: Sage.

Smither, J. (ed.) (1998) *Performance Appraisal: State of the Art in Practice*, San Francisco: Jossey-Bass.

Spitzburg, B. H. and Cupach, W. R. (1984) *Interpersonal Communication Competence*, Beverly Hills, CA: Sage.

Swanson, D. (2001) 'Corporate culture and cross-cultural communication adjustment of American general managers leading in the transitional business society of Guam', in A. Leung, S. Clegg, J. Hollows, V. Luk and S. Porras (eds), *Proceedings of the Asian Pacific Researchers in Organisation Studies: Organisation Theory in Transition: Transitional Societies; Transitional Theories*, Hong Kong: APROS.

Thomas, D. A. and Ely, R. J. (1996) 'Making differences matter: a new paradigm for managing diversity', *Harvard Business Review*, 68, 107–16.

Ting-Toomey, S. (1999) *Communication across Cultures*. New York: Guilford Press.

Triandis, H. (1995) *Individualism and Collectivism*, Boulder, CO: Westview Press.

Veglahn, P. (1993) 'Key issues in performance appraisal challenges: evidence from court and arbitration decisions', *Labor Law Journal*, October, 596–606.

Webster's New World Dictionary (1988) 3rd college edn, Cleveland: Webster's New World.

Wiseman, R. L. and Koester, J. (eds) (1993) *Intercultural Communication Competence*, Newbury Park, CA: Sage.

CHAPTER 2

A best-practice approach to designing a change communication programme

Deborah J. Barrett

In today's business climate it is arguable that however paradoxically it may sound the only true constant is 'change'. The focus of this chapter is change communication, an essential companion to any effective change management programme. At the heart of any successful change communication programme is effective employee communication, for without effective employee communication any change programme will fail.

This chapter illustrates an approach to change communication by using a best-practice model for employee communication called the Strategic Employee Communication Model.

The importance of change communication

Change is difficult, and organizational change is particularly challenging, thus the huge amount of research on managing organizational change, usually called 'change management'. What is change management? Some might say that it is an oxymoron since change is too unpredictable and chaotic to control or manage. However, good managers must attempt to manage it. Change management is the executive skill or art of leading or supervising the people involved in the transformation of or in an organization. People are the heart of change management, and communication is at the heart of people.

Nothing happens in an organization without communication. As Eccles and Nohria say in *Beyond the Hype: Discovering the Essence of Management*, 'Without the right words, used in the right way, it is unlikely that the right actions will ever occur . . . Without words we have no way of expressing strategic concepts, structural forms, or designs for performance measurement systems. In the end, there is no separating action and rhetoric' (1992). Thus, without effective employee communication and a rigid approach to communication during major change, a change programme has little chance to succeed.

Although much research exists on change management, few of the articles or books give adequate attention to the change communication that accompanies any good change management programme; however, at least communication does appear as one component necessary for a change programme to succeed in most cases.

For instance, in Kotter's often cited (1995) approach to successful organizational transformations ('Leading change: why transformation efforts fail'), communication is listed as the fourth of his eight steps:

1 establishing a sense of urgency;
2 forming a powerful guiding coalition;
3 creating a vision;
4 communicating the vision;
5 empowering others to act on the vision;
6 planning for and creating short-term wins;
7 consolidating improvements and producing still more change;
8 institutionalizing the new approaches.

Another frequently cited approach to change management is the ten commandments of executing change found in Kanter, Stein and Jick's *The Challenge of Organisational Change* (1992):

1 analyse the organization and its need for change;
2 create a shared vision and common direction;
3 separate from the past;
4 create a sense of urgency;
5 support a strong leader role;
6 line up political sponsorship;
7 craft an implementation plan;
8 develop enabling structures;
9 communicate, involve people, be honest;
10 reinforce and institutionalize change.

In both of these examples, although the word 'communicate' appears in only one step, the role of communication is explicit in most of the other steps. For instance, how could a manager create a 'sense of urgency' without communicating messages that inspire the necessity to act? How can managers create coalitions, without convincing people (through words) to follow them? How can managers institutionalize new approaches, without instructing people in expected actions? And, of course, we could go on, but these few examples demonstrate how communication is interwoven in all aspects of a change programme. Obviously, without effective employee communication, change is impossible and change management fails.

In 'Leading change: why transformation efforts fail', Kotter lists 'under-communication' as one of the major reasons change efforts do not succeed. As he says, 'Transformation is impossible unless hundreds or thousands of people are willing to help, often to the point of making short-term sacrifices. Employees will not make sacrifices, even if they are unhappy with the status quo, unless they believe that useful change is possible. Without credible communication, and a lot of it, the hearts and minds of the troops are never captured' (Kotter, 1995). Therefore, companies need to apply the same analytical energy and rigour to employee communication and the design of their change communication plan that they give to the financial and operational components of any change programme.

The strategic positioning of employee communication

Employee communication must play a strategic role in an organization to work effectively. That strategic role means that communication must be integrated into the company's strategy and recognized for its strategic implications and effects. Many managers see employee communication as a 'black box'. Communication is either everything in the organization (vision, strategy, business planning, management meetings, information flow, knowledge management, etc.) or it is nothing more than publications intended to keep the communication staff busy and the employees informed of the company news. Many managers see communication as simply process, or the way to get information to people, not as content, the meaningful messages delivered by the process. To be effective, employee communication must be both process and content, which positions communication on more of a strategic level within an organization.

Effective employee communication must be fully integrated into all aspects of a company's business. It is integral to the strategy as well as essential to communication of that strategy. Effective employee communication informs and educates employees at all levels in the company's strategy, and it also motivates and positions employees to support the strategy and the performance goals. During change, communication becomes even more linked to the strategic success. For effective employee communication during major change, the change communication must at a minimum accomplish the following:

1   ensure clear and consistent messages to educate employees in the company vision, strategic goals, and what the change means to them;
2   motivate employee support for the company's new direction;
3   encourage higher performance and discretionary effort;
4   limit misunderstandings and rumours that may damage productivity; and finally,

5   align employees behind the company's strategic and overall performance improvement goals.

The strategic employee communication model and change communication approach are designed to help management accomplish these goals.

The strategic employee communication model and best practices

The strategic employee communication model (Figure 2.1) helps clarify the strategic role communication plays in the day-to-day success of any company as well as during major change and can help overcome the 'everything' and the 'publication-limited' perceptions of communication. The model and its components emerged from research into several Fortune 500 companies to find out what really works when it comes to employee communication.[1] While no company exemplifies each best practice exactly, the better companies demonstrate many of the best-practice definitions. In a change programme, the model and the best-practice definitions can serve as benchmarks against which to measure a company's employee communication strengths and weaknesses as well as a model of effective change communications.

The model captures all of the major components of employee communication, linking them to each other and to the company's strategy and operations. Thus, it works analytically to break employee communication down into manageable, recognizable parts; at the same time, it shows how intertwined and interdependent each part is when employee communication is positioned strategically as it must be to facilitate change. The

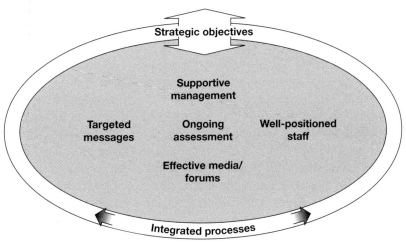

Figure 2.1
Strategic employee
communication model

traditional communication components, such as messages and media are at the heart of the model, but the direct link to the company's strategic objectives and the business planning process plus the overlay of supportive management with ongoing assessment of individual and company communication move the model from the tactical to the strategic level.

From the research into the company examples of effective employee communication, the following best-practice definitions emerge:

1   *Strategic objectives*: In high-performing companies, employee communication reinforces the company's strategic objectives. There should be a one-to-one correlation between what the company has established as its strategic objectives and what is listed as the objectives for the communication. In addition, the communication must be structured to translate the central strategic messages (from vision to performance or financial goals) to all employees.

2   *Supportive management*: Top-level and mid-level management must be directly involved in and assume responsibility for communication up, down and across the organization. In a major change situation as well as for day-to-day operations, communication is not just what the communication staff does. Managers must model the behaviour they expect of their employees, the old adage of 'walking the talk'. They set the tone for an open or closed flow of information. Without them, the channels of communication cannot flow freely.

3   *Targeted messages*: Targeted messages are simply information tailored to the audience (i.e., messages in different words for different people when necessary), so that the information is relevant and meaningful, at the same time that it is consistent. Thus, each business unit or division must tailor the important messages to their employees, and if necessary, convert the overall message of the corporate centre into the digestible and actionable messages the employees can understand and act upon.

4   *Effective media/forums*: Effective employee communication uses all vehicles to reach its audiences, but most importantly, it relies on direct, face-to-face communication over indirect, print or electronic media. Thus, interpersonal communication training, meeting management, and facilitation skills are necessary for all managers.

5   *Well-positioned staff*: The communication staff needs to be close to the most important business issues, involved in the strategic and business planning processes. They must have a 'seat at the table'. Being a member of the senior management team allows the senior communication officer to understand the company's strategy and to participate in the decision making. In addition, the communication staff should be seen as facilitators of change not just as producers of publications.

6   *Ongoing assessment*: The effectiveness of the company's communication needs to be measured company-wide formally and frequently against clearly defined goals on an ongoing basis and throughout the key stages of any major change. In addition, communication effectiveness needs to be evaluated as part of each employee's individual performance appraisal with the appropriate recognition for excellence.

7   *Integrated processes*: Communication needs to be integrated into the business processes with communication milestones included in the business plan and as part of the business planning process. Communication should be placed on the agenda of meetings and built into the management discussion of strategic objectives and planning.

By using the model and best-practice definitions, a company can create very tangible communication goals for employee communication improvement and the change communication programme. The model serves as a tool to approach employee communication as a company would any analysis, that is, breaking the whole down into manageable, carefully defined parts. These definitions can serve as a benchmark against which companies can measure the potential need for communication improvement in their organization so that employee communication will help in facilitating the change programme.

How to design an effective change communication programme

The design of the change communication programme needs to grow out of the size of the change programme and the company's current communication practices. Is the proposed change major or incremental? Is the change company-wide or business-unit specific? How many employees are involved and affected? How effective are the current communication practices? Are they strong enough to carry a major change programme? If the changes are major and essential to company performance, companies cannot afford not to improve the current communication practices if they find them lacking. They must devote the necessary time and resources required to assess and improve employee communication before they launch the change programme; otherwise, the change programme will never get off the ground.

The specifics of any change communication programme are particular to the company; therefore, they must come from inside the organization and not from outside. An approach from off the shelf seldom, if ever, works for any organization. No one should force the strategic employee communication model or any other model on a company from the outside. Instead, the strategic employee communication model and change communication approach should be used to work from the inside of the organization to determine what is needed and to design the appropriate change communication programme to fit those needs. Thus, the model provides an analytical tool to diagnose a company's communication strengths and weaknesses and to frame the change communication plan and resulting programme.

The three-phased action plan below can be looked at as one way to map out a company's programme, one that has been successful and that can be adapted to a company's particular needs (Figure 2.2). Each of the three phases contains the specific actions that are to be taken to implement the change communication programme. They may vary slightly from company to company, and they will evolve as the change programme evolves; the feedback loops indicate information coming in that influences the action plan once the change programme is under way. Any action plan is a living plan although phases and most of the actions represented here will need to occur in most change programmes.

The first phase of analysis and strategy development is critical to the success of any change programme. The analytical phase for change communication is often the phase management will omit or minimize because they fail to recognize its significance, fail to see communication planning as strategic, or fail to see their way clear to allowing the time and attention it needs; however, without the careful analysis of the current employee communication situation, the company is shooting in the dark in developing the change communication programme. They do not know where the communication breakdowns are and how best to reach the organization with the key change messages.

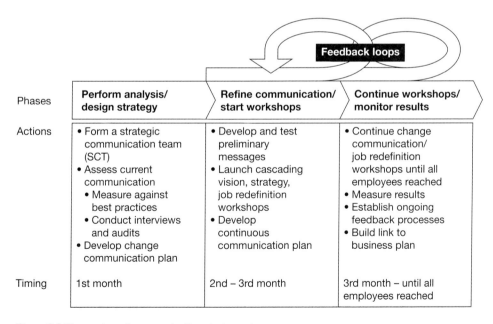

Phases	Perform analysis/ design strategy	Refine communication/ start workshops	Continue workshops/ monitor results
Actions	• Form a strategic communication team (SCT) • Assess current communication • Measure against best practices • Conduct interviews and audits • Develop change communication plan	• Develop and test preliminary messages • Launch cascading vision, strategy, job redefinition workshops • Develop continuous communication plan	• Continue change communication/ job redefinition workshops until all employees reached • Measure results • Establish ongoing feedback processes • Build link to business plan
Timing	1st month	2nd – 3rd month	3rd month – until all employees reached

Figure 2.2 Three-phased communication strategy plan

The three-phase action plan contains four essential actions for an effective change communication programme:

1   forming a strategic communication team;
2   assessing current communication practices;
3   conducting cascading vision, strategy, job redefinition workshops;
4   monitoring the results.

Forming a strategic communication team (SCT)

A full-scale change communication programme requires dedicated resources consisting of not only a few communication staff members, but selected employees and management. The first step in starting any change communication programme is to form a multi-level, cross-functional employee team. The SCT will have four primary objectives:

1   assess the company's current communication practices;
2   address any employee communication improvement gaps;
3   design and implement the change communication programme; and
4   serve as change ambassadors.

The team will need to be fully dedicated since they must address these objectives simultaneously, working fast to make any needed improvements in employee communication when the change programme is launched.

One requirement for having a successful SCT is to have non-communication staff make up most of the team. Although these non-communication people may need some training in the jargon of our discipline, the benefits of having diverse, front-line, operational members clearly outweigh the additional training time required. It can often mean the difference in the employee communication improvements being accepted at all levels. They become additional arms, legs, and brains for the communication staff and often become part of the change programme's mechanism that ensures the changes remain after the 'official' team no longer exists. Although the make-up of the team will differ from company to company, the characteristics of the people selected should be as follows: cross-functional, all levels and geographic locations (if relevant), respected and trusted by their peers, open and honest communicators, skilled at facilitation, and finally, they need a commitment from their supervisors to allow them the time to be a dedicated part of the team.

The SCT will be the heart of any improvement programme and will need to be carefully selected from a cross-section of the organization. They will do the day-to-day work of the employee communication improvement and change communication programmes. After the core team is formed and the preliminary analysis completed, the team can be broken down into sub-teams to focus on the topics of greatest concern. The sub-teams will be needed to manage the workload and to allow in-depth focus on the essential and immediate improvement areas. Figure 2.3 provides an example of how the SCT would fit into the organization and how the sub-teams might be organized. In this example, the sub-teams correspond to the components of the model, but these sub-team topics should grow out of the preliminary assessment to ensure they are the major communication improvement areas. The sub-teams will

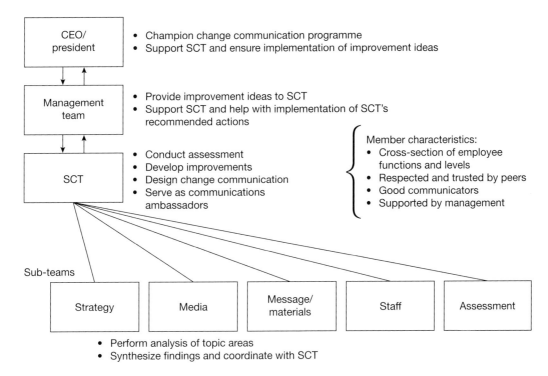

Figure 2.3 Sample SCT structure

work independently, but interact frequently to avoid duplication of effort and ensure no issues fall through the cracks.

The SCT will be linchpin of the development and implementation of the change communication programme. They will provide information from and to the organization, and they will bring credibility to the change communication effort. Just having a cross-functional, multi-level team of non-communication people working on communication sends a message in most organizations that changes are occurring. Communication starts to be seen as the responsibility of all employees, not just a select few. Also, the team members become communication ambassadors who can more effectively reach deep into the organization to ensure widespread understanding of the messages.

Assessing current communication practices

One tool that the SCT can use to facilitate the assessment is the scorecard (Figure 2.4). This scorecard allows a 'quick and dirty' assessment of the company's current communication practices. Also, use of the best-practice definitions and their opposites is one method to begin to educate management in what strategic employee communication means while determining the company's improvement targets.

In addition to the assessment, a few interviews of key managers and a cross-section of employees to gain insight into their perspectives and to start to build their support combined with an audit of current communication vehicles and a review of any employee

Where are the company's employee communication practices at present?
Place an 'x' on the scale below to indicate your preliminary assessment opinion:

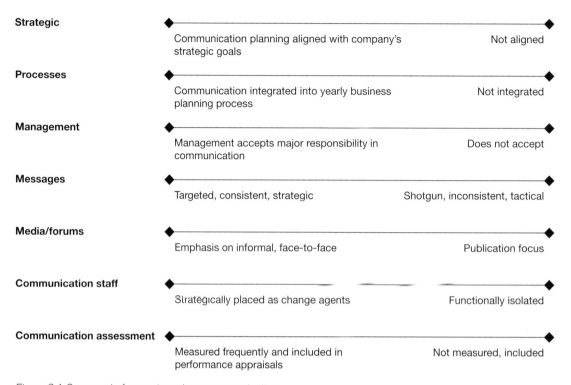

Strategic
Communication planning aligned with company's strategic goals — Not aligned

Processes
Communication integrated into yearly business planning process — Not integrated

Management
Management accepts major responsibility in communication — Does not accept

Messages
Targeted, consistent, strategic — Shotgun, inconsistent, tactical

Media/forums
Emphasis on informal, face-to-face — Publication focus

Communication staff
Strategically placed as change agents — Functionally isolated

Communication assessment
Measured frequently and included in performance appraisals — Not measured, included

Figure 2.4 Scorecard of current employee communication

surveys that human resources may have conducted will reveal enough to gain a sense of the organization's typical communication approach and any communication areas needing particular improvement. This preliminary assessment then can form the foundation on which to build the change communication programme.

Where a company ends up on each component will determine how much time and effort will be needed to improve the current employee communication practices before and during the change communication programme. A couple of the components may need to be addressed before the change programme can be fully launched, but most will

improve as the change communication programme is implemented. If, for instance, the current media are shown to be deficient in reaching employees, the SCT must find new, effective channels immediately. The workshops often serve as one of the new channels once the change programme is under way, but since the cascading workshops take some time to reach all employees, the company will need to find other ways to keep the employees informed and to ensure the change messages are getting to the targets. In addition, if the communication staff is isolated and seen as a 'publications-only' group, they will need quickly to be brought into the change process and moved into roles as facilitators. Finally, if key managers are diagnosed as uninvolved and unsupportive of communication, they will need to be coached and encouraged immediately to become a part of the employee communication improvement efforts.

The model serves as a starting point for the preliminary assessments of the current communication practices and will help determine how much improvement is necessary before the change communication programme can be successful.

Conducting cascading vision, strategy, and job redefinition workshops

The success of any change communication programme will depend on a company having a clearly stated, believed in, understood and meaningful vision statement, which management should be involved in developing and communicating. A 'meaningful' vision is more than a catchy saying on a coffee cup; it is a clear, actionable, realistic and measurable statement of what the company wants to be (Jick, 1989; Collins and Porras, 1996).

If a company already has an acceptable vision, they need only measure its understanding and reinforce it; however, often the vision no longer works for the company, particularly if they are undergoing major

changes. Therefore, the senior management group needs to convene and develop a vision that captures the company's new direction. In addition, management must define the strategic objectives that support that vision. It often helps the organization to understand the changes if they can see the key objectives as they are now and as they will be in the new organization to ensure the success of the change programme. A simple 'from/to' chart can be used to picture the changes. For example, a computer company might have the following as its vision and strategic objectives (sample only):

Vision
To be the market leader in providing high-performing, cost-effective enterprise servers, solutions and services for our customers by:

• providing products at a superior value to meet customer needs from mid-range-level to high-level functionality;
• Creating comprehensive integration of critical solution components.

The strategic objectives can then be broken into their parts to determine what the changes are in line with the new vision. Thus, their 'from/to' might be as shown in Table 2.1

Table 2.1 Strategic objectives

Strategic objectives	From	To
Providing products at superior value	Hardware, software, and solutions for all computers	Hardware and solutions only for servers and complex enterprise systems
	Value to us, low volume at high cost to customer	Value to customer, high volume, low cost
Creating integration	Fragmented products and services in isolated pockets	Connected components within the enterprise system

Once senior management has established the vision and supporting strategic objectives, then the SCT needs to develop two rounds of workshops. The first one is for the first few levels of the organization on the case for change, the major change messages, the vision, and the strategic objectives. This first round should include break-out sessions to test and refine the vision and obtain employee feedback on improvement ideas with the upper-level management across all business units. The SCT should synthesize all suggested changes to the vision and adjust the vision for each subsequent workshop. They should also collect and organize all improvement ideas into groups, arranging them into buckets according to how important and practical they are. Any ideas that can be implemented immediately, should be, which will send a signal that management is open to ideas from all levels of the organization.

Depending upon the size of the organization, these workshops will take a few months with one workshop every two weeks including twenty to thirty employees each. The vision will change somewhat with these employees playing a part in shaping it into something meaningful to all business units and most functions and levels. The key to success in these workshops is that management participates and is open to new ideas. At the same time that the change messages, including the vision and strategic objectives are evolving into something the organization as a whole can understand and act on, management is beginning to buy in to the changes themselves. Senior-level management should kick off each workshop and come back in to close, and management at all levels should be actively involved in the workshops as observers and participants.

This first round of workshops is important to gain employee confidence that the changes are important and the organization wants their support and understanding of what the changes mean. At some point (usually after meetings with 5 per cent to 10 per cent of organization), the change messages will start to receive fewer and fewer suggested changes. At that point, the SCT can consider the new vision, strategic objectives, and any other supporting change materials as established (although some minor tweaking may still be needed once the vision is to become published and communicated externally). The SCT is then ready to move into the next round of workshops.

The second round of workshops consists of a roll-out across the entire organization of the vision, strategy, and idea generation with the addition of job redefinition sessions, which are break-out discussions on how specific jobs will need to change under the new company. These, too, should include as much management involvement as possible. The leaders that emerged from the first round can be recruited to serve as ambassadors and even facilitators for this round of workshops. The more employees participating in these workshops, the better, so that the word is spread and greater buy-in is established. That will also allow faster dissemination of the change messages. These workshops must be held until everyone in the company has participated.

Monitoring the results

The results of the change programme must be monitored frequently. In the first few months, in particular, it is important to keep in close touch with how well the organization is hearing, understanding and accepting the change messages. In addition, the media need to be monitored to determine which are effective.

The quickest way to obtain a picture of the 'what' and the 'how' is to send out very short surveys to a stratified sample of the organization. Depending upon which channels work for the organization and the different groups in the company, these surveys can be distributed electronically through email or on the company intranet or distributed hard copy. Phone surveys work as well, again, depending upon the culture and the preferred way of communicating. The survey should be designed to obtain mostly facts at first. For instance, to establish facts on what messages are being received and by what means, the survey could ask: (1) What is your level of understanding of the changes occurring in the company? (2) What is your most frequent source of information about the changes? The more open-ended questions might be: (1) What is the new vision for the company? (2) What changes do you see occurring in your group that demonstrate the new vision? Only after the cascading workshops are completed would the SCT want to conduct any surveys on attitude or morale since the employees need the workshop interactions to internalize the changes and feel they are part of the new organization.

The four central actions discussed above can influence the level of success of a change communication programme, but at the end of the day, complete success depends upon the following from management:

- senior management commitment to the importance of the change communication and a willingness to devote necessary time and resources to ensure its success;
- emphasis on hands-on interaction between management and employees (small groups, two-way exchanges, idea generation sessions, job redefinition workshops);

- immediate follow-up on employee ideas and rewards for good ideas and good communication;
- barriers to success addressed immediately upon discovery;
- ongoing monitoring of communication effectiveness.

Underlying any of the critical success factors are the continual signals along the way that change is happening and that the change is making a positive difference in the way the company operates. The programme will not be judged a success unless it makes a meaningful difference not only for the employees but for the company overall. And, of course, the managers will ask, 'Was it worth all of the effort?'

One key to building management commitment is the success of the SCT along the way. If the team is functioning as it should, the company will see immediate improvement in communication from the day the team is launched. The team by its very existence demonstrates a change in most companies. The depth of its impact, however, will depend on the supporting mechanisms put in place to reinforce the team's recommended communication improvements and the frequent assessment of individual and company communication performance areas as well as the rewards for 'good' communication throughout the change programme.

Thus, the model helps to bring very specific focus on the employee communication improvement needs and to provide an analytical tool that helps to organize and control the change communication planning. In addition, it can help with implementing the changes in internal communication processes necessary to ensure the success of the change communication programme. It allows the company to determine where it needs to place its employee improvement efforts, at the same time bringing the improvements necessary to support the change programme, such as opening up the communication channels, increasing the role management plays in employee communication, and making communication central to the change programme.

Summary

In summary, change communication consists of the basic components of all good employee communication: targeted messages, selective media and clearly defined audiences, but it needs to be much more to facilitate change. During major change, effective employee communication holds an organization together, allowing the smooth operation of the organization and linking all other processes of the organization, such as the strategic and business planning processes, together to form the foundation for effective change communication. Raising employee communication to the strategic level is essential to the success of any organizational change effort.

The strategic employee communication model and best practices bring employee communication to its necessary strategic level of operation and facilitate the design of a change communication plan that can make a major change programme succeed.

In review, to develop a successful change communication programme, you should do the following:

1   Form a strategic communication team made up of a cross-functional, multi-level group of employees.
2   Assess current employee communication practices against best practices.
3   Target any gaps in communication for improvement immediately.
4   Work with senior management to develop a vision and strategic objectives.
5   Conduct cascading vision, strategy, job redefinition workshops.
6   Monitor the results throughout the change programme and be prepared to make adjustments if you find evidence of breakdowns in communication.

NOTE

1   This research included secondary research as well as interviews of Fortune 500 companies. The resulting data base contains information on the model components as well as information on the communication staff functions, organization, and budget for over 40 companies.

REFERENCES

Ashkenas, R. N. and Francis, S. C. (2000) 'Integration managers: special leaders for special times', *Harvard Business Review*. Nov.–Dec., 108–16.

Collins, J. C. and Porras, J. I. (1996) 'Building your company's vision', *Harvard Business Review Reprint*, Sept.–Oct., 65–77.

Eccles, R. G. and Nohria, N. (1992), *Beyond the Hype: Discovering the Essence of Management*, Boston: Harvard Business School Press.

Jick, T. D. (1989) 'The vision thing', *Harvard Business School Case*, Boston: Harvard Business School Press, 1–7.

Kanter, R. M., Stein, B. A. and Jick, T. D. (1992) *The Challenge of Organizational Change: How Companies Experience it and Leaders Guide It*, New York: Macmillan.

Katzenbach, J. (1995) *The Real Change Leaders: How to Create Growth and High Performance at Your Company*, New York: Random House.

Kotter, J. P. (1995) 'Leading change: why transformation efforts fail', rpt in *Harvard Business Review on Change*, Boston: Harvard Business School Press.

Strebel, P. (1996) 'Why do employees resist change?', rpt in *Harvard Business Review on Change*, Boston: Harvard Business School Press.

CHAPTER 3

Knowledge management for best practice

Stephen A. Roberts

The corporate communicator needs to know how to manage information effectively both individually and within the task/group/organizational setting. In practice corporate communication practitioners are needed who are able to exploit the riches of the world-wide web and other electronic resources with confidence and intelligence, but at the same time realize that traditional information and library skills also have their place in their practical repertoire. Such skills can reinforce strengths in business and organizational information seeking, but today and increasingly in the future this will not be enough. Full professional competence requires a mastery of a totality of capacities and qualities in information. This chapter reveals how the strategic response to this need is being realized through the development of knowledge management: as a key norm within corporate communication theory and practice.

Context

The corporate communicator's work is ethically committed to truthful and verifiable information. So, there is a premium on finding out the facts: getting the right data and information together on clients, events and issues. This contributes to the better understanding of clients' needs and enables the consideration of the right responses to problems and the construction of appropriate messages. It is normative to ensure that corporate communication action is driven by quality information: the best guarantee of quality communication. Information and knowledge management thus become complementary and self-reinforcing to corporate communication practice.

Policy and practice is moving to a state where the total management of information and knowledge resources is a desirable norm and constituent of the corporate communication function. This chapter sets out to address how this strategic goal might be achieved. It will require an exploration of concepts and practices within a considerable spectrum of information, intelligence and knowledge and a reflection on the major constituents of corporate communication practice. Concepts and terminology require definition and models of processes need elaboration to provide some intellectual cohesion.

In practical terms this means *inter alia* the following:

- Corporate communication professionals need to have a good grounding in personal information and knowledge management skills.
- Through their professional education corporate communication professionals need to acquire a good range of transferable information and communication skills to add to their general portfolio of communication and professional skills.
- The corporate communication professional needs to be able to put both understanding and skill in information management at the disposal of the client in every way as an exercise of professional techniques, through ethical and legal responsibility, and as a contribution to meeting client needs as an outcome of quality management.
- Ensuring that the corporate communication practitioner can effectively manage information and knowledge resources within their organization by the establishment of information strategy and policy, action planning and effective management of work, in order to maximise the value of information and knowledge resources and to reduce all risks to themselves and their clients arising from information and knowledge work and communication activities.

Through effective information management corporate communicators are better equipped to exploit their specialist competences in a diverse and complex world, where the understanding of and responding to stakeholder interests and claims is of the highest importance. And, responsive furthermore to the ethical and legal constraints of the environment as well as sensitive to human and social conditions. Transparency of information and communication must be a goal for all in this profession.

The information basis: a foundation for knowledge management

The concept of information provides a useful starting point for this review. Whilst not without challenge to provide a robust scientific and professional definition (as the literature of information science will show) the term has wide colloquial understanding (even misunderstanding) and literary warrant: it means something specific to most people and its meaning is frequently and currently traded. It is a useful term to denote facts, a variety of data, things which inform, things which are useful, an assortment of things which are known and it is even given further significance by statements such as 'information is power' or that information empowers. The use of information reveals it to have properties which can bring about change, transformation and gains.

Information specialists have found it helpful to use the term with greater precision, for instance distinguishing between formal information (usually considered to be published or publishable information, which has been or is going through some processes of transformation) and informal information (often information personally possessed, which is provisional, or imparted through conversation, telling and sharing and so on). Specialists take this further and distinguish between different kinds of formally published information (popular books, monographs, periodical publications and their electronic equivalents) and informal information and communication activities within a social context (meetings, seminars, conferences and even documented contributions which have received less than absolute reviewing and refereeing). Information managers (librarians, information service providers, database providers, webmasters, etc.) have elaborated their competencies and craft on this basis.

All these efforts however have seemed limited in face of the extent of human ingenuity and capacity for thought, endeavour and action. For a long time information professionals had to be content with an operational scope, which however significant, was naturally limited. They could serve their users and provide information but they could not manage their use of information (except in a limited way) and influence the effects information might produce. There were naturally limits to their role in any grand shaping of knowledge (and never did they realistically claim such ambitions). Nevertheless, the impetus to seek greater management capacity over the totality of information has evolved along with the growing complexity of the modern world. Inevitably, the desire and need for a strategic capacity over information has extended to capacities over a more total range of behaviours. The human processing of information towards knowledge gained and retained has indicated where this strategic capacity lies and has suggested necessary and useful responses. The management of information has been progressing towards realizing the capacity to manage knowledge. This movement began professionally in the mid-1970s with the emergence of informa-

tion resource management and by the late 1980s was consolidating around the emergent practices of knowledge management.

Information and knowledge management has emerged as a corporate and business related activity, stemming from initiatives in market research, market, product and competitive intelligence, business information, management information, consulting, modelling, decision support and business and corporate policy. It also continues to have a significant impact on the work of library and information professionals who form a significantly valuable feature of the knowledge supply chain for such communities.

The relevance of information and knowledge management to corporate communication lies in the importance of *information as a resource* in the organization and in the corporate communication process. Successful corporate communication is driven by many other forces and requirements, but the techniques of information and communication used and their management form a common infrastructural element.

The study of corporate communication requires an understanding of both the business and client environments and management principles and practices, as well as issues relating to information *per se*. Information and knowledge management features have evolved concurrently with changes in the business environment: for example, the influence of the information and communication technologies; strategic business and IT; the global marketplace; the virtual corporation and e-business and e-commerce. The current importance and impact of the worldwide web in marketing and corporate communication is now an accepted feature.

Whilst the corporate environment has engendered knowledge management, the future will see wider ramifications in society and for the citizen as a whole: for those who inhabit the global corporate marketplace as citizens, rather than for those who just work in the global corporation or local enterprise.

These trends in information and knowledge management are already impacting on corporate communication, through digital media and electronic business and commerce. Citizens in general and in their roles such as employees and consumers, as well as other stakeholders, are discovering new means of empowerment through the information and communication technologies (ICTs). Such empowerment has to be understood by the practitioner and reflected in new methods, means and balances of communication activity.

The domain and discipline of knowledge management has emerged partly as the information and communication technologies have come to form an infrastructure for many kinds of data and information related activities in organizations and society. It has also emerged in relation to secular and structural changes in markets, business environments, global conditions and new technologies.

Knowledge management extends the already developed concept of *information* (explicit knowledge) and *intelligence* (often a hybrid of explicit and tacit knowledge) as a resource, by incorporating, amongst others, the concepts of tacit and shared knowledge as leading paradigms. Knowledge management extends existing concepts of comparative and competitive advantage in the corporation or firm (based on strategic use of IT and transaction cost concepts) through to the idea of knowledge resources (intellectual capital and intellectual assets), which thrive best in holistic and synergistic environments characterized as the knowledge organization and the learning organization.

The corporate communicator has always been an information worker, and can ever more now be considered a knowledge worker. Corporate communicators will find it vital to incorporate knowledge-related concepts into their professional practice in a more explicit way than hitherto. Knowledge-based organizations and clients will be best served by knowledge-sensitive corporate communicators.

The theories and practices of information management, organizational management and behavioural science as leading tools and techniques provide the tools and techniques for knowledge management as an integrated, hybrid and synthetic methodology which exploits information as a resource, facilitates organizational and individual decision making, and acknowledges the ways in which the *resourcefulness* of information (and knowledge) produces and necessitates change in organizational and individual behaviour as goal fulfilment is sought.

The rationale for this application to corporate communication lies in the progressive evolution of information and communication activities in a global setting. Information systems, information management and information services provide the platform upon which the higher order range of knowledge-related activities are built. In the education of the corporate communicator the incorporation of these studies and practices is a natural progression for intellectual and professional development.

Informational aims and objectives

In developing a programme for knowledge management in corporate communication the following aims can be selected:

- The identification of the concepts of data, information, intelligence and knowledge as they occur and impact on the discipline and practice.
- An exploration of the methods, techniques and circumstances in which information, intelligence and knowledge management principles can be applied to corporate communication.
- The incorporation of the social, behavioural and organizational conditions associated with information and knowledge management in corporate communication settings.
- The development of strategies by which organizations and stakeholders select and promote data and information and to examine the consequences which ensue.
- The identification of the intelligence needs of clients in specific settings and to research, collect and present their findings to their clients.
- The exploitation of the capacities of ICTs and information handling tools to support knowledge management and to meet the knowledge needs of client communities and domains of practice.
- The identification and development of criteria on which the basis of information, intelligence and knowledge activities can be evaluated.
- The evaluation of the impact of information, intelligence and knowledge management strategies, resources and techniques on client communities and domains of practice.

The discussion that follows explores this agenda firstly from a conceptual viewpoint and then develops a practical programme that could help to build the relevant competences for corporate communication professionals.

The information and communication rationale

Information management and the corporate communicator

The principles discussed here are designed to underpin the skills and competences of corporate communicators by providing a disciplined understanding and insight into information and communication. Some familiarity with the professional world of information and knowledge management practice will help corporate communicators explain their information needs to information specialists and provide a body of knowledge and competence to achieve a degree of autonomy in working with information both with corporate communication colleagues and with clients.

This autonomy and competence will increase the efficiency, effectiveness and responsiveness of the corporate communicator. This will help to underpin corporate communication techniques and solutions by providing sound information and communication strategies.

The information and communication cycle

The idea of an information and communication cycle is one of the fundamental concepts of information analysis. The corporate communicator will already be familiar with analogies to the information and communication cycle (ICC) in marketing and media activity. Rowley (1999) offers an interpretation of the ICC from the perspective of information management. Such a model can suggest the intensities and directions of flow of information (for example from a demand and supply perspective) which can be applied to corporate communication settings.

Questions for the corporate communicator include: how much information exists about a given issue; who is in possession of such information; what is the level of quality of the information; what is the nature of the communication activities used and preferred; how can information be processed and managed at different points in the cycle to relate to different needs and conditions; what are the optimum methods to gather, store, analyse and retrieve information; how can relevant information be targeted to the stakeholders and their concerns.

Communication refers to the process of information transfer and the initiation and reception of communicated content. *Information* refers generically to content which can take many forms: data, information, intelligence, knowledge. The variety of forms of both information and communication are numerous. Two related concepts can also be introduced. *Supply* denotes broadly the availability of content. *Demand* implies states of want, need and requirement for content which may or may not be expressed or realized. Demand and supply are also used as more technical terms in economic analysis, and these analyses are also relevant to the study of information.

Information management is concerned centrally with the management of information supply and the mediation of information demand. This information management activity can be carried out individually, collectively and institutionally; in reality the three contexts are frequently simultaneously active. This suggests that information management is a dynamic area; it is active and proactive, rather than passive. The central task is underpinned by techniques in data and information (and document) storage, handling, retrieval,

analysis and exploitation. Nowadays these technical resources can be delivered equally to the desktop and to the field of operation using mobile communications. There are many circumstances where these techniques have to be practised and applied in varied and unstable field conditions. It is in these circumstances that the information and knowledge experienced corporate communicator will have the advantage.

Definitions of information management

Information management is concerned with the selection, evaluation, description, storage, retrieval, manipulation and presentation of information.

(Askew 2000)

Information management (IM) can be defined literally as the formal organization of handling of information.

(Roberts 1997)

These definitions can be realized in terms of activities undertaken by professional information specialists (information manager, library and information service providers, etc.), in terms of personal competences, and in the wider social and organizational setting of corporate communication.

The two definitions of information management are *complementary*. Askew gives emphasis to the process itself, and directly suggests a sequence of functions which have a good fit to parts of the information–communication cycle. Roberts implies the functions denoted by Askew and which are implicated in Rowley's interpretation (1999) but which embodies a general (if abstract) concept of organization (formal, rather than informal; more structured rather than less structured). The lack of formal organization implies disorder, chaos, randomness, chance and suggests inefficiency and lack of effective performance.

However, it may be possible for information management to take place in informal circumstances and still be very effective (e.g. grapevine-style communication that propagates positive information). But such apparently informal environments may have an implicit formal structure embedded in them.

Knowledge is a much more comprehensive and inclusive complex: it has to be defined not only in terms of content but also in terms of time, space, experience, learning and organizational and social activity. What is recognized so far is that information management is a *core contributory element* to the growth of knowledge management as a competence, within the wider knowledge space (of interpersonal frameworks and so-called learning organizations, e.g. enterprises which have adopted knowledge management strategies/practices to contribute to their development, or groups of practitioners in 'communities of practice', who collaborate to share, discover and create new knowledge).

The incorporation of *knowledge management* in the core practice of information professionals reflects contemporary trends as well as potential future goals for information management. IM (information management) and KM (knowledge management) can have separation but are best developed when intimately related.

As previously stated, knowledge management extends the already developed concept of *information as a resource* by incorporating amongst others, the concepts of tacit and shared knowledge as leading paradigms. It is thus possible to talk about knowledge resources (intellectual capital and intellectual assets), which are best disseminated and exploited in a more holistic environment.

In practice knowledge management can flourish optimally in particular kinds of organizational context which are associated with particularly characteristic social behaviours (e.g. Leonard-Barton, 1995; Nonaka and Takeuchi, 1995).

Data, information, intelligence and knowledge: concepts

It is helpful to make clear some distinctions and definitions, especially relating to data, information, intelligence and knowledge. Better awareness of them will help corporate communicators improve, even optimize, their information and knowledge management.

Data can be regarded as the most elemental level of analysis; a 'bit' is the smallest unit of analysis. Data can take various forms. At its most basic, Shannon and Weaver (1949) argued that it can be represented as a binary state (On or Off/1 or 0). In a computer, information (and more complex units of data) is represented as binary data, and can therefore be manipulated in an electronic state through flows of energy in switches, gates and other devices.

Data is also used as a concept and term to represent more complex constructs such as numerical values and linguistic symbols (through alphabets). When these data elements are combined in various ways human beings have the capacity to give them an enriched context and by passing through certain thresholds of presentation and comprehension (which may be conventional or arbitrary) the resulting aggregate is usually called *information*.

For example, as this process is activated data is given greater meaning. When all the cells of data in a spreadsheet are seen as a whole they may be given greater meaning as a set of information (which can be presented to a client, stakeholder or decision maker). For example, statistical analysis of the data would help to increase its meaning or value as data or information. To be more accurate we can say that the probability of this increase in meaning and value happening is greater.

Shannon and Weaver developed their ideas through studies of telephony. Their ideas helped to map out a debate about the nature of information, leading on towards the digital concepts which sustain the present generation of computer based technologies. These technologies are already influencing the ways in which organizations function and within which knowledge management will be a forceful activity. The resulting organizational model is the *knowledge organization* (exhibiting characteristics of learning and experience) or the *learning organization*. Use of technology is significant and necessary in the knowledge organization but is not sufficient. These organizations will be rich in data becoming information, but it will be of little value and significance if such data (and information) is not refined and processed by predominantly social exchanges towards intelligence and knowledge.

Linguistic data when highly structured in the form of language which can convey meaning in spoken words and written text, is certainly to be considered as being more complex. Two people can read the same text and draw widely different inferences and meaning from it.

Information it seems true to say owes a good deal to data of different kinds and to the systems by which data is manipulated. Information, like data, can be freely created, acquired, stored, processed and transferred through different distribution channels. In reality, there is a fierce debate about the nature of information but we can accept it pragmatically as a central operational concept.

Knowledge: how can it be defined?

Arising from the preceding discussion about some precursors of knowledge there is some indication as to how knowledge can be defined in the context of information management and its potential contribution to knowledge management. Pragmatically, other debates about the nature of knowing and knowledge have to be set aside; for example, those prevalent in the fields of philosophy, psychology and sociology.

The capacity to know things and to be conscious of what is known could be defined as Knowledge (with a large 'K'): this is human intelligence itself and the intelligent properties derived from perception, which itself makes use of the psychological and biological processes). Knowledge with a small 'k' comprises the things which can be known in a specific sense and whose intelligent properties are understood through human intelligence.

In practice we can safely use the term knowledge (with a large 'K' or a small 'k') as an aggregate term to mean those things which are perceived to be intelligent (having properties of being known or revealing knowledge) or as intelligence (as a source of knowing). In addition, and very commonly, the aggregate concept of 'knowledge' is used to represent things which are known by people, either individually or collectively. This aggregate 'knowledge' is also endowed with many properties: part of the purpose of knowledge management as a process is to study and act on these properties of knowledge, especially as they occur in and affect organizations and other social complexes.

Intelligence and knowledge

It is sometimes worth differentiating between the *intelligence phase of knowledge* and the *end state of knowledge*, as when things are more completely known (things are never known in full!). This is the case when looking at sources of intelligence (e.g. as in competitive intelligence), and how they are exploited and managed, and how they contribute to forming knowledge. In practical terms much intelligence gathering activity has to be accomplished in order to locate, acquire and create knowledge, therefore we need to be aware and explicit about its contribution to knowledge.

An equation might be of the form:

Intelligence + knowledge (things already known) = More valuable Knowledge

(note the distinction between the sense of large K and small k). Or

Intelligence (potential knowledge)
   + knowledge (existing and known)
   = More valuable Knowledge (large 'K')

Returning to the example of the spreadsheet, we can say that intelligence is embedded in the data plus information in the cells and the matrix as a whole. But crucially it is only realized as intelligence when an external perception is brought to bear on it. The natural intelligence of the perceiver's mind is brought to bear on it within their experience and learning. It is similar to the case of the two people reading the text above and drawing different conclusions from it.

They draw different conclusions by virtue of who they are, what they do, what they already know, their past experience, their future expectations, capacity to learn and so on. It is all relativistic, probabilistic and fuzzy; you may be more right or you may be less wrong – it all depends. You may only know a partial answer to this set, when some decisive event occurs to assist interpretation.

A company's failure to gain market share or the misfortune to go bankrupt is severe indeed, but absolute blame can or cannot be laid on the state of knowledge possessed before the damaging event. Lessons can be learned from this; many businesspeople have become more skilled entrepreneurs and managers after a disaster, from which they have found powers of recovery. On the other hand there are many who do not experience this learning: better knowledge management is clearly what they might require. This rather depressing example is not so gloomy as it seems. It shows that knowledge is also positively correlated with a capacity to learn.

Many knowledge management specialists have come to talk about the 'learning organization'; a knowledge organization is (amongst other things) a learning organization, which manages to apply what it knows and learns and which thus understands how to persistently avoid catastrophes and to capitalize on what it knows.

At the point of an act of reading by two individuals, it would be fair to say that both intelligent readings of the text might have equal potential value. But we come close to a definition of intelligence drawn from the text, as well as acted upon, when the future demonstrates that one reader put the perception to better use than the other. A positive outcome might be regarded as confirming the value of the intelligence gained from a reading of the text.

One helpful practical outcome from this discussion is that it indicates how necessary it is to cultivate skills in intelligence from the point of view of identifying it, capturing and processing it, and putting it to good use. Corporate communication is rich in similar analogies from the business and corporate client field. Determining a client's needs and offering clients advice requires depths of intelligence as well as a thorough sifting of data, facts and information. The same set of information is susceptible to different readings, so corporate communicators weigh up intelligence and draw upon intuition, experience, analogy and metaphor to shape and deliver campaigns. Through the same process they develop their professional knowledge as a variety of intellectual capital.

Definitions of knowledge: a conceptual basis

Some attempt at a working definition of knowledge has already been made through the exploration of data, information and intelligence which leads to an appreciation of knowledge operationally and resourcefully: the sense that a desirable purpose is to consider how to manage it for beneficial ends.

For argument the distinction between small 'k' knowledge and large 'K' knowledge is maintained. The former small 'k' knowledge results as a reaction to known intelligence (derived from information and data). A person will possess knowledge when they have absorbed the potential of a given 'intelligence'. The process of absorption itself is a critical component of knowledge management. Someone will know something to some degree, and furthermore will hope that it will lead to/contribute to positive outcomes when this is necessary (this may protect them from

danger as much as to make an economic, social or political gain).

Knowledge with a large 'K' can be defined as an aggregate of intelligence and knowledge derived from intelligence (which may be traced back to antecedent information and data) and will show states of extension and completion. In usual discourse (and in this chapter) the distinction between 'large' and 'small' is lost. However it is described, knowledge may lead the possessor towards outcomes either positive or negative but both reflecting the resourcefulness of what is known.

Knowledge is now considered conventionally as intellectual capital or assets. Stewart (1997) amongst others identifies customer capital (client embodied knowledge), human capital (especially the competences embodied in the organization's community of practice – its people and human resources), and structural capital (embodied in organizational structures and systems). There is also proprietary intellectual property (designs, patents, agreements, etc.) which seeks to enjoy legal protection as well as other information assets. This intellectual capital is matched by financial capital and physical assets. It is very clear that corporate communication professionals have always worked predominantly with intellectual capital. Knowledge management, as much as information management, should now be seen as a core professional competence enabling the fullest exploitation of intellectual assets and capital.

Knowledge management

Knowledge-based work and management is distinct from, although related to, other situations and people who work with and manage data (statisticians, data processors of various kinds in organizations, data warehousers, etc.) and information (library and information service personnel, library and information service professionals, documentalists, publishers, web page providers and a diversity of content providers, who work across the spectrum from data to knowledge).

In the corporate world it has become increasingly common to define knowledge work and workers as a distinct cluster, which may be supported by data processors, librarians and information managers, to name but a few. It is also clear that many consultants, experts, academics, pundits, journalists and analysts can also be regarded as knowledge-based workers doing knowledge work. We certainly have to include corporate communicators amongst this band.

'Know-what' and 'know-how' criteria

The existence and reality of knowledge can now be understood more effectively as a result of its distinctive contexts and processes. It is not enough to regard knowledge as just a denser form of information and intelligence ('know-what') but as a source of action, potential, capacity for change and competence (often referred to as 'know-how'). Knowledge management is therefore about achieving this state of know-how through intelligence gathering and managing knowledge resources (intellectual capital/assets) and of fostering, maximizing and increasing the stock of it. The reality that the prime exponents of this art in the 1990s and early 2000s are business corporations has led to the idea of the new organizational type: the knowledge organization (sometimes also known as a learning organization, reflecting the role of learning processes in acquiring knowledge).

Many commentators have chosen to make a helpful distinction between *know-what* and *know-how*. As a working hypothesis know-what is raw and less refined information (it may be descriptive, factual, situational, historical, spatial, and so on). As formal information it is typically stored and transmitted in hard copy and electronic documents and databases. Equally, it may have characteristics of informal information (mediated personally, disseminated socially and ranging from the vaguest to the most concrete and specific). It tends to lack or need further interpretation, contextualization and combination with other sources, factors and insights. Higher-order information may show characteristics of intelligence (actual and potential added value, scarcity through limited ownership, confidentiality, conferment of advantage, etc.). Know-what is often equated as the factual, explicit, visible and easily transmissible information.

Know-how has the characteristics of knowledge (source of action, potential, capacity for change and competence) to which the learning organization aspires and which lead it as an organization to acquire, create and maximize the value of the knowledge it possesses. It is likely to reflect experience, evaluation, appraisal, deeper consideration, special insight and so on. These mark out the intangible qualities which define tacit knowledge, and which clearly require further and particular technique to realize its value and resourcefulness. Knowledge management provides the tools and techniques to harness these qualities in a purposeful way. Thus, a very important distinction has emerged in differentiating between 'know-what and know-how.

Knowledge management theorists regard know-what as explicit knowledge. A collection of textual documents can be read by many people who may or may not draw similar conclusions from what they read. The text remains the same and this factual/ informational know-what can be accessed again and again.

By reading, the reader has already started to process the text towards knowledge. This reader/user act of transformation is unique to the reader (unless the reader chooses to share that understanding and knowledge with another agent). The intelligent and thoughtful reading of the text has created a situation of tacit knowledge. This tacitly derived and interiorized knowledge is know-how as tacit (implicit) knowledge. However, tacit know-ledge never exists in the explicit recorded and visible state, although it may be made explicit by telling or recording.

Identifying, extracting, sharing and leverag-ing this hidden knowledge has become the driving task of practical knowledge manage-ment. The world of information is largely the world of explicit and revealed knowledge, although its extraction and management may require very considerable labour and expense. To a degree, the world of information is also preoccupied with making the implicit visible and tangible. Knowledge management thus grows in importance when what is known is largely implicit (and only partially usable) but is needed by the collective. In all this, intelligence stands midway between informa-tion and knowledge: it is knowledge applied to information (and data) with the purpose of extracting meaning and value.

The difference between *explicit knowledge* and *tacit knowledge* is crucial to an under-standing of knowledge management. Arising from this distinction knowledge management theorists and practitioners maintain and build the need for a whole new approach to organ-izational design and behaviour.

Tacit knowledge is locked-in to the knower and to many knowers in an organization. Thus

its location, storage, transfer and use has to be managed in ways different to explicit visible knowledge (better referred to as data and information).

Looking at these ways of dealing with tacit knowledge and with the boundary between tacit and explicit knowledge is at the heart of knowledge and learning organizations which depend on knowledge management strategies for their survival and growth, and are depen-dent on it for their comparative advantage and competitive edge.

Corporate communicators work in an information society and their corporate clients work in knowledge-based environments. Their stakeholders too are increasingly en-meshed in a global information society. The corporate communicator needs to have access to the extensive range of data, information and intelligence resources which represent their clients' and stakeholders' interests. From the basis of these collective resources corpor-ate communication strategy, policy, message and response can be built to develop image, identity and reputation.

Knowledge management: elements of an operational definition

- Knowledge management attempts to rep-resent a comprehensive approach to exploiting what is known in order to gain insight, beneficiality and greater control over actions and their outcomes.
- Knowledge management strategies repre-sent useful approaches to gaining out-comes through knowledge discovery, transfer, sharing, utilisation and creation.
- Knowledge may be derived from data, information, intelligence and above all from experience and learning. Different

tools, techniques, methods and principles and circumstances are used (as methodologies) to support strategies and management.

- Knowledge management, knowledge strategies and knowledge methodologies can operate in both personal and collective domains, and in the private and public domains.

Seeking highly structured, generalized and watertight definitions of knowledge and its practices is neither practical nor realistic. This view is consistent with the tacit, implicit, fuzzy, soft, metaphorical, metaphysical, probabilistic, sticky characteristics of the components of knowing and knowledge; the experiential, the social, the embedded, the partial and the circumstantial aspects.

A programme for practice in information and knowledge management

Suggestions for a programme in information and knowledge management in corporate communication are offered as a basis for practice. The themes presented are based on a module offered in a postgraduate course delivered to students of corporate communication Thames Valley University (Roberts, 2002).

Information management

The preceding discussion has presented the main concepts of information management which form a foundation for knowledge management. The first step is to acknowledge the importance of more formalized information management as a part of corporate communi-

cation practice. This will be assisted by the incorporation of some studies of information and its management in programmes of training and education; the value of journalistic, advertising and similar media skills and training is already acknowledged in corporate communication. This awareness will enhance practitioner skills and in due course will raise a more strategic awareness of information professionalism in the field.

The ever more widespread use of the ICTs in business and professional practice will reinforce information use and personal skill in a variety of ways: word processing, working with databases and spreadsheets, use of websites and search engines, experience with multimedia and so on. Given the appropriate settings and scales of activity, the further professionalization of this usage and a perception of enhanced service based upon them will be seen as relevant. Support for the use of ICTs can lead to a demand for better management of service and the provision of added value and resource enhancing services.

Corporate communicators need access to professional support and expertise to deliver effective information management, but can benefit from personal skill enhancement.

Information resources: producers and users

The information management model will function more effectively where there is greater knowledge of the information resources (the raw material and content) and sources (the forms in which the resources are held). Within the corporate communication process strategic and tactical advantages will be gained when both information and knowledge resources are developed and held more systematically at a personal and organizational level.

Information resources provide the evidence base for the process (data, factual information, published information, etc.) but the major drivers of corporate communication will be intelligence and knowledge based, derived from both internal and external sources. The knowledge based information resource must also be managed; hence strategies and tactics for handling implicit, hidden and individual knowledge are required.

The knowledge based resources show that the users and actors are themselves producers of further resource. Knowledge management has therefore to capture this resource, process it, store it and make it available through sharing, communication and demonstration and so on such that its value is realized. In this way existing knowledge will breed more knowledge. Management of this resource needs to generate explicit evidence of the tacit and implicit features of knowledge. Purposive social and organizational communication, acts of recognition, sharing, analysis, critique and exchange promote tacit revelation. Meetings, acts of recorded communication, archives, databases, indexes, search tools and strategies, intranets and other technology mediated communication form part of this process. Vian and Johansen (in Ruggles, 1997) summarized features of the role of technology: intensive personal interaction, emphasis on the group, users working with producers, the valuing of chance encounters, asynchronous communication and asynchronous thought, divergence, informality, and the acceptance of technology as a participant.

Information and communication skills

Successful corporate communication is indubitably about information and communi-cation skill combined with all the other requisites of knowledge and practice in the field. The assertion made in this chapter is that this has to be supplemented with enhanced *management* capacities: these will be partly at the personal level (in the form of the information and knowledge aware practitioner) and substantially at the corporate level where greater support will be beneficial. Individual knowledge and information resources need to be opened up for sharing and collective appraisal and utilization.

Vital personal skills include knowing about information and needs and requirements, skill in selecting and retrieving information, tools for building messages, selecting communication channels fit for the task on hand, exploiting informal communication and formal information resources, and skills in oral, written and visual communication.

Dissemination, projection and mediation

These three functions are amongst the roots of public relations practice and have a proportionate presence in corporate communication. By defining them as within the scope of information and knowledge management their range of effect is extended.

Whilst the distribution of a press release is an act of dissemination so also is the wider scale of tackling the dissemination of knowledge within the group and between stakeholders. Vian and Johansen's view of computer mediated communication indicates the more extensive scope and effects which can be secured through the use of technology to manage knowledge.

The three functions are also roots of knowledge management: dissemination requires sharing and exchange; projection considers the wider tasks of disseminating knowledge and mediation acknowledges the wide variety of processes through which knowledge permeates and is received. Knowledge management will support a collective responsibility and culture to exercise these functions and extract (leverage) value from what is known.

Organizing information in practice

Whether acting in an individual consultant capacity or within the corporate role there is a need to organize information both in and for practice. All professionals need to exercise personal information management (correspondence, diaries, working papers, archival papers, email, phone logs, etc.) and to manage personal information needs (reading current documents, personal current awareness needs, identifying current project information requirements, etc.).

With increasing task complexity and workload personal information management may prove insufficient and the symptoms of information overload and personal stress may become evident. In these settings supportive and professionally executed information management is indicated. This may take the form of a sharing of information handling burdens amongst colleagues and support staff, but this may not be sufficient. Professional libraries and information services will support some of this burden on an outsourcing or commercial basis, but given the nature and complexity of corporate communication projects this is unlikely to satisfy. Dedicated information management support is the remedy at hand.

What can be used to underpin information management (library and information services, administrative and secretarial support,

etc.) may also assist in the formalization of approaches to knowledge management, but there are limitations. Knowledge management needs more than external support and technological support. It requires a fuller and more active participation of those who work with knowledge to exploit the potential for sharing and exchange – the bases for knowledge creation itself. This participation may become substantially based on supportive technology such as the corporate intranet, data and knowledge warehouses and combinations of information and intelligence handling practice. Yet, it will only thrive on active participation of those involved. An intranet alone will not deliver knowledge management solutions: users have to be active contributors and active exploiters fulfilling both roles extensively.

Models of information and knowledge organization in any field have to move to active and participative mode. Knowledge managers, as autonomous and trained specialists, will be needed to share the burden with the main actors rather than to substitute for them. The corporate communicators have to take the responsibility for the professional practice and solutions, but their burden is to an extent shared with knowledge managers. Burden sharing enables true professional responsibility to be carried.

ICTs and electronic environments

Corporate communication practice is being continually modified and influenced by the development of the ICTs. Its practitioners thus have a significant responsibility to equip themselves to use and exploit these technologies to the full. At the personal level the necessary skills are becoming part of education and learning and are being diffused widely. However, at the project and corporate level the need to secure, invest in and access the hardware platforms is a task of some magnitude. The application of the technology requires support and indicates the need for information strategies tailored to corporate communication and the development of information systems and management skills to comparable levels.

Intelligence gathering and knowledge development

Intelligence can be gathered across the complete spectrum of communication and exchange: it may be gathered deliberately and systematically (as in market and competitive intelligence), circumstances may assist awareness and interception (being in the right place at the right time), and it may be culled in a serendipitous fashion (from a whole variety of inputs, observations, conversations and suchlike). Since the assembly of dissimilar and corroborative information and the scope for reflection and inference are vital parts of intelligence gathering and work, it will be necessary to maximize actual and potential information flows around events and to provide human resource and opportunity to analyse the evidence gathered. The cultivation of environments to generate these requirements and opportunities should be part of the information strategy developed around each corporate communication problem.

Intelligence itself is one of the precursors of knowledge formation. There can be reciprocal action between the two processes. Improved knowledge may clarify the needs for both intelligence and information. Intelligence management supports knowledge management and vice versa.

Writing, editing and publishing

Written communication has played an extensive part in PR and is a substantial tool for corporate communication. Defining messages, crafting them with precision and targeting them effectively are key skills. The sharper and more professional these skills are the better. Corporate communicators need to appraise, critique and value the sources of information they use in written communication: information awareness and information management play their part in this process. The review of information constitutes a significant part of the editing process and leads to the formation of the messages to be communicated through publishing, broadcast and presentation. These tasks require dealing with both content and format. Information management underpins the area of content whilst knowledge management underpins decision making about format, distribution, dissemination and assists evaluation processes. The recruitment market in PR and corporate communication gives a good idea about the centrality of these skills and professional education programmes and training should already provide the wherewithal. Improvements in information and knowledge practice should be sought to strengthen the underpinning and the results achieved measured through changing behaviour, impact of messages, acceptance, market positioning and sustenance of identity, image and reputation.

Networking and contacts

Knowledge activities have a strong social component and in corporate communication, a field characterized by social exchanges, the transition to knowledge based environments and activities would seem to be a natural one to achieve. Rich networks of contacts form a primary resource for knowledge building. But they cannot be assumed to provide lasting effectiveness, and therefore should be maintained and cultivated. The knowledge management culture of the kind sought and proposed for corporate communication should encourage this maintenance as a natural outcome of the adoption of the processes.

Corporate communicators need strategies to sustain communication with stakeholders; they need to track the development of networks and register the resources in the form of indexes of expertise; social networks need to be treated as knowledge networks; for longer-term productivity appropriate etiquette should be followed and networks need to be reinforced, steered and sometimes influenced. Since many networks and contacts are maintained electronically (which is convenient) the fundamental value of personal and face-to-face communication must still be maintained. Networks of contacts should not be taken for granted; reciprocity is essential.

Strategy, policy and planning

Even the individual consultant can find value in a more systematic approach to their information and knowledge management. Personal strategy is a valuable concept especially where it helps maintain a conscious approach to information needs, seeking and value. The larger the group the greater the need for awareness of the acts of individuals and a collective strategy can encourage and support this.

In larger groups with access to professional information support and management sound strategy needs to be developed and should provide a basis for identifying policies and for planning information and knowledge management.

Media and press relations and practice

In public relations and public affairs the use of media, press relations and practice are central to the key processes. Within the strategic vision, which is natural to and effective for corporate communication, media and press relations have a relative and practical importance in a tactical setting. But a common framework of information and knowledge management could, if developed in the settings of practice, serve both complementary specialities to good effect.

Information mediated through PR techniques and released to the audience has to be of the highest standards of quality with respect to source, attribution, currency, accuracy, perspective, objectivity and so on. It can observe these criteria and yet still be persuasive by the way of crafting messages to meet circumstances and audiences.

The better management of the knowledge resource overall can assist in sourcing information, give confidence that the base of information used is unrivalled and ensure that the messages produced are fit for the purpose and robust enough to be defended should they face dissent, contingency or crisis. Good information is not just power but a source of public confidence.

Resourcing information and communication activities

In this context resourcing refers to the financial and budgetary dimension. In the real world of organizations the range of practice and funding is wide. Once the essential goals of information and knowledge strategy and policy have been clarified the funding implications can be considered. Information service professionals will be able to deal with the operational questions raised and make plans, allocate resources and construct budgets according to the constraints. What has to be ensured is that the expected benefits are going to exceed the costs incurred. In this aspect performance measures for information activities and frameworks and methods for evaluation have a crucial role to play.

However, where tangible resources are managed and information is well packaged in services, databases, documents, etc., the linear economics of information provision and resourcing can be managed in practice. On the other hand the worlds of knowledge are non-linear and considerably flexible. Difficulties are bound to ensue as the practice passes from information processes to knowledge processes: from the explicit to the tacit environment. One way to deal with this in practice is to treat the explicit information environment as an overhead for the sequential production and management of knowledge. That is to say that if the focus of attention is adequately resourced from the explicit side the tacit environment can function as a marginally costed activity. Knowledge-seeking-and-using behaviour is not restricted by physical resources and capital, hence its identification as intellectual capital, inexhaustible brainpower. *Know-what* has direct costs but *know-how* is an indirect cost (its overhead cost is infinitely spread) and has potentially limitless value.

Knowledge is thus an inherent resource: it does have to be extracted and there are some costs involved in this process (tacit procedures become explicit) but the ratio of value to cost is frequently going to be positive, although still difficult to measure in monetary terms in many cases.

In operational settings of corporate communication it is prudent to consider informa-tion (and knowledge) activities as a source of expense, requiring appropriate resourcing (institutionally and/or individually) and potentially as an area for targeted investment. This resourcing of information will also serve to lay down bases for knowledge processing and management. But, much of knowledge management is the utilization of accumulated capital in terms of human experience and knowledge. It may be substantially in situ (in mente) and require greater expenditure of time rather than money to extract. This resource then has to be mobilized by behaviour and acts of will rather than through financial expenditure. Data, information and some intelligence activities have to be specifically resourced, but much intelligence and very substantially the knowledge activities require significantly less expenditure to leverage and exploit.

Performance measurement

Corporate communicators have their own sets of performance measures to determine their business success: these are not the concern of the present discussion. However, from an information and communication perspective the effectiveness of information seeking and information and knowledge management should be seen as a contribution to overall corporate communication effectiveness. Information and knowledge delivery to the right person, at the right time, in the right place in sufficient quantity and of excellent quality must be a significant factor in corporate communication.

Haphazard information management and insufficient leverage of knowledge are symptoms of individual overload and stress which can be ameliorated by stepping up information support and professional assistance in management of these resources. There are many professional technologies and methods which can be used to improve information and knowledge handling performance (organized libraries and document collections, classification and indexing methods, retrieval tools, databases, internet use, web technologies, mobile communications, personal information organizers, intranets, knowledge warehouses, expertise indexes and many more). Better information performance will be reflected in raised professional performance.

Evaluation of corporate communication activities

In the fullest sense evaluation is focused on the end user and the ultimate achievement of goals. Clients, stakeholders and publics will be the evaluators of the success of images, identities and reputations. It has been the focus of this review of information tools and processes to indicate the range of possibilities in information and knowledge management which when used will support corporate communication activities and thereby achieve the maximum positive evaluations, measured by problems solved, satisfied clients, restored reputations, favourable publics and well focused and growing organizational capacities.

Information resources, value and technology

However important knowledge is, in the final analysis, its management is likely to be founded best on good information management. Whatever information resources are identified and used in a corporate communication context the information management

task is to maximize the value of the information. Value can be conceptualized as resourcefulness and seen in terms of potential for problem solving and decision making. The corporate communicator as information manager has to identify and select the most potentially resourceful information or to ensure that it is provided for the task on hand.

Information management has increasingly developed around the use of computers and telecommunications (the information and communication technologies: ICTs). The internet and the worldwide web represent the contemporary generation of these ICTs utilizing digitized input, hypertext, multimedia, high-speed data transmission and broad bandwidth.

Within and from this environment the virtual organization has evolved. In popular terms the dot.com enterprise, the e-business engaged in e-commerce. What consequences these new organizational forms will have for corporate communication is still a matter of some debate. Is it a case of new technologies grafted on the older organizational structures and models? Or is the model of the virtual environment radically different?

Some factors are becoming clearer:

- Organizations and stakeholders are becoming more connected by using common technological platforms.
- Information circulation, communication and messaging has become more rapid: good and bad news can travel more quickly to more people.
- Technological diffusion has to some extent created more players and in theory this can create a more 'democratic' environment for corporate communication.
- The boundaries between corporate and personal/individual/private are being readjusted.

- Corporate society is becoming increasingly globalized by its use of new technologies.

If information technology and information management provide a catalyst for communication activity how is corporate communication to be managed in an increasingly information and communication rich environment?

The strategic perspective becomes increasingly important and points towards some practical solutions for corporate communication. The development of information management strategies and policies can be seen as a response for more effective corporate communication in an informatized and globalized world.

The way forward

The impact of the information and communication technologies is shaping the development of corporate communication theory and practice in a substantial way. However, the well tried and tested means of information and communication activity will maintain their importance. The choice of media may have broadened but making the right choices to use and practise is still going to require skill and experience.

Students and practitioners of corporate communication need to gain an understanding of information and communication practice in the round at the level of personal skill as well as an appreciation of its corporate significance.

The kind of programme of information management and knowledge management reviewed in this chapter is a significant step towards developing a strong strand of professional information education in the corporate communication field, drawing on the established disciplines of information and knowledge management.

REFERENCES

Askew, C. (2000) *Database Retrieval Module Study Guide*, London: Thames Valley University.

Leonard-Barton, D. (1995) *Wellsprings of Knowledge: Building and Sustaining the Sources of Innovation*, Boston: Harvard Business School Press.

Nonaka, I. and Takeuchi, H. (1995) *The Knowledge-creating Company*, Oxford: Oxford University Press.

Roberts, S. A. (1997) 'The contribution of librarianship to information management', in J. M. Brittain (ed.) *Introduction to Information Management*. Wagga Wagga: Charles Sturt University, Centre for information Studies, pp. 23–49, Occasional Monographs, 16.

Roberts, S. A. (2002) *Presenting Information: Intelligence and Knowledge Module Study Guide*, London: Thames Valley University.

Rowley, J. (1999) 'In pursuit of the discipline of information management', *New Review of Information and Library Research*, 5, 65–77.

Shannon, C. E. and Weaver, W. (1949) *The Mathematical Theory of Communication*, Chicago, University of Illinois Press.

Stewart, T. A. (1997) *Intellectual Capital: The New Wealth of Organisations*, London: Nicholas Brealey.

Vian, K. and Johansen, R. (1997) 'Knowledge synthesis and computer-based communication systems: changing behaviours and concepts', in R. L. Ruggles (ed.), *Knowledge Management Tools*. Boston: Butterworth-Heinemann, pp. 187–208.

CHAPTER 4

Corporate and government communication: relationships, opportunities and tensions

Kevin Moloney

Business, public and voluntary sector bodies, interest and cause groups can hardly avoid contact with government in modern, liberal, democratic, market-orientated societies. The combined pressures from pluralism of values and of behaviour ensure that contact is always a possibility and is frequently intense.

   This chapter looks at why and how these organizations and groups have to – want to – talk to government; and conversely why government regulates or 'intervenes' in civil society and the political economy. The chapter therefore looks at the context and practice of communication between corporate interests on the one hand and the most powerful communicator in the modern state, executive government, on the other by focusing on media relations (including 'spin'); lobbyists and others.

A background to communicative action in liberal, democratic, market-orientated, capitalist societies

Is there a feature of modern societies which encourages communication *between* business, public sector bodies, voluntary organizations, interest and cause groups, *and* government? The argument here is that the increased pluralism of UK society (publicly expressed differences of values and behaviours) is the stimulus. This pluralism takes two forms and both involve more messaging to and from government.

Since the 1960s, the United Kingdom has witnessed great, observable changes in personal behaviour by its citizens and in collective behaviour by voluntary groups. Jackall and Hirota (2000: 155) note that the greater and lesser tendency of people to come together 'into "intellectual" and "moral" associations for purposes of advocacy' occurs in cycles and they identify the 1960s as a 'flowering'. The personal behavioural changes derive principally from altered values regarding sex, lifestyle, the environment, race, consumption and religion. They in turn generate social pressure for acceptance and tolerance of individuals practising these new behaviours. This pressure frequently leads to collective, group action by like-minded individuals to promote and defend their choices. In this way, increased pluralism of values and groups has been associated with social movements, e.g. feminism, gay rights, environmentalism, consumerism, multiculturalism. These movements are often distinguished by 'contentious collective action' (Tarrow, 1994), such as sit-ins, media events, petitions, demonstrations, all designed to influence public opinion and government. Stonier (1989: 31) argues that 'Social movements are of prime importance to the PR practitioner' and therefore her *alter ego*, the corporate communicator.

Voluntary associations springing from social movements have a long history in the United Kingdom and it would be wrong to argue that vigorous representation of group interests is new. There were the radical political clubs of the late eighteenth century and Chartism in the early nineteenth century. Trade unions, co-operative societies and leisure groups such as association football and the allotment movement grew throughout that century and into the twentieth. They also used techniques which we today would call corporate communication or public relations. The Chartists collected millions of signatures in a petition to parliament and organized a mass demonstration at Kennington, London, in the 1840s. Two hundred unemployed shipyard workers from Jarrow organized an early special event by marching three hundred miles to 10 Downing Street. It was organized by the National Unemployed Workers' Movement. See Black (1973) for the major involvement of the National Union of Local Government Officers in the 1948 foundation of the Institute of Public Relations. What happened in the 1960s, however, was new: it was not so much that there were further public expressions of unconventional, dissident values and behaviours, but that these were publicized by the new mass medium of television in a decade when social deference declined.

But what is the connection of this accelerated pluralism with more communication, and with government? The link lies in the need of individuals for their new values and behaviours to be accepted or at least tolerated by society, and in the pressure on government to react to these changes in civil society. One cannot be gay in an open way if homosexuality is illegal: government is challenged to make same sex legal. One cannot be a sovereign consumer without knowing, say, food ingredients: one would be a dead sovereign consumer unless the government regulates for food safety. One cannot be an informed citizen about the environment if levels of river pollution are not monitored and then published. Employees want workplace rights on health and safety, and on pensions: only government can enforce minimum standards. Individuals and groups, in these examples and in numerous others seen each day in the media, urge involvement by government, and representative, accountable government responds in a liberal democracy. In this way, communication between organizations and groups, and government express the concerns and hopes of the former and the policy responses of the latter. They are the conversations of a liberal democracy. This shift in UK society to more expression by individuals of different values and behaviours via voluntary groups is identified here as value pluralism and group pluralism of a civic kind. Brought together, they will be called civic pluralism.

In addition to this kind, a commercial variant of pluralism has come to the fore in the United Kingdom in approximately the same period. From the middle of the 1970s, it was noticeable that the climate of ideas about markets and business was shifting away from the collective and the planned towards the singular and the autonomous. This altered paradigm for the UK political economy has resulted in business and pro-market interests predominating over their ideological and material competitors. Collectivism and corporatism have waned while individualism and ideas of small government have waxed. Mainstream political parties vie to be more business-friendly. Competition is proclaimed over monopoly; public policy favours consumers rather than producers; markets seesaw where the plan once stabilized; low tax rates privilege private wealth over public goods. As a result, there is now in the United Kingdom a pronounced commercial pluralism. This is the condition where market and business values, ideas and practices prevail over substantial challenges from non-business or anti-business groups. Without it, accelerated pluralism would not affect the lives of all the UK population. Tens of millions are affected by personal and civic value changes: all are affected by market and business changes. This commercial pluralism speaks when we hear calls for the abolition of farm subsidies; when the gaming industry lobbies for the use of credit cards in casinos, and when construction companies want to invest in NHS hospitals.

Overall, the increased emphases on different values and personal behaviours, on voluntary associations for their promotion and defence (civic pluralism), and on the marketable, the entrepreneurial, and the profitable (commercial pluralism) have combined to create a sustained pressure for change in private and public life. In liberal, market economies, popularly elected governments react to change in civil society (voluntary associations outside the family and government) and in the political economy (the wealth creation nexus in society).

Implications for corporate communication

The conditions are now set for a more varied, competitive, argumentative and commercialized public life. It is an outcome which encourages communicative activity as a means to secure advantages for interest and cause groups, for businesses, for public and voluntary sector institutions: and for government to communicate acceptance or rejection of change. It may seem a category mistake at first to have public sector organizations as communicators with government. Are they not part of government? Statutorily they are, but they have executive government as their policy overlord and paymaster and they have to compete against civil service advice, party factions, hostile stakeholders and the treasury for policy and administrative advantages, and for resources.

Accelerated pluralism (both civic and commercial) is an incubator of corporate and government communication. What do these trends tell us about the modern context in which corporate communication flourish?

Pluralism is a competitive condition concerning groups of individuals in society. It is a condition in which the 'one' has to compete for survival amongst the 'many'. Corporate communication are the symbolic and expressive component of this competition and should be seen as competitive activity by transmitters and receivers. The aim of the competition is the search for organizational advantage. It is usually the case that only marginal advantage is available. Exxon is most unlikely to cause the destruction of Greenpeace but it may be able to win more public support over its rival in a particular campaign, e.g. the French courts upheld Exxon's opinion that some environmentalists have amended its logo to give it a similarity with the symbol of the Nazi SS, and that this amendment must not appear in France. Sometimes organizational survival is seriously influenced by communication: witness how a short, scatological remark in 1991 by the eponymous chairman of Ratners ruined his high street jewellery business. There are, however, limits to the pluralist competition which prevent it deforming into a social darwinian struggle for survival at any cost: law, culture, and ethics.

Second, *UK corporate communication come from many different types of organization and group*. Modern British pluralism is a highly variegated and pervasive phenomenon across its civil society and political economy. It would be inadequately descriptive to narrow the term 'corporate' just to business. Friends of the Earth, the Trades Union Congress, and Help the Aged are as structured, hierarchical and stable as McDonalds, the Institute of Directors and EMI. Churches, synagogues and temples are more communicative than many boardrooms. Think of the Board of Deputies of British Jews and the Catholic Media Office. The professional associations for teachers, nurses and police speak to the media and lobby government as often as many industry and trade associations. The definition here of 'corporate', however, does not include anti-globalization, anti-capitalist groupings. Corporate communicators from many sectors are concerned about messages from them, respond to them, and study their techniques, but the anti-globalizers are not the subjects of this chapter as their spokespeople are often anonymous, often speak for themselves, and the fluid combinations of activists around them lack a stable organizational basis. But this exclusion of anti-globalizers as corporate communicators does not deny the importance of their messages. They come from another important tradition in

liberal, democratic societies – anti-establishment thinking and street protests by marginalized, anarchic groups.

Third, *accelerated pluralism is not the same as neo-liberalism*, the ruling conservative ideology of much of the Anglo-American world since the 1980s. Apart from any coincidental identity, they are separate: the pluralism described here is a social phenomenon and process; neo-liberalism is a philosophy. A neo-liberal government may welcome pluralism as an agent for the expression of individualism and free association, but it would also note that pluralism is a process of interest intermediation and that many of these interests are inimical to a neo-liberal government. For example, environmentalism and consumerism have flourished during the period of accelerated pluralism, but they are viewed with suspicion by the neo-liberal as imposed, external costs on markets, and as the cause of increased government regulation. Some industries have ambiguous, if not hostile, attitudes towards free trade. For example, the UK drinks and tobacco trade towards wine and cigarette allowances for holiday makers, and British farmers towards cheap food imports by supermarkets. Pluralism allows views to countervail each other, without regard to consistency with neo-liberal values.

The fourth contextual point is that *corporate communication is, mostly, public activity*, even though its subject matter is sometimes about private behaviour. Corporate communicators are known and accountable officials for their organizations and their work is trackable (mostly). Corporate communication is the *public* relations of communication: public communicative relations of display-for-attention-and-advantage aimed at a distinct public 'other'. Corporate communication sometimes deal with private matters but mostly in a public way. For example, the pay rise of an individual business executive causes controversy but it is defended in terms of policy, if not principle. An individual farmer sows genetically modified seed, but her critics attack the sowing in terms of perceived public welfare. There are exceptions to the publicly known content and delivery of corporate communication. They fall under the communication category known as lobbying and they do raise questions about the transparency and accountability of behaviour by powerful interests and government in modern, liberal democracies.

As most corporate communication, by volume and frequency, is public, *the media is the major channel for the distribution of corporate communication*. This is the fifth contextual point.

The sixth is that it is important to identify the social locations where communication between interests and government is exchanged. There are *three exchange locations for corporate communication*. The first is the media, both old and new, where communication between interests and government is in the mass media and this location is a major focus for this chapter. The second location is civil society which includes the churches, universities, the professions, trade unions, cause groups, sporting organizations. Civil society is a term made to bear many meanings (e.g. educated as opposed to uninformed society; the site of ideological production in capitalist society; the liberal alternative to totalitarian society), as discussed by Kumar (1993). He indicates that the majority British and American usage locates civil society as an area of social activity separate from government, where there is freedom of association, and which excludes the private lives of individuals and of families. Corporate communicators for the various interests in civil society

are in continuous exchange with each other (e.g. trade unions and employers) but those bilateral messages mostly exclude government and are not directly dealt with here. The third location is markets in the usual sense of the term and in the less usual sense of institutions concerned with markets (e.g. market makers such as stock exchanges, and private and public regulators). This location includes marketing communication about goods and services, and messages about corporate life published by stock exchanges, regulatory bodies, government departments and by accountants. The profits and losses, investments and factory closures of car makers, and the statements about model recalls are corporate communication. This marketing and market communication is a focus of this chapter.

It is important to realize that much corporate communication takes place in locations where government is not involved (civil society) or is only involved in a supervisory way (markets), and that this is usually competitive communication – done in public mostly, between allies and critics. It is a reminder that *corporate communicators should always know who their audiences are* – the intended and unintended; the friendly, hostile and neutral; one decision maker or the mass. Government, however, will become interested in these exchanges of views when they generate politics, i.e. when the actions or words of competing interests affect public policy or mass public opinion. An example is the competition between traditional and low-cost airlines: at some stage, the government will be involved over the allocation of takeoff and landing slots. The reference above, moreover, to 'hostile' audiences is a strong reminder that corporate communication takes place in an ideological context and that it is being monitored by critics, if not enemies. This scrutiny lays a research role on corporate communicators. The contemporary period, for instance, is well worth analysing by communicators for there may be a more critical attitude to capitalism developing (Klein, 2000; Monbiot, 2000; Hertz, 2001; Lubbers, 2002).

The seventh contextual point is the internal position of corporate communicators inside their organizations. These professionals are involved with just one corporate resource – the symbolism of words, visual design, sound, and, sometimes, employee behaviour. They work alongside product designers, engineers, accountants, marketeers, fundraisers, planners and fieldworkers responsible for other corporate resources. This is a reminder that *corporate communicators deal only with communication*: they use symbols to represent the beliefs, policies, outputs and behaviours of their organization. A modesty is needed here for there is a professional deformation in some spokespeople: because they write and talk for the whole organization, they can delude themselves that they control its many functions. Instead, they are reliant on their colleagues for the data, knowledge, goods and services out of which to make effective communication, a task onerous enough in its own right to encourage professional modesty. Professional communicators cannot communicate without the 'raw material' of other professionals.

The final contextual point concerns Grunig and Hunt's (1984) categorization of public relations, still probably the paradigmatical typology of corporate communication. Two-way asymmetrical communication is mostly done by large organizations when dealing with their stakeholders: two-way symmetrical communication is found when big business

and powerful professional groups communicate with government.

Why government communicates

Accelerated pluralism, which has been identified as the social stimulus for the increase in corporate communication, has a business; public and voluntary sector; interest and cause group basis. It is the CBI, Virgin Trains, British Airways talking from the capitalist and market corners of UK national life; it is the Consumers' Association, the Citizens' Bureaux, the weights and measures departments of local authorities talking for consumers; teachers, social workers and Age Concern talking for the public and voluntary sectors; the RMT trade union talking for train and station crews. This pluralism creates a great river of self-promoting, biased, repetitive communication, some well founded, some not (media releases; roadshows; briefing notes; exhibitions; conferences; websites; marches; petitions, videos). Why should government pay attention to this accelerated pluralism?

From the government's perspective, the answer is threefold. There is the nature of democracy as a set of ideas (including representation and accountability) about the governance of people; and then the institutional arrangements (elections and secret ballots) which turn those ideas into political behaviour. Third, there is a particular form of pluralism which causes government to respond: the material and ideological power of business in capitalist political economies, a power which is reflected in the rise of the commercial pluralism described above. The early American pluralist writer Truman (1951: 37 and 256) noted that business is a high-status group with much access to government while 'labour organizations' had less access due to 'handicaps in status'. Dahl (1961: 76) calls business people 'economic notables' and observes that 'their authority is particularly great when policies impinge directly on business costs, earnings, investments and profits'. Marsh and Locksley (1983: 1–21) judged that the power of capital was 'qualitatively as well as quantitatively different' from other groups. Dunleavy and O'Leary (1987: 293–7) wrote that 'business interests occupy a position of special importance compared with other social interests when it comes to influencing public policy-making'. The neo-pluralists Lindblom (1997) and Smith (1990) argue that elected governments and business need each other to produce prosperity and employment. (See Held, 1996: 215–18, for a succinct summary of neo-pluralism.) Business people need skilled employees and consumers with disposable income in order to make a profit. Governments need satisfied voters to vote for them. Politicians would be other than representative and accountable – and other than elected – if they do not listen and reply.

The neo-pluralist perspective outlined above suggests that business communicators will be listened to more than others. Another author on pluralism, meanwhile, has calibrated the potential any group has for being listened to. Grant (1995, 2000) puts interest and pressure groups on a scale between 'insiders' (much access and influence) and 'outsiders' (little) and he concludes his 2000 analysis of 'insider' influence with pessimism about the future predominance of democracy over special interests.

How do organizations communicate with government?

The professional cadre employed to communicate are variously titled, with descriptors such as 'public affairs', 'communication', 'information', 'public relations', 'government relations', 'corporate relations' being common; and with government and the non-commercial sectors showing a preference for 'information' and 'communication'. These corporate professionals work with senior decision makers as planners, executives and advisers. It is this coalition of functional communicators plus the dominant coalition inside an organization which 'do' its communication. The values, knowledge, skills and attitudes needed to be a corporate communicator are well set out in various texts (Oliver, 2001; Theaker (ed.), 2001; Heath (ed.), 2000; Harrison, 2000; Kitchen (ed.), 1997; Van Riel, 1996; White and Mazur, 1995).

What can be distilled from this professional practice of communication are some underlying elements on which the superstructure of professional practice rests. First among these elements is issues management – the organizational response to matters in the operating environment which can be either opportunities or threats. An example is a UK government consultation paper (July, 2002) to build four more runways in the south east of England: an opportunity for British Airways; a threat to environmentalists and country life enthusiasts such as the Council for Protection of Rural England (CPRE). The classic role of corporate communicators in issues management is: to scan the boundary of the organization to spot issues; to research them; to plan with others an integrated response by the organization, and then to communicate to stakeholders, government and the general public what that response is. Issues management developed in the 1960s in the United States as a business response to a hostile reform agenda from environmentalists, workers' rights campaigners, and consumers

(Nelson and Heath, 1986; Heath and Cousino, 1990) but is now a strategic planning technique used widely in and outside business. Heath and Cousino argue that it has developed from a 'decide, announce, defend' mode to a 'dialogue, decide and deliver' one. After this primary task of issue analysis and policy response, the next underlying element is a purely communication one: the communication plan.

To develop further the example above of more runways, the communication goal of the CPRE could be (on an illustrative basis only): to persuade government to use existing capacity more intensely instead of building extra runways. Communication tactics to achieve that goal could include:

- a communication alliance with other friendly groups against more runways, e.g. Friends of the Earth, local residents' protest groups, local councils;
- identification of supportive, hostile, and neutral Members of Parliament in areas likely to be affected;
- a lobbying campaign aimed at these MPs above, and, more importantly, at senior civil servants and ministers who will take the final decision;
- the production of a brief for these politicians and officials in written, website, email, video, forms;
- a briefing of senior media editors and journalists covering the proposal by way of regional, local and specialist publications, e.g. planning, environment, air travel;
- liaison with academics, think tanks, industry experts publishing views supportive of the CPRE position;
- liaison with celebrities and local notables who are supportive;

- an ongoing media relations campaign which publicizes the above when it favours the Council's cause;
- an advocacy advertising campaign, backed by direct mailings and tie-ins where appropriate.

With an issues management policy and a communication plan in place, the organization or group is ready to talk to government. The operational style, however, should be cautious for elected governments backed by a popular mandate and a stable parliamentary majority are powerful. There are various points of prudence to consider before speaking to Whitehall and Westminster whether publicly through the media and staged events, or privately through lobbying.

The organization first has to consider whether what it does and says is socially responsible, namely that its policy serves the national interest as well as its sectional interest. Governments invariably talk about governing in the national interest, and they say that they weigh proposals in its light. There was, for example, no point in trade unions trying to argue with Thatcher governments in the 1980s that the right to secondary picketing should be enshrined in law. Organizations must, therefore, avoid being denied access and influence by government because they are perceived only as promoting a self-interest. An organization will know, indirectly, how they are perceived if they have direct access to government decision makers; if they are asked for their views on consultative papers, and are asked to sit on technical committees and task-forces. If the answer is 'yes' to these involvements, the organization is an 'insider' group as defined by Grant (1995, 2000). To stay an insider group, organizations must align their sectional interest with the government's definition of the national interest in their field, or they must at least persuade government that the two are aligned. One policy maker put the official search for the larger interest this way: 'The civil servant's job is to understand what is going on out there [in the non-governmental world] and the art really lies in filtering out the naked self-interests in the points that are being made because . . . that is how policy is formulated' (Moloney 1996: 125).

When governments talk of the national interest, they often encourage some organizational behaviours rather than others. Contemporary UK governments, for example, support ideas of corporate social responsibility by business. The core idea here is that companies defer immediate gains of, say, profit or cost cutting in the short term in order to benefit stakeholders: companies do this in the hope that they will generate more sales or more good reputation in the longer term. An example is the former nationalized British Gas funding village halls in areas where pipelines were laid. The government has a junior minister for corporate social responsibility (CSR) and it supports the work of the promotional group Business in the Community which in turn is supported by the Prince of Wales and by many blue chip UK companies. Whether CSR is a proper business activity is argued by economic liberals (Halfon, 1998; Henderson, 2001) in the tradition of Milton Friedman (1962) who thought that diversions from profit maximization were irresponsible. Hilton and Gibbons (2002), on the other hand, argue that CSR should be further developed into corporate social leadership whereby business gets involved with the delivery of social services to the benefit of the larger community and themselves. Whatever the merit, the second point of prudence in approaching

government is that businesses seeking to persuade government need to be aware of the policy and value environments in which the ruling political parties conduct their politics.

A detailed awareness of major policy commitments is needed in order to frame proposals so that they go with the grain of government thinking. Such an awareness is a necessary condition for successful communication with those more powerful than the message sender, whoever they are. Governments should not be confronted or confounded on their ideology, or their election manifestos. Corporate proposals are persuasive when they reinforce major policy, making it more effective or steering it around unforeseen difficulties. For example, New Labour was committed in its 1997 manifesto to increasing the representative rights of trade unions in the workplace, and it won the election that year with a House of Commons majority of 187. Business interest groups were not going to stop that legislation: instead the Confederation of British Industry (CBI) made its case against more rights in terms of the threshold percentage of trade unionists in a workplace required before representation rights were granted. The implication was that collective rights cannot be given unless there is evidence of widespread support for them. Thus, a technical proposal can sidestep political confrontation and open up space for negotiating an advantage. How this is done is a valuable communication skill. US lobbyists for Japanese car makers selling into the United States showed it in abundance when they got lightweight trucks reclassified as cars in 1989 and saved their clients $500m in tax per year (Moloney, 1996: 16). Where you know that your corporate interest is opposed by government, discuss technical matters with senior civil servants and ministers, especially when they have large majorities. (Most of this technical argument is done by lobbying, a private form of corporate communication described below.)

Status of personnel and organizational size are other matters for prudence when presenting to government. Ministers and senior civil servants expect to see chairpeople, chief executives and finance directors when they are being lobbied. The corporate communicator would be unwise to present alone: he should be there as part of the corporate team, should not speak, and should be present as notetaker and as prompter of the corporate memory. No demotion in any of this: her role has been played out beforehand in arranging the meeting, its agenda and writing briefing papers. As a general rule, ministers and their advisers will not see small businesses or organizations unless their proposal happens to embody some very specialist concern, or an MP has made a strong case for such a representation. This is where trade bodies become agents for corporate communication: their role is to represent small and medium sized firms (as well as large ones), and to aggregate opinions into an industry-wide view. These trade bodies often seek examples and testimonials to illustrate their points in their media releases and this is how small organizations can be identified.

Corporate communication as lobbying

Most of the communication outlined above is delivered in public, either to small audiences at conferences, exhibitions, seminars, roadshows, or through the mass media. But some communication is done privately with government under the heading 'lobbying'. This is corporate communication as direct action:

face-to-face with government and not through the media. Lobbying is 'monitoring public policy-making for a group interest; building a case in favour of that interest; and putting it privately with varying degree of pressure to public decision-makers for their acceptance and support through favourable political intervention' (Moloney, 1997: 175). It is done by organizations with their own staff or with hired-in, commercial lobbyists, working for a fee. Lobbying has become more of a high-risk activity after the 'sleaze' scandals of the late 1980s and early 1990s; scandals involving MPs (most notoriously Neil Hamilton) and hired lobbyists (Ian Greer). These shone an unflattering spotlight on lobbying by businesses and other powerful interests, and led to the appointment of a Committee on Standards in Public Life (the Nolan Committee). Nonetheless, lobbying is a modern expression of the medieval right to petition the sovereign and to seek redress, and if it is done ethically and within the law, it is acceptable corporate communication. It is, moreover, done by a wide range of less powerful interests outside of business but if the reader takes the neo-pluralist perspective on the competition among interests in modern states, the extent of business lobbying is evidence for that view. Miller (2000) and Curry (1999), a former minister, have written authoritatively on how it can be done by business and non-business interests.

The prevalence of lobbying makes it fitting to identify some contextual factors which influence the practice of lobbying and its outcomes. If it is always ill-advised to try to persuade government to make policy against its core values, there is one circumstance which makes governments less clear about what their core values are: a small majority in the House of Commons which is split and cannot be relied upon to always vote with their party.

This was the case with the Major government, 1992–7, which started with a majority of 30 MPs, and ended with 8, and whose supporters were split on European policy. MPs in a governing party with a small majority can lever up their influence on lesser policies if they promise votes on policies vital to the government's survival. In these circumstances, the corporate lobbyist can advance her case through contact with MPs but she will know that when parliamentary majorities are high, persuasion is more effective when aimed at ministers and senior civil servants. (See Moloney, 1996: 96–7, for the witness of a hired lobbyist.)

Whatever the size of a parliamentary majority, corporate lobbyists should calculate how specialized and extensive their knowledge is in areas where government makes policy: government needs personal access to experts to make viable policy. A senior civil servant put it this way: 'It's wrong to assume that Government or bits of Government instantly know their way round the economy, around the public life in the UK: they don't. Even less so when it comes to Brussels . . . and it is a value to a thoughtful civil servant . . . to build up contacts so that when a problem arises . . . you can ring up someone . . .' (Moloney, 1996: 125). Finally, the 'naughty but nice' image of lobbying will not beguile the prudent corporate communicator with prospects of easy success for she will know that governments with large majorities are very powerful, and that for every successful lobbying campaign, there is a failure. A good corporate reputation can easily be squandered. It can be maintained by following what the Nolan Committee listed as the seven principles of public life: selflessness; integrity; objectivity; accountability; openness; honesty; leadership. The middle five have particular relevance for professional communicators.

How do governments communicate with organizations?

Executive government is a powerful professional communicator in modern states like the United Kingdom. Indeed in Britain no other communication set-up can come close to its quantity and quality of output. Perhaps this is as it should be for the government draws its news-making mandate from its elected authority. It also manages the fourth largest economy in the world and exercises a global diplomatic and military role. Its communicative power is a reminder to organizational communicators to be prudent in dealing with it.

The British government employs a thousand professional communication specialists. Over four hundred do media relations and over two hundred publicity and marketing. They are mostly in London and based inside the government functions they serve. The two Blair administrations have extended the power of the centre over these civil servants by having twenty information strategists at 10 Downing Street scheduling a continuous flow of government news. They work upon a planned 'grid' of news releases and comment, often with hourly updates, to a 24 hours media, 365 days a year. The power of this news supply attracts a specialist group of journalists (the Westminster press lobby) dedicated just to reporting it, and to developing non-official and anti-official versions of it (called 'exclusives', 'scoops' and 'leaks'). The government avoids these metropolitan journalists from the 'Westminster village' having monopoly power over delivery of this news supply to audiences by the prime minister briefing the press on television (e.g. 25 July 2002), and by dealing directly with the regional and specialist media.

There are also among the eighty ministerial special advisers some who specialize in media relations. These political appointees give 'policy steers' to the official information teams in their ministers' departments, and they sometimes speak directly on more party political matters to the media. It is no surprise, therefore, that the government's chief professional communicator is considered more powerful than many cabinet ministers. (The BBC2 television programme *News from No. 10*, 15 July 2000, provides insight into the thinking of both journalists and official communicators in the time of Alastair Campbell as the prime minister's press secretary.) It is also no surprise that when this well-resourced news management system breaks down, it is news in itself. (The controversy between special adviser Jo Moore and official director of information Martin Sixsmith in the transport department made headlines in spring 2002, and contributed to the resignation of a secretary of state shortly afterwards.) The UK government has become more communication conscious under the Blair administrations. This is observable in three ways: there are more ministerial special advisers dealing with the media; there is strong central control, and a planning 'grid' delivers news to all media outlets all the time. An emblem of this strengthening of official communication is a new name for the service. After the Mountfield report (1997), it altered from 'Government Information Service' to 'Government Information andCommunication Service' (GICS). GICS includes the Central Office of Information. This is the government's own advertising agency and manager, publicity agent, special events organizer, and public relations consultancy rolled into one entity. It brands itself on its website as 'government's communication expert' (August 2002). It is involved with public information campaigns (communication campaigns for citizen educa-tion) such as no-drink-drive, road safety, stop-smoking.

These thousand civil servants are the official communicators of government, and corporate communicators will have multi-faceted relationships with them: analysing their official statements; judging how to respond, and collaborating on news about joint ventures (e.g. public/private investment initiatives to build hospitals and service railways; running failing schools). But alongside this official structure of communication and civil servants lies politics and elected politicians, producing another stream of communication. MPs and ministers talk to journalists in the Lobby of the House of Commons as well as in their constituencies and in departments. We can say that government has two communication systems and while the constitutional position is that the elected politicians manage the civil servant communication, there is no guarantee that the two systems are giving out the same messages. This is a reminder that government and politics are a 'messy business' often lacking the consistency of the bureaucratic organization. This message of confusion and 'noise' in transmission channels is another reason for prudence when dealing with government. The messages coming from it may be conflicting; are often not traceable to source, and are sometimes conflicting on purpose for tactical political reasons. An example is messages about UK environmental policy. One middle-ranking minister was reported to be critical of New Labour's achievements in the area while his senior claimed that the first minister had not been critical, but had been mis-reported, and that there were identifiable achievements. This 'confusion' sends different signals to business interests and environmentalists who are competing for advantage on policy benefits.

Public silence, private analysis and private lobbying is the best communicative response by those outside government. Much to be avoided is the charge that corporate interests are 'interfering in politics'.

Spin and what to do with it

The term 'spin' is a fashionable one, current in the United Kingdom since the 1990s at least. The favour it finds amongst politicians, however, decreased from 2000 because the approach to news management it represents has serious disadvantages. Instead the term and the approach have themselves become politics. What was once the transmission system for the story has become the story, and not one reflecting favourably on elected politicians.

Spin is the current dominant style of political (as opposed to official civil servant) presentation in the United Kingdom and Gaber (2000) offers an analysis of its features. It is an aggressive, demeaning, exaggerated and uncivil style of presentation used by politicians against the media, and indirectly against other politicians. Rosenbaum notes (1997: 91) that when political press officers were informally called spin doctors, the change denoted a more active, challenging, and hectoring behaviour towards the media. In its contemporary UK form, spin is aggressive, political public relations developed by New Labour to counter hostile media coverage from the right-wing press. It is a euphemism for propagandizing and therefore tends to degrade democratic politics. Politicians should put their spin doctors on half-time contracts – if not sack them altogether – and rebalance their time and energies in favour of policy substance, and more statements in parliament.

The word, however, has taken on a linguistic life far beyond politics. It is now a pejorative term for any public relations, corporate communication, advertising or any publicity disliked by the speaker or writer. Usage has spread even beyond professional territory and into personal relationships: it now conveys dislike of any conversational statement not to the listener's liking. The cause of this popularity is linguistic in that the word has become an easily understandable and culturally rich metaphor in the United Kingdom. It aligns the popular image of the wily politician with that of the crafty spin bowler in a cricket match who is trying to beat the good, honest yeoman of a batsman defending his wicket. The word, however, originated in American baseball and was 1980s jargon for coaches training pitchers to make the ball turn in mid-air in order to confuse the hitter. The transferred meaning into political, corporate and personal affairs, however, whether in America or the United Kingdom, is still the same: to 'spin' is to describe a policy, personality or event with a gloss which the listener disagrees with. You spin what is wrong but I advance what is right.

For all reasons, corporate communicators may be the subjects of spin from government when they deal with the state (car makers as 'rip-off Britain'; trade unionists as the 'enemy within'; banks for making 'windfall profits'). Though they may be objects of the spin accusation from government, they should never themselves employ spin. A corporate campaign may be assertive in that it claims truth for its view but it should show respect, through intent and language, for the views of its interlocutors. It should be reasoned persuasion. It should not use hyperbole of fact or argument or emotion in its messages or behaviour. It should treat the media and the ultimate message receivers in a civil manner. Not to communicate in a civil manner is demeaning for the corporate body and reduces reputation. It should follow what Susskind and Field (1996) have called a 'mutual gains' approach when communicating with an angry public. Applying this approach to government and corporate bodies would produce communication marked, inter alia, by: shared concern; joint fact finding; shared responsibility for the task in hand; trust; and a long-term relationship.

Who has the balance of advantage in corporate communication?

A constitutional answer is that the balance of advantage, defined as the last word on policy in a democratic state, should lie with the elected government. Such governments, especially centralized ones such as the United Kingdom's, are very powerful. They are leviathans, but perhaps democratic ones. Since the 1980s, British governments have dismantled the industrial public sector; reduced the power of trade unions; favoured markets over monopoly and cartels; introduced the 'big bang' of competition into the City of London; reformed the education system, and introduced regulation in all these areas of national life. Corporate interests in the private, public and voluntary sectors have not halted this policy flow: they have only shaped its margins. The constitutional citizen, individual or corporate, may not like it but has to accept it as the consequence of elected government.

Government communication – in structure, volume, frequency and content – reflects the powerfulness of their political sources. Indeed, so powerful is government communication in the United Kingdom that they have been paid a dubious compliment: Deacon and Golding (1994: 3–4) have written about the rise of the 'public relations state', giving the size of the government's advertising spend and of its information service as examples.

But there is a naivety in the constitutionalist's position set out above. It assumes that constitutional rules and conventions in a democracy capture and contain power relations in favour of the many. The Marxist left argues that constitutions do capture these relations but in favour of the privileged few, not the unpowerful many: Marx called the nineteenth-century state the executive committee of the capitalist class. Economic radicals like Dahl and Lindblom (both American) argue that, whatever constitutions say, the business interest is the most powerful one in societies like the United Kingdom and America, and their neo-pluralist perspective (see above) suggests that government has to negotiate with the business interest. From this perspective, business communicators have a powerful message to deliver to government and they do hold the communicative advantage on some key issues. When the Confederation of British Industry, the Institute of Directors, and the Engineering Employers' Federation talk about, say, deregulating labour markets (weakening the bargaining power of employees), or graduate skills for the workplace (more portable core skills), the British government listens. But the neo-pluralists attribute this strong negotiating position to the business interest taken as a whole, and not to individual industries, firms or particular business personnel. Thus chief executives and accountants will find their ethical behaviour more regulated following the American accounting frauds; the British coal industry will face declining state subsidies, and British clothing manufacturers will not be protected from cheap Asian imports.

The tension between these perspectives is another reminder of the need for prudent judgement when corporate interests – private, public and voluntary – communicate with government. There is first the question of whether the corporate communicator has the technical competence to deliver a persuasive message to the most powerful listener in the state. Are you communicating a position which aligns your interest and government's definition of the national interest? Have you identified the most persuasive mix of message forms and channels? Are you communicating publicly or privately or in both modes? Will you be listened to alone or as part of a larger interest? Are political and official channels giving you the same messages?

These questions are the tactics of communication with government: the strategic questions still needed answering as well. Where does your interest lie in the scale of government imperatives and favoured policies? Do elected politicians gain or lose votes by communicating with you? Are you an insider or an outsider to the business of running the country? Your communication can propose but government's invariably dispose.

What have you learnt?

Readers will have noted the following points to aid better understanding and practice:

- Corporate communicators talk publicly and critically to government in liberal, democratic, market-orientated, capitalist societies.
- They communicate in a societal context with distinctive features, chief of which is a high degree of competition amongst interests (accelerated pluralism).

- Communication is done to procure advantage for the organization.
- Without knowing policy and political contexts, communicators are less effective.
- These communicators include those in public and voluntary institutions, and the full range of stable interest and cause groups as well as in business.
- According to the neo-pluralist perspective, business communicators are in a privileged position vis-à-vis government, but one that is challenged and not always on the winning side.
- Elected governments are the most powerful communicators in these societies.
- Most corporate communication is public but some are private and this lobbying raises accountability and transparency questions about dealing with government.
- Governments communicate in both political and official channels.
- Be prepared and prudent when communicating with democratic government.

CorpComs: tracking and analysis

Corporate communication pervades our public messaging spaces (the media, websites, official documents, face-to-face debates) and is easy to track. The strategy and tactics behind it are, however, more difficult to analyse.

Businesses, public bodies, interest and cause groups are always seeking communicative advantage vis-à-vis competitors and government, and a continuous, thoughtful scrutiny of their communication reveals organizational aims and objectives. Here are three tracking exercises.

1   What communication comes from your employer or industry/trade representation body? Specifically, identify the messages; how they are channelled to government; and why they are sent.

2   Discover government's communication on an issue which interests you. Search the websites of the sponsoring ministry, parliamentary reports, and interested MPs. Follow political reports in the media.

Can you identity government's policies and if they have changed over time? How do these policies relate to the organizations you support on the issue?

3   Take a policy of government which you oppose. Identify the businesses or interest and cause groups which are critical of that policy and devise a corporate communication plan for them. Compare your plan with theirs.

REFERENCES

Black, S. (1973) *The Institute of Public Relations 1948–73: The First Twenty-five Years*, London: IPR.

Curry, D. (1999) *Lobbying Government*, London: Chartered Institute of Housing.

Dahl, R. (1961) *Who Governs?*, New Haven: Yale University Press.

Deacon, D. and Golding, P. (1994) *Taxation and Representation: The Media, Political Communication and the Poll Tax*, London: John Libbey.

Dunleavy, P. and O'Leary, B. (1987) *Theories of the State*, Basingstoke: Macmillan.

Friedman, M. (1962) *Capitalism and Freedom*, Chicago: Chicago University Press.

Gaber, I. (2000) 'Government by spin: an analysis of the process', *Media, Culture & Society*, 22(4), 507–18.

Grant, W. (1995) *Pressure Groups, Politics and Democracy in Britain*. Hemel Hempstead: Harvester Wheatsheaf.

Grant, W. (2000) *Pressure Groups and British Politics*, Hemel Hempstead: Harvester Wheatsheaf.

Grunig, J. and Hunt, T. (1984) *Managing Public Relations*, New York: Holt, Rinehart & Winston.

Halfon, R. (1998) *Corporate Irresponsibility Is Business Appeasing Anti-business Activities*, London: Adam Smith Institute.

Harrison, S. (2000) *Public Relations: An Introduction*, London: International Thomson Business Press.

Heath, R. (ed.) (2000) *Handbook of Public Relations*, London: Sage.

Heath, R. and Cousino. K. (1990) 'Issues management: end of first decade progress report', *Public Relations Review*, 16(1), 6–18.

Held, D. (1996) *Models of Democracy*, Cambridge: Polity.

Henderson, D. (2001) *Misguided Virtue: False Notions of Corporate Social Responsibility*, London: Institute of Economic Affairs.

Hertz, N. (2001) *The Silent Takeover*, London: William Heinemann.

Hilton, S. and Gibbons, G. (2002) *Good Business: Your World Needs You*, London: Texere.

Jackall, R. and Hirota, J. (2000) *Image Makers: Advertising, Public Relations and the Ethics of Advocacy*, London: University of Chicago Press.

Kitchen, P. (ed.) (1997) *Public Relations: Principles and Practice*, London: Thomson Business Press.

Klein, N. (2000) *No Logo*, London: Flamingo HarperCollins.

Kumar, K. (1993) 'Civil society: an inquiry into the usefulness of an historical term', *British Journal of Sociology*, 44(3).

Lindblom, C. (1977) *Politics and Markets*, New York: Basic Books.

Lubbers, E. (ed.) (2002) *Battling Big Business*, Totnes: Green Books.

Marsh, D. and Locksley, G. (1983) 'Capital: the neglected face of power' in D. Marsh (ed.), *Pressure Politics*, London: Junction Books, pp. 53–83.

Miller, C. (2000) *Political Lobbying*, London: Politico's Publishing.

Moloney, K. (1996) *Lobbyists for Hire*, Aldershot: Dartmouth.

Moloney, K. (1997) 'Government and lobbying activities' in P. Kitchen (ed.), *Public Relations*

Principles and Practice, London: Thomson Business Press.

Monbiot, G. (2000) *Captive State: The Corporate Takeover of Britain*, London: Macmillan.

Mountfield Report (1997) *Report of the Working Group on the Government Information Service*, London: Cabinet Office.

Nelson, R. and Heath, R. (1986) 'A systems model for corporate issues management', *Public Relations Quarterly*, fall, 20–4.

Oliver, S. (2001) *Public Relations Strategy*, London: Kogan Page.

Rosenbaum, M. (1997) *From Soapbox to Soundbite: Party Political Campaigning in Britain since 1945*, London: Macmillan.

Smith, M. J. (1990) 'Pluralism, reformed pluralism, and neopluralism: the role of pressure groups in policy-making', *Political Studies*, 38, 302–22.

Stonier, T. (1989) 'The evolving professionalism: responsibilities', *International Public Relations Review*, 12(3), 30–6.

Susskind, L. and Field, P. (1996) *Dealing with An Angry Public: The Mutual Gains Approach to Resolving Disputes*, New York: Free Press.

Tarrow, S. (1994) *Power in Movement*, Cambridge: Cambridge University Press.

Theaker, A. (ed.) (2001) *The Public Relations Handbook*, London: Routledge.

Truman, D. (1951) *The Governmental Process*, New York: Alfred Knopf.

Van Riel, C. (1996) *Principles of Corporate Communications*, London: Prentice-Hall.

White, J. and Mazur, L. (1995) *Strategic Communications Management*, Wokingham: Addison-Wesley.

CHAPTER 5

Priorities old and new for UK PR practice

Gerald Chan

In this chapter Gerald Chan has looked to update the 1994 Delphi study on research priorities in the United Kingdom. PR theory and practice has changed since the 1990s, mostly brought on by the phenomenal growth of the internet and new media technologies. Looking at the impact of these changes, and based on a Y2K research report the author asks how has the profession of public relations evolved in the years since the Delphi report and what are deemed to be research priorities.

The current public relations research agenda in the United Kingdom is based on a number of research objectives which developed from White and Blamphin's 1994 study on research priorities in the United Kingdom[1] and an earlier draft report prepared in October 1990[2] including the need to:

- establish priorities for the limited funding available for public relations research in further education;
- tap into the growing interest in the use of research in public relations, drawing from the enlarged resources in the expanded research community.

Public relations in both theory and practice, has changed over the 1994–2000 period, mostly brought about by the phenomenal

growth of the internet and new media technologies. In light of this and the other changing conditions PR practitioners have to operate in, this update has to illustrate how practice has shaped the course of research and vice versa.

A few general questions have been asked to better understand the task at hand. Since the Delphi report, how has the profession of public relations evolved? What are the amendments to the list of research priorities? Are these changes simply a matter of re-arranging the order in which they originally appeared or have there been significant changes in academia/industry that have warranted a reassessment of the research agenda in public relations?

The new project recognizes how developments in industry and the wider environment have resulted in shifts in normative and functional paradigms and thus, by implication, research preoccupations. Key objectives are:

- To conduct secondary research into White and Blamphin's 1994 Delphi study. This report will offer suggestions for new research imperatives in public relations. Some of the previous subject headings from the 1994 study have reached maturity while others were in their genesis. Thus, the original study is far from obsolete, because many of the identified topics are still pertinent. This report will examine the topics that are still relevant and also detect new subject categories for research.
- To provide a basis for future analyses into the theoretical and applied aspects of public relations in the United Kingdom and other countries. A criticism falling on the past study is that it concentrated too much on the United Kingdom's needs. This report aims to widen the scope by receiving input from academics and practitioners operating in centres that have reached a credible level of sophistication in public relations, namely: Europe, Northern America and Australasia. In so doing, it is hoped that the overall body of knowledge in PR theory and practice is expanded, while also increasing the possibilities for co-operation between organizations and countries through comparative and joint research initiatives. Several international initiatives are already in motion and this study will build on their successes.

The research topics that will appear in this report will have to conform to the needs of the academic and professional communities. They will:

- Enhance the existing body of knowledge in public relations by using social scientific research techniques to assemble empirical evidence, in order to better understand the elements of PR theory and practice.
- Relate to the IPR's objectives and requirements, which are: to provide a structure for the understanding of the professional practice of public relations; to provide educational opportunities to meet and exchange views and ideas; and to raise standards within the profession through the promotion of research.

For this study to be truly representative of the current research climate in public relations, it was imperative that the information obtained would assist in drawing up a list of academic questions that mirrored the requirements of industry. Also, to achieve a balanced understanding of current research priorities in public relations, it was decided that both academics and practitioners would be approached to participate in this study.

To comprehend the common topics and problems in PR encountered by academics, researchers and practitioners alike, knowledge of the present state of research was required. This was obtained via a content analysis of the leading publications in PR theory and practice based in the United Kingdom. They were, namely, *The Journal of Communication Management Corporate Reputation Review*, the *Journal of Public Relations Research* and *Public Relations Review*. The volumes consulted were those within the 1994–2000 period. Whilst it is accepted that UK titles do not necessarily offer a world-view of the current state of public relations, it must be pointed out that contributors and the editorial board of these two publications are not solely from the United Kingdom and come from various backgrounds.

Other sources of information were PR trade magazines such as the UK edition of *PR Week*, the IPR's *Profile* magazine and the IPRA's *FrontLine 21* magazine. Clearly this is a limited journal search overall and future developments will widen the literature sourcing.

A programme of PR conferences provided a broad sweep of the issues and challenges facing contemporary PR practice in the world. The conference plans that were examined were the seventh International Public Relations Research Symposium, held at Lake Bled in Slovenia (7–8 July 2000), the IPR National Conference, London (18–20 October 2000) and the Public Relations World Congress 2000, held in Chicago (22–4 October 2000).

From the research conducted, the subject themes chosen are:

- strategic planning and public relations;
- technology and public relations;
- international issues in PR practice;
- the PR role in organizational change;
- the measurement and evaluation of public relations;
- the need to integrate public relations with other communication functions.

Subject headings are generic and each can include other research items as sub-areas for further study. An example would be in the category 'strategic planning and public relations'. Other research subjects that arise from this one topic include managerial roles in public relations and the effects of systems theory on specific PR practice which in turn, considers public relations from an organizational point of view, looking at a range of subjects such as corporate culture and organizational behaviour. Likewise, there is also considerable overlap between the different subjects. Research into strategy in public rela-

tions can extend into the confines of subjects such as 'Technology and public relations' and 'International issues in PR practice'.

A questionnaire was designed based on the findings of the content analysis mentioned above, namely the list of suggested research topics drawn up according to the frequency of their appearance in the journals cited.

Respondents were asked closed and open-ended questions in order for the author to find out as much information as possible. The closed-ended questions required definite answers, such as questions pertaining to the relative importance of a particular subject theme; while the open-ended questions were exploratory in nature. This was the information gathering stage and it was essential to collect information that was both qualitative and quantitative. This initial questionnaire aimed to establish the research interests and personal views of respondents, providing more clues to other research themes that may have eluded the author. Data from the returned questionnaires would have formed the basis for another survey. This second questionnaire would have been more focused and specific in its inquiry into the research priorities of public relations. Subsequently, respondents would have been invited to participate in a focus group to discuss the findings of the survey. However, as the time scale for this project was only two and a half months, a more thorough study was made impossible due to the time constraints and the slow return rate of questionnaires.

A total of 128 six-page questionnaires (two-page introduction to the study, four-page selection of questions) were electronically mailed to participants from the middle of October 2000 to early December 2000. Participants were requested to reply by mid-December. At final count, the total number of answered questionnaires was forty-eight, out of which twenty-three replies were from academics and twenty-five were practitioners. The response rate was thus calculated as 37.5 per cent.

PR academics from Europe and America were approached to contribute to the study. The academics approached are all actively engaged in interdisciplinary research in public relations. Practitioners chosen had a known interest in research and/or education in public relations and held senior positions in the organizations they represented/worked for. They work in consultancy or in-house and have a combined experience in a range of backgrounds, including corporate and financial public relations and political communication. Participants were chosen from the various committees of the IPR, including the Training and Professional Development Committee, or they were selected from international organizations such as Confédération Européene des Relations Publiques (CERP). Speakers at the IPR National Conference 2000 were invited to participate, as were the judges of the *PR Week* Awards 2000.

Despite being based on only one questionnaire, this brief survey provides a comprehensive overview of the changes in the PR environment and profession over recent years. Respondents provided a large pool of information crucial to our perceptions of the theory and practice of public relations in an evolving and dynamic world. As the educator–practitioner divide is fairly equal (48:52, from a total of forty-eight respondents), data gathered has been decisive in giving access into the differences in opinion, which will be discussed throughout this report.

The main concern for some academics was the agenda setting of research priorities. Questions were raised over who determined the new research proposals and the validity of the new list of research subjects. According to one academic, the previous list has not been researched fully and successfully, otherwise huge progress in the field of public relations would have been made. Another academic expressed how there are too many research topics already and the present lack of resources means that it is impossible to do justice to the topics up for research. Overall, the academic view is for research in public relations to focus on PR practice, and in subjects which are relevant to practitioners.

Some practitioners, although recognizing the need for public relations to be theory-driven, were wary about scholastic research into public relations, as such activity runs the risk of reducing PR problems into pedantic arguments, an exercise which has no place in the real business environment as public relations is essentially a practical management function rather than a set of academic conceits. In the words of a practitioner, 'My standard stance on these pseudo-scientific research studies is to decline to participate in order to ensure that no one can suggest that it was anything more than an academic exercise or that it involved people of some experience and expertise who actually practised public relations at management level.' Clearly the long-standing debate over the disparity between practitioner and educator competencies in public relations still forms a bone of contention. However, recent work by Stacks *et al.* (1998)[3] is aimed at dispelling these myths. Similarly, Moloney *et al.* (1999) have researched into the effectiveness of PR degrees and the occupational destination of PR graduates.

The results showed a need for better understanding of the current research milieu in both industry and academia. To follow is a list of the research interests of respondents. The numerals in parenthesis show the number of people from the survey interested in each topic. Response was rich and varied and the common topics were: strategy and public relations (10), PR management (9); ethics (2) and corporate social responsibility (5); issues management (3); research, evaluation and measurement (11); stakeholder relationships (10); globalization issues and public relations (3).

The list below highlights individual research areas which are less prevalent but worthwhile in our consideration since they disclose the hypothetical and technical concerns that confront modern PR practice:

- the interaction of public relations, journalism and the political economy;
- the psychology of communication applied to PR practice;
- managing corporate risk;
- return on communication, intangible assets;
- convergence of new technologies, integration of public relations with IT;
- effect studies;
- change communication;

- public relations and culture;
- social development and public relations.

These groupings are an indication of the interdisciplinary and multi-faceted nature of modern PR practice.

Respondents were asked to rate the chosen topics in order of perceived importance, bearing in mind their relative relevance to current research needs, and also in accordance with the prevailing issues and problems facing contemporary public relations practice.

Table 5.1 contains six subject headings identified as being of importance to research. They have been singled out from the other topics after a content analysis of current research published in academic journals. The high frequency of their appearance as articles is a signal of their significance to the research agenda.

Strategic planning and public relations

There was unanimous agreement over this topic as being important for research.

Table 5.1 Which are the topics most important and relevant to PR research today?

Theme	Ranking in order of importance					
	1	2	3	4	5	6
Strategic planning and public relations	23	8	6	6	1	0
Technology and public relations	5	4	8	10	8	5
International issues in PR practice	1	5	4	7	10	15
Public relations' role in organizational change	1	14	6	8	10	4
The measurement and evaluation of public relations	9	8	10	9	5	3
The need to integrate public relations with other communication functions	8	9	4	5	7	10

Argument over how public relations should be included in the decision-making process continues, though the trend is that it is assuming more responsibility as a management function. As suggested by the last Delphi study, a possible research topic could be on the training needed by practitioners to make this contribution more effective. Research in this area has already been done in the United States by academics such as Dean Kruckeberg, L. van Lueven and Elizabeth L. Toth.

A practitioner commented on how research into this area should focus on the 'Return on Public Relations (in the sense of the return on communication vis-à-vis other management functions)' as it brings together management literature with PR theory through the 'linkage between PR practice and corporate strategy' thereby providing answers to the continued discussion about the management capabilities and requirements for PR practitioners.

An academic who is also an independent consultant remarked that there is the 'constant need to monitor and review . . . (since) strategy is misunderstood by PR practitioners . . . (as they) sometimes have strategies which are either aims/objectives or tactics'.

Public relations' role in organizational change

This was featured in the last report as an important area for future research. The trend in many industries is for consolidation via mergers and acquisitions. Public relations has to respond to this through proactive communication with all stakeholders. New areas in PR practice such as conflict resolution and change communication have elevated the strategic status of PR practice, especially in the growth areas of issues and crisis management.

The measurement and evaluation of public relations

This was considered 'most relevant to practitioners'. By providing better methodologies for the measurement and evaluation of public relations, the result would be higher standards, amidst increasing demands for more accountability. According to the research results of a German academic, there is currently low development in evaluation and public relations, while a British academic noted how for measurement, there is 'already enough there for practice to do it . . . if it wants to'. The PROOF Survey, launched in February 1998, and eventually a collaborative partnership between PR Week, the IPR and PRCA has set out definitive guidelines for the use of research and evaluation in PR.

Technology and public relations

Academics envisage future research in this area along the lines of 'the role and contribution of public relations to the growth of e-business' and the changing skills set of practitioners, as industries conform to new technologies.

A practitioner noticed how 'there is a great deal of confusion or misconception that exists around PR and its role (in the new e-economy). As New Media begins to affect the way we communicate, do business and indeed live our lives, there needs to be a re-alignment of how public relations plays a part and fits in with society.' Current research into the topic has been done by the Institute for Public Relations in Florida.[4] The IPR's Internet Commission has also published a report (Rush, 2000) on the impact of the Internet on communication.

The need to integrate public relations with other communication functions

This continues the debate over the scope of public relations. A comment was 'As professionalism in PR is highly variable . . . lack of understanding within and without PR results from the poor description of the scope of public relations.'

In the eyes of a practitioner, 'There seems to be a lot of disagreement over the scope and meaning of PR. I think this term is becoming outdated as public relations is more than just media relations.' Another practitioner said, 'I see a bifurcation of PR services – on one hand, public relations is losing market value vis-à-vis other communications disciplines (if they can be seen as different), e.g. corporate communication, and on the other hand, I see a broadening of public relations towards "total communication" management (also via concepts like 'reputation management').' An academic's view on this topic on the other hand, is that there is 'too much navel gazing – people there just get on and do it!'

International issues in public relations practice

This topic was considered least important in relative terms for research. A possible reason for this occurrence is because most research in theoretical public relations has so far been done by Anglo-American scholars, thus the high concentration on international issues from such a perspective. There is also conflicting opinion over this subject. A practitioner noted, 'this isn't a matter for proper and structured research – there is an easy list to be provided by anyone heading the function for an international business and/or any CEO of a

multi-national organization'. However, as noted earlier, subject groupings listed are generic and therefore open to interpretation. This topic in particular, does not merely refer to issues concerning the customs and etiquette PR practitioners have to be aware of and sensitive to while doing business in a foreign country. The globalization of the world's economy and the formation of regional centres for trade and development, such as the EU and NAFTA, have resulted in political, economic and social consequences that will affect PR practice, and in consequence, PR theory. There is evidence that academia is beginning to regard this topic as an influential area for scholarly work as seen in the most recent publications (Moss, Verĉiĉ and Warnaby, 2000; Heath and Vasquez, 2001) on public relations.

The numerous international symposia on public relations held each year to bring together practitioners from all around to share and transfer knowledge is a clear indication that more emphasis should be placed on this topic despite its poor estimation in this survey. Table 5.2 illustrates the headings from the recent study that are still applicable for current research purposes. Participants were asked to tick the subjects that are important

Table 5.2 Which subjects from the old study should still be included in the new set of research priorities?

Theme	Number of replies
The definition of public relations	15
Professional skills in public relations	27
The image of public relations	21
Ethics in PR practice	30
The impact of media content	16
Gender issues in PR practice	7
Features of the market for PR service	12

rather than rank in order of perceived importance. In so doing, a ranking of the results
will surface through participants' answers.
From the survey, it is clear that rhetorical
approaches to public relations are still regarded highly in the research agenda.

Ethics in PR practice

This is considered to be the most important
subject for research. In the words of an academic, 'Ethics underpins the practice being
implemented, which in turn, has repercus-
sions for other concerns in PR such as professional skills levels, the image of PR and gender
issues.' In support of this statement, a practitioner working in public affairs observed how
ethics are 'key to the development of business
without slurs of sleaze . . . key to how politicians and officials act on most issues . . . key
to running a successful and profitable business
– or it all falls apart!' Emerging areas for
research in ethics and public relations are: the
effects of corporate governance and corporate
social responsibility, as their enforcement has
many implications for public relations practice
worldwide.

Professional skills in public relations

This is the second most important topic
since the skills that are required to manage
public relations are undergoing constant and
dramatic change. The growth of the worldwide web and the effects of a globalized economy have resulted in new communication
channels, target groups and techniques. PR
professionals have to meet up with these
challenges if they are to remain competitive,
especially since management consultancies,
law practices and accountancy firms have

begun to wander into the territory of traditional public relations by offering auditing
services in management areas such as organizational change management and risk issues
management (Roberts, 2000). Again, the
overwhelming response from participants is
that public relations is recognized as a management function, but it now remains for
public relations to carve a more tangible role
for itself within its managerial function.

The image of public relations

For this subject, comments centred on the
negative connotations of 'PR'. An academic
reported that it 'is a particularly worrying area
as business/public perception has been damaged by the spin vs. substance debate'.
Concern is not unfounded and it has been
suggested that the best way forward would be
to research into the professionalization of
public relations practice as improving standards in the quality of service delivery and
practitioner development would increase the
credibility of public relations.

An educator commented, 'In thirty-five
years, I have always heard the same complaint: Public Relations has to work on its own
public relations.' Indeed, the poor reputation
of reputation managers is an ironic note that
demands further study.

The impact of media content

In the White and Blamphin's study, the main
area for research into this topic was in the
impact of specific media content, such as the
effects of documentaries on public opinion;
and there was the call for a summary of the
relevant research findings.

According to a practitioner, 'The impact of media content can be misleading. Analysis of impact often paints a different picture from perception of a likely impact.' Another practitioner noted how 'further research into the impact of media content would help every PR practitioner and would interest and impress existing and potential PR users far more than other topics'. Research done by John Hitchins at the College of St Mark and St John in Plymouth seeks to address this issue.

The definition of public relations

This is still considered a relevant subject. Despite many attempts to define what public relations is, a common concept is hard to achieve as public relations is practised differently from sector to sector, country to country. An academic states how 'there is (still) no consensus on the definition of public relations', while another academic pointed out, 'If we don't know what public relations is, how can we achieve excellence in practice? The future of the field depends largely on its ethical practice, on the integrity of PR practitioners.'

The need to derive a universal definition of public relations is near impossible, given the inherent linguistic and cultural differences in the world. Several joint projects since the 1990s have striven to break down these barriers and to enhance co-operation between academics and practitioners across continents. This however, remains a gargantuan and long-term task. The trick perhaps, is to 'think global, act local' and focus research in public relations on specific aspects of practice, in accordance to the demands of the environment and its application. For instance, rather than argue over whether public relations is part of the marketing mix or a completely independent discipline, attention and research should look into the interplay of marketing functions, such as advertising and below-the-line marketing with public relations. By doing so, research will begin to reveal the different layers in PR practice and thereby possibly arrive at generic definitions for specific occasions.

According to a practitioner, 'The definition is key as public relations moves up the boardroom, the traditional roles in marcomms are changing and fast. New developments means that the power of PR is even more far reaching than before.' By researching these different areas of public relations, we can enhance our understanding of the use of public relations in different situations, and how it operates under these different conditions. A practitioner notes that this will help to 'define clearly the scope of the roles and responsibilities assumed by practitioners . . . identifying areas which need attention'.

Features of the market for PR service

According to the last report, it was suggested that research on this topic should be gathered primarily by the professional associations, as they acquire the staff resources to carry out this work.

Currently, surveys of market data and trends (such as cost structures in wage terms) have been carried out by the national members of the International Committee of Public Relations Consultancy Association (ICCO). Consequently, PR services in all their diversity and similarities can be understood, and the PR profession as a whole, will be in a better position to brief clients more effectively when it comes to developing international programmes. This is possible only if the features of the market and their implications for PR services are known.

Likewise, the PRSA and IABC have conducted research into a compensation survey. Further initiatives of this kind will help establish professionalism in public relations practice, in light of the industry's response to changes in the shape and values of the market.

Gender issues in PR practice

This was regarded as the least important topic, relative to the others cited. Understandably, it was female academics who considered this as an area worthy of research. Examples of comments include 'The field is increasingly feminized, in terms of numbers but certainly not in power. To avoid further devaluation of public relations, we need to study how the growing number of women will affect the field and, more importantly, how women can and do contribute if they are not forced into the male model' and 'Gender

issues in public relations is an interesting area and along with management theory, should be developed further in this area'.

Table 5.3 brings together the collection of new research priorities. Participants were required to rank each subject heading according to perceived importance on a scale of 1 to 7. The number of votes for each column would signify the amount of importance attached to the subject.

Technology and public relations

Given the boom in the internet and the dot.com industry since the 1990s, technology and public relations is an area of increasing importance for sustained research, as advances in digital technology result in new communication channels and audiences. Fashionable new terms such as 'convergence' and 'disintermediation' mean that managing communication and relationships has become more varied and complex. Issues such as interactivity (a new dimension to communication as opposed to the Grunig and

Table 5.3 Which topics from the new list do you consider to be most important?

Theme	Frequency of replies						
Ranking in order of importance	1	2	3	4	5	6	7
Technology and public relations	10	5	3	7	9	4	3
Examining specific aspects of PR practice, or new communication areas that come under the remit of the communication professional	6	6	12	8	1	7	2
Reputation and issues management and corporate identity	12	11	5	5	5	3	2
Human resources, internal relations and personnel communication	1	4	7	4	10	5	9
Client expectations, service quality and PR	5	9	4	8	6	1	8
Education in public relations and use of social science research	4	2	7	5	5	9	4
The scope of PR theory and practice	7	5	8	3	1	7	9

Hunt's (1984) long-standing two-way symmetrical model of communication between organizations and their publics), freedom of choice on the internet and respective PR activities designed to respond to this change, are possible research areas.

An academic commented how 'The impact of new technologies is a key issue. The internet has brought enormous changes to the way organizations communicate, and the fragmentation of the media as a result has meant that PR practitioners have to work in a different way.' Another mentioned, '(this) remains a constant area of professional interest especially given the potential impact of technological change on the required skills base of practitioners'.

Examining specific aspects of PR practice, or new communication areas that come under the remit of the communication professional

This topic brings together a combination of concepts from other disciplines from the social sciences (such as psychology and sociology) and analyses how their application in PR practice makes communication more effective. To illustrate, the political equivalent of public relations is public affairs. Possible research in this field of PR can be in political marketing during elections.[5] This topic also looks at special interest groups within the PR profession, such as financial PR or PR in the voluntary/not-for-profit sector.

Suggestions for research into public affairs include 'The impact of public relations/public affairs on business success' and socio-political issues 'applies to all public relations, not simply government affairs, because politics touches everyone sooner or later'.

Public affairs provides a wealth of research opportunities as it includes other activities within the remit of the professional communicator, such as community relations, which according to a practitioner is 'an aspect of corporate social responsibility' and research should be on 'whether it is (or should be) an expectation that good businesses/organisations have a responsibility to government/regulatory consultation to help fashion public interest outcomes'.

Reputation and issues management and corporate identity

As large corporations and organizations struggle to remain favourable in the constant media spotlight, the need for proactive public relations and the demand for services in issues and crisis management have increased. Most research in this area exists in documented case studies of corporate disasters that were controlled or averted, successfully or otherwise. There remains the need to demonstrate empirically the effectiveness of public relations in these situations. A problem however, would be in gaining access to conduct research as the relevant information is usually sensitive and hidden from the public gaze. Indeed, an understanding of the concept of corporate identity and corporate image is essential to the PR practitioner in understanding how reputation is built and formed.[6]

Respondent answers are described below:

* 'Reputation and issues management is the key for methodology development and also for clients/employers of PR.'
* 'Issues such as legitimacy and social responsibility are important in our consideration of reputation management.'

A practitioner claims that research should be in 'defining good corporate responsibility with reference to good communication, e.g. internal and community relations'.

Human resources, internal relations and personnel communication

This topic refers to research into how PR agencies recruit and keep staff, an area which in current management jargon is known as the 'emotional capital' of an organization. Research in the area of 'talent management' has been conducted by recruitment consultants Odgers Ray and Berndtson.

This topic also refers to research into communication programmes with all personnel working for an organization, whether technical, e.g. the monthly staff newsletter, or strategic, e.g. specialized schemes to boost staff morale in the face of a possible crisis. Thus, there are other areas for research for this topic, e.g. issues management (especially in relationships with trade unions) and employee relations.

A practitioner noted: 'I think human resources, internal relations and personnel communications is a clumsy description. We are simply addressing internal audiences and relationships (and indeed the internal organisation aspects of reputation management and corporate identity issues). Yes we know that for historical reasons HR/personnel often inherited internal communication, and external relationships might be allocated to a marketing function. This bifurcation is unwise, and reflects naively about organisational structure and mechanics.'

Client expectations, service quality and public relations

Understandably, practitioners expressed concern for this topic. Interest centred around researching client/agency relationships, from a client's perspective. Research would concentrate on strategic relationships between users of public relations and PR service providers, in the effort to understand the requirements and wants of clients. A practitioner said, 'It's good to know how we should change and develop to meet the needs and wants of our clients, but it would also be useful if, as an industry, we could advise clients how *they* should change and develop to get the most out of PR . . . it would be fair to get both sides of the argument – e.g. clients would say they want more strategic advice from their PR team. The flip side of that might be the PR team saying that they'd love nothing more than to give more strategic advice but rarely have the opportunity to do so.'

This topic can be examined as an extension of the subject 'the measurement and evaluation of public relations'. A practitioner who is also an academic noted, 'I see both clients and students being more concerned with financial results and our capabilities to demonstrate them. And to be honest, as long as we are not capable of demonstrating the financial outcomes of our inputs (which clearly are costs) we have limited growth capacity.' Another practitioner academic commented, 'PR needs to demonstrate its "deliverables" to the organisation . . . (and) evaluation will only be successfully addressed in a pervasive research culture.'

By studying the levels of client satisfaction in qualitative and quantitative terms, researchers will be able to analyse service quality. At present, the issue of quality in public relations is being researched by the International Institute for Quality in Public Relations (IQPR) and their findings have helped to develop ISO 9000 standards in public relations. The demands of this quality standard are high. Briefly, they will cover four key aspects: the responsibility of PR management, the needs of clients, the necessary resources needed to maintain these standards and the structure of the quality system.

Education in PR and use of social science research

This topic ranked highly among academics engaged in research and/or pedagogy. Research into PR education increases professionalism and forms the basis for good educational programmes. Fundamentally, all subjects that have appeared on the last list and this update, are in context, useful for public relations education in a large extent.

Research in this area could concentrate on analysing the different methods of teaching and training for public relations in the different countries. An academic suggested that research should look into forming 'possible guidelines for public relations education at different levels, i.e. undergraduate, postgraduate, postdoctoral'. Presumably, this would entail examining the curricula or syllabuses of PR/PR-related courses in individual countries, or in comparison between different countries, or between different universities that teach public relations. Research in education has already been conducted in media studies and mass communication, done by organizations like the National Communication Association based in Washington, DC, and the Association for Education in Journalism and Mass Communication, Colorado State University, in the United States.

A practitioner suggested that 'the basics need to be attended to first – all theses for which advanced degrees are awarded in public relations by universities should be logged and subject to scrutiny by a practitioner panel (from a national PR organisation, such as the PRSA or IPR) of the highest calibre and used as the basis for further and better research that is libraried and made available to all business and management schools'.

In terms of professional skills in public relations, there is the need 'to fine-tune the educational programmes in line with vocational needs'.

The scope of PR theory and practice

This subject would examine public relations from different perspectives. For instance, public relations as a subject is taught mostly in schools of journalism in the United States, while in the United Kingdom, it normally belongs to faculties of business in universities. Is the subject of public relations a communication or management discipline? Is it marketing led, or has it a strategic role? By examining this topic closely, one of the results would be the definition of what PR practice is, in different circumstances. This being the case, there will be an eventual widening of the skills base of a PR practitioner through knowing what is required of public relations in different contexts.

General comments included: 'There seems to be a lot of disagreement over the scope and meaning of PR. I think that the term is becoming too closely related to media relations. The term that seems to be increasingly in use is communication or reputation'; and 'There seems to be room for further development. In the long term, we shall of course have moreinsights into the topic(s) . . . the findings shall eventually be beneficial for producers and consumers of public relations services.'

This section was included in the questionnaire in order to see if there was any congruence with respondents' stipulated research interests. In the case of the academics surveyed, it serves as a measure of the current trends in learning and the present state of PR theory. As most academics are involved in multidisciplinary research in public relations, looking at it from such diverse subject areas as historiography, sociology, rhetoric, marketing and business studies, it became evident that the result will be a cross-fertilized picture of public relations. From a practitioner's perspective, it exposed the PR problems and patterns that professionals face on a daily basis and perhaps also the urgency felt in the search for feasible solutions. Again, it teased from respondents, questions pertaining to the nature of the business of public relations and helped shed light on the different (and differing) ways in which public relations is approached and applied.

Academic view

There was consensus that research should be conducted into the 'relationship management' aspect of public relations. This concept of public relations is not entirely new (Grunig and Hunt, 1984), forming the foundation of modern public relations theory and practice, but it does mean that the need for a defini-

tion of public relations is still relevant today despite many previous attempts (by national public relations associations especially) to construct a universal meaning for public relations. Most recently, the EBOK project for instance, lists 'communications' and 'relationship building' as major concepts in European public relations. For this study, an academic commented, 'The nature of relationships – how to define and measure them – seems to be the biggest topic today.' This view is in keeping with participants' earlier listing of 'relationship building' and 'social interaction' as an area of research interest.

Some academics were also interested in the role of public relations in other business/mass communication functions, such as its use in integrated marketing communication (IMC). For one academic, it was crucial to study 'organisational configurations supporting integrated communications', as there is the need to institutionalize good communication throughout organizations. While for another, emphasis should be on 'participant observation and in-depth interviews with media organisations, including online news services, to determine the value of different approaches by public relations sources', the rationale being that media relations is the most widely used method by organizations wishing to enhance their reputations.

Other suggestions include:

- PR education and 'the underlying diversity and richness of (different) "schools of thought" ' as this forms the basis of providing practitioners with a 'clear view of the profession';
- the development of effectiveness models that link PR outcomes to organizational performance indicators;

- the equity value of corporate reputation;
- identifying measures on the return on investment (ROI) in PR activities;
- organizational response to activist pressures;
- social implications of unprofessional public relations.

PR education is a continued source of research for academics and the spring (1999) edition of *Public Relations Review* is solely devoted to this topic. Professional bodies such as the Public Relations Society of America have also conducted research into PR education.[7]

Currently, the Swedish Public Relations Association SPRA, along with other private initiatives, are engaged in research on the return of investment on non-material assets.[8]

The social implications of public relations are linked to a range of issues such as culture and organizational behaviour, and are closely aligned on the macro-level with research into interest/pressure group activity and public relations. Most of the work done in this area has been collected in the form of case studies, such as Shell's Brent Spar episode. The growing influence of NGOs, along with the anarchist tendencies of some lobbying groups, as seen at the anti-capitalist protests in Seattle and Prague, and the Nice summit in 2000, and the need to manage these situations proactively while under constant media scrutiny makes ethical issues and activism in the PR environment an increasingly important area for study.

Practitioner view

There was a difference in the way practitioners approached this question. Practitioners are more concerned with business-related issues

encountered on a day-to-day basis and this is clearly reflected in their suggestions.

Obvious suggestions for research emphasis were in strategy and public relations, and the construction of a methodology for issues and reputation management. Most practitioners wanted research to concentrate on specific aspects of PR practice such as public affairs and political communication. As with the academic view, interest/pressure group activity is an important topic, but the focus is on the organization itself and the legal and regulatory perimeters that organizations operate in, rather than the management of possible external threats. For one practitioner, there needs to be research into the 'link between good corporate governance and good corporate communication (for both internal and external audiences)' and defining 'good corporate social responsibility with reference to good corporate communications, e.g. public affairs activity as an aspect of corporate social responsibility in the fashioning of public interest outcomes'. A practitioner remarked that research should look into issues such as, 'is communication global . . . why are NGOs better communicators than anyone else? Is it because they are better politicians than politicians?' As an area of research into the failure of effective communication, examples provided were political lobbying in the anti-abortion, anti-tobacco campaigns. Other suggestions by practitioners included 'measurement and evaluation' and 'client–agency relationships'.

In terms of measurement and evaluation, a practitioner commented that research should go into, 'Practical, low cost research methods for PR – e.g. the validity of case studies, pre-testing, etc. PR seems unaware of the many low-cost and no-cost research tools and still makes the excuse of not doing evaluation because of the cost'. Multinational PR agencies have in place some form of auditing procedure to determine the relative effectiveness of their communications. Likewise, there are market research companies involved in quantitative media measurement and evaluation. A wealth of resources, data and expertise thus exists for further, more detailed research into this area. An interesting note here would be the practitioner–academic divide over this topic. Despite listing 'evaluation and measurement' as still having relevance to PR practice, the general academic viewpoint concerning research into evaluation and measurement is that has been 'done to death', a view not shared by practitioners. Perhaps a likely reason for this is, as with any academic subject, that there will be occasions when certain contemporaneous themes, such as the evaluation and measurement of public relations, become 'hot topics'. Swept by the *Zeitgeist*, the result will be a plethora of research into that topic. A calculation of the number of graduate dissertations written on evaluation and measurement of PR activities, in relation to other research topics at a given period, will confirm this hypothesis. This trend, in turn, signals how public relations has developed and matured as an academic subject.

The question of client–agency relationships can be researched from either perspective, and also in tandem with measurement and evaluation. According to a practitioner, research could focus on the 'elements that PR practitioners believe could change or improve their relationships with clients, and the acceptability of those suggestions could be tested among their clients'. From this suggestion, other issues may be considered such as 'fees for pitches, client funding of measurement and evaluation of PR through research departments'.

It is difficult to draw up a definitive list of research priorities for a variety of reasons. In order to have a more balanced view between theory and practice, it was decided that both academics and practitioners would be surveyed. However, conflicting opinions arose simply because of the different research needs and demands of the respective groups. It was detected that the research priorities of academics depend on personal interest. Similarly, practitioners' research interests were in the area of their particular specialism, or the field of public relations that they work in. Thus, there was a fair amount of bias shown when participants were requested to choose their research priorities from the lists provided.

There were certain points of agreement, such as those relating to questions that are abstract and require critical discourse to appreciate. An example of a question of this nature is the perennial inquiry into the image of public relations. Public relation's roots in propaganda and publicity and its past and present use of persuasion to manipulate and manage provides opportunities for continued research and is also a sign of the evolution of public relations as an object of serious scholarship.

Instead of looking out for consensus, research interests were compared and contrasted so that common issues or points of contention were revealed, thus adding to our understanding of the nature and current state of PR research.

Problems encountered during the analysis of research findings were:

- Some participants provide vague answers to open-ended questions. This made interpretation a complex process. For the closed-ended questions, specific instructions were sometimes not followed. Several respondents ticked instead of rating research subjects according to perceived importance. These answers were obscure as they provided no sense of the particular subject's relative standing to other subject headings. They were discounted as such.

- Some respondents felt that certain subject categories were of equal importance, so there are instances of double rating. This made overall comparison difficult because responses had to be double-counted.

- Some respondents did not rate at all while a few felt that they weren't confident about answering the questionnaire as they were unfamiliar with the original report, or felt that they did not have sufficient expertise in the areas cited to offer a critical or informed opinion. These questions were left unanswered by respondents.

- Several respondents felt that the questionnaire design was poor. According to them, there are areas of overlap in the questions provided, while certain questions needed further clarification. It was felt that the question categories were not in-depth and should have been normative rather than precise. Another criticism was that the questions were too constraining. A respondent felt that the choice of subjects should be reduced. The result was potential confusion for participants.

During White and Blamphin's 1994 Delphi study, participants were asked the question 'Who sets the agenda?' and the general response was that academics and practitioners should deepen their dialogue since theoretical and applied research into public relations are important if public relations is to achieve credibility as a profession and an academic discipline. This short study was such a collaborative effort between these two groups to determine the areas of thought and concern facing present and future public relations research. It has been successful in its objective to understand the PR environment from theoretical and practical perspectives. It has also been successful in gathering opinion from a broad cross-section of participants, and has considered contemporary PR theory and practice from an international standpoint.

This study does not propose to set the agenda for PR research but is representative in expressing the views (collective and otherwise) of its participants. The observations and suggestions mentioned in this report have refreshed the original list of research priorities set out in 1994. In principal, all subject headings from the 1994 study are still relevant to research, and the original list of sixteen subject categories has expanded to include topics previously unidentified. What this report has done is to highlight the changes in and additions to the PR research agenda over the six-year period. It has also considered the differences in opinion from the two groups surveyed, i.e. academic and practitioner, and has outlined the implications of these differences for future PR research.

NOTES

1 Research paper presented by White and Blamphin (1994), 'Priorities for research into public relations practice in the United Kingdom: a report from a Delphi study carried out among UK practitioners and public relations academics in May, June and July 1994', at the Research Symposium held at the Institute of Public Relations, London on 11 November 1994.

2 Wheeler, T., D. Moss and J. White, 'A draft report for the public relations education trust: the strategic options for public relations research in the United Kingdom', October 1990.
3 This paper was the largest and most comprehensive study ever undertaken on public relations education in America, and was presented at the National Communication Association's 1998 Summer Conference on Public Relations Education.
4 A brief summary of each topic is available online from the Institute for Public Relations' website: http://www.instituteforpr.com/projects.html. Wright, Donald K. (1998) *Corporate Communications Policy Concerning the Internet: A Survey of the Nation's Senior-Level Corporate Public Relations Officers*, Gainsville, FL: Institute for Public Relations Research and Education. Pavlik, John V. (1997) *Management Policy Issues on the Internet: The Public Relations Perspective*, Gainsville, FL: Institute for Public Relations Research and Education. Pavlik, J. V. and David M. Dozier (1996) *Managing the Information Superhighway: A Report on the Issues Facing Communication Professionals*, Gainsville, FL: Institute for Public Relations Research and Education.
5 Volume 30 (1996), issue 10–11 of the *European Journal of Marketing* investigates the various ways which marketing communications is employed in politics.
6 Volume 31 (1997), issue 5 of *European Journal of Marketing* explores corporate identity, what it means, what it entails and how it is managed.
7 The PRSA's website (http://www.prsa.org/) provides an online version of its research *Public Relations Education for the 21st Century: A Port of Entry. The Report of the Commission on Public Relations Education*, October 1999.
8 The SPRA (http://www.sverigesinformationsforening.se/) has details on its report *Return on Communications*.

REFERENCES

Berth, Kirsten and Sjöberg, Göran (1997) *Quality in Public Relations*, Copenhagen: IQPR.
Botan, Carl H. and Hazelton, Vincent Jr. (eds) (1989) *Public Relations Theory*, Hillsdale, NJ: Lawrence Erlbaum Associates.
Broom, Glen M. and Dozier, David M. (1990) *Using Research in Public Relations: Applications to Programme Management*, NJ: Prentice-Hall.
Grunig, J. E. and Hunt, T. (1984) *Managing Public Relations*, Hillsdale, NJ: Lawrence Erlbaum Associates.
Grunig, J. (ed.) (1992) *Excellence in Communications and Public Relations Management*, Hillsdale, NJ: LEA.
Heath, R. L. and Vasquez, G. (2001) *Handbook of Public Relations*, Thousand Oaks, CA: Sage.
IPRA Gold Paper No. 3 (1979) *A Report on Public Relations Research*, London.
IPRA Gold Paper No. 4 (1982) *A Model for Public Relations Education for Professional Practice*, London.IPRA Gold Paper No. 12 (1997) *The Evolution of Public Relations Education and the Influence of Globalisation: Survey of Eight Countries*, London.
L'Etang, Jacquie and Pieczka, Magda (eds) (1996) *Critical Perspectives in Public Relations*, London: International Thompson Business Press.
MacManus, T. and Moss, D. (1997) *Public Relations Research: An International Perspective*, London: ITBP.
McQuail, Dennis (1994) *Mass Communications Theory: An Introduction*, London: Sage.
Moloney, K., Noble, P. and Ephram, K. (1999) Working Papers in Public Relations Research 3, 'Where Are They Now?' The Source Book of a Research Project into Six Cohorts of Graduates from BA (Hons) Public Relations, School of Media Arts and Communications, Bournemouth University.
Moss, D., Verčič, D. and Warnaby, G. (eds) (2000) *Perspectives on Public Relations Research*, London: Routledge.
Pavlik, J. (1987) *Public Relations: What Research Tells Us*, Newbury Park, CA: Sage.
Roberts, Patrick (2000) *Reputation Gets Legal: Reputation, Risk and Law Reform and the Challenge to Public Relations Practitioners*, seminar session at the IPR National Conference, London.

Rush, Jonathan (2000) *The Death of Spin? How the Internet Radically Changes the Way Corporations Will Communicate*, London: IPR.

Stacks, D. W., Botan, C. and Turk, J. V. (1999) 'Perceptions of public relations education', *Public Relations Review*, 25(1), 9–28.

Toth, Elizabeth (ed.) (1992) *Rhetorical and Critical Perspectives to Public Relations*, Hillsdale, NJ: LEA.

CHAPTER 6

Communication similarities and differences in listed and unlisted family enterprises

Liam Ó Móráin

In the United States, corporate governance legislation was introduced primarily directed at listed enterprises requiring executives to certify financial statements as accurate and requiring increased oversight of boards and auditors. Private unlisted enterprise however, remains free from such regulatory control and security. This chapter asks if there is a role for corporate communication in governance at enterprise, either listed or unlisted. The chapter will look at some relevant governance issues and outline the historical development of communication in unlisted enterprises.

Introduction

As a communication practitioner (PR, IMC, corporate affairs, etc.) in Ireland this researcher's encouragement to examine corporate communication (CorpCom) in the context of the similarities differences, comparisons and contrasts between listed and unlisted family owned enterprises is to gain a greater understanding of the unlisted family owned enterprise decision makers' motivation towards communication best practice in organizations on the one hand, and, on the other hand, to understand the practised reluctance of these decision makers to apply best practice in their communication. In addition our goal is to investigate real or imagined reasons for the ad hoc approach to communication, i.e.

'PR is press relations, and because we don't talk to the media, we don't need PR'.

Different government agencies' investigations (Ireland and the United States) into certain aspects of how governance and corporate management operate, especially in relation to listed enterprises, has created tighter rules and new regulations in terms of establishing accountability, responsibility and transparency with respect to the interests of shareholder investments and returns. In Ireland, political and business–government bribery scandals and investor tax avoidance scandals, which involved exposing governance and corporate management dishonesty and fraud (the Ansbacher Inquiry, the Flood Enquiry, the Moriarty Tribunal) have led to the establishment of a new director of corporate enforcement (Hegarty, 2002). In the United States, corporate governance legislation was introduced, primarily directed at listed enterprise enforcement, requiring executives to certify financial statements are accurate and requiring increased oversight of boards and auditors (*Sunday Business Post*, 22 December 2002).

Private unlisted enterprise is free from such regulatory control and scrutiny. Crosbie (2000) explains that family businesses tend to be less profitable than other kinds of businesses, and argues that family firms take a long time to build, but that building them, rather than satisfying the short-term dividend, needs of a group of shareholders, is usually the key objective. Crosbie says that: 'Family firms are greatly helped by the fact that they do not have a public AGM at which they have to show shareholders what they have achieved and a public company has to prove, every single year, that it is profitable, while a family [unlisted] firm does not.'

This chapter examines literature exclusively, and in researching the origins, emergence and development of communication in enterprise, focuses initially on CorpCom in management and asks if there is a role for CorpCom at governance in enterprise, either listed or unlisted? In an effort to further examine the opportunities of corporate communication at governance in enterprise, this chapter discusses some relevant governance issues and outlines the historical development of communication in unlisted enterprise.

Although there is a dearth of literature addressing the relationship between governance, CorpCom and directorial duty, and although CorpCom is addressed by academics (Van Riel, Dolphin, Oliver, Grunig, Argenti, *et al.*) in management terms, this chapter believes there is opportunity to develop and apply a CorpCom model at governance, and suggests such a model.

A limited unstructured qualitative research process, involving two Irish based family owned unlisted enterprises – one a group of companies, the other a one-product (brand) company – is under way, and is aimed at challenging and testing the suggested CorpCom–governance model, introduced here. No conclusions are proposed at this time, as the qualitative research is not yet completed nor available, however a specific area of further research is suggested.

Literature review

Existing literature and scholarly work focuses on the strategic, policy and implementation programme aspects of corporate communication, as a management tool, in quoted enterprises. There is limited academic published study in the area of unquoted enterprise specific to corporate communication, although many published academic works discuss governance, ownership, entrepreneurship, and a variety of management disciplines that encompass communication issues indirectly rather than specifically and exclusively addressing research topics in corporate communication.

To date, there appears to be a dearth of study, research or investigation into the corporate communication function in unquoted enterprises, especially unquoted family enterprises. From our study and limited research, this chapter shows that scholarly and investigative research in quoted enterprise is growing in intensity and focuses on areas and issues of corporate communication management disciplines. The corporate communication field of study has been evolving throughout the twentieth century in schools of communication and journalism. Research in corporate communication, outside the realms of mass communications, journalism and organizational communication is sparse (Argenti, 1996). However, there is evidence that research in corporate communication by a variety of writers (Oliver, Argenti, Varey and White, Heath, Grunig, Munter, Van Riel, Dolphin and others) is continuing with an emphasis on quoted enterprises. Dolphin (1999) offers the following definition of CorpCom: 'Corporate communication is the strategic management process by which an organisation communicates with its various audiences to the mutual benefit of both and to its improved competitive advantage.'

A management approach

It would appear that corporate communication is seen exclusively as a management function within the fields of academic debate with leading authorities (Oliver, Van Riel, Heath, Dolphin, Grunig, Argenti *et al.*) examining the authoritative management position or role of corporate communication in quoted enterprises, and arguing how different communication disciplines – strategic, policy and/or programme – may be prioritized as management circumstances dictate. For instance, Oliver (2001) argues that due to downsizing there is increased responsibility for managers and staff to know and be familiar with the company's strategic plan, and that traditional corporate strategy viewed the management system in the following manner: 'Strategic planning as a top level activity, management control as a middle manager executive activity and operational control as a supervisory, or first level management task'. Corporate communication in all areas, says Oliver (2001) is affected by 'the prevailing top-down culture'. Greater understanding, in terms of its application to the unquoted family company, will be

gained from closely examining this view. Van Riel (1995) believes that communication is increasingly gaining the status of a valuable, if not indispensable management tool, together with the obligations that such status carries: 'In common with financial management, production management and human resource management, communication is expected to contribute to the achievement of company objectives. Communication's role in this process can be summarised briefly as follows: "to professionally carry out the window and the mirror function" ' (Van Riel, 1995).

Van Riel (1995) explains that the phrase 'window functions' addresses the preparation and execution of communication policy ensuring that messages show all aspects of an organization in a clear and attractive manner. 'The anticipated outcomes of this portrayal are the changes desired by the company on a cognitive, affective and conative level in those target groups with which it is aimed to build and maintain a relationship' (Van Riel, 1995).

Van Riel (1995) also explains that the phrase 'mirror function' addresses the monitoring process of environments' developments and anticipating how they may affect or impact on the organization's communication policy: 'For instance, the mapping of image-building among relevant stakeholders, publication of actual achievements, (e.g. market shares), evaluations of future trends (issue management) and, in particular, keeping up with changes in the internal organizational climate'.

Corporate communication is an approach rather than a discipline, Dolphin (1999), and it has developed into 'an essential management discipline': 'It is an approach that sets out to ensure the consistency of the corporate message and the transparency of the organisation. It is a function that anticipates issues, events, and crises before they occur. Through its messages and themes the organisation conveys its desired image and persona' (Dolphin, 1999).

Heath (1994) also endorses corporate communication as a management function and argues that an understanding of communication can help managers and their personnel co-ordinate efforts needed to achieve their company's mission. Varey and White (2000) state that the debate continues about that part of the overall management task having to do with the management of important relationships and with communicating with groups in these relationships. Introducing, and critically analysing, this model of the CorpCom system of managing – integrating internal with external communication systems and processes, Varey and White (2000) 'urge stronger, direct linkages between those who need to communicate and those who are charged with enabling and facilitating these interactions'.

None of these academic writers and researchers, from our research and from the information available, appears to draw a distinction between listed enterprise, and unquoted family enterprise, although the emphasis in the literature is clearly weighted in favour of debating issues relating to the functionality of CorpCom in listed enterprise (Van Riel, Dolphin, Oliver *et al.*).

A role for CorpCom at governance?

Academic research appears to have overlooked governance and corporate communication. Research shows there is no debate on the issues as to whether corporate communication should have director responsibility on the boards of listed or unquoted enterprises. Corporate communication as a governance

duty and responsibility for board directors is of specific interest here. As a practitioner working with business and industry in Ireland the challenge is to persuade board directors of unquoted enterprises and their senior management to establish sustained planned business-objective-driven corporate communication programmes aimed at supporting their strategic and corporate business objectives. Oliver (1997) argues that firefighting responses to communication problems are not strategic and endanger the corporate mission at a number of levels. Practitioner experience in Ireland suggests that communication management in enterprises operates as Oliver (1997) terms the current practice, as a 'short-term management imperative'. CorpCom is reflected in Ireland primarily as a media-relations-driven, PR function. Varey and White (2000) make a strong argument in favour of managers' need to recognize the CorpCom managing system 'as central to the work of the enterprise community': 'The corporate communication approach enables the reconstitution of social and economic interests, for business is in reality a socio-economic institution upon which we are all dependent' (Varey and White, 2000).

Corporate community is the new form of organization governance that shifts emphasis from profit to democracy by unifying the goals of all parties and while the old model of business is too limited because it is ignoring the reality that business is both an economic and a social institution, corporate governance can evolve towards collaboration amongst all stakeholders (Varey and White, 2000). They discuss the changes in corporate governance and the growing influence of stakeholders on management and suggest that collaboration with stakeholders is now occurring as the stakeholders gain power and because managers need their support (Varey and White,

2000). Stakeholders with a large stake in a company have a greater incentive to play an active role in corporate decisions because they internalize the benefits from their monitoring effort (Pagano and Roell, 1998). In Europe, most companies are not listed on stock exchanges and when they are, Pagano and Roell (1998) report that a single large stake-holder, or a tightly knitted group of share-holders retains a stake in the company: 'Since this ownership structure makes companies impervious to takeovers, the controlling stake is commonly retained by the founder of the company, and by his descendents, even when the company is large and publicly listed.'

This chapter introduces this perspective in the context of establishing choices for the application of CorpCom at governance level. Pagano and Roell (1998) state that it is quite expensive for a publicly listed company to expand its shareholder base, although there is a large fixed cost to listing and they argue that the initial owner is no longer able to pre-vent changes to the identity of his external shareholders. Their argument concludes that if the initial shareholder wants to sell out to many shareholders he must go public. On the other hand: 'If he keeps the company private instead he cannot sell majority status to more than a few large shareholders. As a result he saves the cost of listing the company on the Stock Exchange but has to accept a degree of monitoring far greater than that which minim-ises ongoing costs' (Pagano and Roell, 1998).

Research into CorpCom, focusing on com-munication of private information and initial public offerings evaluation in Asia, presented a discussion (Eng, Khoo and Tan, 1998) on the role of audit reports as the means of commu-nicating the value of an entrepreneur's firm to key investor audiences, investment bankers, auditors, and empirical tests, carried out on

samples of initial public offerings in the United States and Canada, found that valua-tion is positively related to retained owner-ship, the auditors' report and auditors' quality. No research was found to prove or disprove a perceived opinion in the business community that unlisted firms shy away from CorpCom, as a strategy, because the need to communicate in the wider financial and busi-ness circles is not necessary.

No specific references were found in aca-demic journals to CorpCom and governance with a decided interest in Ireland, although Hegarty (2002) reports the announcement of three of the most significant developments in corporate governance in Ireland in many years. These developments concern the duties and responsibilities of both directors and auditors as well as the creation of the new office of the Director of Corporate Enforce-ment. While these developments are similar to equivalent developments in both the United States and the United Kingdom, the impetus for each of them pre-dates the recent corporate scandals in the United States. Oliver (1997) believes that corporate decision making which addresses public relations as a core discipline rather than a marginal one, produces different outcomes and different environments in the post-bureaucratic organ-ization of today, even where modern man-agers remain addicted to administration and bureaucratization. Strategy-led communica-tion, according to Van Riel, is as essential to an enterprise as prudent strategy-led financial directorship. This chapter argues that com-munication may best be implemented if and when corporate communication takes its place in governance, to underpin the strategic importance of CorpCom, as a strategic support to its current position as a management (only) function, and this chapter will endeavour to address this theory in the context of listed quoted enterprise and unquoted family owned enterprise.

Family enterprise

There is a shortage of scholarly, informed or academic writing and/or study in the specific areas of corporate communication, and governance duty relating to listed or un-quoted family enterprise. In order to better understand the opportunities of functional corporate communication at governance in enterprise (listed or unquoted), it is important to examine the governance issues in both types of enterprise, and to appreciate the historical development of unquoted family enterprise.

Research literature on family business is limited. Goffee (1996):

> This reflects both a bias towards the study of large organisations as well as an assumption that within these ownership is widely dispersed. Even where it is acknowledged that ownership (and control – once the share structure has been analysed) remains largely concentrated within a single private family, such information is rarely applied to explanations of managerial or organisational behaviour.

Westhead and Cowling (1997) define a family company as follows:

1   More than 50 per cent of voting shares are owned by a single family group related by blood or marriage.
2   More than 50 per cent of voting shares are owned by a single family group related by blood or marriage and the company is perceived by the respondent to be a family business.
3   More than 50 per cent of voting shares are owned by a single family group related by blood or marriage and the company is perceived by the respondent to be a family business and one or more of the management team is drawn from the largest family group who own the company.
4   More than 50 per cent of voting shares are owned by a single family group related by blood or marriage and the company is perceived by the respondent to be a family business and 51 per cent or more of the management team is drawn from the largest family group who own the company
5   More than 50 per cent of voting shares are owned by a single family group related by blood or marriage and the company is perceived by the respondent to be a family business and one or more of the management team is drawn from the largest family group who own the company, and the company is owned by second generation or more family members.

Westhead and Cowling (1997) suggest that many family businesses begin as entrepreneurial owners,

> exploiting a market opportunity but failing to develop managerial control systems which can cope with growth. Most will fail as a result of these shortcomings, but a small minority may develop the organisational mechanisms necessary to make a successful transition to managerial ownership. From this position, substantial growth – often to publicly quoted status – is possible.

But over time, both entrepreneurial (if they survive) and managerial owners may slip into the paternal mode often sacrificing market opportunities in order to sustain employment relationships characterised by loyalty and mutual responsibilities.

The unprecedented contribution throughout the ages of family enterprise – rather than non-family enterprise – is well documented (Goffee, Rose, Payne, Habukkuk, Rudding, Chandler, Heath, Neubauer and Lank, Scott, Westhead and Cowling). This chapter briefly endeavours to understand more about this, by beginning at the role of the family enterprise during the development of the industrial era, examining how the family business enterprise played a key role in it, and by looking at how quoted and unquoted enterprises developed in this environment. It also seeks to examine briefly if communication played any role.

Family businesses, which were instrumental in the industrialization of most countries, provide a continuing important dimension in modern economies worldwide (Rose, 1995). Payne (1984) in Rose, (1995) reports that in the British industrial revolution of the eighteenth century the power of heredity and the vitality of the family as an economic group was quite remarkable. Legal, economic and cultural forces of the eighteenth and nineteenth centuries advanced the popularity of the family enterprise, and with the continuous threat of bankruptcy, the influence of common law partnership and unlimited liability meant that many businesses preferred to be associated with their family connections than with outsiders (Rose, 1995). Rose also suggests that the local community was the core of the business because business activity was localized, the causes of action were local and therefore the boundaries of the family firm regarding finance, managers and

labourers were based/drawn from the local community. In explaining the developmental and change management role of the family enterprise in the eighteenth century in Britain, Habukkuk (1955) in Rose (1995) suggests that during the early period of industrialization family firms proved the principal agents of change, their rapid turnover providing the dynamism which fuelled the growth process.

Family firms account for between 75 per cent and 99 per cent of all companies in the European Union, and for 65 per cent of GDP and employment in Europe (Rose, 1995). In the United States, one-third of Fortune 500 companies are family owned (FT 93). Beyond Europe and the United States, the family firm has been, and continues to be, the norm (Rose, 1995). Family businesses – mostly small – are the dynamic in Chinese capitalism leading to the significant transformation of Southeast and East Asian economies since the 1970s (Rudding in Rose, 1995). The corporate communication function, especially as a management tool, is not referred to nor specifically mentioned in the literature. Family enterprise owners and their managerial hierarchies are discussed by a number of writers (Chandler, Heath, Neubauer and Lank) in the context of enterprise development.

Chandler in Rose (1995) says that due to the arrival of the large industrial family owned enterprise in the west the ease with which family management maintained itself in labour intensive fragmented industries was highlighted, and that in the capital-intensive, concentrated industries the recruitment of managerial hierarchies was necessary for enterprises to enter markets, survive in them and extend their market share. Similarly specific facilities and skills were required in other operational areas of the enterprise, e.g. production and distribution. In less complex production and distribution processes in smaller enterprises fewer hierarchies were needed, as with capital requirements:

> This theory suggests that members of the founder's family were able to have a continuing say in top management decision making as either inside or outside directors in less technological less capital using industries, and that representatives of banks, other financial institutions and large investors had more influence as outside directors in the more complex and more capital using industries.
>
> (Chandler, in Rose, 1995)

While Chandler makes no specific reference to the function of communication as a management tool, he introduces it indirectly as he explains the hierarchy theory in referring to capital-intensive industries entering markets, and as he distinguishes the directorship roles of insider and outsider directors in the decision-making process of the larger and the smaller enterprises.

Further indirect reference to communication activity is made by Chandler (in Rose, 1995) as he states that the family owned firm persisted in Britain longer than elsewhere primarily because entrepreneurs in Britain and Ireland, which was part of the United Kingdom at this time in history), were reluctant to make substantial investment in new and other untried processes of production, nor were they progressive in their approach to investing in marketing, distribution, research and facilities, and they were reluctant to turn part of the enterprise's administration over to non-family, salaried managers.

Further evidence of the fundamental contribution family controlled and owned enterprises have made throughout recent centuries is the huge family fortunes that were established from pioneering economic activities in the early days of the United States, including rail construction, banking and manufacturing industry (Neubauer and Lank, 1998).

Even after the separation of capital and management in the nineteenth century, the owning families continued to 'call the shots' when it came to directing enterprises at the highest levels. And in this day and age, when many of the better known corporations are owned by large numbers of dispersed anonymous shareholders (that is, they have lost their family business character), family controlled enterprises still generate between 45 per cent and 70 per cent of GNP of their respective countries.

(Neubauer and Lank, 1998)

During the 1980s and 1990s both in Europe and North America economic recessions allowed enterprises to drive these economies (Neubauer and Lank, 1998). Family-controlled and -owned enterprises created jobs, according to Neubauer and Lank (1998), and these enterprises were among the few that were successful enough to pay taxes and showed an agility and flexibility necessary to manoeuvre successfully in the troubled economic waters of their national economies: 'The situation has been similar in other parts of the world. In Asia, for instance, family controlled enterprises, with their vitality, elasticity and tenacity, have driven the (at least until late 1997) much admired thriving economies of that part of the world' (Neubauer and Lank, 1998).

Scott (in Goffee, 1996) says that family businesses – and no distinction is made between listed or unquoted enterprises – continue to represent an important form of work organization within advanced industrial economies and suggests that most small and medium-sized enterprises are family concerns with a small and important number of very large businesses remaining owned and controlled by private families that generate half of all existing and newly created jobs. Goffee (1996) reflects on the lack of research literature on family business, stating that there is a bias towards the study of large organizations as well as an assumption that within these ownership is widely dispersed: 'Even where it is acknowledged that ownership (and control) – once the share structure has been analysed – remains largely concentrated within a single private family, such information is rarely applied to explanations of managerial or organisational behaviour.'

Goffee says there is a need to investigate further the way in which owners of family businesses pursue strategies, which allow for growth and which help them to retain control, an issue relevant in CorpCom management and in governance. Goffee introduces the *Schein Culture Communication Framework*, a model that allows founders to get their own approaches and assumptions embedded within the actions, thoughts and feelings of others in their business. According to Schein (1985) (in Goffee, 1996), the process involves both conscious and deliberate action in addition to that which is unconscious and unintended. Goffee says there is more to passing on a family business and ensuring continuity than delegation and suggests that the success of this process will 'be shared by the (largely unexplored) ability of the founder to create and communicate a workable culture: one which assists members on coping with environmental realities'. The Schein Culture Communication Framework describes five 'primary mechanisms' for embedding and reinforcing culture:

1   What leaders pay attention to, measure and control;

2   leader reactions to critical incidents and organizational crises;
3   deliberate role modelling, teaching and coaching by leaders;
4   criteria for allocation of rewards and status;
5   criteria for recruitment, selection, promotion, retirement and excommunication.

In addition Schein's culture communication framework has five secondary mechanisms:

1   The organizations' design and culture;
2   organizational systems and procedures;
3   design of physical space, facades and buildings:
4   stories, legends, myths and parables about important events and people;
5   formal statements of organizational philosophy, creeds and charters.

Based on a detailed historical review of family businesses in Great Britain their strengths and weaknesses in terms of economic development are discussed and comparison is made between the performance of independent unquoted family and non-family companies in the United Kingdom. Payne (1984) in Westhead and Cowley (1997) concluded that 'the large public company, which retains elements of family control may retard economic growth; whereas, on balance, the small family business possibly promotes economic growth'.

Daily and Dollinger (1992) in (Westhead and Cowling, 1997) argue that owners of family firms are more likely to outperform management controlled non-family firms, and Demsetz (1983) (in Westhead and Cowling, 1997) justifies and supports this view when he says this is so because owners of family firms are more likely to maximize firm value, enabling them to personally realize any gains.

on the other hand, professional managers of non-family firms may not pursue profit maximisation and growth or oriented strategies because they prefer to maximise their own utility function (and realize financial gains for themselves directly) by pursuing activities which maximise short-run sales revenues. Daily and Dollinger (1992) found sales growth, improvement in net margin and perceived performance relative to the firm's major competitor were higher in family-owned and managed firms than in non-family firms.

Binder Hamlyn (1994) in Westhead and Cowling (1997) examined growth sales revenue, employment, exports, productivity and profitability in 667 private unquoted companies with sales revenues between £2.5 and £25m, in the period 1988–93, and they found that sales turnover growth in non-family companies was four times higher than in family companies. Family companies reported a fall of 3.8 per cent in productivity, while non-family companies recorded an 8.1 per cent increase. No evidence has been found that unquoted family enterprises employ CorpCom as a management discipline (and that is not to say they do not). There is the opportunity for further research to ascertain and evaluate how CorpCom strategies, if applied to these types of enterprises, may impact on their financial and overall performance.

Stoy Howard (1989) (in Westhead and Cowling, 1997) argued that family firms have other objectives in addition to financial performance targets, and Hay and Morris (1984) (in Westhead and Cowling, 1997) suggest that the desire to pass the business on to the next generation is one of the prime financial objectives of family firms in the United Kingdom. Binder Hamlyn (1994) (in Westhead and Cowling, 1997) also noted that:

> family rather than non-family companies were much more likely to desire continued independent ownership of the business by not selling or floating the business on the Stock Exchange. In addition, more family companies reported a desire to pass the business on within the family. They inferred for the latter group of companies that business stability was just as important as business expansion.
>
> (Binder Hamlyn, 1994, in Westhead and Cowling, 1997)

No research exists on CorpCom in family or listed, unquoted family enterprise in Ireland, although Hegarty (2002) reports on three significant developments that may have a profound influence in the future on CorpCom in all enterprises. The development focuses on corporate governance and concerns the duties and responsibilities of both directors and auditors as well as the creation of a new regulatory office – the Directorate of Corporate Enforcement.

Heath (1994) argues that since companies began to increase in size over a century ago, and with the development of large companies, particularly investor-owned corporations (quoted enterprises) employees' work had to be supervised and the function of managed communication emerged as a necessary management task: 'As is true of all instances when humans band together to amplify their individual efforts, communication was instrumental in the endeavour of managers to direct activities needed to create, produce and sell products or to provide services' (Heath, 1994).

While not specifying the differences or

similarities of quoted (listed) or unquoted enterprise, Heath (1994) also states clearly that people are the heart, soul and sinew of companies: 'through communication and the creation of meaning they co-ordinate and focus their efforts' (Heath, 1994).

Argenti (1998) turned to Aristotle's account of the roots of modern communication theory where Aristotle defines the composition of speech and this is later applied to modern communication needs in the *Munter communication theory* (Figure 6.1). Munter extends the Aristotle definition to managerial communication and adds two other elements including channel choice (or media) and cultural context. Belmiro, Gardiner, Simmons, Santos and Rentes (2000), when discussing communication change in organizations, suggested a much higher concern by management to the issue of corporate communication: 'it had been constantly suggested that it is better over-communicating with the workforce than missing opportunity for lack of it'. Young and Post (1994) in Belmiro, Gardiner, Simmons, Santos and Rentes (2000) argue that the more communication the better, the more informed the better, and the better you train the people in operating a feedback system to create discussion, then the better will be the business's performance.

Standards

The Conference Board Europe (1999) preface a comprehensive study of communication practices by US communication officers in forty-one industries and businesses with the comment that failure to communicate effectively can be a competitive disadvantage, and argue that the public, the media, regulators and special interest groups are intensifying their examination of corporate activities and demanding higher levels of accountability. It is clear that in the early 1990s there was concern in financial and corporate America as to the valuable function of business information and public confidence in it. The Jenkins Report, commissioned by the American Institute of Certified Public Accountants (1994) to improve the value of listed enterprises, business information and public confidence in it,

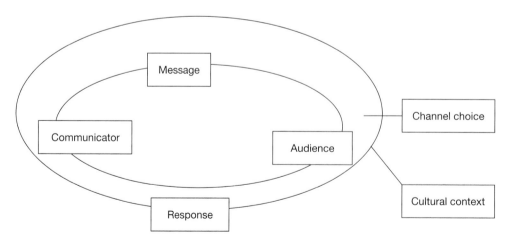

Figure 6.1 Munter communication theory

Source: Mary Munter, *Guide to Managerial Communication*, 4th edn, (Upper Saddle River, NJ, Prentice Hall, 1997) in Argenti, 1998

found that a great deal was right with the present state of reporting in the United States, but identified particular areas open to criticism where feasible solutions were offered. Similarly the Research Committee of the Institute of Chartered Accountants of Scotland (1999) decided to publish a report following their investigation into the needs and expectations of expert users regarding corporate information in the United Kingdom (Westman, Beattie, 1999). The ICAS research committee set out a blueprint for future reporting practices of linked companies (quoted enterprises) focusing on original empirical research work into current practices of users of business information including institutional investors, broker analysts and bank leaders. Their findings identified that: 'the analysis of the decision making process identified for attention the cycle of communication, the importance of maintaining confidence, the ability of expert users to explore and sift data, their selective use of key measures and the importance they attach to information about change'.

In the European Union, member states are required to establish and implement freedom of information acts to ensure greater access to information, decisions and provide for greater accountability in respect to publicly owned organizations, such as government departments, companies run as state owned bodies, and local government authorities. This approach to openness and accountability supported by legislation has not yet spread to include enterprises although regulatory controls on publicly quoted enterprises are established and policed by stock exchange organizations. Non-listed enterprise enjoys little restriction control to communication and freedom of information access. The only information/communication requirement governed by legislation is to submit brief annual

returns to the relevant government company's office (Companies Act, 1963).

Corruption in government by unscrupulous enterprise has come to the fore in some EU countries. Ireland has three major tribunals investigating corruption links between politicians, officials and enterprise on planning-bribery issues. Hegarty (2002) has already outlined the measures adopted by Ireland, specifically. Barnett, Cochran and Taylor (1993) report that legal, ethical and practical considerations increasingly compel companies to encourage employees to disclose suspected illegal and/or unethical activities through internal communication channels: 'Internal disclosure policies and procedures have been recommended as a way to encourage such communication.'

Since the 1960s, the corporate governance battle in the United Kingdom has been focused on accountability of the board and the system of self-regulation (Walker, *Profile Magazine*, IPR, issue 24, 2002). Walker asks whether corporate governance is best achieved through statutory accountability of the board to the shareholder alone or can self-regulation ensure the integrity, probity and transparency society demands and needs? For its part, the UK Institute of Public Relations (IPR) (*Profile Magazine*, IPR, issue 25, 2002) has welcomed the consultation document into the relationship between ministers, special advisers and civil servants by the House of Commons Committee on Standards in Public Life. The IPR's 2002 President, John Aaron, said that the role of the so-called 'spin doctors' needs to be transparent, accountable and clarified as the unregulated actions of a few have damaged confidence in the democratic responsibility of government and enterprise to communicate professionally.

For many years there has been a corporate governance debate and considerable concerns expressed, especially in the United States, about the standards of corporate governance (Pike and Neale, 1993). Arguing that it is generally expected of directors of listed enterprises, in terms of UK company law, Pike and Neale (1993) say that listed enterprise directors are obliged to act in the best interest of shareholders and they point out that there have been many instances of listed enterprise boardroom behaviour that has been difficult to reconcile with this ideal, and they cite listed enterprise collapses (British and Commonwealth Holdings, Polly Peck, Maxwell Communications Corporation) 'often as a result of excessive debt financing in order to finance ill advised takeovers and fraud'. Other standards issues of concern include listed enterprise direction remuneration (Pike and Neale, 1993). In 1992 the UK Financial Reporting Council, the UK Stock Exchange and the UK accountancy profession established the Committee on the Financial Aspects of Corporate Governance with the brief to examine, and make recommendations on the role of directors, executives and non-executives and auditors. Ten key recommendations were made and although widely regarded as 'steps in the right direction' these 'changes' in the rules and responsibilities of directors and auditors were non-statutory (Pike and Neale, 1993). This was 1992.

The year 2002 witnessed major upheaval in the United States with the Enron and the WorldCom scandals. Throughout the United States there was major concern in corporate and financial sectors during the early years of the 1990's as to the value of business information and the confidence people had in this information. A great deal was right with the current state of reporting in the United States, according to the latest report, The Jenkins Report (1994), commissioned by the American Institute of Certified Accountants (AICA), and this US report focused on particular areas open to criticism, and where feasible solutions could be developed and implemented. In Europe, and the UK particularly, a similar report was commissioned by the Institute of Chartered Accountants of Scotland, ICAS, (1999). This Scottish report discussed the results of their investigation into the needs and requirements of expert users regarding corporate information in the United Kingdom (Westman and Beattie, 1999). By focussing on original empirical research work into current practices of business information users, including institutional investors, bank leaders and broker analysts, the ICAS Research Committee set out a blueprint for future reporting practices of linked companies (quoted enterprises). From the analysis of the decision making process, the ICAS Research Committee identified for attention the following (a) the cycle of communication, (b) the importance of maintaining confidence, (c) the ability of expert users to explore and sift data, (d) their selective use of key measures, and (e) the importance they attach to information about change (ICAS Research Committee, 1999).

Relevance of CorpCom in management

This focuses on business reporting and clearly demonstrates the relevance to the management functions of corporate communication. Existing literature defines corporate communication in the context of listed (quoted) enterprises and places it as a senior management function, primarily with ultimate responsibility being accepted at CEO level (Oliver, Diets, Van Riel, Dolphin).

Corporate communication involves the organization's need to communicate in three basic forms: marketing, organization and management (Van Riel 1995). Arguing the management positioning of CorpCom, Van Riel suggests that communication is an indispensable management tool. Supporting the management functionality of CorpCom, Dolphin (1999) says that CorpCom is an approach rather than a technique.

> It has developed into an essential management discipline. It is an approach that sets out to ensure the consistency of the corporate message and the transparency of the organization. It is a function that anticipates issues, events and crises before they occur. Through its messages and theme the organization conveys its designed image and person. Thus through commutation the organization functions, its character and mentality take on a life and form and it becomes known to its various audiences.
>
> (Dolphin, 1999)

Campbell and Yeung in Oliver (1997) purports that

by being clear of the need to have a mission, the need to create a relationship between strategy and articulate behaviour standards, managers avoid the superficial attitude to mission and continue the analysis, thinking and experimentation for long enough to develop the mission that builds 'a great company'. This is CorpCom at its most basic marginalized professional level but being incorporated as a core activity for line management.

Oliver demonstrates this paradigm shift in the assessment framework (Figure 6.2).

Openly (1982) (in Heath, 1994) states that information increases identification and he suggests employees identify with an organization and become committed to it as they feel they have sufficient information to make decisions. Could this theory be adopted and applied effectively to director responsibility in terms of the responsibility for CorpCom at governance in unquoted and quoted enterprises? For this chapter to propose such a view it is important to address the functionalities associated with governance issues in both the listed and unquoted enterprises, and in family

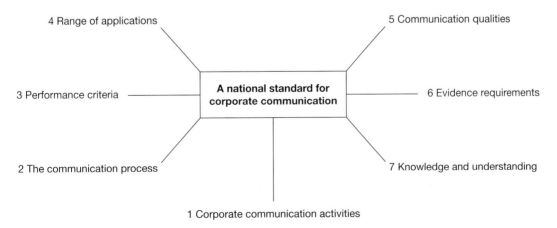

Figure 6.2 Assessment framework
Source: Oliver, S. M. (1997)

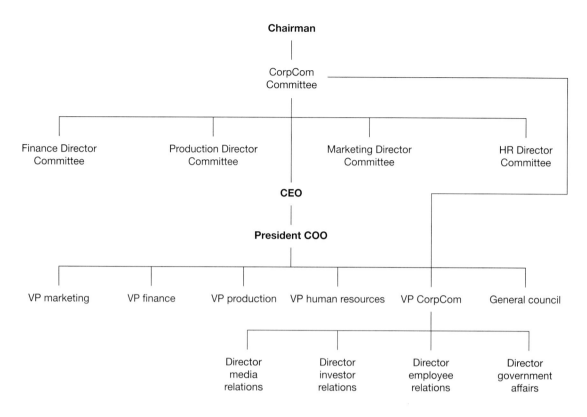

Figure 6.3 Ideal structure for CorpCom function model
Source: Argenti, P. (1998) *Corporate Communication*, 2nd edn, Boston, USA: McGraw Hill

unquoted enterprises. In addition, the relationships between business strategy and management strategy and corporate communication strategy will be discussed.

There is a lack of literature addressing the relationships between governance, and corporate communication and directorial duty. CorpCom academic literature authors address CorpCom in strictly management terms (Oliver, Van Riel, Dolphin *et al.*) and there is opportunity to develop a governance–CorpCom model by drawing on Argenti's ideal structure for CorpCom function model (Figure 6.3).

Argenti (1998) says that a strong centralized function with direct connections to the chief executive officer is the best way for a company to ensure the success of its corporate communication function. This chapter believes that Heath's theory offers a constructive basis upon which unquoted enterprises – drawing on the corporate communication experiences that listed (quoted) enterprises employs – may be helped to improve their corporate communication strategies, policies and programmes implementation and evaluation practices. Yet today, when mistrust, confusion and competition lead communication interpretation, how

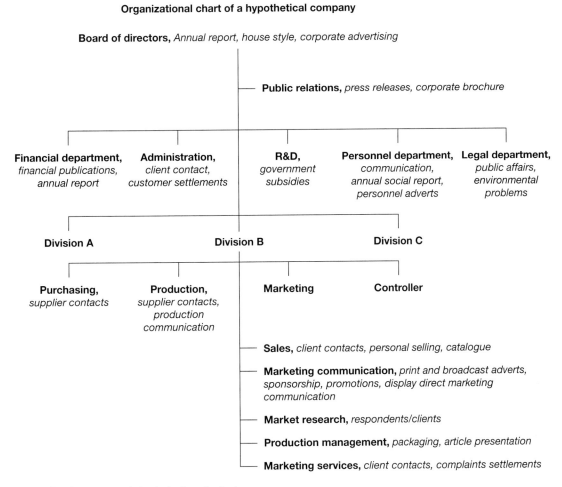

Figure 6.4 Organizational chart of a hypothetical company

Source: Van Riel, CSM (1995) *Principles of Corporate Communication*

can unquoted enterprise view corporate communication as relevant?

No literature appears to address the relationship between governance, director's responsibilities and corporate communication. Because CorpCom writers, from Oliver to Van Riel, address CorpCom in strictly management terms, the various models (Oliver's and Argenti's) offer opportunity to develop a CorpCom governance model.

Argenti (1998) argues that the CorpCom management position should be a strong centralized function directly reporting to and connected to the CEO. Many polls taken over recent decades in the United States, says Argenti (1998), consistently show a huge percentage of CEOs' time spent communicating with various 'constituents' of the company, and he quotes research undertaken by the Tuck School of the Fortune 500 companies in the United States that shows CEOs have spent between 50 per cent and 80 per cent of their time on communication. Argenti (1998) argues that most companies' CEOs 'should have a direct link to the corporate communication function. Without this connection, the communication function will be much less effective and far less powerful.'

Van Riel (1995) outlines forms of internal and external communication that might be employed in a company and he demonstrates that communication as a management tool is used in many areas of the organization other than PR marketing.

Van Riel (1995) believes that the responsibility of communication stretches across all levels of an organization including senior, middle and junior management who use communication to achieve desired results, and he states that externally, management especially the CEO has to be able to accommodate the vision of the company in order to win support of external stakeholders (Figure 6.4). Emphasizing the importance of communication to the success of an organization, Van Riel (1995) states that 'communication is too vital for organisational success to leave it solely to managers' and he argues that experts in communication at various levels and in various areas of expertise may be required and that 'general managers should never consider hiring communication experts as the panacea of organisational communication'. Van Riel (1995) continues this view by stating that

> CorpCom is primarily corporate; it only subsequently encompasses communication; that is to say communication specialists must focus initially on the problems of the organisation as a whole (corpus) and only subsequently should they look at implicit and explicit functions of communication with respect to contributions to the realization of the company's objectives.

No academic research could be found that specifically addresses the roles of the board of directors in this important field, especially as all CorpCom writers address the external issues, the impacts on CorpCom strategies, policy, image, identity and reputation (Oliver, Van Riel, Argenti). Listed companies governance structures offer two options of the position of the Chairperson and CEO as being held jointly or separately. Where joint Chairperson/CEO is concerned we see that Argenti (1998) cites the management reporting structure to the CEO, and where the chairperson is also the CEO (in listed enterprise) there is obviously a governance issue to be addressed – yet there appears to be no literature to examine this. Dolphin (1999) addressing corporate abstention touches on an apparent common approach by companies (listed) in relation to meeting the communication need when he says that some corporations ignore their publics altogether: 'This approach (clearly stemming from the top) may demonstrate the general perception of the CEO and the executive committee of the communication function. It also demonstrates the corporate view of the level of power of strategic communication' (Dolphin, 1999).

Werther, Kerr and Wright (1995) argue that a key impediment to effective and relevant governance activity may be the CEO who generally controls the information flow to the board and its agenda.

> Even if board members pursue an activist approach to their responsibilities, their ability to do so is bounded in large measure by the CEO's control over the amount and type of information they receive. Where the CEO also chairs the board of directors, control extends to the conduct of board meetings. Although the board technically has the ultimate power to sack the CEO or

to facilitate a takeover, these are extreme measures of last resort, more useful in reacting to a crisis than in averting one.

(Werther, Kerr and Wright, 1995)

Boards, usually in response to environmental complexity or competitive turbulence, have witnessed fundamental restructuring of organizations, and according to Werther, Kerr and Wright (1995) these boards have presided over changes designed to improve information exchange and decision making dramatically at every organizational level: 'Yet at the board level, the critical apex of strategic and policy concerns, informational and decision-making practices remain embedded in the structures and protocols of a simpler age' (Werther, Kerr and Wright, 1995).

This conflict between management's approach to CorpCom and the potential CorpCom responsibility at governance must be addressed. Surely it is in the interest (competitive advantage, effectiveness, productivity, profitability, growth, success, reputation and recognition) of firms, listed and unquoted, to employ CorpCom strategically, at governance and management function levels?

Governance offers various definitions and the research exclusively focuses on listed companies with apparently no evidence or academic research material addressing governance in unquoted family enterprise. Tombs (2002) suggests that governance and management are not just about computers and information. They are about attitudes and management culture mixed with information. Taylor (2000) quotes Bohen's (1995) definition of governance as 'the responsibility and accountability for the overall operation' of an organization and he says that 'boards are always charged with this level of responsibility and accountability'. He further suggests that the managing part is further delegated

by the board to the CEO while the board remains responsible for: (1) developing corporate policies and plans, (2) monitoring and measuring organizational performance against these policies and plans and (3) acting as a voice of ownership (Taylor, 2000).

Taylor (2000) also argues that it is important that governing bodies: 'clearly understand what their role is and is not and that their primary responsibility is to oversee and ensure the achievement of their organisational mission and strategic ends, which have been clearly articulated and are shared by all'. Vinten (2000) focuses on recent CorpCom governance concerns including the accountability of those in control of companies (listed) to those with the residual financial interest in corporate success, normally the shareholders, but when the company is approaching insolvency, then also its creditors, as well as widening discussion to consider stakeholders. Among a number of contemporary developments, Vinten (2000) identifies the redistribution of tasks between the public and private sectors, and between public and charitable sectors in the economy in the way companies are run and security markets are organized. Vinten (2000) also suggests as another contemporary development that issues of public confidence can be assessed in terms of the level of managerial remuneration and the effectiveness with which boards of major companies carry out the task of monitoring executive management.

Werther, Kerr and Wright (1995) refer to the attacks on the board's role in Corporate governance and include cronyism, inappropriate remuneration and executive compensation schemes. All these issues fall into reputation, and are directly within the field of CorpCom, which is inherent in the functions of corporate governance yet there is no evidence nor academic research to demonstrate, question, debate the judiciary functions of directors in either listed or unquoted (family) companies, irrespective of size.

This chapter contends that opportunity exists for the elevation of CorpCom from its current exclusive role in management to also be an essential governance function. The Cadbury Report (1992) clearly identified the preferred appropriate structures – board committees involving both directors and non-executive directors. No literature research was found in relation to governance and the management function of CorpCom in unquoted family enterprise. In addition, no evidence was identified regarding CorpCom strategy, policy or programming at management levels in unquoted family enterprise.

Further research

One key area for further research is suggested: CorpCom at governance in listed enterprise.

If, as Van Riel (1994) argues, strategy-led communication is as essential to an enterprise as prudent strategy-led financial directorship, then there is a need for further investigation into the development of governance CorpCom in listed enterprise, particularly as support to the functionality of CorpCom in management. In addition, the limited qualitative research process (which this author is undertaking) in unlisted family enterprise needs to be further researched in greater detail across a variety of different enterprise types, as does research of a similar nature require to be undertaken in state-run enterprises. It is the author's opinion the similarities and differences in CorpCom strategy, policy and programming, the need and role for governance–CorpCom, and its relationship to the organization's mission, and business objectives may provide interesting findings in terms of the future development of CorpCom as a core element for an organization's (listed and/or unlisted) success, survival, growth and wealth.

REFERENCES

Argenti, P. A. (1996) 'Corporate communication as a discipline: toward a definition', *Management Communication Quarterly*, 10(1), 73–85.

Argenti, P. A. (1998) *Corporate Communication*, Boston: Irwin McGraw-Hill.

Barnett, T., Cochran, D. S. and Taylor, G. S. (1993) 'The internal disclosure policies of private-sector employees: an initial look at their relationship to employee whistle-blowing', *Journal of Business Ethics*, 12(2), 127–38.

Belmiro, T. R., Gardiner, P. D., Simmons, J. E. L., Santos, F. C. A. and Rentes, A. F. (2000) 'Corporate communication within a BPR context', *Business Process Management Journal*, 6(4), 286–98.

Coulson-Thomas, C. J. (1983) *Marketing Communications*, London: Heinemann/Institute of Marketing.

Crosbie, A. (2000), *Don't Leave It to the Children: Starting, Building and Sustaining a Family Business*, Dublin: Marino Books/Mercier Press.

Deetz, S. (1995) *Transforming Communication, Transforming Business: Building Responsive and Responsible Workplaces*, New Jersey: Hampton Press.

Dolphin, R. (1999) *The Fundamentals of Corporate Communication*, Oxford: Butterworth Heinemann.

Eng, L. L., Khoo, A. and Tan, R. (1998) 'Communication of private information and the valuation of initial public offerings in Singapore', *Journal of International Financial Management and Accounting*, 9(2), 63–82.

Goffee, R. (1996) 'Understanding family businesses: issues for further research', *International Journal of Entrepreneurial Behaviour and Research*, 2(1), 36–48.

Grunig, J. E. (1992) *Excellence in Public Relations and Communication Management*, New Jersey: Lawrence Erlbaum Associates.

Heath, R. L. (1994) *Management of Corporate Communication: from Interpersonal Contacts to External Affairs*, New Jersey: Lawrence Erlbaum and Associates.

Hegarty, S. (2002) 'Corporate governance developments in Ireland', *Corporate Finance*, Supplement 2, 113, 22–4.

Neubauer, F. and Lank, A. G. (1998) *The World of Family Business*, London: Macmillan Press.

Oliver, S. (1997) *Corporate Communication: Principles, Techniques and Strategies*, London: Kogan Page.

Oliver, S. (2001) *Public Relations Strategy*, London: Kogan Page.

Pagano, M. and Roell, A. (1998) 'The choice of stock ownership structure: agency costs, monitoring and the decision to go public', *The Quarterly Journal of Economics*, 113(1), 187–225.

Pike, R. and Neale, B. (1993) *Corporate Finance: Going Public and Issuing New Equity and Takeovers, Mergers and Disposals*, London: Butterworths.

Quirke, B. (1995) *Communicating Change*, London: McGraw-Hill.

Rose, M. B. (1995) *Family Business*, Aldershot: Edward Elgar.

Schein, E. H. (1985) *Organizational Culture and Leadership*, San Francisco: Jossey-Bass.

Taylor, D. W. (2000) 'Facts, myths and monsters: understanding the principles of good governance', *International Journal of Public Sector Management*, 13(2), 108–24.

Tombs, K. (2002) 'What do we mean by governance?', *Records Management Journal*, 12(1), 24–8.

Townley, P. (1993) 'Managing corporate communications in a competitive climate', *The Conference Board of Europe*, Report 1023, Brussels.

Van Riel, C. B. M. (1995) *Principles of Corporate Communication*, Hemel Hempstead: Prentice Hall.

Van Riel, C. B. M. (1997) 'Research in corporate communication: an overview of an emerging field', *Management Communication Quarterly*, 11(2), 288–309.

Varey, R. J. and White, J. W. (2000) 'The corporate communication system of managing', *Corporate Communication: An International Journal*, 5(1), 5–11.

Vinten, G. (2000) 'Corporate governance: the need to know', *Industrial and Commercial Training*, 32(5), 173–8.

Weetman, P. and Beattie, A. (1999) *Corporate Communications: Views of Institutional Investors and Lenders*, The Institute of Chartered Accountants of Scotland.

Werther, W. B., Kerr, J. L. and Wright, R. G. (1995) 'Strengthening corporate governance through board level consultants', *Journal of Organisational Change Management*, 8(3), 63–74.

Westhead, P. and Cowling, M. (1997) 'Performance contrasts between family and non-family unquoted companies in the UK', *International Journal of Entrepreneurial Behaviour and Research*, 3(1), 30–52.

CHAPTER 7

Strategic challenges for corporate communicators in public service

J. Paulo Kuteev-Moreira and Gregor J. Eglin

What is the role of corporate communication professionals at a national level health service and at a local government level? What are the major challenges to decision making faced by executives and politicians?

The chapter puts into context the specific reality of hospital corporate communication within contemporary public service systems and identifies areas of further research and professional development. It also addresses communication change practices in local government through major issues of public policy, such as transport.

A changing healthcare environment

The policy for 'Health for all in the twenty-first century' (HEALTH21) adopted by the world community in May 1998 and promoted by the World Health Organization (WHO) sets out for the first two decades of the twenty-first century global priorities and targets that will create the conditions for people worldwide to achieve and maintain the highest attainable level of health throughout their lives. The regional policy for Europe was a response to its call for regional and national adaptations on the basis of the global one (WHO, 1999).

The ethical foundation of this strategic policy for the healthcare sector is constituted by three basic values (WHO, 1999: 4):

- health as a fundamental *human right*;
- *equity* in health and solidarity in action between countries, between groups of people within countries and between genders;
- *participation* by and *accountability* of individuals, groups, communities, institutions, organizations and all sectors in the health development movement.

Four major strategies for action have been selected to ensure the implementation of HEALTH21:

- *multisectoral* approaches to tackle the determinants of health, taking into account physical, economic, social, cultural and gender perspectives and ensure the use of health impact assessments;

- *health-outcome-driven* programmes for health development and clinical care;
- *integrated* family-and-community oriented healthcare, supported by a flexible and responsive hospital system;
- *participatory* health development process involving relevant partners for health at all levels – home, school, worksite, local community – and promoting joint decision making, implementation and accountability.

This strategic vision has been adapted by all EU member states and it is now incorporated in its national health systems' policies and priorities for action.

However, the implementation of these four major strategies demands change in the shape of new processes of healthcare delivery. This goal runs into difficulties in a number of healthcare sectors whose strategic interests may not coincide with some of the HEALTH21 proposals.

In this context, managing policy implementation requires a range of complex skills. It involves assessing the environment or circumstances in which the policy will operate, not only to identify possible barriers preventing implementation but also to find supporting arguments or actors to facilitate the change process.

In order to understand and influence the environment in favour of the new policy, the technical ability to manage implementation involves the adoption of a set of essential corporate communication tools and corresponding skills. The confirmation of this premise becomes more evident when we consider the principles of the accordion method as developed by Ansoff and McDonnell (1990) and put into the context of European healthcare reforms by Saltman and Figueras

(1997). This method suggests two fundamental strategies for change:

1   consensus building (resistance reduction)
2   building implementation.

The strategic process of *consensus building* involves a number of alternative actions amongst which we emphasize, in the corporate context of hospitals, the following:

- *Stakeholders* should be *consulted* to find out how they perceive the changes to affect them; this will help in defining messages to minimize apprehension and anxiety by acknowledging their concerns and preferred options.
- The need for *change* should be felt (perceived as necessary) and complemented by the availability of explanations of the purpose of the change. This should minimize hostility and/or resistance.
- Generating positive *support* for change is possible if the corporate communication professionals are able to make clear to stakeholders the benefits that some particular change will bring to them.
- *Alliances* should be built that support change, if necessary excluding, for some time, those stakeholders who are resistant.
- A clear *plan* of the change process should be disseminated within the stakeholders of the organization and include a clear identification of: tasks, responsibilities, resources required and training and development needs. Expected outcomes and a number of milestones against which to monitor progress should be communicated at an early stage of the process.

The second strategic approach to change in the hospital sector is that of *building implementation* which implies three major complementary measures to consensus building:

- The change process should be *incremental* over a period of time and begin with the least contentious changes. As trust amongst stakeholders builds up, the more controversial aspects may be introduced. This will demand image management throughout.
- Stakeholders should be *involved* (or perceived as such) from the beginning. Rewards to support can be communicated but those who resist should not be penalized, since entrenching their resistance may prevent the building of implementation.
- Stakeholders should be informed about *progress*. Evaluating the effects of change and communicating them will allow stakeholders to see the promised benefits and maintain their support.

From this conceptual framework this chapter argues that the corporate communication management function is central for the successful implementation of change in European health systems in general and in healthcare organizations (hospitals) in particular (i.e. NHS hospitals).

Thus, whilst considering the application of communication tools and techniques to help the hospital develop and maintain positive relationships with its audiences, we realize that this purpose demands expertise at all levels of corporate communication: interpersonal, groups, operational and strategic (see Oliver, 1997).

Hence, as noted above, consensus building and building implementation are two fundamental strategies to support change as they define clear priorities for the implementation of the changes expected to achieve HEALTH21 and related reforms.

In this context, we are now going to look into some fundamental corporate communication competencies which need to be developed if the corporate communication function is to contribute to that process. The following sections discuss four levels of corporate communication challenges for practice within the hospital environment:

1   professional and personal;
2   communication with internal audiences;
3   communication with external audiences;
4   preparing for critical media reports.

Professional and personal challenges

The hospital corporate communication function implies communicating with a wide array of very different people on a daily basis: board members, medical, nursing, technical, administrative and clerical staff, volunteers, patients and patients' families, representatives of governmental and other health or social organizations, community healthcare-related organizations, professional organizations, suppliers, potential suppliers, local politicians, the media, etc.

As each of these groups has a different purpose to establish at the encounter, it becomes necessary to learn about their expectations. This is the first step to understanding the nature of the hospital corporate culture. One set of skills required here relates to our own (inter)personal communication practice: listening and negotiating skills, assertiveness and one-to-one communication.

Communicating within the hospital organization demands further practice and development of personal skills like those related to communicating in meetings, making presentations and developing networks within a context of rather volatile and conflicting group expectations and opinions.

In fact, in a corporate environment where the daily pressure, conflicting group and individual attitudes and different professional approaches to problems hamper most prospects of peaceful and stress-free communicational encounters, networking becomes a strategic priority for the development of a corporate communication role. If we are able to develop a network of people who are aiming for a common goal we then have a powerful tool to do our job and help in achieving corporate objectives. Being part of an internal network in the hospital has the following practical advantages:

- provision of relevant comments, suggestions and advice;
- recognition of possible impact and group reactions prior to acting;
- a sounding board for clarifying ideas and strategies;
- extension of support and influence;
- streamlining working relationships;
- improved information flow and knowledge management.

Another fundamental challenge is that of written communication. Contemporary national health systems face a massive multiplication of quantities and formats of written materials published and exchanged via a whole range of channels and technologies: reports, letters, memos, minutes and agendas, briefings, posters and notice boards, patient information leaflets, magazines, bulletins, newspapers, books, faxes, emails, pager messages, web pages, speeches, press releases, backgrounders, etc. In view of all these

options for written communication, we need to develop a practical understanding of effective writing for all of them.

Bearing in mind the paramount assumption that *we write to get a response from the reader*, the absence of response to our writings may anticipate a communication breakdown. When a communication breakdown occurs in the hospital corporate environment, its direct effects may become visible through a series of critical problems: ill-informed patients and families, over-worried relatives, increased complaints, dissatisfied staff, bad publicity, suspicious journalists, loss of staff morale or falling productivity.

In this context, a good understanding of our readers (audiences), a clear idea about our messages and a capacity to adapt messages to different audiences (e.g. transform clinical, technical or management information into plain English) and adjust them to different written formats, become fundamental skills for the corporate communication professional in the hospital environment (see also Albert, 1997).

Communicating with internal audiences: the hospital groups

Involvement in the hospital corporate environment is about maximizing the capacity to create and develop functional networks that promote and guarantee positive interpersonal communication between all professionals. By assisting the development of internal networks, the unifying energy arising from people who collude in contributing to achieve the delivery of a complex service through which lives may be saved, we strengthen the role of the corporate communication professional in the hospital environment. This is one major objective to aim at whilst developing any course of action to communicate with internal audiences.

Most of today's hospital professionals can be described by pointing out their major shared characteristics: they are highly educated, 'territory oriented' and very sceptical about managers (including the corporate communication manager). In fact, within the hospital environment, it is likely that the corporate communication person is one individual amongst a number of strongly self-aware groups of healthcare professionals each possibly comprising hundreds of individuals with their own predefined 'territories' and 'corporate' (group) priorities. The majority of them will be women (especially in healthcare delivery) and increasingly from multicultural backgrounds.

Hence, these professionals are likely to be wary of anybody perceived as representing the board or the administration, as is the case with the corporate communication person. The fact is that healthcare professionals share a very strong group identity and some contemporary proposals for change arising from managers question some of the shared group values and/or priorities (see Harrison *et al.*, 1992). Having said all this, can it become more challenging for the corporate communication practitioner? Yes, it can.

In fact, pressures on the healthcare system include budget strains, litigation and increasing citizen demands. On the other hand, the surge of new technology-related professions demanding similar status to that of physicians and nurses is another communicational challenge as the recognition of that status (or the lack of it) is a potential source of conflict between other hospital professional groups and the board.

Within large and complex organizations such as hospitals, it is natural to find people who are concentrated on the activities and concerns of the particular function or department to which they are assigned rather than on what is happening in other parts of the organization. This corporate reality creates team loyalty but tends to question their individual empathy with the whole organization. This situation adds to the difficulty of creating a shared corporate set of values and behaviours in the hospital environment. In this manner, contributing to effective networking becomes a fundamental purpose for the role of corporate communication as a means to achieving improved shared corporate values by bringing together people from different professional groups and departments.

One could describe the organizational culture of hospitals as 'extremely heavy'. That is to say, it encompasses a diversity of identities and establishes a sense of commitment at two different levels: commitment to the professional healthcare group of origin; and/or commitment to the organization as a whole. The stability of this double identity/commitment will depend on the corporate communication function being able to demonstrate the complementary nature of both (see Harrison *et al.*, 1992). The inability to achieve this purpose will tend to result in conflict and disregard for any effort promoting participation and commitment in activities relevant for the whole but irrelevant to its parts (the professional groups).

Adapted from Huber (1996), who built from several earlier studies, we can identify some major guidelines for the process of building a corporate culture supportive of the need for constant change faced by contemporary hospitals.

• Messages should start from where our internal audiences are in their understanding of the issue.

- Promote the practice (at board and senior management level) of an open style of communication by encouraging discussion.
- Invest time and effort on interpersonal communication: one should meet people in their department and avoid hiding behind email and phone.
- Identify the shared vision of each group, build statements of mission that comply with those 'visions' and then make an effort to 'fit' the values desired for the whole within their 'partial visions'.
- Promote the empowerment of each professional group by valuing and facilitating interaction, co-operation and developing the sense of influence of the group over the whole of the organization.

Further to this, we must also acknowledge a unique group in hospitals: that of the volunteers. Their function may not always be very well defined or known at department level, leaving scope for unhelpful events pertaining to their relationship with the work of other healthcare professionals (especially nurses and ancillary personnel). Our challenge here is to promote their good (group) relations especially with nurses and ancillary personnel. Volunteers need to feel rewarded in other ways than monetary. Thus, group self-esteem uplift tends to be our operational communication theme with this group. Hence, volunteers become a very important network as they can become the extra 'eyes and ears' of the corporate communication professional.

Once we have acknowledged the diversity of internal audiences, we need to consider the purposes of communicating with each one of them. In this sense, we recall the above priorities for consensus building and point out some likely purposes in communicating with hospital internal audiences:

- to establish the perception that 'change for the better' is possible ('it has been achieved elsewhere or even among us');
- to disseminate examples of 'change for better' which occurred in other departments or hospitals (even in other countries);
- to make the need for *change* perceived as necessary and inevitable;
- to disseminate explanations of the purpose of change in order to minimize hostility and/or resistance (adapt this purpose to different groups);
- to generate positive *support* for change by making clear to groups the benefits that some particular change will bring to each one of them;
- to disseminate a *plan* for the change process within all groups of the organization; this *plan* should expose the tasks, responsibilities and resources required;
- to inform all groups about specific outcomes against which the progress of changes can be monitored.

Hence, with regard to specific challenges to do with the hospital internal audiences, we must be aware of the unique complexity of relationships established in a healthcare team (see Figure 7.1). Inevitably the physician is at the heart of the team's propelling energy. In spite of the fundamental contribution of all the other professionals, the number of contacts and requests in the process of patient care directed to the physician is by far higher than any other member of the healthcare team. This fact has three strategic implications for practice: (1) do not send a physician information or request it, if the matter is not important to him/her; (2) until proven wrong, assume that the physician is the most influential member of the healthcare team (for the good and the not-so-good); (3) in spite of the

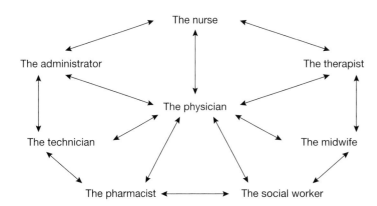

Figure 7.1
Internal audiences – one example of a healthcare team

former being true, never underestimate the influence of other professional groups;

Communicating with external audiences: the hospital stakeholders

Healthcare organizations have a number of stakeholders who confer on these organizations dedicated to caring for people a unique corporate communication environment. The following are the major stakeholders of contemporary hospitals.

Patients and service users are the essence of the hospital's activity. The hospital was created and established to serve them, to satisfy their needs, to guarantee their well-being at all times and to promote harmonious contacts with its premises, technologies and staff. Here we include patients' families and friends (i.e. visitors).

Organizations representing patients and service users are all those non-governmental and voluntary organizations which act as conciliators and negotiators between the specific needs of groups of citizens suffering from a certain clinical condition or socio-demographic characteristic and the hospital's corporate environment within which may

sometimes result contradictory service organizational priorities.

Non-care customers are all those entities to which a hospital may provide non-care services such as renting space to shops in its premises (e.g. flower shop, bank, post office, cafeterias, etc.).

Purchasers (or contractors) are also perceived as customers since they pay (or contract) for the services delivered by the hospital. In the European Union these take different names within the variable ministry of health departments, such as health authorities, contracting agencies or authorities, health boards, primary care groups or trusts, social services, as well as health insurance companies or other life and healthcare private contractors. As the trend towards joint private–public investment in healthcare takes over, this type of stakeholder will become increasingly relevant for the corporate communication practice. Even when one works in a public hospital we may have services for private patients, usually purchased by insurers.

Regulators are responsible for evaluating whether the service provision achieves the predefined quality standards. All over Europe we see that forms of professional and service regulation take either a national standards

approach or a more local-based regional regulation, usually oriented towards specific local
needs and service delivery.

Partners are all other organizations with
which the hospital collaborates in delivering
services. Typical partnerships may include
sharing technical expertise or co-ordination
of service delivery with primary care organizations and diagnosis services (e.g. clinical
exams, radiology, etc.). There is increasingly
the need to establish partnerships with other
service areas like homecare organizations,
community health organizations or the social
services.

Suppliers are the organizations from which
the hospital buys goods and services – from
pharmaceuticals and healthcare disposables
to high-tech equipment, domestic services
and management consultancy.

Competitors/rivals are other organizations
providing healthcare services (with public or
private ownership). If these services are perceived by *regulators* or *patients and service
users* as actual or potential alternatives to
services provided by our hospital, they constitute competition. Hospitals which can demonstrate high and increasing numbers of users
are more likely to guarantee continuing funding and investment whether from public or
private bodies. On the other hand, besides
attracting patients and service users, hospitals
are increasingly under competitive pressure
to attract and retain scarce specialized and
highly skilled professionals who may prefer
some other hospital or similar healthcare
organization.

The *labour market* of the health professions
is made up of individuals who actually possess
the skills and knowledge needed for the
activity of the hospital. Within the healthcare
professions the legal and suitable qualifications needed for the clinical and nursing activities are especially scarce. In this context, the

hospital's reputation becomes fundamental
to assist or damage staff recruitment programmes.

Trade unions and professional associations are
stakeholders whom hospitals find themselves
dealing with over educational or training matters or over wage or productivity incentives
demanded by or offered to staff.

The media must be considered a stakeholder in the sense that they are partners
who are always very interested and aware of
critical events occurring within the hospital
environment. In fact, the media know that
every hospital is a prolific 'supplier' of news
(good and bad) especially captivating for its
audiences (local and national). As in many
cases events at the hospital relate to the
'human-feature' kind of stories, sometimes
even politically sensitive, we must accept and
be prepared for a variable but enduring
media interest and thorough scrutiny. Besides,
as is the case in numerous proposals for
change, the media become the most effective
and powerful source of information for hospital stakeholders and internal audiences.
Contemporary media not only inform but,
most important, also disseminate interpretations, promote opinions and debate about the
changes being proposed or implemented.
One may have been surprised at how many
different groups of stakeholders can be identified as having an interest in the corporate reality of hospitals (Figure 7.2).

The diversity of stakeholders identified in
the hospital organizational environment is a
major factor contributing to its complex
corporate communication challenges. For instance, when the board wants to change one
aspect of a service delivered by the hospital,
each stakeholder may, from its particular
perspective, take a view of the proposed
change. The board may see the benefits to
be gained from such change, but some of the

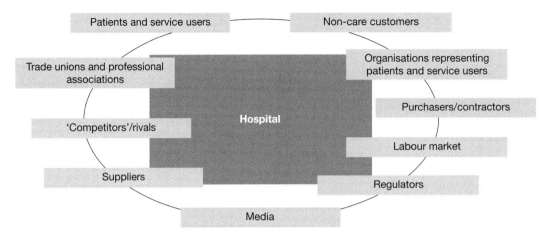

Figure 7.2 A stakeholder environment: the contemporary hospital

stakeholders may emphasize its disadvantages and propose a different way of achieving similar benefits.

As the interests and priorities of stakeholders will vary according to circumstances, we need to take these into account before we communicate a proposed change. Only after considering the nature of the change and its impact from a range of different stakeholders' perspectives is it possible to foresee how each group perceives it and anticipate their attitude and behaviour. This approach is fundamental to facilitating the subsequent decisions on message strategy development.

The awareness of this circumstance leads us further towards the understanding that the contemporary relationships between a hospital and its stakeholders are strongly influenced by the choices and constraints pertaining to the availability of the resources that the organization needs to operate effectively.

Such an analytical approach, as developed by Pfeffer and Salancik (1978), is called the *resource dependence* view. It suggests that no organization is completely independent. In fact, organizations rely on a number of fundamental resources – financial, personnel,

information, technology and, not least, that of reputation.

Thus, it is useful to consider what may be the scarcest resource in a particular hospital context. It may be skilled professionals – including staff with the soft skills pertaining to interpersonal communication with patients and families. In other contexts, the scarcest resource may be hospital beds, community services or simply the money to acquire a particular piece of hospital machinery.

Some resource shortages may be resolved by 'simply' making more money available. This is usually one solution demanded by some sectors of contemporary western societies (hospital stakeholders). However, the 'budget cutback' discourse is dominant in the vast majority of western healthcare systems. Yet, few have managed to invert the trend of escalating healthcare budgets and expenses (see Saltman and Figueras, 1997).

The balance between alternative approaches to solve resource scarcity in healthcare (usually associated with two contrasting political views), is sometimes achieved either by finding *alternatives* to the particular scarce resource (e.g. new rules of financing healthcare to overcome money shortage; or hiring foreign nurses to overcome shortage of nursing staff) or by *changing processes* of delivering care (e.g. delivering healthcare at home is less expensive and potentially more positive to the well-being of the patient; carrying minor surgeries in GPs' surgeries to overcome hospital beds shortages). Any of the alternatives is likely to imply conflict with particular stakeholders.

The resource-dependence view also maintains that the attempts to solve resource shortages oblige the organization to change the balance between its dependencies. As suggested by several authors (see Harrison *et al.*, 1992; Pfeffer and Salancik, 1978), this new balance of dependency may be achieved by one or a combination of four strategic alternatives:

- adapt to the conditions (e.g. influence demand of services or its delivery);
- alter its interdependencies (e.g. merger with an organization that controls some of the scarce resources or growth by developing new services/products so that the organization is no longer dependent);
- negotiate environmental conditions (e.g. create partnerships to deliver joint services or share resources, for instance with social services, voluntary NGOs or even the private sector)
- change by political action (e.g. lobbying politicians to obtain subsidies, favourable regulation and contracts).

Clearly the implementation of any of the four possible ways to change organizational dependency in the hospital sector demands good (public) relations with all its stakeholders (see Figure 7.2). This fact emphasizes the strategic role of the corporate communication function in the hospital environment.

In fact, any hospital may adopt one or more of these strategies to ensure access to scarce resources. However, whatever alternative is taken by the board of directors, there will always be varying support from the various stakeholders. There may be those who will support at one end and those who may be fundamentally opposed at the other end.

In this sense, it is crucial that the course of action of the corporate communication professional keeps in mind the strategic essence and principles of consensus building (resistance reduction) and building implementation (see above).

Yet, as conflict with stakeholders occurs, the media become a central stakeholder since they are a major receptacle for reporting problems at the hospital. Many hospital issues reported by the media occur due to some kind of communication breakdown with one or more of its stakeholders or with one of its internal audiences (i.e. professional groups) who use the media as their advocate. That is the subject of the following section.

Preparing critical media reports

As healthcare reforms become more complex and ubiquitous, the purpose of maintaining stakeholders on good terms with the hospital becomes even more challenging. The complexity of corporate communication practice is most evident when we reflect upon the media approaches to events affecting the hospital. What the media typically report and what challenges for practice arise from it, is one contribution to debate intended from this section.

Table 7.1 presents a set of typical categories of press reports pertaining to hospitals. We need to draw a parallel between these categories and particular key stakeholder(s) with whom a communication breakdown may occur. In other words, we need to understand the nature of typical media reports and relate them to specific communication efforts required to satisfy the needs and expectations of stakeholders affected by any category of media reporting. As media reports alter stakeholders' perceptions, we need to identify the key stakeholders affected by each category so that we can plan preventative measures and procedures. Emerging from empirical data, (Moreira, 2003; Henry, 2002) we identify a number of critical hospital press reports. An introduction to these is presented below.

Management failures

These represent a form of media coverage in which hospitals (especially NHS hospitals) are reported to have failed to achieve one or more of their major social purposes. A hospital may have failed to grant access to healthcare (e.g., being unsuccessful in granting this fundamental *human right* by extensive and long waiting lists), or may have fallen short of its social *accountability* (e.g. unexplained financial mismanagement) or even been accused of wasting resources (thus questioning its contribution to *solidarity*). Keeping

Table 7.1 Categories of press reports

Category	Categories of critical media reports	Key stakeholders (with whom to prevent communication breakdown)
A	Management failures This includes: waiting time, waiting lists, financial mismanagement and waste	Patients and service users Organizations representing users Purchasers/contractors
B	Clinical errors Including iatrogenesis (clinically induced health problems)	Patients and service users Organizations representing users Purchasers/contractors
C	Professional corporate conflicts	Unions and professional associations Patients and service users
D	Staff shortage	Labour market Professional associations
E	Community relations	Organizations representing patients and service users Purchasers/contractors
F	Corporate events	Organizations representing patients and service users Labour market
G	Human stories (features)	Media Patients and service users
H	Community abnormal accidents	Patients and service users
I	Community violence	Patients and service users
J	Introduction of new hospital technologies, therapies or clinical pathways	Patients and service users Organizations representing users Purchasers/contractors Suppliers
K	Hospital originated pollution	All stakeholders

patients and service users (and their repre-sentative organizations) updated on the real capacity of the hospital will help in dissemi-nating realistic expectations. For this purpose, specific corporate media development will be fundamental (e.g. waiting list newsletters) as well as implementing open proactive informa-tion flow procedures directed at the media (especially local) so as to disseminate what the evolution of waiting lists/waiting times is in the various hospital departments. The fact that the media may compare one hospital's data with that of other hospitals will demand an argumentative capacity to justify and place progress in the local context (e.g. refer to local epidemiological data). This approach enhances the purpose of accountability. Concerning the scarce resources dilemma, reports may originate from the reaction of some stakeholder to a change in the balance of the hospital dependencies (see previous section). However, the perception of *solidarity* should never be questioned. All resource re-allocation must be explained under the patient's best interest and, if the media are to report on it, it needs to be presented from the patients' and service users' point of view. Complex management points of view are very unlikely to be conveyed by media reports.

Clinical errors

These are usually grave reports on events affecting a particular individual. Events may be perceived to have been caused by poor clinical performance undertaken by one (or more) hospital healthcare professional. The role of the corporate communication person in these cases may be to gather specific data on the case (e.g. already published), help clinical staff to prepare a public clinical explanation adding a possible announcement

of clinical/legal measures to be taken and/or invite the individuals involved (e.g. patient or family) for a meeting at the hospital so that personalized first-hand information on their case may be provided (rather than inform them through the media). However, a whole set of legal constraints which regulate these cases need to be taken into account.

Professional corporate conflicts

Strikes are the most acute instance of such typ-ical media reports. Often this type of conflict occurs at national level (e.g. the unions versus the health minister) so it may not involve any hospital in particular (except on reports con-firming how many professionals adhered to the strike at that hospital). On other occasions, however, conflict may occur at hospital level between a group of professionals and its board of directors. In these situations we face a divided hospital and a complex challenge to practice: whose side are we going to be per-ceived to be on? From whose point of view are we to pass information to the media? Are there any views likely to ignite conflict and involve other stakeholders?

Staff shortage

This type of media reporting is broad and gen-eral. Media usually refer to it as a national issue although sometimes may refer to the situation at one particular hospital as the evi-dence of one such national problem. Nurses, some medical specialists and specialized tech-nicians are amongst the professionals usually reported to be in shortage. Again the princi-ples presented in the previous section suggest possible strategies the hospital may adopt to overcome this particular resource scarcity. Disseminating an interest in working at our hospital as advocated by the professionals themselves may be a major contribution expected from a corporate communication professional.

Community relations

Problems pertaining to the level of co-ordination and integration of healthcare within local communities are another major area of reporting. In this context, integrating hospital levels of healthcare management (e.g. secondary, tertiary) with those of primary care (e.g. healthcentres or GPs' practices) in order to grant the best patient flow becomes a major pressure to share resources between social and healthcare organizations. The growing complexity of care and the strained financial system put pressure on hospitals to come to grips with the need to plan and manage integrated care plans. These need to include social care organizations and services (e.g. home care, meals on wheels, social alarm) in co-ordination with recent approaches to healthcare services (e.g. telemedicine, telecare). Any breakdown in these complex caring networks can have dramatic consequences for individuals and are of boundless interest to local (and sometimes national) media.

Corporate events

As in any other area of corporate communication practice, corporate events are a favourite approach for originating positive press reporting for corporations. In the hospital environment, this is not so for the media themselves, unfortunately. In fact, it is not easy to get media to cover hospital corporate events. One needs some imagination and a deep understanding of the nature, essence and culture of contemporary media to be able

to create fine-tuned events for the generalist media. However, it is also a fact that clinical, nursing, hospital technology and healthcare management events usually get good coverage from specialized media.

Human stories (features)

Typical reports in this category include the 'miraculous hospital intervention saves baby' kind of story. One should not try to generate this type of media reporting proactively as medicine is not an exact science. Once the media initiates a story of this kind one can never be sure how it will end. Physicians are usually the 'stars' of these stories. Promoting the fact that these physicians work at the hospital is the most certain benefit the hospital can expect from this category of media reporting.

Community abnormal accidents

Traffic and road accidents involving a large number of people, fires, floods or other types of disasters are the nature of this category of hospital reporting. In these situations it is fundamental that corporate communication professionals gather accurate information and facilitate the flow of data to the media (at any time of the day or night). By preparing a good speaker (clinical or not) to announce numbers and clinical progress of the victims it can become an excellent opportunity to project a positive professional image of the hospital.

Community violence

Victims and offenders of community violence tend to end up at the hospital at some point. Again, in these situations, media reporters are eager to get up-to-date information and details (e.g. areas of the body wounded, demographic data about the victims). The name of the hospital comes up in the report and it is important that we are able to provide our colleagues, mostly working for tabloid or local newspapers, with the right information. These contacts facilitate the development of good relationships with reporters.

Introduction of new technologies, therapies or clinical pathways

These reports announce some form of innovation at the hospital. These tend to be positive reports although one must beware if any group of stakeholders feels apprehensive or may have misunderstood the change. This kind of media reporting is fundamental for the progress of incremental changes and gaining support amongst both stakeholders and internal audiences.

Hospital originated pollution

This includes pollution resulting from the incinerator combustion as well as hospital toxic waste. Environmental issues can never be underestimated within contemporary societies highly sensitive and aware of its consequences. Corporate arrogance or facts later found to have been concealed may have a dramatically negative impact on the hospital's corporate reputation. In this event, as in others above, we will need to implement a carefully designed crisis communication plan.

In search of a 'balanced resource dependency'

Hospitals are being challenged to balance the widely acknowledged resource scarcity with

the values of healthcare and the (sub)culture of the healthcare professions (e.g. physicians, nurses, technicians, health services managers and administrators, ancillary personnel, etc.). As these complex organizations begin to rethink themselves and restructure their dependencies, considering corporate communication phenomena becomes fundamental. The longer hospital managers take to invest resources on this function, the more resistance to change and organizational inertia thrives and paralyses its organizational development. Yet preparing professionals for one such challenging corporate environment is not an easy task.

Indeed, a prominent challenge of HEALTH21 is to strengthen the perception of health as a fundamental human right and the activity of hospitals as contributing to social equity and solidarity between communities, groups and genders by promoting the participation of all its stakeholders in its corporate life as argued by several authors (e.g. Seedhouse *et al.*, 1998; Saltman and Figueras, 1997). However, facing the need to change organizational dependency whilst being under daily scrutiny by media eager to sell hospital issues and gain audiences makes the strategic purposes of consensus building and building implementation highly demanding in terms of professional and personal skills.

In this sense, executive priorities for hospital corporate communication involve a number of challenges related to processes of corporate change management in an environment under the constant scrutiny of the 'public eye'. Now we look at this scrutiny through the concept of public participation in decision making via face-to-face meetings with local government officials and politicians on a separate issue, namely transport policy.

A changing local government environment

The government produced its White Paper, 'Modern Local Government: In Touch with the People', in July 1998. This proposed the most radical reorganization of local government for the best part of a century. The White Paper stated: 'Modern councils should be in touch with the people, provide high quality services and give vision and leadership for local communities . . . The old culture of paternalism and inwardness needs to be swept away. The framework in which councils operate needs to be renewed' (Cm 4014, p. 7 L4).

The first set of changes proposed by government was the creation of new political structures, removing the committee system which had been in place for a century and replacing it with a choice of three models (the status quo not being an option). These were:

- a directly elected executive mayor with a cabinet appointed by her/him from the councillors;
- a cabinet with a leader;
- a directly elected mayor with a council manager.

In the event, most councils opted for the cabinet and leader model with a minority opting for the directly elected mayor.

Other reforms proposed included: improving local financial accountability, a new ethical framework and new procedures for allocating capital finance and setting business rates. Also included were arrangements for the replacement of compulsory competitive tendering (CCT) with the concept of 'best value' in the provision of services to the public.

Perhaps the key to these changes were the sections dealing with 'Promoting the Wellbeing of Communities' and 'Improving Local Democracy'. The White Paper contains some interesting statistics on turnout in local elections in EU countries. It quotes figures by Rallings, Thrasher and Downe (1996) showing that the United Kingdom has the lowest turnout at sub-national elections: 40 per cent compared with, for example, France 68 per cent, Germany 72 per cent, Denmark 80 per cent and Luxembourg 93 per cent. It is these figures that persuaded Britain's central government that local government in the United Kingdom needed 'modernising'. 'New structures alone will not bring about renewal of local democracy which is necessary if councils are to be confident that they are reflecting the priorities and wishes of the people they serve. That can only come about if there is higher participation in elections and close and regular contact between a council and local people between elections' (Cm 4014, p. 38, L3). A close reading of the White Paper makes it clear that what the government is trying to re-establish is communication between the local authority and its citizens. This is implicit throughout the document but, surprisingly, is nowhere made explicit.

The modernization was not without its critics and a heated debate ensued within the political classes in the United Kingdom but seemed to engender little interest from members of the public. Although this debate is important and ongoing, it is not the central concern of this chapter. What is of concern is how communication systems changed within local government as a result of the modernization agenda.

The Local Government Bill was laid before Parliament in 1999 and became law in 2000 following the reform that had already taken place as a result of the White Paper.

Elected in 1998, the author was involved in the modernization process in all its aspects and led a study using participative observation research criteria and the findings reflected not only the strengths and weaknesses of that methodology but also the importance of face-to-face communication – an area of growing research interest in employee/organizational stakeholder communication management in this era of computer mediated, information overload.

The pace of change was demonstrated by the fact that all the new arrangements were in place in the borough by May of 2000. The borough itself is, in many ways, a typical outer London borough. In the part of the borough nearest to the centre of London there are social problems akin to those found in inner London boroughs while the areas farthest away from the centre of London contain affluent suburbs. Thirty per cent of its quarter of a million inhabitants are from minority ethnic groups, mainly Asian. At the time of the changes, there was no overall political control of the council. In 1998 there was a minority administration formed by the largest party. In 1999 the second-largest party formed the administration with support from the third party. In 2000 the third party withdrew this support and the largest party regained minority administration.

Public participation

The council had set up a modernization committee of elected members paralleled by a task force of senior officers, so that by the time the Local Government Act came into force, the council already had its reorganized structure in place. The council opted for the leader and cabinet model after consultation with the public. This involved the delivery of a leaflet to all households in the borough explaining what was happening and why and outlining the options. The general public were invited to one of three meetings held in different parts of the borough. Advertisements for the meeting were also placed in the local press. The response of the public was underwhelming. In only one of the meetings did the attendance by the ordinary members of the public reach double figures.

Was this symptomatic of the lack of communication that the government had been so concerned about in drafting its White Paper? The poor attendance was the subject of some debate by the councillors and officers. It should be pointed out, however, that the council had been trying to improve its communication links with the general public for some years and had introduced the facility for members of the public to speak at council and committee meetings. A quarterly borough newsletter had been circulated to all households in the borough for some time. Various views were put forward to explain the seeming lack of interest but the lack of participation seemed to support those sceptical of the modernization process.

One of the most controversial proposals of the modernization committee was the setting up of local area committees. Eventually, their establishment was agreed by the council although the shape and size of these committees was debated at length. Finally, five committees of three wards, one of four wards and one of two were set up. The two latter committees were of non-standard sizes because they related to distinct communities. These committees had executive powers to take decisions on highway schemes, parks/ leisure issues, monitoring local service delivery, transport matters, local housing management and libraries. They also had the power to determine local planning applications.

Act local

Despite the original misgivings, the committees were a success, although it has to be said the degree of success has varied from area to area. The first meeting of the committee, held in the local library, attracted over a hundred people and attendances since have rarely fallen below that. Initially held six times a year, they now meet ten times a year. The layout of the meeting is important, with the councillors sitting in a line facing the public rather than each other in the traditional confrontational way. The first half hour of the meeting is given over to a 'public forum' where members of the public can speak for up to five minutes on issues they consider to be important. Contributions from the floor are also welcomed in the second part of the meeting which looks at policy issues. For the third part, concerned with planning issues, the committee acts in a quasi-judicial manner and the process here is much more formal. Before this latter part of the proceedings a break is taken and all except those concerned with planning matters tended to leave at this point.

The success of the local area committees took everyone by surprise and stood in sharp contrast to the consultation prior to the modernization. It is clear that the public can relate to a local area in a way that they could not to a large borough. The local area was immediate and accessible. People liked the way that they could put their views across at meetings and could hold their local ward councillors to account. The committee established a symbiotic relationship, with local community groups each helping the other to develop.

Officers from a number of departments were in attendance. Each committee had its own 'lead officer' drawn from the senior ranks of the council's full-time staff. It also had a clerk attached to the newly formed area committee support section.

Best practice

How did these developments affect corporate communication? The council was, and still is, organized into departments each with its own chief officer. Some are involved with service delivery, others have staff functions. Communication flows tended to be within departments with co-ordination organized by the chief executive and meetings of chief officers. While the old committee system existed senior officers of departments would communicate with senior members of the committee responsible for their department. Political co-ordination of information flows tended to be within party caucuses. There were also information flows from individual councillors to officers raising matters on behalf of members of the public. Information also flowed the other way with various departments keeping members informed of developments by a variety of methods including the sending of briefing documents and organizing seminars. Communication between the council and the public generally was, as has been mentioned earlier, by newsletters and other circulars. The council has a communication section responsible for public relations, operating with a communication strategy devised by the council.

The replacement of these committees by the area committees has proved problematic for corporate communication. Local people do not regard things in departmental terms. They do not see why, for example, when a decision has been made to put double yellow lines around a dangerous road junction, a six-month delay is necessary so that the legal services department can draw up the necessary traffic orders from a collection of areas. They see local problems and opportunities 'holistically'. It is also the case that the local area councillors also began to see the situation in the same way rather than the former situation of being specialists in a particular service area. Hence, information flows began to develop between the area committees and the cabinet and senior officers in quite a different way from the previous service based ones. Furthermore, while the major spending areas of the council are education and social services, these never feature much as a public concern in area committees where the major issue is the environment. Cleansing, recycling, litter, parks and planning, are regular concerns but above all else is traffic.

The use of traffic management

An interesting case study involved a traffic matter. The area has recently had a major road development designed to link two other major roads and take traffic away from local roads. However, as is often the case, the road development attracted more vehicles and local roads continued to be overwhelmed by through traffic. One particular set of roads became a rat run. At one meeting some 200 members of the public turned up at an area committee meeting to demand that something be done. It was agreed to partially close one of the rat run roads. Shortly after the closure another group of people appeared at the meeting to complain about displacement of the rat running problems to their streets. When both groups turned up at the following meeting it took considerable skills of chairpersonship to control the meeting. Eventually the scheme was reversed and another solution

sought. The only solution to present itself which did not replace the 'rat run' elsewhere involved closing a road at a particular point. This was duly done for an experimental period. However, a third group of residents appeared complaining that car journeys to work or school were being considerably extended by the closure.

A key communication issue arose at this point. Remarkably, the council's highways section undertook to resurface the main through road in the area at the same time as the experimental road closure. Clearly, the departmental priorities conflicted with the area priorities and the two information flows did not register a possible problem. The matter was resolved at a special area committee meeting held in a school sports hall and attended by over 500 people. Some thirty residents spoke at the meeting. The end result was the removal of the road closure.

More than any of the other reforms introduced by the council as a result of the 2000 Local Government Act, the area committee structure has resulted in more communication between the council and its public. This, in turn, has resulted in problems for corporate communication as information flows from the new structure do not fit well with the old departmentally driven ones. It should also be noted that the area referred to in this chapter already had a strong civil society culture. What is clear is that where local people have the opportunity to meet their local councillors in their local community and hold them to account, sound communication will take place. Giving the community the opportunity to comment on and propose policy bring involvement and improved participation. In this area at least, the reforms have been seen to work.

Summary

Both studies indicate the criticality of face-to-face contact with stakeholders at some point in the strategic communication process. It is not enough to issue communication audits via post or internet. People need the opportunity and space to reflect on issues that directly affect their lives for themselves and with others. Communication is key to sound application of policy and the operational techniques that in the longer term are cost effective. (See also Chapter 4.)

REFERENCES

Health services

Albert, T. (1997) 'Doing the write thing', *Health Service Journal*, 107(5562), 29.

Ansoff, I. and McDonnell, C. (1990) *Implementing Strategic Management*, Hemel Hempstead: Prentice Hall.

Benoit, W. L. (1995) *Accounts, Excuses and Apologies: A Theory of Image Restoration Strategies*, Albany: State University of New York.

Harrison, S., Hunter, D., Marnoch, G. and Pollit, C. (1992) *Just Managing: Power and Culture in the National Health Service*, London: Macmillan.

Henry, R. (2002) *The Complete Guide to Crisis and Risk Communications*, Windsor, CA: Gollywobbler Productions.

Huber, D. (1996) *Leadership and Nursing Care Management*, Philadelphia: W. B. Saunders Publishing.

Martin, V. and Henderson, E. (2001) *Managing in Health and Social Care*, London: Routledge.

Massey, J. E. (2001) 'Managing organisational legitimacy: Communication strategies for organisations in crisis', *Journal of Business Communication*, 38, 153–82.

Moreira, J. P. K. (2003) 'Healthcare stakeholders and the resource shortage dilemma: a contribution to corporate communication theory', Proceedings of the Corporate Communication Annual Conference, Wroxton, UK.

Oliver, S. (1997) *Corporate Communication: Principles, Techniques and Strategies*, London: Kogan Page.

Oliver, S. (2002) *Public Relations Strategy*, London: Kogan Page.

Parsons, P. (2001) *Beyond Persuasion*, Chicago: ACHE.

Pfeffer, J. and Salancik, G. (1978) *The External Control of a Organisation: A Resource Dependence Perspective*, New York: Harper and Row.

Saltman, R. and Figueras, J. (1997) *European Health Care Reform*, Copenhagen: WHO.

Seedhouse, D. (ed.) (1995) *Reforming Healthcare: The Philosophy and Practice of International Health Reform*, Chichester: John Wiley.

Seeger, M., Sellnow, T. and Ulmer, R. (1998) 'Communication, Organisation and Crisis', in M. Roloff (ed.), *Communication Yearbook 21*, Thousand Oaks, CA: Sage, pp. 231–75.

World Health Organization (1999) *Health 21: The Health For All Policy for the WHO European Region*, Copenhagen: WHO Regional Office for Europe.

Local government services

Modern Local Government, In Touch with the People (1998) Cm4014 The Stationery Office.

Rallings, C., Thrasher, M., and Downe, J. (1996) *Enahancing Local Electorate Turnout: A Guide to Current Practice and Future Reform*, London: York/Joseph Rowntree Foundation.

PART II CORPORATE COMMUNICATION AT INTERNATIONAL LEVEL

CHAPTER 8

Communication audits: building world class communication systems

Dennis Tourish and Owen Hargie

Effective internal communication by both management and employees alike is a vital prerequisite for the functioning of any organization. In this chapter the authors suggest that the key to building an effective internal communication system lies in managers having an accurate picture of how well they and everyone else in an organization is actually communicating. To achieve this goal the authors believe that all companies must have a focused communication strategy designed to build a world-class system for sustaining internal communication and that this system must be rigorously and honestly evaluated utilizing communication audit techniques.

Introduction

Effective internal communication is a vital prerequisite for the functioning of all organizations. Yet it is a commonplace that communication is poor in most. Employees complain that they neither know nor understand corporate priorities, while frustrated senior managers insist that they have invested a great deal of time in explaining them. There is additional evidence that information transmission from the bottom to the top is also defective, with employees and even managers fearing to articulate their true opinions to those further up the hierarchy (Rosenfeld *et al.*, 1995). Thus, senior managers often have a very limited understanding of the communication dynamics within their own organization. In our own research in this field, we have frequently found that the people most surprised by audits which point to problems are the senior management team (Hargie and Tourish, 2000). The result can be a climate of mutual suspicion rather than trust, with energies that should be focused on beating the competition squandered in internal struggles. In this chapter, we suggest that the key to building a world-class communication system lies in managers having an accurate picture of how well they and everyone else are actually communicating. In a nutshell, we advance a twofold argument:

1   All organizations need a focused communication strategy, designed to build a world-class system for sustaining internal communication.

2   The first step in implementing the above is that current practice must be rigorously and honestly evaluated, utilizing communication audit techniques.

We then discuss in-depth how audits can be implemented, and the data collection options available. While the main focus of this chapter is upon internal communication, audits are also of importance for external communication, and so we raise issues of relevance to the latter area as well.

The nature of a communication strategy

It is a truism that organizations seeking a competitive advantage must design their systems to at least match, and then exceed, world best practice. Organizational communication is no different. It has been suggested (Clampitt and Berk, 2000) that a world-class communication system has five key attributes:

- The leadership team has a strategic commitment to effective communication.
- Employees at all levels have the appropriate communication skills.
- There is a proper infrastructure of channels to meet organizational objectives.
- There are proper communication policies and procedures to meet organizational objectives.
- Information is managed in a way to meet organizational objectives.

Few organizations have systems in place that are consistent with these attributes. Often, the sad reality is that communication is:

- widely touted as a panacea for organizational ills, but allocated minimal fiscal or functional resources;
- all pervasive, but often unplanned; it is often the case that communication is what happens to companies when they are busy doing other things;
- hailed as being of central importance in terms of what managers actually do, but rarely investigated with the same rigour as is reserved for such other functions as finance;
- still regarded as something that managers do to their subordinates; they drop information like depth charges on to those employees submerged in the organizational ocean but make it very clear that they do not expect to receive any feedback torpedoes in return.

(Hargie and Tourish, 2004)

The result is a disabling gap between theory and practice. This is clearly dysfunctional, and can impact adversely upon the workforce, resulting in reduced employee motivation, lower rates of production, greater industrial unrest, increased absenteeism, and higher staff turnover (Hargie and Tourish, 2000).

The schema proposed by Clampitt and Berk (2000) suggests that senior management is not solely responsible for the effectiveness of the entire communication system. All employees have responsibilities in this area. For example, while our own work with communication audits (e.g. Tourish and Hargie, 1998) has often found people clamouring for more information, it has rarely found them insisting that they have any responsibility for transmitting it. A communication strategy built around the five assumptions outlined above will fundamentally challenge such mindsets.

Communication strategies are all about strengthening relationships, sharing ownership of key issues and relating communication priorities to key business issues. If an organization does not develop and implement a coherent strategy to manage its communication, ad hoc and often dysfunctional methods will develop. A strategy provides both a path along which communication can be guided, and a structural set of processes and procedures to ensure success in this field. We have therefore suggested that a communication strategy can be defined as 'A process which enables managers to evaluate the communication consequences of the decision making process, and which integrates this into the normal business planning cycle and psyche of the organisation' (Tourish and Hargie, 1996, p. 12). Flowing from this, what concretely must managers do to develop a communication strategy and implement an audit process that will evaluate its effects? A number of excellent reviews are now available (e.g. Clampitt *et al.*, 2000). Drawing upon this research, we suggest the following process:

1   secure senior management commitment;
2   identify current practice (i.e. audit);
3   set standards to measure success;
4   develop an action plan to achieve the standards;
5   measure the results (i.e. audit again).

We now discuss these steps in the context of outlining a robust communication audit process.

A communication audit process

In broad terms, the key steps in measuring communication can be summarized as follows:

• Audit current levels of performance.
• Disseminate the results of the audit widely across all levels.

• Implement an action plan tailored to rectify identified deficits.
• Conduct a follow-up audit to evaluate the effects of the action plan.

Accurate information about the state of internal communication can best be obtained through the implementation of a communication audit. The main advantage of an audit is that it provides 'an objective picture of what is happening compared with what senior executives think (or have been told) is happening' (Hurst, 1991: 24). The findings provide reliable feedback and this in turn allows managers to make decisions about where changes to existing practice are required. A communication audit sheds light on the often hazy reality of an organization's performance, and exposes problems and secrets to critical scrutiny. It enables managers to chart a clear course for improved performance.

The term 'audit' is ubiquitous. Financial audits are well established, and clinical audits, medical audits, and organization audits are also now widely employed. Three characteristics are, in fact, common to all audits (Hargie and Tourish, 2000):

1   *The accumulation of information*. This is the *diagnostic* phase of the audit. In communication terms, managers need *information* about the quality and quantity of communication flowing between different sectors of the organization.
2   *The creation of management systems*. This is the *prescriptive* phase of auditing. Once information has been gathered, *systems* must then be put in place to further develop best practice, and to remedy identified deficits.
3   *Accountability*. This is the *functional* aspect of the audit process. Specific individuals should be made *accountable* for different

aspects of internal communication, so that when problems are highlighted someone is specifically tasked with ensuring these are swiftly dealt with. If a problem is everyone's responsibility it is usually no one's responsibility.

This chapter argues that assessments of communication effectiveness should match the seriousness of intent evident when such functions as finance are audited. As such, a communication audit has been defined as: 'a comprehensive and thorough study of communication philosophy, concepts, structure, flow and practice within an organization' (Emmanuel, 1985: 50). Various techniques exist to achieve this outcome (Goldhaber and Rogers, 1979; Downs and Adrian, 1997; Hargie and Tourish, 2000; Dickson *et al.*, 2003), and these will be summarized in the next section. Typically, data emerges on information underload and overload, bottlenecks within the organization, examples of positive communication flow, and pressing communication concerns at all levels. For example:

- Do management and staff perceive the organizational world differently?
- What must be done to achieve and sustain significant improvements in communication?
- Where are the greatest threats and the greatest opportunities?
- When, how, and in what way, will future progress be monitored?

A key goal in all of this is to accurately gauge the views of employees. Thus, as noted by Furnham and Gunter (1993: 204), 'A communication audit is a positive and motivating exercise, being in itself an internal consultation process.'

The audit sequence

Relating this to the discussion of communication strategy with which we began this chapter, and based upon the findings of previous audit investigations across a wide variety of sectors (Hargie and Tourish, 2000), we would suggest that the following sequence be adhered to. Auditors who depart from it should have compelling reasons for doing so. Thus, the process of audit implementation should encompass the following key stages.

Engage senior management commitment

A variety of studies has suggested that unless senior managers, and especially the CEO, are actively involved in any change process, and passionately committed to its success, it will fail (e.g. Spurgeon and Barwell, 1991; Pettigrew *et al.*, 1992). The buck usually stops with the CEO as captain of the ship. But the captain also decides upon what voyages will be undertaken and in what ways. Without the CEO on board the audit ship will not sail. New tools designed to assist organizational development will usually appear threatening to some. They require an intense level of senior management involvement, if their use is to yield positive dividends. At the outset of the audit process a problem focused workshop between senior management and the auditors should therefore be held. Such an event serves to achieve the following.

(1) *Improve the management team's understanding of what can be achieved by audits, of how a world-class communication system can be built, and what it might look like in this organization.* It will therefore raise the following questions:

- What are the key business problems that arise through poor communication? It should be noted that this is a different proposition to the identification of communication problems, important as this is. Rather, it is to suggest a focus on the deeper business problems that are caused by the organization's communication difficulties. This ensures that the underlying thrust of a communication review (*to improve business performance*) remains in focus.
- Flowing from this, what are the organization's major communication problems? The audit can then seek to determine whether such problems exist, chart their exact nature, how deep they are, what has caused them, and what can be done.
- What changes in behaviour are required to eliminate these problems? How specific can we be about these changes? How will we know when they have occurred? At the outset, this sets an agenda for action, and primes managers to anticipate that changes in their own behaviour as well as that of others is likely to follow from the audit process.

(2) *Clarify in-depth the value of audits, their role in this particular organization and the commitment required from management if maximum advantage is to be obtained*. For example, the following issues should be addressed:

- What time scale best ties in with the business planning cycle?
- Will other organizational development issues need to be rescheduled?
- How can evaluating communication channels with customers support the marketing strategy?
- What plans can be made to circulate the audit results as widely as possible?

(3) *Identify the top half dozen issues on which people should be receiving and sending information*. An audit cannot examine every conceivable issue, in-depth. Our own research has generally found that information flow on a few key issues tends to be typical of the overall communication climate (Tourish and Hargie, 1998). Restricting the number of issues to be explored in this way is sufficient to provide valid data, while ensuring that the audit remains practicable. For example, if the audit is concerned with external communication, what are the most important issues which the company wants its customers to be aware of? Conversely, what does it want to hear from its customers about? These data can then be incorporated into the materials being used during the audit exercise. If questionnaires are being employed, a section should explore information flow on the key issues identified.

This also offers a good opportunity to delineate the extent of the audit exercise, and therefore clarify managers' conception of the communication process. It is essential, at this stage, to establish what audits both can and cannot do. Managers must have realistic expectations about what can be achieved. Like parents' expectations of a child, it is not good when too much (or too little) is envisioned. The audit will be less likely to achieve its full potential, as a tool for facilitating organizational development, if expectations are unrealistic. For example, it is difficult to use data obtained from focus groups to set statistical benchmarks. If the focus group is the only tool which the organization can use, and there are many circumstances under which this is the case, it is unrealistic to think that future audits will be able to measure precisely the extent of any progress that has been made. Novice auditors may be inclined to promise more than they can deliver, thereby undermining the credibility of the whole process.

(4) *Discuss the communication standards the management team believes they should adopt and live up to.* For example, in the United Kingdom, the National Health Service Management Executive published standards for communication in 1995, and circulated them throughout the main management tiers of the organization (NHS Executive, 1995). This was a summary of best general practice, recommending that commitments be made to:

- board-level discussions;
- regular audits;
- upward appraisal;
- training for effective communication;
- the consideration of communication during the business planning cycle; and
- the identification and reward of good practice.

Having established standards, answers must then be formulated to a number of key questions:

- what do they mean in practice?
- how will every organizational unit be transformed if they are implemented?
- what has stopped such implementation in the past?
- how much can be agreed and how much will remain in dispute for the foreseeable future?
- how quickly can change begin?
- what training needs are essential to implement this change?

The audit can then reveal the extent to which the standards are being implemented; stimulate further discussion on the gap between current practice and the characteristics of a world class communication system; and

encourage overt commitments by the key publics concerned, internally and/or externally.

(5) *The identification of a senior person or persons prepared to act as link between the organization and the external audit team.* If the audit is being conducted in-house, a link between those handling the project and top management is still vital. This is not to suggest that auditors should surrender their independence. However, ongoing contact with key people is vital to keep doors open; prevent sabotage or obstruction; ensure that the audit time scale remains on track; and provide essential information on the organization's structure, history, internal politics, business challenges, main priorities and climate.

Prepare the organization for the audit

Usually, a simple letter is sufficient to inform staff of the nature of the audit process, and the time scale which is envisaged. We would recommend that it be issued by the chief executive, thus putting the authority of this office behind the audit. This helps to ensure that managers facilitate access to audit participants, and generally engage with what is going on. It also binds the top management team into the audit exercise, by publicly identifying them with it. This makes it more likely that the results of the audit will be taken seriously and used to effect improvements in performance. In the case of external audits, a sample of customers or supply businesses can be addressed in a similar manner. Alternatively, internal or external newsletters, videos or team briefing mechanisms can be employed.

Recurring worries which tend to arise at this point include confidentiality, how widely available the results will be, and the time commitment required of audit respondents (Tourish and Tourish, 1996). The most difficult of these issues is confidentiality. Respondents are often wary of honestly expressing their views, in case what they say will be used against them at a later stage. It may be necessary to address these issues during initial communication with audit participants. The following general rules help:

- *Participants should be assured, orally and in writing, that their responses will be treated confidentially.* Research shows that the more often a message is repeated the more likely people are to accept that it is true (Cialdini, 2001). Accordingly, these assurances should be reiterated on a number of occasions – the more publicly, the better. The steps proposed to ensure confidentiality should be explained in detail.
- *Wherever possible, participants should be selected randomly.* This reinforces the message that the aim of the exercise is not to single people out with a view to imposing sanctions. There are hazards to this. When administering questionnaires to a group during one of our audits, one of the people present approached us to remark that it was the third time in six months he had been 'randomly selected' to complete questionnaires, dealing with a variety of organizational development issues. Intense persuasion was required to convince him that we were not part of a management plot against him!
- *Only the audit team should have access to questionnaires, tape recordings or anything else which might identify individual respondents.* All such materials should be destroyed at the conclusion of the audit.

- *Care should be taken, in writing the report, to ensure that it does not inadvertently enable readers to identify particular respondents.* For example, if only one person works in the payroll department the report should not cite comments, good or bad, from 'a payroll respondent'.
- *Audit instruments should be administered well away from the gaze of managers.* Again, during one of our audits, we had just spent some time explaining the confidential nature of the exercise to a group of questionnaire respondents, when a member of the senior management team dropped by simply to see how many people had turned up. Unfortunately, the effect was to discredit our assurances of confidentiality with the people concerned.

Normally, these procedures are sufficient to ensure that this problem is eased. However, it remains one of the strongest arguments in favour of using external rather than internal auditors. If a top manager turns up to administer questionnaires or conduct interviews, or if the person concerned is viewed as being close to managers, confidentiality assurances have low credibility.

Data gathering

This normally proceeds in two phases. A small number of preliminary first round interviews familiarizes the audit team with staff or customer views, as well as management concerns. Typically, respondents will be randomly selected. Feedback obtained by this approach helps in the design of final questionnaires, if this is the main method to be used. A number of issues have been suggested which should be explored in preliminary interviews

(Tourish and Tourish, 1996). The bulk of these are applicable to both internal and external audits:

- how decisions are made;
- communication channels;
- communication relationships;
- communication obstacles;
- organizational structure;
- responsiveness (e.g. the quality of information flow during a crisis).

Finally, the main audit exercise is embarked upon. A pilot test is vital. This makes it possible to detect shortcomings in the design and implementation of questionnaires (Emory and Cooper, 1991), or other approaches being employed. However, as Remenyi *et al.* (1998: 174) pointed out, 'in business and management research there is usually time and considerable financial pressure to get the project started'. Pilots are therefore often selected opportunistically, on grounds of convenience, availability, proximity or cost. We do not view this as a major problem. A pilot is a test case, undertaken to double check the viability of the approach chosen. It should not, even under ideal circumstances, become so elaborate that it develops into a main study in its own right. However, once the pilot is complete, the main study can proceed.

Analysis and action phase

A report is now prepared, which comprehensively describes and evaluates communication practices. Among the key questions that arise, we think that the following are particularly important:

- What targets can be set to eliminate the problems that arise from communication failure?

- What targets can be set to eliminate communication failure itself?
- What behaviours are the senior management team now willing to change, in order to demonstrate a symbolic commitment to improved communication?

For example, targets can be set for:

- increased and sustained knowledge;
- high levels of goodwill and credibility;
- a regular flow of communication (e.g. how much information will flow, on what topics, to what sources, utilizing what channels);
- accurate expectations about future milestones in organizational development (i.e. fewer toxic shocks); and
- satisfaction with levels of participation.

Ongoing audit research tracks the progress of all these factors.

It should be noted that this period presents both opportunities and dangers. Audits arouse increased interest and expectations. As a general rule, people recognize that everyone likes to sing loudly about their successes, while remaining mute about their mistakes. Thus, if an audit is followed by silence it is likely to be widely assumed that managers are either busy burying dreadful secrets in the basement, or meeting in a cabal to plot revenge on certain thankless employees who have criticized them. A key principle when confronted with bad news, if this is what emerges, is that it should be shared openly and quickly, thereby enabling those involved to at least gain credit for their honesty (Payne, 1996).

The results of the audit are, in the first instance, presented to the top management team, orally and in writing. The results then need to be circulated widely, by whatever means are most appropriate. Action plans should also be publicized. In this way, the process of audit, as well as whatever changes to which it gives rise, helps achieve significant strides forward in open and clear communication.

Methods used in the auditing process

There are a wide variety of alternative approaches, and the ones selected should be the 'best fit' for the organization concerned. The methods used should be tailored for the corporate body under analysis, as 'off-the-peg' systems, like cheap suits, are rarely attractive and inevitably fail to fit along some of the required dimensions. Furnham and Gunter (1993) used the term 'organometrics' to refer to the methods used to measure the various dimensions of organizational functioning. We will now briefly review the alternative organometric tools relevant to communication audits.

Survey questionnaires

This is the most widely used approach to auditing. Indeed, Clampitt (2000) pointed out that organizational surveys are now as commonplace as weather forecasts. This was confirmed by Goldhaber (2002: 451), who noted 'The survey, however, has become the dominant method chosen by academics and consultants – mostly due to its ease of development, administration, and interpretation – both for clients and for research publication.' There are several validated audit questionnaires that can be tailored for specific organizations. The two main ones are the *Communication Satisfaction Questionnaire* (Downs and Hazen, 1977) and the *International Communication Association Audit Survey* (Goldhaber and Rogers, 1979; Hargie and Tourish, 2000). The questionnaire method allows the auditor to control the focus of the audit, enables a large number of respondents to be surveyed, and produces benchmark rating scores for various aspects (e.g. 'communication received from senior managers') against which future performance can be measured. The main drawback is that it is limited in the extent to which it can gauge the deeper-level thoughts and feelings of respondents.

Interviews

Another popular audit approach is the structured interview. Indeed, in his text in this field Downs (1988) concluded that if he had to select just one audit method he would choose the interview. This is because it allows for communication experiences to be explored in detail, and as such can often produce interesting insights that surveys may miss. Researchers have increasingly recognized that people form different impressions of the same events, and that chronicling the stories that typify organizational life is a key means of understanding what sense people are making of their environment (Gabriel, 2000). Interviews and focus groups (discussed below) are an invaluable means of tapping into the stories, folklore, myths and fantasies that people develop as part of the organizational sense-making in which we all engage. On the down side, it is time-consuming and expensive. Interviews, which can last up to two hours for managers and one hour for non-managers (Millar and Gallagher, 2000), have to be recorded and transcribed for analysis. As such, it does not readily allow for large numbers to be involved in the audit.

Furthermore, unlike surveys, interviews cannot be anonymous and so may be vulnerable to social acceptability responses.

Focus groups

These are ubiquitous, and have permeated all walks of professional life, from politics to marketing. They can be used to develop insights at a macro level (such as the impact of strategic decision making) or on a micro level (such as detailed responses to particular communication messages) (Daymon and Holloway, 2002). In their comparison of audit methodologies, Dickson *et al.* (2003) argued that the open-ended and interactive nature of focus groups produces insights from respondents that are difficult to obtain through other methods. Participants spark one another into action by sharing and developing ideas. Two main disadvantages are that more introverted staff are reluctant to participate, and some staff may be unwilling to express honest views in the presence of colleagues.

These are the three most widely employed organometric audit tools, although there is a range of other approaches, such as critical incident analysis, ECCO, data collection log-sheet methods, constitutive ethnography, social network analysis, and undercover auditing (for a full analysis of these, see Hargie and Tourish, 2000; Dickson *et al.*, 2003).

For those who conceptualize organizational assessment as a form of collaborative or employee-centred enterprise the two main methodologies employed (Jones, 2002; Meyer, 2002) are:

1   *ethnomethodology*, which seeks to understand how employees construct their interpretations of the organizational world through interaction;

2   *textual analysis* (or hermeneutics), which involves the thematic analysis of written documents of all kinds (brochures, minutes of meetings, mission statements, etc.) as well as transcripts of interviews or group meetings.

In interpretive audits, three main types of data are collected: naturalistic observations, transcriptions of relevant texts, and recorded responses to researcher questions. These are, in turn, analysed using thematic analysis, metaphor analysis or narrative analysis, in order to achieve a symbolic interpretation of organizational communication (Meyer, 2002). The report produced from an interpretive investigation is also different from a traditional audit report, being more in the form of a narrative 'tale' of the researcher's experiences in the organization (Van Mannen, 1988; Gabriel, 2000).

What audits tend to find

There is no substitute for completing an individual audit. Every organization is different and will have specific needs. These can only be identified through a specific, tailored assessment. It is possible to predict certain recurring themes, and a number have been identified in the literature (e.g. Hargie and Tourish, 2003). In general, we have found the following.

Immediate line managers are crucial for effectiveness

In essence, people want supervisors who:

*   take a personal interest in their lives;
*   seem to care for them as individuals;
*   listen to their concerns and respond to these quickly and appropriately;

- give regular feedback on performance in a sensitive manner;
- hold efficient regular meetings at which information is freely exchanged;
- explain what is happening within the company.

In terms of shaping a strategy to deal with such problems, it is therefore important for organizations to disseminate information swiftly to first line supervisors. They should also provide them with comprehensive communication training so that they can optimize the impact they have upon the workforce. Unfortunately, we have often found that many organizations are reluctant to do this, apparently assuming that their managers should be innately capable of sustaining a world-class communication environment. Such assumptions are baseless.

Change and employees

Change is more likely to occur, and will be based on a clearer perception of organizational needs, if the views of employees are regularly and systematically obtained. Employees appreciate a climate in which bottom-up communication is encouraged. This means that systems must be put in place to allow vertical transmission of information and opinions up the hierarchy. Such data must also be acted upon and feedback given on its worth. Thus, Kassing (2000) showed that employees in workplaces where feedback is encouraged have a high level of identification with the organization and openly articulate dissenting views, knowing that these will be welcomed. By contrast, where feedback is discouraged employees have a low level of identification with the organization and are less likely to openly express their views. Repressed dissent leads to resentment and a desire for revenge. Employees are then more likely to try to sabotage management initiatives. Put simply, those organizations that have the most effective communication strategies are open to employee feedback, and spend both time and money in obtaining it.

Information should be widely shared

Staff want to be 'in the know' rather than being ill informed. In their study of over 2,000 employees across 21 organizations in 7 different countries, Shockley-Zalabak and Ellis (2000: 384) found that: 'information reception has a stronger relationship to effectiveness and job satisfaction than other measured communication activities. This supports the importance of planning and monitoring the frequency of messages about organizational performance, practices, policies, and a variety of job-related issues'. In other words, audits are essential tools for measuring and monitoring this pivotal aspect of information flow.

Maximum use should be made of face-to-face channels

It is perhaps a reassuring finding that in our ever-increasing technological world (and indeed even because of it), humans still prefer to interact with one another in person. Employees especially want to meet and talk with senior managers. Interestingly, our findings show that their expectations tend to be very realistic (Hargie et al., 2002). They know that senior managers are busy people and do not expect huge amounts of interpersonal contact with them. However, they do want to see them from time to time. In all walks of life, individuals value being with powerful or famous people (Hargie and Dickson, 2004).

The work setting is no different. Thus, managers who hide permanently in their bunkers, and run their operation by firing out salvos of email directives, are missing out on a potent influencing opportunity. Management by talking with staff is eminently preferable.

Employees value communication training

This finding has two sides. First, employees report that they personally wish to receive systematic training in the communication skills that are central to their work. Second, they want their managers to be trained in the appropriate skills to enable them to manage effectively. Communication skills training has been shown to be effective across a range of professional contexts (Hargie, 1997), yet many organizations fail to realize the full potential of their staff owing to a lack of investment in such training.

Conclusion

Organizations are fundamentally systems for facilitating human interaction. How well people exchange information is often the most critical factor in determining whether a business lives or dies. It is impossible to imagine a highly innovative, customer centred organization coming into existence, or sustaining its pre-eminent position, without its managers, and employees, paying the closest attention to how well they all communicate with each other. Yet, as we noted at the beginning of this chapter, it is often easier to find instances of poor communication than it is to highlight examples of communication excellence.

There are many reasons for this. For example, it is clear that most of us tend to overrate how well we communicate. As with car smashes, communication bumps and collisions are invariably held to be the fault of someone else. We have a vast armoury of self-serving biases, which distorts our perception of the wider social world (Dawes, 2002), and of how well we perform in our roles as managers (Tsang, 2002). Without a system for objective evaluation, people are unlikely to realize that such self-satisfied perceptions are most likely to be distorted illusions. In addition, unless a proper strategic framework is adopted to evaluate and monitor what happens, during difficult times organizations move towards a feeling of helplessness.

We have encountered some managers who shrug aside the view that prevailing systems could be improved. Their view is that communication is like the weather we would all like it to be better, but can't really do anything to bring about such a state of affairs. It is therefore an unfortunate paradox that, while most people admit that communication is vital to the building of successful organizations, most organizations allocate precious few resources to improving it. Some managers convey the impression that they are willing to do anything humanly possible to improve communication – except devote time, energy and resources to it. Few other functions are expected to manage themselves on a similar basis.

This chapter has proposed that it is possible to build a world-class communication system and a front-rank communication strategy. As always, evaluation is critical to success. What gets measured gets done. Organizations that integrate audits into their regular communication planning process, who take the results seriously, and who base their communication strategies on hard data rather than vague hunches are much more likely to succeed than their rivals.

REFERENCES

Cialdini, R. (2001) *Influence: Science and Practice*, 4th edn, Boston: Allyn and Bacon.

Clampitt, P. (2000) 'The questionnaire approach', in O. Hargie and D. Tourish (eds), *Handbook of Communication Audits For Organisations*, London: Routledge.

Clampitt, P. and Berk, L. (2000) 'A communication audit of a paper mill', in O. Hargie and D. Tourish (eds), *Handbook of Communication Audits For Organisations*, London: Routledge.

Clampitt, P., DeKoch, R. and Cashman, T. (2000) 'A strategy for communicating about uncertainty', *Academy of Management Executive*, 14, 41–57.

Dawes, R. (2002) *Everyday Irrationality*, Boulder, CO: Westview Press.

Daymon, C., and Holloway, I. (2002) *Qualitative Research Methods in Public Relations and Marketing Communications*, London: Routledge.

Dickson, D., Rainey, S. and Hargie O. (2003) 'Communicating sensitive business issues: Part I', *Corporate Communications: An International Journal*, 8, 35–43.

Downs, C. (1988) *Communication Audits*, Glenview, IL: Scott, Foresman.

Downs, C. and Adrian, A. (1997) *Communication Audits*, Lawrence, KS: Communication Management.

Downs, C. and Hazen, M. (1977) 'A factor analytic study of communication satisfaction', *Journal of Business Communication*, 14, 63–73.

Emmanuel, M. (1985) 'Auditing communication practices', in C. Reuss and DiSilvas (eds), *Inside Organisational Communication*, 2nd edn, New York: Longman.

Emory, C., and Cooper, D. (1991) *Business Research Methods*, Burr Ridge, IL: Irwin.

Furnham, A. and Gunter, B. (1993) *Corporate Assessment: Auditing a Company's Personality*, London: Routledge.

Gabriel, Y. (2000) *Storytelling in Organisations: Facts, Fictions and Fantasies*, Oxford: Oxford University Press.

Goldhaber, G. (2002) 'Communication audits in the age of the internet', *Management Communication Quarterly*, 15, 451–7.

Goldhaber, G. and Rogers, D. (1979) *Auditing Organisational Communication Systems: The ICA Communication Audit*, Dubuque, IA: Kendall/Hunt.

Hargie, O. (1997) 'Training in communication skills: research, theory and practice', in O. Hargie (ed.), *The Handbook of Communication Skills*, London: Routledge.

Hargie, O. and Dickson, D. (2004) *Skilled Interpersonal Communication: Research, Theory and Practice*, London: Routledge.

Hargie, O. and Tourish, D. (2004) 'How are we doing? Measuring and monitoring organizational communication', in D. Tourish and O. Hargie (eds), *Key Issues in Organisational Communication*, London: Routledge.

Hargie, O. and Tourish, D. (eds) (2000) *Handbook of Communication Audits For Organisations*, London: Routledge.

Hargie, O., Tourish, D. and Wilson, N. (2002) 'Communication audits and the effects of increased information: a follow-up study', *Journal of Business Communication*, 39, 414–36.

Hurst, B. (1991) *The Handbook of Communication Skills*, London: Kogan Page.

Jones, D. (2002) 'The interpretive auditor: reframing the communication audit', *Management Communication Quarterly*, 15, 466–71.

Jones, E. (1990) *Interpersonal Perception*, New York: Freeman.

Kassing, J. (2000) 'Exploring the relationship between workplace freedom of speech, organisational identification, and employee dissent', *Communication Research Reports*, 17, 387–96.

Meyer, J. (2002) 'Organisational communication assessment: fuzzy methods and the accessibility of symbols', *Management Communication Quarterly*, 15, 472–9.

Millar, R. and Gallagher, M. (2000) 'The interview approach', in O. Hargie and D. Tourish (eds), *Handbook of Communication Audits for Organisations*, London: Routledge.

NHS Executive (1995) *Setting Standards for NHS Communications: Consultation Document*, London: NHS Executive.

Payne, J. (1996) 'Developing and implementing strategies for communicating bad news', *Journal of Communication Management*, 1, 80–8.

Pettigrew, A., Ferlie, E. and McKee, L. (1992) 'Shaping strategic change: the case of the NHS', *Public Money and Management*, 12, 27–32.

Remenyi, D., Williams, B., Money, A. and Swartz, E. (1998) *Doing Research in Business and Management: An Introduction to Process and Method*, London: Sage.

Rosenfeld, P., Giacalone, R. and Riordan, C. (1995) *Impression Management in Organisations*, London: Routledge.

Shockley-Zalabak, P. and Ellis, K. (2000) 'Perceived organisational effectiveness, job satisfaction, culture, and communication: challenging the traditional view', *Communication Research Reports*, 17, 375–86.

Spurgeon, P. and Barwell, F. (1991) *Implementing Change in the NHS*, London: Chapman and Hall.

Tourish, D. and Hargie, C. (1996) 'Internal communication: key steps in evaluating and improving performance', *Corporate Communications: An International Journal*, 1(3), 11–16.

Tourish, D. and Hargie, O. (1998) 'Communication between managers and staff in the NHS: trends and prospects', *British Journal of Management*, 9, 53–71.

Tourish, D. and Tourish, B. (1996) 'Assessing staff-management relationships in local authority leisure facilities: the communication audit approach', *Managing Leisure: An International Journal*, 1(2), 91–104.

Tsang, E. (2002) 'Self-serving attributions in corporate annual reports: a replicated study', *Journal of Management Studies*, 39, 51–65.

Van Mannen, J. (1988) *Tales of the Field: On Writing Ethnography*, Chicago: University of Chicago Press.

CHAPTER 9

The Olympic Games: a framework for international public relations

Yvonne Harahousou, Chris Kabitsis, Anna Haviara and
Nicholas D. Theodorakis

The inclusion of properly organized public relations in an organizing committee for the Olympic Games has become a necessity; the Games have evolved, and the complexity of promoting a favourable image for any host city demands strategic planning and organizing. For future organizers to be successful in this task, the knowledge and experience gained from already implemented publicity programmes is vital. In this chapter, PR activities in OCOG's public relations have been recorded and a model has been developed as a reference point for the next Olympic Games PR programme and beyond.

Introduction

The task of a city hosting the Olympic Games is a rather demanding and complicated one, spreading in multiple organizational areas and leaving an apparent impact on the overall image of a whole country for many years following the completion of the Games. At the same time, the preparation period that leads to the Olympic Games is also a significant opportunity for promotion and international exposure.

As image and identity promotion are two sensitive areas (Marconi, 1996), public relations of the organizing body of the Olympic Games should be approached carefully and be developed based on already tested techniques and strategies. The present study aims at presenting the PR evolution in a period of more than twenty years. This permits the reader to have a comprehensive view of the public information needs as expressed by the public and met by organizers.

The PR programmes were presented as evolved through the Olympiads since Los Angeles in 1980 until Sydney 2000, and commendation on the major initiatives was provided. Finally, the best programmes implemented were outlined as a model suggestion for future Organizing Committees (OC) for the Olympic Games. The main hypothesis that this research explores, is whether there has been developed an effective generic model for the public relations in organizing committees which, with certain minor alterations, based on the specific culture for each country and expected evolution, may be adjusted so as to contribute to the success of the Olympic Games.

Public relations involves research and analysis, policy formation, programming, communication and feedback from a variety of publics. The perplexed nature of the field and the sensitivity that characterizes transactions with a public make a PR strategy plan and implementation an absolute necessity for an organization, especially a large-scale one, such as an organizing committee for the Olympic Games. Despite the extensive organizational PR literature and the post-Games reports presenting the PR approach undertaken by organizing committees for the Olympic Games, there is a lack of comparative and evaluative research among these.

Public relations in the organization committees 1980–2000

Los Angeles 1984

The PR department of the Los Angeles Olympic Games Organizing Committee (LAOOC), was formed in late 1979 and included six different sub-programmes that played a key role in shaping popular public opinion for the Games (LAOOC, 1984). These sub-programmes were: community relations division, public information division, audiovisual division, speakers bureau, Olympic spirit team and publications division. Several other operating departments within the OCOG, many of which had their own public relations or publicity staff, supplemented the work of these PR department divisions.

The PR programme of the LAOOC was generally designed to keep people informed of what the OCOG was doing rather than to sell the Games. The philosophy of the OCOG was that the Games would spontaneously sell itself, as the world's most anticipated sporting event. The structure and responsibilities allocated in LAOOC were clear and based on a thorough organizational planning. The projects that contributed the most to the overall success of the Organizing Committee's PR programme were the public information and the speakers bureau.

Members of the speakers bureau played a vital role in shaping the positive feelings of the people of Los Angeles, which culminated in their enthusiastic support, and resulting success of the Games. The Olympic spirit team, which made systematic use of former Olympians, an idea originally launched from the Munich organizers back in 1972, was also a success. The individuals making up the group not only had considerable media appeal, but they were strongly motivated, articulate and enthusiastic, able to inspire many youngsters, volunteers and entire communities by giving their time and energy to promoting the Olympic Games.

What is remarkable for the Los Angeles PR implementation is the fact that importance was given to developing a two-way communication programme, for the first time in Olympic Games PR history. The structure of the PR department contributed to that. The public information division filled a need for more direct contact with southern California residents by creating a telephone hotline that the public could call to voice concerns, ask questions or offer support. The speakers bureau and the Olympic spirit team offered even more personal contact by dispersing staff members and Olympians to share information and experiences with the public. The Los Angeles Games were of decisive importance to Olympic PR evolution, as they applied a well-structured department format, providing future organizers with a lot more than just a new idea for publicity. A brief description of LAOOC PR practices is presented in Table 9.1.

Seoul 1988

The basic goals of the Seoul PR programme as stated in the official post-Games report were: to create an atmosphere for the maximum public participation and stimulate public awareness domestically, and to win global support for Seoul's hosting, ultimately drawing the participation of as many nations as possible (SLOOC, 1988). Public relations

programmes were classified into: direct public relations, intended to support Games programmes themselves, including activities undertaken directly by the OCOG at home and abroad, and those aimed at creating a favourable environment and atmosphere, that included support of direct PR programmes through the media, various administration channels and activities to raise people's public consciousness.

The SLOOC took charge of direct public relations while the Ministry of Culture and Information along with other governmental offices and private organizations handled public relations aiming at the creation of a favourable atmosphere.

Table 9.1 Los Angeles 1984

	PR practices	Description
1	Community relations	The Community relations' staff opened two 'satellite' offices, in combination with the Olympic neighbours programmes provided Los Angeles residents direct and easy access to the OCOG.
2	Public information	The need of the OCOG to assemble and disseminate information and respond to inquiries and requests was the reason for the set up of this division that handled telephone and written requests, remote ticketing, info booths and info kiosks.
3	Audio visual, radio and TV	The division produced tapes and films that would help foster understanding of the Organizing Committee's planning, and promote public enthusiasm and support on the Games. More than 24 films and radio messages were realized.
4	Speakers bureau	In the five-year period during which the bureau operated approximately 2,000 speeches were made to an estimated audience of 560,000 people. The majority of speeches were during lunch or dinner hours to local businesses, chambers of commerce, professional organizations, schools and service clubs; 150 speakers from the local community and staff from the OC were used.
5	Olympic spirit team	Some 250 contemporary Olympic athletes voluntarily participated in an effort to promote personal involvement and the support for the Games.
6	Publications	Regular publications, such as the *Olympic Update* newsletter, informational brochures, and other major projects, such as the *Official Olympic Guide to Los Angeles* were designed and produced in collaboration with the *Look of the Games*, and led a further step forward the Olympic publications history.

Seoul followed the PR philosophy successfully launched in Los Angeles, and gave importance to the two-way communication model, aiming at stimulating public awareness and involvement in the Games. A significant novelty launched by the Seoul organizers was the collaboration with an overseas public relations agency, something that emphasized the professionalism required for the international relations of an OCOG. Special attention was also given to community relations, due to the Korean culture and traditions. The Pansanghoe information sessions, public information allocation, events and local media relations consisted of particularly important means for the formation of favourable opinion of the OCOG in the community. A brief description of SLOOC PR practices is presented in Table 9.2

Barcelona 1992

Barcelona organizers having studied the previous two Olympic Games communication activities realized that the scope of public relations grew at a considerable rate, expanding to each and every single department of the organization. The Barcelona OCOG was the first one not to use public relations as a title description of one of its main programme areas. The acknowledgement of the contribution the organization structure made to the public image of the Olympic Games Committee, led to the creation of a broad Image and Communication Division, that co-ordinated all the different sub-programmes included. The Image and Communication Division arranged for public attention and support for the Barcelona Olympic Games, significant issues for the Spanish organizers who worked to that end, through: promotional campaigns, distribution of promotional

material, media relations, the Alcatel project, the official newspaper and other publications and public information.

A change from the previous Olympiads, due to technological progress and the increasing information demand by the media was the Alcatel project. The need for a central information system, that would allow frequent updates at a considerably lower cost compared to constantly revised publications, was evident. Spanish organizers, being technologically oriented, implemented a pioneer project, available to the Olympic family, other VIPs and media. The project however, was recorded as a forerunner of the idea for an Olympic Games official website, that would allow international access and good value publicity. A brief description of BOCOG PR practices is presented in Table 9.3

Atlanta 1996

The Atlanta Olympic Games Organizing Committee (ACOG), chose to allocate tasks that were previously executed in the context of public relations to two different programme areas: communication, and government relations (ACOG, 1996). Communication staff were divided into four areas: media relations, press operations, press information and public information. Government relations of the Atlanta OCOG included: federal government relations, local government relations and community relations.

The Atlanta PR programme was one of the most inclusive, combining some of the most successful and well-tested projects, based on the effective two-way communication model. Technology and the Barcelona innovation led Atlanta to operating the internet website, which served as a highly successful ambassador of the 1996 Olympic Games to the

Table 9.2 Seoul 1988

	PR practices	Description
1	Production of informational materials	The OCOG produced various publications for use at PR exhibits and for distribution to national and international publics. Overseas information materials were distributed through either PR exhibits operated at major events, overseas delegations or individual mailing.
2	Periodicals	Three regular periodicals were published (quarterly, weekly and monthly). During the Games an official daily newspaper was distributed to the Olympic family and tourists.
3	Non-periodic publications	Informational folders and booklets were published in many language editions, carrying stories about Korean culture as well as information on Games, cultural programmes and Olympic Games tickets. Small information items such as posters, stickers, badges, etc., were also produced, as well as a pictorial publication titled 'Games of the XXIVth Olympiad'.
4	Audiovisual material	Five documentaries were produced, along with seven videos and multiple slides. The films and videos that followed until the opening of the Games also included information on tourism and accommodation, cultural events and venue facilities.
5	Information centre	A year before the opening of the Seoul Games, a public information desk was established at Kimpo International Airport. The desk served more than 600 people on an average-day basis, both Koreans and foreigners. A few days before the opening of the Games, 23 information centres started operating at the entrance of each Olympic venue.
6	Information and educational public relations	Several sessions were organized regularly in cities and provinces on the progress of planning and preparations, as well as the effects of the Games for Seoul and Korea. Sessions were held in 14 cities. Other activities were the distribution of Olympic educational materials, speeches by leading figures, a 24-hour telephone audio text service and the distribution of information in neighbourhood meetings.
7	Public relations on special occasions	A significant opportunity for public relations was the organization of events linked to the Games. The concept of countdown days to the opening of the Games was also widely used for PR goals. Three large-scale events were organized 500 days, 365 days and 100 days to the opening of the Seoul Games. The inauguration ceremony of the olympic stadium was also such an event.
8	Use of overseas PR	Among the tasks taken over by the international PR agency was the monitoring agencyof the trend of public opinion in many areas and the arrangement of press interviews during major events. The agency also published a quarterly full-colour newsletter, prepared major speech texts for senior officials, provided counselling in media issues and prepared documents, articles and scripts in English for publications and videos issued by the Seoul OCOG.

Table 9.3 Barcelona 1992

	PR practices	Description
1	Promotional campaigns	In 1989, two information campaigns were staged; 'Barcelona '92, three years before', and 'We're getting on with it', aimed at the people of Barcelona and Catalan to justify the inconvenience caused by the works. Also specialized campaigns were organized for the support of sponsors and licensees, the promotion of the state lotteries, increased awareness on the torch relay route, and ticket sales.
2	Promotional materials	Licensed products were given away to journalists, schools, university and other community groups for PR purposes. Olympic families received a promotional item token from the organizers.
3	Media relations	The press department organized a wide range of activities for the media such as press conferences, publications (a daily bulletin, a weekly newsletter, an updated press dossier every six months), PR events (e.g. Olympic tours) and a welcoming campaign designed for reporters from all around the world.
4	The Alcatel project	The aim of the Alcatel project, named after the joint partner of the Barcelona OCOG, was to set up an information hotline to the world's leading media, institutions and VIPs related to the Olympic Games, through nine information databases devoted to various subjects such as Spain today, Catalonia today, history of the Games, etc.
5	Publications	During the day a daily newspaper was distributed for free in two languages. A monthly magazine, booklets for volunteer recruitment and training, information editions for all sports of the OG, guides, official programmes and official Games results book.
6	Public information	Staff of the public information dept were responsible among other things for the information booths project, a series of information points in Barcelona and its suburbs for the public.

world public. The internet website was the optimum method for transmitting PR information about the Atlanta Games to worldwide destinations, speeding up communication in a sophisticated way (Oxley, 1987). Thus, there was a further expansion in the national and international target publics, while at the same time community relations strengthened PR messages to ensure effective community support and involvement.

Atlanta organizers had the unique opportunity to plan their Olympic Games public relations, based on the expertise acquired by the Los Angeles Games in 1984. This, in combination with the advances in the technological environment enabled them to improve on the already successful programmes and take these one step further. A brief description of ACOG PR practices is presented in Table 9.4.

Sydney 2000

The Sydney Organizing Committee (SOCOG) was mainly based on the example of Atlanta in the organization of its PR programme, taking it a little further with the technological help of the internet and the electronic databases. In addition, the Sydney 2000 public relations made the transition from PR

Table 9.4 Atlanta 1996

	PR practices	Description
1	Media relations	During the 1996 Games, media relations worked also with press and broadcasters on non-sports issues of the Games (Longhurst, 1996). Media relations' staff collaborated with all appropriate ACOG functional areas to determine the best communication strategies for issues that would affect the public. Publicity campaigns were also implemented to promote ticket and merchandise sales, Olympic arts festivals, test events and recruitment of volunteers. Main tasks and achievements included: the press guide, news conferences and news releases, venue tours, media information line and issue management.
2	Press information	Press information was given the responsibility to expand the scope of information that would be provided to the media (Jefkins, 1993). Additionally, press information was responsible for the Atlanta Olympic News Agency, which served as a single news source during the Games and ensured delivery of news and information to the media.
3	Press operations	Press operations department planned and installed facilities that the press would need during the Games, managing at the same time Games services such as accreditation, accommodation and transportation.
4	Public information	The public information division managed several programmes oriented to general public inquiries. These were: The Olympic experience (a public info gallery), speakers bureau (informed more than 1,500 groups), information requests, worldwide website (the first official site and a big success, 200 million visits during the Games), call centre (24 hours, 7 days per week) and Games time operations.
5	Government relations	The primary missions of government relations were to facilitate communication and co-operation between the various department of the OCOG and the federal and state government. Second, the government relations aimed at educating public officials on all aspects of the Olympic Games.
6	Community relations	This programme area was committed to improving all community areas affected by the Games and for that purpose several projects were developed such as: committee on disability access, Olympic environmental support group, youth programmes, Atlanta University centre legacy, interfaith advisory group and neighbourhood job training and employment programme.

strategy to PR structure. The expanded structure introduced was a reflection of the organizational PR enhanced strategy (Mintzberg, 1990).

Public relations evolution was based on the acknowledgement of the importance of a consistent and well-communicated overall organization image to a variety of publics. The complexity of this task, and the increasing demand for targeting effectively the messages of the OCOG could not be satisfied through a single department in SOCOG, no matter how wide in scope that would be.

Communication and community relations incorporated the basic PR methods and principles, contributing to their evolution

Table 9.5 Sydney 2000

	PR practices	Description
1	Community and public relations	The management of community based PR activities and raising awareness of the 2000 Olympic Games among all Australians. National publicity was furthered for key programmes such as the national education programme, ticketing and consumer products through events and activities. The operation of the call centre was also among the projects undertaken by this department. The call centre operating since 1998, enabled Australians to obtain all the information they needed about the Games for the cost of a local telephone call.
2	Olympic communication speakers bureau	Professional speakers were provided at a range of public events, from community meetings to corporate conferences. Speakers communicated desirable SOCOG messages and informed the public on their involvement opportunities in the Games.
3	Olympic 2000 national education	The programme reached over three million Australian students, through a range of education projects. These included distribution of Olympic publications and CD-roms promoting the Olympic ideals and enhancing the notion of volunteerism. Additionally, the 'share the spirit' art competition was organized for Australian students up to 12 years old, while a special section for students, named KIDS was introduced in the Sydney 2000 Olympic Games website.
4	Multicultural affairs programme	This programme was a special addition in the organizational structure due to the special multicultural Australian environment (Banks, 1995). The programme ensured that all SOCOG Programmes incorporated the needs of Australia's diverse communities in their planning for the Games. Through a multicultural affairs programme, SOCOG reached out to multicultural communities through newsletters, community briefings and events and the mainstream of ethnic media.
5	Public information co-ordination	The public information co-ordination (PIC), provided a centralized store of public information services and systems. The PIC oversaw the development and maintenance of SOCOG's key internal communication database, Athena, which carried regularly updated information for use across the organization, and externally through the official website and the call centre.
6	Publications	This programme managed and produced hundreds of publication projects, as was the case in previous Olympiads.
7	Internet	The official Games internet website enabled worldwide access to. information and gave people the potential to buy tickets and licensed products of the Sydney 2000 Olympic Games. The public information department was responsible for feeding the website with constant information and news updates.
8	Research and information	The programme maintained SOCOG's archives and library collection, providing access to online databases that facilitated research.
9	Other programmes	Other programme areas that contributed to SOCOG'S success were: media information, government relations, aboriginal and Torres Strait Islanders relations and international relations.

according to the specific Australian cultural needs. Nevertheless, it was the active and long-lasting involvement of more than that one department that actually Sydney offered to the PR evolution of the Organizing Committees for the Olympic Games. Communication and community relations, however, was the main division responsible for managing the SOCOG's communication with corporate businesses, community and sporting groups, tourism bodies, venue and host councils, schools, ethnic communities, media and the general public. The division also managed SOCOG's PR agency, Capital Public Relations, briefing the company on the SOCOG's major communication and promotional campaigns and overseeing project delivery.

The objectives set by the Sydney 2000 Olympic Games OCOG PR programme may be summarized as: (1) the co-ordination, facilitation or provision of the necessary mechanisms and material for SOCOG interactions with government, community groups and the public; (2) provision, for all SOCOG divisions and programmes, of service and advice on public relations, issues management and government relations, and assistance to the media relations programme on matters of public and media interest; and (3) co-ordination of the material used for SOCOG publications for consistency of information and messages (SOCOG, 1999) (see Table 9.5).

Conclusions and suggestions for future organizers

The roots of public relations for the Olympic Games extend deep in the ancient Games. Generating publicity for the Olympics in ancient Greece demanded the same skills as it does in the modern Olympics (Wilcox *et al.*, 1998).

Public relations evolved through the years, changing from one prevailing model to another. In theoretical terms this evolution can be described through the models proposed by Wilcox *et al.* (1998): (1) *The model of public information*: this primary form of public relations was focused on the dissemination of information, not necessarily with a persuasive intent. It was based exclusively on one-way communication, viewed only as transmitting messages, without any interaction with the publics, as little, if any, research was undertaken. (2) *Two-way symmetric*: the purpose of this model is gaining mutual understanding, and communication is two-way with balanced effects. The model includes feedback from the publics. Research is used both to learn how the public perceives the organization and to determine what consequences the organization has for the public, resulting in the counselling of management about policies. Evaluative research is used to measure whether a PR effort has improved both the understanding publics have of the organization and that which management has of its publics. It is to be noted that the Los Angeles Olympic Committee attempted first to develop a two-way communication model in the history of the Games.

As previously presented, public relations in organizing committees should not be viewed as simple publicity and one-way communication, but as a strategic process of negotiation with a number of key publics. Taking into consideration all the above, a framework for future organizers is presented in the following paragraphs.

PR research

Effective public relations are processes, and the essential first step is research. In basic terms, research is a form of listening. Before any PR programme can be undertaken, information must be gathered, data collected and interpretation done. Then, the organization can begin to map out policy decisions and strategies for effective communication.

Communication within the organization

Taking as an example the organizational structures in Sydney and Atlanta, it is understood that public relations could no longer be conceived as an individual part of the organization. On the contrary, communication links should be developed among the different divisions in future Olympic Games organizing committees that would allow the imminent flow of information and promotion of messages. Athena, the electronic database operated by Sydney OCOG, containing media releases, a weekly workforce newsletter, and several reports, accessible by all Sydney employees, could provide a basis for internal communication advancement. An electronic information database would result in saving considerable time and effort for interested parties, and providing accurate and updated information starting from each organizational division and reaching a wide range of publics.

Public information

Featuring interactivity in communication has proved essential for actually capturing and involving people in the Olympic Games. Publications were a well-known long-lasting tool for Games organizers to promote their messages; however, they could no longer be solely used to accomplish the PR goals set.

Publications and audiovisual material should always be considered as a complementary way to approach publics, through a series of projects that encourage active participation from the public (Epov, 1986).

Communication projects

Internet website
The term 'interactivity' is usually used in connection with the latest technology achievements, as these are two-way communication oriented. As interaction is a necessity for current public relations, an official Olympic Games website is a lot more than desirable. The internet secures information penetration to a global public in a direct and effective way. An OCOG should definitely take advantage of this low-cost opportunity for international exposure, which could also be used for commercial exploitation (Howard, 1998).

Call centre
The call centre operation is a project of significant sensitivity. People employed in the call centre should have advanced communication skills and be well trained and constantly updated on major issues that could raise public interest. Call centre employees offer for many people the only immediate contact with the Games OCOG. Therefore, the impressions formulated after contacting the Games call centre often influence public disposition towards the overall OCOG and the Olympic Games themselves. The success of the call centre, however, is dependent on two factors: the use of a large and dedicated volunteer workforce and a flexible staff structure, which would combine both centralized and venue-oriented responsibilities. The amount of cross-training and dual responsibilities shared

between venue operations and the phone bank should allow for maximum intercommunication and exchange of information. An overall programme for similar direct communication between future Olympic organizing committees and the local, national and international publics is strongly encouraged.

Speakers bureau

The establishment of a speakers bureau allows spreading of information to interested parties in a more active and detailed way. The OCOG would be able through its speakers to reach an extensive variety of groups, of different interests and concerns, carrying enthusiasm for the Games and aiming to found public support. This project underlines the substantial attention given to community understanding and acceptance, enhancing the community profile of the OCOG. Training and constant news updates to speakers, as well as suitable speakers selection are essential to the success of the programme. Los Angeles OCOG being the first to have introduced a speakers bureau, did so with careful planning and selection procedures, which should be followed by future organizers as well (Macnamara, 1996).

Events

Public relations events should be optimum to generate enthusiasm and promote favourable messages (Haberman and Dolphin, 1988). Media coverage is an important prerequisite for the success of the events, which should be organized in a special context, as could be Olympic Games countdown days, first launched by Seoul OCOG.

Events should be organized by as many departments of an OCOG as possible, in order to raise public awareness and communicate the multiple dimensions of the Olympic Games organization.

Community relations

Community involvement opportunities

Two major projects that require community involvement are volunteerism and torch relay. Special publicity, including speeches, publications and events should be organized to inform the public of these opportunities to participate in the Games (Burke, 1999).

Educational programme

In co-operation with the government the OCOG should give emphasis in educating people and particularly students on the Olympic Games values. The example of Sydney organizers who realized the importance of supporting an educational programme should be taken further. Additional features of the programme could include lectures and seminars, film projection and publications distribution, and motivation for participating in less popular Olympic Games sports. To conclude, as the ultimate purpose of public relations is to generate publicity, media exposure is considered vital for the success of any PR project. For that purpose, *media relations* should never be overlooked. On the contrary, all opportunities for promoting PR activities through the media should be exploited.

The completion of this research has confirmed the original hypothesis that there is connectivity among the various public relations programmes as exercised by OCOGs. Furthermore this connectivity is expressed in an evolutionary pattern. Each organizing body for the Olympic Games has introduced at least one new public relations programme. This may be justified due to the cultural differences among the different host cities. The only country to host two Olympic Games in the twenty years of observation was the United States. Los Angeles and Atlanta, in 1984 and 1996 respectively, contributed significantly to the evolution recorded. This enables us to realize that the organization of the Games in one country every four years would benefit the overall progress of the Games. However the multicultural dimension of the Games allows the integration of a model that could be adjusted to every culture, however different this could be.

As observed the current tendency in the organizational PR field is related to technology. Internet and other communication appliances will play a vital role in the advancement of public relations, to a far wider audience in a significantly shorter time frame. The co-operation that started through the transfer of knowledge programme under IOC co-ordination is also an effective way of communication and easier issues resolution. In the era of communication explosion and globalization, public relations could only grow towards this direction, according to the original universal spirit of the Olympic Games.

The present research opens additional fields for exploration to future researchers as well. A more detailed analysis of specialized PR areas such as media relations, press relations, government relations and community relations is required, to name but a few.

Additionally, crises management issues should be addressed, in conjunction with reactive PR and media predisposal to the Games. The effect of technological advancements in public relations could also comprise a research topic.

Finally, it should be taken into account that this research was completed before the Sydney 2000 Olympic Games, which does not allow an overall appraisal of the practices performed by the public relations of SOCOG. This specific time frame was chosen with the aim of maintaining objectivity towards the PR programme, as developed, irrespectively of the Games impressions. However, the fact that the research took place during the preparations for the Sydney Games could raise a question of subjectivity. The research was completed one day before the opening of the 2000 Olympic Games. This allowed for as extensive as possible a coverage of the PR practices implemented and any problems related to these. The lack of related research studies in the field of public relations both in OCOGs and sport organizations does not allow comparative evaluation. The literature reviewed for that reason derives from the broader organizational PR area. In the end it is to be noted that this chapter has referred only to the specific PR requirements of Olympic Games organizing committees.

REFERENCES

Atlanta Organizing Committee for the Olympic Games (ACOG) (1996) *Official Post Games Report of the Centennial Games*, Atlanta, GA.

Banks, Stephen P. (1995) *Multicultural Public Relations: A Social-interpretive Approach*, Thousand Oaks, CA: Sage.

Barcelona Organizing Committee for the Olympic Games (BOCOG) (1992) *Official Post Games Report of the 25th Olympiad*, Barcelona.

Burke, E. (1999) *Corporate Community Relations: The Principle of the Neighbor of Choice*, Westport, CN: Quorum Books.

Epov, P. (1986) *The Marketing and Public Relations Manual*, Lidcombe, NSW: Peter Epov Sports Marketing Pty.

Haberman, D. A. and Dolphin, H. A. (1988) *Public Relations: The Necessary Art*, Ames, IA: Iowa University Press.

Howard, S. (1998) *Corporate Image Management: A Marketing Discipline for the 21st Century*, Singapore: Butterworth-Heinemann Asia.

Jefkins, F. (1993) *Planned Press and Public Relations*, Glasgow: Blackie Academic and Professional.

Longhurst, J. (1996) *Making the News: A Media Relations Manual for Nonprofit Organizations*, Winnipeg: Windflower Communications.

Los Angeles Olympic Games Organizing Committee, (LAOOC) (1984) *Official Post Games Report of the Games of the XXIIIrd Olympiad*, Los Angeles, CA.

Macnamara, J. R. (1996) *Public Relations Handbook for Managers and Executives*, revd edn, New York; Sydney: Prentice Hall.

Marconi, J. (1996) *Image Marketing: Using Public Perceptions to Attain Business Objectives*, Lincoln-wood, IL: NTC Business Books.

Mintzberg, H. (1990) 'The design school: reconsidering the basic premises of strategic management', *Strategic Management Journal*, 11, 171–95.

Oxley, H. (1987) *The Principles of Public Relations*, London: Kogan Page.

Seoul Organizing Committee for the Olympic Games (SLOOC) (1988) *Official Post Games Report*, Seoul.

Sydney Organizing Committee for the Olympic Games (SOCOG) (1999) *Annual Report*, Sydney.

Wilcox, D. L., Ault, P. H and Agee, W. K. (1998) *Public Relations: Strategies and Tactics*, 5th edn, New York: Longman.

CHAPTER 10

Facets of the global corporate brand

T. C. Melewar and Christopher D. McCann

This chapter discusses some of the issues surrounding the use of corporate branding in an international context. It examines the issues of communication of corporate values to a global audience and the importance of establishing corporate brands is considered through analysis of a case study. Makita Corporation in Japan is an 85-year-old established company that operates in the global small power tools and accessories market. The authors suggest that three key facets of global corporate brand are: communication of a consistent message; organizational support of brand image; and control and standardization to add value to new products and entrance into new markets.

Introduction

Why are there so many television programmes, books and magazines devoted to business? A large part of it is because business has such a profound influence on our lives. Business is a spectacle; a drama filled with excitement and adventure. The actors in this drama are the companies who use their image or actions to create the drama and intrigue in order to get people on their side. We interpret companies by their outward signs, such as advertising brochures and reported performance. As in successful drama, businesses need to communicate their message effectively to be successful. A number of factors contribute to this success. First, images determine people's attitudes and behaviour; a positive image can help create and support a company or its products. Second, the image is a mixture of appearance and behaviour – one needs to support the other. Lastly, to succeed one needs to be a good communicator. As soon as one extends this drama/business analogy to an international environment these success factors become even more complex and challenging. One way international companies could reduce the complexity is through corporate brands. Corporate brands provide effective and consistent communications that have an increasing role to play in the drama we call business.

Meaning of the corporate brand

Corporate branding is generally considered important, but at the same time difficult to define. Both of the words 'brand' and 'corporate' carry certain connotations. 'Corporate' implies organization – both profit and non-profit. What defines it as corporate is its cohesion; the idea of people coming together and working towards a common goal (Stuart, 1999). At the same time there are factors, particularly of large organizations, that serve to diffuse this meaning of corporate. Different parts of the organization can develop their own, often contradictory, directions. This implies the need to understand the organization as a part of the term 'corporate brand'. Traditionally, a brand is a descriptor applied to a good. It is distinct from the idea of a product in that with a brand there is the notion of values that go beyond mere functional performance. When tying the two words together one suggests a new way of looking at

organizations and what values they bring to a brand. In the next few sections we discuss the facets of corporate branding in the international context (see Figure 10.1).

Communication of consistent message

In an effort to create tangibility, communication for corporate brands should operate on both the micro and macro levels. On the macro level, a key part of the corporate brand is determining what values the company wants to be known for, then communicating them outward. When we buy a product brand we can touch or feel the product. We may not know or understand its make-up, but we can describe its attributes. Even though each individual has a unique perception of the company, there is still the need to try to build a consensual image. In reality we often glean information from a company's communication,

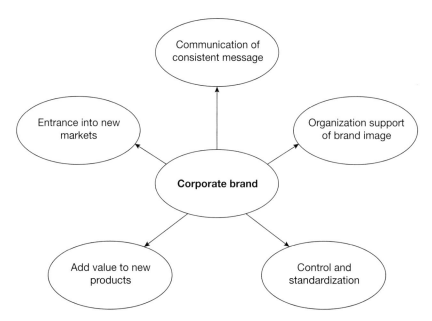

Figure 10.1 Facets of the global corporate brand

its people and its products, and we make judgements. We see and hear a company's message and experience its products or people and we construct an image of the organization. Research indicates that the more familiar we are with a brand the more favourable we view it (Ind, 1997). This requires a consistent message to all stakeholders.

Although a brand has some tangible elements, a company is often seen as very remote. Corporate branding allows organizations to communicate one message as to what it is and how it wishes to be represented (Sellers, 2002). With product brand a unique message for each brand is communicated. Consistency in communication is, therefore, vital. On a micro level, the brand needs to build an interactive relationship with each individual stakeholder. This involves providing a product that meets the needs and wants of the customer. In the international context and on the micro level this can prove quite challenging. In contrast, on the macro level this is an advantage in that it is easier to uniformly convey the corporate values such as quality, value for money or reliability. These terms are easier to communicate than product differences that may be difficult to adapt to international tastes. Because of this, corporate brands can only truly be successful if there is a relationship established at an appropriate micro level.

The effectiveness of corporate brands internationally is, to a large extent, improved through globalization. Several global drivers support this. First, demographic trends across the developed world are very similar; an ageing profile, an increase in single-occupant households and a declining population (Hassan and Katsanis, 1991). Second, global products and advertising help to ensure that people are aware of the same things and able

to buy the same things around the world (Jain, 1989). Third, global media helps to define more universal lifestyles (Jallat and Kimmel, 2002). All of these factors favour corporate brands, particularly western brands, that allow them to be easily adapted to international markets.

Entrance into new markets

Generally, in any company there is a clear association between products and the organization that produce them (Olins, 1989). The nature of the product influences an organization's culture and identity, while the identity in turn influences the nature of the product. This link between product brand and company brand allows these two entities to easily enter markets where that brand is already somewhat known. When considering international expansion there are traditionally two alternatives – the 'waterfall' and 'sprinkler' methods (Keegan, 1989). The 'waterfall' method is a trickle-down model where products are launched in countries based on level of development – prioritizing the most developed countries first. This method ensures that the product is exactly suited to the customer. The disadvantage is that it can take up to several years to fully enter new markets globally.

The contrast to this is to develop a product and simultaneously introduce it to world markets (sprinkler model). The difference between the two methods is based on the assumptions about the nature of the world markets. The sprinkler approach recognizes the trend of globalization and that markets develop simultaneously around the world. This requires substantially less time and is viewed by many as the only realistic option in today's fast paced global competitive environment (Riesenback and Freeling, 1991). The use of the corporate brand with the sprinkler method of product introduction allows more consistent product introduction into the international markets.

Adds value to new product

As people have become more aware of the world around them they also have become more confident as consumers. People have far less inhibition about exploring new experiences and trying out new brands for different occasions. In other words, people are no longer loyal to their brands. This lack of loyalty is a challenge for companies and much promotion is spent to address this issue. Many corporate brands have begun loyalty programmes or relationship marketing initiatives. The goal here is for consumers to have an emotional attitude towards a brand or a company. This is not the same relationship we have with families or friends but a 'business' relationship built around mutual benefits. These mutual benefits are ultimately transferred via a product or service.

The purchase of a product is only the beginning of the relationship – it is the use of the product over time that either cements or dissolves the relationship. The implication of this is that the consumer builds a relationship not with the product itself but more with the company that provides it (Eales, 1989). As a result, well-regarded corporate brands are able to deliver products with ready-made goodwill. Companies can use this to introduce new products more easily. At the same time, it is easier to diversify their product portfolio by introducing completely new, or new to the company, product fami-

lies. As we have mentioned earlier, globalization has resulted in people having more information on brands from around the world. By combining this goodwill with global familiarity corporations can easily leverage this brand into international markets (Ekuan *et al.*, 2001).

Control and standardization

When considering a corporate brand in the global context a number of consolidation issues become relevant. Unified marketing communication ensures a consistent message worldwide that can lead to increased sales (Buzzell, 1968). Furthermore, research by Sorenson and Wiechmann (1974) concluded that 'standardisation makes consumers familiar with the company and its products and services, and helps establish a uniform corporate image'. Standardization of marketing efforts is often achieved through a centralized corporate function. These two statements support the overall use of a corporate brand in the marketplace. This is an important issue in the international context as a study indicates that centralization often flows from the needs of globalization (Melewar and Saunders, 1999). Very often centralization is seen as a necessity in determining corporate communication. Consistency is possible only when there is a single and sufficiently powerful source of authority. In the end, someone must decide an approach and then impose strict control over this communication.

Implementation has to take into account the organizational structure. If the individual countries enjoy significant autonomy then trying to impose central control will be difficult. Hence, the degree of centralization influences the degree of standardization of the corporate brand identity of multinational companies. Even though the literature is somewhat divided as to the degree of centralization, most do agree that it is an important factor when considering corporate branding (Roellig, 2001; Walton, 2001; Rosen et al., 1987).

The financial arguments in using a standardized corporate brand are fairly straightforward. Economies of communication can be achieved by producing advertising campaigns and other promotions which can be run anywhere in the world with only minor changes. However, the scale of these savings is still under debate (Riesenback and Freeling, 1991). Companies with a large advertising budget felt the cost savings from standardization were a small percentage of the total budget. On the other hand, companies with a small advertising budget felt that the savings from standardization were high. In successful global campaigns, it is outstanding creative ideas, not budget dollars, which are truly in short supply. Thus, the meaningful goal is to seek to increase sales through consistency, rather than to reduce costs by compromising the focus of the marketing effect.

As discussed above, it is this consistent corporate message that is important in the international context. By and large, things such as names and logos should be seen as integral to the corporate brand and should be co-ordinated centrally (Topalian, 1984). As we move downstream (towards the end customer) the case for adaptability becomes greater. The communication objectives may be different depending on the situation. When entering new markets the communication may need to solidify or build brand awareness. In countries where the brand awareness is higher, brand owners may want to concentrate on highlighting those factors that can be seen as differentiators.

Organization support of brand image

People are the corporate brand (Hatch, 1993). They interact with audiences and each other, make the products and perform the services that the organization sells, and define and create marketing communication strategies. Perceptions of an organization are determined, directly and indirectly, by managers and staff. It is their values and their perception of what the organization and the corporate brand stand for that give it cohesion and meaning (Hatch and Schultz, 2000).

It follows then that an organization's corporate brand can be maintained and often improves by concentrating on its relationship with its employees. Key to the success of this is the employee identification with the strategy of the organization. To some extent this requires an empathy with the organizational values so that there is a match between the individual's beliefs and the employer's (Ind, 1997). This empathy can be developed through a number of ways including effective communication and employee development.

Effective internal communication needs to concentrate on developing a feeling of involvement and empowerment. Effective employee development ensures that consumers and other audiences will interact with better-educated and more committed individuals. As well as improving the image of the organization, employees can help the organization adapt to a changing environment and learn new ways of doing things. This becomes even more important as a company begins to expand internationally. Managers need to build awareness for their new brand and consequently need information regarding the local environment (Simoes and Dibb, 2001). This process is facilitated by technology, notably the corporate intranets. This allows managers and employees to keep up with what is happening in various parts of the organization that can influence them. In the next section we discuss the issues that have been raised in the context of a company called Makita Corporation.

Makita Corporation

> Makita's aim is to become the best supplier of electric power tools world wide, including battery operated power tools, wood working machines, pneumatic tools and garden tools all of which makes living much more comfortable and enjoyable.
>
> (www.makita.co.jp)

Makita is a global producer of professional-grade electric power tools. The company makes jigsaws, planers, drills, hammers, grinders, sanders, stationary woodworking machines, garden tools, and other household products. Already having a worldwide presence, Makita has made significant gains in market share in the Americas, Asia, Europe, and Australia/New Zealand, where it is an industry leader. Sales in 2001 were over one billion US dollars with a sales growth of 25 per cent. More than three-quarters of sales are outside Japan. Makita operates with about eight thousand employees in more than thirty international subsidiaries.

Makita began operation in Nagoya City, Japan in 1910 producing lighting equipment, transformers and motors. After the Second World War the company moved to Sumiyoshi-Cho, Anjo-City and began producing electric planing equipment, the first in Japan. The company continued to produce innovative products and in 1960 changed its name to Makita Corporation. The company grew steadily during the 1960s and 1970s and in 1970 established its first outlet outside Japan – in the United States. Makita continued to expand internationally during the 1970s and 1980s setting up operations in most of continental Europe. Through the 1990s the company established itself in Eurasia as well as China. The company presently has sales subsidiaries in over thirty countries and production facilities in the United States, Canada, United Kingdom and China.

Communication of consistent message

Since its creation in Japan the goal of Makita was to produce products of superior quality. This goal is communicated very strongly through a large proportion of their marketing communication. The brand and logo used are the same around the world. The advertising for Makita is fairly consistent in design and message where it highlights quality as the differentiating factor over the competitors. High quality is supported internationally through its subsidiary network of service centres. In larger countries (United States, Australia and Mexico) there is a regional centre owned and operated by Makita in addition to approved service providers. This allows Makita to ensure consistent quality and the company can boast one of the fastest turnaround times for repair and delivery in the industry (www.makita.com). The key market for Makita products is the construction industry and advanced DIY. Both of these industries are fairly consistent globally, which allows Makita to use a strong corporate brand. On a micro level, they establish a relationship characterized by high quality and effective after sales support and service.

Entrance into new markets

Makita began its expansion internationally at the beginning of the 1960s. From the beginning the company goal was to produce and sell products of the highest quality and provide superior service. In order to achieve this, Makita had a policy of manufacturing the products close to the customer. After Makita had sufficient production in Japan it began expanding in Europe by setting up Makita subsidiaries. The subsidiaries in turn began establishing a network of approved service providers. Makita expanded in this fashion since it recognized that in the electric power tool market word-of-mouth communication is one of the most effective ways of promoting a new brand. Following its general policy regarding close production and as demand and the number of subsidiaries increased, Makita established production facilities in Europe and North America. Overall, Makita grew its corporate brand by establishing consistent values and used these values to enter new markets and expand globally.

New product development and standardization

In the late 1980s Makita firmly established itself in the North American market. Their brand was successful in that it represented quality and service. During this time their main competitor was Black & Decker who had substantial market share. Black & Decker had similar products of a slightly lower quality. Their products and marketing were not, however, standardized throughout North America. Black & Decker had different products in different parts of the world under various smaller brand names. This lack of standardization, particularly in the area of R&D and

product innovation resulted in varying degrees of quality as well as higher production costs. Makita successfully entered this market by following their strategy of producing and marketing globally standardized products worldwide. This allowed them to establish themselves as a low-cost producer and allowed them to steadily increase market share. This situation continued until Black & Decker adopted a similar process using central R&D and product development.

Control and standardization

The Makita logo is used consistently throughout the organization. The logo and its use are the same on all marketing materials. Most decisions regarding logo and marketing of the brand are centrally taken in Japan. At the subsidiary level, advertising is adapted through local language with limited changes to the other elements of the promotion. All products are designed following similar design themes and have a very consistent 'look'. One product characteristic that has emerged as part of the brand is the use of colour. Makita uses a 'blue-green' colour as a consistent design element in most of its marketing materials. More importantly, all of its products, to a large extent, use the same 'blue-green' colour as well.

Overall, Makita has successfully used its corporate brand to communicate its values of innovation and quality on a global scale. It has complemented this with establishing a relationship on the micro level with its stakeholders based on its high level of service. It has used its brand to effectively expand to other regions while at the same time managing the same value proposition to its customers. Makita has supported these corporate values – innovation and quality – through central R&D and product development resulting in innovative products of a consistently high quality.

Conclusion and recommendations

This chapter has highlighted some of the issues surrounding the use of a corporate brand in the international context. The corporate brand is distinct in that it has a very diverse audience that it needs to interact with. Corporate brands need to balance between the needs of the employees and customers as well as investors. To be successful, it needs to make the most of the employees' and organization's abilities, attract the goodwill of investors and meet the demands of customers.

To facilitate the above, corporate brands need to maintain familiarity. Familiarity is partly formed through products but often is the result of marketing communication and interaction with the organization. Because of this, consistency is very important. From a communication perspective consistent organizations are more likely to achieve recognition and understanding if they keep saying the

same thing. This is particularly acute in the international context. This is also supported by the growing trend of globalization in that people travel much more, making familiar global brands more effective.

The final requirement of an effective corporate brand is interaction. To make sure that an organization is meeting the need of its customers and that its communication is relevant, it needs to build relationships with its audiences. This is particularly true in an international context. With a global organization it needs to listen to the different perspectives and requirements from both the customers and its employees in each country. Without this the organization will lack the fundamental ingredients necessary to make a strong corporate brand.

The secret of building an effective corporate brand is not complex, but rather it is through doing simple things well: listening to and involving customer and employees, developing relationships and integrating consistent internal and external communication. The challenge internationally is finding the right balance of adaptation of all these simple elements.

REFERENCES

Buzzell, R. D. (1968) 'Can you standardise multinational marketing', *Harvard Business Review*, December, 102–12.

Eales, R. (1989) 'Multinational report: multinational corporate communications, a growth sector', *Multinational Business*, 4, 28–32.

Ekuan, K., Francey, P., Van Niekerk, R. and Butler, D. (2001) 'Powerful brands: perspectives of design managers from around the globe', *Design Management Journal*, 12(1), 57–67.

Hassan, S. S. and Katsanis, L. P. (1991) 'Identification of global consumer segments: a behavioural framework', *Journal of International Consumer Marketing*, 3(2), 11–28.

Hatch, M. J. (1993) 'The dynamics of organisational culture', *Academy of Management Review*, 18, 657–93.

Hatch, Mary Jo, and Schultz, Majken (2000) 'Scaling the tower of Babel: relational differences between identity, image and culture in organisation' in Majken Schultz, Mary Jo Hatch and Mogens Holten Larsen (eds), *The Expressive Organisation*, Oxford: Oxford University Press.

Ind, Nicholas (1997) *The Corporate Brand*, London: Macmillan.

Jain, S. C. (1989) 'Standardisation of international marketing strategy: some research hypotheses', *Journal of Marketing*, 53, 70–9.

Jallat, F. and Kimmel, A. J. (2002) 'Marketing in culturally diverse environments: the case of Western Europe', *Business Horizons*, July–August, 30–6.

Keegan, W. J. (1989) *Global Marketing Management*, New York: Prentice Hall.

Melewar, T. C. and Saunders, J. (1999) 'International corporate visual identity: standardisation or localisation', *Journal of International Business Studies*, 30(3), 583–98.

Olins, W. (1989) *Corporate Identity: Making Business Strategy Visible Through Design*, London: Thames and Hudson.

Riesenback, H. and Freeling, A. (1991) 'How global are global brands?', *The McKinsey Quarterly*, 4, 3–18.

Roellig, L. (2001) 'Designing global brands: critical lessons', *Design Management Journal*, 12(4), 40–5.

Rosen, B. N., Boddewyn, J. J. and Louis, E. A. (1987) 'US brands abroad: an empirical study of global branding', *International Marketing Review*, 6(1), 7–19.

Sellers, L. J. (2002) 'Building corporate brands', *Pharmaceutical Executive*, 22(1), 38–44.

Simoes, C. and Dibb, S. (2001) 'Rethinking the brand concept: new brand orientation', *Corporate Communications: An International Journal*, 6(4), 217–24.

Sorenson, R. Z. and Wiechmann, U. E. (1974) 'How multinationals view marketing standardisation', *Harvard Business Review*, May–June, 38–54 and 166–7.

Stuart, H. (1999) 'Towards a definitive model of the corporate identity management process', *Corporate Communications: An International Journal*, 4(4), 200–7.

Topalian, A. (1984) 'Corporate identity: beyond the visual overstatements', *International Journal of Advertising*, 3, 55–62.

Walton, T. (2001) 'The nuances of designing for global markets', *Design Management Journal*, 12(4), 6–9.

www.makita.co.jp

www.makita.com

Differing corporate communication practice in successful and unsuccessful companies

Colin Coulson-Thomas

When we discuss corporate communication we generally assume that effective communication is a 'good' thing. But what do we mean by 'effective' in the reality of today's turbulent and competitive marketplace? How vital are corporate communication activities?

In this chapter the author looks at how communicators actually behave in practice. He examines what winners, people in successful companies that cope with changing circumstances and grow, do differently from losers, their colleagues in business that struggle and fail. The chapter looks at differing attitudes and approaches in order to distil some critical success factors for managing change, competing and winning and considers the role that external and internal communication plays in relation to winning competitive bids, relationship building and managing change. It also considers the issue of differentiation and the international dimension before drawing out some key differences between attitudes, behaviours and approaches of winners and losers.

Many businesses win a significant proportion of major new contracts through some form of bidding process. Competitive markets and falling barriers to entry have strengthened the negotiating position of buyers. As more contracts are put out to competitive tender and new entrants to markets are invited to bid, the prospects of a supplier winning a particular opportunity can decline unless performance is improved.

As expectations rise, invitations to tender also become more demanding. Proposals get larger and more expensive to prepare. The cost of lost bids has to be recovered out of a squeezed margin on those that are won. Companies that win too few bids find themselves driven out of business. Corporate survival can depend upon success in competitive bid situations.

Yet some companies – according to the flow of reports from the Winning Business Research Programme at the Centre for Competitiveness (see www.luton.ac.uk/cfc) – are much more successful than others at winning business. Studies which have been undertaken cover many sectors, particular sectors (construction, engineering and manufacturing, IT and telecoms) and eight professions ranging from lawyers and accountants to engineering and management consultants.

The findings are consistent and compelling. Let us consider the evidence of a study of how people in 293 companies set about 'winning major bids' (Kennedy and O'Connor, 1997). A wide gulf exists between winners and losers. The two groups appear distinct species with different personalities. Losers are undisciplined, unimaginative and reactive. They pursue far too many opportunities, and they focus primarily upon their employers' immediate concerns and sales priorities.

Members of 'loser' bid teams respond mechanically to invitations to tender. They are preoccupied with the practicalities of producing proposals and problems such as obtaining cost information and up-to-date CVs from busy colleagues. They find themselves under pressure to meet submission deadlines. Yet they ignore tools that could speed up their basic activities and free up thinking time.

Little effort is put into distinguishing the approaches or 'solutions' they recommend. Specific product related information is communicated. Broader corporate credentials that might suggest opportunities for a wider relationship are not presented.

Losers 'hold back'. They only commit significant effort when a prospect is 'seriously interested'. They describe their roles in terms of 'submitting bids'. Although they may claim to be 'winning business' they devote the majority of their effort to losing potential business as most of the proposals they send in are rejected.

In businesses with below average success rates bid team members are left to 'get on with it'. Senior managers may talk of proposal preparation as a 'boring' chore and one best avoided. They are rarely involved in individual opportunities.

Losers measure success by the number of proposals they submit. They make little effort to learn from either their experience or best practice. Rejection letters enable them to 'close the file' and move onto the next proposal. Above all, they don't mind losing. Failure is accepted as the norm. It is rationalized with phrases such as 'you can't win them all' or 'someone has to lose'.

Winners who submit successful bids and make effective presentations behave very differently from the losers just described. They are far more confident, energetic and proactive. They identify prospects with growth potential, organizations that are likely to do well and which would make good business partners. They take the initiative. They approach those they would most like to do business with. They carefully target their communication.

Winners are very selective. They ruthlessly prioritize available opportunities. Turning down some invitations to bid allows more effort to be devoted to those that are retained and pursued.

Winners want their customers and prospects to do well. They think about them. They become absorbed in their problems and opportunities. They focus responses upon the needs and priorities of their prospects and structure their proposals around the selection criteria likely to be used in purchase decisions.

When winners do respond it is with commitment and clear objectives. They think through the outcomes and relationship they would like to achieve. From the moment an initial contact occurs they position themselves as a potential business partner. They hit the ground running, and allocate sufficient resources early on to build up an unassailable lead.

Senior managers in the more successful companies participate in pitches. They are interested, understand the importance of business development activity and want to be involved. The visible and active support of senior management can be decisive in close contests. It demonstrates the importance attached to a particular order and/or potential relationship.

Winners try to understand how buying decisions are made within a prospect's organization. They identify influencers, opponents and allies. They consider the personalities involved and remain sensitive to how buyer concerns may change during the course of a particular procurement. People like to work with individuals and organizations they feel comfortable with. Winners work hard to establish empathy, build trust, and match the culture of prospects.

Where possible, winners automate the more mechanical aspects of proposal production. Time freed up is used to tailor responses, differentiate offerings and build relationships. Thus sales representatives could use a laptop-based tool for accessing presentational information, assessing requirements, configuring and pricing suggested solutions, and generating proposal documentation (see www.cotoco.com).

At the end of the day the crucial differentiator between winners and losers is that the winners want to win. Prospects are not 'items in their in-trays' as is often the case with losers. Winners are devastated when they lose. Win or lose, they also regularly review their processes, submit their practices to inde-

pendent or peer review, and debriefs are held to learn from both successes and failures.

The results of the Winning Business Research Programme (www.luton.ac.uk/cfc) suggest the winners among the companies examined could do even better. The 'super bidders' – the 4 per cent who win more than three out of four of the competitive races they enter – are only very effective at less than half of the 18 critical success factors identified by the 'Winning Major Bids' report (Kennedy and O'Connor, 1997). There is enormous opportunity for most businesses to significantly improve their performance. 'Win rates' are directly related to how many of the identified key factors a company is good at.

Many of the changes that may be required to increase bid win rates can be put in place relatively quickly and at a modest cost. Guidance is also available in the form of 'winning business' reports for particular industries and professions (see www.ntwkfirm.com). These spell out the relevant critical success factors. They also contain best practice case studies and commentaries by industry experts. A bespoke benchmarking service accompanies the eight reports covering individual professions.

Sales support tools can also be used. A laptop-based solution reduced the sales cycle of one company by up to 50 per cent and won the 1999 Award for Knowledge Management. The original investment was returned within four months by just one order. The knowledge management framework used (www.K-frame.com) won the 2000 eBusiness Innovations Award for Knowledge Management and is used to communicate complex and technical messages.

Processes and practices for winning business should be regularly subjected to an independent review. Even though there is enormous potential for improvement many companies re-engineer just about every one of their processes except those for winning business.

Business development teams generally – and bid teams in particular – are frequently overlooked when training budgets are allocated. The report 'Bidding for Business, the Skills Agenda' (Kennedy, 1999) identifies the top twenty bidding skills and how they can be obtained. A thirty-tool 'Contract Bid Manager's Toolkit' (Bartram, 1999) is also available. People can avoid being 'losers' by consciously setting out to become 'winners'.

Differentiating your communication

Survey participants define success at bidding in terms of winning orders at an acceptable price (Kennedy and O'Connor, 1997). Differentiation and tailoring can enable a supplier to justify a premium price (Coulson-Thomas, 2002a). A differentiated offering may also attract attention and stand out. People are often distracted by events and confused by conflicting messages. Individual communication that is not distinctive may fail to register.

Smart communicators establish the extent to which services, skills and experiences are unique, special or distinctive. When colleagues seek new business do their presentations and proposals stand out? What is being offered that people cannot get elsewhere? Does an organization have a compelling reason for existing? Why should people want to join it or use its services? What would the world lose or miss if it ceased to exist? Would anyone notice or care?

People's interest in communication should not be taken for granted. 'Me-too' organizations that imitate others often struggle to be noticed, and they usually find it difficult to make a mark. Differentiation or standing out from other available alternatives is a major challenge for many sales, marketing and communication teams.

Many purchase decision makers suffer from information overload. They are inundated with claims from various suppliers, and often find it difficult to discriminate between the possibilities on offer. Too often they are confronted with similar options in different wrappings rather than genuine choices. When we strip away advertising claims we may find that several suppliers offer essentially the same product. 'Minimum differentiation' sometimes seems the prevailing approach to marketing.

Although customers demand greater responsiveness to their particular requirements, and they often have more options for innovation and scope for enterprise than any previous generation in history, many suppliers play it safe. They all target the largest market segments and alternative sets of requirements are ignored. They also make similar assumptions. Thus all cars within each category and price bracket seem to have the same general aerodynamic shape.

The potential exists to produce many more goods and services that reflect our individuality and particular requirements. For example, in relation to cars many people would happily incur the penalties of greater wind resistance if they could step into a more distinctive design. Visitors to motor museums encounter an enormous range of different early car models produced by a variety of small manufacturers.

Today's boaters are quite willing to wait between eighteen months and two years for a new narrowboat. Most of the steel shells are hand built. Craft workers lovingly fit them out according to the personal requirements and individual designs of proud owners. People happily pay a premium for individuality.

Most businesses have the potential to be unique and special. Yet, to take another example, we are encouraged to buy standard software packages. They give us the same capabilities as everyone else when bespoke development might enable us to be different, might provide competitive advantage and could create additional intellectual capital.

Losers follow the herd, play catch-up and copy others. However, 'me-too' activities are not the route to market leadership. Communicators can help their employers and clients to identify potential differentiators and thus become more distinctive. For example, an organization's aspirations, intentions, vision, goals or values might be unusual or interesting.

A management team is not required to seek the same ends as other groups. Nor should it feel compelled to emulate their achievements. People ought to be able to think for themselves. They should consciously set out to do something different.

An organization and/or its offerings might already have a distinctive image and reputation. If not, the communicator should set about trying to build one. There are many ways of making greater impact, from dress and language through design and style to original ideas. Thought leaders tend to be associated with particular ideas, views or concepts.

People may be distinguished by their appearances, backgrounds, competences, experiences, special skills and viewpoints. Winners assess perceptions. They ask third parties to tell them what stands out when they meet colleagues, competitors and peers. Do they work, learn or otherwise behave in a noticeable and particular way?

A company might be structured differently from other firms. Maybe its products and services are distinctive. Alternatively, it may offer more of the same. It may work and function as others do, or it might have its own distinctive approach, tools or methodology.

Interesting angles can create interest. An organization's terms of business might be unusual or novel. How it operates, the basis upon which it charges for services, or the relationships it forges with clients could also be a source of differentiation. Perhaps it partners in a certain way or has a particular approach to sharing risk.

There may be many potential differentiators and various combinations of them that could be adopted. But whatever approach is used needs to be relevant to the particular situation and appropriate for the circumstances in which a group finds itself.

Differentiation is an attitude of mind. Confident communicators probe prevailing assumptions. Like winners, they ask challenging questions. Are new alternatives being created? Is choice being extended? If the organization stopped operating would customers simply buy similar offerings from other suppliers? What would be established to fill the gap, and how would it differ from what currently exists?

Losers often limit themselves. They become imprisoned behind imaginary bars and fall into traps of their own making. In order to stand out, make a mark and have an impact winners look beyond the norm. In many companies more imaginative thinking is required to craft marketplace offerings for the unfulfilled and those who aspire to be different. Collectively they may constitute distinct communities that might support new enterprises.

Copying is often a self-imposed constraint. There are usually alternatives to bland consensus, middle ways, and lowest common denominators. However, differentiation requires a willingness to reflect, debate and challenge; a desire to innovate; and the urge to discover. Effective communicators distinguish fundamentals from fads, substance from surface and reality from illusion (Coulson-Thomas, 2001).

Exercises exist for formulating new marketplace offerings and there are checklists for challenging the relative importance of action and reaction, complexity and simplicity, activity and reflection and change and continuity (Coulson-Thomas, 2001). Shifting the balance between them can result in genuine alternatives. Not everyone has the same speed or time preferences. Given the chance, many customers would make different trade-offs from those that suppliers decide on their behalf.

Winners are often sensitive souls and restless spirits who create distinctive offerings for particular groups. Because these are different they get noticed. 'Viral marketing' or 'word of mouse' brings them to the attention of other people with similar passions and shared obsessions.

People with complementary aspirations can form model communities, share facilities and provide care and cover for each other. Just as individuals work with natural materials to craft unique items that attract commissions from consumers who rebel against mass manufacture, so companies can offer alternatives to contemporary bandwagons.

Thinking through the implications of where the great majority of people are headed allows entrepreneurs to identify opportunities. For example, instead of adding to the various ways of communicating with others an astute operator could provide intelligent devices that screen, prioritize and respond to the many approaches sought after individuals receive and structure and manage subsequent relationships.

Creative companies attract characters and inspire rebels rather than reward conformists.

Corporate cultures should encourage discussion; stimulate thought and inspired innovation (Coulson-Thomas, 1999). Imaginative entrepreneurs recognize diversity, explore contradictions and foster individuality. Winners generate distinctive options, create alternative models of operation and establish new markets.

Working and learning environments need to offer variety – perhaps peace and solitude for one task and interaction and stimulation for the next. Communicators searching for a 'big idea' may need to forsake anaemic offices, avoid the distraction of mobile phones and seek out quiet areas where they can sit, dream, meditate and think.

Building strategic relationships with customers

Having won a new customer the next challenge is to build a relationship that will result in a flow of repeat orders and follow-on business. To do this requires effective customer relationship and key account management, another area that has been examined by a team from the Centre for Competitiveness.

Researchers examined how people in 194 companies set about 'developing strategic customers and key accounts' (Hurcomb, 1998). They identified a variety of critical success factors that distinguish 'winners', the companies in the top quarter of achievement that realize the benefits of strategic customer relationships, from the 'losers' in the bottom quarter that do not.

There is a general dissatisfaction with performance. Less than one in six of the participants consider themselves 'very effective' at increasing profitability through strategic relationships, and fewer than one in seven are happy with the way they develop them. Yet, a clear majority of the respondents believe the proportion of their sales due to key accounts will increase beyond the current level of over two-thirds.

The survey reveals a wide gulf between the attitudes, approaches and results of the winners and losers. For example, winners consider three times as many of the key processes identified by participants as 'very important', and they are five times as likely to be intending to make use of emerging technologies (Hurcomb, 1998).

Losers tend to live for the moment. They are driven by the prospect of immediate business. They apply the 'key account' label to their most important current customers, and when they deal with them they focus upon their own requirements. In essence they seek to use their customers to achieve short-term internal targets. Key account relationships are also left to sales and marketing staff and hence contact may be lost when particular individuals change jobs or move on.

Losers mouth generalizations about the importance of building closer relationships with customers. However, they do little in terms of concrete actions to make them happen. They avoid commitment, discourage tailored responses and shun integration. They fear that departing from a standard approach might cause process and systems problems, while establishing electronic links might expose them to viruses and hackers.

Open book accounting is another 'no go' area. Information and knowledge is jealously guarded. Overall, losers are very reluctant to change corporate procedures to accommodate bespoke approaches. Little effort is made to categorize accounts or 'do things differently' to help particular customers in view of the 'hassle' involved.

Losers use a range of traditional sales and negotiation techniques to win orders that fail to recognize 'buyer power'. Terms of business are used as a selling tool. If all else fails they will offer discounts to secure new business (Coulson-Thomas, 2002a). Customers derive few benefits from being upgraded to 'key account' status. However, when they learn of their importance to a supplier they may demand price reductions.

When it comes to locking out the competition (and locking customers in) the contrast between winners and losers is particularly stark. The winners rank 11 out of 17 lock out factors while the losers do not rank any (Hurcomb, 1998). Quite simply the bottom quarter of companies examined do not appear to be taking any steps to protect their key accounts. Not surprisingly, they fail to realize strategic relationship benefits.

In contrast, winners look ahead. They take a lifetime view of relationships and consider future potential when categorizing accounts. They value their customers and are prepared to put themselves out for them. They are open and build personal relationships. Their focus is upon customer requirements and buyer expectations. They endeavour to understand their customers' businesses, industries and buying processes and look out for opportunities that might benefit them.

Winners encourage a broader range of contacts at multiple levels between their own staff and those of key account customers. Hence relationships can survive re-organizations and changes of staff. At the same time, senior managers are involved in important negotiations.

Winners are prepared to differentiate and depart from the norm in order to deliver greater value and benefit their customers' businesses. They regard processes, systems and procedures as a means to an end rather than as ends in themselves. They ignore traditional 'hard sell' and 'win–lose' sales techniques and endeavour to influence buying rather than overtly sell.

Rather than mouth generalizations, 'winners' concentrate upon specific and practical steps to build relationships. They are prepared to commit, to extend partnership to the terms of business, and to integrate processes and systems. As a consequence of their attitudes and approach winners realize the many benefits of strategic customer relationships that elude the losers.

Overall, these findings reveal a wide spectrum of effectiveness and considerable potential for improvement. By their own admission, even the winners could do much better (Hurcomb, 1998).

Improving key account management

Turning to what needs to be done, in many companies key account managers (KAMs) have prime responsibility for customer relationship management and business development through cross-selling and winning new accounts within the sectors for which they are responsible. A first step would be to review their responsibilities in relation to those of other staff in order to address any gaps, overlaps and boundary issues.

A profile of the competences and 'role model' behaviours required by an effective KAM could be developed and agreed, and KAMs assessed against it to identify personal and team development needs. Important next steps might be to define and agree a key account development process, a customer relationship management process, and a process for winning business in competitive situations.

It may be necessary to develop or acquire the approaches, tools and techniques needed to cross-sell and win and retain accounts.

These might include the thirty tools in the 'The Contract Bid Manager's Toolkit' (Bartram, 1999), the twenty skills profiled in the 'Bidding for Business, the Skills Agenda' (Kennedy, 1999) report and a suggested systematic approach to key account management (Hurcomb, 1998).

Customer relationship managers and KAMs may require training, individually or as a group. Collaborative arrangements can supplement skills, experience and reference sites in areas of relative deficiency. Communicators ought to be able to provide help and support in the development of communication and relationship building skills.

The allocation of existing customers and eligible prospects to individual KAMs should reflect the sectors in which they and the company and its partners have particular expertise and distinctive strengths. Rules, arrangements and terms covering access to the staff of partners and the use of their know-how for business development, customer support and service delivery purposes may need to be negotiated.

Revenue and profitability targets for each sector and KAM should reflect corporate strategy and priority objectives. Specific business development and marketing plans may be needed for particular sectors. Communicators may wish to participate in the formulation of account development plans for existing key accounts, and account capture plans for eligible target accounts.

The Winning Business Research Programme (see www.luton.ac.uk/cfc) has produced reports on the critical success factors for winning business in particular business sectors and various professions. KAMs could use these to identify 'best practice' approaches. Specific sector and cross-sector applications, offerings, events and marketing materials may also need to be developed.

Sales and business development teams should establish mechanisms for capturing, sharing and learning from positive and negative experiences. Deficiencies should be addressed. For example, arrangements with potential non-national partners to support the winning of international accounts could be negotiated.

Each KAM should be responsible for prioritizing new business opportunities and prospects, allocating and managing available business development resources, and achieving account and sector business development and profitability targets. The assignment of accounts to KAMs offers the customer a point of contact with someone who ought to have a holistic insight into the totality of their requirements.

Partnering

The growth of partnering, the spread of e-commerce, and the desire for strategic alliances are important issues for both business development teams (Hurcomb, 1998) and the purchasing community (FitzGerald, 2000). There is therefore considerable scope for the sales and purchasing communities to work together for mutual benefit. However, winners and losers are adopting very different approaches to this opportunity.

Losers are cautious and wary. They seek refuge in small print and are reluctant to open up. They avoid risks by not straying beyond what they know. Companies that adopt legalistic and protective approaches are likely to end up as low-margin commodity suppliers. Playing 'win–lose' games will ensure that they lose.

Winners are likely to earn higher returns. They are more flexible and innovative. They are more willing to accept challenges and embrace new ways of working and learning. Winners adopt a partnership approach. They are prepared to share visions and risks. They strive for 'win–win' outcomes by agreeing to mutually beneficial objectives, and they consciously endeavour to remain relevant and add value.

Winners are restless and eager to innovate and try out new approaches. They are prepared to commit to continued and measured improvements in whatever they supply or provide. Savings achieved are shared between the parties concerned.

Winners are also prepared to practise 'open book' accounting and to share information and knowledge relating to the achievement of common objectives. They recognize that differences can and do arise. However, within the partnering relationships they foster there are simple and quick processes for handling disputes at the lowest possible levels.

The international dimension

The horizons of ambitious managers today embrace the globe. Deregulation, privatization and market forces have eroded trade barriers. The end of the cold war has created new opportunities.

Work can follow daylight around the world allowing twenty-four hour a day operation. Resources can be accessed and activity undertaken locally, regionally or at global level depending upon requirements and comparative costs. Even sole traders use websites and email to make direct contact with foreign customers.

However, operating in the international business environment also presents new challenges. There are commercial, legal and financial risks. There might still be obstacles of distance, culture and time that communicators and their colleagues may need to address.

It is important to retain a sense of perspective. Business people around the world watch the news on CNN. Global media is shaping their attitudes and perceptions. But even MTV has its regional offerings, and requirements for products can vary greatly between national markets. The significance of borders will depend upon the nature of the activity being undertaken.

Successful international operators and businesses that struggle to build foreign relationships adopt very different approaches (Coulson-Thomas, 2002b). Losers tend to 'continue as before' with the addition of overseas names on circulation and distribution lists. Winners adapt their behaviour and practices as appropriate. They are aware of what is happening abroad, open to new influences, and receptive to alternative ideas.

Some losers are overawed or disheartened by the claims of others. However, many so-called international companies are essentially national enterprises that trade internationally. People who travel a lot may hold onto their stereotyped views or exaggerate their national characteristics. Living and working abroad can reinforce existing prejudices.

Winners recognize that appearances can be deceptive. Some make an effort to adjust and adapt, while others do not. Attitudes, approaches and perspectives distinguish internationally aware mangers. They are alert to developments in the global business environment.

True internationalization is much more than an ability to speak foreign languages. Winners are open to alternative viewpoints, tolerant of national differences and actively support cultural diversity. They seek opportunities for foreign travel, participate in overseas exchanges, swap jobs, and join international project groups, task-forces and teams.

Companies like countries can have distinct cultures. Communicators need to be sensitive to differences and similarities in national assumptions, attitudes and motivations. They should try to reconcile conflicting interests while recognizing that particular local requirements might create opportunities for bespoke offerings.

Customer segments may or may not co-incide with national borders. Experienced international managers are intuitive. They have cross-cultural awareness. They are able to handle diversity, run joint ventures and build relationships with overseas colleagues. Mutual expectations need to be realistic and compatible. There may be practicalities to address, such as whether the differing technologies of the various parties will connect and work together.

Some individuals and organizations have little choice but to go global. The people who are likely to be interested in what they have to offer may be widely scattered. Losers stunt the growth of their businesses by keeping opportunities to themselves, trusting no one and operating alone. Winners expand internationally by forming relationships with complementary collaborators.

Some managers have a distorted understanding of overseas situations and naive expectations of international initiatives. Communicators need to be realistic and should think through the implications of what they are setting out to do. Winners anticipate likely consequences, probable outcomes and possible reactions. They are prepared to address potential problem areas.

Losers often fail to recognize fundamental

national differences, and they may say one thing and do another. For example, they might use the rhetoric of diversity and then insist upon common approaches. Some executives talk about internationalization but make sure that all key positions are in the hands of nationals of the 'home country'.

Winners avoid the imposition of standard solutions that are inappropriate in particular locations. Wherever possible, they tailor their approach to local circumstances and individual requirements. They communicate with customers and prospects in ways and using languages that are acceptable to them.

Diversity can be a spur to creativity. Successful companies recruit and develop a multinational cadre of managers. Opportunities go to those who are best qualified for each role. Internationalization is not forced down people's throats. It occurs naturally and problems are tackled as they arise.

Losers tend to sweep difficulties under the carpet or hope they will go away. Winners let people network. They allow them to forge whatever cross-border relationships will best enable them to achieve their objectives.

Losers also impose a single corporate culture on employees, customers and suppliers regardless of differing local conditions and unfavourable circumstances. Winners strive to adjust their management style to match how the people they wish to develop closer relationships with operate.

People should be equipped to handle joint ventures with overseas businesses before they are set up. Time has to be devoted to making them work. Because of the effort involved winners select their prospects with care. They also learn both from their own mistakes and from their customers, suppliers and business partners.

Communicating for change

More demanding customers, competitive markets and tough trading conditions may trigger reviews of corporate aspirations, approaches, capabilities, structures and operations. Change is generally assumed to be necessary, desirable and beneficial. The 'management of change' has become a priority for many organizations.

During the recent downturn in economic fortunes many companies initiated a new wave of restructuring and redundancy. Despite a decade of re-engineering, a succession of management fads, heavy investments in new technologies and the extensive use of external management consulting services many boards and management teams were caught flat-footed.

Communicators need to address the reality of the context in which they operate. Despite the rhetoric about flexibility, the ambitious claims made by corporate leaders and the hype of their advisers, many companies struggle to cope with adverse circumstances. Because so many corporate change programmes have failed to produce greater resilience and responsiveness, sudden and dramatic readjustments may be thought necessary.

Employees are laid off and contracts are cancelled. Recruitment, training and the placing of advertisements are frozen. People are expected to do more with less. As a consequence they may feel jaded and insecure. Many managers do not seem to have learned from previous experience of the consequences of severe cutbacks.

There might be various reasons for individual and collective amnesia. People may be overloaded with initiatives, inundated with information, and confused by competing claims. Many people work very hard and for long hours, but on peripheral activities. They do not focus upon the critical success factors for managing change, competing and winning (Coulson-Thomas, 2002b).

If too much is changed at once people may lose a sense of identity, belonging, direction and purpose. Change can disorientate and disrupt, and some individuals can only take so much of it. Business leaders need to think carefully about how much change can be handled before negative consequences wipe out any desired gains. Enough continuity should be provided for people not to feel threatened and insecure.

In some companies change has been ubiquitous and indiscriminate. Managers are assessed and rewarded according to the amount of change they bring about. Yet change is rarely neutral and it is not always beneficial. It can be unsettling and disruptive. When mismanaged it can also be stressful and destructive. It can distract people who should be focused upon other priorities.

Communicators need to be sensitive to the impacts of changes. Introducing them without first assessing their consequences is risky and may prove very harmful. Altering a task at one point in a process, or introducing a new activity, may cause problems for those operating elsewhere, either within the same process or in a related or dependent one. An end-to-end perspective is required.

Few changes affect everyone in the same way. Some may benefit while others are disadvantaged. Those who are satisfied – and they may include key employees and important customers – may favour a status quo, while frustrated colleagues and unhappy individuals may prefer an alternative. Opinion within a board, management team or work group may be divided between those who are for or against particular changes.

The impacts of some change may not be immediately apparent. Their consequences might be delayed or hidden. For example, they might result in the loss of strategically important knowledge and understanding. There may be pressure to conform. For a variety of reasons people may be reluctant to speak up against change. Corporate media may not give them a voice. Only one side of an argument may be presented.

While enthusiasts may champion change, determined opponents might endeavour to undermine it. When the benefits of change are widely spread the advantaged may not even register them. Marginal beneficiaries may lack the motivation to prevent blocking action by those who are strongly disadvantaged. People who are indifferent or ambivalent may simply 'go with the flow'.

The Centre for Competitiveness has examined the approaches and practices of both 'winners' who successfully manage change and 'losers' who do not. The attitudes, behaviours and priorities of the two groups are fundamentally different (Coulson-Thomas, 2002b). What is clear is that change helps or harms depending upon what is changed, how it is changed and for what purpose.

The findings are similar to those for winning business and building relationships with customers. Losers are indecisive and oblivious to the needs of others. They are cautious, wary of commitments and fail to inspire or motivate. They are also reactive. They respond to events and often fail to anticipate the requirement to change. When they do act it is often in peripheral areas. They overlook what is important.

Losers hoard information. They are reluctant to delegate and trust. Although driven by their own agendas they often end up playing other people's games. They adopt standard approaches and are rigid and inflexible. They imitate and copy others rather than think for themselves.

Losers utter opinionated assertions and make self-serving observations. They confuse activity with progress. They train by sheep dipping. Individual needs are not addressed. Immediate priorities take precedence over longer-term aims. They are complacent, secretive and defensive. They try to do everything themselves, and they resist new evidence and external ideas.

Losers are indifferently led and confuse operational and strategic issues. People are offered bland generalizations rather than a compelling vision. A combination of destructive attitudes, mistaken approaches and wrong priorities locks losers into a negative spiral of decline towards commodity product supplier status.

Winners in the struggle to change, transform and reinvent are very different. They understand that goodwill can be steadily eroded by the imposition of a succession of changes that are not justified and which appear trivial. Thinking managers tread warily. They avoid diversions, panaceas and single solutions. They only alter what needs to be changed to achieve the results they seek.

Winners appreciate that change can disrupt valued relationships. They distinguish goals, values, objectives, policies and activities that need to be reviewed and revised from those that should be continued. They also recognize that some people 'follow the herd'. Once a clear majority accepts a particular course of action the uncommitted may climb aboard the bandwagon.

Some communicators instinctively favour consensus to the extent of excluding minority views. Yet the members of a majority may be naive or mistaken regarding their best long-term interests. Also preferences and priorities can change. Nothing is more frustrating than

to find that certain options have been lost because a selected course of action cannot be reversed.

Much depends upon the purposes of change and the capacity to adapt of those involved and directly affected. Confident communicators are not afraid to question the rationale for proposed changes. They ask whether an impact analysis has been undertaken of their likely implications. They also advocate an adequate assessment of the potential consequences for employees, customers, suppliers, business partners and investors.

Winners tell those likely to be affected by them why changes are thought necessary. People should only be expected to make demanding changes for valid reasons. Pain and disruption should be justified rather than rationalized. The visions and arguments offered by many boards are excessively general and economical with the truth.

Management action and communication support should be applied where they are most likely to make a difference. Justifiable changes could be those that focus upon the critical success factors for achieving key corporate objectives and delivering greater customer and shareholder value. Winners have a longer-term and more strategic perspective. They set out to enhance capabilities, deepen relationships, develop additional options and remain relevant.

Winners are also confident, positive and pro-active. They build and release individual talent. They explore, pioneer and discover. They encourage enterprise and innovation. They trust other people and share information and opportunities with them where this is likely to prove mutually beneficial.

Winners address the specific realities and practicalities of what they need to do to manage change and achieve their objectives.

They inspire and motivate people. They prepare and equip them to achieve the changes they are expected to bring about. They avoid wasted effort and concentrate upon the areas of greatest opportunity.

While open to ideas, winners select people, business partners and opportunities with care. They are persistent but pragmatic, and determined but adaptable in pursuit of their aims. They take calculated risks, experiment with new ways of operating, and create new knowledge, options and choices.

Risks to relationships, standing and trust are especially important. A growing business may need to build upon an existing reputation and safeguard core values. Steps may need to be taken to protect what is important and prevent the compromise of cherished beliefs. Communicators should know the anchor points of a business, the cement that holds its people together.

Some companies incur a high and continuing penalty for modest and transient reductions in a cost base. Winners value relationships. They try to protect rather than disrupt them. They empathize and invite feedback. They probe and debate, and listen and learn. They collaborate on the basis of openness and transparency with complementary spirits who share their vision and values.

The boards of companies that successfully manage change tend to avoid the distractions of trappings. They endeavour to inspire, enable and support growth, development and transformation. They aim to cut through blather and hype in order to get down to the fundamentals of what needs to be done.

Winners prefer simple solutions and direct action. They regard review, renewal and transformation as normal activities. They think before they act, and ensure that existing and potential customers are not disadvantaged by change. They push back the boundaries of what is possible and become sought after and trusted business partners.

Managers in the more successful companies work with colleagues to foster winning attitudes and behaviours. They strive to attain a balance between strategy and capability. They also ensure all the pieces of the jigsaw puzzle required for successful transformation and sustained competitiveness are in place (Coulson-Thomas, 2002b).

Alert communicators look out for the telltale signs of losing attitudes and approaches. Typical symptoms are self-contained and incomplete change and transformation programmes initiated with little confidence of success and without the necessary capabilities for effective implementation.

Losers sometimes give themselves away by ducking questions and avoiding confrontation. They manage 'communication' rather than achieve results. Communicators should avoid being drawn into activities to sidetrack critics, conceal disappointments or rationalize failure.

Successful change managers check that colleagues are clear about what they are trying to achieve and are visibly committed to agreed objectives. They make sure people both understand what they need to do and are enabled to act. Barriers to change should be identified and tackled.

Directors and senior managers cannot become directly involved in the many and varied activities that more bespoke and imaginative responses to changing circumstances will demand. Different business units and venture teams should be empowered and enabled to bring about whatever changes are required to enable them to achieve their objectives and deliver value to *their* customers.

At any stage of the change process new areas of risk can arise as structures, processes and systems are altered. Communicators will be particularly concerned with threats to image and reputation and to relationships and trust. People should understand what is at stake and be equipped to respond. Problems will arise. Their absence could indicate a lack of ambition. Learning from them and re-enforcing success helps to maintain progress.

Winning and losing approaches to communication

Modern corporations are essentially networks of relationships based upon trust. When a reputation for fair dealing and accurate reporting is compromised the consequences can be dramatic. The experience of WorldCom illustrates how quickly meltdown can occur.

Executives sometimes go to considerable lengths to conceal the true state of their companies' affairs. Association with the perceived misrepresentation of Enron's financial standing sealed the fate of Arthur Andersen. A key question for regulators is whether such widely reported cases are isolated instances of deception or symptoms of a wider crisis in corporate communications.

The foundations of effective communication are often in place. Many corporate value statements advocate openness, while professional codes of practice champion integrity. Managers are expected to have 'communication skills'. Substantial investments have been made in communication technologies. Senior executives recognize that a distinctive vision, stretching goals and clear objectives can inspire, excite and energize people.

However, in many companies there is a wide gap between management rhetoric and corporate reality (Coulson-Thomas, 2002b). People are drowning in irrelevant information. They are overloaded, overworked and insecure. With little time to think many people do not see the wood for the trees. The various studies of the Centre for Competitiveness reveal considerable differences in the communication practices of successful and unsuccessful companies and the attitudes and behaviour of their communicators. These can now be summarized.

Let us start with vulnerable companies, or the losers, and practices that should trigger alarm bells. Communication is largely top-down and one-way. Communicators simply pass on whatever messages their bosses wish to communicate. They do not question a brief, challenge assumptions or ask whether information they are handed is accurate or fair.

Losers only communicate when *they* feel they need to. They become preoccupied with messages that they would like to put across. Recipients are just targets. Smart communicators in some floundering companies pride themselves on their ability to distract, exaggerate or keep a situation under wraps. They avoid speaking to people directly and hide behind technology. Sanitized summaries are posted on intranets.

The communication of struggling companies is often insipid and non-committal. They give little away. Bad news is hidden under the carpet. Slick packaging encourages passive acceptance. Communicators mouth motherhoods and repeat slogans. Their work is often of a high technical standard. But the focus is upon form and style rather than relevance and impact.

Communicators in stagnant and dying companies can be emotionally detached. They often display little personal commitment to corporate messages. Their communication can be cold, clinical and bland. Many are sophists and cynics. Communication for them is a game to be played. They may consider scoring points to be more important than helping others to understand the reality of a situation.

In ailing companies corporate communication is more likely to be a distinct activity undertaken by dedicated specialists. Communicators do the chief executive's bidding. They work mechanically and struggle to highlight what is different, special or unique about their employer. Not surprisingly they fail to connect with key stakeholder groups and they spend much of their time rationalizing failure. When rumours start and adverse publicity occurs few are sympathetic. Those who have been tricked or feel duped look the other way.

Communicators in successful businesses are more confident. They have less to hide and they behave very differently. They share information, knowledge and understanding with people whose co-operation is needed to achieve corporate aspirations. They engage in two-way communication and they encourage, welcome and respond to feedback.

Good communicators are not preoccupied with themselves. They focus on the people they would like to establish, build and sustain relationships with. They try to understand, empathize with and reflect their aspirations, hopes and fears. They make direct and personal contact. They feel. They may stumble over the words, but they demonstrate they care.

Communicators in winning companies consciously build mutually beneficial relationships. They forge long-term partnerships. They are both sensitive and flexible. They listen. They monitor reactions and are alert to changing requirements. Communication activities evolve, as changes are made to ensure greater relevance.

Effective communicators identify unmet needs, analyse communication barriers and address problems. They recognize the import-ance of symbols and are visibly committed. They understand that they and their colleagues will be judged by their actions and their conduct. They endeavour to match words with deeds.

In companies with prospects communication is an integral element of management. It is built into work processes and the roles of managers. Communicators think for themselves. They question motivations, probe sources and assess likely implications. They take steps to ensure the veracity of corporate messages. They assume responsibility for what they communicate.

Winners are able to explain with conviction the essence of what they are about. Their communication celebrates and sustains success. They engender allegiance and foster relationships that can withstand market shocks and survive the traumas of economic downturn. People trust them and will put themselves out for them.

Effective relationships depend on openness, trust and respect. Lasting partnerships are based upon a shared vision, common values and goals, and agreed objectives. Winners consciously create arrangements that benefit all the parties involved. They celebrate, enjoy and sustain success.

Investors, employees, customers, suppliers and independent directors should never take corporate communication for granted. The intelligence, standing and bravado of corporate leaders and their professional advisers are no guarantee that the full story is being told. People should be alert to telltale signs of whether communication approaches and practices indicate likely failure or herald future success.

Many more communication professionals need to engineer a revolution in their role. Hitherto they may have been charged with passing on top-down and one-way messages from business leaders to the people of organizations. They must become involved as advisers, coaches and enablers in achieving culture change and corporate transformation.

Outcomes sought must go beyond understanding and include involvement, ownership, buy-in and more imaginative and entrepreneurial responses.

REFERENCES

Bartram, B. (ed.) (1999) *The Contract Bid Manager's Toolkit*, Bedford: Policy Publications.

Coulson-Thomas, C. (1999) *Individuals and Enterprise: Creating Entrepreneurs for the New Millennium through Personal Transformation*, Dublin: Blackhall Publishing.

Coulson-Thomas, C. (2001) *Shaping Things to Come: Strategies for Creating Alternative Enterprises*, Dublin: Blackhall Publishing.

Coulson-Thomas, C. (2002a) *Pricing for Profit: The Critical Success Factors*, Bedford: Policy Publications.

Coulson-Thomas, C. (2002b) *Transforming the Company: Manage Change, Compete and Win*, London: Kogan Page.

FitzGerald, P. (2000) *Effective Purchasing: The Critical Success Factors*, Bedford: Policy Publications.

Hurcomb, J. (1998) *Developing Strategic Customers and Key Accounts: The Critical Success Factors*, Bedford, Policy Publications.

Kennedy, C. (1999) *Bidding for Business: The Skills Agenda*, Bedford: Policy Publications.

Kennedy, C. and O'Connor, M. (1997) *Winning Major Bids: The Critical Success Factors*, Bedford: Policy Publications.

CHAPTER 12

Communicating with 1.3 billion people in China

Ying Fan and Wen-Ling Liu

As a country with sustained high economic growth since the 1980s, China has been dubbed 'the world's last and largest market'. This chapter presents the Chinese dimension of integrated communication through an overview of the advertising and PR industry with some of the latest statistical information, and through an examination of renaming global brands in different cultures. The authors also illustrate the benefits and drawbacks of using promotional events and sponsorship as a new type of media activity for China, especially in the increasingly affluent youth sector.

China is undoubtedly a large and important market with 1.3 billion consumers. The economic reform and open-door policy since 1979 has set off an unprecedented consumer revolution, which has significantly changed the living standards and lifestyle of millions of people. The phenomenal growth in the market economy is mirrored by the dramatic development in integrated communication in the country, particularly in the advertising industry. A virtually non-existent sector until the early 1980s, the advertising industry is now the second largest in Asia after Japan and employs more than half a million people.

Contemporary advertising in China dates back to the 1920s. Since then, it has experienced many ups and downs. After the first advertising boom in the 1930s, its develop-ment suffered restrictions after the communists founded the People's Republic in 1949 and began to practise the Russian-style centrally planned economy. During the Cultural Revolution (1966–76), advertising virtually disappeared being branded as 'evil' and 'deceptive'. It returned to business in 1978 when China started the economic reform and open-door policy.

The last decade of the twentieth century witnessed a dramatic growth in the sector with average annual growth rate of 39.8 per cent. The total advertising revenue increased more than thirty-one times from 2.5 billion RMB to 79.5 billion RMB (US$ 10 billion) between 1990 and 2001, putting China into the top 10 largest markets for advertising services (see Table 12.1). By the end of 2001,

COMMUNICATING IN CHINA   185

there were 78,339 firms involved in the industry, employing 640,000 people, including 46,935 advertising agencies (60 per cent) as compared with fewer than 10 agencies in 1976 and 6,000 people in 1980. Geographically, the advertising industry is concentrated on three centres: the capital Beijing, the largest commercial city Shanghai, and Guangdong Province, which borders Hong Kong and has the most dynamic economy. The three areas account for 50.7 per cent of all advertising revenue. Table 12.2 shows the top 12 largest advertisers by product category. The top 10 advertisers by brand were all local companies whose expenditure accounted for 7 per cent of the total advertising spend.

Types of media

The four major advertising media are television, newspapers, radio and magazines (Tables 12.3). In 1990 television accounted for 17.7 per cent of the total expenditure, ranking third after outdoor (39 per cent) and newspapers (31 per cent) in advertising spend. Since the 1980s, every type of media in China (radio, television, newspapers, magazines and other media) has increased in number and expanded in scope. They have become more segmented and diversified in content and style. For example, there were 202 television stations in 1985; ten years later the number had surged to over 1000, plus more than 1,200 cable stations. There are now 2,895 television stations, 2,128 newspapers and 723 radio stations that take advertising. Television is the most powerful medium, reaching more than 1.1 billion viewers (90 per cent of the population) and accounting for around 40 per cent of advertising revenue in China. China's TV stations in 2001 broadcast an estimated 9.56 million hours of pro-

grammes, whilst only producing 2.02 million hours of programmes. The media sector has been dominated by a few important players. For example, one leading TV channel CCTV 1 attracted 28 per cent of all advertising revenue on TV. Similarly, *Guangzhou Daily* had an 18 per cent share of all newspaper advertising income. *Elle* proved to be the most 'sellable' magazine in China with 21 per cent of all advertising revenue for magazines (*China Daily*, 06–11–2002).

In recent years the internet and mobile phones have emerged as the new media with great potential. By the end of 2002, China became the largest mobile phone market in the world with 206.6 million subscribers (compared with only 10 million users in India). Chinese mobile customers sent nearly 80 billion text messages in 2002, a five-fold increase over the previous year. During the 10-day period of the Chinese New Year holiday in 2003, 6 billion text messages and more than 1 million multimedia messages were sent (*China Daily*, 02–11–2003).

Production of TV programmes, development of cinemas and distribution of newspapers and magazines will become the most profitable investment areas in China's media industry, according to 'China Media Investment Report 2002–03' (*China Daily*, 02–11–2003). In its third year of WTO membership the government has loosened its control on foreign media entering the Chinese market, and will open up TV, book and newspaper sectors to foreign investors.

International firms and their strategies

Entering China in the early 1980s, international advertising agencies have seen their market share increasing from 5–10 per cent in the middle of the 1980s to 55.4 per cent in 2000. The primary motive of these multinational agencies in entering China was to provide a service to their international clients who were eager to tap the large consumer market there. But now they have also attracted more accounts from Chinese domestic companies. China has presented a great challenge to both international agencies and their clients: a language based on ideograms, different cultural values with regional variations, the huge divide between urban and rural areas, remaining ideological restraints, to name a few. In contrast to the notion that standardization is enough for low-income markets like China, a recent survey of 873 international advertisers in China found that most companies used the combination strategy (Yin, 1999). Although the Chinese market is still less affluent, it is a highly competitive one that requires international advertisers to recognize the cultural differences and to adapt. However, studies on how advertising in China should be adapted remain inconclusive. On the one hand, Chinese consumers have shown great responsiveness to advertisements that emphasize concrete, functional and utilitarian product benefits rather than symbolic themes. They will read even the fine details of product print advertisements. On the other hand, Chinese consumers are becoming increasingly sophisticated. Urban, young and affluent viewers prefer the advertisements that are interesting, entertaining and that communicate new lifestyles and western values.

PR industry

In 1980 PR practice first appeared in China in some foreign-funded enterprises in Shenzhen and spread gradually from there to the rest of the country. The year 1985 witnessed several firsts in the PR industry: the first PR department set up in a pharmaceutical company, the first PR company founded by the state news agency and the first PR degree programme. Since the 1980s the PR industry has grown from zero into an established sector. By the end of 2000, there were 150 PR organizations and more than 1,000 PR agencies employing around 100,000 people, including 5,000 qualified PR professionals. The total turnover reached 1 billion RMB in 1999 and was expected to reach 2 billion (240 million US dollars) in 2001. The first international PR firm coming to China was Hill & Knowlton in 1984, followed by Burson-Marsteller in 1985. Now 15 international PR firms (including the top 10) are operating in China. International PR firms have apparent strengths in strategic planning, branding and crisis management, whilst Chinese PR firms are good at media relations, event planning and exhibition design. Despite its short history, PR has played an important role in China. For example, in the aftermath of the Tiananmen massacre in 1989, the Chinese government employed an international PR firm to improve its image in the west. A more recent case is the use of PR to help China's Olympic bid.

Despite its rapid growth since the 1980s, the advertising industry still accounts for only 0.7 per cent of China's GNP, as compared to 3–4 per cent in the United States. The industry is expected to continue to grow at double-digit rate and China is predicted to become the second-largest market after the United States (but before Japan) by 2020. China is the world's largest market with 1.3 billion consumers. More than 350 million people (the size of the European Union) are expected to become relatively affluent 'middle class' with an annual income above US$ 4,000 in the near future. With the country's entry into

Table 12.1 Advertising industry turnover and growth

Year	Turnover RMB bn	Annual growth (per cent)
1990	2.5	25.1
1991	3.5	40.3
1992	6.8	93.4
1993	13.4	97.6
1994	20.0	49.4
1995	27.3	36.5
1996	36.7	34.2
1997	46.2	25.9
1998	53.8	16.4
1999	62.2	15.7
2000	71.3	14.6
2001	79.5	11.5
Average annual growth (1990–2001)		31.8

Source: *Economic Daily*, 6.11.2002

Table 12.3 Advertising expenditure by medium, 1997

	Turnover RMB bn
Agency	19.4
Television	11.4
Newspaper	9.2
Other	4.1
Radio	1.1
Magazine	0.5

Source: A. C. Nielsen (China) Ltd

Table 12.2 Advertising expenditure by product category, 2001

Rank	Product	RMB bn	Annual growth (per cent)	Share in total ad spending (per cent)
1	Medicines	9.67	29	12.2
2	Food and drinks	9.0	30	11.3
3	Home appliances	6.59	−10.4	8.3
4	Property sales and lease	6.95	16.6	8.7
5	Cosmetics and skin care	6.33	33.4	8.0
6	Alcoholic drinks	4.12	69.3	5.2
7	Health services	3.26	6.9	4.1
8	Fashion	2.43	14.5	3.1
9	Cars	2.29	−46.2	2.9
10	Medical instruments	1.87	−13.4	2.4
11	Tourism	1.58	22.6	2.0
12	Tobacco	0.91	5.9	1.1
Others		24.5	8.3	30.8
Total		79.5	11.5	100

Source: *Economic Daily*, 6.11.2002

the World Trade Organization and the 2008 Olympic Games to be held in Beijing, there will be a huge influx of foreign goods and capital investment into China as the market becomes more open with many trade restrictions being removed. This will provide international advertising and PR firms with great opportunities (see Tables 12.1, 12.2 and 12.3).

Brand communication

Lux is called 'Strong Man' in China, a name contradicting the image of a young lady on its package. When the brand first entered the Chinese market in the early 1980s, a Hollywood actress was employed in one of the earliest western TV commercials. While bathing herself in a large bathtub (certainly an exotic scene to the Chinese viewers at the time), she said in a soft seductive voice 'I only use *Strong Man*. How about you?' This proved to be a huge success and Lux became a household name within weeks. In Taiwan Lux is called 'Beauty', a name that matches with the image of young lady. Both names are pronounced with exactly the same sound and tone. In the end Lux has two different names with totally different images in the same language and culture. An explanation can be found from the ideological differences existing in the two parts of China. While 'Beauty' would be an acceptable name in China today it was certainly a problem back in the 1980s. Under the orthodox communist doctrine, 'beauty' was related to the decadent bourgeoisie aesthetics.

The need to have a new name

For many international companies entering the Chinese market, the first barrier they encountered was the language. As the Chinese use characters based on ideograms and the majority of people are unfamiliar with the Roman alphabet, the international brand has to choose a proper Chinese name. This is a complicated task that requires a thorough understanding of Chinese culture as well as linguistic skills. Three methods are commonly in use to translate a foreign name into Chinese:

1   *Direct translation or transliteration*. The Chinese equivalent sounds close to the original, but has no specific meaning.
2   *Free translation*. The foreign name is translated according to its meaning or meaning in Chinese, regardless of its original pronunciation.
3   *Mixed translation*. Both sound and meaning are considered. The pronunciation of the original name dictates the sound (phoneme/syllable) of the new name. The meaning of the name is chosen after the sound.

There are some cases when foreign brands are left untranslated either deliberately or due to difficulty in finding a suitable name. Typically these brands have the following characteristics: short product names (M&M); or in the business sector (IBM); or have an upmarket image (Bang & Olufsen).

A recent study examined 100 international brands and their adopted Chinese names (Fan, 2002). It found that the mixed method was mostly used (46 per cent), followed by free translations (29 per cent) and direct translation (25 per cent). Direct translation maintains the phonetic link between the two names, i.e. the new name sounds like or close to the original, but it has no specific meaning in Chinese. Free translation, on the other hand, gives a meaningful Chinese name but loses the phonetic link with the original. The mixed method seems to be the most popular one among the three as it creates a new name in Chinese that both sounds like the original and has a meaning. This result confirms that the sound of the original name is the starting point in the translation process, but the meaning of the new name is a more important concern. Three-quarters of the sample used either mixed or free translation.

Factors affecting renaming

Reflecting product benefits and brand positioning are the two largest groups. It is inter-

esting to note the use of folklore or idioms in renaming car brands such as: BMW as a horse, Citroen as a dragon and Rover as a tiger. All these animals are powerful symbols in Chinese legend. The horse is related to speed, the dragon to power and the tiger to prestige. It is also worthwhile to compare Coca-Cola with Pepsi Cola. In their Chinese names 'Palatable and enjoyable'[1] and 'Hundred things enjoyable', the last two characters are the same. However, the difference in the first two characters sets them apart. Coca-Cola's name has a clear link with product benefits; the repetition of a character makes the name rhythmic which enhances the name recall. In contrast, Pepsi's name is a poorer imitation

Table 12.4 Factors influencing the new name

Factor	Brand	Name in Chinese	Meaning	Total = 75
Reflecting product benefits or industry characters	Nivea Pampers Ikea Polaroid	妮维雅 帮宝适 宜家 拍立得	Girl keep elegance Help baby fit Good for home Shoot get instant	18
Quality/brand positioning	Saab Gucci Goodyear	绅宝 古姿 固特异	Gentleman's treasure Classic looks Strong, special unique	16
Lucky names	Kellogg Heineken Carrefour	家乐氏 喜力 家乐福	Home happy Happy power Family, happy fortune	13
Traditional values	Ericsson Prudential	爱立信 保诚	Love build trust Protect honest	5
Beliefs/customs	Rover	路虎	Land tiger	3
Linking to logo or packaging	Wrigley's	箭牌	Arrow brand	4
Patriotism	Aiwa Henkel	爱华 汉高	Love China China high	3
Country of origin effect	L'Oreal	欧莱雅	European elegance	3
Other	Microsoft	微软	Tiny weak	6
Same or similar to the original meaning	Volkswagen	大众	The masses	4

Source: Fan, 2002a

without any distinctive feature. In all 100 cases, Glaxo-Wellcome is the only long name with five syllables. Despite its length, the name itself is unique and easy to remember. For Glaxo the last character used in Chinese represents medicine names. The second part Wellcome is rendered as 'keep healthy', clearly describing the product benefits. Other examples are shown in Table 12.4 (p. 189).

Balance between sound and meaning

Chinese names place more emphasis on meaning than sound. A meaningful name is crucial in developing both a mental image and favourable associations. Mercedes Benz is a good example. Its official name in the People's Republic of China is 'Speed on'. The sound and visual image of two characters indicate a horse with associations of speed, dynamism, performance and capability – the exact attributes that the brand symbolizes.

Brand positioning is another important consideration. In the case of Canon, its new name 'Best calibre' is *strategically desirable*: it sounds appealing and generates associations of quality. The new name has the inherent ability to be recalled easily from memory and establish a distinctive, quality brand positioning. Renaming a brand in another language/culture involves more than simple linguistic issues. Brand positioning is perhaps a more important consideration here. A good localized name like 'Best calibre' with 'Built-in' image could add value to its original brand equity and make brand communication in that market a relatively easier task.

Brand renaming in a foreign culture is notoriously difficult due to the complexity in linguistic and cultural differences. It has to take into account various factors and weigh up any subtle differences between alternatives. Examples in Table 12.5 demonstrate that a poorly conceived name could create confusion in the consumer or harm the brand's equity. Although no simple rule guarantees the finding of a good name, an understanding

Table 12.5 Names with potentially negative connotations

Brand	Name and meaning in Chinese	Comment
Peugeot	标致 Pretty	Too feminine, no link to product benefits
Pizza Hut	必胜客 Must win customers	Sounds desperate, confusing
Dunhill	登喜路 Ascend happy road	Philistine, incompatible with the upmarket image
Compaq	康柏 Healthy cypress	Cypress symbolizes the aged or old, incompatible with a hi-tech image
Microsoft	微软 Tiny soft /weak	Implies 'tiny and weak', contrary to its status of the world's largest firm
Olivetti	好利获得 Good profit gained	Who gains profit? What about customers?

Source: Fan, 2002a

of the issues discussed here will help the company prevent the costly blunder of choosing a wrong name.

The global–local paradox in brand communication

Brand image refers to the perception of consumers, a picture in the mind of the beholder. A brand's name is the foundation of its image. Though global brands may exist, it remains a question whether there is any global image as the perception of global brands is conditioned strongly by various factors at national level such as cultural and socio-economic market environment (Ross, 1995). The translation process gives an international brand not just a Chinese name, but also a distinctive local image. Take BMW as an example. To millions of Chinese consumers, BMW is a 'treasure horse' rather than *the ultimate driving machine*'. A horse is generally perceived as a heroic creature in Chinese culture: there are dozens of idioms and legends describing its feats and it is a popular subject in traditional Chinese paintings. By adopting such a name, the brand can tap into the rich cultural deposits and create a favourable mental image in the consumer's mind.

Although some research has found ample evidence that consumers in Europe and the United States increasingly favour national brands over brands from other countries, the situation in China is different and more complicated. On the one hand, Chinese consumers prefer localized international brand names that carry positive meaning as examples from this study showed; on the other hand, they also favour international brands over real local brands as the former are perceived to have either better quality or higher status. No wonder hundreds of indigenous Chinese companies deliberately gave their products a brand name that sounds like a translated foreign name to benefit from the appeal of foreignness. Some went even further by simply adopting an English name; for example, TCL is the leading consumer electronics brand in China. The dilemma faced by the international brand is not about whether to choose a suitable Chinese name (it is a necessity in the majority of cases), but whether to maintain a western image or to create a more localized image. For example, Nike and Reebok have adopted very different brand image strategies. Nike maintains a standardized 'fitness and performance' image in all of the markets it serves. Nike is translated into Chinese as a name that has no specific meaning (though its first character means 'durable') but has a distinctive foreign or western image and sounds more appealing. Its rival Reebok, on the other hand, customizes its image on the basis of national differences. It is rendered as 'dashing step', a meaningful name but without a foreign image.

From a broader perspective, the global brand–local image paradox is part of the debate of globalization and adaptation (for example, see Levitt, 1983; Quelch, and Hoff, 1986). The challenge for international branding is to find a fine balance between the two strategies, as there are risks at both extremes. A pure global image that is alien to the national culture will not appeal to local consumers. On the contrary, a totally localized image will not benefit from brand assets of the original and find it hard to differentiate itself from the local competition. Unilever is a good case in point. A global brand, according to its chairman Michael Perry, is simply *a local brand reproduced many times* (quoted in *AdWeek*, 14 December 1992). The company has been for years actively pursuing localized branding strategy in China, localizing all its international brands and acquiring successful local brands. Most Chinese consumers probably have no idea about Unilever's origin, it is perceived as a multinational company with a Chinese identity, namely 'united benefit China'. The company launched its first localized corporate identity programme in China in April 2001. The new logo places the original Unilever logo against the shape of a house with the slogan on the top 'Where there is a home/family, there is Unilever'. This is in accordance with Chinese emphasis on family values (Fan, 2000) and provides an example of a well-balanced and integrated global–local image.

Emerging new media for integrating communication

Consumption is a relatively new experience for Chinese consumers, who began to enjoy shorter working hours and more official holidays in recent years. With more spare time and additional disposable income consumers now demand a wider choice of products and services, particularly in sports, leisure and entertainment. This is in line with the experience of other southeast Asian countries where economic development drove growth in the leisure industry.

As the market becomes more competitive, it is crucial for international companies to find a better way to cut through the competition and reach the target audience. Event sponsorship provides companies with alternatives to the cluttered mass media, an ability to segment on a local or regional basis and opportunities for reaching targeted lifestyle groups whose consumption behaviour can be linked with the sponsored events. On the other hand, the huge growth in sports activities, music and art events, and other forms of entertainment

offers a vast potential in sponsoring such activities and events.

Music is probably the most universal means of communication nowadays, instantly traversing language and other cultural barriers. Popular music reflects changes better and faster than any other genre. And it is usually reflective of what is happening in society as a whole. Finding a way to link a message to popular music in order to reach a target segment of Chinese consumers is what music event sponsorship is pursuing. Younger people living in big cities consume popular music through MTV and the Chinese MTV channel called Channel V. They also listen to the radio, regularly attend music events and go to clubs and discos. In Shanghai there are a variety of discos and clubs that are equipped with the latest laser, light and sound systems and provide enough space for 2,000–3,000 people. Some discos specialize in hosting big music raves featuring famous DJs from the United States and Europe, attracting young people who can be classified into what Wei (1997) called 'Modern' and 'Generation Xers' lifestyle segments. These two segments are characterized as being more affluent, better educated, hedonistic and pursuing a fancy and distinct lifestyle. They become core target groups for international companies in consumer goods and sports fashion markets.

The sponsorship of such events offers the sponsor good opportunities to reach and communicate directly to target audiences by means of free samples, prize draws and information gathering, etc. For Chinese young people the latest techno rave, house and hip-hop music events are a means of expressing new lifestyles. At the same time such events give them the opportunity to taste/experience new things (products, ideas, fashion and lifestyle) portrayed through the music. Music raves reflect younger people's contemporary wants and attitudes, something that is highly valued by a specific type of audience. Event sponsors can develop positive effects in building favourable associations and links to the brand. For example, Carlsberg had co-operation with MTV in which they sponsored special programmes. In addition, Carlsberg organized special music event parties in Shanghai. The sponsor benefits not only from the impact generated from the events them-selves, but from wider coverage in the local media.

One of the most important benefits is that events offer opportunities to establish direct contact with opinion leaders and innovators. Chinese culture value systems place emphasis on uncertainty avoidance and conformity (Fan, 2000). To a Chinese person, any un-certainty, ambiguity and risky or undefined situation is viewed as threatening and must be avoided. The innovator takes over the social and financial risk in trying for instance, new products/fashion or lifestyles. Other mem-bers in the group make use of the reference of the opinion leader/innovator. As a result per-ceived risk for other group members dimin-ishes. They may also feel discomfort at being left behind in the new fashion and are easily seduced into following what the innovator has tried. Innovators in this case become opinion leaders who develop important links between members in the diffusion cycle of new prod-ucts because they introduce the new product and lifestyle to early adopters, who go on to influence a larger minority.

Group conformity is another important cultural variable among Chinese people and has a strong impact on consumer behaviour. The product/fashion or lifestyle must reflect the values and norms deemed as acceptable by the group. In this regard, event sponsor-ship plays a key role in forging links with opin-ion leaders and in reaching target audiences.

This becomes particularly important to many foreign companies who find themselves facing difficulties in identifying and reaching target segments.

How are international companies practising event sponsorship in China? What benefits and problems are they encountering during the process? These are some of the questions investigated by Fan and Pfitzenmaier (2002) in an internet-based survey with an online questionnaire. Forty-five companies were selected from wide business sectors including automobile, beverage, sport apparel, airline, bank, hotel and entertainment. The names and email addresses of contact persons were obtained mainly through personal contacts and from a German agency's website. All the companies have their headquarters in Europe or the United States and are currently operating in the Chinese market. A total of thirteen completed, usable questionnaires were received, a net response rate of 29 per cent. Among those responding were two sports marketing firms, three companies in brewing or wine trading businesses, one advertising agency, one estate agency and one TV channel. Geographically, twelve were from Shanghai (China's largest industrial city) and one from Chengdu (capital of Sichuan Province). Due to the exploratory nature of the study and small sample, generalizations should be made with caution. However, the main findings from the survey are summa-rized in the following tables.

From Table 12.6 it can be seen that tradi-tional forms of media such as TV, print and (to a less degree) billboards are still most used. However, a majority of respondents acknow-ledge the importance of the internet as a new media. The highest concentration of promo-tion budget is on direct marketing, followed by sales promotion and point of sales. Long-term brand-building tools seem to have a low

Table 12.6 Which is your most used marketing medium?

Rating	1 Most used	2	3	4	5 Least used	Replies
TV	5	1	1	0	3	10
Radio	0	2	2	3	4	11
Internet	0	3	3	5	1	12
Print	5	3	2	1	2	13
Billboards	2	1	4	0	3	10

Source: Fan and Pfitzenmaier, 2002

Table 12.7 What kind of event(s) would you consider sponsoring or hosting?

T = 13	Per cent	Replies
Music	46.2	6
Sports	64.5	8
Arts (theatre, galleries, dance)	46.2	6
Company events, celebrations	46.2	6
New product or collection introduction	15.4	2
Local culture/lifestyle events	46.2	6
Education (schools, university, grants)	30.8	4
Others (specify)	7.7	1

Source: Fan and Pfitzenmaier, 2002

Table 12.9 How did you build an association or link between the sponsored event and your brand/company?

	Per cent	Replies (T = 13)
Event signage	61.5	8
Event title	30.8	4
Official event sponsor	53.9	7
Company brand, logo, name on:		
1 Event poster	53.9	7
2 Event ticket	46.2	6
3 Other print media	23.1	3
Others	7.7	1

Source: Fan and Pfitzenmaier, 2002

Table 12.8 What event(s) have you sponsored in the past three years?

Christmas parties	Annual tournaments (basketball, tennis)
New year parties	Soccer games
British embassy balls	FA cup final
Opening of new British consulate	Rugby
Receptions of ambassadors	Shanghai frisbee league
Belgian business association event	Ultimate frisbee
American chamber of commerce event	Hash house harriers
Canadian business forum event	Shanghai darts league cup
	TV shows, music concerts
Company openings	Theatre production
Opening ceremonies of official institutions	First Shanghai Asia music festival
Release of new movies	DJ swing in rojam (music)
	DKD DJ parties
Local charities	Jazz concert in Park97
First Shanghai international food festival	Wine tasting
Rave parties of various scales in east and south China	Company events (e.g. Shanghai-Suzhou outing)

Source: Fan and Pfitzenmaier, 2002

Table 12.10 How did you integrate the event
sponsorship into your marketing mix
or campaign?

	Per cent	Replies (T = 13)
Event logo integrated into own ad campaign (TV, print, etc.)	38.5	5
Event logo or name on product package	23.1	3
Competition and lucky draw with event related involvement	38.5	5
Sales promotion	38.5	5
Direct marketing	30.1	4
Merchandising	38.5	5
PR	23.1	3
Others	0	0

Source: Fan and Pfitzenmaier, 2002

priority in the budget, as event sponsorship received a low percentage of the budget with two exceptions.

Table 12.7 presents the most favourable events that the companies would consider to sponsor or host. Sport is considered to be the number one (64.5 per cent). The next three have same ranking: music, arts and local culture events. This is confirmed by the listing of events that these companies have actually sponsored in the past three years. Table 12.8 clearly shows the majority of events sponsored are sport or music related.

Table 12.9 reveals that event signage is regarded as the most important method (61.5 per cent) for building the association and links between the sponsored event and the sponsor's brand. Official event sponsorship and company/brand logo on poster come next (53.8 per cent). Event title sponsorship is considered less important (30.8 per cent). A finding in Table 12.10 indicates that event sponsorship is integrated into the

marketing mix by combining it with other tools from advertising and sales promotion (38.5 per cent) and packaging and PR (23.1 per cent). The ratio of the expenditure for event sponsorship and sponsorship-linked promotion indicates that spending on the latter is quite low. Only one company has a ratio of 1:2, five companies spending 1:1 and below. The two most important objectives in the sponsored events reported are enhancing brand awareness (88.9 per cent) and reinforcing brand image (55.6 per cent), followed by brand positioning (44.4 per cent) and providing a platform to increase sales and market share (44.4 per cent). Forging links with opinion leaders and strengthening corporate image through PR are also viewed as important objectives.

The unique business environment in China creates some difficulties in achieving set objectives according to some organizations (Table 12.11). They cite problems with bureaucratic regulations and corruption. One respondent highlighted differences in

Table 12.11 What difficulties have you experienced in reaching the objectives?

- Brand loyalty does not seem to depend on promotions. Chinese regard promotions as a chance to have something for free and it usually ends there
- Competition, budgets
- Government regulations
- How to increase the real news value of the sponsorship and make it interesting to media, trade and regular consumers
- Being effective in reaching the consumer with the least expense possible
- China itself in every way is difficult: corruption, lying, cheating, empty contracts
- For parties involved to abide by the agreed terms
- Target groups not clear
- Opinion leaders were not identified

Source: Fan and Pfitzenmaier, 2002

perceptions among Chinese consumers of brand loyalty and promotion. When asked about whether the outcome of the objectives are measured or researched, the responses were divided with four saying 'yes' and five 'no'. This shows there are difficulties in measuring and monitoring objective outcomes, a problem not peculiar to China.

The key factors facing companies when making decisions about event sponsorship are cost and efficiency (Table 12.12), followed by reach of target prospects. Respondents also emphasize the importance of Chinese culture. They acknowledge that promotional events management should adapt to the local culture and language to give the brand a local identity. Table 12.12, on the other hand, indicates that the majority of respondents clearly believe that event sponsorship does give advantage, compared to traditional advertising.

Table 12.13 on future strategies for event sponsorship indicates that companies want to have a sharper focus on two objectives, namely 'maximum exposure to target audience' and 'to enhance image and create distinct brand identity. Cost control and budget

Table 12.12 Does event sponsorship offer you an advantage in the following factors compared to traditional advertising?

	Yes %	No %
Adapt to Chinese culture/ language	38.5	30.8
'Buy into' (create brand associations related to) Chinese popular culture and lifestyle	53.8	15.4
Give the brand a local identity and fit	53.8	15.4
Reach target prospects and get into direct contact with them	53.8	15.4
Cost advantage and efficiency of communication tools	53.8	15.4

Source: Fan and Pfitzenmaier, 2002

Table 12.13 What is your future strategy for event sponsorship?

- Focus on small scale parties and events where your product is purchased but some free samples are given in support
- We will be involved in a minor way in the events that allow us maximum exposure to the target market at a minimum cost
- Our key focus will be to enhance the brand image and create a distinctive brand identity among specific target consumers instead of boosting the brand awareness in general
- We want to reach the persons passionate about sports through being active in sporting events. Especially related to young people. Limited budget
- Large parties, co-operation with multiple- sponsors
- High quality ones which closely link to brand position
- Continue to focus on music and sports and to promote British culture

Source: Fan and Pfitzenmaier, 2002

implications are another major concern. When asked about the role that event sponsorship plays in the integrated marketing communication mix (Table 12.14), respondents were divided in their opinions. Seven organizations replied that event sponsorship plays a minor role at this point. Six claim that it has already played an important role and would become even more important in future. In the words of one respondent, event sponsorship is a critical part of promotional programmes in the marketing mix. It is seamlessly combined with sales promotions and always 'PR-ed' in a well-branded manner to enhance brand image/positioning.

There seems to be an agreement that event promotion has a potential for growth (Table 12.15). Though events management is regarded as still being in its infancy, there is no doubt that 'all major marketers will pay more attention to below-the-line programmes'. The importance of establishing direct contact with

Table 12.14 What role does event sponsorship play in your integrated marketing mix?

- At this point a minor one
- To remind the community of our presence, to develop potential contacts and to support activities that we believe in
- More and more important
- In fact, event sponsorship is a critical part of promotional programmes in our marketing mix. It is seamlessly combined with sales promotions and always PRed in a well-branded manner to enhance brand image/positioning
- Event sponsorship has been the major way to market our name and product
- Important, but one has to bear the costs in mind

Source: Fan and Pfitzenmaier, 2002

Table 12.15 Comments on the future development of event marketing in China

- Direct contact with consumers is becoming increasingly important in the China market. All the major marketers will pay much more attention to below-the-line programmes instead of above-the-line advertising. Event marketing will play a key role to build contacts
- Event marketing is just at the infant stage with a great deal of growth to be had
- Growing but painfully, no big events to come off yet
- Event marketing is considered to be a good marketing tool, yet any blind following without right strategy is dangerous. Measurement of the efficiency is needed
- It should increase in usage
- The above questions are all relevant to a company that sells products or services in China. We are the largest sports marketing company in the world including China. We do very little above-the-line promotion of our company
- Sports and music as a means to bring people together
- One must consider the socio-political context in China (marketing mix) and the feasibility of using event sponsorship does depend on the product of the company in question (i.e. there are restrictions for tobacco companies, etc.)

Source: Fan and Pfitzenmaier, 2002

consumers will play a key role as will the impact of local environment on any PR activities. For example, Marlboro's much-publicized promotion campaign in 1998 was cut short after strong criticism from the press. In 1999 the company was forced to give up the title sponsorship of China's premiere football league after the government tightened up legislation on tobacco and alcohol advertising.

International companies in China today are facing stiff competition not just from other foreign firms but also local brands which may have moderate or even matching quality but sell at far lower prices. They also find it more difficult to reach increasingly sophisticated markets. Communication through traditional mass media such as TV and press becomes more expensive and less effective. Events management, though still at an early stage, can provide companies with a good alternative, if used in co-ordination with PR and other principal elements in the integrated marketing mix. The sponsorship of popular sports, music and local cultural events would appear to be particularly effective in forging direct contact with the opinion leaders, gath-

ering PR intelligence and encouraging product trials.

The threat of growing competition from foreign multinational corporations combined with knowledge and identification of culturally related differences are of critical concern. Cultural change, combined with an increased desire for material goods, is stimulated partly by new integrated communication, including strategic advertising (Costa, 1991; McCracken, 1988) but might recognize that people are committed to their own culture's value systems, attitudes, beliefs, and this in turn influences people's perception processes.

For example, young Chinese adults aged between 18 and 24 years, in common with other demographic groups worldwide, are highly driven achievement-oriented individuals. Individualism in the fast-growing Asian markets is manifested by an eager embrace of new freedoms and western values. These young adults show strong drive and ambition and tend to be free-spending and self-indulgent. They have a carefree attitude, a short-term focus, a marked self-centredness, with strong drives towards materialism.

The desire for different types of branded goods and company information (Table 12.16) shows in advertisements to improve living standards and lifestyles in China, through demand for cars, fashion, computers, books, education, home interior and entertainment information. Electrical appliances such as fridges, microwaves, etc. are no longer the most popular items in China. Nevertheless, young UK adults also require more information on audiovisual equipment, entertainment, fashion. In particular, they ask for more medicine and health information. As housing plans in China's major cities have increased, Chinese young adults appear to demand more interior design information, while young UK adults show less or no interest in it. Table 12.16 compares requirements for more product information from the two countries.

Thus, general information about advertising exposure in the United Kingdom and China combined with semantic issues relating to language and culture, has provided important branding information based on the viewpoints of UK compared to Chinese peoples, especially young Chinese adults. Such PR intelligence will inevitably expand in the current economic climate to inform multinationals, Chinese organizations and consultants alike, on how best to communicate with this large and important global sector.

Table 12.16 Advertisement by branded product information

	China	UK
Cosmetics, sanitation and hygiene products	M	
Advertisements for medicine, nutrition and health		M
Advertisements for consumer electrical appliances, e.g. fridge, microwave, etc.	O	O
Advertisements for household appliances, e.g. detergent, shampoo, soap, etc.	M	
Advertisements for daily necessities like watches, glasses, bikes, etc.	O	O
Advertisements for carpets, furniture and other interior decoration	M	
Advertisements for food and drink	M	
Advertisements for cars and motorcycles	M	
Advertisements for computers, photocopiers and other office products	M	
Advertisements for books, magazines, schools and education, etc.	M	
Advertisements for audiovisual equipment, eg. hi-fi, Walkman, TV, VCR, etc.	M	
Advertisements for fashion information, e.g. clothing, shoes, jewellery, etc.	O	O
Advertisements for entertainment like music, movie, travel, cameras, etc.	O	O

Source: Wen-Ling Liu (2003)

Notes: M indicates that the country demands more product information, $p < .001$. O indicates that both countries have no significant differences, $p > .05$.

NOTE

1   The Chinese names of international brands in the study have been reverse-translated into English literally. The translation may appear odd in English because (1) they are coined in such a way as a brand name; and (2) Chinese characters used in these names may have various interpretations in meaning.

REFERENCES

Fan, Y. (2000) 'A Classicification of Chinese culture', *Cross Cultural Management: An International Journal*, 7:2, 3–10.

Fan, Y. (2002a) 'The National image of global brands', *Journal of Brand Management*, 9:3, 180–192.

Fan, Y. (2002b) 'Globalbrand.com: standardised or localised communications?' Academy of Marketing Conference, Nottingham.

Fan, Y. and Pfitzenmaier, N. (2002) 'Event sponsorship in China', *Corporate Communication: An International Journal*, 7:2, 110–116.

Levitt, T. (1983) 'The globalization of markets', *Harvard Business Review*, May-June, 61:3, 92–102

Quelch, J. A. and Hoff, E. J. (1986) 'Customizing global marketing', *Harvard Business Review*, 64:3, 59–68.

Roth, M. S. (1995) 'Effects of global market conditions on brand image customisation and brand performance', *Journal of Advertising*, 24:4, 55–75.

Usunier, Jean-Claude. (2000) *Marketing across Cultures*, 3rd edn, London: FT Prentice Hall.

Wang, J. (1997) 'From four hundred million to more than one billion consumers: a brief history of the foreign advertising industry in China', *International Journal of Advertising*, 16:4, 241–260.

Wei, R. (1997) 'Emerging lifestyles in China and consequences for perception of advertising, buying behaviour and consumption preferences', *International Journal of Advertising*, 16:4, 261–276

Wu, X. (2002) 'Doing PR in China: a 2001 version – concepts, practices and some misperceptions', *Public Relation Quarterly*, Summer, 10–18.

Yin, J. (1999) 'International advertising strategies in China: a worldwide survey of foreign advertisers', *Journal of Advertising Research*, 39:6.

ACNielsen, www.acnielsen.com.cn

China Daily, www1.chinadaily.com.cn

China PR, www.chinapr.com.cn

Economic Daily, www.economicdaily.com.cn

Unilever, www.unilever.com.cn

CHAPTER 13

Today's corporate communication function

Michael B. Goodman

This chapter looks at a variety of management functions in relation to an organization's communication strategies for both internal and external stakeholders. It recognizes that technologies such as the internet underscore the global character of communication and that corporate communication has become a strategic tool for a corporation to gain competitive advantage. The chapter explores current trends in corporate communication and a variety of other important issues such as the role of business and communication; tools for communication practitioners; the building of relationships; and communication during change management.

Corporate communication (Goodman, 1994 and 1998) is the term used to describe a variety of management functions related to an organization's internal and external communications. Depending on the organization, corporate communication can include such traditional disciplines as: public relations, investor relations, employee relations, community relations, media relations, labour relations, government relations, technical communication, training and employee development, marketing communication, management communication. Many organizations also include philanthropic activity, crisis and emergency communication, and advertising as part of corporate communication functions.

Technologies such as the internet underscore the global character of communication. In practice, corporate communication is a strategic tool for the corporation to gain a competitive advantage. Corporations use it to lead, motivate, persuade, and inform employees – and the public as well. Understanding corporate communication provides the vision a company requires in an information-driven economy for strategic planning.

Corporate communication is more art than science. Its intellectual foundations began with the Greeks and Romans – with rhetoric. Its body of knowledge is interdisciplinary, drawing on the methods and findings of: anthropology; communication; language and linguistics; management and marketing; sociology; psychology.

Strategic importance of corporate communication

Communication has become vital to business growth since our economy has firmly based itself on information, rather than manufacturing. Customers, employees, investors, suppliers, and the general public now expect a high level of communication and candour from the companies that operate in their community.

Even in an environment that extols the virtues of decentralization to meet customers' needs quickly, the value of a central management structure for communication makes sense for many organizations, particularly ones with global operations. A central group responsible for communication develops, projects, and maintains the corporation's image and culture. A communication group within an organization sets policy and guidelines to meet the strategic goal of developing and perpetuating a corporate image and culture, to project consistent messages, and to communicate with its various publics on a routine basis, as well as in emergency and crisis situations.

Current trends in corporate communication

Data from the Corporate Communication Institute's (CCI) Benchmark Study conducted November 1999 to March 2000, and the Council of Public Relations Firms (CPRF) Spending Study conducted February 2000 to April 2000 points to the trends in corporate communication. The Corporate Communication Institute conducted a study to set a benchmark for the practice of corporate com-

munication. The CCI surveyed corporate communication executives from Fortune 1000 companies and asked eighteen questions. Several of these focused on the functions of their work and the budget responsibilities for those functions. Other questions were asked about the executives themselves – age, educational background, gender, salary. The CCI also conducted phone and email interviews with selected respondents.

The Council of Public Relations Firms commissioned the CCI to conduct a study of the relationship between spending on corporate communication functions and its reputation as reported by Fortune in its annual ranking of the 'Most Admired'. These studies have implications for corporate communication practitioners:

- *Relationships with your community matter a great deal.* The CPRF Study indicated a positive, statistical relationship between what a corporation spends on its 'foundation activities' and its reputation ranking.
- *Culture is vital to organizational health.* Intangibles such as the culture of the organization form an inviting environment that can attract and retain quality people; or create one that encourages people to be less productive or to leave. A positive culture has become a standard for global corporations, such as: American Express, Boeing, General Electric, IBM, SONY, Johnson & Johnson.
- *Communication is strategic – now more than ever.* Many company executives consider communication as purely tactical in both its nature and its execution. In an information driven age, communication is an integral part of the corporate strategy. Strategic issues include an orientation of communication to an organization's pri-

orities, as well as toward the external environment. Integrity and credibility are the pillars of strategic communication. Realistic measurement systems and processes for improvement are strategic tools for success.

- *The age gap between managers and employees must factor into communication planning.* Sixty-eight per cent of corporate executives in charge of public affairs and employee communication (internal and external) – a large majority – are between 40 and 55 years of age. The workforce they manage is overwhelmingly younger. A 'generation gap' exists, but can be mitigated by applying the basic communication process, by conducting an audience analysis, and by focusing on the concerns of the workforce and the generation.

- *People in the workforce care more about themselves than the company.* Members of the contemporary workforce have been told since high school, and by parents and elders, that corporate life is not forever and no job has a guarantee. Is it any surprise they practise enlightened self-interest? How can a company expect employee loyalty in such an environment?

- *A company is expected to be a good corporate citizen, as well as to make money.* In the wake of diminished power among almost all power structures in our society – religion, government, the family – corporations have by default taken on a greater role in solving many of the ills of society. Social problems – substance abuse, sexual harassment, child care, elder care – have fallen to the corporations by default.

- *Media relations is more complex – no more old boy system.* In a 24/7/365 environment with scores of media outlets from

newspapers to broadcast to the internet, relationships with the media are no longer a matter of contacting a few old friends over a leisurely lunch. Each channel, each reporter, demands a professional relationship built on credibility.

- *The internet is just a tool; the internet is a strategy – truth is on the continuum.* Any anthropologist will tell you that a new tool in a human system changes that system. So the internet has changed dramatically the way people in corporations communicate internally and externally. It has at once created a sense of liberation, and also represents a constantly present taskmaster.

- *Speed is faster that it ever was.* Experts compare an internet year to a 'dog' year. Is it any wonder that people seem much older than their years? The speed of life has us live several lives in one lifetime.

- *Every company will have a crisis; prepare for it.* Crisis planning is informed by the Boy Scout motto: 'Be prepared'. The Boy Scouts, however, did not conceive that their court victory (a decision allowing the organization to bar gays from its ranks) could have resulted in a crisis of their own – donations from corporations drying up and communities barring their use of public facilities. Be prepared, indeed.

- *Writing is still the core skill for corporate communication.* The internet has underscored that writing of the highest order is still the major talent required of those who create and send the messages in and from our major corporations.

Some of the findings of our research indicate some changes in how we communicate at work. Others indicate changes in relationships between you and your workforce, as well as changes between you and the community your company is in. This brings us to our next question.

The role of business and communication

Communication is a constant corporate function and that role has changed. It is more complex, strategic and vital to the health of an organization than it was yesterday, and will only gain in importance in an information driven economy. It is tied to the messages created for all audiences – internal and external, paying and non-paying.

What are the functions of corporate communication? The CCI Benchmark Study asked whether or not corporate communication executives' responsibilities and budgets included twenty-four communication func-

Table 13.1 Corporate communication functions

Function	Responsibility (%)	Budget (%)
Communication strategy	95.6	N/A
Media relations	93.4	88.3
Public relations	93.4	80.3
Executive speeches	90.5	86.1
Crisis and emergency	89.8	77.4
Communication policy	86.9	N/A
Annual report	79.6	69.3
Corporate identity	75.2	67.9
Internet communication	73.7	59.1
Intranet communication	72.3	58.4
Community relations	66.4	56.9
Issues management	58.4	48.2
Advertising	56.2	42.3
Marketing communication	52.6	26.3
Corporate culture	48.9	39.4
Corporate philanthropy	46.7	41.6
Employee relations	43.8	82.5
Mission statement	38.0	29.9
Investor relations	27.0	19.7
Government relations	21.9	19.7
Ethics code	8.8	N/A
Labour relations	3.6	1.5

tions such as annual report, crisis, employee relations, internet, intranet, media relations, policy, strategy, and public relations. Some of the results are shown in Table 13.1.

These figures (Table 13.1) indicate the substantial involvement of corporate communication executives in communication actions central to corporate growth and survival. The responses also indicate substantial budgetary responsibility for traditional communication functions and a shared or matrix role in forging important corporate relationships with customers, vendors and investors.

And just how big are the corporate communication budgets of the Fortune 1000? According to the benchmark study:

Up to $500,000:	19.1 per cent
Up to $1,000,000:	14.0 per cent
Up to $5,000,000:	27.2 per cent
Up to $7,500,000:	14.7 per cent
Up to $10,000,000:	4.4 per cent
Over $10,000,000:	20.6 per cent

The Council on Public Relations Firms Spending Study asked more detailed questions about spending in the Fortune 500. The Spending Study found the following.

The 'typical' corporate communication department in the study had a budget of $7.5 million and a staff of ten professionals and three support staff. It was headed by a VP (often a senior or executive VP) who reported to the chief executive or chief operating officer, and expects next year's budget and staffing will both increase.

The range of spending on corporate communication was very large: $285,000 to $100 million. The mean was $21.6 million.

Among those companies whose budgets included them, the following were the largest line items:

- corporate advertising ($11.4 million);
- foundation funding ($8.1 million);
- social responsibility ($4.65 million, including community relations, non-foundation funding, etc.);
- government relations ($4.2 million);
- employee communication ($2.6 million);
- investor relations ($2.1 million).

These figures underscore that playing the communication game at the Fortune 500 level requires substantial resources in professional staff and financial commitment.

Importance of a corporate communication philosophy

Corporate mission statements and company philosophies are the products of executives who recognize the strategic value of a clear statement of what the corporation stands for, its goals, and its practices. Clear understanding and articulation of the company mission is the cornerstone for building an image in the minds of employees and the public.

Organizations committed to communicating with employees and the community have a definite communication philosophy. Companies may refer to it as their communication policy, or their mission statement. The philosophy may be articulated through statements of commitment to employees, customers and other stakeholders. The written statement of corporate commitment to goals and values is often the external manifestation of the communication philosophy. It is not necessary for a written statement to exist to have a philosophy, but if the written statement does not represent corporate behaviour and values, its hollowness will be apparent to everyone.

For companies operating globally, a strong corporate communication philosophy can offer the foundation for a code of ethics that applies throughout the world. Most corporations have an ethics code with a section on international business ethics.

The written mission statement defines the corporation, its goals and operating principles, and its values and beliefs. The first of these three parts is clear and brief. The presentation of goals and operating principles calls for more detail. The expression of a company's values and beliefs is difficult because people associate values and beliefs with philosophical or religious activities, not commercial ones. These statements cover a company's commitment to:

- quality and excellence;
- customer satisfaction;
- stockholder return on investment;
- profits and growth;
- employee relations;
- competition and competitiveness;
- relations with vendors;
- ethical behaviour;
- community relations and corporate citizenship;
- diversity in the workplace;
- preservation of the environment and resources.

A corporate code of conduct, ethics policy guidelines, or handbook of business practice expands the company mission statement. The written code acts as an implementation guide, and may include:

- policy regarding general business conduct; disclosure; compliance;
- workings of the corporate business ethics committee;
- compliance with laws;

- securities – insider information; financial inquiries
- disclosure of company information
- political contributions
- relations with government officials (domestic and foreign)
- commercial bribery – kickbacks, gifts
- record keeping
- anti-trust – Sherman and Clayton Acts
- mergers and acquisitions
- international operations.
• bidding, negotiation and performance of government contracts;
• conflict of interest;
• equal opportunity;
• working conditions;
• the environment.

Ethics and corporate citizenship

Professional organizations and societies, such as the Public Relations Society of America (PRSA), also issue standards of ethical practice for their members, and for the profession or industry as a whole. The American consumer has become highly sceptical of business practices and intolerant of companies that operate unethically. Maintaining the highest standards for propriety and ethical behaviour is the best approach to developing a reputation for honesty and integrity.

Over a quarter century ago in *The New York Times* Milton Friedman called corporate giving the equivalent of theft, 'spending someone else's money' to solve social problems that are the province of government. He defined a manager's moral mandate to 'make as much money for the stockholders as they can within the limits of the law and ethical custom'. A new generation of managers views Friedman's position as out of step with corporate citizenship. (Goodman, 1994, 1998) Put simply,

corporate citizenship is the acceptance of the corporation's role as a responsible and significant member of the community it is in.

Add to this the changes in the nature of stockholders since the 1987 crash from individuals, to institutions such as the enormous pension funds of TIAA and the states of New York and California, and the concept of responsibility meets the profit motive in a partnership that works for Levi's, L. L. Bean, Microsoft, and other successful companies. The message also came from over a decade of financially conservative government funds for social programmes which were prime candidates in the slashing of public budgets. So if government was out of the business of solving social problems, who would? Members of the community. They have increasingly come to include organizations and businesses. No longer was it sufficient for a business to only pay taxes and stay out of the affairs of the community.

Corporations who defined themselves as good corporate citizens overwhelmingly link their giving programmes to their business goals. Such corporate citizens supported education programmes, recycling and other environmental support programmes. Good corporate citizens measure and report their corporate efforts by:

• mentioning the activities in their annual report;
• publishing a 'public interest' report;
• featuring the activities in the company newsletter;
• issuing press releases;
• linking their citizenship actions to advertising and marketing themes.

Companies that have a long-term commitment to social responsibility are rewarded with greater name recognition, more productive employees, lower R&D costs, fewer regulatory hurdles, and stronger synergy among business units (Goodman, 1994, 1998). Acting as a good citizen, modern corporations have provided social services such as health care; or have funded public facilities such as parks, playgrounds, recreation buildings; or have entered a partnership with the community to maintain the infrastructure of highways and bridges. For corporations with research and development ties, the corporation often demonstrates its citizenship by support of employee membership and participation in professional, scientific, and scholarly societies and organizations. Such support includes attendance at conferences and encouragement to take leadership roles in the organizations.

Tools for the corporate communication practitioner

Organizations use personality profile instruments to find the right person for the job. A corporate communicator should have:

- written and speaking communication expertise;
- understanding of the communication process;
- interpersonal skills: face-to-face and telephone;
- media savvy;
- an understanding of customer, stakeholder, and community needs;
- curiosity;
- active listening skills;
- an understanding of advocacy.

In addition to excellent writing expertise, superior interpersonal skill, the ability to create media products – press releases, video,

web pages, magazine articles, newsletters – other tools need to be in the professional's toolbox to meet the challenge of change. A professional needs the ability to:

- teach;
- absorb and comprehend vast amounts of complex information quickly;
- create and build relationships internally and externally;
- build trust in all your audiences;
- build a corporate culture.

In addition, corporate communication demands an ability to solve problems in groups, to understand media and communication technology, to work ethically, and to feel comfortable in a global business environment. The elements of communication continue to exert substantial influence in all transactions from simple customer questions of front-line sales and retail personnel, to the pressure negotiations involved in a multinational merger.

Writing for organizations is growing in the form of web pages, newsletters, press releases and speeches, etc. All those are still there. Now much more work for individuals acting as vendors is the result of 'outsourcing'. The CCI Benchmark Study asked how corporate communication executives used vendors and agencies for their work. The most commonly cited were:

- advertising: 75.9 per cent
- annual report: 73.7 per cent
- internet: 46.0 per cent
- public relations: 43.1 per cent
- identity: 43.1 per cent
- media relations: 40.1 per cent
- marketing communication: 38.7 per cent
- crisis communication: 28.5 per cent
- intranet: 22.6 per cent
- investor relations: 18.2 per cent

Only 8.8 per cent use a vendor for community relations and for issues management, and 6.6 per cent use a vendor for employee relations and for labour relations. Less than 5 per cent of companies use vendors for communication policy, corporate culture, mission statement, corporate philanthropy. Creation of messages remains the work of the corporation itself with its own resources. It appears that vendors help with technology, production, distribution and execution.

Corporate communication has evolved into a complex profession, yet writing remains the central talent to create any communication in a corporate context. No matter what the medium of the final message, the ideas more often than not begin in writing. Understanding the writing process is fundamental to communication and media applications.

The writing process also serves as a model for the communication process, and emphasizes three main areas of analysis:

- audience,
- context,
- content (message).

Corporations routinely target a message for a particular audience, meeting their needs while achieving the company goals. Successful communication puts human interaction at its centre, and in a collaborative corporate environment seeks to win both for the organization and for its customers.

The type of person who has the ability to collaborate is someone who can see an issue from several perspectives and create a message based on analysis rather than on personal bias.

The ability to see a message as a graphic image, or series of images, is also essential. No one can deny the impact of visual media on how people gather and process information.

Curiosity is also a valuable personal attribute for professional communicators. The communicator must first have an interest in what is happening in the company and to its people and customers to be able to communicate that interest to others. Without interest, the writer's message is bland at best, at worst phoney and hollow.

Active listening is essential to effective communication, and builds a relationship of trust. Communicators understand the need for this fundamental business practice: listen to your customers and employees. Consideration of the ideas of others places value on them and on your relationship with them.

Understanding advocacy communication is also essential to corporate communicators. A company spokesperson may be called upon to put aside personal opinion in favour of a company position. Because of this fact of corporate life, the ideal corporate communicator is someone who has been with the organization for a long time.

Integrity is extremely valuable for any organization, and any corporate spokesperson should instil trust in the audience. Without trust, the message is unlikely to have the desired impact or much positive impact at all. Integrity and trust are built over time through attention to detail, consistency in message, follow-through on promises. It is reinforced in face-to-face contact with customers and employees through body language and eye contact, as well as words. Integrity and trust are built with every act and every message of an organization.

Groups and presentations

Corporations and organizations function through groups, and as collections of groups. Note the language: management team, quality circle, quality action team, management committee, board of directors, product management group, crisis committee.

Whether an organization emphasizes old-style hierarchical leadership techniques, what have been called Theory X, or more contemporary consensus management styles – Theory Y or Z, the ability to work effectively in and with groups is an essential element in a broader definition of corporate communication. The reengineering and quality programmes are built upon a foundation of shared commitment to corporate goals. Most communication at work occurs in small groups.

People give numerous presentations related to actions and projects. Companies and industries have their own particular presentation style. In engineering and high-tech firms, the presentations are straightforward and factual. Engineers prefer an analytical presentation of the facts. Visuals tend to be overhead projections, or slides in formal situations.

Management presentations, on the other hand, tend to be brief and direct with the use of slides and video. More effort, however, is spent on the form of the presentation than would be for an audience of technical experts. Managers expect a presentation of the options, alternatives, and solutions, rather than an analysis alone, because they need to see the results of an analysis. Decision makers, then, expect a polished presentation, not a slick one.

Increasingly, meetings are on interactive video networks, computer networks, and by email. Meetings can occur through computers, changing familiar patterns of eye contact, facial expression, and body language in face-to-face communication. Like the telephone, computer-mediated communication calls for a new etiquette of human interaction. As these customs and rules develop, the corporate communicators will be in the vanguard of the change.

Selecting media

Corporate communication requires professionals to determine the best media for both the message and the audience: high-technology digital multimedia to low-technology posters in the company lobby; a new company logo to a 'dress-down' day for employees are possible media for corporate messages. Selecting the right medium for the message plays a central role in the success of the communication. The corporate communication professional selects media, keeping in mind the message, the desired effect on the audience, and the corporate environment. Cost is always a factor since resources – time, talent, money – are limited and budgeted.

Negotiation skills for advocacy communication

Contemporary management experts identify at least six patterns of interaction in negotiations: win–win, win–lose, lose–lose, lose–win, win, or no-deal. Even though contemporary business is highly competitive, it is also extremely co-operative and interdependent. Win–win thinking seeks benefit in interactions, and selects agreements or solutions to problems that are mutually beneficial and satisfying. The contemporary business environment is one in which today's competitor is tomorrow's partner. Win–win builds an environment of trust since the solution is not your way or my way, but a better way.

Building a corporate communication culture

Forces within organizations shape and influence the behaviour of individuals in subtle, yet powerful ways. These forces, like the wind and the tides in natural environments, are often unseen and unnoticed themselves, but their effects can easily be observed. These forces combine to create the culture. Corporate culture (Deal and Kennedy 1982; Ott 1989; Goodman, 1994, 1998) has become a concept that, used appropriately, offers the intellectual tools for an insightful analysis of a organization's beliefs and behaviour. Used improperly, it devolves into jargon and faddism. In an anthropologist's terms, all human groups by their nature have a culture – the system of values and beliefs shaped by the experiences of life, historical tradition, social or class position, political events, ethnicity, and religious forces. In this context, a corporation's culture can be described, understood, nurtured and coaxed in new directions; but rarely created, planned or managed in the same way a company creates a product or service.

Nevertheless, an organization's culture plays a powerful role in its success, and in its failure. For this reason, the discussion of a corporation's culture offers a foundation for understanding the group's behaviour, and suggests ways to either perpetuate or change the cultures.

Deal and Kennedy popularized the term corporate culture in 1982. A corporation's culture, exhibits three levels:

1 artefacts and patterns of behaviour which can be observed, but whose meaning is not readily apparent;
2 values and beliefs which require an even greater level of awareness;
3 basic assumptions about human activity, human nature and human relationships, as well as assumptions about time, space, and reality; level three is often intuitive, invisible, or just below the level of awareness.

Examples of artefacts and behaviours abound: corporate logos, the company headquarters, annual reports, company awards dinners, the annual golf outing, the business attire at the main office. The artefacts and behaviours can be observed. Often these are outward manifestations of what the corporation believes and values, no matter what it says its values and beliefs are.

Examples of values and beliefs may be articulated in a slogan or an ad campaign, such as Ford's decades old, 'Quality is Job 1', or GE's 'We bring good things to life.' These are simple, yet effective ways to put into words what may be complex and difficult concepts. Both examples present a complex pledge from the company to its customers to create products that improve their lives. Companies that actually write a values statement find the task difficult because the written presentation too often sounds like the values statement of almost any company. Cliches and platitudes can make the most honest presentation seem hollow.

Basic assumptions, the third level, is even more difficult to articulate because it requires the analysis of both what the company says and an observation of what it does, then a synthesis to determine conflicting areas. One example of a fatal conflict between the projected basic assumption and what lay beneath the surface was the demise of investment houses E. F. Hutton and Drexel Burnham in the 1980s. Both companies quickly lost clients' trust when scandals surfaced which undermined the integrity a client expects from an investment bank.

Signs of a culture in trouble

Can a problem with corporate culture be identified? Weak cultures have no clear values or beliefs. Members often ask for an articulation or written statement of the mission of the group. When a mission statement is available, people in the organization routinely ridicule it as a fantasy having little to do with what the company really does. Weak cultures also exhibit many beliefs. That may appear to be tolerance, but no agreement on the most important beliefs plants seeds of confusion and undermines motivated employees. Some beliefs may develop into an ingrown and exclusive subculture, and the subculture values then pre-empt the company's. Destructive and disruptive heroes are apparent in cultures in trouble. In direct conflict with the organization's stated beliefs and values, an executive's abusive, harassing, or uncivilized behaviour may be ignored because he or she looks great on the bottom line. Other signs include disorganized rituals of day-to-day life resulting in a pervasive sense of fragmentation and inconsistency. People in the organization do not know what to expect from one day to the next. As a result, the organization develops an inward, short-term focus. Signs of such deterioration can be observed in low morale, emotional outbursts and subculture clashes.

Perpetuating corporate culture

If corporate culture can be understood through analysis and observation, and if it can be modified through change programmes, then corporate training can be used to nurture and perpetuate a culture that is desirable. Several methods on how a culture perpetuates itself, afford an opportunity for training:

- preselection and hiring of new employees;
- socialization of members;
- removal of members who do not fit in;
- presentation of behaviour appropriate to the culture;
- justification of behaviour that is beyond the norm;
- communication of cultural values and beliefs.

Many corporations have a clear idea of the kind of people they wish to hire and that profile provides them with a guide for recruiting. The analogy is a sports team that drafts players with certain talents and skills, but also with the ability to fit in with the other players. A corporation does the same thing.

Once a person is recruited and hired, the corporation requires the socialization of its new members through a formal orientation programme, followed by less formal socialization in the first few weeks and months on the job. Some organizations go further by instituting a mentoring programme to reinforce the corporate culture. Sometimes the match does not work out, so the member who does not fit must be removed. This is usually done within an initial probationary period. The performance appraisal has come to be the instrument for perpetuating the corporate culture. Appropriate behaviour is generally written in a formal employee handbook, a guide to ethical behaviour, and a company code of conduct. These documents function as the formal presentation of the company culture. The informal code is in normal activity, tradition, and company custom. When a member of the company breaks the customs, the corporation must justify this apparent deviation from acceptable behaviour.

Perpetuating the culture is vital to survival. Of the hundreds of automobile makers in

America some seventy years ago, only three major ones remain. Since chance and luck can happen to anyone, the survivors must have developed a culture that evolved with the changes in the market and technology.

Building relationships

Corporate relations

Corporate identity is more than the sum of these parts: mission statement; logo, letterhead, and annual report; advertising; internal perception programmes; external communication and public perception of company image. People learn to recognize a company by everything it does, from the products and services it sells, to its buildings and employees. Mergers and acquisitions, downsizing, and restructuring have treated corporate reputation and image rather roughly. From GM to IBM the face of business has changed dramatically. The need to build corporate identity through corporate culture has never been more important to a company's survival than it is leaving the twentieth century and entering the twenty-first. Corporate identity can be demonstrated through a traditional relationship with various publics. With the change in the American economy and way of life from rural to urban during and after the industrial revolution, the role of the organization in a community changed. No longer was it sufficient for a business to only pay taxes and stay out of the affairs of the community. Its presence there had a strong impact on the lives of the people. Public relations has come a long enlightened way since its beginnings when wealthy company owners handed out nickels to the crowds. The role of public relations is now a strategic element in the business plans of most corporations. Public relations plans contain clearly articulated goals, methods and measurements that coincide with larger corporate goals.

Community relations, or outreach programmes are now more closely allied to the core business. For instance, the public utility may sponsor and run a series of seminars at retirement homes and villages on coping with power outages due to a thunderstorm or hurricane. The same utility may offer courses for home owners in how to handle and repair electrical appliances safely. Other companies may donate services like a telephone bank or computers to help with fundraising. Often a company will set aside a day to help the local community by building a community playground or renovating a park. And more and more organizations are sponsoring a section of a highway for litter control, their participation indicated by signs along the roadside. Outreach programmes also include corporate education programmes in communities, schools and universities. Sometimes outreach programmes may include adult courses in first-aid, water-safety, crime prevention, recycling. Company representatives often speak at high schools or colleges about a career in an industry and one at the company in particular. Blood drives for the local Red Cross depend on corporate participation, as does the United Way. Companies also offer in-kind gifts such as used, but useful, office furniture and equipment to local charities and schools. During natural disasters, corporations are a valuable source of volunteers, as well as equipment, food, clothing and medical supplies. Such activities are often done with little or no fanfare depending on the corporate attitude toward volunteerism.

Government relations is the meeting with local, state, federal and in some cases international agencies to advocate for the corporation on matters in its interest. Some corporations will provide legislators and agency professionals with position papers and information designed to inform and persuade the agency. In the marketplace of ideas, such advocacy efforts often make the decision clear. Individual corporations have in recent years avoided direct lobbying efforts in favour of joining an industry advocacy group that does that work for all companies in a given industry. Because of abuses in the past in trying to influence the government decision-making process, this area of corporate communication demands the highest ethical standards. Each company develops its own code of business conduct which often includes standards and procedures for ethical practices with fellow employees and subordinates, with customers, with vendors, with the community and with the government.

Customer relations is considered the 'front porch' of the corporation. How a corporation routinely treats customers and vendors, as well as how it handles an angry customer's complaint about a product or service, form the foundation on which the corporation's image is built in the minds of individuals. It can be inviting and co-operative, or cold and impersonal. Successful companies make every effort to meet customers' needs. The old cliché, 'The customer is always right', is not a cliché for most companies. It is an informing philosophy. It is also a central principle in the quality movements that have infatuated American businesses through the 1980s and 1990s. Satisfied customers come back again. Disgruntled customers do not; and they also tell at least ten others about their bad experience. Good customer relations depends on positive word-of-mouth. The service industry has made customer relations not only central to the company business strategy, but an art form. In a market driven economy, companies with close relationships with their customers have a better chance of surviving difficult periods than companies that do not listen to their customers. Solid, positive relations with customers is a fundamental part of the quality revolution in America.

Media relations

Creating good media relations requires constant effort and attention, and a mature corporate attitude toward the public and the media. The contemporary business environment is awash with media – newspapers, magazines, professional and industrial journals, TV, business radio, multimedia, the worldwide web. Corporations spend millions on marketing and advertising so their message can reach their current and potential customers. If the press sees a corporation's product or service as news, then it will write or broadcast a story. Many organizations measure the media coverage in terms of the equivalent cost of advertising. Coverage is the goal of any media relations plan. Good relations with the press result when the reporter checks with the corporation to validate statements and facts. Their contact offers an opportunity to set the record straight, or put the facts into a clearer, more objective, context. Rumours and inaccuracies can be corrected.

Developing a media strategy

A media strategy is important locally and globally. The process follows a four-step problem-solving model.

- *Define the problems*. Write a problem statement, and analyse the situation. The analysis requires gathering, processing and interpreting information. Listening and observing are fundamental methods. The interpretation of information helps to confirm the problem statement, or to restate it in a new light. The analysis should lead to planning.

- *Plan.* Articulate goals and objectives, and develop a programme of actions to achieve them. Identify the audiences or 'publics', the goals for each, and the message and media strategies determined to meet the goals. Budget time and other resources that must be committed to the programme. Planning also involves the evaluation of the performance of the programme.

- *Implement plans and communicate messages.* The fundamentals of the communication process offer the key to successful implementation. Understanding the corporate goals and objectives, fitting them to the audience needs and expectations, and being mindful of the context in which the communication occurs applies. The goal is to change the thinking and behaviour of the audience.

- *Evaluate.* Evaluation of the effectiveness of the programme can vary from the number of column inches or the number of minutes on the air the effort generated; to the increased awareness of the issues measured in the target audience; to changes in attitudes, opinions, or behaviours; to evidence of economic, social or political change. The criteria and evaluation methods must be determined as the programme is planned and as it evolves.

Table 13.2 offers some suggested actions as guidelines for meeting the press. The information in the table is often cited by scholars and practitioners.

Investor relations

Building relationships with the investment community, a central function of corporate communication, demands clear, honest interaction. Not only is it good practice, but laws and regulations require full and fair disclosure of material information to the marketplace. The goal of this flow of information is to give analysts and investors the best information possible so they can fairly assess the value of your company. The information allows informed decisions about the strengths and prospects of companies.

Communication builds a company's mutually beneficial relationships with investors, analysts, and stockbrokers. Information about a company that is candid, complete, timely and honest is the foundation of a strong positive relationship. Companies help investors develop realistic expectations by providing accurate information for analysing results and making forecasts. The relationship keeps big surprises from occurring. Investors and analysts prefer companies that have predictable performance and provide reliable information. Once communication establishes the company's credibility, investor confidence in management grows.

A strong relationship with investors can help in flat or down quarters. Investors accept explanations, are more patient, and may be more inclined to hold the stock. Communication vehicles for investor relations are:

- *Printed matter*: company prospectus, annual reports, quarterly reports, 10K and 10Q reports, press releases, fact books, corporate background or overview statements, Securities Exchange Commission filings, the proxy statement.
- *Oral presentations*: annual meetings, briefings, conference calls, telephone contacts, audio tape reports.

Table 13.2 Meeting the press: some guidelines

Suggested action	Rationale
Be prepared	In an information society such as ours, having accurate data and timely statistics is expected. Not only are you giving your valuable time to discuss issues and events with the press, but their time is valuable also. So, do your homework, and prepare wisely for a press interview
Make your points	Have three main points you wish to get across. Just as you would in an executive summary of a report, or in a marketing communication, identify clearly the main ideas that make up the message you want communicated
Be concise	But avoid yes, no. Show awareness of the space and time limitations of the media by presenting positions clearly and concisely. Although brevity is a virtue, the press also looks for interest. Yes and no answers make the story difficult to write, and uninteresting for TV or radio
Get comfortable	Remember that movements and eye contact communicate non-verbally. When meeting face-to-face with the media prepare for the discussion by making sure that you will not be interrupted. A conference room set aside for outside guests is a good idea
Tell the truth	Building credibility with the media begins with their perception of you as a source of accurate and truthful information. Integrity is a valuable attribute. People react positively to people they perceive to be genuine. Being yourself is linked with telling the truth and is part of building corporate integrity
Use the printed word	Prepare for press encounters with a printed statement or press release. The document helps reporters get facts straight: figures, statistics, the spelling and titles of people mentioned. Remember the reporter's job is to report the facts, and getting accurate information includes often complex and detailed data
Keep your composure	The media must attract readers and viewers to sell advertising. Such pressure translates into the search for unusual or controversial angles. Journalists call this the 'hook', the means to capture the audience's attention. Offbeat, even offensive questions are a common tactic to elicit an emotional reaction that would make a good headline. So be cool under pressure
Think of the reader or viewer	Remember the importance of the audience in any communication. Consider how remarks would appear on the front page of the *New York Times* or the *Wall Street Journal*, or the local TV news, or on the national news
Say you don't know	When asked a question that stumps you, or requires information or data you do not have at hand, say you don't know. Follow up immediately with plans to get the information, and an offer to contact the reporter later, preferably before their deadline
Hypothetical questions, third-hand information	Reporters may ask questions that lead to speculation. Such questions are particularly common when corporate officers are asked to comment on possible mergers, anticipated layoffs, or restructuring. Also, if reporters cannot identify the source of their information, politely decline to discuss rumour and hearsay because of your company press policy
Sensitivity to deadlines	The daily production of newspapers and TV or radio broadcasts places strenuous demands on reporters to file their stories on time. It is a common courtesy to ask at the beginning of an interview when the reporter's deadline is
Accessibility	Give reporters a contact number, an email address, and a fax machine number to indicate that you will be available for follow-up questions as the story is being written, and later as a source for other stories
Forget 'off the record'	If you don't want something to appear in print, or broadcast, then don't say it
'No comment'	Finally, the press universally interprets the response 'no comment' as a ploy to hide something. Say clearly the company does not discuss proprietary issues, or matters that have personal impact on employees
Be human and tell the truth	

- *Electronic means*: email, broadcast fax, videotape reports, online information services and databases, the internet.

The annual report is the primary publication that is given freely to introduce the company to the outside world. It provides information on the company's progress and accomplishments for the investment community, stockholders, employees and the general public. An indirect but essential goal of the annual report, and one other way to justify its expensive production is its role in perpetuating the image and identity of the organization. Copies of the report not only go to all registered stockholders, but also to Wall Street analysts, the business press, students, libraries, vendors, trade associations and professional groups. The report is often a requirement in new business proposals to clients and the government, and frequently used for employee recruiting.

Given all these uses, every element of the annual report is designed to contribute to the positive image of the company:

- artful covers, excellent photography
- CEO's letter
- summary of accomplishments
- discussion of plans for the coming year
- auditors' statement and balance sheet
- ten-year comparison of financial highlights
- footnotes to satisfy Securities Exchange Commission regulations.

Communication in crisis

This section discusses stages of a crisis, planning for and managing a crisis, and responding during the crisis and after. The remainder covers crisis preparation through issues management.

Stages of a crisis

Many people who write about crises and management use a medical analogy. In the First World War, medics developed *triage* for rendering aid on the battlefield:

- not seriously wounded who could be treated and released;
- those near death for whom no amount of effort could make a difference; and
- those who would most likely recover if something were done immediately.

The *triage* model applies to communication and actions during the crisis itself, when time to contemplate and analyse is all but non-existent. The triage approach fits the management principle of applying limited resources for their greatest impact. Another model identifies the development of disease through stages: (1) prodromal, (2) acute, (3) chronic, (4) resolution to a normal state. In practice you can refer to (1) the precrisis stage, (2) the clear signs of a crisis, (3) the persistent reemergence of the crisis, and (4) the resolution. Airlines, utilities, computer operations, hospitals plan for the unthinkable because they have learned from painful experience that the unthinkable has a nasty habit of happening.

Crisis communication plans

In the past what happened in a business was literally no one else's business. Corporations cut off questions with a curt, 'No comment'. Such closed door policies create an information vacuum. With the trend toward sensationalism, many reporters will do just that, often in ways damaging to the organization.

Employees also fill the information vacuum, fuelling the rumour mill within an organization. Combine one disgruntled employee and one ruthless reporter and the result can be a major headache for the company, which can become the catalyst in a media feeding frenzy with unpredictable outcome. Co-operation with the media and employees is a much more prudent and mature policy for any organization to take in normal times and in times of crisis.

Planning for a crisis as a fact of corporate life is the first step in its resolution, and a subsequent return to normal operations. No one can predict when an event will occur, only that sometime in the life of an organization a product will fail, markets will evaporate because of a new invention, stock will fall, an employee may be caught doing something illegal, the CEO will retire, the workforce will go on strike, a natural disaster will occur, a terrorist will plant a bomb.

It is perfectly normal for executives to avoid thinking about a crisis. Positive thinking is embedded in the way managers are taught to be effective. Problems are opportunities; one person's misfortune is another's fortune – and so it goes. Admitting that a crisis could occur is to entertain the greatest of corporate sins: failure.

The tendency to ignore the worst also recognizes that people cannot control events. Being unable to control the forces of nature certainly does not mean weakness on the part of managers. It merely indicates that people must plan to deal with emergencies and their consequences. Weakness comes only when people do not prepare for events. Companies which get into trouble are often the ones which never considered that bad things would happen to them.

Emergencies, disasters, bomb threats, criminal charges, executive misconduct . . . None of these may happen, but a well run corporation develops plans in case the unthinkable occurs. Even the best run companies can and do have difficulties. Gerald Meyers identifies nine types of crises: (1) public perception, (2) sudden market shift, (3) product failure, (4) top management succession, (5) cash flow problems, (6) industrial relations, (7) hostile takeover, (8) adverse international events, (9) regulation and deregulation.

Planning for a crisis implies the people in the company can recognize a crisis when it occurs. People experience generally the same stages when faced with adversity or catastrophic loss: denial or isolation, anger, bargaining for time, depression and grief, and finally acceptance. An organization is no different since it is made up of people. Organizations experience: (1) shock, (2) a defensive retreat, (3) acknowledgment, (4) adaptation and change.

Responding to pressure groups and crisis preparation

Interest groups can make corporate life difficult for companies either through public demonstrations staged to capture media attention, through announced boycotts of products and services, through direct harassment of company executives and employees, or through terrorist acts directed at the corporation.

The conflicting power of *money* and *morality* is at the heart of understanding the social fabric of contemporary business. Freedom of choice, freedom of religion, free markets pull and tug at one another over the issues of the environment, sexual behaviour and practices, and behaviour that could corrupt the individual and the community. These issues represent the sharp edge of social change, potentially valuable in a dynamic free society, or a grave danger to the health of the corporation.

People on their own and in organized groups have been, and continue to be, extremely vocal on these social issues. They express their position with their pocketbooks. Monitoring social change is the best way a company can prepare itself for new markets, and for changes in existing customers' attitudes. Social change is often not indicated on the traditional balance sheets, but its power can be felt as changes influence the corporation and the community it serves.

During the 'greed' decade of the 1980s, the drive for profit forced many companies to rank very low the impact of their actions on customers, employees, and the greater social good. Driven by corporate councils and a philosophy that adhered to the letter of the law rather than its spirit, many corporate leaders asked 'Can we do it?' as opposed to 'Should we do it?' The environmental icons and popular culture symbols of disaster such as Chernobyl and Bhopal are the result. Companies can have their image tainted, and by extension their brands, through a simple act of indifference. According to Ottman, 'In this new marketing age, products are being evaluated not only on performance or price, but on the social responsibility of manufacturers' (Ottman, 1998). Consumers now look at the long-term impact of the product on society after it is used. The concept of quality in products now incorporates their environmental impact. Customers' needs, laws and regulations, and the reality of technology to simultaneously create new solutions to clean up the mess and also to cause a new mess, are the forces driving companies to include a 'green position' in their marketing, advertising and corporate communication.

Communication technologies

Knowledge is power. Electronic media offered the productivity and communication tools to usher in the information age to organizations. It was simultaneously a lever to flatten hierarchical organizations and to provide the means for an empowered and informed workforce. However, 'the paradise of shared knowledge and a more egalitarian working environment just isn't happening. Knowledge isn't really shared because management doesn't want to share authority and power' (Zuboff, 1996). Are these the signs of a failed revolution, or are they more likely the end of a cycle in which the organization and the individual continue the struggle for dominance?

Since the 1920s and 1930s, and through the depression, organizations worked toward the realization of a human relations model, described by Elton Mayo and expanded by Abraham Maslow.

These theorists articulated the twentieth century conflict between the needs of the individual and the needs of the organization. Then as now, this conflict remains the irreconcilable force of the industrial revolution, the post-industrial revolution, and of the information age. Our electronic communication tools highlight the paradox. A single person can influence the course of large organizations, such as in the case of Intel's troubled introduction of the Pentium chip in the winter of 1994–5. Such David and Goliath tales of organizational life make headlines. More often than not, though, it is the organization that still wields such power and influence that most contemporary Davids are overwhelmed almost effortlessly. Today David can be downsized, restructured, press-released, or budget-cut into submission. Or David can be worked into submission, his support staff replaced by productivity software, groupware and internet access.

Impact of electronic media

Tools, as anthropologists know, are the artefacts of a culture. Add a new tool to an existing culture, and it changes that culture. Our media technologies now allow us to communicate anytime, anywhere. The impact of a global, 24-hour workday has profound implications on our lives (Perugini 1996) and on how communication technology influences our society. Gates (1996) and Negroponte (1995) to the contrary, the change is not always positive. New media technologies – the tools of communication – continue to have a profound impact on corporate communication. By their nature innovations are tools, which may or may not require us to change our behaviour. Technologies that require us to change, Moore (1991) calls 'discontinuous innovations' and these tools are not user-friendly. As such they are often doomed to failure, or require several iterations to attract acceptance.

The issues that face communication professionals focus on human interaction – both with machines and with other people. The use of contemporary communication technologies in an environment of accelerating change, political uncertainty, economic stress, and uncertain corporate direction places new demands on the communication professional. No longer is mere superior talent with the written word sufficient. Understanding the ethical conflict of individual rights and corporate goals is necessary for survival. With increased emphasis on team action and the proliferation of empowerment programmes through TQM and re-engineering, the need to work effectively with others, rather than in isolation, is also a fact of corporate life for communication professionals.

Information technologies have changed the way we create, archive, access and distribute information. New technologies have made the access to, and use of, information more egalitarian, less proprietary. Gatekeepers have been eliminated and new classes have emerged – the information haves and the information have-nots. Some experts (Zonis, 1996) see a global destabilization as a result of these technical advances, for example, a rapid breakdown in the power structure of business, the family, and political organizations. However, the equalizing power of information has flattened the hierarchical nature of organizations. With hierarchies disappearing, egalitarian and collaborative structures are emerging. The workplace, the nature of work, and the fabric of our society entered a change cycle that is rapid and unrelenting. Once the relationship between individuals and the institutions of our culture could be relied upon. A bond existed that engendered trust and loyalty; however, contemporary executives find these rare commodities indeed.

Email links computers to send messages from one computer to another. The systems have global reach through various networks such as the internet and commercial providers. These electronic communication channels save time and distribute costs. Messages can be posted on a general bulletin board which anyone on the system can have access to, or sent to a distribution list, or to one person on the network. In many organizations email has replaced the use of and the need for informational memos. Using email to replace paper memos and physical distribution of those documents has substantially accelerated the communication within organizations.

LANs (local area networks) function similarly to email, but they are several computers in a particular location linked to form a network that allows the users to share data and programmes. LANs have the outward appearance of a centralized computer, but the system functions more like a bundle of cells.

The internet and the worldwide web came into wide commercial use after 1994. Companies have built web pages for fear of being left out of this technological revolution. The internet may fulfil the predictions as interfaces improve, the infrastructure gets better, security becomes tighter, bandwidth becomes higher, and full motion video is added. Sceptics see the open architecture of the internet and the worldwide web as its reason for success, as well as its commercial weakness. Designed by the Defense Advanced Research Projects Agency (DARPA) to be able to withstand the catastrophic damage of a nuclear holocaust, its strength is in its open nature. So security of proprietary company data cannot be protected in this environment with high confidence. Nevertheless, almost every company has an internet address, up from fewer than half in 1995.

Communicating change

What has changed in audiences and communication channels? Globalization, women, Gen-X, Gen-Y, Gen-Z, Gen-Jones, the digital generation . . .

The need to develop and maintain the organization's culture has added to the challenge of corporate communication. Employees are no longer captives to the organization. They move often from job to job. They learned their lesson well from the experience of the decades of downsizing, restructuring, mergers and acquisitions.

They were told in school and observed from their parents that corporations and organizations would not have a job for them for life. They were taught in high school and college to see each job as a learning experience for them to prepare for the next job in their career path. Service was self-service, so they have no role models for understanding the concept of the value-added nature of customer relations.

Enlightened self-interest was the appropriate way to think about their place in the world of work. They saw what happened to their fathers and mothers who committed themselves to work and a life of delayed gratification – downsized at 55 just short of their pension and other benefits.

Now the challenge is to motivate a generation of workers who have priorities vastly different from the priorities of the company. The work/life balance for corporations places work first. For the new workforce, the work/life balance means *life balance.*

The change process

The change process emphasizes a rethinking in management practices from hierarchical, authoritarian relations among managers and employees, to a consensus approach. The focus is on teams empowered to identify and solve problems, and implement solutions. Communication and a new customer orientation are the cornerstones of the change in both company attitudes and practices, requiring corporations to make massive changes in the way people communicate within the organization and with those outside. Corporations continue constant and unrelenting change – reinventing, rethinking, transforming and re-engineering themselves. Change also brings chaos, uncertainty and renewal. For everyone involved, change represents a threat to security, or an opportunity to move forward.

New and powerful forces are at work in changing corporations:

- *New sophistication in customers or audience*. The force of the customer is felt everywhere from consumer electronics, to the use of new management tools such as integrated product development (IPD) in traditionally conservative, hierarchical organizations. Customers at all levels demand quality products and are hungry for information about the products they want. They are also looking for stimulation and entertainment, which has profound implications for such fields as software interfaces and the development of the information super highway.
- *New media technologies*. The number of communication channels available is increasing: email, fax, voicemail, desktop publishing, personalized magazines and journals, networking software and groupware, the worldwide web. Because there are more tools and more choices, consumers need more information than ever before.
- *More widespread ethical environment*. Since the tools of our technological age have enormous social and economic impact, the ethics of the workplace must be considered. No longer can a corporation make a product and not worry, or care, about its impact on the community. Companies now function as 'corporate citizens'. New methods of regulation and new laws underscore the responsibility customers expect of providers. The workforce in America is becoming more diverse in ethnicity, race, gender and age. The need for individuals to work in groups or teams at work has increased as a result of greater technological complexity in the nature of work itself. Even before the building of the pyramids of Egypt large projects demanded group efforts. Technological effort in the 1990s and into the twenty-first century implies that individuals from a wide variety of backgrounds work together in groups. The quality process itself depends on groups of professionals and technicians at all levels working together to achieve the common goals of the group. Interpersonal communication skill which begins with understanding and respect for each of the people in the group is the key to successful group performance. In a corporate culture of decision making by consensus, the efficient and effective interaction of members of a group is essential for communication. Prejudice and bigotry have no place in corporate America.
- *Stronger economic factors*. Competition has been the strongest economic factor for change in corporations. It has forced the quest for quality and efficiency as co-equal goals in a company's strategy. It has also forced the rapid growth in globalism.
- *New strategic alliances*. Ventures, partnerships, reorganizations, mergers, acquisitions, buy-outs, re-engineering, downsizing, rightsizing – more than buzzwords, these are the codes for a workplace in upheaval. Almost every organization has undergone, or is undergoing, a profound change in structure or ownership. The new alliances, if managed well and communicated clearly, signal a different way of thinking about work in general, and about the workplace itself.

Qualities of organizations and people necessary for successful change

An individual who sees the challenge of widespread changes in work processes and outcomes is best suited for technical innovation and change. This person comes to work smiling, often arriving early and leaving late. No matter how much chaos the organization is in, this person appears to respond well to the situation.

Others in the organization respond less well to change and exhibit dysfunctional behaviour. There are degrees of dysfunctional behaviour related to change. For instance, examples of a low degree of dysfunction are: poor communication, reduced trust, blaming, defensiveness, increased conflict with fellow workers, decreased team effectiveness, inappropriate outbursts at the office. Moderate dysfunction: lying or deception, chronic lateness or absenteeism, symptoms such as headaches and stomach pains, apathy, interpersonal withdrawal. A high degree of dysfunction: covert undermining of leadership, overt blocking, actively promoting a negative attitude in others, sabotage, substance abuse, physical or psychological breakdown, family abuse, violence, murder, suicide.

The person who responds well to change exhibits buoyancy, elasticity, resilience – the ability to recover quickly from change. Such people possess a strong, positive sense of self, which gives them the security and confidence to meet new challenges, even if they do not have all the answers. They are focused on a clear vision of what they wish to accomplish and they are tenacious in making the vision a reality. In addition, these people tend to be accommodating and flexible in the face of uncertainty, and organized in the way they develop an approach for managing ambiguity.

They engage the circumstances, rather than defend against change.

Such a person practises fairness, integrity, honesty, human dignity – the principles that provide the security to adapt to change.

Understanding and managing expectations helps an individual or an organization through the change cycle. Rather than lower expectations, manage them. In doing so, consider that in responding to positive change most people go through phases:

1   uninformed optimism or certainty at the start;
2   informed pessimism or doubt – people may quit publicly, or more destructively they quit privately and continue to work, allowing the negative feelings to generate dysfunctional behaviour;
3   hope emerges with a sense of reality;
4   informed optimism results in confidence;
5   satisfaction closes the cycle of change.

The good news is the cycle is predictable and can be used to manage expectations by helping people prepare for the rough periods. The bad news is most people feel they are an exception and they will not follow the cycle from beginning to completion. People neglect to consider that change carries an equal opportunity for failure.

The language of change

Often people react to new situations without fully realizing their true feelings; nor can they articulate them. The metaphors they use reveal and shape their understanding of events. The metaphors of change can be roughly aligned with four types of organizational change: *maintenance, developmental, transitional, transformational*.

- In *maintenance*, change is equated with something broken or poorly maintained. Change means that something is wrong and needs to be fixed. The metaphor provokes a fix and maintain image represented by agents such as a mechanic, maintenance worker, or 'repairperson'.
- In *developmental*, change builds on the past and leads to better performance over time. In this environment teamwork is the key to build and develop. The agent is often called trainer, coach, mentor, facilitator, or developer. You might hear metaphors borrowed from sports, 'There is no 'I' in 'TEAM'.
- *Transitional* change involves a move from one condition to another. For instance an operation goes from manual to automated. The image is often one of movement and relocation and the agents are often called planners, guides, or explorers. In such environments you might 'need to create a map for unexplored territory'.
- *Transformational* change implies the transfiguration from one state of being to a fundamentally different one. An example might be a business or industry that changes from a regulated monopoly to a market-driven competitive business. The image is one of liberation, and the agents are called visionary, creator, liberator.

Understanding and using the language of change benefits everyone involved, and helps them perceive change as an opportunity to move forward, rather than as a threat to their well-being.

Communication in international environments

'Act local, think global' has become a familiar business mantra. The simplicity of the phrase can lure the unsuspecting into a simple-minded interpretation. Much has been written on the need to compete in global markets. The reality is that doing business in another country is complex and difficult. For a start, it demands familiarity with the history, the politics, the alliances and treaties, the art and literature of a country. An effective approach to learning about the transnational environment also includes an understanding of: language, technology and the environment, social organization, contexts and face-saving, concepts of authority, body language and non-verbal communication, concepts of time (Goodman, 1995).

Language

Doing business successfully demands attention to cultural, social, political and religious practices, in addition to technical, business, legal and financial activities. Communication is the key to each. Real communication – not cookbook do's and don'ts. The first step is to make every effort to learn the language. Almost all people notice your effort to learn their language. This is more than just symbolic. Language encodes culture, and making an attempt to understand the words leads to trying to understand the way people think. Learning the language helps to understand the way the people who speak it view their world. In addition to its power to convey information and ideas, language is also the vehicle for communicating values, beliefs and culture.

Technology and the environment

The way people view technology and their environment is culturally defined and has an impact on international business communication. The way people view human-created work environments differs in the perception of lighting, roominess, air temperature and humidity, access to electricity, telephones and computers. People perceive their relationship to the physical environment differently. For some, nature is to be controlled, for others it is neutral or negative, and for others it is something for man to be in harmony with. Even climate, topography, and population density have an impact on the way people perceive themselves, and that has an impact on the way they communicate, their concepts of mobility, and the way they carry on business. Western managers expect a clean and relatively quiet office; one with dependable lights, telephones, copiers, networked computers and email, temperature control. However, many countries ration essential services such as electricity. Transportation and housing may not meet western standards. The natural environment may be much hotter, colder, more humid or dryer than anticipated. Daylight in northern countries may be limited in winter, and almost endless in summer. Heat and rain may change the daily routine, particularly in the tropics. Be prepared to adapt.

Social organization

Social organization, or the influence of shared actions and institutions on the behaviour of the individual, has a strong impact on business communication. Institutions and structures reinforce social values – the consensus of a group of people that a certain behaviour has value. Familiarity with the major works of art and literature opens a window to the social organization of the country you are working in. These social structures influence business:

- family relationships;
- educational systems and ties to business;
- class and economic distinctions;
- religious, political and legal systems;
- professional organizations and unions;
- gender stereotypes and roles;
- emphasis on the group or the individual;
- concepts of distance and attachment to the land;
- recreational activity.

Contexts and face-saving

Contexts and face-saving refer to the way one communicates and the situation in which the communication occurs. Cultures are high-context, like the Japanese, and low-context like the German. In a high-context culture like the British, details about class and education and even the place of birth are apparent in one's clothes and accent. On the other hand, low-context cultures require almost photographic detail for clear meaning. People all over the world seek to preserve their outward dignity or prestige – face-saving. Cultures, however, differ in the emphasis on it. High face-saving cultures have these general characteristics:

- high context;
- indirect strategy for business communication;
- toleration of a high degree of generality, ambiguity and vagueness;
- indirect communication considered polite, civil, honest, considerate;
- direct communication considered offensive, uncivilized, inconsiderate;
- few words used to disclose personal information.

Low face-saving cultures have these general characteristics:

- low context;
- a direct strategy for business communication; confrontational;
- very low tolerance for generality, ambiguity and vagueness;
- indirect communication considered impolite, unproductive, dishonest, inconsiderate;
- direct communication considered professional, honest, considerate;
- written and spoken words used to disclose personal information.

Saving face is allied with concepts of guilt and shame. Shame is associated with high-context cultures; guilt with low. Low-context cultures value rules and the law; breaking the law or a rule implies a transgression – sin-and-guilt – as a mechanism for control. High-context cultures use shame as the agent of controlling behaviour through face, honour, dignity and obligation.

Concepts of authority

The concept of authority, influence and power, as well as how power is exercised in the workplace, differs from culture to culture. In western cultures power is the ability to make and act on decisions – an abstract ideal discussed and debated by philosophers and theorists. In Asian cultures, power and authority are almost the opposite of the western concepts. Power results from social order. Asians accept decision-making by consensus, and decide to be part of the group rather than the leader. Understanding the concept of power helps shape a business communication strategy. The direct approach to communication,

so effective in the west, may prove crude and offensive elsewhere.

Body language, nonverbal communication

Body language and nonverbal communication are just as important in international and cross-cultural communication as they are in communication within a homogeneous culture. Important elements in international communication are: kinesics (body movements); physical appearance and dress; eye contact; touching; proxemics (the space between people); paralanguage (sounds and gestures used in place of words); colours; numbers; alphabets; symbols (such as a national flag); smell.

Concepts of time

Concepts of time differ from culture to culture. Physicists such as Albert Einstein and Stephen Hawking, have demonstrated that time is relative. For purposes of communication across cultures, it helps to consider time as a social variable too. Time is defined culturally, and by shared social experience.

Corporate communication: meeting the challenge of the future

What is corporate communication, and who does it? Corporate communication is the total of a corporation's efforts to communicate effectively and profitably. It is a strategic action practised by professionals within an organization, or on behalf of a client. It is the creation and maintenance of strong internal and external relationships. The actions any particular corporation takes to achieve that goal depend in large part on the character of the organization and its relationship with its suppliers, its community, its employees and its customers.

Enormous changes in the workplace have had an impact on the communication practices of corporations and organizations. Avoiding print, broadcast and electronic media no longer suffices as adequate communication policy or even effective corporate communication. A policy of developing strong channels of communication both internally and externally has become a standard for most organizations.

Not only has the nature of corporate communication changed over the last few decades, the type of people who create the company messages has changed as well. The typical corporate communication professional is college educated with a degree in the humanities. A major in journalism, English, marketing, public relations, communication, or psychology is common. Generally, practitioners are loyal company people with a long record in the organization. This reflects the importance of the strategic nature of the organization's communication.

Often the professional has had a minor in economics or business, or depending on the company's core business, some related technical discipline such as engineering or computer science. This may be in stark contrast to a previous generation of business professionals with a background in law or accounting who have handled the company communication.

Using a communication professional underscored another shift in corporate communication emphasis from a total focus on the investment community or shareholders – any owner of the company's shares or stock – to a broader interpretation of community which now includes all 'stakeholders'. A stakeholder is anyone who has a stake in the organization's success: vendors, customers, employees, executives, the local barber and the kid on the paper route.

The explosion in the number and type of media available for communication has also had an impact on the communication professional. In the past, mastery of the written word was more than enough. Writing is still the core skill on which all others are built. But a mastery of essentials of broadcast media is now essential to the creation of corporate messages for TV, radio, email, cable news programmes devoted to business topics, multimedia and digital communication on computer networks, and public speeches.

When all is said and done

With all the changes in the nature of work, the tools, the people, the companies, maybe some simple guidelines might be helpful. How about Nordstrom's? They have two:

1   Use your best judgement
2   See rule 1.

Judgement, wisdom, understanding, integrity – develop and rely on them.

REFERENCES

Belkin, Lisa (2000) 'Life's work', *New York Times*, 5 July, G1.

Chronical of Higher Education (2000) 'Remember when? This fall's freshmen may not', 8 September, A10.

'Corporate Communication Benchmark Study' (2000) Corporate Communication Institute, (www.corporatecomm.org)

'Corporate Communication Spending Study' (2000) Corporate Communication Institute for the Council of Public Relations Firms.

Deal, Terrence and Kennedy, Allan (1982) *Corporate Cultures*, Reading, MA: Addison-Wesley.

Deal, Terrence and Kennedy, Allan (1999) *The New Corporate Cultures*, Reading, MA: Perseus Books.

Gardyn, Rebecca (2000) 'Who's the boss? The new American worker', *American Demographics* September, 53–9.

Gates, Bill (1996) *The Road Ahead*, New York: Viking.

Goode, Erica (2000) 'How culture molds habits of thought', *New York Times*, 8 August, D1 and 4.

Goodman, Michael B. (1994) *Corporate Communication: Theory and Practice*, Albany: SUNY Press.

Goodman, Michael B. (1995) *Working in a Global Environment*, New York: IEEE Press.

Goodman, Michael B. (1998) *Corporate Communication for Executives*, Albany: SUNY Press.

McClain, Dylan Loeb (2000) 'Forget the raise, give me some time off', *New York Times*, 12 July, G1.

Meyers, Gerald (1986) *When It Hits the Fan: Managing the Nine Crises of Business*, Boston: Houghton Mifflin.

Moore, Geoffrey (1991) *Crossing the Chasm*, New York: Harper.

Negroponte, Nicholas (1995) *Being Digital*, New York: Knopf.

Ott, J. Steven (1989) *The Organisational Culture Perspective*, Pacific Grove, CA: Brooks/Cole.

Ottman, Jacquelyn (1998) *Green Marketing*, Lincolnwood, IL: NTC Business Books.

Perugini, Valerie (1996) 'Anytime, anywhere', *IEEE Transactions on Professional Communication*, 39(1), 4–15.

Tahmincioglu, Eve (2000) 'To shirkers, the days of whine and roses', *New York Times*, 19 July, G1.

Tapscott, Dan (1998) *Growing Up Digital: The Rise of the Net Generation*, New York: McGraw-Hill.

Wellner, Alison Stein (2000) 'Generational divide', *American Demographics*, October, 52–8.

Wellner, Alison Stein (2000) 'Generation Z', *American Demographics*, September, 61–4.

Zonis, Marvin (1996) Speech at Chicago Graduate School of Business's 'Business Forecast '97' New York, December.

Zuboff, Shoshana (1996) In *The New York Times*, 4 November, D1.

CHAPTER 14

Assessing integrated corporate communication

David Pickton

With the expanding remit of corporate communication and the realization that much of its function overlaps the boundaries of other established professions, how can corporate communication professionals provide to key stakeholders such as sales and marketing specialists, a coherent and synergistic approach to communication? One answer, perhaps, lies in an integrated corporate communication (ICC) strategy which can provide a practical guide. Standard assessments of any ICC strategy can be made through the use of two suggested frameworks: namely dimensions of integration and continuum of integration, both of which 'add value' to the employer and offer a way of looking at the communication role functionally, strategically and managerially.

Corporate communication spreads its tentacles throughout and far beyond the marketing function to the organization as a whole. Defining and delineating its boundaries is difficult and can be arbitrary. Overlaps exist between corporate and marketing communication and arguments are rife as to which subsumes the other. Some of the debate is semantic and superfluous. Other aspects are born out of the development of 'functional silos' (Schultz, 1993). What is not contested is the multifarious nature of corporate communication and in recent years a spotlight has turned towards a deeper understanding of the synergistic benefits of *integrated* communication. However, the full extent of the integration process is rarely fully articulated or understood. Wolter (1993) has complained (at least in the past) that it suffers from superficiality, ambiguity and rigidity. Whilst ensuring the effectiveness and efficiency of each aspect of corporate communication is clearly important, so too is the need to manage and evaluate the impact and efficacy of the myriad communication activities that come together (White, 1997) either to work in harmony or disrupt one another. This can be considered at a variety of 'levels' from the individual campaign to the holistic corporate communication effort (see Figure 14.1).

Integrated corporate communication (ICC) is not a new concept and the simple argument

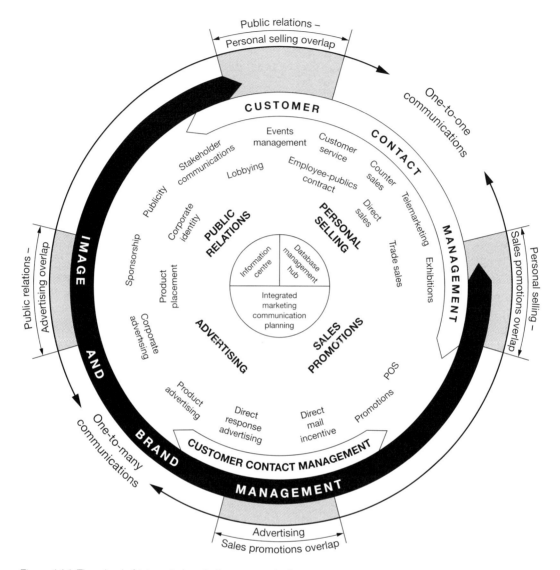

Figure 14.1 The wheel of integrated marketing communication

for integration is that there are financial, competitive and effectiveness benefits to be achieved through the *synergy* afforded by the process of integration (Pickton, 2001).

Yet it is not easily achieved as there are many difficulties that stand in its way. As Van Riel (1995: 3) comments, 'In practice, the large variety of internal communication "sources" can lead to fragmented, sometimes even contradictory, external manifestations of the company as a whole . . . It thus becomes clear why it is possible to observe a tendency to strive for increased mutual coherence between all forms of internal and external communication.' Integration has to be operationalized and to do so involves the development of working relationships with groups that may, in the past, have been antagonistic towards each other. 'Elitist' attitudes are commonplace (Robbs and Taubler, 1996; Gonring, 1994; Swan, 1993) with each communication 'specialism' claiming greater significance over the others (e.g. Varey, 1998). For integration to succeed, the perspectives of all involved need to be viewed together but the very fragmented nature of organizations, their management and the agencies within the communication industry impose problems. Varey and White (2000) argue for a total stakeholder perspective and the need to integrate communication activities around constituent–constituent relationships.

A consequence of integration should be that corporate communication is coherent. This was recognized by Meffert (1979), an early protagonist of integration, and consistency should exist between all elements involved. Corporate communication should become both more efficient and effective and this is all the more imperative when it is argued that it plays a dominant role in achieving organizational growth (Varey, 1998). Linton and Morley (1995) list ten potential benefits of integration which they relate to marketing communication but the benefits can be equally applied to corporate communication as a whole. Within their list are included creative integrity, consistency of messages, better use of media, cost savings and operational efficiency. An example of an integrated campaign that worked very successfully was that for the Tunisian Tourist Board. Despite a fast-developing infrastructure, research showed that people in the United Kingdom and Ireland believed it to be a long-haul destination with poor hotels and little more than a few camels for entertainment. The Tunisian Tourist Board employed a new agency who simultaneously strove to

create a new image for the country while convincing travel agents in the United Kingdom and Ireland that it was a competitive destination in order to drive up bookings. The agency redesigned the Tunisian tourist logo and developed a new range of literature to convey a more modern feel than previous brochures. They devised the new strap line, 'More from the Mediterranean', to reinforce the message that Tunisia is as close as many popular Mediterranean resorts. To bring the trade on board, the agency briefed operators on the campaign and ran a series of initiatives to stimulate interest. They sponsored the premiere of the movie *The English Patient* which was filmed in Tunisia. To target consumers, the agency leafleted cinemas and ran a PR programme to highlight the appeal of Tunisia and its culture. Tunisia's first TV advertising for a decade was created. Selected press and poster advertising was underpinned by a new website. In all these ways, a variety of audiences was reached with a variety of media with consistent and coherent messages in a very cost efficient way. The total communication process was managed as an integrated whole. The outcomes were changed attitudes by consumers and trade alike and increased tourism resulted. The Tourist Board was voted best in the UK annual awards. Bookings to Tunisia from the United Kingdom and Ireland increased by almost 30 per cent year on year.

Whilst it is argued that corporate communication should be integrated, the extent of integration can vary enormously. Corporate communication activities can vary from very small, 'one-off', discrete pieces of communication (such as the mailing of a corporate brochure), to the development of a larger campaign which involves many promotional tools, and even to the development and co-ordination of multiple campaigns intended to achieve a greater goal possibly over an extended time period in many countries. The need for integration and the scale of that integration becomes greater as the size and number of campaigns increase. It is necessary to determine just how important it is that all messages and images should be consistent or whether they can remain completely detached and, if so, what impact this is likely to have on total effect. Particularly sensitive times are when organizational crises occur and the corporate communications 'machine' has to be mobilized for damage limitation and, if possible, gain positive attribution.

Key features of integrated corporate communication

In its simplest form, integrated corporate communication (ICC) is the bringing together of all relevant corporate communication activities. However, this belies the rather more complex and significant managerial implications of integration that affect the entire organization together with its relationships with its communication agencies and external audiences. Van Riel (1995) recognized these implications when he described corporate communication as the integration of management communication, marketing communication and organizational communication. What, then, might integrated corporate communication incorporate?

Features of integrated corporate communication

- Clearly identified corporate communication objectives that are consistent with other organizational objectives.
- Planned approach which covers the full extent of corporate communication activities in a coherent and synergistic way.

- Coverage of a range of target audiences embracing all relevant stakeholders and publics.
- Effective management of all forms of contact which may form the basis of corporate communication activity.
- Effective management and integration of all communication activities and people involved.
- Identification and recognition of the impact of all product/brand communication on corporate communication efforts.
- Exploitation of a range of promotional tools – all elements of the communication mix including personal and non-personal communication.
- Use of a range of messages – brand (corporate and products) propositions should be derived from a single consistent strategy. This does *not* necessarily imply a single, standardized message. Integrated corporate communication effort should ensure that all messages are determined in such a way as to work to each other's mutual benefit or at least minimize incongruity.
- Use of a range of media – defined as any 'vehicle' able to transmit corporate communication messages and not just mass or printed media.

The challenge to management is to assimilate the various facets of corporate communication identified above in a way that appears seamless and co-ordinated. This is integration, or what some prefer to call 'orchestration' and 'joined-up thinking'. As will be shown later, any evaluation of the success or otherwise of ICC should involve an assessment of how well these features are brought together. While many may comment on how common-sensical is the list of features above, there remain practical difficulties in achieving their orchestration.

Barriers to integrated corporate communication

The concept of integration is warmly embraced by some but argued against by others, sometimes for what they consider to be the sheer impracticality of integration. What is indisputable, however, is the fact that the whole communication business is going through a period of change which is having a significant impact upon working practices and philosophies. Developments in database technologies are encouraging and facilitating integration but as Fletcher et al. (1994) have discovered there are major organizational barriers which can arise when a company attempts to move towards database management in any significant way. There has been growth in international communication and global branding requiring a much more integrated approach. Companies have become more sophisticated in their understanding and in their demands for communication services involving the whole organization targeted towards multifarious audiences. There has been increasing awareness of brand value and brand equity and the role played by corporate reputation. Despite such impetus for integration it is not easily achieved. While the problems of integration are not insurmountable they are significant for a variety of reasons and these present barriers to the process.

Mindset

The mindset built up over many years of practice has rewarded specialization and overlooked the need for, and benefits of, integration. Gonring (1994) has identified the fear of change and loss of control felt by individuals associated with the communication

business. Robbs and Taubler (1996) have highlighted creatives' aversion to integration and their lack of willingness to work across the media and communication mix. Schultz (1993) has commented on the cult of specialization and the history, tradition and experience of companies as limiting factors to the fulfilment of integration.

Moreover, there is the question of what it is that we wish to integrate. Hartley and Pickton (1997), for example, have discussed the developments in direct 'personal communication' and their inter-linkage with 'nonpersonal communication'. Exacerbating the problem, many organizations relegate communication activities to the tactical level and fail to appreciate their strategic significance. Any comprehensive approach to integration has to take the widest view, both strategic and tactical. A 'totally integrated communication programme accounts for all types of messages delivered by an organisation at every point where a stakeholder comes into contact with the company' (Moriarty, 1994: 38).

Taxonomy and language

The very taxonomy and language that are used to describe the communication mix have a detrimental effect on the integrative process (Hartley and Pickton, 1997). The result is that we perceive and encourage the uses of communication as discrete activities. This taxonomy (albeit it in simplified form) which typically identifies the mix as personal selling, advertising, sales promotion, sponsorship, publicity and point-of-purchase communication (Shimp, 1997), is increasingly inadequate in expressing the range of activities it seeks to describe and presents major classification difficulties. It is difficult, for example, to know where to place within the mix categories such varied activities as direct mail, product placement and endorsement, exhibitions, internal forms of communication, etc.

Structure of organizations

The structure of organizations may make it difficult to co-ordinate and manage disparate specialisms as one entity. Organizations have typically subdivided their tasks into subunits (departments) in order to cope with the magnitude of operations. Management's response when faced with large, many faceted tasks has been to disaggregate them and give them to specialists. While project teams and cross-functional assignments can help to break down organizational barriers there still remain problems of hierarchical structures, vertical communication, 'turf battles', power and 'functional silos' (Gonring, 1994; Schultz, 1993) in which individuals and groups are protective of their own specialization and interests. Significantly, the increasing use of database technology and systems offers new structural mechanisms for facilitating organizational integration.

Elitism

Not only do organizational structures encourage separatism, there is a sense of perceived elitism exhibited by individuals within each communication specialism. Public relations specialists extol their superiority over advertising specialists who likewise extol their virtues over public relations, direct mail and sales promotion, etc. (Varey, 1998). For as long as such views are held it is not likely that they will come as equals to the 'communication discussion table' to determine what is best for the total corporate communication effort.

Magnitude of task

It is very difficult to conceptualize the 'big picture' and to muster all the organizational influences needed to achieve integration. There are many levels and dimensions to integration which all pose their individual and collective difficulties. To be implemented, integrated corporate communication requires the involvement of the whole organization and its agents from the chief executive downwards. It needs consideration from the highest, corporate, strategic level down to the day-to-day implementation of individual tactical activity. Among the most significant findings from a collaborative study by Edelman Public Relations Worldwide, Northwestern University and Opinion Research Corporation in the United States were that the effectiveness of corporate communication was critically dependent on the level of the most senior communication executive and that there was too little corporate communication with employees (Morley, 1998).

Manager ability

The need for cross-disciplinary skills creates a barrier to ICC. The skills required are wide, with few possessing the ability to master them (Moriarty, 1994).

Dimensions of integration

There are many dimensions of integration. If integration of corporate communication is to be achieved the problem must be addressed in each dimension and between the dimensions. These dimensions or elements of integration range from ensuring that the communication mix and messages are integrated and targeted towards a variety of audiences to ensuring that integration is achieved between the many individuals and organizations involved in the process. Nine dimensions in total have been identified and these will be explained in more detail shortly.

Output vs. process measures

Measuring communication effects has been notoriously difficult. While some elements are relatively straightforward, others are less so and, because of the multiplicity of variables involved, spurious cause-and-effect relationships can be (incorrectly) claimed. In assessing communication, attention has previously tended to focus on 'output' measures to evaluate the results of communication; whether the activity has worked and to what extent – is the sale made, at what contribution; what coverage is achieved, how many column inches; what are the customer reactions, what is their recall of the latest campaign; how have the range of publics responded, to what extent do they hold positive attitudes; how are employees affected by internal communication, do they know the corporate mission and objectives; what impact have financial disclosures to the City had on share values; and so on.

Public relations utilizes an extensive array of communication tools each with its own purpose and outcomes and each requiring different means of assessment. Advertising is seen as a strong force by some (e.g. Jones, 1995), having a direct bearing on sales, whereas it is seen by others (e.g. Ehrenberg et al., 2000) as a weak force principally affect-

ing recognition and reinforcement. There is no agreement on how (or whether it is even possible) to use output measures to satisfactorily assess the full array of all the individual elements of corporate communication, let alone their combined effect. What should be used as appropriate measures of assessment is hotly contested. Furthermore, while a plethora of measures exist, it is the interplay and interaction of numerous variables that ultimately have an impact on the success or otherwise of the communication; consequently, arguments abound concerning the best use of output measures (important though they are).

An alternative perspective exists in which one might look at the 'process' of communication rather than its 'outputs' as a way of assessing its management and effectiveness. Duncan (1994) has observed that there are two ways to measure and control most operations – through the use of *output* controls and through the use of *process* controls. 'Output controls evaluate the results of programmes ... Process controls evaluate how programmes are developed ... Up to now, however, process controls have seldom been used in marketing (*and corporate*) communication' (p. 26). Having previously identified the importance of recognizing that integrated corporate communication is a managerial activity, it seems highly appropriate under these circumstances to adopt a 'process' driven approach to its assessment. To make sense of this and to 'map' the total integration process, two frameworks are presented below which will then be combined together to create an assessment profile (Figure 14.3) that can be used by managers as a development, evaluation and control tool. The first framework (Figure 14.2) is the 'Continuum of Integrated Corporate Communication'. The second is 'Dimensions of Integrated Corporate Communication'.

Continuum of ICC

Integration permits the opportunity for all corporate communication activities to build together to create a greater positive 'added value' than would otherwise be achieved by a loose collection of unconnected activities. It is rarely the case that corporate communication is either fully integrated or not and Figure 14.2 illustrates the concept of a 'continuum of integration'. On the right hand side of the figure, as a greater degree of integration is achieved, the greater the synergy in which more positive benefits result. At the central point there is limited integration of campaign elements but this results in only a neutral effect. Beyond this point and to the left there is an increased likelihood of each activity detracting from the others which can result in dysfunctional communication. The greater

the degree of separation and dysfunction, the greater the negative value of the corporate communication effort. The development of corporate communication which lacks integration therefore not only fails to add overall value through lack of *synergistic effects* but also runs the risk of having a negative impact through dysfunction. This is the cost of not integrating – producing communication that is counter-productive and which produces negative effects when one piece of communication contradicts or is at odds with another. The extent of integration deemed to be necessary is further complicated by the 'level' of integration required which can vary from the corporate down to the product brand or even to very local, one-off promotions. It is a matter of managerial decision and strategy as to what extent the corporate brand interacts with the product brand (contrast, for

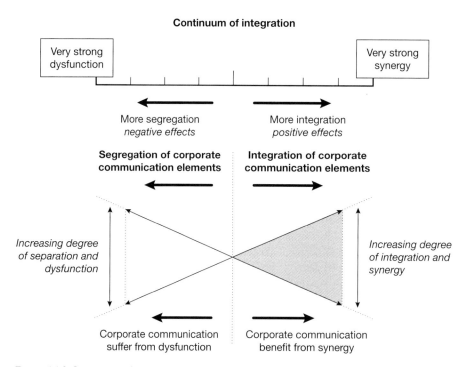

Figure 14.2 Continuum of integrated corporate communication

example, the different strategies adopted by Cadbury and Mars in the confectionery market) or how much freedom is given to local initiatives versus total central control.

Dimensions of integrated corporate communication

By considering the various features of ICC identified earlier it is possible to summarize and represent them as different 'dimensions' of integration. It is clear from even a casual perusal of these dimensions described below that a significant proportion of them are related to organizational issues. It may be argued that the most important implication of ICC is the impact it has on organizational structure, systems, relationships and management. Unless these facets are addressed it is unlikely that any true sense of integration can be achieved. It is possible that organizations and their agencies are misleading themselves currently if they believe they have taken anything more than the first tentative steps towards the integration of corporate communication. The way is clear for those who wish to fully embrace ICC to achieve strong competitive advantage over those who are only 'tinkering around at the edges'. But they will only achieve this if all those involved become willing partners in the process.

Communication mix integration

This is integration of the elements of the communication mix. Integrated corporate communication can be described as a 'concept of corporate communication planning that recognizes the added value of a comprehensive plan that evaluates the strategic roles of a variety of communication disciplines, e.g. general advertising, direct response, sales promotion and public relations – and combines these disciplines to provide clarity, consistency, and maximum communication impact' Such a description emphasizes the roles of each communication tool and its inter-relationship with the others. Implicit within this description is the need to integrate the objectives of each communication mix element and *all* the media used. Media should be recognized as any medium used for the transmission of messages.

Communication mix with marketing mix integration

This is integration of the elements of the communication mix with those of the marketing mix. Not only is it necessary to seek integration between the communication mix elements but, also, it is necessary to integrate these with all the other elements of the marketing mix and to integrate the objectives of them all while ensuring consistency with other organizational objectives. It should be recognized that each marketing mix element has a potential communication value. For example, the price charged, or the nature of the distribution, or the materials used in the manufacture of the product all have something to say about the brand and all have a communication impact. True integration involves integration of all marketing and communication elements.

Creative integration

This is integration of creative themes, concepts and messages across the myriad corporate communication activities. Creative integration need not imply the development of a single theme and message although in many cases this is the preferred approach because of the advantages generated by having a single coherent message. There are occasions, however, where such an approach is not necessary, for example where there are clear distinctions between the audience groups targeted, or where there are distinctive and separate product offerings, or where there are distinctive corporate entities (strategic business units or SBUs) even if they are part of a single conglomerate corporation. What is important is recognition that themes and messages should be planned together with an understanding of the impact they may have on each other.

Intra-organization integration

This is integration of all the relevant internal departments, individuals and activities *within* an organization which generate and impact upon corporate communication. Such integration may be achieved through restructuring or otherwise ensuring that communication between all parties is facilitated and managed. This includes the interlinking and integration of relevant management and business objectives and the provision of resources and budgets to facilitate integrated corporate communication. This might be described as the area of 'internal marketing'. Also included here is the *internal* management of all 'contacts' between stakeholder groups and the organization. Many believe this is a fundamental and distinguishing part of integrated corporate communication that can play a major role in achieving and sustaining competitive advantage.

Inter-organizational integration

This is integration with and between all external organizations involved in corporate communication on behalf of an organization.

This includes all relevant companies within a corporate organization, members of its distribution chains and the various agencies that work on their behalf, both above-the-line and below-the-line. By way of facilitating this, there has been, to some extent, a growth of agencies claiming to be 'through-the-line' providing a full range of corporate communication services 'under one roof'. There are arguments for and against such an approach.

Information and database systems

There is little dissent about the value of information and a well-managed database for integrated corporate communication. The role of database management is well recognized, 'As you integrate communication you must integrate marketing activities. To integrate marketing you must integrate sales and selling, and to integrate those functions, you must integrate the entire organization . . . The goal is to align the organization to serve consumers and customers. Databases are rapidly becoming the primary management tool that drives the organization's business strategy' (Schultz, 1997: 10). The focuses of corporate communication are the company's stakeholders and target audiences among whom are the consumers and customers. The more that is known about them, the more effective the organization's communication is likely to be. Today's databases can be very sophisticated. Computing power has created the ability to store and cross-analyse vast amounts of data such as service and sales data, all forms of transactional records, and attitudinal and behavioural data. There are many fields of data covering millions of relationships. Without this information it is unlikely that truly integrated corporate communication can exist.

Integration of communication targeted towards internal and external audiences

A variety of audiences, 'publics' and 'stakeholders', need to be considered within the context of a corporate communication campaign or variety of campaigns. The audience members may be both external and internal to the organization. They will represent a variety of potentially disparate groups. Integrated corporate communication needs to consider the roles and impact of each in order to manage the total process successfully.

Integration of corporate and 'unitized' communication

Corporate communication such as corporate identity is often perceived as a separate activity from 'unitized' communication (e.g. product, brand, personality, or trade communication) and it usually has different people responsible who act as 'corporate guardians'. Despite the separation, organizations clearly recognize the strategic and tactical impact of corporate identity on all their other promotions. However, some achieve this integration better than others. Some organizations use their corporate identity as the 'umbrella' under which they place all their brands. Other organizations choose to let their brands stand independently. Whichever the choice, the total corporate communication process has to be carefully controlled to ensure integration, consistency and clarity across all its different forms.

Geographical integration

This involves integration across national and international boundaries. Geographical inte-

gration is complicated through language, religious, cultural and regulatory variations. Whilst it may be obvious that corporate communication takes different forms in different countries, language, religious and cultural variations should also be recognized within national boundaries as well, sometimes within very small geographical areas. Belgium has the French and the Flemish; Spain has the Basques and the Catalans; Malaysia has the ethnic Chinese and the Malays; China has Mandarin speakers and Cantonese speakers; America has ethnic groups of many different origins. The task of successful integration and national and global branding is made significantly more complex because of these features.

The ICC assessment profile

By combining the concepts of the 'dimensions of integration' and the 'continuum of integration', it is possible to develop an instrument for assessing the 'quality of integration' of corporate communication. Figure 14.3 illustrates such an approach to the assessment of integration. This is presented as an assessment profile. The profile provides the basis for evaluating the overall extent to which integration of corporate communication has been achieved. It does not represent an objective output measurement but is based on subjective appraisal of the various facets and process of integration. Output measures may be included in the use of the profile if so wished.

The degree of integration may vary from being strongly dysfunctional to strongly synergistic and an assessment of these degrees can be made for each of the dimensions identified. A tick or a cross can be placed in the box considered most appropriate for each dimension of integration. The resulting assessment

Dimensions of integration	Very strong dysfunction	Strong dysfunction	Weak dysfunction	Very weak dysfunction	Very weak synergy	Weak synergy	Strong synergy	Very strong synergy
Communication mix integration								
Communication mix with marketing mix integration								
Creative integration								
Intra-organization integration								
Inter-organization integration								
Information and database systems integration								
Target audience integration								
Corporate and unitized integration								
Geographical integration								

Figure 14.3 Integrated corporate communication assessment profile

creates a 'profile' of the integration achieved. The further right that more crosses appear, the greater the overall quality of integration that has been achieved. If the profile is completed by a single individual, the results would be somewhat subjective, however, it is recommended that the approach should involve a number of assessors who, through the activity of assessment, are more likely to produce an accurate and more objective profile. The very act of discussing the issues is, itself, of great benefit to the managers involved. In this way, the ICC assessment profile can be described as a management development tool.

Scores could be assigned to each level of integration for each dimension of integration. These scores could then be summed to provide a grand total score. While this is entirely feasible, it is *not* recommended. The alloca-

tion of scores would be somewhat arbitrary and is exacerbated by the fact that the relative importance of each dimension is likely to vary. A simple, unweighted summation of scores would, therefore, not be particularly helpful. A profiling approach is favoured over a grand total score as it makes more obvious the principal areas of weakness and strengths. More focused development action can be taken as a result.

Figure 14.4 illustrates a completed profile. The profile shows that there is room for improvement on all dimensions and this would not be a surprising result as the general quality of integration of corporate communication across organizations tends to be poor. What is relevant to note from the profile is that the weakest area and one that is most in need of improvement is that of 'intra-

Dimensions of integration	Very strong dysfunction	Strong dysfunction	Weak dysfunction	Very weak dysfunction	Very weak synergy	Weak synergy	Strong synergy	Very strong synergy
Communication mix integration						X		
Communication mix with marketing mix integration					X			
Creative integration							X	
Intra-organization integration	X							
Inter-organization integration			X					
Information and database systems integration		X						
Target audience integration					X			
Corporate and unitized integration		X						
Geographical integration			X					

Figure 14.4 Completed integrated corporate communication assessment profile

organization integration'. This suggests that there are benefits to be gained by paying more attention to the ways in which the various parts of the organization work together in the context of corporate communication. Together with the results for 'inter-organization integration', 'information and database systems integration' and 'corporate and unitized integration', the profile indicates that significant improvements could result from a complete appraisal of the internal and external organization relationships, communication and management of the corporate communication process.

This analysis is all the more significant when it is realized that the level of integration achieved for 'communication mix integration' is relatively high. It is this single area which is most likely to be considered when attempting to achieve corporate communication integra-

tion, yet it is clear from the profile that attention to this aspect alone would be inadequate. Assessment of this single dimension may lead to the inaccurate conclusion that a reasonable degree of integration is actually being achieved whereas the full picture indicates something quite different. Moreover, because of the interrelatedness of all the dimensions of integration it may only be possible to achieve further improvements in the area of 'communication mix integration' through improvements in the other dimensions. In this instance, it is highly likely that improvements in the levels of 'inter-organization' and 'corporate and unitized' integration would have a significant effect on the 'communication mix integration'.

Recently this profiling technique was successfully used with managers in a large international company whose worldwide headquarters is in Germany but has 'local' sales and marketing headquarters in a variety of countries. As part of a larger research exercise the profile was used by two groups of managers assessing two separate campaigns involving multiple communication activities, a range of internal staff, a range of agencies and channel members, targeted towards a number of different communication audiences. Assessment profiles for the two campaigns were also completed by managers not directly involved in the campaigns and the results were compared.

Preliminary findings from this work highlighted a general degree of consistency and agreement between the managers involved in the assessment and a general willingness for them to be open, critical and 'objective'. While there was a slight tendency to over-inflate the assessment by the managers directly involved in the campaigns compared with those who were not, the differences were considered insignificant. Moreover, it was quite clear that the major benefits described by all concerned had less to do with the 'fine detail' of the evaluations and more to do with the discussions and development that took place in completing the profiling exercise. The managers saw benefit in using the profile as part of their deliberations when formulating new corporate communication plans, monitoring plans as they were being implemented to 'track' progress (and modify where appropriate), and evaluating at the end of a programme. They perceived the ICC assessment profiling approach as a management development opportunity as well as an evaluation and control tool. They anticipated the learning that took place would also be the basis of improved performance and continuing development for future corporate communication activities. They believed that the profile related most easily to specific and discrete campaigns although there was recognition that the same approach could be applied to the total corporate communication effort which would span across campaigns and extend over a period of time. The managers emphasized the importance of care being taken to ensure that all those involved should use the profile in a positive, mutually supportive way. They expressed concerns that criticism, implied or explicit, could be perceived negatively by individuals.

Summary

The principal aim of this chapter was to elucidate the different aspects of integrated corporate communication and to propose a means by which an assessment could be made of the quality of integration attained. Two frameworks were suggested which identified the 'dimensions of integration' and a 'continuum of integration' along which the degree of integration could be assessed. By combining both frameworks, a composite framework was developed which can be used as a profiling instrument to highlight the relative strengths and weaknesses of integration. The profiling approach has been used successfully in practice.

A method by which the profile can be used was suggested which favoured assessment along each dimension rather than a determination of a total score. The profile creates insights into areas where further improvement may be focused and effort channelled to greatest effect. Assessing integrated corporate communication in this way provides opportunities for all relevant mangers to be involved in the development activity.

It should be particularly noted that the frameworks proposed are not prescriptive of any particular course of action and the profile is an assessment tool. The resulting analysis does not suggest a particular strategy but may be used to formulate both strategies and tactics in a focused way by concentrating on areas of most need.

The chapter is predicated on the presumption that integration of corporate communication is a good thing which can offer the benefits of synergistic effect. Importantly, it was recognized that a lack of integration is likely to have dysfunctional consequences. Lack of attention to ICC is not a neutral position but a negative one. The assessment profile proposed makes no attempt to measure these effects or to justify the value of integration. The ICC profiling approach proposed is 'process' driven, not outcomes driven. This is seen as the most practical and appropriate approach to adopt to assess integration. However, managers may make use of relevant 'output' performance measures in determining their responses to each of the dimensions and may seek to highlight particular sub-areas of each dimension for this purpose.

REFERENCES

Duncan, T. R. (1994) 'Is your marketing communication integrated?', *Advertising Age*, 64(4), 26.

Ehrenberg, A. S. C., Scriven, J. A. and Bernard, N. R. (2000) 'Advertising established brands: an international dimension', in S. O. Monye (ed.), *The Handbook of International Marketing Communication*, Oxford: Blackwell, Chapter 13.

Fletcher, K., Wheeler, C. and Wright, J. (1994) 'Strategic implementation of database marketing: problems and pitfalls', *Long Range Planning*, 27(1), 133–41.

Gonring, M. P. (1994) 'Putting integrated marketing communication to work today', *Public Relations Quarterly*, 39(3), 45–8.

Hartley, R. A. and Pickton, D. W. (1997) 'Integrated marketing communication: a new language for a new era', *Proceedings of the Second International Conference on Marketing and Corporate Communication*, University of Antwerp, April.

Jones, J. P. (1995) *When Ads Work: New Proof That Advertising Triggers Sales*, New York: Simon and Schuster.

Linton, I. and Morley, K. (1995) *Integrated Marketing Communication*, Oxford: Butterworth Heinemann.

Meffert, H. (1979) *Praxis des Kommunikationsmix*, Münster: BDW.

Moriarty, S. E. (1994) 'PR and ICC: the benefits of integration', *Public Relations Quarterly*, 39(3), 38–45.

Morley, M. (1998) Corporate communication: a benchmark study of the current state of the art and practice', *Corporate Reputation Review*, 2(1), 78–86.

Pickton, D. and Broderick, A. (2001) *Integrated Marketing Communications*, Harlow: Financial Times, Prentice Hall.

Robbs, B. and Taubler, D. (1996) 'Will creatives prevent agencies from adopting integrated marketing?', *Marketing News*, 30(20), 4.

Shimp, T. (1997) *Advertising, Promotion, and Supplemental Aspects of Integrated Marketing Communication*, 4th edn, New York: Dryden Press.

Schultz, D. E. (1993) 'How to overcome the barriers to integration', *Marketing News*, 27(15), 16.

Schultz, D. E. (1997) 'Integrating information resources to develop strategies', *Marketing News*, 31(2), 10.

Swan, A. (1993) 'One-stop debate', *Marketing*, 1 Apr, 42–3.

Van Riel, C. B. M. (1995) *Principles of Corporate Communications*, London: Prentice Hall.

Varey, R. J. (1998) 'Locating marketing within the corporate communication managing system', *Journal of Marketing Communication*, 4(3), 177–90.

Varey, R. J. and White, J. (2000) 'The corporate communication system of managing', *Corporate Communication: An International Journal*, 5(1), 5–12.

White, R. (1997) 'Shouldn't we be assessing the effectiveness of total communication campaigns rather than individual techniques?', *International Journal of Advertising*, 16, 118–22.

Wolter, L. (1993) 'Superficiality, ambiguity threaten IMC's implementation and future', *Marketing News*, 27(19), 12–13.

CHAPTER 15

New technology and the changing face of corporate communication

Martin Sims

How often have corporate communicators heard the mantra that the information highway will change core businesses like never before and that contact with stakeholders will allow instant access and the possibility of real time information exchange if not quality symmetrical communication?

In this chapter the author looks at these and other issues relating to the question of whether new technology is changing the face of classical corporate communication. He challenges some of the current tenets of ICT by balancing out the practicality of the new technologies against traditional media formats, such as print, and reflecting on the professional role carried by corporate communicators.

Every year spending worth billions of pounds is based on our assumptions about new information and communications technologies. Outlay on software and hardware to increase business efficiency is just part of this. New information and communications technologies (ICTs) play a role in social change and so our assumptions about their effects are a main plank of forming long-term corporate strategies. How many times have you heard things like: 'find new ways of reaching our stakeholders'; 'brands are under threat as never before'; 'corporations are at the mercy of special interest groups'; or 'we can now talk directly to customers'?

'The internet changes everything' was a common cry during the dot.com boom, usually as an opener to claims that this new technology would turn the business world upside down. Three years after the bursting of the internet bubble, most of the fêted dot.com 'pure plays' have collapsed and the biggest sites on the net are owned by familiar names like BBC and AOL Time Warner.

'People want interactivity' is an assumption which has underpinned much recent debate about the digitizing of communications technology: the idea being that the way people want to communicate has changed. The argument is that technological change has demassified the mass media: the one-to-many model of broadcasting is slowly but surely being replaced by video on demand.[1] Consumers are active, individuals want to be empowered: people want to choose what they watch and they want a two-way relationship with it. In fact, in Europe and the United States the utterly non-interactive national terrestrial TV networks continue to deliver the sort of audiences satellite, cable or the internet can only dream of. The tragedy of modern politics is that people *do not* want interactivity. Across the western world countries report a decline in voter turnout and in membership of political parties. In this most crucial area fewer people are demanding the two-way relationship which would give them greater control over their own lives.

Implicit in all these arguments are simplistic assumptions about the effects of new ICTs, often put forward by less than disinterested parties.

One cause or many?

The most common problem is to assume that new communications technology is the sole or at least major cause of social or behavioural change. As many academics have pointed out this is not a simple cause and effect relationship between the two, but a complex intertwining of factors.[2] Gutenberg's invention of the printing press did not singlehandedly bring about the Reformation, but it was an important factor, along with wider political and social change.[3] With the technology boom behind us and the internet as a commercial medium now past the toddler stage many of the visionary's claims have been tested by human experience and deserve a measured reassessment.

So what are the implications of developments in ICTs for the PR professional? The answer is a complex one. It is rare for the power of technological change to force society in one direction only. Human beings are complex animals, actions have reactions that make the end result hard to predict. In the 1960s the satellite era gave birth to MacLuhan's dreams of a global village. In technological terms that is closer than ever, but have the nations and regions of the world become more intimately connected or are they more inward looking? The answer is probably both, globalization as we now call it having contributed to political and national insularity and facilitated greater international interaction. Let us examine some of the common claims about the effects of new ICTs in detail.

Empowering the individual?

Has the balance of power changed between the individual and the corporation, between big organizations and small organizations or between the individual and the state? The most common argument is that the nature of new ICTs has changed the relationship by putting more power in the hands of the individual. Take for example someone seeking information about the health risks associated with radon, a gas released naturally from certain types of rocks. Until the advent of the internet he or she would have had to wait for information to appear in a newspaper, magazine or on the broadcast media. Otherwise they would have to go to a library to search out a book on the subject. With the internet it is much easier for individuals or small groups to get their views into the public domain. An internet search will generate a wealth of material, though not all of it may be reliable.

However, there are also strong arguments in the opposite direction: that new ICTs have empowered the state and corporations at the expense of the individual. The increasing sophistication and integration of databases, which now contain a mass of information on everything from credit history and medical information to TV viewing has made individual behaviour open to state and corporate scrutiny in a way unimaginable some thirty years ago. Mobile phone technology means that for the first time very accurate positional data is available for every caller. The internet offers immense possibilities for surveillance. The US government spent $34 billion on the Information Awareness Office, which aims to improve national security by using the surveillance possibilities of the internet and other new ICTs.[4] Wanting to make use of these new sources of information for national security or crime prevention is a common reaction for governments and can been seen in the United Kingdom in the Regulation of Investigatory Powers Act (2000).[5]

So there is a potential to both empower the individual and diminish their privacy and liberty. In practice empowerment is subject to several qualifications. First, individuals are only empowered if they have a desire to find something out. It is tempting to imagine that with all that information at our fingertips we must be inexorably moving towards a society where people are increasingly holding government and corporations to account and where the barriers to humans' thirst for knowledge, creativity and personal development have finally been removed.[6] Sadly this optimism is misplaced.

Developments in ICTs have been accompanied by other social developments which tend to work in the opposite direction. Political participation is declining; many argue that news coverage is moving away from serious consideration of policy issues towards a tabloid obsession with celebrities, ignoring international news in favour of domestic news. All the evidence suggests that the internet has not revolutionized media consumption but rather built on existing patterns of behaviour. A combination of cross-promotion, the enormous power of the existing media and the search for trust in a environment of limitless choice means the 'old' media dominate the 'new' media: the UK's most popular site is that of its most popular broadcaster – the BBC.

To summarize: the internet empowers those with a desire to find out. By itself it does not motivate people. The urge to find out more or to campaign on a particular issue comes largely from the same real world impetuses as ever: personal experience, friends, family, interaction through clubs, unions or political parties, and what we hear, see or read *in the mainstream media*. If you are already a shareholder in corporation X, or are an environmental activist in a field in which corporation X operates, the internet usually gives you access to much more information. If you have never heard of corporation X the wealth of online information is unlikely to have any effect.

In practice, for PR professionals this means that putting information on a corporate website, desirable though this may be in terms of transparency, has next to no effect on the population at large. It will be seen by those who have a connection with the organization (whether as enemies or friends) but it will only get through to the general public if it is picked by journalists from the 'traditional' media, for it is the 'traditional' media which dominate the online world.

An accurate picture of social trends is vital if PR professionals are to strike the right tone and adopt effective long-term strategies. Although the most common reaction in the developed world has been to emphasize the potential of new ICTs for individual empowerment, there has been mounting public concern about attacks on civil liberties. In the developing world a common reaction has been concern about the potential of new ICTs to further increase the gap between rich and poor nations. It is more fruitful to think of the relationship between the individual and state or corporations as having changed in several ways rather than having shifted in one direction only. The emphasis then becomes redrawing rights and responsibilities to take account of the changed circumstances.[7]

Putting the internet in perspective

Access to communications clearly affects wider social power structures, though it certainly does not determine them. We need a measured assessment of how technologies have tipped the balance.

Twenty years ago Tomita argued that there was a 'media gap' (see Figure 15.1). The broadcast media provided almost instantaneous communication to large groups of people (10,000+); the telephone gave instant communication between individuals; printed media, from letters to newspapers, allows everything from one-to-one to one-to-millions communications but with a significant time delay, varying from a day to a month. The gap is for quick communication to

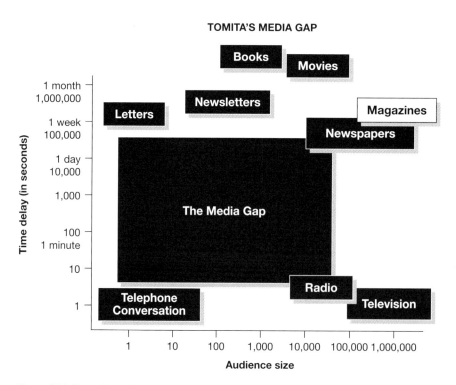

Figure 15.1 Tomita's media gap

Source: Adapted from *The Future of the Mass Audience*, W. Russell Neuman (1991)

smaller groups of people, i.e. from tens to tens of thousands.

This gap has been filled by websites, email and to a lesser extent other new technologies like bulk SMS messaging and telephone and fax broadcasting (sending the same recorded or written message to many people). However, to get the full picture it is necessary to consider another characteristic of the different communications channels – their cost.

The cost of communicating

Broadcasting is expensive, requiring expensive infrastructure, technology and many personnel. Printing is also expensive, though owning a printing plant is not a necessity this is balanced by the high costs of distribution. Writing in February 2003 in the United Kingdom the bare minimum cost of professionally printing and distributing a subscription-based black and white 40-page magazine to 1,000 people was £2000 per issue.[8] At the cheapest end of the market this is outside the scope of many organizations, certainly on a regular basis and without advertising support. At the other end of the scale the cost of national newspapers is well known, Of the United Kingdom's two most recent market entrants one of the world's richest media moguls, Rupert Murdoch, was unable to bring *Today*, a middle-market tabloid with hundreds of thousands of readers, into profitability and avoid its eventual closure. The *Independent* struggles from crisis to crisis and from rescue bid to rescue bid, despite both newspapers employing the latest technology and having the resources of large media groups to fall back on.[9]

Not only do websites and email allow near instant communication with smaller groups, they also bring a huge cost reduction. For only the price of a computer and an internet connection an individual could send emails and create a basic website using free software and free server space. Professional web design software costs a few hundred pounds and your own web address and server space can be bought for less than a hundred pounds. At the most basic level an individual can disseminate information for a one-off cost of less than a thousand pounds – much cheaper than the ongoing costs associated with printing.

However, it is often mistakenly assumed that the low cost of basic web production means anyone with a home computer can create a site to rival the BBC or Amazon. Simple sites may be cheap but large complex sites are every bit as expensive as the traditional media. Sites which compile lists of users or restrict access by the use of unique passwords require integrated databases which greatly increase the design costs. In the United Kingdom quotes for sites with this sort of functionality currently start at £10,000, and cost far more during the dot.com boom.[10]

Furthermore, the technical characteristics of websites mean unlike broadcasting there is a significant marginal cost. The costs for a radio station are exactly the same whether they broadcast to one person within their coverage area or one million. But with websites adding users increases the costs, most significantly if we are talking about creating a mass audience site with millions of hits. It requires a higher bandwidth connection to the internet backbone and larger numbers of more powerful servers running more expensive software.[11] For the managers of big websites the number of users who can access the site without it crashing – particularly during national emergencies like 9/11 – is a matter of great pride and testament to the site's expensive technical capabilities.

Neither can it be forgotten that the media is a labour intensive industry and for an enterprise of any size this is equally true of websites. Even the smallest local paper requires at least a couple of journalists, as would a small magazine-style website, but it would also need IT staff, as do printers and newspapers. The United Kingdom's biggest site, www.bbc.co.uk, reportedly employs 200 people and cost £100 million in 2002,[12] but the true figure would be much higher if it took into account the cost of sourcing the material it recycles and repurposes from BBC radio and television.

Table 15.1 Top 25 US web properties by parent company

	Parent	Unique audience
1	AOL Time Warner	76,353,004
2	Microsoft	72,891,223
3	Yahoo!	66,217,672
4	Amazon	28,115,562
5	Google	27,863,289
6	eBay	27,120,841
7	Terra Lycos	22,999,754
8	RealNetworks	22,805,779
9	United States Government	21,694,762
10	About-Primedia	21,004,816
11	Viacom International	15,022,286
12	eUniverse	14,935,148
13	Walt Disney Internet Group	14,688,910
14	USA Interactive	14,624,792
15	Sharman Networks	13,519,847
16	CNET Networks	12,604,100
17	Landmark Communications	11,716,856
18	Apple Computer	11,669,656
19	Classmates	11,145,862
20	InfoSpace Network	10,983,618
21	AT&T	10,523,768
22	The Gator Corporation	10,000,792
23	EarthLink	9,459,880
24	American Greetings	8,710,937
25	Wal-Mart Stores	8,645,168

Source: Nielsen//NetRatings Audience Measurement Service, December 2002

Table 15.2 Top 10 UK web properties

	Property	Unique audience
1	MSN	8,750,554
2	Yahoo!	6,959,887
3	Google	6,737,921
4	Microsoft	5,726,141
5	AOL Time Warner	5,568,160
6	Wanadoo	5,067,551
7	BBC	4,762,173
8	British Telecom	4,454,923
9	Amazon	4,188,153
10	eBay	3,995,562

Source: Nielsen//NetRatings Audience Measurement Service, January 2003

The economics of the internet reinforce the 'media gap' theory – websites and email are a highly cost-effective way of communicating with relatively small numbers of people but once audience numbers reach hundreds of thousands or high functionality is required, then costs spiral. It is also important to note that websites and email can communicate internationally as easily and cheaply as nationally (Tables 15.1 and 15.2).

Assessing the effect of ICTs

The internet has made little impact on the economic realities which shape the mass communications landscape. As a way of reaching national audiences of hundreds of thousands there is no significant cost saving over the 'old' media. It is unsurprising that the most popular sites in most countries are run by either big companies like Microsoft or national telecoms providers; or well established media organizations like the BBC or AOL Time Warner. These are complemented by start-ups like Yahoo! and Google who had sufficient funding and a good enough product to challenge the big boys. Mass communication continues to be dominated by a handful of huge companies and is likely to remain so.

The implication for PR professionals is that the internet has changed little in terms of disseminating a message to a mass audience. The only effective way to get a message across to non-specialist audiences in the tens of thousands and above is the traditional print and broadcast media. Even for specialist audiences a trade or special interest publication and its associated website is still likely to be the best channel, though there are a few examples of online magazines which are leaders in their field: http://www.drudgereport.com/ for US political exclusives and www.popbitch.com for showbiz gossip in the United Kingdom. Disseminating information via the internet will never have the same impact as traditional mass media relations.

Where the internet can have a marked effect on corporate communication is in utilizing its ability to communicate quickly and cheaply with relatively small numbers of people, i.e. in the low tens of thousands and below. To return to the earlier example, a developer who built houses in an area where the rock is known to release large amounts of radon could achieve a great deal by setting up a website which provides the latest information about whether the gas is harmful. A large company is likely to have the resources to produce a more comprehensive and regularly updated site than small groups of campaigners. Add to this an email blitz directed at people who have expressed interest in buying the properties and you have a cost-effective campaign, though one that would need to be complemented by coverage in the local media.

Brand and reputation

It is often said that new ICTs have made corporate brand and reputation more vulnerable.[13]

Rumours can fly at lightning speed via email and receive unwarranted global credibility via swiftly constructed websites. Mobile phones have allowed protest groups to organize with unprecedented efficiency. Pictures and video can now be sent around the world in a way that only the richest broadcasters could afford ten years ago.

However, there is a tendency to accept these assertions without question: ICTs are usually a double-edged sword. It is easier and cheaper to organize small campaign groups but it is also easier and cheaper for corporate bodies to monitor these groups and develop their own relationship with stakeholders. Well-funded corporations that prioritize stakeholder relations should be in at least as strong a position as any campaign group.

If the internet has given a new credence to unsubstantiated rumour and implausible conspiracy theories which previously only circulated via word of mouth is this necessarily a bad thing? Is open public dissection of these rumours better or worse for public bodies? It leads to many being disproved, like claims that an airliner which crashed in the Atlantic had been hit by a stray US missile. When these rumours are examined by the mainstream media it gives corporates the chance to put their case in a reasonably fair fight, and when the rumours exist only on message boards or websites it is often easy to have them removed. In the United Kingdom ISPs are so afraid of being sued that most remove postings as soon as there is a complaint, much to the alarm of free speech campaigners.

However, the speed of current communications does mean that crises can flare very quickly. Perhaps the best strategy is to be proactive, as Hayes has argued: 'Organisations that wait for issues to occur before managing their communications with key stakeholders often end up with a crisis on their hands.'[14]

There is a paradox here: as well as making brands vulnerable to attack, the internet has also strengthened them. In an almost limitless universe of information, much of it unreliable, with always a danger of fraud, invasion of privacy or offensive content, people naturally seek out trusted and reliable sources from the offline world. Hence the success of big media organizations and of familiar names like Wal-Mart. So what has been taken with one hand has been given with the other, weighing the balance is practically impossible.

New ways of reaching the public

Scepticism about the impact of new ICTs is essential because the field is over-hyped. Computing, telecoms and technology companies have huge marketing and PR budgets dedicated to talking up the potential impact of ICTs. Those who talk down the impact or argue for a measured assessment have no budget at all and are mainly quite isolated academic voices. In fact the general mood in academia has followed the wave of enthusiasm for all things web related.

This article has looked at the evidence for dramatic change so far, this is not to say that great changes in communications patterns may not emerge over the next decades. This can happen very suddenly, as we saw in Europe with text messaging (or SMS), and there are many more technological possibilities to be explored. Marketing using the very accurate positional data captured by mobile phones is a fascinating prospect, and one that mobile companies may be pushed towards if their margins continue to fall. Imagine being able to alert people walking past a renovated park that this was paid for by a corporate social responsibility programme. Moreover, 3G networks would even be able to send a short video clip. Equally, imagine how difficult it would be to overcome public resistance to disclosing personal information like your location at a given moment.

Interactive television is another developing medium, which uses digital television's return path to allow viewers to access 'microsites'. These are similar to websites. They potentially overcome some of the limitations of TV advertising – the inability to offer detail, difficulties in measuring the success of the campaign and the lack of opportunity to collect information about viewers. The most successful interactive adverts have included offers like the chance to book a test drive for a new car. The initial buzz of enthusiasm for this technology has given way to disappointment about its effectiveness, but these are early days and the prospect of adding to the capabilities of the most powerful medium could be very attractive to PR professionals.

The internet is certainly having a growing impact and is becoming ubiquitous in work and education. The online advertising agency i-level say the internet's share of all media consumption by the average adult in the United Kingdom is about 7 per cent – impressive for such a young medium.[15] It will certainly become more relied upon as an information source, but whether that means most people will simply go to the same mainstream media online rather than offline is a moot point: whether the balance of power between individuals and institutions will change significantly is dependent as much on economics and wider social change as on technology. It also depends on human nature – do we have a limitless capacity for interaction, choice and finding out for ourselves, or do most of us, most of the time, want the sort of entertainment which currently dominates the TV schedules? The growth of the internet and the gradual increase in multi-

Figure 15.2
The changing face of Coca-Cola: a poster from 1931 and an interactive TV advertising campaign from 2001. (Photos courtesy the Coca-Cola Company and Respond TV)

channel penetration in the developed world suggests the former, but the continued domination of the terrestrial TV networks suggests the latter.

This chapter has often qualified and downplayed claims about the social impact of ICTs, but there is no doubt that they are agents of change to a greater or lesser extent, and some of these changes are potentially damaging to corporations. This is reason enough for organizations to embrace these new technologies and the multiple possibilities for dialogue with stakeholders which previously would have been impracticable. Success in the new media environment depends on trust because it involves access to increasingly personal information. Institutions must seize every opportunity to build that trust.

NOTES

1   One of the earliest versions of this argument is Gilder, G., *Life after television*, New York: W. W. Norton, 1994.

2   See *inter alia* Williams, R., *Television, Technology and Cultural Form*, London: Fontana, 1974.

3   For an explanation that gives this debate the subtlety it deserves see Briggs, A. and Burke, P., *A Social History of the Media*, London: Routledge, 2002, chapter 2.

4   See Beckett, R. and Rogerson, S., 'E-democracy, rights and privacy in the age of information', *Intermedia*, March 2003.

5   See www.fipr.org/rip/ for a summary of (mainly critical) press and public reaction.

6   An argument made by Gilder (1994).

7   The Beckett and Rogerson article above is a good introduction.

8   Printing costs in the UK are approx. GBP 1400 and distribution GBP 700 at 70p per copy. Based on quotes received in 2002 for the printing of the IIC's journal, *Intermedia*.

9   See Curran, J. and Seaton, J., *Power without Responsibility*, fifth edn, London: Routledge, 1997, pp. 101–5.

10   A complicating factor is that the cost of computers, web design and web hosting is coming down. Design software is becoming increasingly sophisticated allowing non-experts to add increasing functionality to their sites. However, the gulf between a home designed site and a professionally designed and well-funded site remains marked and is likely to remain so.

11   For more details, see Wessberg, A., 'Challenges and opportunities in the internet age', *Intermedia*, April 2001.

12 BBC Annual Report 2001/2 Notes to the
    Financial Statements http://www.bbc.co.uk/info/
    report2002/pdf/facts_finance_notes.pdf
13 See among others Hayes, R., 'The importance of
    crisis management', *Intermedia*, Sept. 2001.

14 ibid.
15 'Sizing up the web', *Guardian* 20 Jan. 03.

PART III MANAGING IMAGE, IDENTITY AND REPUTATION

CHAPTER 16

Reputation and leadership in a public broadcast company

Sandra M. Oliver and Anthony Clive Allen

In this chapter, the concepts of image, identity and reputation are explored theoretically through Grunig's excellence model prior to addressing them in relation to the case of the British Broadcasting Corporation (BBC). Three issues illustrate public perception of this organizational icon: the statutory licence fee; the use of infotainment trails; and employee responses to a former director general's memoirs. While all three issues have come together in the United Kingdom to present a national debate about public broadcasting *per se*, it is outside this chapter's frame of reference to discuss issues of state propaganda and control. What is of interest for best practice, is whether or not an organization such as the BBC, with its well established worldwide reputation developed over many years, can be eroded or indeed stand up to today's vigorous but democratic public debate and challenges from diverse stakeholders at home and abroad, including government, journalists and employees alike.

From its beginnings in 1922 as the United Kingdom's first domestic broadcaster the BBC established itself as one of the leading international media players, first with the World Service Radio and more recently with television channels such as BBC World or BBC Prime. As a public corporation the BBC has always been formally independent of government, and to this day its main source of revenue is a licence fee payable by everyone who owns a television set. However, the level of the licence fee is determined periodically by parliament, as is the general regulatory framework within which the corporation operates. The BBC's remit has always been to 'inform, educate and entertain' by providing a mixed schedule of high quality programmes to the population as a whole (Birt, 2002). As such it has been responsible for providing a model of public service broadcasting which has had a far-reaching influence at home and abroad. The BBC has built its global reputation above all on the fairness, impartiality, accuracy and authority of journalism. But its output extends far beyond simply news programmes to cover all categories of programming and various modes of delivery – it supports amongst other things, two national analogue television channels, one international, five national, three national and thirty-nine local radio stations, a range of digital television channels and 600,000 pages on BBC online, (the most visited non-portal website outside the United States). Today the BBC is one of the best-known media brands in the world. ('It's Creative Darling', Internal Communications Practice at the BBC, 2001).

Yet this venerable institution still has its critics. Even before the advent of the digital age criticism had been growing over the funding of the organization and in particular the principle of the licence fee. Most vocal have been the BBC's media competitors, notably by newspapers owned by Rupert Murdoch's News International, which also has a 40 per cent stake in BSkyB, the subscription based satellite broadcaster and direct competitor to the BBC. Many politicians have also condemned the licence fee as a regressive tax (*Sunday Times*, 20 October 02) and even journalists are jumping on the bandwagon crying for reform (*Guardian*, 7 November 02). With the emergence of the third age of communication (Blumler, 2001), e.g. the explosion of new digital channels, commercial and political groups are asking the question 'Why should the BBC continue to be treated as a special case?'

Critics both inside and outside the BBC cite the corporation as being overstaffed, bureaucratic and out of touch (*Sunday Times*, 3 November 02). Even the BBC's chairperson, Sir Christopher Bland, in the corporation's annual report said: 'We must be more open and accountable, finding better ways of interacting with the public' (BBC Report, 2000). In recent years the BBC's high-profile loss of broadcasting talent and sporting rights to commercial rivals, e.g. *Match of the Day* to ITV,

has provided its critics with yet more ammunition. It has also done little to restore the low morale of many staff resulting from the management culture of the 1990s.

In recent years UK television broadcasting organizations have increasingly come to realize the importance of building relationships with their various stakeholders. The reasons for these changes are not hard to find. Technological developments, an increasingly deregulated media environment and fiercer competition for audiences, advertisers and staff, have challenged much of the world the UK media once operated in.

Before the advent of satellite broadcaster BSkyB in 1989 there were just four UK terrestrial channels (two run by the BBC) plus a small number of moderately successful cable stations. In the intervening period satellite and cable penetration has been substantial: in 2001, nine million households had domestic dishes and connected cable out of a total of 23 million homes (*Media Week*). Digital technology capable of offering hundreds of channels of viewing has been available since 1998, further fragmenting audiences, and it is expected to replace analogue services before 2010. This is the environment that the BBC now operates in.

In this competitive age in which the BBC now finds itself, its stakeholders are increasingly faced with a plethora of alternatives to the BBC. In such a competitive market, it is clear that any stakeholder's decision to support the BBC will only be successful if they identify positive reputation of the corporation through the corporation's image of an organization producing quality services and identifying that quality with value for money. Knowing that a strong identity has a number of potential benefits for an organization, e.g. adding value, generating consumer confidence and loyalty, stimulating investments, attracting high-quality personnel and breeding employee motivation (e.g. Balmer, 1995; Van Riel, 1995; Van Riel and Balmer, 1997) in-house communication specialists have always sought to keep the issue of identity on the board agenda and PR budgets. Moreover, with growing journalistic attention and increasing critique of private business corporations by various interest groups, organizations have recognized and costed the price of developing a socially responsible, *ergo* a positive, corporate image. But what is organizational image? Or organizational identity? How do these terms interrelate to present a measured view of a corporation's reputation?

Identity and image

In spite of the growing attention given to identity and image there is no definitive definition for these pseudo-psychological terms. Identities and images are volatile social constructions that, although seemingly 'objective', base their existence and significance largely on the interpretative capabilities and preferences of their audiences (Christensen and Askegaard, 2001). Although literature abounds with different definitions of corporate image and corporate identity, there are some commonalities. We find a sense of convergence around the idea that corporate identity is a set of symbolic representations, sometimes organizational behaviour (Abratt, 1989; Van Riel and Balmer, 1997). Corporate identity can then be seen as an assembly of clues, or as Abratt (1989) puts it: 'by which an audience can recognise the company and distinguish it from others and which can be used to represent or symbolise the company'. On the other hand, we find corporate image typically viewed as the total impression of an organization that it makes on its various audiences (Bernstein, 1992). Corporate image, in other words, describes the reception of an organization in its surroundings (Christensen and Askegaard, 2001).

Identity, however, is the visual manifestation of image as conveyed through the organization's logo, products, services, buildings and all other tangible bits of evidence created by the organization to communicate to its various stakeholders (Argenti, 1998). Some researchers see these definitions as opposite ends of the same communication process (Margulies, 1997). Others suggests that identity is what is created and sent from an organization to its external world, with image as something which emerges outside of the organization's boundaries and is eventually 'sent' back to the organization via external analysis (Stacks, 2002). This perspective is seen in models that depict the interplay between corporate identity and corporate image to the extent that they allow some overlap between different audiences (Balmer, 1995). Today, however, the dividing lines are becoming more blurred between senders and receivers of messages and, consequently, a clear distinction between inside and outside organizational boundaries is increasingly problematic to uphold. Employees, for instance, interact with 'outsiders' and are also members of external groups that encounter organizational symbols in their lives outside their workplace. It is this partial inclusion within organizations that arguably has led to organizations recognizing that workforces also belong to multiple memberships of groups within the workplace that form impressions of the organization, a fact that has been explicitly recognized in the consolidation of corporate communications functions in a number of industries (Cheney and Christensen, 1999).

Conversely, and of equal importance, many organizations have come to realize that organizational practices which traditionally have been thought of as strictly internal, e.g. organizational structure, use of resources, ethical issues and the practice of leadership are now becoming themes in public discourse, and thus become part of the communication that the organization, sometimes unwillingly, carries on within its surroundings. When customers start boycotting organizations that function according to unethical principles and when employees begin choosing their workplace on the basis of its reputation in society traditional distinctions between internal and external with respect to identity and image break down in terms of stakeholder theory (PC) and mass communication theory (audiences) (Cheney and Christensen, 1999). Indeed, the actions and statements of top managers simultaneously affect organizational identity and image (Hatch and Schultz, 1997).

Reputation

The rationale for acquiring a favourable corporate reputation is that it is likely to mean that an individual is more predisposed to buy a company's products or services (Van Riel, 1995) or as Fombrum (in Argenti, 1998) states, 'Reputation is a source of competitive advantage.' Equally, a well-managed and carefully nurtured corporate reputation can be stored over time to the extent that banked goodwill cushions the adverse consequences of bad publicity (O'Rourke, 1997), a view supported by research in reputation which often emphasizes the historical nature of reputation formation. Herbig and Mulewicz (1995), for example, define reputation as the 'estimation of the consistency over time of an attribute of an entity . . . based on its willingness to perform an activity repeatedly in a similar fashion'.

However, like image and identity and despite numerous attempts at semantic and meaningful clarification, there remains no unambiguous definition of corporate reputation acceptable to the communication industry. The term is defined in the Oxford dictionary as 'what is generally said or believed about a person or thing', but over the years, practitioners and writers have adopted different, sometimes even contradictory, definitions for corporate reputation (Gotsi and Wilson, 2001). Academics such as Fombrun and Van Riel emphasize the effects of this ambiguity, by suggesting in their writings that the lack of a single common definition explains partly why although corporate reputations are ubiquitous, they remain relatively understudied. Many early writers concentrated on the concept of corporate image in a way that appears synonymous with corporate reputation. Martineau (1958) regarded the term image as the sum of functional qualities and psychological attributes that exist in the mind of the consumer, while Boulding (1973) defined image as subjective knowledge. Later, writers like Dowling (1993) and Dichter (1985) saw the terms corporate image and corporate reputation as identical, defining image as 'the total impression of the company'. Finally, Ind's (1997) definition of corporate image as 'the picture that an audience has of an organization through the accumulation of all received messages' illustrates that the author sees no distinction between the term corporate image and corporate reputation.

Recently, several authors (Balmer and Greyser, 2003; Grunig et al., 2002) have considered the terms corporate reputation and corporate image as separate concepts whereby organizations should be focusing on the management of corporate reputation and not of corporate image: when, for example, Scott Cutlip says 'We in PR must be concerned with that good, old fashioned word reputation – not image', he fails to consider key monitoring and control factors such as critical path analysis and integrated programme evaluation.

Generally, it is accepted that the concepts of reputation and image are interrelated and that there is a dynamic relationship between the two, even if measurement is difficult as, for example, in Gotsi and Wilson's (2001) statement . . . 'A corporate reputation is a stakeholder's overall evaluation of a company over time. The evaluation is based on the stakeholder's direct experience with the company, any other forms of communication and symbolism that provides information about the company's actions.'

Towards excellence

Grunig *et al.* call their theory of best practice the Excellence Model. But like perceptions of identity, image and reputation, how is excellence defined, particularly in relation to an organization? Before Grunig *et al.*'s study there were various attempts at defining excellence depending on the context. Hobbs (1987) identified excellent companies by measuring return on sales and return on owner's investment. However, Carroll (1983) criticized the use of financial measures for identifying excellence in management by pointing out that factors such as proprietary technology, market dominance, control of critical raw material, and national culture and policy also affect financial performance regardless of the excellence of management. Kanter (1989) on the other hand defines excellence as innovation,

whilst Hickman and Silva (1984) suggest that each organization creates its own unique criteria for excellence and then suggest how leadership can help the organization meet those criteria. However, no one set of criteria can be used to identify every effective organization (Grunig and Hunt, 1984). As a result, excellence in management may produce different results, for each organization defines its own criteria for success. In Grunig's excellence model (1984) he went much further, suggesting twelve factors that contribute to the excellence of an organization to include: human resources (HR); organic structure; intrapreneurship; symmetrical communication systems; leadership; strong, participative cultures; strategic planning; social responsibility; support for women and minorities; quality as a priority; effective operational systems; a collaborative societal culture. These factors were standard practice in UK-based multinational organizations in the 1960s and 1970s. No strategic PR plan would have got through the board had any factor been missing. The importance of the excellence model lies in its aid as an industry focus, if not a universal standard.

In this study of the BBC, Grunig's factors of excellence are interrelated with definitions of image, identity and reputation through the context of three specific issues namely, the licence fee; the use of commercial trails by the BBC and the impact of the memoirs of the former director general of the BBC to see how, or if at all, the BBC could be said to be functioning as an 'excellent' organization.

The importance of building relationships through their various stakeholders has increasingly exercised the hearts and minds of the BBC as the arrival of digital technology offers yet more opportunity and threat for fragmentation of audiences. Furthermore, changes to the United Kingdom's regulatory framework open up new competitions in what were once safe markets; and stiff competition from internet computer games and radio challenges the BBC to prove that it is capable of delivering excellence in all its activities throughout the organization. How one national institution like the BBC is orchestrating its response to a changing environment is worthy of longitudinal studies that require deeper analysis over a longer period of time than this chapter allows. With the proliferation of academic courses, it will be an inevitable research development.

The licence fee

Unlike most commercial broadcasters the BBC has neither advertisers nor shareholders with whom to concern itself. Its principal stakeholder groups are its viewers and listeners who as licence fee payers also provide over 90 per cent of the corporation's income. The licence fee is periodically reviewed by parliament as is the BBC's charter, the legal basis by which it operates. A second key stakeholder is therefore the government of the day and politicians more generally. The constitutional position of the BBC virtually guarantees that relations between it and government will be difficult at times. During the 1980s, for instance, when Margaret Thatcher was prime minister, the BBC came in for sustained criticism and was forced to accept a reduced level of funding. The Blair government is less antagonistic. Indeed in 2000, Chris Smith, the then minister in charge of culture, cited the BBC as 'the UK's important cultural institution'. In the full glare of publicity, the BBC continues to fight hard to retain its reputation in the face of its 2002 and 2003 annual reports; and its handling of intelligence relating to Iraq and weapons of mass destruction which con-

tributed to the suicide of a notable government scientist.

The British statutory licence fee invokes strong feelings. Sir David Attenborough, in an article in the *Independent* newspaper (November 2002) said, 'the licence fee is the key to important broadcasting, almost everything you can think of that you and I admire about the BBC is due to the fact of the licence fee'. However, this view is contradicted by a poll conducted by the *Daily Telegraph* newspaper in which more than half the people polled believed the licence fee should be abolished (BBC News website). In the year to March 2001 the BBC earned £2.533 billion sterling from the licence fee – a sum substantial enough to explain perhaps why the BBC is keen to continue its funding through a licence fee (*Guardian*, 22 July 2002). So funding too has been a key issues with its stakeholders in respect of image and reputation for excellence.

Corporate trails as infotainment

One of the best examples of relationship building concerns what is being called corporate trails. Corporate trails are generally programmes that are longer in length than a television commercial but briefer than a short programme. They share the same high production cost and value of a good commercial, because they compete for attention with these in the periods between programmes and because they are intended to be viewed on more than one occasion. Their characteristic is to blend together a corporate message with visual/aural pleasure. They may be conceptualized as a type of 'infotainment', blending information with entertainment.

The BBC has used 'infotainment' to deliver the corporation's message to stakeholders at various levels of perception in an effort to highlight the maintenance of the high standards of programming traditionally identified with the BBC. One method, taken directly from commercial advertising is celebrity endorsement (as seen in the latest BBC advert extolling the fact that 'Television is Evolving' (more precisely, BBC television is evolving)) using celebrities from the world of art, sport, music and news to present an image to the public that the BBC is 'evolving' into the digital age. This message seeks to build the BBC's image and identity as a 'change leader' (Kanter, 1989) in new technology together with identifying to stakeholders the variety and quality of entertainment that the BBC produces.

The Excellence theory could be applied to the use of this 'infotainment' as an example of corporate PR excellence under a number of headings: strategic planning, necessary to ensure that quality is not just spoken about but that action takes place; the utilization of a strong participative culture where employees share a sense not only of the mission but also of its success. Furthermore, by utilizing women and minorities in its 'infotainment' the BBC also seeks to show itself as an organization that recognizes the value of diversity, another factor in Grunig's model.

Arguably, this 'infotainment' message works on two levels. First, it is inextricably linked to the important message of funding. The licence fee is what makes possible the production of programmes of high ambition and the public is asked to recognize this through the medium of celebrity endorsement. Second, the 'infotainment' medium also seeks to engage the emotions of the BBC's own employees and contractors by trying to create, through the images of these endorsements, a corporate reputation that people will feel proud to be associated with.

An example of where the development and production of 'infotainment' meets the criteria identified in Grunig's Excellence Model, is the BBC's 'Perfect Day' production. It became one of the most successful UK corporate trails ever made, and was a BBC innovation concerning the corporation's musical output. 'Perfect Day' (1997) was a celebration of the corporation's public service commitment to the broadest range of music programmes (Meech, 1999). Broadcast in its full four-minute and one-minute cut-down versions, it quickly became something of a cult. It was shown originally between September and December 1997, though sales of a CD version contributed significantly to the BBC's annual national charity appeal for Children in Need that year (Annual Report 1997). The concept of the trail was arguably to project to the BBC's stakeholders the image of the BBC as a champion of excellence across a wide spectrum of music, a spectrum that it could achieve only through its vast resources, paid for by stakeholders' licence fees. The trail also provided synergy between the BBC's promotional work and its corporate social responsibility work. Thus Grunig's factor of social responsibility, in the sense that excellent organizations have an obligation to serve societal needs (Chung, 1987), would seem also to have been met.

'Perfect Day' was revived in May 2002 to promote a five-day, national music festival, BBC Music Live, which featured more than 1,000 hours of television, radio and online broadcasts. The sheer size of the undertaking was arguably something only the BBC with its huge infrastructure (Grunig's HR and organic structure factor) and creative flair (intrapreneurship factor – necessary for innovation) could reasonably claim to have been capable of producing in a UK context. The festival ended, on a national holiday, Monday 29

May, with 24 hours non-stop music broadcast culminating, appropriately, in a rendering of 'Perfect Day'. On this occasion it was sung and played simultaneously at venues throughout the United Kingdom and edited live into one continuous broadcast performance. The corporate trail, which had started out in the BBC's own words as a 'licence payers' information film' achieved its zenith. On a national holiday one day in May it became, for a short time, an alternative national anthem, identified and sung by large groups of people across the United Kingdom with the images seen by millions of others beamed directly into their homes – via the BBC – creating such a sense of community and a sharing of values, that the BBC could be said to have fulfilled its public service role in one moment and arguably in the next, created a new genre in the field of reputation management. This one trail showed almost all the factors identified in Grunig's Excellence Model. It took intrapreneurship and innovation to think up the idea – the hallmark of excellence according to Peters (1987), leadership to see the task through (Peters and Austin, 1985), a participative culture capable of integrating human resources, organic structures and symmetrical communication to ensure that employees shared a sense of the mission and of the success, strategic planning as Kanter (1989) describes it – the vision to see the opportunity and ability to set up strategic partnerships with the various stakeholders necessary to see the vision through, and as already discussed, a social responsibility – what Chung (1987) saw as an organization's obligation to serve societal needs. An effective operational system combined with a collaborative social culture were also required to ensure that resources were transformed as effectively as possible to develop the mutual trust and teamwork necessary to ensure the event's success.

Memoirs

However, as O'Rourke states: a well-managed reputation can be stored over time to cushion the adverse consequences of bad publicity. As a national icon, the BBC comes under critical scrutiny not only from outside the organization but also from within. Perhaps the most damning reaction is that seen in BBC employees to the memoirs of the former Director General of the BBC, John Birt. Both the media and BBC employees were critical of the direction of the BBC under John Birt. Birt has been held responsible in some quarters for the damage to the reputation of a vital institution in the life of the nation (*Daily Mail*, 11 October 02). Ironically, for a man brought in to breathe new life into the BBC (Birt, 2002), he appears to have been cast as the antithesis of Grunig's Model of Excellence. Michael Grade, then Director of Programmes for the BBC, damned Birt as a poor communicator, who created a culture of secrecy through editorial dictatorship (as opposed to Grunig's view that organizations should have symmetrical communication). Finance Director Rodney Baker-Bowles cited Birt as a man that did not understand human behaviour (*Daily Mail*, 11 October 02). He was not alone, a poll of 4,000 BBC employees in 1996 showed that 97 per cent were unhappy with Birt's regime (*Daily Mail*, 22 October 02) – predictably he dismissed the survey as meaningless, as opposed to Grunig's view of HR where employees' views and participation are actively sought. In Birt's apparent opinion, size seemed to equal greatness. By diverting £63 million sterling from mainstream programmes, he expanded the news operation, but audiences quickly shunned the sterile, predictable bulletins. Deprived of money, the BBC's drama and comedy departments began to wither. At the end of his career, the government was outraged that Birt's BBC was 'dumbing down' and increasingly dependent on American imports. Many of the BBC's best creative talents left the organization and a survey by accountants Price Waterhouse showed that 25 per cent of the corporation's income, i.e. the licence fee, had disappeared in bureaucracy (*Daily Mail*, 11 October 02). All of these factors are the antithesis of Grunig's factors for achieving excellence in an organization, and unsurprisingly this litany of British innovation was soon terminated by his successor, Greg Dyke. But the effects are still being felt.

The British people want to trust and believe in the BBC as 'one of the world's most trusted and valued broadcasters' (DG's Comment in Annual Report 2001/2002) but a different BBC will create different long-term image and reputation issues to manage – issues which lie at the heart of its corporate strategy.

REFERENCES

Abratt, R. (1989) 'A New Approach to the Corporate Image Management Process', *Journal of Marketing Management*, 5, 1.

Argenti, P. A. (1998) *Corporate Communication*, 2nd edition, Boston: Irwin/McGraw-Hill.

Balmer, J. M. T. (1989) 'Corporate identity and the advent of corporate marketing', *Journal of Marketing Management*, 14, 963–96.

Balmer, J. M. T. (1995) 'Corporate branding and connoisseurship', *Journal of General Management*, 21, 1.

Balmer, J. M. T. and Greyser, S. A. (2003) *Revealing the Corporation*, London: Routledge.

Bernstein, D. (1992) *Company, Image and Reality. A Treatise in the Sociology of Knowledge*, London: Doubleday, Anchor Books.

Birt, J. (2002) *The Harder Path*, London: Time Warner.

Blumler, J. G. (2001) 'The third age of political communication', *Journal of Public Affairs*, 1(3).

Boulding, K. E. (1973) *The Image*, University of Michigan Press.

Carroll, D. T. (1983) 'A disappointing search for excellence', *Harvard Business Review*.

Cheney, G. and Christensen, L. T. (1999) *Identity at Issue: Linkages between Internal and External Organisational Communications*, Thousand Oaks, CA: Sage Publications.

Christensen, L. A. and Askegaard, S. (2001) 'Corporate identity and corporate image revisited', *European Journal of Marketing*, 35.

Chung, K. H. (1987) *Management: Critical Success Factors*, Boston: Allyn and Bacon.

Dichter, E. (1985) 'What's in an image', *Journal of Consumer Marketing*, 2, 75–81.

Dowling, G. R. (1993) 'Developing your corporate image into a corporate asset', *Long Range Planning*, 26, 2.

Fombrun, C. J. (1996) *Reputation*, Cambridge, MA: Harvard Business School Press.

Gotsi, M. and Wilson, A. M. (2001) 'Corporate reputation: seeking a definition', *Corporate Communications: An International Journal*, 6(1).

Grunig, J. E. (1992) *Excellence in Public Relations and Communications Management*, New York: Lawrence Erlbaum Associates.

Grunig, J. E. and Hunt, T. (1984) *Managing Public Relations*, New York: Holt, Rinehart and Winston.

Grunig, L. A., Grunig, J. E. and Dozier, D. M. (2002) *Excellent Public Relations and Effective Organisations*, New York: Lawrence Erlbaum Associates.

Hatch, M. J. and Schultz, M. (1997) 'Relations between organizational culture, identity and image', *European Journal of Marketing*, 31, 5–6.

Herbig, P. and Mulewicz, J. (1995) 'To be or not to be . . . credible that is: a model of credibility among competing firms', *Marketing Intelligence and Planning*, 13, 6.

Hickman, C. R. and Silva, M. A. (1985) *Creating Excellence*, London: Allen & Unwin.

Hobbs, J. B. (1987) *Corporate Staying Power*, Lexington, MA: Lexington Books.

Ind, N. (1997) *The Corporate Brand*, London: Macmillan.

Kanter, R. M. (1989) *When Giants Learn to Dance*, New York: Simon and Schuster.

Margulies, W. P. (1997) 'Make the most of your corporate identity', *Harvard Business Review*, 55, 66–74.

Martineau, P. (1958) *The Personality of the Retail Store*, Cambridge, MA: Harvard Business Press.

Meech, P. H. (1999) 'Television clutter: the British experience', *Corporate Communications: An International Journal*, 4(1).

O'Rourke, R. (1997) 'Managing in times of crisis', *Corporate Reputations Review*, 1, 1–2.

Oliver, S. (1997) *Corporate Communication*, London: Kogan Page.

Oliver, S. (2002) *Public Relations Strategy*, London: Kogan Page.

Peters, T. (1987) *Thriving on Chaos*, New York: Knopf.

Peters, T. and Austin, N. (1985) *A Passion for Excellence*, New York: Warner.

Stacks, D. W. (2002) *Primer of Public Relations Research*, New York: Guilford.

Van Riel, C. B. M. (1995) *Principles of Corporate Communications*, London: Prentice Hall.

Van Riel, C. B. M. and Balmer, J. M. T. (1997) 'Corporate identity: the concept, its measurement and management', *European Journal of Marketing*, 31, 5–6.

Other sources

Daily Mail, 11 Oct. 02.

Guardian Newspaper, 22 Jul. 02; 7 Nov. 02.

The Independent, 19 Feb. 02; Nov. 02.

Media Week, 1 Jun. 02.

Sunday Times, 20 Oct. 02.

BBC Annual report and Accounts 2001/2.

www.bbc.co.uk/Info/report2000/pdf/bbc-summary.pdf

A presentation to the Internal Audience at the BBC entitled 'It's Creative Darling' by R. Grossman (2001).

CHAPTER 17

Corporate reputation

Philip Kitchen

Corporate reputation, or the management and communication of the corporate brand, is playing an increasingly important role in terms of the ability of corporations to build and sustain market share, and influence the minds, and hearts of customers and stakeholders all over the world. Corporate reputation also significantly impacts upon share values, and on the ability of the business to attract and retain excellent employees.

This chapter discusses and outlines some findings from recent empirical research. It provides a foundation for the view that corporate reputation has significant meaning for CEOs in sustaining global performance at national and international levels.

The backdrop behind the emergence, rising importance, effective management, and more appropriate communication of corporate reputation is the interconnected and omnipresent global economy. As early as 1967 McLuhan said: 'The new electronic interdependence re-creates the world in the image of a global village' (McLuhan, 1967).

By 1994, Jack Welch stated: 'In the environment of the 1990s, globalisation must be taken for granted. There will be only one standard for corporate success: international market share ... winning corporations will win by finding markets all over the world' (Welch, 1994).

In an earlier book (Kitchen and Schultz, 2001a), we argued that, by virtue of competing in a globalised interactive marketplace or marketspace:

that a multinational or global firm's personality and image [*inter alia its reputation*], will become the biggest factors in consumer choice between its products and services and those selected from competitors. But, personality and image do not just impact on consumer choice and behaviour, but also on a variety of publics or stakeholders, whose views and behaviours can impact markedly on overall corporate performance and simultaneously exert a positive or negative influence on consumers, governments, and shareholders.

Table 17.1 The best corporate reputations in the United States

Rank	Company name
1	Johnson and Johnson
2	Coca-Cola
3	Intel
4	Ben and Jerry's
5	Wal-Mart
6	Xerox
7	Home Depot
8	Gateway
9	Disney
10	Dell
11	GE
12	Lucent
13	Anheuser Busch
14	Microsoft
15	Amazon.com
16	IBM
17	Sony
18	Yahoo!
19	ATandT
20	FedEx

Source: Featured in the *Wall Street Journal*, September 1999

Notably, the Reputation Institute has shown that the best corporate reputations in the United States – the world's major market (Fisher, 2000) – also means that the companies perform significantly better than others in terms of market share and share value (*Wall Street Journal*, 1999). The top twenty corporate reputations are shown in Table 17.1.

Despite the positive influence exerted by good reputation, good reputation occurs within environmental circumstances and the market environment over the past three to four years has borne significant resemblance to a tremendous storm out at sea. For example:

- There are no more stable marketplaces, only turbulent ones.
- If one compares stock market valuations using four major indices (e.g., UK (FTSE 100 Index), USA (S&P 500), Japan (Nikkei 225), and Europe (Dow Jones Euro STOXX 50), all markets are dropping overall, and individual share values enjoy significant volatilities.
- Investors (corporate and individual) are searching for 'safe haven' investments, and corporate reputation plays a significant role in invest/divest decisions.
- Chief executive officers are literally in the 'firing line' if targets are not reached, or markets respond badly to organizational initiatives.
- Board room doors seem to be continually revolving.

In this scenario, corporate ability to present sustainable corporate reputation stories to consumers, customers, business analysts, industry analysts, and other interested and savvy publics and stakeholders, is of crucial importance. Among many quotations that could be cited, the following summarize the current [academic and practitioner] position:

> Good reputation is very useful for an organisation; it may enable it to charge premium prices for its products, enter into favourable financial arrangements with banks, attract graduates from top universities, get in touch with customers easily, and so on, such that good reputation constitutes a valuable asset to the organisation.
>
> (Fombrun and Shanley, 1990; Shapiro, 1983)

In contrast, an organisation with bad or no reputation is likely to encounter situations where the opportunities open to it are few and the constraints imposed on it are many.

> (Podolny, 1993; Vendelo, 1998)

One could liken corporate reputation to a flag. Given any particular corporation in Table 17.1, and using apperceptions associated with the flag metaphor, where on the flagpole would the flag actually be? What colour would it be? What condition would the flag be in at this point in time? As the chapter unfolds, please keep the flag metaphor in mind.

Global issues and global problems with corporate reputation

We live in a world awash with corporate promises. The promises not only come from business corporations though that is the major focus here. But they also come from political parties – spokespersons and spin doctors; and they come from corporate entities of all types with the profit axe to grind. Often such promises and assertions are associated with individuals – in the corporate sense it is usually the CEO (e.g., Richard Branson, Anita Roddick, Bill Gates, etc.). *But*, are such promises to be believed? Perhaps a jaundiced perspective on corporate reputation may have long preceded the modern era, but still have recognizable meaning for corporations and the consumers they ostensibly serve – in our day:

> those who have known how best to imitate the fox have come off best. But one must know how to colour one's actions and to be a great liar and deceiver. Men are so simple, and so much creatures of circumstance, that the deceiver will always find someone to be deceived.
>
> (Machiavelli, *The Prince*)

Machiavelli's statement has resonance in today's world. For our world offers many promises of ethical corporate behaviour. However, as we turn to the current literature in all medias concerned with reporting such behaviour, there is a nagging suspicion that many business executives may have made Machiavelli current bedtime reading. Certainly Enron, WorldCom, Marconi, financial traders, investment bankers, and trusted individuals in positions of authority have all recently had their corporate reputations revealed as more concerned with rhetoric than with reality. Meanwhile, tens of thousands of people and organizational investors have either been badly let down, lost (£$millions), and consumer and stakeholder confidence and goodwill has been further eroded. For example: 'Enron, the American energy trader and self-proclaimed "world's leading management company" went spectacularly bust. Financial management (or mismanagement) was to blame for the $17 billion black hole in its accounts' (*Observer*, 23 December, 2001, p. 4).

The focus on fraudulent dealing will be most unwelcome for the accounting industry. In summer 2001, Arthur Andersen had its corporate reputation mauled for shredding 'literally tons of documents' relating to Enron (see *Guardian*, 2002). Similar mismanagement (though not fraudulent) is also evident in the case of Marconi whose shareholders are to receive one-twentieth the share value of their stock (2003). WorldCom has also had its reputation shattered. Even J. K. Galbraith emerged from semi-retirement with a new book due to be published in 2004. Its title: *The Economics of* 'Innocent Fraud' (emphasis added). And yet, reputation – so clearly important in the field of corporate activity – is also exposed to criticism even at the individual level. In the past few years, the following names and reputations have also been severely dented in society: Jeffrey Archer, John Major, Peter

Mandelson, Henry McLeish, and Slobodan Milosevic. Thus, reputation of either a corporate or individual nature is evidently an opportunity for rhetorical public proclamation, but perhaps also of private renunciation, hence the use of the quotation from Machiavelli. Moreover, 2002 will be remembered as a year of corporate crime, the year President George Bush – on behalf of a nation – embraced the notion of 'corporate responsibility'. Remarkably, the ten worst corporations of the year, are also avid promoters of the concept of corporate reputation. These ten corporations were described as: 'polluters, dangerous pill peddlers, modern-day mercenaries, enablers of human rights abuses, merchants of death, and beneficiaries of rural destruction and death' (Mokhiber and Weissman, 2003). For a full list of these ten businesses and their corporate activities, please access http://www.multinationalmonitor.org

Despite poor examples of reputation in practice, corporate reputation is on the global agenda of virtually every corporation, it has almost become a form of mantra for twenty-first century corporations, and – as said earlier – a strong reputation equals a healthy bottom line and a robust share price.

Given this widespread position of acceptance of corporate reputation, we will now consider three related principles:

1   Modern corporations must demonstrate accountability to all stakeholders.
2   Corporations should embrace the market's growing perception of the CEO as the personification of a company's ideals and goals.
3   Corporations should use the internet as a mass communications tool.

However, what a corporation knows it should do and what it actually does do, may be very different. Moreover, it is difficult to turn such broad brush strokes into a detailed strategic picture. The major question is:

•   How do companies perceive and manage corporate reputation?

Let us first take a look at why these three reputation principles have assumed such pre-eminence in the corporate reputation debate.

Principle one: greater accountability

Businesses are becoming ever more accountable (*Marsh Topic Letter*, 2001). Just as they face more complicated national and international business environs, which occasion more business problems, within those environs they are scrutinized by sophisticated shareholders, and by involved publics, stakeholders, and consumers. Businesses have to abide by rigorous regulation and rapidly evolving standards. They are always encouraged to grow, be profitable, and provide excellent ROI. But these are no longer enough. Growth, profits, and ROI will always be business necessities. But, the businesses are also part of the societies in which they operate, and they have to consider the impact their behaviour has on these societies. The impact businesses may have upon society can be likened to 'dropping a stone into a pond'. The three stages of 'ripple effect' (derived from Harrison, 1997) – which one expects to be sustained and accelerated – are:

•   *Level one*: businesses are expected to pay taxes, observe all legal requirements, and deal fairly.
•   *Level two*: concerned with organizational issues in which the corporation seeks to

minimize all potential negative effects, and to act, not just in accord with the letter, but also the spirit of the law.

- *Level three*: concerned with societal issues such as the concern for health, and to help remove or alleviate societal inequities. This third level extends well beyond financial and operational issues.

But that was 1997. Corporate responsibility has now come under the microscopic attention of governments, institutional investors, opinion formers, best-practice organizations, customers, consumers, and other informed streetwise, sophisticated, and savvy groups. Stakeholders seek to understand and, if necessary, criticize the social and ethical performance of corporate entities in which they have an interest (Fombrun, 1996). This interest extends beyond financial and operational issues. Marsh further indicates: 'Corporate social responsibility addresses both the sustainability of an organization's activities and the moral acceptability of its actions. Management would do well to integrate these considerations into their thinking.'

In the global environs of the twenty-first century, the old exchange process is insufficient. Brands and branding are insufficient. Monies changing hands is insufficient. Stakeholders want to know the company behind the brands. And companies have a desire to amortise communication cost across brand portfolios. Thus, they need to raise the corporate umbrella (see Kitchen and Schultz, 2001a). However, as noted elsewhere (see Kitchen, 1997), expenditure in the field of corporate communications is dwarfed by traditional brand marketing communication budgets. Significant financial investment is necessary to promote the corporate brand; significant management time is required to develop and sustain corporate reputation;

significant investment is required in gaining the required senior personnel and providing excellent support infrastructure. But all these factors would be to no avail, without principle two.

Principle two: the chief executive officer

The chief executive officer (CEO) is the person charged with responsibility to communicate the reputation of the business (Bennis, 1997; Koch, 1994; Zorn, 2001). CEOs do not operate alone. They must be supported by, or build around themselves, corporate communication specialists who develop programmes in a manner consistent with the corporate identity. The tools used by corporate communication personnel include: public relations, public affairs, investor relations, government relations, labour market communications, issues management, social responsibility programmes, corporate advertising, and media relations. But all of these mechanisms to support and sustain reputation are merely rhetoric if the organization or its personnel act unethically, are seen to damage the societies where they do business, or simply do not develop appropriate relationships with stakeholders. Faced with recalcitrant corporate entities, investors invest elsewhere, consumers prefer competing alternatives, and legislators force change.

Businesses, led by the CEO, must be seen to be acting in a socially responsible manner. There are at least two reasons. First is the overarching need to develop the corporate brand to sustain and maintain the corporate reputation (Herbig and Milewicz, 1995; Ettore, 1996; Vendelo, 1998; Schultz and Kitchen, 2000; Kitchen and Schultz, 2001a; Kitchen and Schultz, 2001b; Kitchen and

Schultz, 1999). The second reason is the requirement to protect and nurture strategic business units and their associated brands to enable them to grow. Strategic business units, as indicated by planning grid matrices (McCarthy and Perrault, 1994) are the powerful building blocks of corporations. They are powerful corporate assets, the brands they manage are powerful corporate assets too (Brand Finance, 2000). SBUs and their brands need a powerful business backing them. Business leaders everywhere see a positive corporate image as an absolute prerequisite for achieving strategic business objectives

Kitchen and Schultz (2001b) described the chief executive officer as 'holding the handle of the corporate umbrella'. This means that the CEO is not only the chief instigator of all communication activity; he/she is also the person responsible for personifying such information. CEOs such as Bill Gates, Anita Roddick, Richard Branson, Jack Welch, Dave Thomas, and Lee Iacocca help create and sustain a positive corporate image that has resonance for stakeholders, including the all-important triumvirate of customers, investors and employees. Zorn (2001) points out that such 'leaders' represent not only their own companies, but also sets of values and positions on prominent social issues: 'Effective leaders – particularly in highly visible positions – must be skilled communicators.' He goes on to say: 'A handsome or pretty face will only go so far these days. It is not enough to make a few cogent remarks from time to time. These must be related to the core values associated with the corporation and what it stands for in society' (Zorn, 2001: 27). In today's global marketplace, CEOs are necessarily cast in the role of influential corporate reputation influencers. They do not stand alone, but have a wide range of corporate communication resources and personnel to assist them. But

they themselves must communicate personally, effectively, and well. This is an absolute must.

Given the two related strands – increased accountability and CEO communication – corporate reputation becomes an essential component of national, international, and global success. Failure to communicate, or worse – miscommunication, can do much to damage corporate reputation and simultaneously brand sales, market share, and share values. It is too important a subject to leave to chance. But, there is still a third principle which companies ignore at their peril.

Principle three: the power of internet communication

By year-end 2003 it was estimated that there were six hundred million users of the internet globally. Notably, these users were statistically spread as one would expect in a global economy with the United States at 36 per cent; Japan at 11 per cent, Germany 6 per cent, and the United Kingdom at 5 per cent. Kitchen and Laurence (2003) state: 'the increasing power of global media, consumer and shareholder power, and the shifting public role of corporations underpin the new dynamic agenda for building and maintaining corporate reputation. But there is a place ("space" might be a better word) where these issues have come to a head faster and with greater impact – the Internet'.

The internet has the capacity to facilitate or damage corporate reputation. Of the millions of sites accessible and available, many are geared to detailing and reporting the activities of specific corporations and industries. Unlike other more traditional media, information can span the internet almost instantaneously with almost no effort. Company boundaries, once tightly sealed, are blurring. Internal mail is no different from external mail. It is no longer necessary to sneak sensitive subversive or confidential information out of buildings. It is necessary only to press the 'attach' and 'send' buttons. There is no real hierarchy between 'official' and 'unofficial' websites, they all have the same status on the web. A simple UK search for BT, revealed that the 'official' website, the one owned and marketed by BT, was ranked 33 in the list. In terms of corporate reputation, the internet has the power to break all the bulwarks of scale, obstruction, and distance that has allowed corporations to control stakeholder communication in the past. Information posted on the web (possibly hearsay and speculation) can make and break share prices in today's global interconnected economy.

In relation to the three factors we have discussed: accountability, CEO communication, and the internet, the findings from an ongoing international corporate reputation study may be advantageous.

Setting the scene

Each year since 1997, Hill and Knowlton/ Harris Interactive (2001) have carried out a study considering executive opinions and views relating to corporate reputation in many nation states. For example, in a paper written by Kitchen and Laurence (2003) on which this chapter is based, corporate reputation in eight nation states is explored. In this chapter though, we will extrapolate the findings from that study to understand and explore the following issues or questions relating to corporate reputation:

- its importance;
- whether it is measured formally;

Table 17.2 Primary industry (%)

Manufacturing	27
Business services	19
Technology/telecom/IS	9
Distribution	8
Consumer durables	8
Consumer products	6
Financial services	4
Construction	4
Energy/utilities	4
Health care	3
Transportation	3
Other	5

Source: Hill and Knowlton/Harris Interactive (2001)

- the most meaningful measures;
- key influencers;
- relationship to international expansion;
- CEO reputation;
- ability of CEO to protect and enhance reputation;
- responsibility for managing reputation.

The study concerned executive perceptions of corporate reputation by attempting to measure and benchmark the role and importance placed on a company's reputation by executives in the eight countries. A secondary and related purpose was to identify and explore the role of key influences on corporate reputation, both internal and external to a company. The primary industries involved in the study are shown in Table 17.2.

The demographic profile of respondents was as follows:

- 8 per cent were CEOs
- 7 per cent were chairs/vice chairs, or chief operating officers
- 25 per cent were corporate financial officers
- 17 per cent were general managers
- 22 per cent were managing directors

Table 17.3 Revenue (%)

Less than $100 million	50
$100 million to less than $500 million	26
$500 million to less than $1 billion	6
More than $1 billion	9
Refused to divulge	9

Source: Hill and Knowlton/Harris Interactive (2001)

- 21 per cent were regional CEOs or regional managers

Of these respondents, 17 per cent of respondents were members of boards other than that of their own company; and 78 per cent were from private, as compared to public, companies.

Revenue from these firms is reported in Table 17.3. The demographic criteria indicate that a widespread response was obtained from board-level personnel. Given the self-directed nature of response, however, the study can be viewed as exploratory and as a prelude to more in-depth analyses.

Research findings

Given that the study has been carried out annually, the findings reveal that corporate reputation, its measurement and its management, is high on the agenda of leading companies and executive minds in many countries around the world. Corporate reputation is of significant importance to CEOs in achieving corporate objectives. More and more companies are developing and putting into place formal systems to measure corporate reputation. Table 17.4 indicates that while the importance of corporate reputation has apparently not changed in at least three years, its importance is highlighted by firms as they develop and implement formal reputation

Table 17.4 Corporate reputation

	1998	1999	2000
Importance of corporate reputation[a]	94	94	94
Implementation of formal reputation measurement systems (in place)	19	37	42

Source: Hill and Knowlton/Harris Interactive (2001)

Note: [a] The importance of corporate reputation increases with firm turnover

measurement systems. What seemed to be carried out on an ad hoc or unsystematic basis in 1998, was far more sophisticated in 2001.

Corporate reputation was seen as of great importance relating to the achievement of business objectives in all countries (see Table 17.4). Thus, 'marketing' or 'creating exchanges' would just be one (albeit extremely important) element in developing and maintaining a sound corporate reputation. A second related element concerns the gathering of research data that monitors and measures corporate reputation on an ongoing basis.

A major trend in the 1980s and 1990s was for businesses to augment marketing and latterly corporate communication departments with in-house analytical services (McDaniel and Gates, 1993; Van Riel, 1999). The current measurement devices used in terms of corporate reputation, however, can all be applied informally, rather than structured into business activity in a formalized manner. However 'custom research' is invariably ranked first in order of importance, but much greater analysis is needed on a case by case basis to discover what such custom research actually entails and the contribution such research makes.

What influences corporate reputation the most? The findings from the study indicate that customers, employees, and the CEO (*in that order*) are all most highly ranked in terms of maintaining corporate reputation. By nigh on unanimous vote, *customers are by far the most important influence on corporate reputation* (see Kitchen and Schultz, 2001a). However, this point is not unremarkable in that it has been hammered home in innumerable text books and articles derived from the marketing discipline. Customers are important for at least five marketing reasons as listed by Schultz and Walters (1997), but note however, that each of these terms also has resonance for corporate communication and reputation.

1   *Buying rate*: a base measure of loyalty which allows the firm share of market, mind and heart.
2   *Customer retention, in total and by class*: the percentage of customers retained in a specific accounting period.
3   *Customer advocacy*: increases in customer referrals as a percentage of total customers is also a key indicator of loyalty.
4   *Price elasticity*: where customers are willing to accept price increases with little or no effect on their behaviour, strong loyalty is presupposed.
5   *Customer-switching costs and barriers to competitive entry*: where a brand creates customer-switching costs, loyalty is more likely to be achieved. The greater the switching costs the more difficult it is for competitors to 'pull' customers away from the brand.

The Schultz and Walters range of criteria, however, is supported by a range of measures from the corporate communication literature. For many firms, the brand is not just the product(s) customers learn about, consider, value, purchase, consume, and are loyal to. Customers increasingly want to know about

the corporate entity that ostensibly owns the brands in terms of:

*   What does the parent company do?
*   What doesn't it do?
*   What values does it personify?
*   Which personalities are running the company?
*   How do they treat employees globally?
*   Are they 'good' corporative citizens?

The issue of how employees are treated can become important media news all round the world. As Nike has found to its cost, it is one thing to subcontract work to factories in Southeast Asia, and quite another to square sweatshop wages with premium prices in western markets. Bennis (1997) makes the claim that for corporate vision to be meaningful it has to be shared at all organizational levels. Sharing a vision implies a sense of belonging, support given to corporate goals and positive behaviour and word of mouth. Fombrun (1996) indicated that corporations that employees would like to work for promote trust, empower people and inspire pride. It is remarkable how few organizations are able to achieve these seemingly simple objectives.

In a wider international context, corporate reputation plays an important role in terms of generating sales in new overseas markets. But, Dunning (1993) considers that reputation extends well beyond sales performance. From a multinational enterprise context he asks:

*   Is its impact on economic welfare a good thing?
*   If it is (already) good, how can it be made even better? (brackets added)
*   Do we wish our country to be tied to an international division of labour fashioned or influenced by foreign MNE activity?

While there is little doubt that good reputation precedes market entry and market growth rates, of even more importance is the 'insider' phenomenon, where the corporation needs to be inside the economic firewall such as the European Community, ASEA, or NAFTA, for example (Ohmae, 1985, 1989; Czinkota and Ronkainen, 1995).

a) CEO reputation enjoys a significant correlation with corporate reputation, though this varies from country to country within the Hill and Knowlton study. When CEO's retire the ability of the proposed new incumbent is carefully scrutinised in terms of his/her impact on reputation (see also Van Riel, 1999; Pincus et al., 1991).

In the twenty-first century, managing corporate reputation is a global responsibility, which means that whatever is planned or communicated must be done on a national, international, or global basis.

Discussion and conclusion

As seen from the findings of the Hill and Knowlton study, and in the preceding review of literature, corporate reputation and its management has become increasingly important to firms of all types and sizes. Reputation management is thus a topic of great importance to corporations, and many other organizations and their leaders in this new century. New buzzwords may well include: correlation, CEOs, communication and connectivity insofar as reputation is concerned. While the old executive issues of managing resources, capital, labour, and technology will always be there, alongside these traditional managerial issues will be that of managing the corporate brand. Whatever else

CEOs do, or do not do, this is the most important task of CEOs in today's environs. Why? Because the perceptions, beliefs, and feelings of stakeholders (including the all-important customers) impacts on the current and on-going success of the company. Surely, these perceptions, beliefs, and feelings need to be targeted by effective integrated corporate and marketing communication?

Reputation – at least in presentational and rhetorical terms – has become part of the warp and woof of everyday corporate activity. Based on the theoretical evidence presented, and that of a limited empirical nature, corporate reputation is here to stay. It will be a dominant theme of corporations in the twenty-first century, together with its sub-themes of corporate identity and the measurement of corporate image among stakeholders who could impact organizational performance. It is not enough to have a corporate reputation, such reputation must also be planned, managed, and capable of evaluation. In the mind of any reader must be misgivings. Maybe the earnest statements of behavioural intent found on the websites and literature of corporations are no more than Machiavellianism translated to the twenty-first century, with all the believability of political rhetoric. Reputation is, in the end, no more and no less than a reflection of what is believed to be ethical in a particular society at a specific point in time. The fact that so many fall below even stated expectations is a problem for students and business practitioners to ponder over.

This chapter commenced with a metaphor. I asked readers to imagine that corporate reputation was like a flag, and then asked three questions:

1 *Where on the flagpole would the flag be positioned?* The best estimate may be

that corporate reputation is somewhere close to half mast or below. It is reality for some corporations and rhetoric for others. And in between, perhaps – the rest drift to and fro.

2 *What colour would the flag be?* Rather than bright colours on a pristine white background, corporate reputation may be a somewhat unwashed or rather grubby grey.

3 *What condition would the flag be in at this point in time?* Not in pristine condition, perhaps a little bedraggled and torn.

The responsibility for improvement, and the need for further research, is clear.

NOTE

This chapter is dependent on material derived from various sources and we acknowledge the kind permission of Harris Interactive, Hill and Knowlton, Marsh Limited, Palgrave Publishers, Yankelovich Partners, and *Corporate Reputation Review and Forum*, to utilize and cite some of the materials in this chapter.

REFERENCES

Bennis, W. (1997) 'Becoming a leader of leaders', in R. Gibson (ed.), *Rethinking the Future*, London: Nicholas Brealey Publishing.

Brand Finance (2000) 'Brand Valuation' June, p. 3.

Czinkota, M. R. and Ronkainen, I. A. (1995) *International Marketing*, 4th edn, Fort Worth: The Dryden Press.

Dunning, J. H. (1993) *Multinational Enterprises and the Global Economy*, Wokingham: Addison-Wesley Publishing Company.

Ettore, B. (1996) 'The care and feeding of a corporate reputation', *Management Review*, 85(6), 39–43.

Fisher, K. L. (2000) 'All a broker needs to succeed', *Research*, July, 41–5, (www.researchmagazine.com)

Fombrun, C. and Shanley, M. (1990) 'What's in a name? Reputation building and corporate strategy', *Academy of Management Journal*, 33(2), 233–58.

Fombrun, C. (1996) *Reputation: Realizing Value from the Corporate Image*, Harvard, MA: Harvard Business School Press.

Guardian (2002) 1 March, p. 5.

Harris Interactive (2001) 'The Hill and Knowlton/ Harris Interactive International Corporate Reputation Report: C-Suite Executives on the Value of Corporate Reputation, the Internet and Reputation Influencers', May.

Harrison, S. (1997) 'Corporate social responsibility: linking behaviour with reputation', in P. J. Kitchen (ed.), *Public Relations: Principles and Practice*, London: International Thomson, pp. 128–47.

Herbig, P. and Milewicz, J. (1995) 'The relationship of reputation and credibility to brand success', *Journal of Consumer Marketing*, 12(4), 1–6.

Kitchen, P. J. (1997) *Public relations: Principles and Practice*, London: Thompson.

Kitchen, P. J. and Laurence, A. (2003) 'Corporate reputation: an eight-country analysis', *Corporate Reputation Review*, 6(3).

Kitchen, P. J. and Schultz, D. E. (1999) 'A multi-country comparison of the drive for integrated marketing communications', *Journal of Advertising Research*, 39(1), 21–38.

Kitchen, P. J. and Schultz, D. E. (2001a) *Raising the Corporate Umbrella: Corporate Communications in the 21st Century*, London: Palgrave.

Kitchen, P. J. and Schultz, D. E. (2001b) 'A comparative analysis of integrated corporate and product brand communications', *Journal of Global Competitiveness*, 9(1), 438–41.

Koch, J. (1994) 'In search of excellent management', *Journal of Management Studies*, 31(5), 681–99.

Machiavelli, N. (1995) *The Prince*, tr. G. Bull, London: Penguin, p. 55.

Marsh Topic Letter (2001) 'Social and Ethical Risk', London: Marsh Limited, www.marsh.com

McCarthy, E. J. and Perrault, W. D. (1994) *Essentials of Marketing*, 6th edn, Chicago: Irwin, p. 105.

McDaniel, C. and Gates, R. (1993) *Contemporary Marketing Research*, 2nd edn, St Paul, MN: West Publishing Co.

McLuhan, M. S. (1967) cited in W. J. Keegan (1999) *Global Marketing Management*, New Jersey: Prentice Hall, p. 1.

Mokhiber, R. and Weissman, R. (2003) 'The 10 worst corporations of 2002, available at http://www.multinationalmonitor.org downloaded 2 January; cited here with permission.

Observer, (2001) 23 December, p. 4.

Ohmae, K. I. (1985) *Triad Power: The Coming Shape of Global Competition*, New York: The Free Press.

Ohmae, K. I. (1989) 'Managing in a borderless world', *Harvard Business Review*, 67, May–June, 152–61.

Pincus, J. D., Robert, A. P., Rayfield, A. P. and DeBonis, J. P. (1991) 'Transforming CEOs into chief communication officers', *Public Relations Journal*, 47(4), 87–92.

Podolny, J. M. (1993) 'A status-based model of market competition', *American Journal of Sociology*, 98(4), 829–72.

Schultz, D. E. and Kitchen, P. J. (2000) *Global Communications: An Integrated Marketing Approach*, Chicago: NTC Business Books; London: Macmillan.

Schultz, D. E. and Walters, T. (1997) *Measuring Brand Communication ROI*, Chicago: American Marketing Association.

Shapiro, C. (1983) 'Premium for high quality products as returns to reputations', *Quarterly Journal of Economics*, 98(4), 659–81.

Van Riel, C. (1999) *Corporate Communications*, New Jersey: Prentice Hall.

Vendelo, M. T. (1998) 'Narrating corporate reputation', *International Studies of Management and Organisation*, 28(3), 110–28.

Wall St. Journal, (1999) 'The best corporate reputations', September.

Welch, J. (1994) cited in W. J. Keegan (1999) *Global Marketing Management*, New Jersey: Prentice Hall, p. 1.

Yankelovich Partners (2001) Hill and Knowlton – Third Annual Corporate Reputation Watch: CEOs on Corporate Reputation.

Zorn, T. (2001) 'Talking heads: the CEO as spokesperson' in P. J. Kitchen and D. E. Schultz (2001), pp. 26–7.

CHAPTER 18

Communicating a continuity plan: the action stations framework

Sandra M. Oliver

Restructuring during the 1980s and 1990s often saw functional areas such as investor relations and government relations become the remit of finance or treasury departments, while internal or employee management communication found itself positioned as a low priority activity in human resource departments. During a disaster, this often left responsibility for corporate affairs such as image, identity and reputation management in a vacuum and without reference to corporate PR and communication strategists other than as an afterthought by marketeers responsible for customer relations or product promotion. The result was often a long-drawn-out damage limitation exercise or worse.

The chapter focuses on three banks to illustrate how emergency communication structures and processes are critical components in forward planning. The role of corporate communication/PR director is pivotal in any organization's continuity planning, carrying as it must for optimum performance, board-level authority and accountability, as illustrated by the co-dependency Action Stations Framework.

Introduction

At this critical point in the history of corporate communication management theory and practice as it evolves from PR disintegration, in parallel with the convergence of technology, the role of integrated communication management in industry and commerce is once again attracting a higher profile, particularly in the banking industry. The principal activity during a crisis for communication specialists is media relations, yet titles and roles of communication practitioners in British organizations vary. In banks, for example, operational and strategic organizational functions, including crisis management, may appear as shown in Table 18.1.

In 1986 a Gallop survey of Britain showed that only 3 per cent of the general population trusted bankers, which suggests that in a crisis situation, banks are likely to attract more adverse publicity from the media than other

Table 18.1 Operational functions of banks

Banks	Department	Functions
Abbey National	Corporate Affairs	Media relations; public relations; internal communication (newsletter, video)
Barclays Bank	Communications	Shareholder communications; employee relations; support for community – young people; the arts and the environment; press relations
Co-operative Bank	Public Relations	Press information; opinion survey; publicity; policy development; community projects; funding for charity works; internal communications
Lloyds Bank	Corporate Communications	Environmental policy; community support; internal communication; information service to the public, in particular students; corporate sponsorship; press information
Midland Bank	Corporate Communication	Monitor corporate identity; corporate brochure; internal communication; media relations, public relations; ethnic and environmental policy
Nat West Bank	Corporate Affairs and Communications	Co-ordinate internal communication; group media relations; develop public and ethical business policies; investor relations; community relations; campaign for plain English; 'green policy' – best practice; staff suggestion scheme; school programme – financial literacy, personal money management, opinion formers (politicians, business leaders) relations; advise business unit on advertising
Royal Bank of Scotland	Corporate Communications	Community relations; corporate sponsorship of sport and cultural events; environmental policy – energy conservation; guides to services and products
TSB Bank	Group Corporate Communications	Corporate advertising; press relations; investor relations; corporate identity; internal communication-newsletter and special events
British Bankers' Association	Communications and External Affairs	Communication strategy; media relations; 'educating' the publics; identify target audience; opinion research; banking seminar and conferences

professions. Although Liew's (1997) research indicated that Britons were largely satisfied with the performance of the banks and were less antagonistic than the media indicates, an integrated communication strategy is essential in managing relationships with all stakeholders and that 'effective relationship management requires corporate action or change. Corporate communication – including the research function – plays a role in shaping a bank's course of action, how it is structured and its decision making process.'

Banks perhaps more than most have had to address the sheer scale of environmental change brought about by technology, globalization and social change, so although Liew found no significant anti-bank bias in the media, he argued that 'the weakness in existing bank/media relations in the United Kingdom is a glaring knowledge gap that will expand as the nature of banking business increases in complexity' (1982).

Thus tactical, empirically derived evidence for communication programme planning and budgeting is no longer good enough. Strategy also informs tactics at both research and evaluation levels to a very high degree, which is why the professional studies programme at Thames Valley University in London is one of the first, if not the first European University to incorporate knowledge and information management as a core learning module in its masters degree programme in addition to the ability to critically analyse best practice models of performance.

What the books say

Given the limitations of empirical research underpinning the professional era of public relations between the post-war period and the present day, academics have attempted to apply business or corporate strategy models to the management of communication as a value added component of linked organizational mission and goals. However, awareness of the need for companies and investors to maintain relationships with all stakeholders in the interests of corporate performance, puts pressure on companies to reassess levels of influence which could be reliably measured in respect of the bottom line. Gaved (1997) argues that 'a new model of corporate change and evolution needs to be developed, which enables management teams to be renewed without major discontinuity. This need is quite independent of the issue of takeovers. What we currently have is a system of informal influence, which increases the pressures on companies – which normally means the CEO and chairpersons – in response to deteriorating performance. For most companies, most of the time there is very little of this 'behind closed doors' influence, but when it does take place, it is the largest shareholders who get most involved and who have disproportionate influence on the company, board and senior management team.

Table 18.2 identifies and distinguishes the difference between routine emergencies and disasters. For an international bank experiencing, say, cyberspace terrorism as a result of systems intervention from a hostile hacker, dependency on a geographical measure to define the scale of such crisis is unlikely to be very helpful. Prior to the mid-1980s, PR practitioners thought in terms of 'routine emergencies' and suggested that a crisis has five stages. Fearn-Banks argues that crisis management is strategic planning to prevent and respond during a crisis or negative occurrence, a process that removes some of the risk and uncertainty and allows the organization to be in greater control of its destiny. However, if as she says a crisis has five stages, the banking culture has to create for itself an anticipatory model of crisis management which 'guides practitioners toward a position in which they can proactively investigate their organization to determine the most likely cause of technological crisis'. With a foundation in anticipation and empowerment, each bank's model would optimize the precautionary abilities of the organization to prevent and cope with a crisis, 'routine emergency', but would they be adequate for a 'disaster'? Table 18.3 suggests the range of routine emergencies and disasters which might occur.

Olaniran and Williams (2001) argue that 'crisis prevention requires a thorough understanding of the technology and the context in which the technology is being used'. This includes processes of enactment and expectation as well as vigilant decision making and they suggest there are two key issues involved, namely rigidity and control.

Table 18.2 Differences between routine emergencies and disasters

Routine emergencies	Disasters
Interaction with familiar faces	Interaction with unfamiliar faces
Familiar tasks and procedures	Unfamiliar tasks and procedures
Intra-organizational co-ordination needed	Intra- and inter-organizational co-ordination needed
Roads, telephones, facilities intact	Roads blocked or jammed, telephones jammed or non-functional, facilities damaged
Communications frequencies adequate for radio traffic	Radio frequencies often overloaded
Communication intra-organizational	Need for inter-organizational information sharing
Use of familiar terminology in communicating	Communication with persons who use different terminology or speak another language
Need to deal mainly with local press	Hordes of national and international reporters
Management structure adequate to co-ordinate the number of resources involved	Resources often exceed management capacity

Source: Auf der Heide (1989)

Table 18.3 International terrorism incidents, 1968–79

	Number	%
Type		
Explosive bombings	1,588	48
Incendiary bombings	456	14
Kidnappings	263	8
Assassinations	246	7
Armed attacks	188	6
Letter bombings	186	6
Hijackings	100	3
Theft/break-ins	78	2
Barricade and hostage	73	2
Snipings	71	2
Other	87	3
Target		
Business executives/facilities	487	36
Diplomatic officials/property	273	20
Other government officials	217	16
Military officials/property	204	15
Private citizens	166	12

Source: US Department of Defense and Central Intelligence Agency in Regester (1989) *Crisis Management*

Rigidity is the degree of inflexibility built into a particular action or process. This is important in terms of interaction and successful outcome because it recognizes that individuals will view problems during any crisis in different ways; through different perceptions people select different options from those available and the consequences will determine the quality of the outcome. Control on the other hand is viewed as 'the degree of influence that organisational members have at their disposal. Control is often elusive because it has to do with individual perception especially when the influence is indirect in nature.' Olaniran and Williams quote the case of ATAT's crisis episode in which 'a software glitch caused a power outage that disrupted its nationwide services for nine hours in January 1990', causing 'an inter-dependent effect on other organizations'. The authors suggest that

the anticipatory model of management can be likened to the law of probability indicating that the less frequent the occurrence of an event, the greater the probability that the event will occur in the future. Therefore, organisation should and must continue to evaluate reliance on technology and to prepare for crises in advance. The anticipatory model of crisis management suggest the possibility that crises could be held in check through an understanding of preconditions and instituting action plans to counteract the precondition effects.

'In nearly every global disaster situation, it is the case that at some level or another, information was available which could have prevented the disaster from happening', wrote Allison in 1993. However, the information was either possessed by those with authority to act upon it but who did not act; or it was not possessed by those with the authority to act and it was not sought out by those in authority; or it was possessed by those who did not have the power to act on it but not shared by them with the parties who did possess the authority to act upon it; or it was shared with the parties who possessed the authority to act on it but the parties with the requisite authority did not take the information seriously enough (p. 40). Thus the will to communicate relies to some extent on the existing culture of a bank and its available expertise not only in speaking and providing information through the media during the crisis and afterwards but also in taking responsibility for ensuring the existence of free flowing information through excellent continuity planning.

This responsibility relies heavily on an understanding of chain of command when the informal system of influence mentioned earlier is clearly inappropriate due to the impact of uncontrollable time constraints. During a crisis and particularly during a disaster, each individual in the communication operational chain must know to whom s/he is

responsible and there should be units of different managerial sizes for different purposes and all units will have been simulated and practised under health and safety regulations. Clearly this span of control must not be excessive but must be organized so that real control is maintained like an army in war time. In other words, the open system of normal management practice will click into a closed system based on military-style organization and co-ordination principles. In wider civilian terms where organizations must liaise with local authorities, this means that the scalar concept which views an organization as a group of grades arranged in sequence with the superior grades carrying authority and the lower grades carrying no authority, becomes irrelevant. The unity of command will belong to the people trained as members of special emergency communication and continuity planning teams.

On 19 June 2003 the British government's cabinet office released a draft 'Civil Contingencies Bill'. For the first time this will provide a single statutory framework for civil protection and emergency planning in the United Kingdom. When enacted it is highly likely that the bill will impose a duty to undertake risk assessments in respect of emergency planning. At local authority level, a major emergency plan (MEP) is drafted in accord with the agreed procedures and practices given in the *Major Incident Procedures Manual* published by the London Emergency Services Liaison Panel (LESLP). The manual is made available to all on the Metropolitan Police website.

The MEP provides guidance to those responsible for managing and co-ordinating the council response to a major emergency. It is geared towards the set up of the Emergency Co-ordination Centre and the roles of key personnel internally and externally.

Due to the wide range of circumstances which a council may be called upon to deal with, it is neither event nor site specific but is generic in nature. The flexibility that this approach assumes has stood the test of time.

The MEP is supported by a department emergency plan, which outlines the procedures to be adopted within each department. Those departmental plans and those of their contractor partners, standardize the layout and ensure a corporate style which everyone understands. MEP and departmental plans are reviewed annually.

For a local authority a major emergency exists where the required council response, at the scene or elsewhere, is in excess of that which can be provided by the council operating under normal day or night conditions and/or where special mobilization and organization of council services is necessary.

Many emergencies are dealt with by departments under their own departmental emergency arrangements, without the need to activate the major emergency plan. However, whilst events which occur during normal working hours may be dealt with perfectly adequately from within available resources, the same event arising during the early hours of the morning, or at the weekend, may require a major emergency response due to the reduced resources immediately available to deal with it.

Back in 1916, the concept of forecasting and planning were called 'purveyance' by Fayol who saw it as one of five divisions of the administrative function, while administration was one of six operations to be found in a business, namely technical, commercial, financial, security, accounting and administration. Together these activities are what today we term management. However, Fayol could never have imagined the complexity of managing organizations today when routine organizational activities are disrupted not only internally but externally by what Florence and Kovacic (2001) call 'the interconnected actions of the major stakeholders' and when 'organisational crisis truly become the public concern when defined and influenced by the mass media'. They quote Thurow's conceptual framework of 'punctuated equilibrium', which depicts an organizational crisis as 'rapid developments characterised by flux, this equilibrium and uncertainty'. Zhu and Blood (1997) offer a four-stage universal model:

1   The build up or pre-crisis period where the symptoms are detectable, such as repeated messages or persistent sets of clues.
2   Crisis breakout – acute crisis which are the initial stages.
3   Abatement or chronicity of the crisis with charges, counter-charges, demonstrations, inquiries, legal actions and the continuing coverage by the mass media.
4   Termination where the organization attempts to get back to normal and where the crisis is no longer a threat to an organization's operational environment or its constituent publics. The media set the agenda in terms of communication during the crisis lifecycle.

Third parties such as the media, play a key role in assessing risk which evolves from research and corporate intelligence. This requires a high degree of trust and confidence as Figure 18.1 indicates.

Managerial perception

Communication managers often confuse risk assessment with risk perception during message design and implementation, (Susskind

Public confidence in scientists working for:

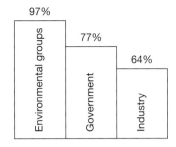

Media confidence in scientists working for:

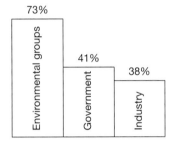

Who would you trust more to make the right decisions about the environment?

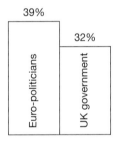

Figure 18.1 Monitoring the trust factor
Source: Mori, 1995, Third party information expertise

and Field, 1996). Perception plays an important part at every stage of monitoring and evaluation of public response. For example, Susskind and Field (in Florence and Kovacic, 2001: 84) suggest six types of anger requiring different responses, namely: when people have been hurt; when people feel threatened by risks not of their own making; when people feel their fundamental beliefs are being challenged; when people feel weak in the face of powerful others; when people believe they have been lied to or duped; and when people strategically display anger to manipulate the reactions of others.

Thus, confidence in the quality of information provision and in the perceptions of management relies on what Sopow (1994) calls the critical issues audit based on recognition of the main points (recognizable in key phrases such as unique, new, first, only or last); in quality support through research, evidence, studies and testing methods; and through public linkages which emerge through what people say, what the public demands and strong support (Regester and Larkin, 1997: 32). UK consultants Regester and Larkin's 1995 UK research audit suggests the organizational priorities based on cost and choice shown in Figure 18.2. A 1994 survey of 250 British companies indicated that employees thought a crisis was more likely to be triggered from outside the organization, rather than inside by management, as shown in Figure 18.3.

Florence and Kovacic (2001) suggest three models of crisis communication management. Their market place model argues that crises are caused and solved by economic, political and legal competition; ideologically based models evolving new or evolving social movements; and a public participation model based on co-operation among governments, private industry and the public. Because of the significance of mass media involvement, these authors stress the importance of message strategies; by identifying stages in a crisis, message strategies can be more appropriately put together, up to a point. Of course, unknown variables make a positive risk-theoretical view virtually impossible and so as with models of forecasting, empirical knowledge is built up with experience so that an understanding of the 'probabilities consequent to

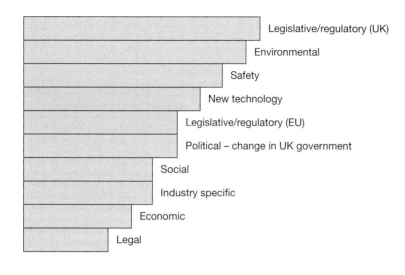

Figure 18.2 Information costs and choices

Source: Regester and Larkin (1997)

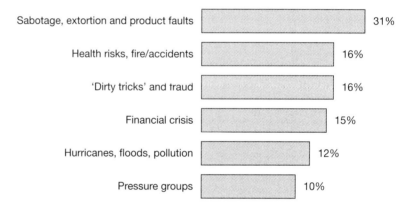

Figure 18.3
Likely causes of crises

certain actions' takes place. The media affect people's perception during the very first moments that they see or hear about a crisis and so one aspect is indisputable. The facts have to be reliable and the attitude credible no matter how different the communication code systems and styles are.

The literature up to the mid-1980s focuses on tactical PR activities and to a lesser extent, on PR strategy as banks became increasingly technologically dependent. But something else happened in the United Kingdom to create a paradigm shift and it begins here – with corporate governance.

Corporate governance

With the rise of banks and other organizations as techno-organizations, the significance of corporate governance is a popular media topic. Williams suggests that directors' oaths would consist of sets of statements to 'reflect the director's strong commitment to his or her employees, the top priority of safety, the high ethical importance of communication and the protection of that communication. A director's oath might include statements that he or she as director is morally responsible for seeing to it that both a will to communicate and a structure for communication are present in the organizations.' Ten years earlier, Allison had suggested 'the establishment of a ten-ured, independently funded safety board which would possess veto power over opera-tional decisions which placed the lives of employees or the general public at risk'. Allison's views were based on all of the disas-ters which he studied where serious com-munication breakdown occurred during the crisis which had been openly acknowledged by 'totally separate judges and investigative committees'.

The Institute of Chartered Accountants in England and Wales (ICAEW) established the Turnbull Working Party to provide assistance to companies in implementing internal con-trol requirements including crisis management strategies; a report was drafted in April 1999, published on 28 September 1999 and be-came a statutory requirement in December 2000. It represents the final element in a combined code on corporate governance and full compliance with the code became a requirement for listed companies from 23 December 2000. The combined code incorp-orates the Turnbull Report, the Cadbury Report and the Hampel Report and suggests key performance indicators as follows:

- Obtain management co-operation.
- Prepare a plan.
- Identify objectives.
- Prioritize the risk to the achievement of the above objectives.
- Establish a risk management policy.
- Consult through the organization.
- Improve the culture of the organization, where and if appropriate.
- Keep the whole plan simple and straight-forward.
- Monitor.

- Incorporate the Turnbull plan in the organization's management and corpor-ate governance processes.

The author of the Report, Nigel Turnbull, states 'we have focused on producing practi-cal guidance that will ensure that the board is aware of the significant risks faced by their company and procedures in place to manage them. Executive management is responsible for managing risks through maintaining an effective system of internal control and the board as a whole is responsible for reporting on it.' Public Limited Companies are expected to have a solid internal control system in order to safeguard the investments of shareholders and the assets of the company.

The effectiveness of internal controls has to be reviewed at least once a year and the risks and issues a business faces should be regularly evaluated. Risk management, operation and compliance and financial controls should be part of a company's review and the entire board of directors is responsible for risk management. An organization has to keep under review the requirement of an internal audit department and the contingency plan of the Turnbull Report was put together so companies can focus on internal controls and specifically their crisis management pro-gramme. The report states that 'social and environmental factors should be included in risk assessments along with conventional/financial threats'. The report also recommends that listed companies radically review their risk management programmes. Thus Nick Bent of Burson-Marsteller, a large PR consul-tancy, stated 'the Turnbull Report means that companies will have to take a broad, sophisti-cated approach to risk, explicitly including environmental matters and threats to reputa-tion. Reputation is a key element of the intan-gible assets of a company and hence its value.'

The Turnbull Report encompasses issues relating to electronic media now that stakeholders expect and demand information in real time and email has raised the expectations of shareholders regarding how quickly companies respond. A typical contingency plan to meet the demands of the Turnbull report can be seen from Accenture's business risk management process.

- Establish goals.
- Assessment of the risk.
- Develop risk solutions.
- Design and implement controls.
- Monitor and feedback.
- Improve the process.

For the above six stages to be successful Accenture notes that the quality of information is crucial for sound decision making. Each of the above stages must 'generate and use time relevant and reliable information'.

Crisis management specialists, Regester and Larkin, state 'in today's complex environment, organizations have to understand and respond rapidly to shifting public values, rising expectations, demands for public consultation and an increasingly intrusive newsmedia. This is particularly crucial when things go wrong.'

Brian O'Connell writing in the *Investor Relations Journal* suggests 'the internet has an estimated 2 billion pages of information and is growing at a pace of 100 million pages per month'. The main crisis arising from this trend is the growth of bulletin boards or chat rooms. It is now possible for an individual to post any sort of information, accurate or inaccurate, on one of these sites and therefore spear illicit and inaccurate information about the company and the management. This suggests the need for these sights to be monitored

closely and outsourcing companies now exist who will undertake search and monitoring on behalf of organizations such as banks. The Investor Relations Society states 'mishandling bad news creates a crisis of confidence in the ability of a company to manage its affairs properly. The result can be disastrous for investors, employees and customers. In some cases a company may never recover.' The society recognizes that it is the responsibility of the communication department to handle events in a professional manner.

The London Stock Exchange points to two levels to crisis management. The first level is where a company should look for anything within its business that may cause a crisis, the second level concerns preparation for specific issues. For example, where a bank may be in the middle of talks concerning a takeover or merger with another bank, it should be assumed this news will be leaked to the media. This sort of issue is relatively predictable and therefore plenty of preparation should and could be undertaken in the form of pre-prepared or holding statements for the press and other media groups and preparations and training of management on what to do and say approached by the media or other parties requesting information. In a report by the UK Department of Trade and Industry 'Creating Quality Dialogue' (1998) it was stated that only 21 per cent of fund managers think that smaller quoted companies, for example, are proficient at communicating information. Imagine how much worse that could be during a crisis.

The organizational crisis matrix in Figure 18.4 suggests the extent to which different parties have control over different types of crises at any given point in time. Each of the crises detailed has the potential to damage an organization's reputation if the amount of control a company has over the outcome of different types of crises is not recognized, understood and addressed accordingly.

The Financial Standard Authority (FSA) states in rule 39 'a firm should have in place appropriate arrangements, having regard to the scale, nature and complexity of its business, to ensure that it can continue to function and meet its regulatory obligations in the event of an unforeseen interruption. These arrangements should be regularly updated and tested to ensure their effectiveness.'

Companies face increasing amounts of regulatory information concerning disclosure of information, which if not handled competently by corporate communication experts will attract attention during a crisis from financial journalists and other interested parties. For example, the Y2K Regulation Fair Disclosure (Reg. FD) prohibits selective disclosure and requires the simultaneous disclosure of material information to the general public with disclosure to analysts or any other group. The aim is to ensure a fair and consistent flow of information to all stakeholder groups where previously certain parties received privileged information from which they accrued considerable advantage. It also aims to discourage 'mosaic' information which the UK Financial Services Authority describes as 'information which, when pieced together with other like matter, creates a material insight into the affairs of a company'. This carries considerable significance after a crisis and for its reporting in a company's quarterly reviewing and annual report and accounts.

The continuity planning industry

It is interesting looking through the case studies available through established business continuity planning websites such as Global Continuity.com to observe how only now are organizations beginning to understand that even though many may have continuity plans in place, the strategic and operational demands being placed on human corporate

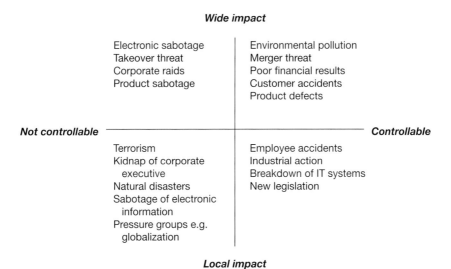

Figure 18.4 A crisis impact model
Source: Adapted from Fill, C. (1999)

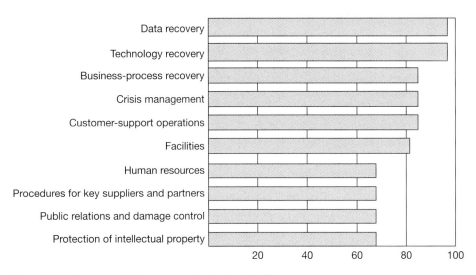

Figure 18.5 Elements of a business continuity plan (BCP)

Note: Multiple responses allowed. Base: 245 companies with business continuity plans. Data: *Information Week* business continuity survey of 350 business technolgy managers.

Source: Information Week in Luftman (2003) p. 164

communication in the event of an invocation are not being addressed (Figure 18.5).

Crisis management is often referred to as issues management by organizations in order for a threat to appear less dramatic to prevent over-reaction by the media and panic by susceptible stakeholders (Table 18.4). The most frequent potential crises many industries face, especially the banking industry, are computer viruses with the fear that one might one day cause the collapse of all computer systems throughout the world. This Y2K crisis failed to materialize but large sums of money were spent by companies panicked into putting contingency plans in place. This involved emergency training of staff and paying over-time rates to IT employees for holiday pay. One Canadian bank for example, held a full-day simulation in their residential training centre where nearly 500 senior staff participated. They used two of their PR staff to simulate the press, complete with professional video camera to inject a level of realism into the situation and to provide a tool for use at subsequent

debriefings via their own training video. Luftman (2003) argues that 'recovery and management plans should be tested at least annually or twice yearly, with performance

Table 18.4 Nine steps to managing BCP performance

1	*Visualize* the business functions (top-down approach)
2	*Itemize* the tasks involved (bottom-up approach)
3	*Prioritize* work only on critical functions until they are substantially complete
4	*Categorize* and organize the problems into management pieces of work
5	*Minimize* the risk – the ultimate goal of business continuity planning
6	*Organize* staff to react to emergencies as they occur
7	*Rehearse* events so that staff are familiar with the planned responses
8	*Sponsor/champion* participation to demonstrate and communicate the importance of the recovery plan
9	*Vigilant monitoring* of supply chain and partners' plans

Source: Giga Group in Luftman (2003)

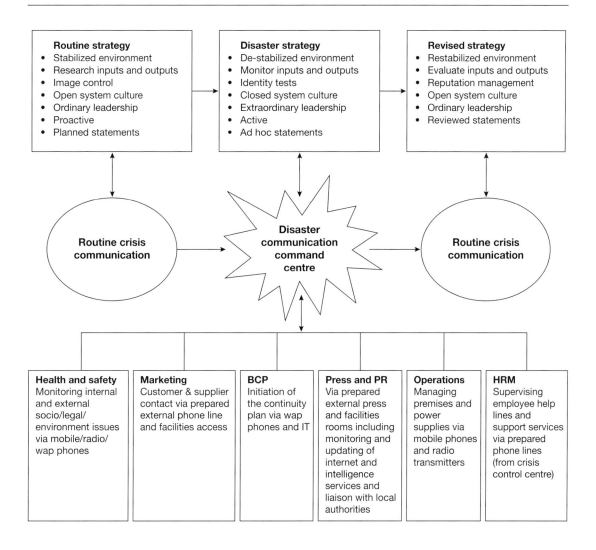

Figure 18.6 The action stations framework: a co-dependency model (see also www.ukresilience.info

gaps identified and actively managed for remediation'.

From a banking perspective, the Y2K threat went through a number of phases in the United Kingdom as it did in Canada and elsewhere. The first was the fear that each bank's own computer system would fail. This resulted in a massive effort to inspect and if necessary correct every line of code. However, opera-

tional contingency planners through Canadian Bankers Associations and the PR industry worked in co-operation with very effective results. They recognized the interdependency with all types of financial institutions, the stock markets and the specialists who move money around. They worked closely with other co-dependent organizations who were important to the industry's infrastructure such as electrical supplies, voice and data communications experts, transit systems for staff, building, heating and air conditioning experts, elevator or lift service companies (Figure 18.6).

Another area of concern was public perception. Although the industry appeared to be on top of the problem, naturally banks could not anticipate the degree to which the public might draw out cash and overload individual banks' ability to respond. The Canadian Bankers Association, traditionally a low-profile damage control type of organization, became proactive in developing a strategy to make sure it had well briefed representatives wherever banking issues of Y2K were likely to be discussed, whether in national media or in schools. It developed a new website and issued explanatory leaflets through their Y2K public affairs working group. While one of the benefits of new technology has been the 24/7 facility that databases provide via websites, cyberspace can also be a threat. While the internet may be a useful monitoring tool for information gathering it also creates narrow costing and a demand for highly skilled practitioners who can monitor and disseminate proactively, critical intelligence that will affect an organization's reputation or security.

For example, the fastest growing crime in the United Kingdom currently is identity fraud. The UK fraud prevention service, Cifas, reported 75,000 cases in 2002 alone, an increase of 55,000 in just three years. It is almost solely due to non-personalized banking communication where security measures lag behind criminal activity. It could be seen as tantamount to negligence by the banking industry – possibly a typical case of bringing to a competitive market something before it or management is ready. With call centres set to increase in number but moved to economically weaker countries, the

longer-term implications are clear. UK bank accounts will be hard for internal and external fraudsters to resist if sophisticated 'man and machine' security measures are not embedded in corporate communication plans underpinning continuity planning training policies.

Corporate communication lies at the heart of all commercial operational activity but especially where organizational security is concerned. This demands excellence in internal communication practices from the top as well as excellence in driving external PR programming and everyday corporate affairs. An organizational climate that can demonstrate that its people work well together, stays together during a crisis and overcomes setbacks more quickly. Sabotage born of internal strife or unethical behaviour, can rarely be dissociated from an organizational culture which may have preceded or triggered a crisis in the first place.

Three learning organizations

Case 1: First Interstate Bank

At the First Interstate Bank in the United States, a fire which rates as one of Los Angeles' biggest, took hold at their premises in Los Angeles' tallest building. The bank came close to losing the entire building and although the incident took place in 1988, it is still used as a training case study because for the business continuity community, this fire rates as perhaps the earliest, it not the best documented example of a business continuity plan in action. Being in an earthquake-prone area, First Interstate had set up a business resumption planning unit and developed a business resumption plan which had been tested just weeks before the fire. They were helped by a consulting group who had had experience during the NorWest Bank fire in Minneapolis six years previously. Over two thousand staff had to be relocated during the outage.

First Interstate's plan centred on an emergency operation centre (EOC) as the hub for decision making. They had six EOCs across California which included regular conference rooms with enhanced communication and media watching equipment. They had a regular staff of about six who would service the EOC and this was increased to twenty around the clock, using volunteers during the incident. Public affairs and employee information were seen as a single responsibility given that employees and their families would see what was in the media and so should get the same message from the bank. Because public affairs and internal communication staff were regarded as a special team within the business resumption plan and because they had recently participated in business disruption exercises, they were called soon after the incident at 1 am on the night of the fire.

This would be normal practice in PR terms but often gets forgotten during a disaster when the corporate culture is tested to its limit. The plan decided upon was as follows:

- There would be a general policy of honesty.
- There was a need to anticipate areas of vulnerability, such as the issue of having no sprinkler system. The bank was installing one at the time.
- It was important to deal with perception issues such as the loss of headquarters and therefore the loss of the bank's ability to serve its customers.
- They must proactively provide the media with a 'we're still in business' angle so the incident became a positive story rather than a negative one.

Practical measures followed which included the setting up of a media centre with twenty phones by 6 am the morning after the fire, including a customer hotline and arrangements that allowed cameras and reporters to interview and take photographs. One witness said 'I seem to remember that they had the CEO being interviewed for American AM outside the burned building at 6 am.' They were able to be confident because the personnel involved knew the business continuity plan and the people running it and were party to new information as it became available. Despite the fact that the bank did not have the full picture when they went to press, it felt confident enough to initiate an interview that went out live and uncut. Thus the media were able to put the emphasis on recovery to counter the visual image of the burning building. This is only possible if there is confidence that the facts can and will back up the story. The image portrayed was that of a wounded giant getting back on its feet because it had a plan to do so. The media also became important in messaging the thousand staff in the tower not to go into work, but to wait for instructions. After this success by the First Interstate PR department a new phenomenon arose. The media's attitude changed and questions were raised. Was this arson because some traders had been dismissed before and the fire started in the trading room? This was never proved. Another question related to the structure of the building. Was it now sound, because it had to be stripped back to bare steelwork. This proved to be okay. The media centre was updated with news every twenty minutes and briefed about the approach to take in response to the questions that were being asked. The small PR department had to suddenly grow and deal with searching questions over a prolonged period. It had to consistently anticipate which direction the media would take so that they could be ready and proactive. While dealing with the media, there were other stakeholders to deal with, such as customers. First Interstate anticipated what we now term call centres by at least ten years. Some of the most frequently repeated dialogues related to customers concerns about the safety of their savings and access to their safe deposit boxes. It is on such fundamental enquiries that longer-term reputations hinge.

The bank had 10,000 employees who played a critical PR role during the crisis ensuring that journalists were referred to the media centre, for example. Wrong or inappropriate responses to the media can be dangerous to an organization's credibility rating, not to mention that of the employee. There are also legal and insurance implications which often focus on statements to the press and film recordings of the first three days. The first news employees and their families get is often from the media who may set the tone for an entire recovery period which in Interstate's case was up to 18 months. Public perception naturally also has investor implications. In this case, while the stock market went down 16 points on average the day after the fire, First Interstate shares only dropped three-quarters of a per cent. Messages to the media were factually based and the bank had a plan for ongoing media interaction over a prolonged period. Employees can make or break the best of plans where the psychological impact of a prolonged outage is great but the effect can be mitigated by effective communication. Internal employee communication must be consistent with external communication and what is heard through the media. Families have a major influence during a crisis and are often less tolerant than the staff themselves.

Indeed at Interstate some family members tried to stop staff returning to the building

after restoration because they feared it was still unsafe. Other issues which emerged related to an initial requirement for the majority of staff to stay at home. There were managerial concerns that staff would not pull their weight, while families were anxious as to whether they might not get paid. Information had to be provided on a regular basis to show that they were not forgotten and a contact number issued for staff to call to raise any question, however trivial. The questions raised by staff were monitored so that the concerns could be identified and addressed collectively or individually. As a consequence First Interstate Bank established an employee communication co-ordinator in each division who was reliable, available and accessible on a 24-hour basis. They compiled lists of home numbers of all staff with priority for core management. Within eight days of the fire, a newsletter was circulated to all affected employees and this continued on a twice weekly basis for the first few weeks. Copies were sent to recovery centres and continued to be issued on a regular basis until all had returned to the damaged building with the question and answer section proving to be of great value. However, although employee morale was high on their return in the first few days after the fire, this soon deteriorated when they found they were working in unfamiliar locations, in makeshift workstations or not working at all. Many also had different travel patterns, longer or different hours of work and apart from direct assistance where necessary, the newsletter came to be an essential way of counselling (Figures 18.7 and 18.8).

The communication and PR staff themselves were not immune from fatigue and depression, so directorates need to be aware of the impact on all staff and themselves. This positive case study is very different from that

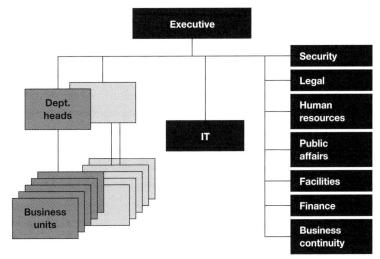

Figure 18.7
First Interstate: normal
organization

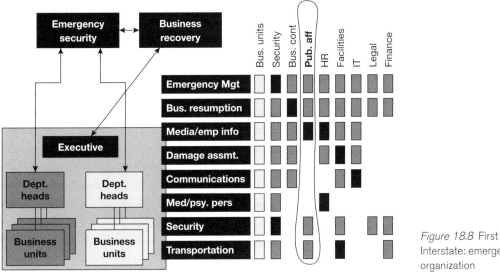

Figure 18.8 First
Interstate: emergency
organization

of another bank fire which took place in the centre of Philadelphia in 1991. The Meridian Bank, situated in a 38-storey bank tower with the Meridian Bank logo prominently displayed and only 300 staff in the building, were not able to defend themselves from bad publicity when a fire got out of control. Three firemen died and there was considerable media concern for customers that the bank and their money were in trouble. Even though the bank were not the major tenant, nor responsible for the fire, their trademark was on top of the building. Meridian were frequently maligned by the media, resulting in loss of public confidence and market share.

First Interstate was organized much as any other major corporation with business units delivering customer service and specialist departments providing support, all under the watchful eyes of the CEO. Public affairs and human resources staff supported the media and information team.

For business continuity to work, it has to be accepted as a management discipline that takes a commitment of resources.

First Interstate: lessons

- Business continuity is a management discipline – not a project.
- Business continuity is a multidiscipline concept requiring buy-in from all areas of risk management.
- It is not enough for individual business units to have their own plans – co-ordination is required for major incidents.
- Plans must be flexible to handle unexpected events.
- Develop experts and trust them to activate the plans.
- Trust comes from exercising the plan.
- Executing a plan well is not enough – all stakeholders have to know that their interests are being taken care of.

Although it might be thought possible to create a specialist unit to manage the practice of business continuity in the organization – it cannot operate in isolation. It must be a cog in a risk management machine. Many organizations that succumbed to the marketing edicts of the 1980s pushed business continuity responsibility down to individual business units, forgetting that a major incident calls for overall co-ordination through the corporate communication or public affairs department. Interstate's plan was flexible enough to be adapted to an unthinkable situation and first Interstate's executive didn't get in the way of the execution plan. The worst thing that can happen is that executives, who have not gone through the training, pull rank and overrule the experts right in the middle of the crisis itself.

Case 2: Allied Irish Bank

The AIB group (UK) plc is a wholly owned subsidiary of Allied Irish Bank plc and is incorporated in Belfast. The company operates in Britain under Allied Irish Bank GB and under First Trust Bank in Northern Ireland. It is the largest Irish banking and financial services group and is made up of four main areas: AIB Bank, United States of America, Capital Markets and WB Kay/Bank Zacodni (Poland), AIB ranks among the top 25 banks in Europe and was quick to recognize that in a crisis its main concern would be to manage its reputation. The bank has won the forum for best business bank four times in succession. This was carried out by a survey of nearly eight thousand businesses and they ranked Allied Irish Bank number one, well ahead of other high street banks. The bank relies on its reputation and by winning this award are able to market this aspect of their image and identity. The bank has stringent procedures in place for dealing with evacuation, salvage and recovery in the event of a crisis. These procedures should be seamless, that is, the changeover should not be seen from the outside. However, it does not deal with major crises and the handling of media, where staff have been injured or customers affected. They therefore use case studies guidelines from the British Home Office and the global continuity websites to develop their policy and guidelines; they used a step approach such as the one described above to do a qualitative analysis and then address the issues of worst case scenario in managing crisis communication such as only starting work on a potential crisis after it is made public, letting your reputation speak for you, treat the media like the enemy or getting stuck in reaction versus being proactive and many others. They looked at corporate behaviour, interpersonal and group communication, the organizational culture, the formal levels of communication and the problems that may bring during a crisis, although the bank had communication guidelines for their public relations strategy, they found the exercise and existing policy did not deal with the communication media relations in the event of a major international crisis in respect of a media relations policy.

In April 2001 they submitted a communication and media relations policy, specifically for business continuity management, which is an integral part of Allied Irish Bank's operational risk management strategy. The policy established an effective and consistent framework for BCM communication and media relations across Britain in line with leading best practice to meet regulatory requirements and observe internal standards and obligations. The policy was both practical and applicable to all businesses within Britain, while sufficiently flexible to cater for change and the impact it has on the continuity risk. The policy was endorsed by the group BCM Committee as providing a process for the consistent delivery of a proven, documented and up to date business continuity.

The chair of the BCM steering group activates the communication team who will keep abreast of potential issues through monthly or quarterly meetings. The Steering Group has communication organizational structure and people in place so that after a decision is made to activate crisis capability, internal teams meet to determine the actions and the implementations of assignments. Once the plan is activated the team maintains constant contact updating assignments and plans as necessary until a decision is made to deactivate.

It was decided that the invocation procedures would be as follows. Business would continue as normal if the system or building failed or was down for a portion of one day. However, the BCM team would meet if

Table 18.5 Communication channels

| Medium | Internal only | | | | | | Stakeholders |
	Instruct	Inform	Listen	Consult	Involve	Empower	
Alimail	•	•	•	•	•		Internal only
E-mail/internet	•	•	•	•	•		All
Video	•	•					N/A
Telephone	•	•	•	•			All
Newsletter	•	•					All
Letter	•	•					All
Circulars/memos	•	•					Internal only
Team meeting	•	•	•	•	•	•	Internal only
Briefing	•	•	•				All

Source: Fill, C. (1999)

the system/building failure was down for a full day and the communication team would meet with crisis management to authorize invocation if systems or building failure went beyond one day. A communication personnel decision-making tree was established for both inside office hours and outside office hours and the communication channels established as shown in Table 18.5.

The checklist identifies tasks that teams or individuals may be called upon to perform and the performance measures expected from the team were also established. Press briefing locations to be used were identified and the stakeholder contact list was issued, which included television news agencies, the press, the regulators and others. A training programme is in place for taking control of a crisis, understanding initial response options and other general guidelines such as co-ordination, briefing the news media, including likely media questions and enquiries, the rules for radio interviews and press releases, training for the spokespersons and interview record keeping with questions and answers to be used for evaluation and research for continuing improvement.

Case 3: Scotiabank

Scotiabank is a $240 billion international bank, operating across Canada and in fifty-five foreign locations. It is one of ten office buildings in downtown Toronto housing about 6,000 staff. It has sixty-eight floors compared to First Interstate's sixty-two.

They set up a permanent BCM unit in 1989 after analysing a series of major events in the United States and overseas which they examined for business continuity issues and lessons to be learned.

A series of incidents

United States

- World Trade Centre bomb
- Oklahoma city bomb
- Earthquakes (LA and SF)
- Hurricanes Andrew, Fran
- Midwest floods

Canada

- Days of protest
- Red River flood
- Great ice storm
- Brush fires
- Demonstrations
- Power outages
- Telecom failure
- Christmas tree fire

Overseas

- Hurricane – Jamaica
- IRA bombs – UK
- Power outage – NZ

Y2K

The Y2K preparations brought these to a head, not only within their own organization, but as a collaborative effort for the whole Canadian and international financial community. The interesting thing to watch was the progression of the threat from that of a technology failure, to that of an infrastructure failure, to one of public confidence failure leading to the banker's traditional nightmare – a sudden huge demand for cash. Thus the emphasis in the final months of 1999 in Canada was on aggressively managing public attitudes – which led to an unprecedented joint PR exercise for the Canadian Financial Institutions orchestrated by the Canadian Bankers Association.

Thus, a number of the bank's informal relationships developed which were reinforced by a number of actual operational incidents. Past semi-formal relationships between the business continuity management unit and PR unit had to be formalized to the process as part of the Scotiabank emergency response plan. The plan involves the use of two teams which look after Scotiabank's interests as a tenant when incidents occur in their main office towers in downtown Toronto. One team, Scotiabank InformationCommunication and Analysis Team (SICAT) collects information on the situation, analyses it for validity and implications to the bank and presents it to the second team (Scotiabank Emergency Response Team, SEMT) for them to determine the best overall strategy for the bank for that particular situation. SEMT has two components. The prime team is made up of the main decision-making responders and includes security, facilities, insurance, business continuity and the vice president. SEMT secondary members are called if the situation warrants it and include public relations, human resources, general council and IT.

Under the plan, each department provides a main member and two alternates who are on call 24 hours, 7 days a week, contact is made at random once a month, and the time to establish contact is recorded to ensure it is within acceptable time frames, members also undertake to take part in two exercises a year using realistic scenarios, the plan is tied into that of the building managers where they are located to ensure that all share the same information and is thus formalized. This is particularly important if the bank's spokesperson and the building management spokesperson are to give the same story and not create confusion in the media. For example, there was a fire in the electrical feed vault outside the building adjacent to the bank which was occupied by one of their competitors, the Royal Bank. In order to put water onto the fire, the fire chief ordered the electrical supply to be cut which also cut power to the smaller of the two towers belonging to Scotiabank, because it is fed from the same transformer. In fact, both Royal and Scotiabank immediately activated their business continuity plans. Scotiabank evacuated twelve hundred people and Royal Bank evacuated nearly a thousand people. The media greatly underestimated the number of people affected but also assumed that everyone was simply sent home. The PR spokesperson called the reporter and explained the situation after being briefed by the business continuity planning director, Rex Patterson. The result was a much more positive report the following day. In the meantime Royal Bank had not proactively managed the media and did not come out of the incident so well. In the *Toronto Globe and Mail* dated 22 June 2000, they quoted the Scotiabank's senior manager of public affairs as saying 'the fire has been an inconvenience, but it hasn't been disruptive' whereas the newspaper said of the Royal Bank that the incident had a silver lining for at least one resident: 'I got in and found out I had the day off. It's the first day of summer. You can't go wrong', one Royal Bank employee said.

Scotiabank has set the standard in Canada after being given a brief to develop a comprehensive formal emergency management capability in autumn 2000. Their first job was to come up with a methodology that would underpin their plans, which made sense if they broke them down into nine distinct stages as shown in Figure 18.9. Some of these may run concurrently and some may never be invoked if the emergency does not develop into a major outage. However they were able to develop protocols for each stage that provided them with common starting points.

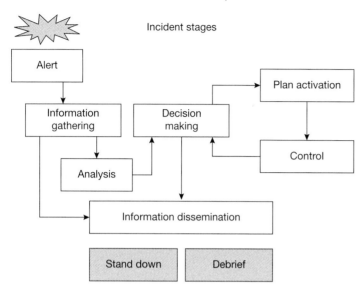

Figure 18.9 Scotiabank's incident response

Scotiabank's emergency management organization (Figure 18.10) bears a strong resemblance to the First Interstate model. It has a core group of *decision makers* made up of senior members of their real estate (facilities), security, insurance and operations departments. This core group can be rapidly expanded to pull in senior members of public affairs, human resources, communication services, network support, and legal departments. Designated members of these teams, and their alternates agree to be on 7/24 call.

For the decision makers to make effective decisions they must have the best available information and if the decisions are to have an impact they must be communicated. This only works if there is a group *dedicated* to this task and not involved in responding to the incident. Known as SICAT it is made up of the members of the business continuity management (BCM) unit plus a number of volunteers who train with BCM and are also on call 24/7.

Neat diagrams are not enough to provide an emergency response capability. Some of the issues the bank came across in turning the model into a reality meant having teams that can convene rapidly in time of need. Team members have to agree to being on call on a 24-hour basis, 7 days a week, and part of that agreement is to participate in random contact tests on a regular basis.

The bank realizes that it is possible to teach theory but instincts (or panic) tend to take over in a crisis. They issue each team member with a red book of checklists and other information to guide them when called. This information is now downloaded onto Blackberry hand-held devices. Decisions must be made on sound information. Typically in a major incident there is an overload of information and very reliable facts. It takes knowledgeable and dedicated people to create 'intelligence' from the information available and this, of course, is a key discipline in the armoury of the professional communication specialist, who knows that gathering information is one thing – making sure it gets to those who need to know is another.

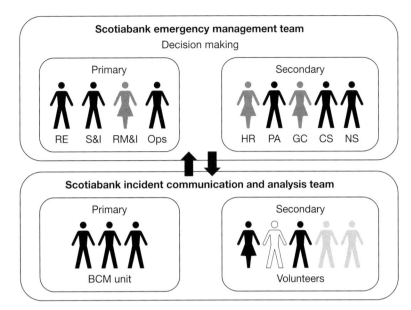

Figure 18.10 Scotiabank's approach to emergency management

Five stages of an incident

Each team member has all the instructions for carrying out their tasks either on a hard copy 'red book' or on a Blackberry hand-held device. Somehow, somewhere, someone becomes aware of an actual or possible incident and calls a member of one of the teams (or both). The person contacted uses their checklist to review what they have to do and how to do it. There will be a contact between the two teams and a decision to activate the alert. A time for a conference bridge is set. Scotiabank use a broadcast telephone alert system (Alertcast) to rapidly alert all team members. At the same time they activate their status line so staff can check that the BCM Unit are aware of a situation. Designated team members have the information at hand to do this. Once the teams are alerted they usually need more information. The Blackberry provides a list of what information may be important and who might be best to obtain it.

This information is fed to the communication and analysis team who also monitor the media and internet as appropriate (Figure 18.11).

Raw information is not enough. It has to be checked for accuracy and relevance to the bank by the communications and analysis team. They will also check on the business units' BCPs and if they are being actioned and this information is put onto the standard status format and transmitted to the Blackberries and PCs of the emergency management team. A meeting of the emergency management team or another conference bridge is initiated and an overall assessment of the situation made in a standard format. From this an overall strategy is drafted (using a checklist) to provide overall guidance and support to the impacted business units. This is presented to the bank's executive for approval (Figure 18.12).

Now the organization is ready to get a consistent and proactive message out to all

Scenario: phases 1 and 2

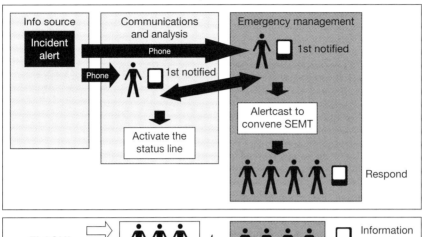

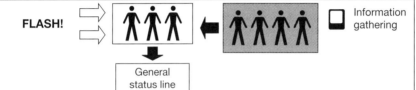

Figure 18.11
Scenario: phases
1 and 2

Scenario: phases 3 and 4

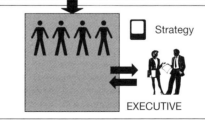

Figure 18.12 Scenario: phases 3 and 4

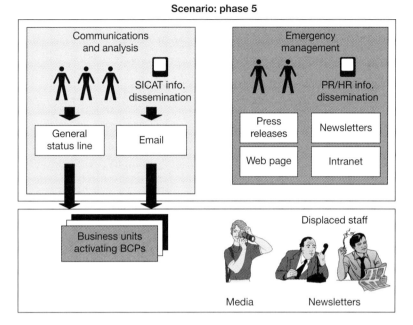

Scenario: phase 5

Figure 18.13
Scenario:
phase 5

stakeholders. If you have had to face the media before this point you have been able to say with some confidence that your organization has plans in place to deal with any disruptive situation and that those plans have been activated. Now you are armed with an approved strategy to deal with this particular situation which you can show is being managed – not just reacted to. The bank works to checklists that have been developed through experience. Several methods are used – all using the same source, namely corporate communication and PR interfaces with the media. For a prolonged outage, human resource management will interface with staff, including those who have been told to stay at home. Meanwhile the communications and analysis team is interfacing with the business units making sure that they are kept abreast of what is going on, using predetermined guidelines (Figure 18.13).

The remaining four phases deal with the management and control of a prolonged outage, the return to normal and debriefing.

All are important but the crucial communication element continues to maintain, monitor and prioritize relations with all stakeholders.

Organizations are conscious of the importance of business continuity capability to cope with increasing numbers of business disrupting incidents.

Scotiabank found that individual plans are not enough. Responses must be co-ordinated and that depends on excellent communication. Many organizations put such a capability in for Y2K only to abandon it afterwards.

Best practice

Corporate communicators realize that recovery demands that all stakeholders know about it and the organization must go beyond damage limitation if it is to profit from any disasters afterwards. The lesson learned is that strategic communication strategy is only as valuable as the organization's culture and capacity to cope functionally during a disaster.

As vice president, Rex Engstrand, director of Wells Fargo and Company corporate business continuity planning office, once said about the value of uninterrupted service:

> our mission is to contribute to the continued success of the bank by providing guidance and support to each business unit. Our BCP plans are designed to safeguard and protect personnel, customers, cashflow and long-term market share in the event of an unplanned interruption to our business. The advancement of technology has driven new solutions that were not available in recent years. I believe as we proceed into the future, we will see continued blurring of what differentiates the technology plan and a business unit plan.

Interestingly what he does not refer to on his webpage article, published in February 2001, is the role of corporate communication.

The corporate communication industry is very aware of this and specialist services are popping up overnight in recognition of the fact that wherever human dramas or tragedies are played out, the press will be there. The Press Alert Organization have issued a press pack of do's and don'ts which offers advice and information that they say applies just as well to the financial crisis, whether involving fraud, business collapse or a hostile takeover bid. They offer a checklist of twenty principles or questions that need to be asked when planning communication as part of a business continuity plan:

- Why should my company be of interest to the media?
- How can my company prepare, in advance, to deal with the media?
- In a crisis how quickly will the media respond?
- What is the impact of this instant press response?
- How should my company deal with the media in the immediate aftermath?
- What should the response of our senior spokesperson be?
- What happens if we refuse to co-operate with the press altogether?
- Who should tell the press any really bad news?
- How should my company help the relatives of anyone killed or injured where the press are concerned?
- How should we handle the recall of products?
- What about the practical side of dealing with the media on the ground?
- What are the pros and cons of radio, television and newspaper interviews and how do they differ?
- What do the local/regional press want from us and what is their role?
- What do photographers want from us?
- What if the international press are involved in covering a crisis?
- What should we do when the press point the finger of blame at us?
- What happens when a VIP visits the crisis scene?
- How should my company react to a concerted media campaign from a pressure group?
- How will the story be reported in the long term?
- What should be done after the crisis to media plan for the future?

Source: Press Alert

Conclusion

These three cases indicate the level of strategic underpinning that is critical to organizational disaster management. The corporate communication strategy should operate like clockwork. Organizations must have simulated training events to ensure that all members of the emergency and continuity planning team know how to behave and conduct themselves in relation to the corporate communication director, who is accountable for best practice for the duration of a disaster and immediately afterwards. This includes updates and changes to previously evaluated PR policy schedules. Like regular fire drills, simulated events should be seriously undertaken and assessed on a regular basis, with all staff involved including the core group of continuity planning, communication and PR professionals and main board directors. (See Action Stations Framework on p. 289).

The reward will be that the monitoring and evaluation of organizational performance before, during and after a disaster through first-class communication could be seen to be not only best practice, but impressive. Post-disaster feedback from all stakeholders should be audited and measures of image, identity and reputation carried out on a regular follow up basis so that quantitative and qualitative data can be fed into future communication decision-making processes and plans.

Based on classical theories of action centred leadership and occupational psychology principles of co-dependency approaches to corporate governance, competent continuity planning performance management would include training models such as the action stations framework (Figure 18.6).

NOTE

The author is greateful for the contribution made to the case studies by practitioner colleagues at Bank of Nova Scotia (Canada) and AIB (UK).

BIBLIOGRAPHY

Allison, R. E. (1993) *Global Disasters: Inquiries into Management Ethics*, New York: Prentice Hall.

Fayol, H. (1949) *General and Industrial Administration*, London: Pitman.

Fearn-Banks, K. (1996) *Crisis Communications*, Mahwah, NJ: Lawrence Erlbaum.

Fill, C. (1999) *Marketing Communication*, 2nd edn, New York: Prentice Hall.

Florence, B. T. and Kovacic, B. (2001) 'Intersections between crisis and management', in D. P. Cushman and S. S. King (eds), *Excellence in Communicating Organisational Strategy*, New York: State University of New York Press.

Gaved, M. (1997) 'Corporate governance: The challenge for communication practitioners', *Corporate Communication International Journal*, 2(2).

Hutton, J. G. (2001) 'Defining the relationship between public relations and marketing: Defining the practice', in R. L. Heath (ed.), *Handbook of Public Relations*, Thousand Oaks, CA: Sage Publications.

Liew, J. (1997) 'Banking on a sharper image?', *Corporate Communication: An International Journal*, 2(2), 76–86.

London Stock Exchange (2000) *A Practical Guide to Listing on the London Stock Exchange* and *A Practical Guide to Investor Relations*, London: Stock Exchange.

Luftman, J. N. (2003) *Managing Information Technology Resource: Leadership in the Information Age*, Harlow: Pearson/Prentice Hall.

Olaniran, B. A. and Williams, D. E. (2001) 'Anticipatory model of crisis management: "A vigilant response to technological crisis"', in R. L. Heath (ed.), *Handbook of Public Relations*, Thousand Oaks, CA: Sage, Chapter 41.

Oliver, S. (1997) *Corporate Communication: Principles, Techniques and Strategies*, London: Kogan Page.

Oliver, S. (2000) 'Symmetrical communication: does reality support rhetoric?', *Corporate Communication: An International Journal*, 5(1), 26–33.

Oliver, S. (2001) *Public Relations Strategy*, London: Kogan Page.

Pearson, C. M. and Mitroff, I. I. (1993) 'From crisis prone to crisis prepared', *The Executive*, 7.

Price Waterhouse Cooper (2000) *The Technology Race: the 2000 European Benchmarking Study for Technology Companies*.

Regester, M. and Larkin, J. (1997) *Risk Issues and Crisis Management*, London: Kogan Page.

Sopow, E. (1994) 'The critical issues audit', in Register and Larkin (1997).

Susskind, L. and Field, P. (1996) *Dealing with an Angry Public: the Mutual Gains Approach to Resolving Disputes*, New York: Free Press.

Thurow, L. C. (1996) *The Future of Capitalism; How Today's Economic Forces Shape Tomorrow's World*, New York: William Morrow.

Williams, H. M. (1997) 'Financial relations', in O. W. Baskin, C. Aronoff, D. Lattimore (eds), *Public Relations: the Professions and the Practice*, Madison, WI: McGraw Hill.

Zhu, J. H. and Blood, D. (1997) 'Media agenda setting; telling the public what to think about', in B. Kovacic (ed.), *Emerging Theories of Human Communication*, New York: SUNY Press.

CHAPTER 19

Crisis management in the internet mediated era

David Phillips

This chapter looks at crisis and issues management from an internet mediated perspective. It examines how transparency, porosity and agency influence both the nature of issues and crisis and how they extend the range and speed which such corporate problems can materialize. By reviewing how internet tools such as email and web pages can be deployed in an escalating crisis situation, the author shows how the internet can be applied (or not as the case may be) to aid crisis management. Finally the chapter looks at a range of internet crises faced by a variety of organizations that have occurred in recent years and offers some ideas for planning against such eventualities.

The nature of crisis

The nature of organizational risk has two elements and it is worth dwelling on them and their nature to help understand the range of concerns that need to be considered in crisis and issues management. The elements are:

- crisis which threatens the survival of the company/organization;
- an issue which is a normal process of management which is an exception to daily routine.

Crisis

A crisis can be sudden and unexpected which can be handled by a person on the spot with direct responsibility and training or, often, good common sense. It may be an event that requires the co-operative effort of more people and which may require bringing people in to work from home or it may require a team of colleagues and outside agencies/contractors. At its worst, a crisis can be because of a major sudden disaster.

Alternatively, a crisis can be caused through an issue running out of control. This form of latent crisis is by far the most frequent cause for corporate disaster and is also, by far, the most difficult to manage.

The best defence against most crises is in the effective day by day management of issues.

Issues

Issues management is part of the daily process of PR practice. The *situational theory of publics* defined by Grunig (1982)[1] outlines three characteristics that affect how publics react to issues: problem recognition, constraint recognition and level of involvement.

1   In *recognizing* a problem, he proposed, people will actively seek information about the issue that concerns them and/or record (or *process*) information that comes to them unsought.
2   *Constraint* recognition describes the extent to which people believe there are obstacles that limit their ability to fulfil their plans.
3   Level of *involvement* means the extent to which a person feels connected to a particular situation and will determine whether they are likely to *act* or not.

Grunig and Hunt (1984)[2] say that when an organization or its publics behave in a way that has consequences for each other, they create PR issues. When affected people choose to react, they become members of a public. Publics form around issues.

By preparing for, and managing issues corporate response reduces the probability of crisis threatening the organization.

The internet information structure

The Rand Research Brief 'Strategic War in Cyberspace' for the US National Defense Research Institute in 1995,[3] says *'National Security is becoming progressively more dependent on and identified with assets related to the "Information Revolution".'* As for the United States, so for every organization. Company security is becoming more dependent on

and identified with assets related to the information revolution. This can include a website, email, SMS, WAP and downloads and viruses. In addition, the wider public can quickly form pressure groups and affect corporate security.

The public's perception of internet information security focuses on external online gossip, rogue sites and hacking (which are, nevertheless, a problem), the Rand organization identified that the majority of online compromise comes from within.

The insider with access and authority to information can, through incompetence, inadvertence, accident, purposefully or maliciously compromise an organization very easily. In addition, information now flows through organizations as never before and many employees are not trained or conversant with their online responsibilities. Lapses in security are a very common cause of the emergence of issues. Preventing digital security lapses is incumbent on all employees (and external contractors and agents). This can be as simple as not sending emails to external people that include prior content from someone else. Occasionally, organizations will find that a hacker is intent on breaking into corporate information and so good defences by way of firewalls and virus protection are very important. With the advent of internal email, information flows between departments and up the hierarchy of organization with great ease. Historic departmental and seniority barriers have come down (Figure 19.1).

In addition multidiscipline groups are formed on a project basis using internal email and other technologies which provide for greater information flows between departments and also offer the means for information to 'leak' to the outside world into trusted partner organizations (e.g. supply schedule)

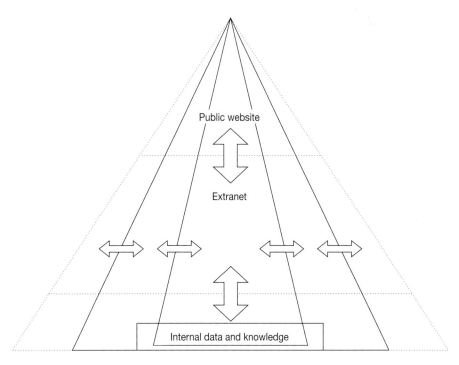

Figure 19.1 Information flows in an organization

as organizations become more transparent. These easy communication lines create opportunities for sensitive information to 'escape' and this can be the cause of varying degrees of embarrassment and corporate compromise.

Our organizations are becoming much more transparent. Companies publishing press releases for the convenience of the press and public automatically make them available to competitors. This is just one example, there are hundreds including comparisons of price, product and service that can be made by competitors as well as consumers, employees and many other publics.

Information that 'leaks' out of organizations is called porosity. Examples of porosity can be found in emails leaked to the press (the Martin Sixsmith/Stephen Byers debacle in the United Kingdom included emails being leaked

from the Department of Transport, Local Government and the Regions).

People using newsgroups and discussion lists at work and at home, frequently comment about their companies to people they do not know and who may live on the other side of the world or a street away. People (and technologies) can use, amend, annotate and juxtapose this information, the internet can act as an agent of change to alter, spread and misapply corporate messages and information(Figure 19.2).[4]

Protecting organizations with employee awareness campaigns

We can learn lessons from the US government's approach to crisis and its analysis of the threat.

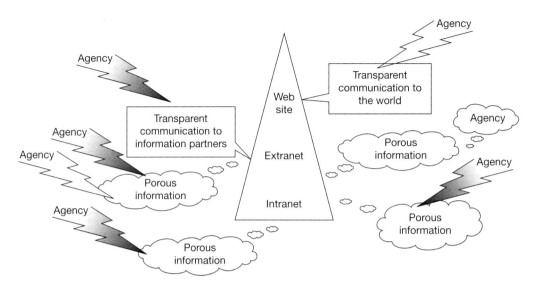

Figure 19.2 The flow of information to the outside world making organizations more transparent and porous, offering greater opportunities for internet agency to take effect

It made it clear that technology in the form of security systems and firewalls is not enough. It identified that organizational policies, practice and processes as well as technology are important. It noted that, in an environment where most employees are trustworthy, there is a lesser threat but pointed to the need for policies, practices and processes to be implemented and adhered to, to reduce the threat.

This is where the PR practitioner has a role to play. Employees who are aware of the value of reputation (which can be worth as much as, if not much more than, the capital value of buildings, machines and many intellectual properties) will be much more aware of the need to mind corporate reputation, if for no other reason than self-interest. In addition, employees who are aware of the ethical mores of an organization will be much less tolerant of compromise by colleagues.

There is a greater threat from disaffection. This can be because of slight (imagined or real), unhappiness (over working conditions,

pay, or frustration with colleagues) or availability of work equipment. A typical response may be from frustration caused by dated computer equipment at work (especially when a home computer will often be more powerful and running the latest software while a work computer and its software can be comparatively dated). Frustration will lead employees to 'short circuit the system' by, for example, working from home or by adding pirate software to a work station leading to security lapses. It is then a short step to sending insecure information externally. A spiral of compromise results and opens the gateway to more dangerous outcomes until this issue becomes a crisis.

An actual case in August 2001 occurred when Cisco implemented major cost cutting throughout the organization. An employee, unhappy and frustrated by a cutback in the budget for supplying mineral water (kept refrigerated and available to everyone), created a website[5] with a number of spoof posters (see example in Figure 19.3). In a very

Figure 19.3
Cisco found itself subject to very public satire after displaying posters asking employees to drink less water as a cost saving exercise – a more than usual example of corporate porosity

short time this site was quoted across the internet. It was light hearted but nevertheless embarrassing for Cisco, if amusing to the rest of the world.

In examining such motives, an organization will heed the report of the joint findings by the US Computer Sciences and Telecommunications Board, the National Research Council and the National Academies in the United States.[6] This group identified that there was little distinction between the vulnerabilities of classified and unclassified data and systems. They found they were both subject to motivations as diverse as coercion to personal conviction prompting unhelpful or dangerous responses by malcontent employees.

In addition, the committee identified that as organizations became more transparent

(it cited the US Department of Defense, with over 200 gigabytes of publicly accessible data) much can be inferred and conclusions drawn of an unhelpful nature by employees and external activists. There are many advantages for organizations when making up-to-date information available on websites but equally there is the opportunity for it to provide raw material for close external analysis and conclusions to be drawn.

Once again, it is the senior PR manager who has to balance the needs of website users and the advantages of transparency against the occasion of unwarranted or misleading conclusions being drawn to damage an organization. As many websites are large, it is usual to discover out-of-date information juxtaposed with apparently conflicting modern website content. Such lack of website maintenance discipline can cause some serious problems for organizations. The internet is responsible for only a small proportion of corporate crises.

Management caused crisis

According to the Institute for Crisis Management,[7] management decisions/indecision still rank highest as the cause for corporate crisis. Human error, mechanical problems and acts of god, are, in descending order, the remaining principal causes.

What the internet does, is offer fast and extensive reach of information about such disasters. It is on the internet that the consequences of management decisions/indecision are most evident in creating issues. In 2001, Microsoft was involved in a direct mail lobbying campaign. Its managers decided to aid the distribution of letters to be sent to government representatives ostensibly from the public pleading the company's cause. The

campaign was undermined and Microsoft's reputation was tainted when it was discovered that some of these letters had been received from people who were dead. For most Microsoft users, this story is a 'little local difficulty' in the United States. While the story broke in the *Los Angeles Times*, the reach and speed of the internet meant that the story was out across the world in minutes (Figure 19.4). Knowing where crisis is most likely to emerge is very helpful for crisis management.

Planning to handle sudden crisis

The four key attributes public relations brings to crisis management are:

1   The practitioner who is able to bring to crisis planning a dispassionate, broad and considered balance to potential hazards. Being able to understand the danger and not be sucked into a panicked response is the most important quality of the professional practitioner. The most effective

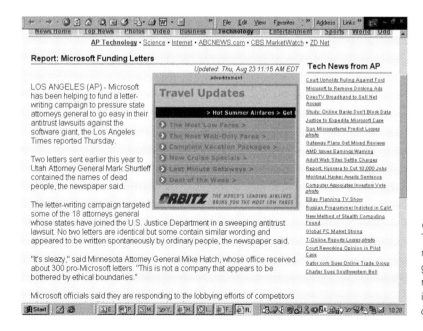

Figure 19.4
The Microsoft lobbying misadventure is available to a global public because of the reach of the internet. The internet aids the transparency of the *Los Angeles Times*

practice comes from taking the broad view and planning. The process of planning will expose vulnerabilities and reduce risk.

2   It is cause for little surprise to find otherwise competent managers are unskilled in communication. A PR practitioner will always respond by reviewing the communication needs of a wide range of different publics. They will weigh up the consequential effect of different forms of communiqué on different and tertiary publics. Most managers have a much narrower view. Thinking about consequences for employees, shareholders, communities, suppliers, the media and other relevant publics is a key asset.

3   The third and most valuable asset is a practitioner who is prepared and who has considered a wide range of scenarios and necessary responses.

4   The fourth asset is the practitioner who can, in peacetime, inspire people to think the unthinkable, plan, prepare and practise. It may never happen but developing teams to manage crises makes them better managers for day to day work and makes them aware that even small issues can escalate, and so they see why they have to manage them ever more effectively.

Planning responses

Planning responses for crises will fall into perhaps four levels of preparation and response. The key to managing crises is to construct plans in such a way that they can be managed on an escalating scale. From management of a potential dangerous but contained event to a full-scale disaster, the plan will need to change. In a real crisis, the first rule is to be

calm and as dispassionate as possible. The following provides some guidance as to how responses can be in place for increasingly serious events. Events may require a pick and mix approach to the use of these crisis tools but they form a process for escalating response, as follows.

1 Sudden and unexpected events which can be handled by a person on the spot with direct responsibility and training or, often, good common sense. This is the most common form of crisis. This might be to put out a small fire, or set off an alarm. The practitioner will want to prepare for responding to such an effort by developing an internal briefing plan and an external communication routine for delivering information to relevant publics. This will mean that the practitioner will have a list (database) of publics such as employees, departmental or section heads, other and external stakeholders and the media. While traditional means for communication are to be included (letter, memo, telephone, press release), it is important to have email addresses available too. It may be useful to have a webpage (and draft content) ready to add to the relevant intranet or website which can be quickly populated and posted to the server. The key issue here is the modernity of the lists and an ability to manage such a crisis from a different location. In addition, the practitioner will need to be wary of turning a local incident into a global issue. The circulation of information needs to be circumspect. The BBC will leap at a fire story and a small incident can be akin to a national disaster on a slow news day! Be wary of using email. It is all too easy to 'forward' an email to hundreds of friends. An employee using email can make his 'exciting day at the office' sound like Armageddon!

2 An event that requires the co-operative effort of more people and which may require

bringing people in to work from home is the next escalation step in planning responses. More people are involved and so more information and even wider interpretation of events is normal. In addition, there will be wider spread about news of the incident.

The practitioner may be away (even PR people take holidays) and even the most appropriate managers may be too far away or incommunicado. The practitioner will want to have in place all the arrangements identified above but will additionally be responsible for alerting more colleagues and external agencies. Once again, the most appropriate list of contacts will need to be available. The logistics will now be more cumbersome and the temptation to use email even more compelling. The need for the plan to work even when key people are absent is now a significant consideration.

3 An event that requires a team of colleagues and even outside agencies or contractors raises the incident profile considerably. An attendant fire engine or horde of 'inspectors' create excitement, interest, and the interpretation of events will have an aura of gossip forming round knowledge, debate and conjecture. There will be the additional need to have people in place who can act as one or more (trained) spokespersons. This person (people) should not be the responsible PR practitioner (he/she will have far too much to do). The CEO should not be in the front line either. Senior managers should be protected from media calls because the business will continue to need management, and press calls are an unnecessary distraction. The key to being effective under such circumstance is to ensure managers are briefed with facts (and only facts) and are up to date.

Crisis is a distraction and even in competent hands some will want to 'meddle'. If the briefing plan is well conceived and updates are regular and reassuring (even when the crisis is worrying), the practitioner and the crisis team will have greater freedom for action (and more productive time) if the briefing process is effective. In this circumstance, the plan calls for both offsite backup of the organization's intranet and website (a mirror site) and will require pages prepared that can be uploaded quickly. A major incident may mean that the organization's web server is affected and so cannot be relied on. For the same reasons, there need to be alternative and offsite telephones ready to come into play. Personal cellphone numbers are not a very good idea. They quickly become inundated with incoming calls. Making outgoing calls becomes a nightmare. Work with a nearby call centre to see if their facility can cope with sudden and significant pressure.

In an event such as this, there will be a call for a lot of supporting information by many publics and the media. It should be remembered that corporate websites are now the first port of call for journalists. Background information and key contacts need to be very visible from the front page of the website but a new and direct emergency page needs to be posted quickly. Pre-prepared pages that can be populated and posted to the site quickly will point to other of the organization's (often already existing) pages. Contact information, maps and personnel profiles plus added information such as local services (hospitals, police, and the fire brigade PR departments may be included). It may be that the organization's emergency site will point to government departments and specific relevant official web pages. But the pages posted in such events need to be flexibly constructed. There is no point in publicizing the fire brigade when your crisis is the demise of a key employee in a far off land. The new additions to the organization's site will offer contact information (with alternatives). One form of contact is not enough. Phone is fine, email is essential, instant messenger for a selected few and even web cam broadcast can all be a plus. This is the hardest time to handle email requests for information and, at the same time the most critical time. Email turnround has to be swift. There is nothing more impressive than an organization with a major incident on its hands that is providing good information and contacts via the web page and apparently very in-control. If everything is dead . . . everyone knows this is not an incident – it's a disaster. On one hand, the organization's reputation sours and, on the other, it is driven into the realm of management incompetence.

Why email? For a big incident, and because news spreads very fast through the web, relatives, journalists and friends will want to be kept informed from around the world. With telephone facilities too stretched (or significantly disrupted) email is a very useful communication tool and will relieve pressure on other, more critical communication resources. It is useful to have a number of people who can manage email. The use of call centres for telephone enquiries can also be used as a template for a significant email response resource. In the plan (and on your website), it is possible to offer different email addresses for different needs. Some for the press, some for shareholders and another for employee or family enquiries. In an email centre and in a call centre, one of the most helpful assets is an ability to construct web pages on the fly. When a question keeps coming up, it is quite efficient to offer a web page that offers information for the centre's staff and for the caller/email enquiry. Websites and intranets can give information to staff responding to enquiries that they may not know about. It is a quick and effective form of briefing for many people.

Information and planning available to all in normal times can become inaccessible in an emergency. Information availability during a crisis needs to be considered in the planning process. This size of event may well need prepared positions with outside stakeholders. Hospitals, police, fire, ambulance, call centres, stress councillors, community leaders can be in a position of readiness from prior consultation, but there are some other refinements that the internet will offer the prepared.

4 Major disaster happens infrequently. It is hard enough keeping internal lists of employees. To be as well informed for a whole external community is far too difficult. Using the internet, it is possible to make information available that can be a combined introduction, call for help, and a list of things that you need done. This can be delivered by email or (and much better) made available (when and if the time comes) in a website that has a specific and hitherto unavailable address. In this way detailed information, links to related data, instruction, organizations and people can be posted to the site and will require little maintenance for days after the event, to free key people for more urgent work.

Because crisis hits unexpectedly, the process of keeping plans and the necessary facility both up to date and flexibly available to a number of key individuals is very important. Consideration should be given to maintaining a layperson's guide. One of the best ways of doing this is on a CD disk. Updated each quarter and distributed both on and off site (even globally), it can guide even the least well trained to handle a crisis professionally. In addition, it is relatively simple to keep CDs safe and secure and confidential.

The biggest incidents can overwhelm all these preparations; or may mean that not all the planned responses can be (or need to be) deployed. In addition, the consequences of events may call for prolonged responses.

The case where employees have to be stood down or suppliers have to be turned away can become a big problem. Planning for such events will require the deployment of a lot of information.

The big issues are not from the most highly protected information. This should already be backed up and supported offsite. The intellectual properties and corporate information will already be well guarded against disaster (unless this is the crisis you face). The real problem will be the simple daily routine. Employee addresses that have been destroyed or (worse) revealed to the population at large is not an untypical event. A simple headcount of employees can become a living hell when a worried family is uncertain about the safety of an employee. Inadequate response at such times can be a reputational disaster as well as a human (if temporary) tragedy. When such issues have to be managed, there will need to be a contingency plan. Using the media to aid recovery may become an important part of the practitioner's job.

Other information, often contact information, order information and many departmental plans can be held on intranets or PCs where it can become inaccessible. Of course, organizations have backup facilities, but in a real disaster, it becomes evident where organizational loopholes leave organizations wrong footed.

The UK government, faced with a foot-and-mouth disease disaster, was subject to high levels of criticism for not deploying resources as proposed in the public inquiry to the 1967 epidemic. In that case, the crisis plan seemed to be rather dusty.

There is a further problem which is a mismatch of paper-based and information-era data management which can leave crisis management planners re-inventing systems to manage its crisis. It is important to translate paper-based crisis management with digital tools.

In a big crisis, there will be those who will try to publish everything and those who will attempt to hush everything up. In addition, there is a natural desire to express hoped for outcomes rather than facts. There has to be fine judgement as to when 'going public' will be the lesser of two evils or even a real advantage. There is no case for offering anything but accurate information. The consequential loss of confidence can be traumatic.

One of the big problems organizations face under these kinds of pressures is the combination of creating helpful facilities for the media (and some other onlookers) and, at the same time the means for reducing trespass. Press centres are helpful and should be a place where all statements are made. It avoids confusion and ensures that the media is frequently in one place. It has to be reasonably comfortable, must have many telephones and there is a need for a room to hold press conferences separate from where the media foregather. In a real crisis, photographers, and not a few journalists, can be very rough. Some beefy security is often needed.

There is also a state of mind that allows some managers to think in terms of turning a disaster into an advantage. This can be a real boon. A TV crew in a school temporarily used for this work can be a story about a company striving to overcome disaster to the comfort of employees, community, suppliers and shareholders.

When issues escalate into crisis

In every organization there are incipient disasters waiting to happen. The practical and pragmatic practitioner will plan for such eventualities. A crisis management team will be advised to prepare against events getting out of hand. In every sphere of organizational management, there will be a weak spot. A leaking tank, unresolved claim, incomplete accident form, unexpected litigation, whistle blower, government inquiry, new legislation, etc.

The process for planning against such issues gaining crisis proportions and, should they escalate, minimizing the damage, is a practical management one. The escalation path can follow a route from daily event to major crisis, passing issues management on the way.

1 At their least dangerous issues are mostly dealt with as part of everyday management. Disgruntled employees, customers, suppliers, competitors, government regulators, pressure groups, activists or local communities can have issues as simple as quality control concerns, minor accidents, inadvertent exposure of confidential information, and these are part of day-to-day operation. In the internet-mediated era it is quite simple for an employee's 'bad day' to become an evening internet chat room discussion. Such information will be almost innocently shared with complete strangers a few miles away and across the world. The practitioner will be aware of the implications and will be well advised to ensure effective employee training about their responsibilities and the consequences of such actions implicit in such exchanges. For the most part these alarums and excursions are dealt with by line managers and are little cause for concern when dealt with at the time.

2 Because it is very simple to contact an array of authorities and interest groups, an employee, customers, suppliers, competitors, government regulator, local communities,

pressure groups, activists or the simply malicious can instigate all manner of enquiry. A simple phone call or email can start a very dangerous hare running. This will involve more than a line manager and, while it may not overly disturb the business of the organization, may require sensitive handling and a reporting line to alert the PR practitioner. For the most part, such events can be handled by straight dealing with the relevant authority. A corporation with a good relationship within the local community will, mostly, be unaffected save for the cost of managing such activity. A regular flow of such incidents will be a different matter and will require both internal relationship management developments and closer, more focused, dealing with the affected authorities. Enhanced transparency is called for.

This added transparency can use many different communication channels. It may be on an intranet or via a website and may be there just to be reactive such that an enquirer can find the information if interested. It will probably be the case that proactively promoting such information will not be part of the chosen plan at this stage. Some companies have such pre-emptive strategies evident to the world. The extent to which a supermarket has to be prepared is freely available on the Tesco website (see Figure 19.5).

There are alternative strategies where organizations assist employees to resist the work of people who would disrupt the organization. The 'Miami University Resources for Dealing with Hate Crimes and Bias-Motivated Incidents'[8] makes a clear statement as to what it will do in cases of threats to students and personnel and also offers help and advice.

In addition the practitioner will need to possess lists of relevant statutory, industry association, academic, government and issues

Figure 19.5
Tesco has statements about
many of the issues the
company manages on its
website

organizations ready to aid communications as appropriate. It is important that these lists include information about relevant websites (and the appropriate webpage), email addresses and, if available, instant messaging and online conferencing capability. Part of the practitioner's job is networking with such organizations for normal exchanges between an organization and its publics and in readiness for issues management at this level. Such contacts should not be managed in a haphazard way but as part of a structured approach to management of issue. Good record keeping is essential and a schedule of contacts maintained.

The employee that offers confidential information in order to hold the company accountable or to gain unfair benefit or even as blackmail will require a wider range of expertise on the part of the practitioner. This may be available in-house, with a third party (such as ACAS) and may require a response that is more robust with police or legal partici-

pation. As the number of people involved grows, so the organization moves closer to crisis.

3 Issues really escalate when the threat looks as though it will become evident in different communication channels. A threat to a mediated channel, such as a newspaper, government department, or established institution, has the benefit that such organizations tend to seek more information, the truth or at least a good story. Good issues management and effective press relations will keep an issue in proportion. When the channel for expressing an opinion or even fact has moved from internal reporting, conjecture or gossip to a journalist, discussion list or usenet is a change of communication channel and is serious. The issue is now a crisis. The easy way to spot a crisis is that point in time when information jumps channels.

The internal (and in many cases associated external) people involved in this crisis are often very vulnerable. They will need help (as will their families in many cases). They will need somewhere to go away from the glare of publicity. They will need time to think and reflect as well as to plan. These facilities need to be considered well in advance. The media will look very hard and are good at finding 'secret locations'.

Today there is a more dangerous option and it is much easier than talking to a journalist. For example, an employee considering publishing information in a usenet newsgroup or email discussion list or who may consider publication in a personal website is very easy. A threat of a person (external or employee) opening up new channels to express their angst may require counselling and/or external (often legal) help. At this stage the practitioner will need to have available a range of internal and external communication processes. The contacts identified above are now more important and may be needed as part of the issues management plan. Added transparency by way of factual information available to employees and other stakeholders becomes significant.

Once again, having the means for using web-based information can be very helpful for both a growing number of internal and external managers and advisers and also to be made available to the public at large. Some of this information can be promoted to relevant publics as part of the plan.

The organization's virtual press office (VPO) is now a very important resource. There needs to be a direct link from the home page (and many other pages) into the VPO. In addition, where the organization has created some form of barrier between unregistered journalists and the favoured (and interested) few, this needs to be removed. In a crisis, a whole new range of journalists will take an interest in the organization and will need very fast access.

A prominent (if risky) example of going public when innocent as the means for managing a crisis was used by Neil and Christine Hamilton in the United Kingdom in 2001. The whole story is available at the BBC (http://news.bbc.co.uk/hi/english/uk/newsid_1513000/1513921.stm) and offers a case study of how such a strategy can work. Being able to withstand the pressures, especially from the media, in this scenario will have to be thought through very carefully before embarking on such a process.

4 Issues as they escalate to major crisis proportions require the full use of all the crisis management capability mentioned above. Much of the media and especially photographers will be hard to handle. They will always be looking for an angle that juxtaposes people with a 'slant' on the story. *Panorama*, the UK investigative programme broadcast by the BBC made a habit of signing off stories with a journalist posing in front of government ministerial buildings to give otherwise flaky accusations the apparent authority of the government.

Crisis management processes at this stage will really be worrying all the organization's stakeholders. They will seek information and will be happy to accept it from anywhere. Silence can be an option but not often.

This does not mean that the media, web or email communication should be the only options for communication. Some pretty old communication techniques are very powerful. A letter (preferably personally signed), private meetings of interested groups and the telephone are all significant forms for communication in a real crisis.

At this stage, when survival really is on the line, there will be no other activity in the organization which is more important. Taking resources from all departments in the organization is something that has to be done when needed. Demarcations and traditional lines of communication may have to be short cut to be effective.

Planning for issues-led crisis is very rewarding. It helps the practitioner's organization understand its vulnerabilities on a day-to-day basis. It is able to examine quality issues from a risk and reward perspective. It enables the organization to examine corporate social responsibility policies from the perspective of the risks involved from disgruntled employees, employees' mistakes and poor decision making, customers with a complaint, upset suppliers, competitors, government regulators and inspectors, pressure groups, activists and local communities.

Simple scenario brainstorming round these publics will help the organization understand such organizations. In preparation for such activities, there are some valuable resources to be researched such as:

- Institute For Crisis, Disaster and Risk Management: http://www.seas.gwu.edu/~icdm
- One World: http://www.oneworld.org and http://www.oneworld.org/ni/index4.html
- Urban75: http://www.urban75.com and http://www.urban75.com/Action/squat.html and http://www.urban75.com/Links/index.html
- Managing Reputation in Cyberspace: http://www.hawkesmere.co.uk/auto/titles/158.html
- Risk Issues and Crisis Management: http://www.ipr.org.uk/Products/pr_in_prac/riskissues.htm
- Steven Van Hook's Issues management pages at About PR: http://publicrelations.about.com/cs/crisishelp/index.htm and http://publicrelations.about.com/cs/crisismanagement/index.htm

- Company Ethics: http://www.companyethics.com
- Urban Legend: http://www.snopes2.com

What crisis to plan for

Every organization will want to plan for different crises but it is helpful to have a starting point. The list below is published on the Issues and Crisis Management pages of the ICM website http://www.crisisexperts.com.

Adverse government actions
Computer tampering
Anonymous accusations
Damaging rumours
Competitive misinformation
Discrimination accusations
Confidential information disclosed
Equipment, product or service sabotage
Misuse of chemical products
Industrial espionage
Disgruntled employee threats
Investigative reporter contact
Employee death or serious injury
Merger/acquisition rumour
Employee involved in a scandal
Labour problems
Licensing disputes with local officials
Lawsuit likely to be publicized
Extortion threat
Security leak or problem
False accusations
Severe weather impact on business
Incorrect installation of equipment
Sexual harassment allegation
Legal injunction
Special interest group attack
Grassroots demonstrations
Strike, work stoppage
Illegal actions by an employee
Terrorism threat or action

Arrest or legal action of an employee
Illegal or unethical behaviour of an
    employee
Major equipment malfunction
Union organizing actions
Nearby neighbour, business protest
Whistle blower threat or actions

Some online crises

The following cases are extracts from *Managing Your Reputation in Cyberspace*[9] and offer the practitioner a range of scenarios to ponder and imagine how well prepared their organization may be to manage such circumstances.

A pornographer's attack

What do Disney, Barbie, CNN, Honda and Mercedes have in common? They topped the list of the ten brands most commonly associated with pornography on the internet, according to a study by Cyveillance™,[10] who specialize in online brand protection. The other five brand names most often found in pornographic websites were Levi's, ESPN, NBA, Chevy and Nintendo, respectively. These popular brand names appeared in hidden or visible text on the sites identified and in metatags in 25 per cent of the sites suspected of containing pornography – presumably without the brand owners' knowledge.

Meta attack

In the United Kingdom a company discovered a sudden drop in visits to its site. On investigation it found a competitor had used its name in the metatag, thus steering search engines towards the competition.

In another case, a company used competitor comparisons naming specific brands in its web pages to seduce search engines to bring competitor enquiries to its site.

Front organizations

Some companies have used front organizations to attack brands: they are often noticed because they attack only one type of product when others exist in the market niche. Sharon Beder who wrote *Global Spin* mentions a corporate front group called 'Mothers Against Pollution', which campaigned against plastic milk bottles. It was discovered that this was initiated by the owner of a company which produced cardboard cartons.

Counterfeit marketers

'Children's toys are not the only items being counterfeited and sold over the Internet' said Brandy Thomas, CEO and chairman of Cyveillance. 'The Internet has become a hotbed for the sale of counterfeit luxury items that you might typically find on any street corner in New York City – watches, pens, sunglasses, leather goods, you name it. Like in the streets of New York, prices that seem too good to be true, usually are.'

Politician on the take

By combining the databases that track the voting and investing information with a network that distributes the information, in this case a website, it becomes possible to provide a citizen's guide to who owns who in Washington.

Mojo Wire,[11] is the website which connects the databases into a 'Taking Stock in Congress' section where citizens can follow the stock transactions and voting records of '83 members of Congress who purchased or sold stocks near the time of Congressional votes or other government actions relevant to the stocks' value'.

There have been some interesting revelations.

Senator Alfonse D'Amato (R-NY) bought up public utilities stock just two days before President Bush signed the National Energy Conservation Act, which deregulated energy transmissions, offering growth opportunities for many utilities.

Newt Gingrich (R-GA) helped kill amendments to cut funding for the space station programme just three weeks after buying stock in Boeing, which was subsequently named the prime contractor for the station.

Protect your employees

Since February 1997, Bill Sheehan has operated a website which contains four general types of content: (1) Sheehan's grievances against government officials and private parties, most of them credit reporting agencies and debt collection services; (2) strongly worded expressions of opinion (e.g. referring to a corporation as 'criminally insane', etc.); (3) allegations about corporations and persons which were claimed to be defamatory; (4) information about employees of companies.

After Sheehan filed his lawsuit, he added to the website information regarding defendants' outside counsel.

The information about employees includes: home addresses; street maps identifying the locations of the addresses; home telephone numbers; fax numbers; social security numbers; photographs of automobiles and their licence plates which appear to have been taken in public; and photographs of people which appear to have been taken in public. Sheehan declares that he obtained this information lawfully, from such public information sources as the Washington Secretary of State and other internet sites. Sheehan's website contains no explicit encouragement for readers to engage in any specific conduct, or to use the information about employees or attorneys in any specific way.

Iffy analysts commenting on your share price?

There are a host of scams. Professional internet promoters, some with elaborate briefing sites and any number of ways to avoid regulators.

Masquerading as 'Analysts' they offer a range of services. And look very appealing. The content of www.financialWeb.com/stockdetective is packed with scams and promotion devices, names people and companies and shows website URLs. It has a marvellous page of alleged scams called 'Stinky Stocks'.

Using your site for scam?

Turner Phillips found a novel way to make it appear as though it was a member of the Investment Dealers Association of Canada, three Canadian stock exchanges and the NASDAQ Stock Market in the United States.

It copied all the information on the website of an unnamed Canadian investment dealer that is a member of these self-regulatory agencies and superimposed the name Turner Phillips onto that firm's data, then posted the material to its own site. Turner Phillips contacted prospective victims over the telephone and then referred them to the website for more information on the firm. Although Turner Phillips said it had its head office in Vancouver, all it had in the city was a mail drop and a telephone answering service. Calls placed to the Vancouver number were forwarded to a location in Washington State and then from there to another location. Mail was forwarded to somewhere in Ontario.

Employee share scam

A phoney Bloomberg tip, part of a disguised webpage hoax about a purported takeover of PairGain Technologies, prompted online speculators into a feeding frenzy and sent shares of the company's stock soaring 34 per cent on 7 April 1999. A Yahoo chat room visitor publicized the page's existence. A lot of people visited it and decided to buy the stock.

The whole scam was invented by Gary Dale Hoke of Raleigh, N.C. Hoke, a PairGain employee, who owned stock in the company, which makes high-speed internet connection products. The story falsely claimed that an Israeli company was acquiring PairGain for $1.35 billion in cash. Shortly after the story was posted, PairGain's stock surged from $8.50 per share to $11.25. The stock later dropped after the hoax was exposed.

New human rights acts: do they change the threat?

In the Raython case, the company asserts that employees leaked proprietary technical and financial data via the internet. While an employment contract may bar employees from discussing company secrets in public (and confidentiality law is more widely applied in Europe), the First Amendment may give employees a right to do so. Sobel says: 'The Supreme Court has said the First Amendment protects the right to communicate anonymously, so I do see a First Amendment problem with these cases.' A company may be protected in the United Kingdom but not in the United States and as a result the story will be available everywhere.

Conflicting national laws affecting your business?

The prominent US Jewish group, the Simon Wiesenthal Centre, asked Bertelsmann to make sure that books like Hitler's *Mein Kampf* are not sold in Germany through barnesandnoble.com, Bertelsmann's joint venture with US bookseller Barnes and Noble. The distribution of such books is illegal in Germany, but allowed in the United States.

Of course banning books in the United States is illegal and so Bertelsmann is taking the lead in getting multinational corporations to help unify national regulations relating to global electronic commerce.

Someone got your copyright: you got someone else's?

Copyright is the right to copy in any form (reproduce, perform, adapt, publish, publish translations, convert to a different format, communicate by telecommunication, rent, exhibit in public, etc.), in whole or in part, an original creative work. Original creative works include literary, dramatic, musical and artistic works, and computer programmes. A few things, which are not protected by copyright, are: names, titles, slogans, short phrases, factual information, plots, characters, and methods or techniques. Some of these, however, can be protected in other ways. For example, names or slogans can be trademarked and in some states like the US 'registered' ®.

Usually copyright is owned by the creator of the work. If, however, you create the work as part of employment, the copyright belongs to the company unless there is an agreement specifying otherwise. In any case, in the UK copyright applies automatically and does not have to be explicitly registered.

Passing off as you?

Global Asset Management, a London based investment company, created four websites and found that the GAM name was being used by a company based in Ghana to the extent that search engines would find the Ghanaian company before the real GAM sites.

A hate site?

It was a chill morning in London on 16 October 1986 and a day that was to create one of the pivotal events in internet activism. It was the day when a campaign was started to place McDonald's at the centre of anti-corporatism by a number of activists.

It gave rise to the longest civil court case in history between David Morris and Helen Steel and McDonald's.

The appearance of a website created by the activists came in February 1996 when Morris and Steel launched the McSpotlight internet site from a laptop connected to the internet via a mobile phone outside a McDonald's store in central London (Figure 19.6). The website was accessed more than a million times in its first month. It was headline news across the world.

By any standards, the McSpotlight site is big and has an amazing amount of content. A large part of the content is critical of McDonald's and some is allegedly libellous.

On 19 June 1997, after a case said to have cost the company over £10 million and a £60,000 settlement against Morris and Steel, the website was accessed 2.2 million times.

Activists

A number of activists believe: 'there is a dynamic of struggles between competing groups to establish their perspective as absolute truth. For this reason it is important to look at the actions and motivations of actors who seek to halt the progress of environmental groups.'

There are a number of well known books which deal with activism including: *Global Spin* by Sharon Beder, *Toxic Sludge Is Good For You* by John Stauber and Sheldon

Figure 19.6
McDonald's

Rampton and *Green Backlash* by Andrew Rowell.

They are up-to-date, says Simon May, Shell's internet manager. He is reported as saying he believes that activism on the internet should not be viewed as a 'menace', but rather as a 'challenge' for corporates. Companies should adopt the internet for the same reasons and utilize some of the same strategies as activists, but with a more planned and professional approach. Furthermore, full advantage should be taken of the potential of the internet to monitor grassroots opinion and activities (Lubbers 1998:net).

Unhappy employee

Name: Witheld
Email: n.a.
Comments: I have been a Chase employee since 1992 (old Chase). Since the Chase–Chemical merger in 1996, I have seen this bank go down hill. The bank became trashy and the Chase name which at one time I was proud to work for, means nothing.

The Chemical senior managers took the Chase name and ran it through the mud: http://www.chasebanksucks.com

Unfounded accusation

In March 1997, a well-known US fashion designer, Tommy Hilfiger, was accused of making racist remarks during an appearance on *The Oprah Winfrey Show*. Tommy Hilfiger denies ever making such remarks. This is not hard to do. Both he and spokespeople for Ms Winfrey maintain he has neither appeared nor been asked to appear on *The Oprah Winfrey Show*. This did not prevent a mass of comment in dozens of newsgroups pointing at Tommy Hilfiger and branding him as racist.

Even the most exhaustive PR campaigns cannot easily refute rogue information which is allowed to spread too long. In spite of well-publicized responses the newsgroup talk online still disparages Tommy Hilfiger's supposed remarks to this day.

Not included in internet exchanges?

In another study by IRS, during June 1999, in only three discussion groups (support. asthma, uk.local.surrey and games. miniatures) there were 3,500 comments on quality pertaining to UK supermarkets. The subject of quality associated with named supermarkets appeared in 36 UK newsgroups. By extrapolation, it might be said that there were 30,000 public comments available for the whole world to see about the quality of UK supermarkets.

In addition, there was an audience who did not actively comment in numbers, maybe vying with the Sun newspaper in total audience size. By any measure this represents a sizeable number of people prepared to make a comment and elect to spend time reading such comments. A sample of the postings showed 63 per cent of commentators recommended a particular retailer and 37 per cent who were critical. Notably, some retailers came out well ahead of the others with little criticism and much praise.

The steps of the plan

- For each of the above potential threats it is worth undertaking a risk assessment.

- Consider the organization's strengths, weaknesses, opportunities and threats.
- Develop a series of realistic scenarios.
- Begin to develop lists of people and contacts both internal and external who are important to you and your organization.
- Develop plans in a number of scenarios from the least threatening to the most threatening – an escalation plan.
- Prepare key materials, messages, and the means for communication and include electronic media.
- Select and train the crisis team.
- Involve the team in risk assessment.
- Simulate.
- Ensure you have the means to manage when key people are away and if the operation is not possible on site.
- Find a way of ensuring that for both issue and crisis management there is a good management reason (preferably other than crisis) to keep your information and capability up to date.
- For each of your issues use a step by step approach on how to handle a crisis – see the crisis management plan (Figure 19.7).

Conclusions

Issues have to be managed. The practitioner role is pivotal and there is a significant cross over from the public relations role to corporate management. Being prepared, planning and training and then teambuilding with dispassionate and calm people who can work under pressure in difficult circumstances goes without saying. It is the skills of the PR professional that are most significant, which include the ability to assess the impact of events, actions and statements on many publics. This is a critical skill.

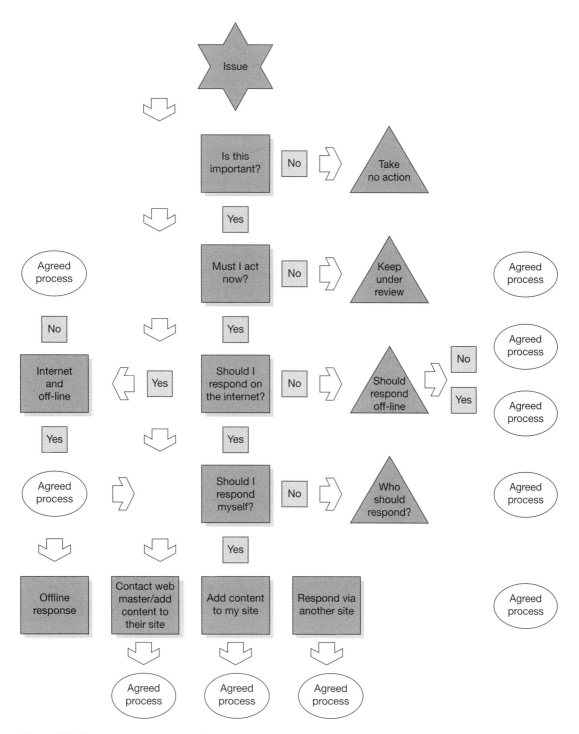

Figure 19.7 Crisis management plan

NOTES

1 Grunig, J. E. (1982), 'The message–attitude–behavior relationship: communication behavior of organisations', *Communication Research*, 9, 163–200.
2 Grunig, J. E. and Hunt, T. (1984), *Managing Public Relations*, New York: Holt, Rinehart and Winston.
3 Molander, R. C., Riddile, A. S. and Wilson, P. A. (1995), *Strategic Information Warfare: A New Face of War*, Washington Rand Distribution Services.
4 The United Kingdom PR industry Internet Commission identified the nature of this transfer of information in terms of: *porosity*, being the enhanced leakage of information from organizations; *transparency*, in which organizations make information available and *internet agency* where people (and intelligent machines) act as an agent in changing the nature of messages.
5 The Cisco parody site is located at: http://www.angelfire.com/ego/frugal (August 2001).
6 *Summary of Discussions at a Planning Meeting On: Cyber-security and the Insider Threat to Classified Information*, chaired by Jones, A. K., and Quarles, L. R., Washington, DC, November 2000. Published by the Computer Science And Telecommunications Board (2000) Washington, DC.
7 Institute of Crisis Management: http://www.icm.org (August 2001).
8 The 'Miami University Resources for Dealing with Hate Crimes and Bias-Motivated Incidents': http://www.muohio.edu/nohate/Resource.htmlx (August 2001).
9 Phillips, D. (1999) *Managing Your Reputation in Cyberspace* London: Thorogood.
10 Cyveillance, 1555 Wilson Blvd, Suite 404, Arlington, VA 22209 2405 (www.cyveillence.com).
11 www.motherjones.com

CHAPTER 20

The impact of terrorist attacks on corporate public relations

Donald K. Wright

This chapter explores how the corporate communication and public relations professions were affected by the September 11, 2001 terrorism attacks on the United States. Data were gathered between September 2001 and March 2002 in several stages involving both quantitative and qualitative methodologies. Results found two-thirds of the corporate PR executives surveyed thought the events of September 11 have changed how their companies communicate. This suggests that the terrorist attacks have had an impact on their organization's PR and communication function. The author explains how the terrorist attacks have precipitated a paradigm shift advancing public relations into a more significant role in corporate America and how company executive teams have since become more aware of the importance of communicating openly, effectively, and in a timely manner.

Many things have changed since September 11, 2001, when terrorists hijacked four aeroplanes and attacked the United States destroying the World Trade Center, causing significant damage at the Pentagon, and killing thousands of innocent people. Immediate emotional reactions of horror, anger, shock, sadness and disbelief appeared to lead to a realization the nation was vulnerable. This, in turn, stimulated enhanced security, increased patriotism, renewed interest in religion, and a greater sense of family throughout America.

Given the large publication time gap for most scholarly articles, there is limited aca-demic literature discussing their impact. However, the popular literature reports on a number of research studies involving a variety of general public audiences, and echoes the reality that these terrorist attacks had a huge impact upon American opinion. Kohut says they 'brought unparalleled national unity and patriotism', 'elevated the importance of nationhood', and 'changed the way (Americans) view the world'.[1]

A CNN/*USA Today*/Gallup poll conducted on the evening of September 11 found Americans considered the events of that day represented 'the most tragic news event' of their lifetimes.[2] A study by CBS News and the *New York Times* discovered the American public's trust in government doubled in the weeks immediately following the attacks.[3] This tragedy had a huge impact upon the approval ratings of President George W. Bush. His CNN/*USA Today*/Gallup poll scores hovered around 50 per cent in early September, but surged to 90 per cent by 22 September and remained in the 85 per cent range in mid-January, 2002.[4] And, according to the *International Herald Tribune*, 79 per cent of those outside the United States claim the events of September 11 'marked a new chapter in world history'.[5]

Six months after the attacks, CNN/*USA Today*/Gallup poll research continued to find most Americans thought September 11 represented 'the most tragic event of their lifetimes', and most (76 per cent) did not believe the nation's 'wounds' resulting from the attacks had been healed.[6] American support for increased defence spending in March 2002 was nearly three times higher than it had been four years earlier.[7] At the same time, however, this research found Americans less affected by the attacks in March 2002 'than they were in the immediate aftermath of Sept. 11'.[8]

With the passing of the immediacy of September 11, the *New York Times* opined that since that day, 'Almost all the news – economic, political, international – seems to have spun from that one day, although that one day was merely a single episode in a global struggle that has taken years to develop.'[9] The Associated Press reported 'the attacks altered the attitudes and assumptions of most Americans', but also stressed 'there is no real consensus about the nature and permanence of the changes'.[10] Nearly half of those interviewed in a March 2002 CNN/*USA Today*/Gallup poll said they thought September 11

should become a national holiday.[11] A Gallup Organization study said more Americans think the attacks have changed the country than they have impacted individual lives.[12]

Purpose of the study

The major goal of this research was to explore the impact the September 11, 2001, terrorist attacks have had on corporate communication and public relations in the United States. The study sought answers to questions concerning whether or not the events of that Tuesday changed how organizations communicate, and whether or not the attacks have had any impact on corporate PR and communication functions. In a related line of analysis, the study explored several additional, but closely related, questions. The momentous nature of the September 11 terrorist attacks raised the possibility that any research of this nature might discover an immediate, or primacy, effect. Consequently, data were gathered through a variety of different quantitative and qualitative research methods and over a six-month period of time from September 2001 through March 2002.

A second and equally significant purpose of this research examined theoretical implications, in particular those that might link any of the study's empirical findings to excellence theory, the behavioural model theory, and the communication executive role.

Methods

Data were gathered between September 2001 and March 2002 in several stages involving both quantitative and qualitative methodologies.

Quantitative methods

The study's quantitative measuring instruments consisted of two, short, email questionnaires distributed to senior-level, US-based, PR and corporate communication executives. The first of these questionnaires was disseminated on 10 October 2001, one month after the attacks. The second was circulated on 9 March 2002, six months after the tragedies. Sampling was purposive and intentionally small in an attempt to restrict participation to only the most top-level corporate and agency professionals, and, in the case of some very large companies, the second and third people in the communication function. Anonymity was promised to all participants.

Short email questionnaires were selected for data gathering based upon our previous, successful experiences conducting survey research with senior-level, PR and corporate communication executives. Our research has found communication executives rarely complete mail questionnaires, and are extremely difficult to pin down for telephone interviews. And in terms of electronic surveying, we have found return rates significantly higher when questions are asked as part of a regular email text message as opposed to situations where subjects are invited to click upon an embedded link which would take them to a web-based survey questionnaire.

Another limitation in surveying truly senior-level communication executives is the reality that there are very few of them. Wright claims there are only 250 to 300 communication executives in the United States.[13] Working carefully with membership rosters of the Arthur W. Page Society, the Public Relations Seminar, the Public Relations Society of America College of Fellows, and the International Public Relations Association, a sample of email addresses of 55 senior-level professionals was selected. Responses were received from 37 subjects during the October 2001 data-gathering phase and from 38 respondents in March 2002, representing respectable return rates of 67 per cent and 69 per cent respectively.

While critics might suggest this study's population was small, the purpose was to focus on truly senior-level corporate communication and PR professionals. In academic terms, we were interested in what communication executives – not everyone in the United States who practises public relations – thought about the impact of the September 11 terrorist attacks.[14] In addition to representing names of some of the most senior-level professionals in the United States, respondents included four past presidents of the Arthur W. Page Society, a select membership organization for senior public relations and corporate communication executives, and nine members of the Page Society's Board of Trustees. The study's participants included many of the leading corporate and agency professionals in the United States as well as three past presidents of the Public Relations Society of America (PRSA), and a past president of the International Public Relations Association (IPRA).

Anonymity and confidentiality were promised to all participants. Participants in this research have approved all quotes attributed to them. The October and March questionnaires both asked four, closed-ended questions on a set of five-point Likert-type answer scales ranging from 'Strongly Agree' to 'Strongly Disagree'.

The four closed-ended questions in the October 2001 questionnaire were:

- Do you agree the events of September 11, 2001 will change how your company communicates?

- Do you agree the events of September 11, 2001 have had any immediate impact on your organization's PR and communications function?
- Do you agree managed, strategic communications and public relations can be effective weapons of war?
- Do you agree the United States will implement a managed, strategic communications and public relations campaign in the current struggle against terrorism?

October respondents also were invited to add open-ended comments following each question. The first two questions focused directly upon the events of September 11 – one asking how the terrorist attacks might change how companies communicate; and the other asking about any immediate impact on the PR and communication function.

Two of the October questions were designed to measure thoughts and opinions regarding how strategic PR and communication campaigns might impact military retaliations the United States was taking in an attempt to combat terrorism. The United States has a long history of effectively implementing managed and strategic communication and PR campaigns when the country has been at war. This was particularly evident during the First World War when President Woodrow Wilson asked crusading journalist George Creel to establish the Committee on Public Information (CPI).[15] And, in the Second World War years when Elmer Davis was head of the Office of War Information (OWI).[16] Steinberg says US public relations efforts in the First and Second World Wars, 'provided the stimulus for the development of public relations into what many of its contemporary practitioners like to call a full-fledged profession'.[17] In spite of this success during the two world wars, the United States did not imple-

ment any noted, strategic public relations effort during the Vietnam conflict years of the 1960s and 1970s.

Although the two noted world war communication campaign efforts received considerable praise for keeping the American public behind the cause of those wars, such was not the case during the Vietnam era when a large percentage of the US population opposed the military action. A major reason the October questionnaire asked questions about the use of strategic public relations during war was to measure how important senior-level communication executives thought these might be in the campaign against terrorism.

This study's first questionnaire was distributed on 10 October 2001, four weeks following the terrorist attacks and three days after the first round of US military retaliation in Afghanistan. Responses received up to 22 October 2001 were included in the analysis.

An obvious methodological concern about research of this nature focuses upon whether the initial – and potentially emotional – reactions of PR executives remain constant over time. For example, did the fact that so many US civilians were savagely murdered in the September 11 attacks prompt initial concerns that would diminish as the nation, and the world, adjusted to the tragedy? In an attempt to control for this possibility, all US-based subjects in the study were surveyed again in late March 2002, six months after the attacks.

The March questionnaire also contained four, closed-ended, Likert-type questions. Two of these were similar to October questions with two minor changes necessary with the passing of time. Those questions were:

- Do you agree the events of September 11, 2001 changed how your company communicates?

- Do you agree the events of September 11, 2001 have had any impact on your organization's public relations and communications function?

Analysis of the October data suggested the terrorist attacks might have precipitated a paradigm shift advancing communication and public relations into a more significant role in corporate America. Furthermore, some evidence suggested the events of September 11 triggered some executive leadership teams within many companies to become more aware of the importance of communicating openly, effectively, and in a timely manner. Consequently, these two questions became part of the March questionnaire.

- Do you agree the September 11, 2001, terrorist attacks precipitated a paradigm shift advancing communications and public relations into a more significant role in corporate America?
- Do you agree your company's executive teams have been more aware of the importance of communicating openly, effectively, and in a timely manner since September 11, 2001?

March respondents also were invited to answer this open-ended question: 'In the space below, please feel free to offer any comments regarding the impact the events of 9–11–2001 have had on public relations and corporate communications.'

Qualitative methods

In addition to the study's quantitative measures, data also were gathered through a variety of qualitative methods. These included responses to open-ended questions on the

October and March email questionnaires; email conversational interviews with subjects who entered into periodic, electronic dialogue with the researcher; plus several telephone and personal interviews with subjects in this study. Qualitative data gathering began in September 2001 and continued up to March 2002.

Data analysis

Quantitative responses were imported from the author's emailbox and data were coded and entered into the Statistical Programme for the Social Sciences (SPSS). Responses to each question were then broken down into frequency response percentages and means. This yielded most of the information necessary to describe the study's findings. Finally, multiple statistical tests were run on the data in an attempt to measure for any significant differences between October and March responses. Specifically, a t-test was run comparing both of these groups of respondents. Qualitative data were analysed via informal content analysis.

Results and discussion

RQ1: Do senior-level corporate public relations executives believe the events of September 11, 2001 changed how their companies communicate?

As Table 20.1 shows, roughly two-thirds of the senior-level, US-based, corporate communication executives surveyed in this study agree the tragic events of September 11, 2001 have changed how their companies communicate. Differences between perceptions in October 2001 and March 2002 are minimal, although

Table 20.1 Responses of senior-level, US PR and corporate communication professionals to the question: 'Do you agree the events of September 11, 2001, changed how your company communicates?' (%)

	Strongly agree	Agree	Uncertain/ no opinion	Disagree	Strongly disagree	Mean
Responses from survey of October 2001	19	50	6	23	3	3.59
Responses from survey of March 2002	17	50	17	17	0	3.67

Note: Mean scores were calculated on five-point, Likert-type answer scales ranging from '1' for 'strongly disagree' to '5' for 'strongly agree'. Consequently, in this and all subsequent tables, the higher the mean score, the greater the agreement

the March mean score is slightly larger. Open-ended comments related to this first research question clearly suggest these changes will alter many aspects of future internal and external communication.

As far as internal communication is concerned, immediately following the September attacks a number of companies reviewed their employee communication practices and policies in an attempt to develop methods that could help get information to employees more quickly. Results of the March follow-up survey provide every indication this trend is continuing. Respondents to both surveys pointed out more information is being demanded by employees, and some companies stress these employees now want it delivered in the most expedient fashion. This is forcing a number of organizations to reconsider traditional internal communication printed documents such as brochures and newsletters in favour of email and intranet delivered information. Respondents to the March survey particularly stressed they have seen an increased interest in disseminating internal information regarding security issues more frequently and more expeditiously since the September 11 attacks.

Although neither as extensive nor as immediate, a number of companies also made changes in how they communicated externally as a result of September 11. As one senior-corporate officer said, September 11 'has put many issues in a different perspective'. Another pointed out, 'The tone of communications will be balanced against a backdrop of daily reminders about how precious and fragile freedom is.' Several March survey respondents stressed the terrorist attacks appeared to serve as the catalyst to help corporate officers recognize the importance for organizations to have and maintain open channels of communication. Both sets of survey responses contained comments predicting companies will be facing reduced levels of urgency around certain issues, petty matters, and small agenda items. Some anticipate American business will show, 'a much stronger resolve to succeed in the face of a difficult economy as a way of not letting terrorism win'.

In terms of specific communication channels, respondents to both waves of the study's survey suggested internet and intranet systems were becoming more important because they have the ability to enhance information dissemination more quickly and more efficiently than other communication media. Others pointed out corporate PR and communication professionals now are making greater use of the internet and intranet systems and are going beyond simply communicating with publics to a point where they are trying to develop relationships with them. Many believe the attacks caused companies to revisit their crisis communication plans. In October, some predicted future business might be conducted in a more serious mood with fewer jokes and much more emphasis on patriotism. March responses appear to validate that this is happening within some organizations.

There were those who, in the October survey, did not anticipate change resulting from September 11. As one said then, 'once people get past the horror of 5,000 deaths, the crisis will pass and things will settle down again'. Other October respondents thought the attacks might impact what is communicated, but not how messages are disseminated. Results of the March survey find fewer sceptics. A few March respondents thought, as one subject reported, 'it's pretty much back to business as usual except for those companies that were devastated by the attacks'. However, the majority disagreed and suggested the events of September 11 had changed how their company communicates.

RQ2: Do senior-level corporate public relations executives believe the events of September 11, 2001 have had any impact

on their organization's public relations and communications function?

As Table 20.2 reports, the study found exceptionally strong agreement that the September 11, 2001 terrorist attacks have impacted the corporate PR and communication function. In October, 88 per cent agreed with this suggestion while 92 per cent agreed in March. Relative agreement was higher in October given a larger number of responses in the 'strongly agree' category.

The October survey found 88 per cent of the respondents thought the events of September 11 had an immediate impact on their company's PR and communication function. This figure increased to 92 per cent in March, but the latter survey's mean score was slightly lower on this item because the intensity of agreement was not as strong as it had been five months earlier. The need to communicate quickly to employees and other strategic target audiences appears to be significant here. Results to both survey waves discovered a number of respondents indicating the terrorist attacks provided PR and communication functions with opportunities to take on roles that CEOs and other executives now view as more important and more central to organizational success. Following the attacks, communication and PR functions now appear to be responsible for more

Table 20.2 Responses of senior-level, US PR and corporate communication professionals to the question: 'Do you agree the events of September 11, 2001, have had any impact on your organization's public relations and communication function?' (%)

	Strongly agree	Agree	Uncertain/ No opinion	Disagree	Strongly disagree	Mean
Responses from survey of October 2001	25	63	6	3	3	4.03
Responses from survey of March 2002	9	83	4	4	0	3.96

important and more significant assignments than was the case prior to September 11. As one October respondent wrote, 'The horror that took place that day gave communications a chance to help senior managers in my company lead.' Another pointed out, 'Our public relations and communications function is in a stronger position, because we were able to serve so effectively September 11 and every day since then.' And one offered this comment, 'We are now discussing everything, and our corporate communications professionals have been thrust right into the center of virtually everything the company does.' A high-ranking officer in one of the world's largest public relations agencies said, 'We have changed how we communicate to our employees and how our clients communicate to all of their publics.' Open-ended comments to the March survey echoed and reinforced these thoughts. One such comment, from a senior-level, chief PR officer, was, 'Following the attacks the CEO and others turned to us for help much more frequently than ever before. And, because we were able to deliver when called upon, those people continue to seek our assistance. 9–11 really changed the communications milieu in our company.'

In some instances, the initial new-found appreciation for public relations and communication developed out of having corporate communication professionals take the lead in organizing fundraising and relief assistance efforts during September and October. In other 2001 situations, CEOs and executive heads of other corporate functions sought advice from communication and PR professionals before taking actions that previously had been considered fairly routine. Immediately following the attacks, organizations appeared to be much more sensitive about what they said and did, how they put things forward, and whether actions were appropri-

ate given time and place. March survey results suggest this had softened some, but corporate public relations officers clearly thought the situation was better in March 2002 than it had been prior to September 11. In October, the PR and communication function appeared to be playing a more significant role in helping companies decide what they should do and how they should do it in addition to helping them decide what to say and how to say it. This also appeared to be the case in March.

A number of March respondents thought the impact of September 11 might have been escalating over time. Senior-level consultant, E. Bruce Harrison, said, 'The CPRO role is escalating. It's logical. All corporate top executives are now extraordinarily sensitized to the potential for sudden events, including a crisis. During times of crisis, CEOs and others in top management instinctively turn to communications and involve the CPRO. This lights the entire communications board.' Matthew P. Gonring, who at the time had recently stepped down as Vice President, Corporate Communications, Baxter International Inc., said the impact of September 11 continued to have a huge influence upon a variety of aspects closely related to corporate communications. Included on Gonring's list are a greater use of the internet and intranet systems, greater relevance of messages and impact, increased corporate security, reliance on alternative means of travel, and the opportunity for corporate PR executives to exhibit leadership qualities.

Analysis of various open-ended responses in both waves of the survey suggests impact for the corporate public relations and communication function in the following areas:

- mobilizing organizational change;
- influencing policy making;

- participation in decision making;
- advising CEOs;
- advising other senior executives;
- gaining more access to CEOs;
- helping the value of public relations to be better understood;
- demonstrating that communications is vital to the business;
- enhancing the counsellor role for chief PR officers;
- awareness of the potential impact on all businesses;
- increased security, exposed vulnerability, more secretive operations;
- much greater reliance upon internet and intranets;
- appreciation and understanding about relevance and impact of messages;
- appreciation of the importance of timeliness re information dissemination;
- many are now avoiding opportunistic behaviours;
- much more emphasis upon corporate social responsibility;
- many are re-evaluating the need to travel;
- rapid growth in non-travel communication – web casting, online chats, voice and video teleconferencing;
- family, god and country have become much more relevant to many;
- more effort on shoring up existing customers rather than attracting new ones;
- greater need for improved internal communication;
- more interest in crisis services including planning and drills, outsourcing of crisis needs;
- new appreciation of biotech's role in combating possible bio terror;
- advertising revenue spending is reducing the journalism 'news hole';
- noted staff cutbacks in many media operations;

- greater reliance on non-traditional media, especially by those under 40;
- greater focus on safety, security, family, home, personal heath, etc.;
- many unprecedented opportunities to lead through communication.

RQ3: If senior-level corporate PR executives believe the events of September 11, 2001 changed how their companies communicate and/or impacted their organization's public relations function, will the intensity of these beliefs have changed between October 2001 and March 2002?

On the question asking whether or not the events of September 11th changed how companies communicate, mean scores were identical (3.59) for the October and March respondents. Results of t-tests displayed in Table 20.3 suggest no statistical differences between the respondent groups.

In terms of the question asking if the terrorist attacks had any impact on 'your organization's public relations and communications function', the October mean score (4.03) was slightly higher than the March mean (3.90), but results of t-tests, as shown in Table 20.3, indicate no statistical significance.

As the statistical tables suggest, the October wave of this study's survey found considerable evidence suggesting the September 11 terrorist attacks precipitated an immediate impact upon corporate public relations and communications. Results of the March follow-up wave provide every indication this impact continues. Consequently, differences between answers to both of these questions in October and March are minimal.

When results of all qualitative data gathered between September 2001 and March 2002 were analysed, findings revealed four uniquely different groups of communication

Table 20.3 Comparing mean scores between responses from October 2001 and March 2002

	Mean scores		Levene's test for equality of variances		t-test for equality of means	
	October 2001	March 2002	F	Sig.	T	Sig.
Question						
Do you agree the events of September 11, 2001 changed how your company communicates?	3.59	3.67	0.533	0.469	0.080	0.937
Do you agree the events of September 11, 2001, have had any impact on your organization's public relations and communications function?	4.03	3.96	1.78	0.188	0.591	0.558

executives. A small minority did not believe the terrorist attacks were having any lasting impact upon corporate communication and public relations. The other three groups included those who suggested the impact of September 11 upon corporate public relations was highly pronounced, respondents who said an impact was evident but moderate, and those who thought that the terrorist attacks had served as a catalyst for change along with other contributing factors – mainly the Enron scandal and the sluggish economy. Those who perceived the impact of September 11 to have been the most prominent were most likely to have been relative newcomers to the position of an organization's chief PR officer.

> *RQ4 and RQ5*: (4) Do senior-level corporate public relations executives believe the events of September 11, 2001 precipitated a paradigm shift advancing communications and public relations into a more significant role in corporate America? (5) Are corporate executive teams more aware of the importance of communicating openly, effectively, and in a timely manner since September 11, 2001?

There was only moderate agreement and a fair amount of uncertainty in terms of findings to research questions 4 and 5. As Table 20.4 shows, a majority (52 per cent) of the March respondents agreed the September 11 attacks had precipitated a paradigm shift advancing communication and public relations into a more significant role in corporate America. However, 23 per cent disagreed this was the case and 27 per cent were uncertain. There was slightly greater agreement (64 per cent) regarding whether or not corporate executive teams have been more aware of the importance of communicating openly, effectively, and in a timely manner since September 11.

Qualitative results

A careful examination of open-ended responses combined with the realization of which subjects agreed with these statements and which respondents did not, sheds an interesting and important light on the situation. More than half of those who disagreed with the two questions articulated in Table 20.4, did so mainly because they believe that

Table 20.4 Responses of senior-level, US PR and corporate communication professionals to additional questions in March 2002 (%)

Question	Strongly agree	Agree	Uncertain/ no opinion	Disagree	Strongly disagree	Mean
Do you agree the September 11, 2001, terrorist attacks precipitated a paradigm shift advancing communications and public relations into a more significant role in corporate America?	18	32	27	23	0	3.45
Do you agree your company's executive teams have been more aware of the importance of communicating openly, effectively, and in a timely manner since September 11, 2001?	18	46	14	23	0	3.59

prior to September 11: (1) corporate public relations had established a strong tradition of playing a significant role in their company; and (2) their organization's executive teams recognized years ago the importance of communicating openly, effectively and in a timely manner. Given the reality, these respondents essentially were not disagreeing with the questions reported on in Table 20.4, the level of agreement actually would be considerably higher – nearly 65 per cent for RQ4 and greater than 75 per cent for RQ5. Furthermore, while taking precautions not to violate the study's promises of anonymity and confidentiality, it is important to point out that several of those who disagreed with these two questions are very senior-level corporate communication officers who have earned the utmost respect from their professional peers. Essentially, then, their responses to these questions might need to be overlooked. They disagreed with the paradigm shift thesis because corporate public relations already was extremely significant in their organization. And, they disagreed with the executive teams question because that kind of open

communication has been taking place in their company for many years.

Although this research was conducted with promises of anonymity and confidentiality, several subjects identified their responses and provided additional permission to be quoted directly in results reports. This included five very senior-level corporate public relations professionals. Each of these individuals was asked to provide a direct quote in October 2001 assessing the impact the September 11 terrorist attacks were having on their jobs. The same five senior-level professionals were asked to review their quotes in March 2002 and explain how, if at all, their opinions might have changed.

Quotes from these five professionals follow.

Bill Nielsen, Corporate Vice President, Public Affairs and Corporate Communications, Johnson & Johnson

October 2001

My company's employee communications came to the forefront following September

11th because stockholders and employees demanded to know more about what was going on throughout the organization.

March 2002

Employee communications are still extremely important. Interestingly, the Enron matter has probably also heightened the interest of employees in knowing what is going on.

Matthew P. Gonring, Vice President, Communications, Baxter International

October 2001

It enhanced the role of the communications executive especially as it applies to being a counselor and advisor to senior corporate management.

March 2002

I still feel much the same way, but I would expand upon this and say the events of 9/11 brought greater attention to the relative importance of communications, especially the role of senior counselor and advisor.

Curtis G. Linke, Vice President, Corporate Communications, Deere & Company

October 2001

The terrorist attacks prompted Deere & Company to propel the communications function into the lead of a senior management, policy making team. Now headed by me, this group consists of five of the company's most senior executives, and has pledged to keep employees informed on anything that might affect their workplace or their home place.

March 2002

The only difference now is that one of the five retired, so it is four senior executives. Otherwise still accurate, but the sense of urgency has abated.

E. Ronald Culp, Senior Vice President, Public Relations and Government Affairs, Sears, Roebuck and Company

October 2001

The September attacks created a demand for faster communications, especially around employees and issues involving security.

March 2002

My October quote still appropriately echoes how I feel.

E. Bruce Harrison, President, E. Bruce Harrison Company and Senior Consultant, International Truck and Engine Company

October 2001

As the result of what happened September 11 the CPRO (Chief Public Relations Officer) role is escalating. It's logical. All company top executives have become extraordinarily sensitized to the potential for sudden events, including a crisis. During times of crises, CEOs and others in top management instinctively turn to communications and involve the CPRO. This lights the communications board. It starts with employee communication but spreads quickly to stakeholders throughout various channels – security, sales, stockholders, investment advisors, supply, transportation, parts, etc. As the expert on communicating – two-way, symmetric – the CPRO is at more tables and more important tables.

March 2002

The basics of relationship and reputation have not changed. However, I see chief communications officers putting new energy into their continuous evaluation of the impact of external conditions on critical stakeholders. There is a mandate for excellence in the communicator's role as counselor to others in the company on the interactions (which are not achievable without two-way communications) that sustain trust. If there were ever a time for the CPRO to become 'chief trust officer', it is now.

Intervening variables

Evidence of two potentially significant, intervening variables surfaced a number of times in analysis of the March results. One of these concerned the impact the economic recession of early 2002 might have been having upon corporate public relations. The other involved the potential impact precipitated by issues such as organizational mismanagement, lack of corporate trust, etc., arising out of the Enron Corporation scandal. Although not prompted to do so in any of the March questions, about half of the subjects who provided open-ended responses to this wave of the survey suggested that either or both of these two variables might be more significant for changes in corporate communication behaviour than reactions to the September 11 terrorist attacks. In terms of the economy, US public relations was facing a steady downturn in business prior to the attacks and this trend was continuing into March. In some cases corporate staffs had faced layoffs, but even more pronounced were cutbacks at technology companies and within many public relations agencies.

Additional findings

Nearly every respondent (97 per cent) to the October survey agreed managed and strategic communication and public relations can be effective weapons of war. And an equal number (97 per cent) thought the United States would implement such a campaign in the struggle against terrorism. Neither of these questions was followed up in the March research in order to accommodate queries about the paradigm shift and executive teams recognizing the need to communicate openly, effectively and timely.

Summary

This research study of senior-level, American, corporate PR executives explores how corporate communication and public relations were impacted by the September 11, 2001 terrorism attacks on the United States.

Data were gathered between September 2001 and March 2002 in several stages involving both quantitative and qualitative methodologies. The study's quantitative measuring instruments consisted of two, short, email questionnaires distributed to senior-level, corporate PR executives in October 2001 and again in March 2002. Sampling was purposive and intentionally small in an attempt to restrict participation to only the most top-level corporate and agency PR professionals. Short email surveys were used because our previous research has discovered communication executives rarely complete mail questionnaires, and are extremely difficult to pin down for telephone interviews.

Additional data were gathered through a variety of qualitative methods, including responses to open-ended survey questions, email conversational interviews with subjects, plus telephone and personal interviews with a small number of subjects. Results found two-thirds of the corporate public relations executives surveyed thought the events of September 11, 2001 have changed how their companies communicate. The intensity of feelings on this question increased slightly between October and March. Findings also reflect strong agreement (88 per cent in October; 92 per cent in March) suggesting the terrorist attacks have had an impact on their organization's public relations and communication function. When data were submitted to t-tests, no significant differences were determined between October and March responses.

The study also found moderate agreement suggesting the terrorist attacks precipitated a paradigm shift advancing public relations into a more significant role in corporate America. Two-thirds of the respondents agreed their company's executive teams have been more aware of the importance of communicating openly, effectively, and in a timely manner since September 11.

This research also found a number of exam-

ples showing evidence of implications of excellence theory and behaviour model theory in the perceived impact the terrorist attacks have had on corporate public relations. The study reports on a number of theoretical implications of both theories based upon both quantitative and qualitative findings. Specifically, the research found a number of instances where the events of September 11 have served as examples of 'latent readiness' and 'triggering events' as articulated in the behaviour model. Also, a number of examples were found relating to 'two-way asymmetrical' and 'two-way symmetrical' communication as described in excellent theory literature. A number of implications vis-à-vis the excellence theory concerning the role public relations plays in an organization's dominant coalition also are expounded upon in the study's results and discussion section.

All in all, the senior-level corporate PR executives surveyed in this study report the September 11, 2001, terrorist attacks have had a significant impact not only upon how companies now communicate but also on how many corporate PR departments function.

NOTES

1 Andrew Kohut, 'Nationhood, Internationalism Lifted,' a report for the Pew Research Center, February 14, 2002. Available at http://people-press.org/commentary/display.php3?AnalysisID=44 (27 February, 2002).
2 Frank Newport, 'Americans Still Consider Sept. 11 Most Tragic Event of their Lives', Gallup Organization Poll Analysis Report, 11 March, 2002. Accessed online, 11 March, 2002 at http://www.gallup.com/poll/releases/pr020311.asp.
3 Kohut, 'Nationhood'.
4 Jill Lawrence, 'Bush has more challenges lined up in 2002,' USA Today, 18 January, 2002, p. 5A.
5 David Ignatius, 'Commentary: a changed world,

perhaps, but no apocalypse now', International Herald Tribune, online version, 11 March, 2002. Accessed at: http://www.iht.com/cgi-bin/generic.cgi?template=articleprint.tmphlandArticleId=42409.
6 Newport, 'Americans'.
7 Kohut, 'Nationhood'.
8 Newport, 'Americans'.
9 'Six Months Later,' editorial, New York Times, 11 March 2002, p. B7.
10 David Cary, 'Americans differ on how Sept. 11 changed them', Associated Press, 11 March 2001. Accessed online 11 March 2001 through America Online.

11   Patrick McMahon, 'Holiday wins grass-roots favor', *USA Today*, 12 March, 2002, p. 3A.

12   Newport, 'Americans'.

13   Donald K. Wright, 'validating credibility measures of public relations and communication: interviews with senior-level managers and executives from other corporate disciplines', *Journal of Communication Management* (1998), 3, 105–18.

14   For information about the communication executive role see, Donald K. Wright, 'The role of corporate public relations executives in the future of employee communications', *Public Relations Review* (1995), 21, 181–98; and, Donald K. Wright, 'Validating credibility measures of public relations and communications: interviews with senior-level managers and executives from other corporate disciplines', *Journal of Communication Management* (1998), 3, 105–18. For information about other roles public relations professionals function in see, Glen M. Broom and David M. Dozier, 'Advancement for public relations role models', *Public Relations Review* (1986), 7, 37–56.

15   James O. Mock and Cedric Larson, *Words That Won the War*, Princeton, New Jersey: Princeton University Press, 1939. Also see, George Creel, *How We Advertised America: The First Telling of the Amazing Story of the Committees on Public Information That Carried the Gospel of Americanism to Every Corner of the Globe*, New York: Harper and Row, 1920.

16   Alan M. Winkler, *The Politics of Propaganda: The Office of War Information 1942–45*, New Haven: Yale University Press, 1978, p. 4. Also see, Robert L. Bishop and LaMar S. Mackay, 'Mysterious silence, lyrical scream: government information in World War II', *Journalism Monographs*, 19, (May, 1971).

17   Charles S. Steinberg, *The Creation of Consent*, New York: Hastings House, 1975, pp. 29–30.

CHAPTER 21

Public relations and democracy: historical reflections and implications for practice

Jacquie L'Etang

In this chapter some key criticisms against public relations are examined. From 'spin doctors' to 'champions of discourse in society', the debate on the role of public relations shows no sign of abating. Indeed today's media hungry society seems only to fuel the debate. Using a historical analysis of the PR profession in the United Kingdom, the author seeks to explore some of the factors that have challenged the role of public relations through empirical evidence in a variety of political, social and economic contexts. She identifies some precise contributions to democratic as well as anti-democratic practices and provides deeper insight and broader understanding of public relations today; its interpolation within the deep structures of society; and sources of the mythology that plagues the PR profession.

'Spin doctors', 'hidden persuaders', invisible persuaders', 'charlatans', 'anti-democratic': these are typical contemporary criticisms of public relations. What lies behind such accusations appears to be the fear of manipulation and the secretive and inappropriate access to power, subterfuge and the employment of hype and selective silences to enhance the case of the organization on whose behalf the practitioner works. Criticisms are aired in the popular press and in the academic journals and books of media researchers. Indeed, an increasing amount of popular argument is being marshalled against the legitimacy of PR practice and the ethics of its practitioners. The

defence of the industry has been somewhat lacklustre and a little unconvincing, partly because the industry is unregulated and the large majority of practitioners are not members of the professional body. This makes the task of professional bodies in the United Kingdom, the Institute of Public Relations and the Public Relations Consultants Association, very difficult since they cannot claim to represent all practitioners, and while they have well publicized codes of practice, they certainly do not control the practice. This in turn reduces their potential as a media source, the media often preferring to turn to individuals such as publicist Max Clifford whose undoubted personal charisma and connections with the worlds of celebrity, entertainment and politics make him irresistible. As a non-professional occupation the parameters of practice are still unclear and barriers to practice (as opposed to membership of professional bodies) still do not exist. Historically, since public relations emerged as a discrete occupation in the United Kingdom, its practitioners have been challenged by journalists. In its defence, PR practitioners and some academics have argued that public relations enhances discourse in society and thus in fact contributes to democracy. This chapter explores some of those ideas through historical analysis both of the pattern of development and of some of the occupation's intellectual history.

The chapter focuses on the history of public relations in the United Kingdom. History provides empirical evidence of the role of public relations in a variety of political, social and economic contexts and it is possible to identify some precise contributions to democratic as well as anti-democratic practice. Such an analysis provides a fuller understanding of the role of public relations and its interpolation with the deep structures of our society. It also permits some analysis of the sources of mythology about public relations: both its demonology and its evangelism.

Literary antecedents and intellectual history of public relations

There is an assumption in much of the existing PR literature that public relations was first developed in the United States and then exported elsewhere, a view that this article challenges. Another feature of historical reviews within PR literature is the way in which PR practice is defined as akin to activities carried out by the Greeks or the Romans, as well as journalists and activists such as Jonathan Swift, Daniel Defoe, Charles Dickens and William Wilberforce. Such definitions imply that persuasion, rhetoric, sophistry, advocacy and lobbying are a central part of PR practice. There is an inevitable tension between this acknowledged heritage and the contemporary professional notion of public relations as part of management, a move which suggests a respectable, technocratic, neutral function.

Historically, embryonic ideas about a formalized information occupation emerged from debates about the implications of widening democracy. Political elites recognized that public opinion management (and communication) was now crucial to ruling in a democracy but feared the rule of the mob as franchises were widened. In the 1920s the American political writers Lasswell and Lippman were key in developing a number of important analyses. Lasswell expressed serious concerns about the development of propaganda in the First World War which he saw as marking 'the collapse of the traditional species of democratic romanticism' (Ewen, 1996: 174). It was Lasswell who introduced the Taylorist metaphor of engineering to PR work and his compatriot, Lippman introduced another – the manufacture of consent. Lippman's pessimistic view of mass society led him to recommend the creation of a cadre of communication specialists who would be given privileged access to elites and events and who would subsequently be responsible for briefing the media (Lippman, 1998). It could be argued that this rather Platonic arrangement was an early example of the notion of neutral, technocratic communicators, having access to, yet separate from, elite power, and charged with responsibility for public communication. This class of people would be responsible for educating the masses about public policy options. This theme of education became important in PR discourse. It was taken up strongly by the influential Scottish film documentarist and communication expert, John Grierson, who wrote extensively on problems of democracy and the importance of public relations in facilitating democratic practice. Grierson had been influenced by Lippman, under whom he had studied in the United States, and shared much of his pessimism, writing, for example, that he had

> noted the conclusion of men such as Walter Lippman, that because the citizen under modern conditions, could not know everything about everything all the time . . . democratic citizenship was therefore impossible. We . . . turned to the new wide-ranging instruments of radio and cinema as necessary instruments in both the practice of government and the enjoyment of citizenship.
>
> (Grierson and Hardy, 1946: 78)

Grierson wrote extensively during the 1930s and 1940s about the problems of communication in an increasingly complex and technologized world. Although he was a film expert his thinking went far beyond the merely technical. For him, public relations and propaganda were overlapping notions that offered a solution to the threat of alienation and the possible breakdown of society. An analysis of the Institute of Public Relations (IPR) journals from 1948 demonstrates that much of Grierson's idealism influenced the post-Second World War generation of practitioners who began to professionalize the field. Professional status requires social legitimacy, so Grierson's grandiose notions of the important role for public relations in society (drawn from Lippman) thus resonated with practition-

ers' emerging ambitions for status and influence in an increasingly sceptical post-war world (L'Etang, 2000: 91). The idea that public relations should be a powerful force in society was therefore rooted in the early ideas about the practice in Britain.

Grierson's influence was enhanced by his connection with Sir Stephen Tallents, an extremely influential mandarin in the civil service who had the concept of a 'school for national projection' to promote Britain abroad. This subsequently became the blueprint for the British Council, a body whose cultural diplomacy remains important to British interests overseas, targeting elites and the 'successor generation' in a wide variety of countries. Tallents commissioned members of the British Documentary Film Movement, of which Grierson was the acknowledged leader, to make a number of important educational and propaganda films on social and political issues and helped ensure the survival of the film unit.

The context within which Tallents operated was one in which issues of communication had been debated since the propaganda efforts of the First World War. Within local government there was an important contribution made by officials who, due to increasing social, educational and welfare provision (a trend begun by the Great Reform Acts of the early nineteenth century), needed to communicate more, and more effectively, with local communities. The intellectual contribution in terms of the history of public relations in the United Kingdom was significant. Local government officials in Britain in the 1920s and 1930s developed key PR concepts and contributed in an important way to PR ideology, particularly in relation to concepts of professionalism in the articulation of their own public service ethos. Their ideas were expressed in a range of articles published in the specialist journal *Public Administration* and demonstrated their understanding of the importance of monitoring the wider environment to aid and influence public policy. Public relations was seen as a tool to facilitate smooth administration. It was local government public relations officers who formed the nucleus of those responsible for setting up the IPR for which task they clearly possessed the appropriate administrative skills. The contribution of British civil servants to the development of public relations in the United Kingdom was substantial both in terms of practice but also intellectually and ideologically. A prime value for them was that of government responsibility for the public interest and in their writings we can see a clear articulation of what could be called 'the public interest model of public relations'. The idea that public relations should work in the public interest remains today and is alluded to in professional codes of conduct. The notion of professional neutrality remained an important value in the British Government Information Service after the Second World War and was an important contrast to the heavily politicized American counterpart. Latterly, however, there is evidence of the erosion of that principle.

It was not until 1949 that the first British book on public relations was published (Brebner, 1949). It was written by the practitioner J. H. Brebner whose distinguished career included public relations at the Post Office; membership of the committee which set up the Ministry of Information (MoI) in 1937; Director of the News Division, MoI; special overseas operative 1943–5; Director of Press Communications at Supreme Allied Headquarters; public relations at the British Transport Commission. Apparently influenced by management writers Taylor and Barnard, Brebner's argument for the existence and

justification of the role of public relations was that it was an administrative or managerial tool both to counteract the negative results of specialization within organizations, and to motivate the workforce. This seems to have been the earliest explicit claim in a British context that the role of public relations is to support management. Like Lippman and Grierson, Brebner argued that the PR practitioner should have senior status and access to the policy makers in an organization.

Thus we can see that the shape and trajectory of British public relations has been influenced partly by intellectual developments originating in the United States but also by some key home-grown thinkers and policy makers.

Critical issues

Intrinsic to the concept of contemporary democracy is the idea of popular debate and the resolution of issues via discussion and negotiation. However, in a free society debate between the organizational actors, publics and individuals is a consequence of specific, directed intentions, usually focused on persuasion, and not conducted as an end in themselves. In other words, corporate communication has to support the goals of an organization and is not explicitly conducted to support democratic values, although sometimes this might be a side-effect of such communication. Thus, communication in modern democracies is a haphazard and contingent affair in terms of democratic practice, however focused and goal-oriented it may be in organizational terms. To claim that public relations is either specifically promoting or undermining democracy is overstating either case since it is an outgrowth of fundamental political and social structures and international flux and transformations. So while the concept of a valuable role for public relations in facilitating the 'free market place of ideas' in a capitalist, competitive context might seem attractive, it always has to be remembered that public relations activities may be utilized to support some potentially anti-democratic ideals. In an open society it is inevitable that different causes will utilize public relations to advance their positions, and it seems increasingly the case that in times of organizational or organizational–public conflict communication will include a meta-argument about the nature of communication, both by the participants who may hurl the slur of 'propaganda' against their opponents and by the media who will be searching for examples of 'spin' or hypocrisy.

The concerns of media academics have largely focused on structural inequalities in complex society that privilege corporate and government institutions at the expense of smaller organizations and causes. For example, while tending to conflate advertising, marketing, propaganda and public relations Chomsky's analysis that the media serve the interests of state and corporate power 'framing their reporting and analysis in a manner supportive of established privilege and limiting debate and discussion accordingly' does imply the need for elite networkers, wheeler-dealers, rhetoricians and lobbyists who can put their case across (Chomsky, 1989). One argument is that those with 'deep pockets' can fund expensive public relations campaigns which disadvantages 'resource-poor' groups and this is the line taken by Gandy in his notion of information subsidies which illustrate that structural inequalities in society can be reinforced by public relations and the media (Gandy). Another approach is that those with resources clog the channels of communication and dominate the limited

space available for individuals and less well-off groups to debate issues of importance to them. The relationship between sources and the media explored by a number of media sociologists (Hall, 1969; Schlesinger, 1990; Anderson, 1993; McNair, 1996; Miller, 1998; Dinan, 2000; Davis, 2002) has focused on the implications for citizens to the public sphere. Such analyses rely to some degree on the notion that the moral principle of fairness, which seems important for democracy, is potentially infringed by PR practice. In other words issues, and the way they are framed are done so in terms of government and corporates, and competing interests and lines of argument are not heard. It is worth pointing out, however, that there is still a limited amount of empirical work in the field. It is also the case that media sociologists on the whole focus on relationships between the media and public relations to explore and condemn the extent of their influence. Such a focus omits an exploration of the non-media aspects of PR work and its influence in the public sphere and upon publics, public opinion and society more widely. It is also the case that the substantial academic critiques emerging from media sociology have not been addressed by the PR discipline which has until relatively recently largely excluded critical debate as being 'unhelpful' to the practice. Media academics to varying degrees reflect the prejudices of journalists and may therefore regard PR academics as either nefarious or unthinking functionaries operating in an atheoretical and thus inferior environment. Consequently, debate is still polarized into opposing camps which inhibits analysis of what is actually a very complex practice. Even at the level of basic definitions the history of public relations has led to considerable confusion over terminology, the relationship between the various related occupations such as public relations, design, advertising and marketing, not to mention the confusion over the degree of overlap or distinction between public relations and propaganda. In short, much that is written conforms to existing disciplinary conventions and agendas and as such inhibits our understanding of the role of public relations in democracy.

A very valuable revisionist approach is taken by Davis (2002). He identifies a number of gaps and contradictions in media sociology literature, not least its strong bias towards examining political public relations at the expense of corporate (though this may be somewhat corrected by the output of an ESRC study currently under way at the University of Stirling). Davis's empirical work shows that the assumption that larger resources necessarily lead to better media coverage is flawed in relation to corporate public relations. Specifically he points out that,

> Direct corporate source influence on national news production in the UK has been significantly weaker than most accounts assume. The logics that guide both journalist routines and business communication objectives each suggest that companies are neither able, nor strongly inclined, to concentrate their efforts on influencing the output of mainstream news texts. Rather, they tend to pursue public promotion through advertising and political objectives through direct contact with policy-makers. Thus, if public relations is benefiting the corporate sector it cannot simply be on account of its ability to influence national journalists and public opinion.
>
> (Davis, 2000: 45–6)

Instead he argues that corporate goals are better served by advertising and through discreet access to policy makers.

The substantial critiques emerging from media sociology have not been addressed by the PR discipline, as will now be discussed. Existing narratives of the origins and development of the PR occupation are largely American. One interpretation has come to dominate – that developed by J. Grunig and Hunt, which suggests that public relations has passed through four developmental stages: publicity, public information, asymmetrical and symmetrical communication. Somewhat simplistically, the first two stages are described as 'one-way' communication in comparison to the 'two way' types of which the asymmetrical variety employs research techniques to support its persuasive efforts, while the symmetrical type is motivated to achieve consensus between an organization and its publics. The models are focused on organization-publics and therefore do not take account of the broader 'public interest', and so have a somewhat different approach to the British tradition. Much of the literature promotes the idea that this evolutionary model is universally applicable both as a historical explanation and as a typology that satisfactorily explains professional practice. Yet it fails to take account of significant cultural and political factors in non-US settings and its monolithic application in deductive research and status as a worldview has inhibited the development of research grounded in the daily practice of public relations. Historically speaking it is a rather superficial account of developments, perhaps because the main interest is in characterizing types of practice rather than piecing together the complex collage of human endeavour in mass communication.

The dominant paradigm is broadly liberal pluralist and sees public relations as supportive of democracy, opening up channels of communication and facilitating dialogue between organizations and publics. According to this view, public relations is neutral, benign and broadly utilitarian. The dominant paradigm therefore chooses to ignore the intrinsic self-interest necessarily present in the representation of an interests and advocacy on behalf of an organization.

The major contribution of the American PR theorist and historian, Scott Cutlip, should not be ignored. His approach differs from that of Grunig and Hunt as he argues that,

> The history of public relations cannot be told by simply saying that it grew out of press agentry. Nor can it be fully told in terms of people such as Ivy Lee or Arthur Page. Efforts to communicate with others and to deal with the force of public opinion go back to antiquity; only the tools, degree of specialisation, breadth of knowledge, and intensity of effort are new.
>
> (Cutlip, et al., 1994: 89)

Cutlip et al. (1994) identify a number of key periods in American history focusing on the twentieth century showing the important links between events in international affairs and politics, economics, technology and the growth in both the media and public relations. But as Cutlip pointed out in his groundbreaking volume *Unseen Power* (1994), writing the history of public relations in the United States is impossible without also writing a history of the United States itself. The sheer scale and impracticalities of writing a complete American history led him to take a more biographical and consultancy-based approach. Cutlip's admission shows that the emergence of public relations is clearly tied to democratic structures.

Significant scholarly American corporate histories have been tackled by Tedlow (1979), Olasky (1987) and Marchand (1998) and it is clear that the devil is in the detail in terms of illustrating the real implications of public relations for democratic practice. To date equivalent work has not been tackled in the United Kingdom.

Evolution of public relations in the United Kingdom

Public relations in the United Kingdom developed primarily in the state sector as a consequence of political, economic and social changes. The approach taken here is to link the evolution of public relations to those broader changes. This is in contrast to some histories of public relations which give much emphasis to individuals, thus taking Thomas Carlyle's approach that 'History is the biography of great men.' Historiographically speaking, this type of analysis can lead to the exaggeration of the importance of individual, creative effort and the idolization of the few. A classic example in the literature is the treatment of the American practitioner Edward Bernays, whose real historical contribution is rather obscured, not least because Bernays was such a self-publicist and lived to the age of 104, his good genes thus enabling him to enhance and promote his contribution long after most of his contemporaries. Of course this is not to say that at certain points in history the contribution of one or two individuals produces a particular crux in PR history but it is important to recognize the reasons why those individuals had the opportunities they did to develop their skills and not to overplay their significance. Individual opportunism could only flourish in certain conditions. Analyses that focus on the identity of 'the father of public relations' (one wonders about the mothers) seriously limit our understanding of the relationship between public relations, environmental factors and the consequent institutional structures that shape our lives.

The reason that the state contribution in the United Kingdom was so paramount was two-fold: first, Britain's international position as a colonial power (L'Etang, 2003) required the management of a host of domestic and worldwide publics; second, social reform gathered pace from the early nineteenth century which required a major shift in the climate between the government and its subjects. Unlike the isolationist United States, Britain's history dictated close involvement in European areas and particularly with the other major colonial powers of France and Germany. Communications were needed to support diplomacy. For example, it required substantial propaganda efforts on Britain's behalf to persuade the United States to become involved in both world wars (even so, the United States did not participate until 1917 and 1941). The two world wars, and the international unrest which preceded them, facilitated the growth of what was, initially unproblematically, termed 'propaganda'.

Modern war and the advances in communication technology contributed greatly to the development of propaganda. The increased democratization of society necessitated public opinion management in times of war. Government needed to control and censor unfavourable information that might harm morale; to penetrate enemy communication networks in order to confuse or demoralize; and to win and maintain alliances from which political, economic or military support might be forthcoming. In wartime the British government made substantial propaganda efforts both at home and overseas. The wartime experience sensitized civilian and military populations to issues of propaganda, information and intelligence. While Britain cultivated notions of media independence and truthful information, there was an extensive internal and external propaganda effort. 'Black' propaganda (defined as communication which entails deception and untruths) was considered morally justifiable in the circumstances and somewhat romanticized. The head of SOE's 'F' Section was Colonel Maurice Buckmaster who had worked for Ford Motor Company prior to the war. After the war he became Director of Public Relations at Ford and subsequently went freelance representing the French champagne industry. He became a fellow of the IPR in 1954 and was president in 1955. The career of such a man clearly demonstrates the overlap between public relations and propaganda and the difficulty in separating the two terms.

The emergence of totalitarian politics in continental Europe in the 1930s and the growth of home-grown versions stimulated an ongoing policy debate about the British response to such developments and the necessity of a propaganda policy to respond to the perceived threat. Thus it was at this point in history that the term 'propaganda' began to be tarnished and associated with particular political structures and ideologies. There was much debate in British political circles about the appropriateness of a propaganda policy in a democratic society in peacetime (its use in wartime was deemed inevitable and justifiable) and whether it was right to adopt such tactics in order to compete with the totalitarian states. The idea that propaganda was a necessary adjunct of diplomacy began to prevail.

In terms of domestic politics there was an increasing awareness by politicians of the need to manage public opinion (and their own personal image) in an increasingly democratized state. Consequently, some civil servants became specialized in media relations. Some of these took their skills into the private sector. For example, one of the earliest PR consultants in the United Kingdom was Sydney Walton, who set up business in 1920, having previously worked as press officer for Lloyd George. Another, who has been credited by some as being Britain's first fully fledged PR consultant was Basil Clarke, a former *Daily Mail* journalist who later directed the Special Intelligence section at the Ministry of Reconstruction, then moved to the Ministry of Health and finally became Director of Public Information in Dublin Castle until he left in 1926 and set up his own agency, Editorial Services, which he founded jointly with two practising consultants, R. J. Sykes of London Press Exchange (LPE) and James Walker of Winter Thomas. Some have argued that Basil Clarke was the 'father' of public relations in Britain in the 1920s partly because of his well-established and impressive record in government and partly because he drafted the first detailed code of practice, much of which formed the basis of codes of the Institute of Public Relations for many years. Basil Clarke's son claimed that his father had known Ivy Lee but it is difficult to check how much contact the two men had and Ivy Lee junior wrote to me in a letter in 1998 that, 'I don't remember ever having heard of him [Basil Clarke] . . . neither my brother nor I have any recollection of my father having contact with any British practitioners.' On the other hand, the Scot, John Grierson, suggested a terminological influence when he wrote that in Britain in the 1920s, 'The word publicity itself was set aside: the concept of public relations took its place, borrowed oddly from the Chicago Transit Company under that old thug Sam Insull . . . the key to public relations . . . was the dramatisation in every way, not of the end-product, but of its sources' (Grierson, 1956: 8) so perhaps we should remain cau-

tious of the extent to which US practitioners exported their ideas to the British.

Nevertheless, Britain's international PR and propaganda efforts taken together with the intellectual and practical efforts of British civil servants show that British public relations emerged in its own unique way arising from the immediate context and was not purely the consequence of imported ideas from America.

Public relations and the media: a troublesome and troubled relationship

The emergence of public relations immediately threatened the professional role and freedoms of journalists. Although PR practitioners saw their role as helping the media, journalists could not but see them as a barrier to access to policy makers. Tensions grew rapidly after the Second World War as the PR occupation expanded against a backdrop of rapid change in the media. The end of paper rationing in 1956 meant that advertisers, now using market research, could target audiences more effectively. Newspapers that could not deliver audiences were subject to closures and the industry began to contract (Williams, 1998: 213–20). In this context, public relations appeared to offer what seemed to be free publicity. Thus the post-war generation began to focus more on publicity and stunts. Out-of-work journalists were well qualified to move into such jobs and were also influential in shaping the role of the occupation at this time in terms of practice, norms and values. Ex-journalists could offer clients the ability to de-mystify the media as well as protecting them. They therefore offered more tangible benefits than the other major category that formed the post-war influx into public relations – the ex-army types who could generally only offer bonhomie and social contacts plus some administrative skill.

Post-war media criticism of public relations presented a problem for PR practitioners since the IPR was trying to establish the occupation as respectable. Media criticism focused on the perceived incompetence of practitioners and ethical issues such as: apparent attempts to bribe the media with lavish hospitality; the development of parliamentary lobbying; work carried out on behalf of foreign interests some of which were opposed to British government policy or interests. The rapid expansion of public relations meant that sources had a better ability to raise issues and frame news stories so the power balance between sources and the media was altered in a way that journalists naturally perceived as unfavourable, both in terms of their professional status, but also, to some degree, democracy.

Historically, perhaps the most significant aspect of the media–public relations tension is the durability of the arguments over half a century. Reading the stinging criticism by journalists in the 1960s (L'Etang 2003) it is clear that there are recurring themes and tensions between the two occupations and while it could be tempting to assume that such tension is healthy in a democracy the revolving doors between journalism, public relations and politics seem less than desirable in terms of creating a privileged elite who share information and power in a way that prohibits citizen debate.

Post-war economic recovery: the emergence of consultancy and corporate rhetoric

Post-war there were several opportunities for public relations to become an established part of the socio-economic framework: the large amount of new social legislation needed to be explained to citizens; goods had to be promoted, initially to export markets and then, with the increase of consumer durables, to the home market; finally, the new administration's interventionist economic policies required some explanation and triggered opposition from business in ideologically motivated rhetorical campaigns, for example, those conducted by Aims of Industry (L'Etang, 2003).

The emergence and growth of PR consultancies marked a distinctive historical development in terms of the professionalization of public relations since it presumed sufficient hold on certain crafts, knowledge, experience and a sufficiently coherent identity for business to survive, indeed thrive in the marketplace. Such a development represented a major shift in terms of public relations' place in the British economy and signals the point at which there was a major uptake of PR services and thus public recognition of the practice. The growth of consultancy was important for the process of professionalization and eventually culminated in the formation of the Public Relations Consultants' Association in 1969.

The situation in Britain was very different from that of the United States where all the big advertising agencies had public relations departments in the post-war era. Consultancy had much slower growth in the United Kingdom, partly because it took so long for the British economy to recover after the Second World War (Britain finished the war as the world's largest debtor nation). Economic expansion in the late 1950s and early 1960s stimulated the consumer and retail industries which in turn demanded editorial publicity to support advertising and marketing.

By the late 1950s and early 1960s many PR consultants left their umbrella advertising organizations to establish their own clients. The interplay between consultancies, consumerism and the economic growth of the 1960s was crucial. With hindsight we can see that the growth of consultancy foreshadowed the exponential growth of public relations that, 'has played a key role in the transformation of British political and economic life in the 1980s' (Miller and Dinan 2000: 5).

Conclusion

This brief review has highlighted some of the key features of the evolution of public relations in the United Kingdom. It has demonstrated that British public relations had its own distinctive trajectory derived from its unique long history and colonial position. It is clear that PR practice evolved largely from different aspects of international and domestic policies in a democratized context and that civil service values made a substantial stamp on the British brand of public relations. Nevertheless, it can be seen that different intentions fuelled practice with some efforts specifically designed to improve democratic practice and much else to improve the position of particular organizations. While the critiques of journalists can reveal nefarious practice in terms of media relations, there is still much that is hidden from view in terms of undue influence behind the scenes and this remains a problem for PR ethics.

REFERENCES

Anderson, A. (1993) 'Source–media relations: the production of the environmental agenda', in A. Hansen (ed.), *The Mass Media and Environmental Issues*, Leicester: Leicester University Press.

Brebner, J. H. (1949) *Public Relations and Publicity*, London: Institute of Public Administration.

Chomsky, N. (1989; 1993) *Necessary Illusions: Thought Control in Democratic Societies*, London: Pluto Press.

Cutlip, S. M. (1994) *The Unseen Power: Public Relations History*, Hillsdale, NJ: LEA.

Cutlip, S. M., Center, A. H. and Broom, G. H. (1994) *Effective Public Relations*, Prentice Hall.

Davis, A. (2002) *Public Relations Democracy: Public Relations, Politics and the Mass Media in Britain*, Manchester: Manchester University Press.

Ewen, S. (1996) *PR! A Social History of Spin*, New York: Basic Books.

Gandy, O. (1992) 'Public relations and public policy: the structuration of dominance in the information age', in E. Toth and R. Heath (eds), *Rhetorical and Critical Approaches to Public Relations*, Hillsdale, NJ: LEA.

Grierson, J. and Hardy, F. (eds), (1946) *Grierson on Documentary*, London: Faber & Faber.

Habermas, J. (1989) *The Structural Transformation of the Public Sphere: an Inquiry into a Category of Bourgeois Society*, Cambridge: Polity Press.

Hall, S. (1969) 'The technics of persuasion', *New Society*, December, 948–9.

Herman, E. S. and Chomsky, N. (1988) *Manufacturing Consent: The Political Economy of the Mass Media*, New York: Pantheon Books.

Lasswell, H. D. (1927) *Propaganda Technique in the World War*, New York: Knopf.

Lippman, W. (1998) *Public Opinion*, New Brunswick: Transaction.

L'Etang, J. (2000) 'Grierson and the public relations industry in Britain', in J. Izod and R. Kilborn with M. Hibberd, *From Grierson to the Docu-soap: Breaking the Boundaries*, Luton: University of Luton Press.

L'Etang, J. (2001) 'The professionalisation of British public relations in the twentieth century: a history', PhD thesis, University of Stirling.

L'Etang, J. and Pieczka, M. (eds) (2003) *Public Relations: Critical Debates and Contemporary Practice*, Hillsdale, NJ: LEA.

L'Etang, J. (2004) *Public Relations in Britain: A History of Professional Practice in the Twentieth Century*, Hillsdale, NJ: LEA.

L'Etang, Jacquie and Muruli, George, (2004) 'Public relations, decolonisation and democracy: the case of Kenya', in D. Tilson and E. Alozie (eds), *Towards the Common Good: Perspectives in International Public Relations*, Allyn and Bacon.

L'Etang, J. and Pieczka, M. (eds) (1996) *Critical Perspectives in Public Relations*, ITBP.

Marchand. R. (1998) *Creating the Corporate Soul: The Rise of Public Relations and Corporate Imagery in American Big Business*, Berkeley: University of California Press.

McNair, B. (1996) 'Performance in politics and the politics of performance: public relations, the public sphere and democracy', in J. L'Etang and M. Pieczka (eds), *Critical Perspectives in Public Relations*, ITBP.

McNair, B. (2005) 'PR must die: spin, anti-spin and political public relations in the United Kingdom, 1997–2002', in J. L'Etang and M. Pieczka (eds), *Public Relations: Critical Debates and Contemporary Practice*, Hillsdale, NJ: LEA.

Miller, D. (1998) 'Public relations and journalism: promotional strategies and media power', in A. Briggs and P. Cobley (eds), *The Media: An Introduction*, London: Longman.

Miller, D. and Dinan, W. (2000) 'The rise of the PR industry in Britain 1979–98', *European Journal of Communication*, 5(1), 5–35.

Moloney, K. (2000) *Rethinking Public Relations: The Spin and the Substance*, London: Routledge.

Olasky, M. N. (1987) *Corporate Public Relations: A New Historical Perspective*, Hillsdale, NJ: LEA.

Schlesinger, P. (1990) 'Rethinking the sociology of journalism: source strategies and the limits of media centrism', in M. Ferguson (ed.), *Political Communication: The New Imperatives: Future Directions for Research*, Thousand Oaks, CA: Sage.

Tedlow, R. S. (1979) *Keeping the Corporate Image: Public Relations and Business 1900–1950*, Greenwich, CT: JAI Press.

Toth, E. and Heath, R. (eds) (1992) *Rhetorical and Critical Approaches to Public Relations*, Hillsdale, NJ: LEA.

Williams, K. (1998) *Get Me a Murder a Day! A History of Mass Communication in Britain*, London: Arnold.

PART IV THE FUTURE IS NOW

CHAPTER 22

Visualizing the message: why semiotics is a way forward

Reginald Watts

Any concept that defines itself as the science of signs must offer a rich seam of new ideas for the corporate practitioner. The author asks 'if applied semiotics (the science of signs) can inform the way non-linguistic images in corporate literature are analysed'. Non-linguistic refers to anything from page design, logos and photographs to the choice of material, print fonts and even to the binding itself. Despite the importance of the visual component in communication, managers appear to find difficulty expressing themselves when commissioning print material with non-written elements. This chapter aims to show that semiotics can be used to reduce uncertainty in decision making by encouraging practitioners to focus on individual elements that transfer meaning. In this way unstructured decision-making can be reduced. Corporate practitioners also need techniques to achieve consistency regardless of which executive signs off their material.

Social semiotics within the context of corporate communication

The term 'semiology' derives from the work of Ferdinand de Saussure[1] who stated that 'a science that studies the life of signs within society is conceivable; it would be part of social psychology and consequently of general psychology: I shall call it semiology [from the Greek semion "sign"].'

Saussure attempted to explain the processes by which meaning was possible through language and stressed that such signs were composed of signifiers and signifieds which are connected arbitrarily. This connection was by conventions which had to be accepted by the reader. This indicates that in part, meaningful communication arises from the relationships between elements in a system of language, some elements of which are more fixed than others. In this chapter I extend this concept to a wider arena of signs discussing how non-written or visual elements transfer meaning to a viewer.

The tradition of semiotics is not monolithic nor even an agreed body of theories and concepts. It is a way of assessing the process by which signs transfer meaning. A template is developed in this chapter as an aid to analysis for managers who lack training in semiotic theory.

The application of semiotic theory to the visual

Kress and van Leeuwen[2] in their seminal work *Reading Images*, examined ways in which images communicate meaning. By looking at the formal elements and structure of design, colour, perspective, framing and composition they developed a visual grammar.

Visual representation not only expresses meaning that is separate from, and often different from, written text but it can have its own grammar. Meanings arise out of the society in which people live. There is a plethora of differences between societies and the people in them but messages replicate these differences through contrasting codings.

Communication takes place in social structures which are inevitably marked by power differences. This affects how each participant understands the notion of understanding. The commercial sign-maker needs to understand what social changes are at work and whether they are understood in their interrelation. Language has always existed as only one mode in a total list of modes which can be used in the production of a text. For the majority of communication specialists, many of them trained in the skills of journalism, the language mode has been paramount and the one in which they received training.

As a starting point we must accept that what in language is described in words such as 'action verbs' are in pictures realized by shapes or elements that can be termed vectors. These may be realized, for example, by a figure pointing, an outstretched arm or the line of a building, roof or road. The visual structuring and the linearity of the story set the foundation of the visual text. When participants are shown to be doing something to each other they are connected by a vector which forms a narrative that can show class, ideology, and other meanings. Because of their size or position in the picture, the actor and the goal are often the most salient of the participants. They contrast against the background, the colour and its variations, the sharpness of focus of the picture, and possibly through the psychological salience they have for the audience to whom the picture is intended.

Kress and van Leeuwen use the word 'participants' within a picture because it suggests something is actively happening by virtue of the participants' involvement. There are two types of participant, the 'interactive participant' who appears to be speaking or listening or is in some way in the act of communication, and a subset which can be described as 'the implied interactive participant', who is silently instructing us, the viewer, through the design of the picture.

It is important how the participants relate to each other. One set of participants can, for example play the role of 'subordinates' to at least one of the other participants who is termed 'superordinate'. Equivalence may or may not exist between subordinates and this can be visually realized by symmetrical or asymmetrical composition. The subordinates being placed at equal (or not) distance from each other, given the same size (or not) and the same orientation (or not) towards the horizontal and vertical axes.

Kress and van Leeuwen say that 'When represented participants look at the viewer, vectors are formed by participant's eye-lines' which connect the participants with the viewer. Contact is established, even if it is only on an imaginary level. There may be a further vector formed by a gesture in the same direction. This visual configuration can create a visual form of address by acknowledging the viewer explicitly or it can constitute an 'image act' whereby the producer uses the image to do something to the viewer. This type of image is termed 'a demand'. There is a demand that the viewer enters into a relationship.

The relationship is often signified by other means, perhaps by the facial expression of the represented participant. The converse of the demand is 'the offer', where the picture addresses the viewer indirectly. The viewer is not the object but the subject of the look. No contact is made. The viewer's role is that of an invisible onlooker. It offers the represented participants to the viewer as an item of information as though they were in a glass case. The contrast between the offer and demand is a choice which can be used to suggest different relations with different others to make viewers engage with some and detach from others.

It is normal for viewers to attach more credibility to some kinds of message than to others. Although reality is in the eye of the beholder the eye has had a cultural training and is situated in a social setting and a history. Realism for a particular group is an effect of the practices which define that group. A particular kind of realism is itself a motivated sign in which the values, beliefs and interests of that group find their expression. Different realisms exist side by side in the same cultural context. What is expected and accepted as real in one mode, say in a glossy magazine about the countryside where naturalism is as close as the picture editor can achieve, may differ from the case of photographs of cars in an automotive manufacturer's brochure. Even

here there may be a form of idealized reality which is accepted as idealized by the viewer. They may identify with the participants, despite the fact they know objectively it is a fantasy environment where the sun always shines and every car is in showroom condition.

Kress and van Leeuwen argue that the modern densely printed page has ceased to be a significant textual unit of meaning because words and concepts flow from one to the next and the flow can be broken by the typesetter (or computer) at any point in the text without changing its meaning. The page becomes a single semiotic unit structured not by its linguistic content but by its visual composition. When the readers scan the page of a corporate brochure they are not necessarily linear in the direction and movement of their eyes. The eyes may go from centre to margin, in circular fashion or vertically and it becomes a 'nonlinear composition', a form of page design which encourages multi-directionality.

In western society it is assumed that what appears on the left is the given in informational terms and what appears on the right is new or not yet known to the reader. There is thus a sense of continuous movement from left to right following societies' left–right reading pattern. The word 'given' in this case refers to what can be assumed to be known by the viewer and the word 'new' is what is assumed and cannot yet be known.

Composition of a picture or a page involves different degrees of salience and, as such, salience can create a hierarchy of importance among elements which can change the value between the 'given' and the 'new'. The perception of salience in speech results from a complex interplay between a number of auditory factors such as pitch, loudness, vowel colouring and so on. Salience in visual composition can be judged by visual clues which form a trade-off between a number of factors such as size, focus, tonal contrast (borders perhaps between black or white), colour contrast (saturated versus soft colours), perspective, human faces or cultural symbol. The use of depicted elements such as structural buildings lead the eye, abstract graphic elements lead the eye, tilting of photos lead the eye and different styles of photography, drawing, etc. all lead the eye.

The application of semiotic theory to corporate literature

During the sign-making process the social, cultural and psychological backgrounds of the executives involved will combine and fuse in terms of the pressures on them of their commercial training. The composite influence will guide the selection of what they, as a team, see as the criterial aspects of the text. They are, in fact, looking for the most plausible signifiers to express a previously agreed signified. Commercial literature is usually 'signed-off' by a senior manager before passing to 'production' and it will be the executive who 'signs-off' who is most likely to use the templates described here.

Our objective therefore is to create a template valid in terms of semiotic theory but transmuted (perhaps translated is a more apt expression) into a format that is simple to use and meets commercial needs.

Commercial managers need systems that demand a short time frame consistent with the cost/time equation which dominates an executive's life. The template here has been developed therefore with questions structured around the generally accepted AIDA (Attention, Interest, Desire and Action) model.

The AIDA model and application

Having caught the attention of the viewer a commercial brochure needs to offer information relevant to the interests of the target cohort. It must generate a desire to do something, to excite the recipient to take a specified action. This may be to 'buy' the product or accept a change of opinion (as in the case of public affairs), or change an attitude towards, say, smoking, the use of narcotic drugs or to take more exercise.

Questions have been clustered, therefore, in the template as to whether, or not, they will produce data which relates to the A, attention getting function, or A + I where attention and interest are closely merged. In corporate material the need to gain attention is less than in a selling leaflet because there may have been an approach by the viewer for corporate information. However, there is still the need to hold the attention at first glance.

One area, for example, where sufficient research has been carried out to argue its attention getting validity is in the use of colour. Marketing psychologists advise that a lasting colour impression is made within 90 seconds and accounts for 60 per cent of the acceptance or rejection of an object, place, individual or circumstance. The colour consultant Georgiana van Walsum[3] has written that as those within the commercial world become scientifically literate, there is a move towards a recognition of the power of colour beyond the purely aesthetic. Colour can be used as an effective shorthand for conveying the values of a company and associating its services and products. It can be used to persuade and motivate, to convince and persuade, to induce trust or create excitement. The colour red, for example, is highly charged. Jakobson[4] argues that primary colours have a meaning similar to that of vowels and they suggest strength or weakness. The 1960s fashion designer Mary Quant[5] 'sees red as expressing raw energy: hard, hot, alive, sure, pushy and crude, blood and guts, cruel, sex . . . and it always works'.

Colour is only one of the factors that concern us. The attention factor in the AIDA model is difficult to achieve when the primary function is to obtain sales but at corporate level there is a more subtle, a more complex interaction created by a matrix of processes. This does not mean the attention gaining process does not require the same level of analysis as a sales brochure, but it does suggest we should be aware of semiotic functions that may come into play at first viewing and those more likely to be decoded later.

The template developed below takes account of the AIDA objectives. Those elements most likely to be seen or noted first, such as colour or the materiality factors where its physicality is immediately apparent are grouped under Attention. Elements concerned with the totality of the meaning such as narrative and contextuality and its interaction with the viewer are grouped later.

The words Attention and Interest as headings have been used for the first two groups but Desire and Action have been merged into one heading as a final stage. Action need not be physical. The desire to change may be no more than a change of attitude or opinion which although an action, is difficult to isolate within the psychological process.

A brochure may arrive in the hands of the target recipient by post or from a company representative. The recipient will glance at the product quickly and if the 'attention' gained is strong may either read it or put the text aside. At a second stage (Interest) a further examination is made of the brochure, reading parts of the text which 'catch the interest'. If sufficient 'interest' is aroused it is likely the recipient will read more slowly and if the 'desire' is created consider whether to take 'action'.

The three stages of the model thus vary according to the interactive environment between the sign-maker and the representative of the company. During the interaction, power will change from the superordinate to the subordinate participants and back again as the mental negotiation proceeds. In the first instance the end viewer (perhaps a potential customer, a journalist, a financial analyst, or a parliamentarian) may have instigated the dialogue because of a need for information. The company representative or the artefact moves into a superordinate position as the supplier of the information. Different elements in the semiotic relationship come into play.

Questions regarding salience, contextuality, ellipsis, dimensions and non-compositional influence, because they are less likely to resonate when the viewer is only 'glancing' at first sight in a showroom, have been included within the third section. It is then that the reader's/viewer's interest may concentrate on a full examination. The elements that reinforce, add to or delete from earlier meanings but only transfer meaning after a slower more considered analysis (Desire-Action) have been positioned in the last section.

To help in the understanding of how the questions might be used, the template has been applied to a single-page photograph (Figure 22.1) taken arbitrarily from a Toyota Annual Report (1995, p. 13). Following each question is a typical response we might expect from the analytical team if they apply the concepts discussed.

"We're squeezing waste and inventory out of our sales operations, just like Toyota has been doing at its plants for years."

"Every encounter with a customer is a chance to make a sale," enthuses Katsumi Hashimoto, a service manager at a Toyota dealership in Tokyo. "Maintenance and repair work is as important for us as selling vehicles. It's a great opportunity to cement ties with customers who bought their cars from us. It's also a chance to win over customers who bought their cars elsewhere."

Toyota dealers in Japan are working systematically to raise efficiency in filling customer orders for cars and also in providing maintenance, repair, and inspection services. They are borrowing readily from the Toyota Production System:

• implementing just-in-time principles to trim inventories and respond promptly to customer needs,

• standardizing work procedures to provide a basis for continuing improvements,

• distributing work evenly through the day and week to make optimal use of personnel and equipment.

Those measures are speeding turnaround time for customers and raising profitability for the dealers.

"We built a sales-and-service network that was second to none—as long as the market kept expanding," observes executive vice president Hiroshi Okuda. "But Japan's market has matured. We now must deal with a pattern of alternating upturns and downturns. Our dealers and we have got to come up with more-efficient ways to sell and service cars."

Figure 22.1 Toyota

Source: Permission has been given by the Toyota Motor Corporation to reproduce this page (13) from their 1995 annual report

---

Analytical classification

Attention
(1) Identify signifiers/signifieds and their causal relationships.

Response
The following signifiers are apparent:

• two human figures;
• white Toyota saloon with raised bonnet showing black engine;

- Toyota name in red on rear display wall heart-shaped logo with word Tecno in close proximity;
- participant in white shirt, no coat, clipboard held under arm by one participant who is also holding a pen;
- second participant in dark suit, blue shirt;
- both participants wear dark ties. One participant without coat;
- in metalinguistic terms, page is gloss coated paper in full colour;
- the background display panel performs framing role.

(2) Identify narrative sequence, interactive participants and their vectoring (actor, goal, recipient and the transaction.

Response
The picture represents two males leaning over the raised bonnet of a car. One male is pointing with his pen to an engine part while looking at the second male. The elements are arranged symmetrically against a neutral background.

Reading from left to right from the 'given', or the 'authority', the actor acts upon the engine (the goal) which is a metonym of the whole which is the car and the car is a metonym for the Toyota company. The car extends the meaning by this act of pointing which adds further attributes to the car. The engine then becomes the actor which forms a transaction with the second male as goal. There is thus a double transaction which is apparent to the viewer who is invited to assume a detached scrutiny.

There are a number of vectors which appear to control the meaning. They are: the gaze of the left side human figure which 'eyeballs' the second, thus demanding the goal's full attention. The left arm of the actor on left is pointing to a part in the engine which creates a vector that meets a vector running from the eyes of the goal male who is looking at the point the left male is touching. There is thus an inverted triangle formed by the vector from the top of the heads of the two humans which continues to its apex where the arm of one meets the eye-line of the second.

Other vectors apparent are the humans who form two sides of a rectangle joined by the front edge of the bonnet. The fourth side of the rectangle opposite the bonnet is closed by the bottom edge of the picture.

The central concentration is reinforced by two vectors formed by the underside of the car, this leads the eye to the central bottom point of the picture and by the roof of the car leading the eye into the central rectangle.

Further vectoring establishes a sense of framing.

(3) What are represented participants (people, places and things in the picture? They can also be abstract concepts which could be a subject about which the images are produced)?

Response
The represented participants are:

- *People*: Two males, the younger between twenty and twenty-five and an older, between thirty and forty years. The generational interaction is significant in terms of the power relationship and the image projected.
- *Places*: A single room, possibly an automotive showroom.
- *Things*: From top-down the name of the manufacturer Toyota is carried in prominent sanserif lettering which is the same depth as, for example, the heads of the human participants. A secondary logo of a heart accompanying the words Tecno in same typeface but half the size. A saloon car with bonnet up, a clipboard, a pen/pencil, and a tie clip.
- *Abstract concepts*: The picture carries no caption except words in white reversed out on blue rectangle saying 'We're squeezing waste and inventory out of our sales operations, just like Toyota has been doing at its plants for years.' This quasi-caption appears to relate through its adjacent positioning in the text yet does not relate to the contents of the picture nor to the actions of the participants.

(4) What are implied interactive participants who silently instruct viewer through design of picture?

Response
There are two implied participants. The first reinforces the central concentration of meaning because viewer becomes the third or implied participant drawn into the transaction as an observer. The second is the designer of the picture who has used vectoring to hold the attention of the viewer in one place.

(5) Identify the carrier and possessive attributes. How do the participants fit together to make a larger statement? There is usually a low degree of modality if background is plain or out of focus. Their purpose is still interactional but the interaction is with the viewer.

Response
The human participants are not the primary subject but they are the creators of the meaning through their concentration on the third participant, the car. Without the human presence it would simply be a car with a raised bonnet. The pointing of one human participant to a part of the engine could be pointing to a fault or a problem. This possibility is removed by the smile on the face of the goal human participant whose stance of relaxed concentration shows him to be impressed and not concerned by the action of the actor who despite his youth has an assured air of confidence created by the symbol of management efficiency, a clipboard. The fact he does not wear a coat establishes his 'hands on' approach to his work.

(6) Note subordinate and superordinate participants.

Response
Although there is no covert taxonomy in the accompanying text we might assume that as the written subject is sales the right side human is a customer and could therefore be referred to socio-culturally as the superordinate participant. At the viewer's first glance the superordinate participant is the left side human who is pointing, looking serious and carrying the authority of a clipboard and indeed a pen as an extension to his hand.

(7) What are participant demands (image/viewer relationship/offer)?

Response
The viewer as an implied participant receives no direct demand. The modern technique of selling is to avoid direct demand but to include the prospect in what is intended to feel like an objective analysis. A similar psychological positioning has been created by the viewer as an implied participant watching a technical discussion between two authoritative participants.

(8) Trace vectors and transactions (NB eye-line reactions and 'circumstances of means', i.e. tools and user becoming one).

Response
The pen is a 'circumstance of means' and in being so takes an additional iconic authority through advertising and other culture specific situations where executives around tables in discussion are shown with a pen pointing at a document.

(9) What is the process of change (the 'given' and the 'new')?

Response
The left side participant is established in the picture as the 'given'. He is shown here as an authority on the subject of the engine and is thus in a power relationship. He is the representative of the company who can transfer knowledge to what the picture suggests is a buyer. The process passes from left to right through the car to the 'new'.

(10) What are the transitory spatial arrangements/concepts? Is participant a generalized essence of: class; structure; meaning?

Response
The human participants represent a generalized essence of class through the classic clothing. Both are in suits and ties although one has removed his coat. The third participant, the car, is shiny, white and would be seen as a symbol of a wealthy lifestyle. There are no other participants in the picture that reduce this meaning.

(11) Is the linearity (position of one object in relation to another):

- Spatial? *Response*: The objects are spatial yet so tightly related through vectoring and composition as to establish a single purpose.
- Locative? left/right. *Response*: The linearity is left to right.
- Locative? top/bottom. *Response*: The positioning of the company name establishes its importance as an overarching 'given'.
- Locative centre/margin? Does centre unify the information or provide meaning from which the surrounding elements draw their own meaning? *Response*: The centre does unify the information but the surrounding elements do not draw their meaning from it although it is the reason for their existence in the picture.
- Is there a 'locative circumstance' which relates other participants to a specific participant in a setting? *Response*: No.
- Define the reading paths. *Response*: The reading path takes a circular route which starts at the intersection between the pointing hand and the eye-line of the second participant. From there the eye runs back up the two vectors and down again but within the context of the powerful presence of the car.
- Indicate any motion (i.e. cat climbs tree). *Response*: There is an implied assumption that the left side human will follow with further pointing to other parts of the engine.
- Identify co-operative interaction. *Response*: There is a co-operative element in that the vectoring draws the right side human who is probably before the 'action' in this picture a stranger to the left human, into a close relationship based on mutual technical interest.
- Discuss multimodal and materiality in terms of typeface, quality of paper, shape/size of text and colour. *Response*: The modes in use in this brochure include the following: high gloss paper, full colour, hard spine binding, paper size A4, use of variable type size, colour (part of modality marker list): score on 1–5 basis, colour saturation (scale full colour saturation (5) to absence of colour (0)). *Response*: Score saturated full colour 4. Colour differentiation (scale maximum range (5) to monochrome (0)). *Response*: Score colour range 4. Colour modulation (scale full modulation (5) to plain unmodulated (0)). *Response*: Score colour modulation 4. Colour contextualization (scale absence of background (0) to full articulation/detail (5). Note level of degrees of focus, muddy dark background, high degree (5) low (0). *Response*: Score background context 1. *Response*: Score background focus 4. Representation (scale maximum abstraction (5) to maximum representation of pictorial detail (0)). *Response*: Score representation 4. Depth in perspective (scale from absence of depth (0) to maximum deep perspective (5)). *Response*: Score perspective 3. Illumination (scale full play of light/shade (5) to absence (0)). *Response*: Score illumination 3. Brightness (scale maximum degrees of brightness (5) to black and white (0)). *Response*: Score brightness 3.
- What are the criterial factors in socio-economic terms? *Response*: The sign-maker has ensured only resonance for viewer will be one of affluent, traditional middle-class

lifestyle. This resonance is created by the suits and ties of the human participants which transfer to the car.

- What are power relationships, (sign-maker to viewer)? *Response*: The sign-maker has created the viewer and rejected any other potential purchaser. For example, there may be wealthy purchasers from the world of film, pop music, academia, or even design, who could and would be interested in the car but have, by a paradigmatic choice, been rejected.
- What is icon and symbol usage? The symbol attribute may have salience through placement, focus or colour. *Response*: The only icon used is that of the heart placed beside the sub-brand name TECNO with no explanation. The heart with its representation of warmth may be an attempt to humanize the technological hegemony.
- What is representation of detail and tonal shades? *Response*: The representation of the criterial elements is emphasized through the detail, locative positioning, depth of colour and use of neutral tonal shades. The three participants are thus emphasized as such with each participant separated through the use of colour contrast, foregrounding and involvement in a network of vectors.

Interest
(1) Identify if and how people, places and things combine into meaningful whole which is/is not an extension of the meaning

Response
The 'people' and 'the thing' (the car) combine through the use of vectors and foregrounding. The 'place' is less meaningful. It may be the collection point for a car whose maintenance has been completed or a stand at an exhibition where one enthusiast is discussing the technical elements with another.

(2) Unisemic or polysemic?

Response
The picture is polysemic with each meaning unidirectional, one strengthening the other. The meanings are apparent within the context of the text which accompanies the picture and which refers to the sales operation. The left participant must be assumed, in the absence of a caption, to be a salesman who is identifying sales strengths within the engine. By pointing at one element and showing his own authority a second level of meaning is adumbrated. The part of the engine to which the participant points is well engineered so, therefore, is the rest of the engine and through that the sense of quality is suggested for the rest of the car which is not visible. The expression of acceptance on the face of the right participant is of pleasurable involvement in the discussion. Although the picture is polysemic the second and third layers of meaning are not easily identified and to the viewer may not be as readily accepted as by the right side participant.

(3) What is the integration of different semiotic codes? Is there an overarching code providing a logic of integration such as:

- A code of spatial composition, i.e. texts where elements are spatially co-present such as painting, magazine pages, etc?
- A code of temporal composition in which texts unfold over time such as in speech, drama, opera?

Response
All elements are co-present but the over-arching code is social and cultural because the viewer is expected to identify with the right side participant and, like him, become satisfied with the explanation given. Alternatively, to be party to what would then be a three-way discussion in which one person, the left participant, leads while the other equal partner, the right participant accepts the point of view of the left participant and the viewer should do so also.

(4) What are the locative circumstances and relationships regarding:

- foregrounding?
- backgrounding?
- is there foregrounding to create stress/contrast?
- is locative function realized by overlap, gradient of focus, colour saturation, angles, curves and other geometrics?

Response
The locative circumstance has been created through foregrounding, reinforced by colour contrast and vectoring, with geometrics playing a significant role in reinforcing the importance of the central transaction. Overlap is used to place the right participant in front of the car to make clear that although the car is the point of the discussion it is the right side participant who is the goal and participant of decision.

(5) Is there social meaning present through coding especially regarding modality as:

- technological coding where concern is visual representation?
- sensory coding where the pleasure principle is dominant as in art, fashion, cooking which conveys high modality?
- is abstract coding used by elite talking to other elites?
- what is the naturalistic norm where coding is generally accepted?

Response
The text selects a model reader through its choice of code, style and assumption of a specific competence. A number of concurrent social codings are working within the

picture. There is an implied technological coding as one participant appears to be emphasizing what is possibly a technological sales plus. There is a minimum of sensory coding.
For the fourth implied participant there is the sense of being a member of an elite
group of the two represented participants. This is an implied abstract coding. The overall
modality is created, however, through the accoutrements of the left side salesperson and
how the low modality normally associated with a salesman is reversed by the efficient,
hands-on stance of that participant.

(6) Note the different meanings created compositionally by multi-modality through
interrelated systems such as the informative value through placement of elements
(participants and syntagms that relate to each other and the viewer). Note the salience
elements such as participants and representation, the presence of interactive syntagms
which attract viewers to different degrees and which can be realized by placement in the
foreground or background, their relative size, contrasts in tonal value (or colour), differences in sharpness, and any framing that creates dividing lines, or frame lines that
disconnect or connect elements of the image, signifying they belong or do not belong
together.

Response
The subject of the syntagm is placed centrally. The surrounding elements lend information
and purpose to that subject who is both actor and goal, creating a relay effect by passing
additional information to the third participant on the right side, who becomes the goal.
Salience is generated through the placement of the three participants in such a way that
they create their own framing, a rectangle that holds the viewer's attention centrally
within the picture.

Desire/action
(1) Are there any trade-offs between discrete social cultural groups?

Response
The identifiable human participants in upper socio-economic groups make a reference
contextually to comfortable lifestyles which can be enhanced through the purchase of
what the sign-maker sees as a metonymic symbol of 'good living'.

(2) What is the salience of participants, by colour contents, human faces or cultural
symbols?

Response
The colour content is above the naturalistic in terms of saturation but normal if compared
to the saturation levels of television and some advertising.

(3) What is the relationship between text and visual, which comes first?

Response

The text is concerned with the sales operation and dealerships. The picture has no caption although a sentence concerning the squeezing out of waste does take the quasi-function of a caption. There is no reference to the picture to explain the meaning of the actions or dialogue within it.

(4) Visual ellipsis (what is left out but assumed).

Response

What has been left out is any reference to why one part of the engine is being identified without any statement of what it is or why it has been selected. There is a visual ellipsis without an assumption of meaning.

(5) Is there an apparent strategic deviance, whereby the cultural classification rejects an over arching strategic message?

Response

There is deviance as a result of the clothes and classical style of the human participants who form an established sense of who the target should be. In doing this they are excluding potential customers who have high disposable incomes yet do not subscribe to the classical form of dress and posture. Many in the media, the arts or even entrepreneurs reject such visible icons yet buy 'high-end objects' such as the car in the picture.

(6) What are the non-linear compositional factors? Readers may read a magazine from back to front or fall into their own reading pattern. Is there a non-linear composition created by the producers for their own agendas?

Response

There is no opportunity for non-linear compositional factors with the exception of what appears to be a reflection of the car in a mirror, plus marks on the background display panels which engage the eye and create an unknown factor due to the lack of cohesion with other items.

Commentary and summary

The example above shows some of the analytical tools available within the semiotic armoury. Such an extensive deconstruction would not be practicable if applied to a full brochure. In such cases each item on each page has to be assessed within the context of the full page, and for the purpose of identifying narrative the full brochure has to be viewed as one.

It behoves the practitioner to select his/her own critical semiotic elements, assemble them within the AIDA model (TV and film pose a different set of requirements because there is normally only one opportunity to view) and create a template for use by the public affairs team.

The underlying fact remains, within semiotic theory there exists a range of analytical tools with direct relevance to the work of the corporate communication practitioner and which, in an age where the visual has become increasingly important, should be used in day to day practice.

NOTES

1   Saussure, F. de (1993) *General Course in Linguistics*, New York: McGraw-Hill.

2   Kress and van Leeuwen (reprinted 2001) *Reading Images: The Grammar of Visual Design*, London: Routledge

3   Georgiana Van Walsum, unpublished report (1998) Commissioned by RW on behalf of Wace Plc.

4   Jakobson, R. (1968) *Child Language, Aphasia and Phonological Universals*, Hague: Mouton.

5   Quant, M. (1984) *Colour by Quant*, London: Octopus Books.

CHAPTER 23

Methodological issues for corporate communication research

Richard J. Varey

This chapter contributes a review of typical methodological commitments in corporate communication research, highlighting significant limitations and biases in the general field of applied communication 'research' in the corporate situation. The purpose served by management research with its particular outcomes is scrutinized. Popular 'theories' commonly in use in UK business and management schools are identified as are other theories that are obscured or omitted from research practice when 'human communication' is treated as no more than an informing control technology. The orthodoxy of instrumental managerialistic empiricism is characterized, highlighting the constraining dogma, and challenged. A balanced (or alternative) social science is proposed.

The epistemic domains of communication theory in management studies

When management researchers make claims to warranted knowledge, they necessarily make epistemological commitments with implicit or explicit theories of what constitutes appropriate description and explanation of what goes on in people's lives. Such claims, although often not actually 'spoken', tell the 'reader' to 'listen' and to take the work seriously as legitimate, justified and authoritative.

Wilber (1996) shows that we make claims to know internal 'things' (intentions) and external 'things' (behaviour) about individuals (personal, cultural things) and collectives (communal, social things). The warrants to know 'good' knowledge are, respectively, truthfulness, truth, mutual understanding and functional fit. Validity is conferred by pursuing and demonstrating, through method, respectively, integrity, a correct account of nature, a right worldview and system functionality. The phenomenon of people communicating is generally treated as an 'I' or 'It' occurrence. Yet, only in the cultural domain of intersubjective production of a right worldview can we truly speak of the 'We' action of communicating.

But, almost all managerially applied communication theory is rooted in a cognitive epistemic domain drawing fundamentally from an objectivist epistemology with an objectivist ontology (Anderson, 1996). Thus, most knowledge of 'communication' is produced positivistically, premised on a purpose of control. Anderson identifies eighteen communication theories that prevail in contemporary textbooks on human communication – they all fall into the positivist science domain of knowing. These include the main theoretical explanations in marketing, public relations, advertising, brand management, HRM and other fields of management studies:

- agenda setting;
- dissonance theory;
- social judgement theory;
- source credibility;
- uncertainty reduction theory;
- diffusion of innovation;
- theory of reasoned action;
- uses and gratifications;
- cultivation analysis;
- meaning;
- communication pragmatics;
- spiral of silence.

This is a deeply worrying veiled limitation on knowing in this realm of human action and experience.

Beyond the gates of managerialistic hegemony

Anderson (1996) identifies a range of theoretical resources from cultural studies, critical theory, narrative theory, dramatism, social action theory and structuration theory, that move beyond the cognitive domain to take account of the social action and discourse of the lived world. To what extent do researchers of corporate communication draw upon these?

Of course, we have a ready explanation for the relative dearth of application of these alternative knowledge-making approaches – instrumental rationality.

Management is understood as a knowledge enterprise, increasingly with an emphasis on the management of trading relationships. Our experience can show us that the thinking and talking of many practitioners, academics and educators is largely unreflective, uncritical, and poorly theorized. Management, now almost ubiquitous in its application, remains largely a normative endeavour, with students almost universally concerned with 'how to?', rather than 'why?'.

In taking a critical reading of management (see, for example, Alvesson and Willmott, 1992, 1996), we find cause for concern in the discourse, conception of knowledge, model and way of seeing human relating. Fundamentally, we see a politically motivated explanation for the common conception of communication for management that is hidden from scrutiny.

Taking a Foucaultian view, the management idea can be seen as a professional ideology and a particular discourse, as well as a set of practices. These are each promoted and taken for granted and have become a common sense ('truth') of market-based capitalism (i.e. a consuming society). Management continues to colonize further domains of society as this knowledge is deployed for the management of 'markets'.

Almost the entire discipline of management (both practice and academy) is premised on a technical-rational view of the nature and purpose of knowledge. This positivistic and normative explanation of knowledge drives a functionalist view of society and a scientistic pursuit of control through empiricist examination of phenomena defined in microeconomic fashion.

The whole management endeavour is thus cast by the prevailing 'technicists' as a neutral instrumental technology of control. The possibility of a social (political) process is unrecognized or ignored. A managerialistic[1] view is universally discussed, whilst a wide range of alternative schools of thought lie undiscovered or discarded (even denounced). The challenging books remain unread – the questions remain unasked or unanswered.

The unseen menace in this unreflective pursuit lies in the location of managerialism within the process of constituting a particular kind of society. Specifically, humans are treated as things (to be observed and manipulated), personal identity is reduced to ownership of commodities (brand), social relations are conceived in marketing terms (buyer–seller), and the question of the contribution of management work to the social good is unasked by most.

In the field of 'managing relationships', thinking is almost universally stranded in very particular entitative taken-for-granteds. Personal characteristics of the individual person and context are treated as entities that exist separately and independently of each other. Relationships are understood as between discrete entities, viewed as either subject or object. The subject is understood to act by gathering 'knowledge that' the other has certain characteristics and to achieve 'influence over' the other (as object) (Hosking, 1995). A relational approach to organization, on the other hand, takes the unit of analysis to be relational processes as the vehicle by which person and culture are produced and reproduced. Subsequent talk of person and context then cannot treat them as independent entities but as outcomes of participation in conversations that construct identities, meanings, and knowledge (Deetz, 1992). Thus, a relational perspective assumes multi-

ple, socially constructed realities – constructed in the social processes of discourse. Meanings, local knowledge and ongoing meaning-making processes are explained. This alternative constructive participatory explanation of human interaction is not generally found in the managerialistic (control-oriented) literature.

The technology of manipulation that we call management incorporates a particular way of seeing relationships and of relating to people (agents), objects (products) and events (exchanges in 'consumption situations'). Thus, 'organizations' are not understood as social systems, but as technologies of governance. This way of thinking favours those who manage by neglecting structures of domination and exploitation. Social relations are then ignored or objectified as variables to be managed.

This leaves us to ask, among other questions, what mental model prevails in management education, scholarship, research and practice? In an email discussion with David Ballantyne, he commented 'I do see dialogue as a "creating value" term, whereas communication is a "circulating value" term.' Dialogue is proposed as 'reasoning together' (drawing on Bohm, 1996[2]) – a special kind of communication, which is itself a special kind of interaction. Communication operated as a participatory social action is constructive of identity, meaning and knowledge (Deetz, 1992, 1995), whereas the 'conduit metaphor' conception of communication that is a foundation of managerialism, places it as no more than an informing technology. Then, there is no free exchange in a value-creating interaction. Rather, this possibility is precluded, to result in reciprocal manipulation. It is time that both the dominating management discourse and underlying ideology were more widely challenged.

What's wrong with empiricism?

Empiricism and positivism are often conflated. The positivist inquirer tests theory against empirical observation. The empiricist researcher tries to construct empirical generalizations or causal connections from data and logic in observing empirical association. Thus, experiment and surveys are unreflectively prevalent. For many, survey *is* field research. Theories are accepted or rejected on their correspondence with facts 'seen' in the objective world. Management research has tended towards empiricism, paying all too little attention to theory building.

The positivist social scientist in the investigations of social action claims to emulate the natural scientist, and thus takes the social world to be a single, observable, factual reality that can only be known scientifically. Yet, the natural sciences and 'cultural sciences' do not share, and should not be organized around, the same beliefs and principles. Immanuel Kant (1781) showed that empiricists wrongly assume that the world provides meanings to us, whereas it is people who endow the world with meanings. Our minds are not passive receivers of data from our sensorium. Facts and experiences cannot speak for themselves.

Today, critical social psychology (Stanton Rogers et al., 1995, for example) does not accept that the knowable world can be sensibly limited to what can be empirically demonstrated through rational inquiry. In our technological world we are promised WYSIWYG. The unfortunate result of the inherent bias in much empirical work is that 'What You Get Is What You See' (or 'I'll see it when I believe it').

Concepts are muddled in the unreflective practices of 'knowledge takers' who assume inscrutable epistemologies, producing far too much 'kitchen sink' thinking that accretes and confuses, when coherence, integration and creativity are needed. Social science is taken to be just like natural science in treating observer-independent features of the world 'objectively' (science is, by definition, objective, it is claimed). There is all too little knowledge making.

In pursuit of methodological sophistication

Implications of the inadequacy of much management studies research (in terms of complexity, intricacy and versatility in making knowledge) are serious. First, the misnomer of 'methodology' – simplistic description of methods employed, that does not engage in the study of method for producing warranted knowledge, and does not recognize choices to be justifiably made. Thus, mode of inquiry is not clearly matched to the nature of the research question and how it is to be posed. Competing (perhaps incommensurate) knowledge claims are not dealt with adequately. Such research practice lacks scholarly reflection.

When researchers unreflectively speak of their research methodology, they are (almost always) guilty of a misnomer that reveals their bias and narrow thinking. It is alternative epistemologies that are at stake. Methodology (or 'metascience') is the inquiry that reveals the presuppositions, assumptions, beliefs and set of methods and practices of an ontological-epistemological commitment, as well as the philosophy of knowledge 'paradigm' within which that approach is located (Gebhardt, 1978).

In epistemological reflection we examine how it is that we can know that we know. Discussion of such matters produces increased awareness of what is involved in inquiry so that we may recognize the virtues and limitations of our claims to knowledge.

Empirical and scientific knowledge is but one form of belief. Positivist 'research' practices suppress epistemological issues, and result in the making of bold and hegemonic claims to knowledge. This is commonplace in management studies. Empirical study is taken to be about *things* that happen, and even non-empirical claims may have empirical consequences. 'Much of what is considered positivistic management research may not actually represent positivism as it remains under-theorized and conceptually lacking, thus perhaps being better described as naïve empiricism' (Johnson and Duberley, 2000: 60).

Tudor (1982) suggests general criteria for the acceptance of knowledge. For knowledge to be accepted it is shared by a body of 'significant others' (an epistemic community, Holzner, 1972) (intersubjective legitimation). The knowledge has to be congruent with what that epistemic community already knows (coherence with accepted preconceptions). In principle, the truth is publicly demonstrable. Pragmatically, what gives good practical results is considered 'good' knowledge (contribution). Only positivists would insist on correspondence with the 'facts' of 'reality'. Yet the will to pragmatism can bypass coherent theoretical foundation.

> For us, being *critical* does not mean standing outside management and exposing its flaws and weaknesses. It entails an active and passionate commitment to improving managers' abilities to deal with the problems they face, and helping them to discover how to manage better. This involves both sustained investigation at the practical level and equally sustained critical activity at the level of theory and analysis; it also

> entails a requirement of both managers and academics to be self-critical. A critical capacity then is not something which is outside and opposed to management – on the contrary, it is the very condition for management to be able to learn, adapt and influence the rapidly changing world conditions of the coming century.
>
> (Fulop and Linstead, 1999: 1–2)

In reflecting on management education, I recognize the significance of the anthropological notion of a complex 'web of belief' (drawn on by Quine and Ullian, 1970). The philosopher Kant wanted to abolish knowledge to make way for belief. In mindlessly pursuing 'science', maybe that is largely what we have achieved! Is too much of our so-called 'research' no more than the 'discovery' of evidence to confirm our own beliefs-in-use of the moment, or can we really aspire to use some rigorous and systematic process to change our beliefs and values for the better?

'Teaching' methodology for communication research

The traditional rationale is to teach research methods – sophistication and proficiency in using (the right) method is taken to be the (only) path to warranted knowledge. I wondered how well what happens 'between people' could be treated entirely with scientific method. 'From a purely positivist point of view man (sic) is the most mysterious and disconcerting of all the objects met with by science. In fact we may as well admit that science has not yet found a place for him (sic) in its representations of the universe' (Teilhard de Chardin, 1959: 181).

Since this comment, the fields upon which corporate communication researchers might draw (cognitive psychology, social psychology, managerial economics, and so on) have been further built upon a scientific foundation. Management researchers have taken for granted that they can 'stand on the shoulders of giants' to apply 'tried and tested' ways to treat management problems. But, perhaps, in general, corporate communication researchers are too tied to an instrumental purpose of helping managers to 'manage'. Is there sufficient critical reflection on what is produced in the name of academic knowledge (as a resource for authoritative management – MBA, etc.) and how such work is conducted?

I have encouraged masters and doctoral students to reflect on their presuppositions of what constitutes research for managerial purpose, and not merely to seek research skills. I have reflected on my alternative approach to a class on research methods for managing communication. My aim is to produce greater awareness to allow managerial researchers to more carefully choose which of the 'innumerable mutually uncomprehending groups talking to themselves in esoteric jargon' (Wheatcroft, 2002: 63) they prefer to engage with and be a part.

The statement of the class rationale follows, to illustrate.

Part-time MSc./MBA programme

Communication research methodology

The aim of this module of study is to understand and challenge orthodox managerial theories-in-use in conducting research on managing human communication. This will be accomplished by drawing on critical social psychology as the basis of a scholarly critique of the hypothetico-deductive science tradition in communication research.

By producing a rigorous written critical review on a research study, each member of the class will address practically, and relevantly, the significant issues in planning, doing, and writing their own research (as a knowledge producer), and in finding, reading, using, and evaluating others' research (as knowledge taker and user).

The module tutor will provide a theoretical framework for critical reflection and will advise on significant methodological issues as the projects progress.

A distinction is to be drawn between research as 'fact finding' (description and measurement for problem-solving and developmental activity) and research as the 'systematic making of knowing' (inquiry for understanding and scholarly production).

Assessment will examine the extent to which the written work is coherent in presenting a rigorous, practically relevant critique of communication research.

Following Tudor's (1982) suggestion, I wish to promote a simple framework for a knowledge creation interaction process that emphasizes the interactive nature of enquiry and recognizes that a knower always knows what is known in a particular human and natural context.

Research as coming to know

- *Experience* a significant and/or problematic aspect of the world.
- *Interpret* through applied preconceptions derived from earlier experiences, interests, already accepted knowledge, social situation and so on.
- *Relate* interpretations to other experiences and interpretations derived from significant others.
- Intersubjectively *establish* 'true' knowledge.

- In making sense of the world, use to *explain* further experiences.

So what?

Where does corporate communication research lie? Is it part of management studies (in the United Kingdom) or a specialist-applied branch of communication studies (in the United States)? How coherent is the field in drawing upon psychology and sociology (and other epistemic communities)? What form of bounded social science provides our disciplinary matrix? It would seem sensible to suggest that the several epistemic communities address aspects of the phenomenal world at various levels of abstraction. This presents an expectation of shared discourse as well as direct conflict. It is in the confrontations that creative insight and advancement is possible.

Carey (1975) defines communication as 'a symbolic process whereby reality is produced, maintained, repaired, and transformed'. How well does our research treat this rich picture of what happens between people?

The scholar is intellectually responsible (Kennedy, 1997) in self-consciously reflecting on methodology. We must neither disable ourselves, with methodological meanderings, from pursuing our academic duty to apply our critical intelligence in original exploration for scholarly production, nor resign ourselves to methodological disinterest or ignorance.

Bernstein (1976) argues that an adequate, comprehensive political and social theory must be empirical, interpretative *and* critical. Almost all of what is published in the field of corporate communication research (and related, including corporate reputation, brand management, public relations, and so on) is empirical but not properly interpretative, and certainly not critical. So to return to my central question. Do researchers of corporate communication wish to pursue no more than a managerialistic endeavour, in which communication is merely an 'instrument' or 'technology' to be used for commercial ends, or do some at least have the courage to challenge the orthodoxy as constructive mavericks? Perhaps the extent to which membership of epistemic communities is recognized as limiting is what distinguishes scholars from technician-scientists? Some make intellectual tools, whilst others strive only to proficiently use them. There needs to be more aspiration to the former, as well as more care in using such tools in making claims to warranted knowledge.

Unfortunately, still far too much so-called research is conducted by earnest reductionist-specialist technicians in the Department of Detailed Quantification of Not Very Important Problems (Faculty of Traditional Hegemonic Scientism). Where from will much needed creative insights stem? Corporate communicators must become creative generalist integrators. Naive empiricism in the pursuit of power and the treatment of politics as no more than a variable to be accounted for in some machine model of 'organizations' is unsatisfactory.

Sciences may be learned by rote, but Wisdom not.

(Laurence Sterne, 1713–1768, *Tristram Shandy*)

NOTES

1 Deetz (1992) defines managerialism as 'a kind of logic, a set of routine practices, and an ideology'. He specifies that it is 'a way of conceptualising, reasoning through, and discussing events' (a discursive genre) and it involves 'a set of routine practices, a real structure of rewards, and a code of representation', and 'It is a way of doing and being in corporations that partially structures small groups and conflicts with, and at times suppresses, each group's other modes of thinking.'

2 There is an irony here – David Bohm was one of the greatest physicists of the twentieth century.

REFERENCES

Alvesson, M. and Willmott, H. (eds) (1992) *Critical Management Studies*, London: Sage Publications.

Alvesson, M. and Willmott, H. (1996) *Making Sense of Management: A Critical Introduction*, London: Sage Publications.

Anderson, J. A. (1996) *Communication Theory: Epistemological Foundations*, New York: Guilford Press.

Bernstein, R. J. (1976) *The Restructuring of Social and Political Theory*, Oxford: Basil Blackwell.

Bohm, D. (1996) *On Dialogue*, ed. L. Nichol, London: Routledge.

Carey, J. (1975) 'A cultural approach to communication', *Communication*, 2(2), 1–22.

Deetz, S. A. (1992) *Democracy in an Age of Corporate Colonization: Developments in Communication and the Politics of Everyday Life*, Albany, NY: State University of New York Press.

Deetz, S. A. (1995) *Transforming Communication, Transforming Business: Building Responsive and Responsible Workplaces*, Creskill, NJ: Hampton Press Inc.

Fulop, L. and Linstead, S. (1999) *Management: A Critical Text*, London: Macmillan Business Books.

Gebhardt, E. (1978) 'A critique of methodology', in A. Arato and E. Gebhardt (eds), *The Essential Frankfurt School Reader*, New York: Basil Blackwell, pp. 371–406.

Holzner, B. (1972) *Reality Construction in Society*, Cambridge, MA: Schenkman.

Hosking, D.-M. (1995) 'Constructing power: entitative and relational approaches', in D.-M. Hosking, H. P. Dachler, and K. J. Gergen (eds), *Management and Organization: Relational Alternatives to Individualism*, Aldershot: Avebury Books, pp. 51–70.

Johnson, P. and Duberley, J. (2000) *Understanding Management Research: An Introduction to Epistemology*, London: Sage Publications.

Kant, I. (1781;1934) *The Critique of Pure Reason*, tr. J. M. D. Meiklejohn, London: Dent.

Kennedy, D. (1997) *Academic Duty*, London: Harvard University Press.

Quine, W. V. and Ullian, J. S. (1970) *The Web of Belief*, New York: Random House.

Stanton Rogers, R., Stenner, P., Gleeson, K. and Stainton Rogers, W. (1995) *Social Psychology: A Critical Agenda*, Oxford: Polity Press.

Teilhard de Chardin, P. (1959) *The Phenomenon of Man*, New York: Harper & Brothers.

Tudor, A. (1982) *Beyond Empiricism: Philosophy of Science in Sociology*, London: Routledge & Kegan Paul.

Wheatcroft, G. (2002) 'Two cultures at forty', *Prospect*, May, 62–4.

Wilber, K. (1996) *A Brief History of Everything*, Boston, MA: Shambhala Publications.

CHAPTER 24

Communication for creative thinking in a corporate context

Glenda Jacobs

It is widely recognized that organizational growth and even survival in a changing business environment relies directly on the creative ability to question, adjust and at times re-invent accepted processes, services and products.

This chapter argues that, given the demands of today's business environment, both the ability to think creatively, and a rigorous understanding of how creative thinking should be managed and developed in organizational environments. are for corporate communication managers not only useful talents, but also professional responsibilities. The chapter seeks to demonstrate how a clearer understanding of the close relationship between corporate creativity and corporate communication allows organizations to more effectively manage creative opportunities, as well as to integrate creative thinking processes into existing corporate structures.

The need for creative thinking in organizations

It is only during the second half of the twentieth century that 'creativity' as a concept ceased to be perceived as the province of the eccentric, the gifted and the artistic, and has gained legitimacy in the realms of academic research and effective business practice (Drucker, 1985; Ford and Gioia, 1995; Getzels, 1987; Isaksen, 1987; Sternberg, 1999; Wehner et al., 1991). In addition, international surveys (by, among many others, the American Management Association, Arthur D. Little, Fortune 500, Digital Strategies and the Centre for Research in Employment and Technology in Europe) consistently reveal that both SMEs (small and medium-sized enterprises) and leading multinational companies recognize creativity to be an essential priority for survival in the twenty-first century. Consequently, the period since the 1960s has seen an escalation of investigation into how best to encourage, develop and manage creativity and innovation in organizational settings.

The relationship between communication and corporate creativity

While definitions of creativity vary, underpinning both past and current research is the recognition that communication is central to it. In fact, in his seminal paper categorizing types of creativity in 1961, Mel Rhodes goes as far as to define the term as 'the phenomenon in which a person *communicates* a new concept' (p. 216; my italics). Implicitly and explicitly, communication is consistently identified as both a creativity-relevant process, and a domain-relevant skill (Amabile, 1983), since it is essential as a means not only of creating, facilitating and managing creative environments, processes and outcomes, but also of acquiring the knowledge on which corporate creativity and innovation need to be based (Collins and Amabile, 1999; Csikszentmihalyi, 1990; Hallman, 1963; Locke and Kirkpatrick, 1995).

It is therefore not surprising that studies of business creativity invariably also provide unique insights into principles of organizational communication – for example, those underlying employee motivation, evaluation and feedback; collaboration and networking; communication of corporate vision, values and climate, as well as problem solving, change management, negotiation and persuasion (see for example Collins and Amabile, 1999; Gryskiewicz, 2000; Kanter, 1988; Sternberg and Lubart 1999; Treffinger, 1987).

This chapter will show that recognizing, examining and mapping out these areas of influence will allow organizations more effectively to harness and manage creative opportunities, as well as integrate creative thinking processes into existing corporate systems and structures. The term 'creative thinking' will be used in this chapter to encompass both the successful production of 'new and relevant' (Amabile, 1983; MacKinnon, 1978; Stein, 1984) ideas and products, as well as the mental processes that underpin and contribute towards that production.

Corporate language choices and creative thinking

At its most simple level, effective incorporation and management of creative thinking in organizations is fundamentally influenced by the language used to identify it. Even the most commonly used terms 'creativity' and 'innovation' both carry connotations that can either inhibit or enhance what people perceive as the kind of activities and thinking they would embrace, and this in turn affects how valuable they seem to corporate goals. For example, the term 'creativity' is preferred by psychological theorists who have in the past dominated the field of creativity research (Lehrdahl, 2001). However, the term is also often perceived as carrying with it broader suggestions of liberal arts, design, subjectivity, eccentricity and even dishonesty, which may influence and limit its perceived acceptability in many corporate environments.

By way of contrast, business discourse tends to prefer the more outcome-oriented term 'innovation', which, even when it is used interchangeably with the term 'creativity' (Amabile, 1983; Andriopolos and Lowe, 2000; De Bono, 1989; Peters, 1991), implies practicality, strategy and a shift in focus to successful outcomes such as 'new products, new services, and new businesses' (Jonash and Somerlatte, 1999: 6; Wehner *et al.*, 1991). However, the problem arises that, while avoiding the possibly vague and unbusinesslike connotations of the term 'creativity', a discourse emphasizing innovation simultaneously de-emphasizes the value of the early preparation, incubation and provocative thinking stages on which creative outcomes are based. Consequently, in corporate environments, which tend to be outcomes-based by default, it would be easy unwittingly to downplay or overlook the degree to which the creative thinking process contributes in its own right to ongoing corporate growth and learning – whether or not specifically identifiable outcomes result.

One may argue that this caution places too much weight on a simple vocabulary preference, yet the tendency to emphasize outcomes at the expense of process can clearly be observed in studies where 'innovation' is deliberately defined as referring only to the practical implementation – 'the successful exploitation' (Tidd *et al.*, 1997: 25) – of creative ideas, as opposed to either the method of producing the ideas or even the ideas themselves (Isaksen, 1987; Lampikoski and Emden, 1996).

A primary challenge, for communication managers then, would be to find a method of naming or labelling the notion of creative thinking in a way that that is both unambiguous and free of negative connotations in the corporate environment. In addition, caution would be necessary when interpreting and attempting to apply the results of studies and reports on organizational innovation, since it would first be important to take into account the sense – inclusive or exclusive – in which the term is being used.

A second communication challenge is that of legitimizing and incorporating into corporate discourse the types of verbal interaction that support and encourage creative thinking processes. For example, corporate discourse tends to place considerable value on vocabulary reflecting deductive and inductive logic, and emphasizing what is rational, practical,

valid, possible and likely. By way of contrast, the distinguishing purpose of creative thinking is to escape the confines of conventionally accepted logical and rational trains of thought. This requires openness to ideas that are seemingly irrational, illogical, impractical, invalid, impossible and unlikely – even bizarre – in order to explore their potential and exploit their generative power. Practically speaking, this means that language and vocabulary choices that reflect and promote suspension of evaluative logic, resistance to closure and openness to generative exploration have to become part of what is accepted and valued as 'normal' in everyday verbal exchanges. Initial evidence of where this has begun to occur can be found in expressions such as 'blue sky', 'black hat' and even 'brainstorm', which have already become part of organizational linguistic repertoires.

Of course, the value of traditional forms of logic and critical reasoning to corporate decision making, planning and management is not under dispute. Nevertheless, in any organization wishing to learn from and co-ordinate both creative as well as logical/evaluative thinking styles and systems, it remains important to recognize how easily seemingly sensible comments such as 'That's not practical' and 'Let's be reasonable' will (often unintentionally) shut down creative thinking opportunities.

Organizational culture and creative thinking

In order to survive, organizations must strike a balance between order and change. On the one hand they can only function effectively if members perform their roles consistently, carry out routine tasks and maintain ordered systems. On the other hand, they need to remain open and flexible enough to respond to and pre-empt the shifting demands of their changing business environment.

The role of communication in managing the tension between these two goals is highlighted when approached from the relational perspective of Carl Weick (1979), who proposes that organizations are essentially the products of communication interactions. Organizations, according to this viewpoint, are created out of the communication actions and interpretations of the individuals that comprise them. Organizational learning guru Peter Senge expands on this relationship when he defines a learning organization as one where people are continually discovering how they create their reality, where they continually expand their capacity to create the results they truly desire, and where new and expansive patterns of thinking are nurtured (1990).

Approached from this perspective, one of the most significant responsibilities of a communication professional would be the maintenance of a communication culture that encourages the discovery, examination and questioning of existing thinking patterns, and that allows and supports the airing and consideration of new and unconventional ones.

A primary characteristic of such a communication culture would be its capacity to accommodate conflict, since new ideas by their very nature will suggest change that could call into question existing (and valid) ways of doing things. Conflict in a corporation that values creative thinking would need to be generally recognized as an opportunity for clarification, learning and improvement, rather than as a negative phenomenon to be avoided in the interest of maintaining the status quo and of encouraging superficially 'positive' employee morale.

This would require:

- communicating to all employees – not just executives and managers – their responsibility to examine, reflect upon, challenge and suggest alternatives to accepted organizational attitudes and practices. To this end, communication of corporate vision and values that depend on these activities, as well as feedback and reward systems that reinforce them, would be pivotal;
- facilitating corporate systems that can accommodate ambiguity and that encourage (or at least do not inhibit) exploration of new and extemporaneous ideas at both individual and group level. This would require communication management that supports a transition from 'command and control' to 'freedom with responsibility' models of leadership;
- providing a variety of communication channels for expressing individual ideas, managing diverse viewpoints and for confronting existing – however successful – routines, practices and products. Recent advances in communication technology both considerably increase opportunities in this regard, and add to their complexity;
- ensuring that all members of the organization both understand and develop the interpersonal skills necessary for open discussion, disclosure and negotiation. This would include training employees in interaction styles as well as in creative thinking approaches and strategies.

Vision, values and leadership

The focus of creative effort, if it occurs at all within an organization, will be determined by what the organization values and how commitment to those values is communicated to the workforce. This creates a significant leadership responsibility to make sure that, as Jones (1995: 199) points out, the elements of corporate 'winning behaviour' are unambiguously defined, and that creative thinking is seen to be one of those elements.

A corporate vision that depends on and articulates the need for creative effort from all members of the workforce would be an essential starting point. Moreover, the vision would need to be one with which the workforce is able to identify, which they own, and which they feel instrumental in constantly reinforcing and recreating. Instilling this sense of empowerment requires understanding of the link between information and creative effort. When employees are kept informed they are more likely to feel trusted and respected, and this in itself encourages the self-confidence necessary for risking the exposure of new ideas. Furthermore, the more informed all employees are about organizational functions, processes and systems, the greater their sense of ownership is likely to be and the better equipped they will be to engage imaginatively with and participate in the pursuit and (where necessary) reinvention of corporate goals and aspirations. Indeed, merely providing information about where creative thinking is needed would improve the likelihood of it occurring. Lastly, from a purely practical perspective, the creative ability to make associations, apply unusual perspectives and synthesize knowledge would naturally increase relative to the breadth and depth of employees' information base.

In addition to promoting and requiring the informed participation and initiative of all members of the organization, a corporate vision that values creative thinking needs to be reinforced by congruent control structures, operating procedures, reward systems and resources. For example, the most creative of corporate visions will be undermined and nullified by authoritarian leadership, bureaucratic procedures, reward systems that encourage maintenance of the status quo and short-term, bottom-line outcomes, and lack of practical resources such as money and time.

Conversely, the identification and definition of creative thinking as 'winning behaviour' would be communicated by corporate leaders through, for example:

- modelling creative thinking techniques in their everyday management routines (such as during meetings);
- providing examples and stories that reinforce creative values;
- replacing hierarchical and rules-orientated control structures with flatter and more flexible ones that emphasize individual initiative as well as freedom to determine how objectives are met;
- developing problem-solving procedures that make it possible to resist the organizational survival instinct towards immediate solutions, and to tolerate ambiguity while pieces fall into place or links emerge from unexpected sources;
- providing feedback that reinforces and further stimulates creative thinking initiatives. The part played by feedback and reward in communicating the value of creative thinking to a corporate workforce is much debated, not least because studies have suggested that external rewards which motivate employees to be more productive may under certain circumstances negatively influence creative performance. These issues are discussed in more detail in the following section.

Influence of feedback and reward on creative thinking

Inevitably, much of the feedback given in corporate environments tends to be negative in tone – identifying weaknesses and enforcing accepted standards where they seem to have been overlooked. However, repeated negative feedback inhibits creative thinking by placing recipients on the defensive and discouraging them from suggesting or undertaking tasks that challenge accepted ways of doing things and make them vulnerable to further criticism.

On the other hand, withholding negative feedback where it threatens accepted norms or corporate attitudes – often in the guise of 'not rocking the boat' and 'maintaining a positive attitude' – also promotes uncritical conformity and perpetuates unthinking adherence to the status quo.

Even positive feedback can discourage creative endeavour if, for example, it measures successful performance against the performance of others (Amabile, 1983; De Bono, 1989). This could act as a powerful disincentive to ambitious individuals with a record of past success because engaging in creative initiatives and untried processes could place their reputations at risk should they not succeed. Likewise, if positive feedback emphasizes and is focused exclusively on successful outcomes, employees will be disinclined to engage in creative thinking activities that by their very nature may produce uncertain or unpredictable results.

Furthermore, extrinsic rewards used as positive feedback can also discourage creative productivity, according to Teresa Amabile's intrinsic motivation hypothesis (1983). She argues that the motivation to be creative comes from the enjoyment to be gained from engaging with the challenge of a task, from the strong internal desire to do something based on interests and passions, and from the internal satisfaction when that challenge is met. Follow-up studies further support the value of intrinsic motivation by indicating that, where external constraints exist, emphasizing internal motivational factors can make individuals more resistant to their negative effects (Amabile and Gryskeiewicz, 1989; Amabile, *et al.*,1994). Naturally, however, where external factors actually serve to build up internal motivation – clear goals, for example, and recognition/rewards that build confidence – they too serve to heighten creative thinking capacity and performance.

In order to encourage and stimulate creative thinking, therefore, feedback within corporate contexts would need to concentrate on:

- providing opportunities for employees to experiment and take risks, with failure treated as a learning opportunity and generating opportunities for improving ability;
- increasing employees' intrinsic motivation by emphasizing the value of their work, and making the work process rewarding in itself;
- increasing employees' confidence, raising their consciousness of their value and of their ability to make a difference;
- encouraging further feedback, with questions and responses that elicit information about motives, reasons, underlying assumptions and that reinforce awareness of the genuine value placed on reflection;
- encouraging and respecting minority views, since these spark questioning and encourage further independent thinking.

Opportunities for providing a variety of channels that allow feedback to be given and received in the most accessible, convenient and appropriate form have been considerably enhanced by the development and adoption of new communication technologies. These are discussed in the following section.

Communication technology and creative thinking

For many years it was assumed that using computers as a communication medium would foster impersonal, even aggressive, task-oriented behaviours of a kind that would discourage creative thinking. However, early research was frequently conducted using zero-history, inexperienced participants engaged in short, inauthentic tasks under laboratory conditions. Subsequent studies reveal that computer-mediated communication produces both social and task effects that contradict early findings completely (Baym, 2002; Lea and Spears, 1991; Walther, 1997; Lea et al., 2001; Scott, 1999), and demonstrate that communication technology can be highly supportive of – and indeed in several ways enhance – group communication and collaboration.

For example, electronic brainstorming has been repeatedly demonstrated to outperform the face-to-face kind in large groups, owing to the absence of production blocking and also to reduced social loafing. Larger electronic brainstorming groups have further been found to generate more high-quality ideas than their non-electronic counterparts (Gallupe et al., 1992; Dennis, 1994; Briggs, 1995; Valacich et al., 1994). Other specialist group-oriented computer-mediated tools that enhance creative thinking include software for mind-mapping and three-dimensional mental modelling, which allows users to share and reflect upon visual representations of their thinking patterns and approaches. An additional advantage is that these applications can instantaneously integrate and display input from a variety of sources, further transcending limitations of paper-based – and even whiteboard-based – methods.

Of course, one of the most obvious advantages afforded by communication technology is its potential to allow collaboration between teams comprising widely dispersed members, unlimited by organizational, geographic or even time constraints. These networks also provide opportunities for individuals to participate in multiple teams and projects, increasing the likelihood of creative cross-fertilization of ideas.

Recent studies involving computer-mediated decision-making groups whose sole contact is online, however, suggest that if group salience is high (in other words, if the members of the group regard their group identity as of primary significance to them), group members tend to demonstrate greater normative behaviour and are more likely to conform than when members' individual identities are salient (Lea et al., 2001). This would have implications for leaders of virtual groups, who may at times want to hold off tendencies toward consensus in the interest of provoking a wide range of contrasting perspectives. In such cases, deliberately highlighting members' consciousness of their individuality – while naturally still encouraging supportive, social and co-operative behaviours – would be an important strategy. It is to be remembered, however, that these findings apply only to groups whose sole contact is online, and short term. As Walther (1997) points out, there comes a time in all extended-term groups when members start sharing personal information, and group salience is eroded. For the majority of corporate users, though, the online medium would be one of many channels used for communication between participants, so individual identities would remain salient and participants' tendency to conform or disagree would be as unaffected as if they were face to face.

Technology that could facilitate creative thinking is not limited to groupware and the internet, however. For example, visualization, an important ingredient of the creative process, is enhanced by the advent of interactive 3-D virtual image displays, webcams and increasingly high-resolution flat panel displays. Furthermore, increasingly sophisticated computerized knowledge management systems nowadays provide employees with easy access to resources and information that add to their capacity and increase their inclination to engage in creative thinking. In fact, communication technology overall provides vitally increased capacity for the immediate capture and subsequent sharing of information and ideas, whether synchronously or asynchronously, anonymously or allowing for personal recognition.

In all these ways, far from being cold and impersonal inhibitors of imagination, communication technologies provide systems and channels for organizations and their members to use their creative potential more fully, by allowing them to rise above the constraints of bureaucracy, geography, memory and time.

Collaboration and creative thinking

While radical creativity may at times depend on the initiative of an individual, leading figures in creativity research agree that collaborative and team processes are essential to ongoing and consistent practice of creative thinking by the workforce as a whole. On the one hand, teams are necessary for pursuing and developing radical individual creative initiatives, and on the other hand they are vehicles for the 'incremental' creative thinking necessary for corporate success, particularly in organizations with complex, changing business environments (Amabile and Gryskeiewicz, 1989; Csiksezentmihalyi and Sawyer, 1995; Hunt, 2002; Lehrdahl, 2001; Qvale, 1995).

Consequently, communication management strategies intended to encourage creative thinking would need to concentrate on fostering, maintaining and developing collaborative problem solving, teambuilding and networking opportunities within – and outside – the organization. Interestingly, extensive studies demonstrate that while win–lose competition has a negative effect on individual creative performance, competitive pressure can enhance creative thinking within teams when that pressure is perceived as meaningful rather than arbitrary (Amabile, 1996). The reason for this seems to lie in the energized, cohesive climate created within a team in the face of a meaningful challenge, without the stresses associated with individual evaluation. In other words, a sense of competition in a collaborative team environment could work to the creative advantage of an organization, and need not be assumed automatically to discount the possibility of accommodating creative processes within corporate contexts *per se*.

Once again, the importance of communicating a culture of 'belonging' is clear. However, while constant open communication within and between segments of an integrated organization is recognized as a basic requirement of creative production (Kanter, 1988; Gioia, 1995), the additional importance of networking outside immediate corporate confines is often overlooked. Studies in communication networking pointedly indicate that links with colleagues and acquaintances outside employees' normal professional circles have the effect of broadening their knowledge base, as well as exposing them to new ideas and different perspectives (Garton *et al*.,1997; Haythornthwaite, 2001; Harasim *et al*.,1995; Pickering and King, 1999). As such, these 'weak ties' are important sources of divergent and non-redundant information on which creative thinking thrives. Exposing employees to these connections could be facilitated by setting in place opportunities for cross-functional workshops, inter-organizational team projects and (using increasingly advanced groupware and other digital communication channels) project-based virtual collaboration between dispersed – and probably transient – work groups. At a more basic level, though, they are encouraged and maintained by such simple measures as the provision of swift and immediate networking channels such as email, as well as access to specialist discussion groups on the worldwide web.

For the benefits of collaborative environment to be fully realized, however, opportunities for both executive and workforce training in group leadership and participation (both onsite and particularly virtual) would need to be provided. These and other professional development requirements necessary to underpin and promote creative thinking in corporate contexts are identified in the following section.

Training needs

Critical and analytical thinking techniques are routinely taught and evaluated as part of undergraduate degrees in business and management, and rightly so. However, despite the wide recognition of the value of creative thinking in modern business environments, prospective managers and aspirant executives are expected to pick up the techniques and approaches intuitively, or, if they are lucky, to have a creative instinct or talent that they are never formally required to harness, account for, or constructively communicate to others.

Thus the need for relevant education in creative thinking skills and management remains unmet. Although there has been a proliferation of corporate training courses claiming to improve employee creativity in the workplace, the value of such programmes is open to question on the grounds that the full spectrum of organizational needs is rarely catered for, while application of principles of creative thinking research and theory seem perfunctory at best.

For example, corporate training programmes to improve employees' creative abilities tend to be of short duration (typically, a half to two days), and most frequently focus on identifying creative thinking barriers, practising uninhibited idea generation such as brainstorming, and/or doing exercises to activate various sections of the brain. Some controversy surrounds the effectiveness – and even the validity – of some of these techniques (Epstein, 1996; Efron, 1990; Weisberg, 1993). More important, however, is that such courses seldom if ever provide either follow-up on the subsequent progress of course attendees, or ongoing maintenance or monitoring of how (or indeed whether) the new processes are integrated into the workplace.

Research also shows that, while some forms of training can indeed have some positive effect on attitudes toward using creative thinking techniques (Basadur *et al.*,1990; Hall and Lin, 1984; Hipple, 2001), significant knowledge transfer from such brief exposure is unlikely (Rickards, 1993; Weisberg, 1993).

Nevertheless there is some value to be gained from exposure to training in creative thinking approaches, if it

- increases employees' openness to experimenting with a wider range of thinking approaches;
- increases employees' belief in their ability to think creatively; and
- provides teams with a common vocabulary and system for either identifying creative thinking opportunities or identifying occasions where creative thinking is being obstructed.

Equally or more important, however, would be training in the skills that make creative thinking possible and practically manageable within the stresses and complexities of corporate environments. As this chapter has argued, these skills would encompass:

- group collaboration and negotiation;
- conflict management;
- virtual team participation and leadership;
- software and technology for information sharing, collaboration and networking.

Summary

In this chapter we set out to examine the importance of creative thinking in corporate contexts, and the extent to which it is dependent on effective and insightful corporate communication policies, systems and strategies. In order to do this, we identified the communication principles and processes central to inspiring, developing and managing not only the techniques but also the attitudes and tensions resulting from introducing creative thinking behaviours into necessarily structured and bottom-line oriented organizational frameworks.

The role of language and its influence on the perceived value of creative activity was identified and discussed, as was the importance of a clearly communicated corporate vision, supported by an organizational culture that encourages and values experimentation, discovery and the challenging of established norms. Furthermore, it was proposed that while corporate leaders play a critical role in modelling, managing and constructively acknowledging and rewarding creative behaviour, it nevertheless remains of primary importance that all members of the corporate workforce feel able and motivated to recognize, seize, and act upon creative opportunities when they arise. This sense of empowerment and ownership would be enhanced by the establishment of communication channels that cut across traditional organizational hierarchies, and that create means for intra- and inter-organizational networking, collaboration and information sharing. Finally, existing forms of corporate 'creativity' training were discussed, and suggestions made as to how this could be improved by incorporation of communication skills, approaches and principles.

Overall, this chapter demonstrates that a clearer understanding of the close relationship between corporate creativity and corporate communication would allow organizations more effectively to harness and manage creative opportunities, as well as integrate creative thinking processes into existing corporate systems and structures.

Activities

1   Select three established writers of corporate 'self-help' texts on creative thinking (several appear in the reference and bibliography sections below). Compare and evaluate their contributions to the available pool of 'language and vocabulary choices that reflect and promote suspension of evaluative logic, resistance to closure, and openness to generative exploration'.

2   Investigate and evaluate creativity training programmes in your city/region, using the criteria in this chapter as a guide, and adding to them where appropriate.
3   Download a demo version of any example of popular communication groupware (e.g. MeetingWorks, LotusNotes) and assess its capacity for enhancing or inhibiting corporate creativity.
4   Write a critical analysis of the contents of this chapter, using your own company (or a client) as a case study.

REFERENCES

Amabile, T. (1983) *The Social Psychology of Creativity*, New York: Springer-Verlag.

Amabile, T. (1996) *Creativity in Context*, US: Westview Press.

Amabile, I. and Gryskeiewicz, N. (1989) 'The creative environment scales: work environment inventory', *Creativity Research Journal*, 2, 231–53.

Amabile, T., Hill, K., Hennessey, B. and Tighe, E. (1994) 'The work preference inventory: assessing intrinsic and extrinsic motivational orientations', *Journal of Psychology and Social Psychology*, 66(5), 950–67.

America's Most Admired Companies (1999) *Fortune 500*, 139(4), March.

Andriopolos, C. and Lowe, A. (2000) 'Enhancing organisational creativity: the process of perpetual challenging', *Management Decision*, 38(10), 734–42.

Argyris, C. (1994) 'Good communication that blocks learning', *Harvard Business Review*, July–August.

Baer, J. (1993) *Creativity and Divergent Thinking: A Task-Specific Approach*, Hillsdale, NJ: Lawrence Erlbaum.

Basadur, M., Wakabayashiu, M. and Graen, G. (1990) 'Individual problem-solving styles and attitudes towards divergent thinking before and after training', *Creativity Research Journal*, 3, 22–32.

Baym, N. (2002) 'Interpersonal life online', in S. Lievrouw and S. Livingstone (eds), *The Handbook of New Media*, London: Sage, pp. 62–75.

Collins, M. and Amabile, T. (1999) 'Motivation and creativity', in R. J. Sternberg (ed.), *Handbook of Creativity*, Cambridge: Cambridge University Press, pp. 297–312.

Connolly, T. (1997) 'Electronic brainstorming: science meets technology in the electronic meeting room: In S. Kiesler (ed.) *Culture of the Internet*, USA: Lawrence Erblum & Associates, pp. 263–76.

Csikszentmihalyi, M. (1990) 'The domain of creativity', in M. A. Runco and R. S. Albert (eds), *Theories of Creativity*, Newbury Park, CA: Sage, pp. 199–212.

Csikszentmihalyi, M. and Sawyer, K. (1995) 'Shifting the focus from individual to organizational creativity', in M. Ford and D. A. Gioia (eds), *Creative Action in Organisations*, Thousand Oaks, CA: Sage, pp. 167–73.

De Bono, E. (1989) *Lateral Thinking for Management*, London: HarperCollins.

Drucker, P. (1985) *Innovation and Entrepreneurship*, London: Heinemann.

Efron, R. (1990) *The Decline and Fall of Hemispheric Specialisation*, Hillsdale, NJ: Lawrence Erlbaum Associates.

Epstein, R. (1996) *Creativity Games for Jumpstarting Workplace Creativity*, New York: McGraw-Hill.

Ford, C. M. (1995) 'Creativity is a mystery', in M. Ford and D. A. Gioia (eds), *Creative Action in Organisations*, Thousand Oaks, CA: Sage, pp. 12–51.

Ford, C. M. and Gioia, D. A. (eds) (1995) *Creative Action in Organisations*, Thousand Oaks, CA: Sage Publications.

Gallupe, R. B., Dennis, A. R., Cooper, W. H., Valacich, J. S., Bastianutti, L. M. and Nunamaker, J. F. Jr. (1992) 'Electronic brainstorming and group size', *Academy of Management Journal*, 35(2), 350–69.

Garton, L, Haythornthwaite, C. and Wellman, B. (1997) 'Studying online social networks', *Journal of Computer-Mediated Communication*, 3(1). www.ascusc.org/jcmc/vol3/issue1/garton.html

Getzels, J. W. (1987) 'Creativity, intelligence and problem finding', in S. Isaksen (ed.), *Frontiers of Creativity Research*, New York: Bearly, pp. 88–102.

Gioia, D. (1995) 'Contrasts and convergences in creativity', in C. M. Ford and D. A. Gioia (eds), *Creative Action in Organisations*, Thousand Oaks CA: Sage, pp. 317–29.

Gryskiewicz, S. (2000) 'Cashing in on creativity at work', *Psychology Today*, September, 63–6.

Hall, R. and Lin, H. (1984) 'A meta-analysis of long-term creativity training programmes', *Journal of Creative Behaviour*, 18, 11–22.

Hallman, R. (1963) 'The necessary and sufficient conditions of creativity', in G. S. Nielson (ed.), *Proceedings of the SIV International Congress of Applied Psychology*, 2, 11–39.

Harasim, L., Hiltz, S., Teles, L. and Turoff, M. (1995) *Learning Networks*, Cambridge, MA: MIT Press.

Haythornthwaite, C. (2001) 'A social network theory of tie strength and media use', *Proceedings of the Hawai'i International Conference on System Sciences*, 3–6 January, Maui, Hawaii. http://alexia.lis.uiuc.edu/~haythorn/HICSS01_tiestrength.html (September 2002)

Hipple, J. (2001) 'The Future of Corporate Innovation Centers, Processes and Champions', http://www.innovation-triz.com/papers/corporate.html (May 2002)

Hunt, J. (2002) Interview, *Innovation update*, June, http://iexchange.london.edu/html/int_j_hunt.html (July 2002)

Isaksen, S. (1987) *Frontiers of Creativity Research*, New York: Bearly Ltd.

Johnson, C. and Hackman, M. (1995) *Creative Communication: Principles and Applications*, Long Grove, IL: Waveland Press.

Jonash, R. and Somerlatte, T. (1999) *The Innovation Premium*, New York: Perseus.

Jones, F. B. (1995) 'The changing face of creativity', in M. Ford and D. A. Gioia (eds), *Creative Action in Organisations*, Thousand Oaks, CA: Sage, pp. 195–200.

Kanter, R. (1988) Change-master skills: what it takes to be creative', in R. L. Kuhn (ed.), *Handbook for Creative and Innovative Managers*, New York: McGraw-Hill, pp. 91–9.

Lampikoski, K. and Emden, J. (1996) *Igniting Innovation*, Chichester: John Wiley and Sons.

Lea, M. and Spears, R. (1991) 'Computer-mediated communication, deindividuation and group decision-making', *International Journal of Man-Machine Studies*, 34, 283–301.

Lea, M., Spears, R. and De Groot, R. (2001) 'Knowing me, knowing you: anonymity effects of social identity processes within groups', *Personality and Social Psychology Bulletin*, 27, 526–37.

Lehrdahl, E. (2001) 'Staging for creative collaboration in design teams', Doctoral thesis, Trondheim.

Locke, E. and Kirkpatrick, S. A. (1995) 'Promoting creativity in organizations', in M. Ford and D. A. Gioia (eds), *Creative Action in Organisations*, Thousand Oaks, CA: Sage, pp. 115–20.

MacKinnon, D. W. (1978) *In search of Human Effectiveness: Identifying and Developing Creativity*, Berkeley: Creative Education Foundation Ltd.

Peters, T. (1991) 'Get innovative or get dead', *California Management Review*, 33(1), 9–23.

Pickering, J. and King, J. (1999) 'Hardwiring weak ties', in G. Desanctis (ed.), *Journal of Computer-Mediated Communication*, 33(2), 214–21.

Qvale, T. (1995) 'Organising for innovation: from individual creativity to learning networks', in M. Ford and D. A. Gioia (eds), *Creative Action in Organisations*, Thousand Oaks, CA: Sage.

Rhodes, M. (1961) 'An analysis of creativity', in S. Isaksen (ed.), *Frontiers of Creativity Research*, New York: Bearly Ltd., pp. 216–22.

Rickards, T. (1993) 'Creativity from a business school perspective: past, present and future', in Scott Isaksen, Mary Murdock, Roger Firestien and Don Treffinger (eds), *Nurturing and Developing Creativity: The Emergence of a Discipline*, Norwood, NJ: Ablex Publishing Corporation.

Robinson, A. and Stern, S. (1997) *Corporate Creativity: How Innovation and Improvement Actually Happen*, San Fransisco: Berrett-Koehler Inc.

Senge, P. (1990) *The Fifth Discipline*, New York: Doubleday.

Scott, C. (1999) 'Communication technology and group communication', in L. Frey (ed.), *Group Communication Theory and Research*, Thousand Oaks, CA: Sage, pp. 432–72.

Shepherd, M., Briggs, R., Reinig, B. and Yen, J. (1994) 'Social loafing in electronic brainstorming: invoking social comparison through technology and facilitation techniques to improve group productivity', *Journal of Management Information Systems*, 12(3), 155–70.

Stein, M. L. (1984) 'Creative: the adjective', *Creativity and Innovation Network*, 10, pp. 115–117.

Sternberg, R. J. (1999) *Handbook of Creativity*, Cambridge: Cambridge University Press.

Sternberg, R. J. Lubart, T. I. (1999) 'The concept of creativity: prospects and paradigms', *Handbook of Creativity*, Cambridge: Cambridge University Press.

Tidd, J., Bessant, J. and Pavitt, K. (1997) *Integrating Technological, Market and Organisational Change: Managing Innovation*, Chichester: Wiley and Sons.

Treffinger, D. J. (1987) 'Research on creativity assessment', *Frontiers of Creativity Research*, New York: Bearly Ltd., pp. 103–19.

Valacich, J. S., Dennis, A. R. and Connolly, T. (1994) 'Idea generation in computer based groups: a new ending to an old story', *Organisational Behavior and Human Decision Processes*, 57(3), 448–67.

Van Gundy, A. B. (1986) 'Organisational creativity and innovation', *Creativity and Innovation Network*, 16, 201–18.

Walther, J. (1997) 'Group and interpersonal effects in international computer-mediated collaboration', *Human Communication Research*, 23(3), 342–69.

Wehner, L., Csikszentmihalyi, M. and Magyari-Beck, I. (1991) 'Current approaches used in studying creativity: an exploratory investigation', *Creativity Research Journal*, 4(3), 261–71.

Weick, C. (1979) *The Social Psychology of Organising*, Reading: Addison-Wesley.

Weisberg, J. (1993) *Beyond the Myth of Genius*, New York: W. H. Freeman.

BIBLIOGRAPHY

Amabile, T. (1988) 'A model of creativity and innovation in organisations', *Research in Organizational Behavior*, 10, 123–67.

Csikszentmihalyi, M. (1999) 'Implications of a systems perspective for the study of creativity', in R. J. Sternberg (ed.), *Handbook of Creativity*, Cambridge: Cambridge University Press, pp. 313–35.

Herrmann, N. (1996) *The Whole Brain Business Book*, London: McGraw-Hill.

Johnson, C. and Hackman, M. (1995) *Creative Communication*, US: Waveland Press.

Kaplan, A. (1999) 'The Development of Capacity' http://ngls.tad.ch/english/pubs/dd/dccontents.htm (July 2002)

Kiely, T. (1993) 'The idea makers', *Technology Review*, January, 32–40.

McDonough, E. (2000) 'Investigation of factors contributing to the success of cross-functional teams', *Journal of Product Innovation Management*, 17(3), 221–35.

Michalko, M. (2001) *Cracking Creativity*, US: Ten Speed Press.

Nemiro, J. (2001) 'Connection in creative virtual teams', *Journal of Behavioural and Applied Management*, 2(2), http://www.jbam.org/Articles/article2_8.htm

Peters, T. (1991) 'Get innovative or get dead', *California Management Review*, 33(1), 9–23.

Polland, M. (1994) *The Evaluation of Creative Behaviours* (CD-rom) ERIC item: 369539.

Stein, M. L. (1986) *Gifted, Talented and Creative Young People*, New York: Garland Publishing.

Staw, Barry. (1995). *Psychological Dimensions of Organisational Behaviour*, Upper Saddle River, NJ: Prentice-Hall.

Von Oech, R. (1998) *A Whack on the Side of the Head*, US: Warner Books.

CHAPTER 25

Language as a corporate asset

Krishna S. Dhir

With corporations operating in an increasingly globalized environment, many are paying attention to the languages in which they conduct their business. This chapter introduces the concept of language as corporate asset. Analogies between money and message and between, currency and language, form the basis of the ideas developed here. The role of language in emerging knowledge economies, globalization of business and workforce diversity is examined while the economics of corporate vocabulary and language is discussed from the perspective of corporate planners. Finally, an example illustrates how a global corporation may formulate its language policy.

Introduction

With increased globalization, corporations are paying attention to the languages in which they conduct their business. Businesses that operate globally bring together people from different cultures and traditions, who were educated through different learning processes, and who operate in different political systems in regions with different levels of industrial development. Language affects the ability of multinational organizations to function in the global market. Yet, the need for corporate language policies has not been adequately recognized in strategic management literature or communication literature. Research in the field of the economics of language was rare

prior to the 1960s. Until the mid-1960s the concept of the economics of language was not well understood or articulated. Since the mid-1960s, however, linguists have begun to pay attention to the link between language and economics. As of 1996, there were reportedly just more than a hundred academic articles and books published by economists on language matters. Interestingly, a majority of these works had the specific focus of exploring the evolution of language status and language use in business organizations within Quebec, Canada (Grin, 1996: 18; Dhir and Savage, 2002). Although the business of foreign language education continues to thrive today due to growth in international trade, scientific co-operation, tourism and the increasing demand for cultural insight (Coulmas 1991: 1), linguists have published relatively fewer works. Corporate planners, too, have generally not paid much attention to the important role played by languages in the conduct of modern business. In this chapter, some of the emergent conditions that necessitate corporate foregrounding of language in the formulation of business strategies are discussed. Language is presented as a corporate asset that offers means for information and knowledge management.

Language as an asset

Although interest in academic research of the economics of language is of recent origin, by the end of the seventeenth century many philosophers already had started to recognize the relationship between economics and language. Coulmas (1992: 2) observes, 'The analogy of money and language which is so conspicuously encoded in language itself has often been regarded as mere stylistic decoration.' He translates an example from the early seventeenth-century thinker, Stefano Guazzo, who used the analogy in making the point that in public speech the valuable must be separated from the worthless, as follows: 'Just as all sorts of coins – golden, silver and copper – issue from a purse, expressions and other words of greater and lesser value come out of the speaker's mouth' (Coulmas, 1992: 2).

Late in the seventeenth century, Locke referred to *word* as 'the common measure of commerce and communication' (Locke, 1959: 154). Locke's contemporary, Leibniz, alluded to the link between language and money, drawing an analogy between words as aid to thought and logic and counters as aid to computation (Leibniz, 1983: 5). He was looking for precision in valuation through both linguistic nomenclature and economic measurement. According to Coulmas (1992): 'Leibniz did not believe that, as a matter of principle, the expressive power of one language was greater than another. Nevertheless, he realized the advantage of precision. The smaller the unit, the greater the exactitude of the transactions that can be carried out in a system that uses it' (Coulmas, 1992: 3).

A few decades later, Hume (1964) moved beyond the metaphor. He saw parallels in the development and functions of language and money: 'In like manner are languages gradually establish'd by human conventions without any promise. In like manner do gold and silver become the common measures of exchange, and are esteem'd sufficient payment for what is of a hundred times their value' (Coulmas, 1992: 3).

According to another seventeenth-century thinker, Adam Smith, the currency of a country 'is the exact measure of the real exchangeable value of all commodities. It is so, however, at the same time and place only' (Smith, 1904: 39). Correspondingly, explains Coulmas (1992: 4), 'the value of words is contingent upon temporarily and locally limited common practice'. Coulmas quotes Hamann, a contemporary of Smith, to make his point:

> Money and language are two objects whose investigation is as profound and abstract as their use is common. Both are more closely related to each other than should be conjectured. The theory of the one explains that of the other; they seem to issue from common grounds. The wealth of all human knowledge is based on the exchange of words . . . All treasures of civic and social

life, on the other hand, are related to money as their universal measure.

(Coulmas, 1992: 4)

Coulmas (1992: 4) goes on to explain that 'words do not derive their meaning from their material substance . . . but from the purpose they serve in transmitting nonmaterial content, and likewise the value of money is not based on its material embodiment, but on the function it fulfils as a common means for the exchange of goods'.

As described above, in the literature the analogy is generally drawn between language and money. However, better analogies may be drawn between (1) *message* and money, and (2) language and *currency*. In all economic communities, *money*, in one form or another, is used to exchange economic assets between parties engaged in economic activities. Similarly, in all social communities, *messages* are used to exchange ideas, information, or knowledge between parties engaged in social discourse. Economists typically emphasize three functions of currency as: (1) a unit of exchange, (2) a unit of account, and (3) a store of value. As a unit of account, it is used in invoicing trade and in denominating financial instruments. As a medium of exchange, it is used to settle trade and financial transactions. As a store of value, it serves as an investment asset. A language, too, may be seen as performing three analogous functions of (1) exchanging information and knowledge, (2) accounting through narratives, and (3) storing value of knowledge and knowhow.

In different economic communities, different *currency* may be used to transact business. Similarly, in different social communities, different *language* may be deployed to communicate ideas. The value of a currency to an organization operating in an economic environment may be affected by such considerations as the demographic range in which the currency is used, the degree of investment made in that currency by the economic community, general demand for the currency, and so on. Similarly the value of a language to an organization may be affected by the degree to which the language is used in the demographic community defining the organization's strategic environment, the investment in the language relative to other available languages, demand for the language as a commodity within the organization's strategic community, and so on. Just as different prevailing economic trends have implications for strategies devised for the management of currencies held by a company, different social trends have implications for the management of a corporation's language assets. We will now briefly explore some of these trends.

Evolving trends

In the prevailing social context, three distinct trends are evolving that characterize the challenges facing corporate planners in managing language as a corporate asset. These are: (1) the evolution of the knowledge economy, (2) the globalization of business and economy, and (3) diversity of the workforce. As we shall see, each of these point to the importance of the development of an organizational culture that is conducive to the creation and application of knowledge, free flow of organizational information and empowerment of its constituent members. We also shall see how language plays a critical role in the formation of the organizational culture through its role in knowledge creation and application, flow of information and functioning of the organization. A brief review of each trend is presented below.

The evolution of the knowledge economy

The traditional paradigm of organizational theory views an organization as a system that processes information and solves problems through decision making. It seeks to improve the efficiency with which information is processed within the context of decision making in an uncertain environment. Recently, however, an alternative paradigm has emerged. This new paradigm suggests that organizations in the contemporary environment should be viewed as systems that create and manage both information and knowledge (Nonaka, 1994; Kolodnyet et al., 1996; Scarbrough, 1996; Amidon, 1997). This paradigm is the basis of a growing body of literature on the knowledge creation process and its management. Within the framework of this paradigm, information-driven organizations and knowledge-driven organizations anchor opposite ends of a continuum (Sveiby, 1997; Dhir and Harris, 2001). Nonaka (1994) has attempted to develop the essential elements of a theory of organizational knowledge creation.

Information-driven organizations sell knowledge as a package. They focus on knowing facts acquired through information that is often obtained by formal education. Information is independent of the individual creator. Its transfer is quick and mass oriented. Means of communication may include lectures and audiovisual mediums. Information-driven organizations, such as software companies, bundle information into standardized packages for a mass of customers. Major costs of communication are developmental. The cost of increasing volume is minimal. At the other end of the spectrum, knowledge-driven organizations sell knowledge, the capacity to act, as a process of knowing. They focus on learning by doing through training, practice, mistakes,

reflection, and repetition. The transfer of knowledge may be slow and individually oriented. The means of transfer is person to person, with the aid of games, simulation models, and role-playing that require learners to recreate skill. Knowledge-driven organizations, such as consulting firms, sell processes to solve problems for individual customers. Major costs relate to delivery of services. Costs increase with volume (Sveiby, 1997: 24–50).

Complex organizations have elements of both information-driven organizations and knowledge-driven organizations. In the context of a knowledge model, reflecting about the purpose of an organization reveals the importance of intangible assets in fostering corporate competences. This realization acts to render visible new concepts of assets and desired competences. Five factors that motivate the demand for new corporate competencies, as enumerated by Dhir and Harris (2001), are:

1   *New stakeholders*. New stakeholders are calling for a focus on relevant corporate competences including a general understanding of local and global environments, communication skills, interpersonal and team skills, and stakeholder orientation.
2   *New expectations*. Corporations are expected to develop processes that add value to organizations. This requires that corporations focus less on activities designed to convert events into information (e.g. collecting, classifying and summarizing activities) and focus more on activities designed to transform information into knowledge (e.g. analysing, interpreting, and evaluating activities that drive the decision-making process). Competences basic to value enhancement are: analytical skills; advisory skills; organizational pro-

cesses and model building understanding, including sensitive analysis; and operational definitions of concepts and design of appropriate measurement techniques development that lend themselves to decision making and process intervention.

3   *New technologies*. Emerging computer-based technologies offer enormous potential for efficiency, innovation, and value creation to society. Value derives from knowledge, and human capital is the most critical corporate asset. Vital competences include hardware and software development, problem solving, encryption and communication.

4   *New time horizons*. The environment in which today's organizations exist is in a continual state of flux. Complex changes occur at an ever-increasing pace. Given the rapidity of change, corporations must invest heavily in lifelong learning skills to enable individuals to maintain current knowledge, skills, and essential competences to facilitate agile response. It is necessary that continuing education emphasize intellectual capacity and professional development.

5   *New competition*. As information becomes accessible across national boundaries, global markets are becoming dominant. Organizations need to develop the ability to understand emerging problems, and to rapidly develop and deploy cost-effective services. Required competences include marketing and selling, understanding stakeholder needs, problem solving, designing and deploying effective solutions, and communicating.

Communication, and therefore language, is an important competency implied by each of the five factors described above.

There is considerable interest in the study of organizational design for effective knowledge creation and management. Blackler (1995) has reviewed concepts of knowledge, classified them, and examined processes for generating, storing, and applying knowledge. He has developed a typology of knowledge organizations. Other writers have discussed various aspects of management of knowledge (Peters, 1992; Skyrme and Amidon, 1997; Sveiby, 1997), including designs of work systems for knowledge workers (Pasmore and Purser, 1993), organizational learning in knowledge-intensive firms (Starbuck, 1992), and power and control of expertise (Reed, 1996). Unfortunately, the relationship between language and knowledge in the context of organizational design has not been studied. Let us examine the role of language in knowledge management.

For effective management of the knowledge creation process, it is important to comprehend the difference between knowledge and understanding. Schwandt (1999) expresses the difference between knowledge and understanding in German through the questions, 'Woher weibetat du das?' and 'Wie verstehen Sie das?' In English one would ask, 'How do you know that?' and 'What do you make of that?' It may be argued that to effectively use or apply information, as knowledge, to strategic advantage, an organization should *understand* the knowledge, as evidenced by its *making* something of that knowledge. To compete effectively, a multinational corporation, operating at a global scale, must acquire the ability to make something of its knowledge, through its core competences, including communication in different historical, cultural and linguistic milieux. In the 1990s, 97 per cent of US export growth came from small- to medium-sized businesses, but only 10 per cent of these companies were exporting their products. In testimony before the US Congress, lobbyists seeking increased funding for foreign language instruction explained that the most frequent reason cited by those not exporting was a lack of background knowledge and language skills required to understand foreign markets (Peterson, 2002). This is by no means a uniquely American problem. In a recent survey of 1,000 German small- to medium-sized exporters, 60 per cent of those interviewed have no business connections with enterprises in the United Kingdom, but if they were to establish them, 80 per cent would prefer to correspond in German. Only 20 per cent would even be prepared to use English. Of those who trade with the United Kingdom in English, half said that they would definitely prefer to use German and look more favourably on UK companies that have made the effort to learn German (Coleman and Cree, 2002).

When a person comprehends the socio-economic culture of a market, that person is able to engage and participate in what Gadamer refers to as the 'art of conversation' (Gadamer, 1975). Knowledge and understanding become possible when a person overcomes prejudices that prevent new understanding, and allows transformation through whatever is revealed through the course of conversation (Zeddies, 2002). The same may be said for a group of people, or an organization. An organization must be willing to participate in the socio-economic culture of the local market, and through adaptation, be transformed by the socio-economic realities it encounters. Language is the fundamental medium through which culture, tradition and custom are transmitted. Moreover, the capacity of language is not limited to designation, discovery, reference, or depiction of situations. Language also is used to carry out or perform actions and to reveal how things

are presented to us as we deal with them (Schwandt, 1999; Zeddies, 2002). Darlington-based Adrenalin-Moto is a small firm in the United Kingdom with three staff members, supplying motorbike parts and accessories. Its owner, Debbie Purdy says: 'France is our second-biggest market, and when the French are selling to us, language isn't a problem. When we are selling to them, however, it is a different matter. It can be frustrating. We knew that unless we addressed the problem we would miss out on a lot of trade.' Adrenalin-Moto set up a second, French-language website at a cost of £2,000. Almost immediately, online enquiries began to arrive (Coleman and Cree, 2002).

Globalization of business

Even as corporations are adapting to the evolving knowledge economy, business and economy are becoming increasingly globalized. In response to this trend, corporations bring together people with different cultural orientations, who are educated differently, operate in different political environments with different levels of industrial development, and do not all speak the same language. Nevertheless, they work toward a common organizational mission. Language affects the ability of multinational organizations to function in the global market. However, the need for corporate language policies has not been adequately explored in the strategic management literature. Also, the issue has not been discussed in the broader communication literature (Dhir and Goke-Pariola, 2002). In the following sections, we examine some of the factors that would define the development of a corporate language policy in a global market. We begin with a brief literature review.

Early in research on internationalization of corporations, Wiedersheim-Paul (1972) cited the importance of psychic or cultural distance between the locations in determining how a multinational company's operations get organized. Language has consistently been recognized as an important factor contributing to cultural distance (Johanson and Vahlne, 1977; Fixman, 1990; Petersen and Pedersen, 1997). More recently, it has been argued that the issue of language should be addressed in terms of the strategic management of multinational corporations (Marschan et al., 1997; Dhir and Savage, 2001; Dhir and Goke-Pariola, 2002; Dhir and Savage, 2002). In a global organization that operates in diverse locations and cultures, the challenge of deriving synergy from a set of activities performed by individuals who speak different languages can be daunting. Hood and Truijens (1993) studied a Japanese manufacturing company in Europe and found that language was one of the dominant factors considered in their decision to locate in an English-speaking environment. However, such strategies can be limiting, and work only in the short term. As suggested by Marschan-Piekkari et al., (1999), 'a Canadian firm moving into the United States, then Australia, New Zealand and the United Kingdom, can postpone language complications of international growth for some time'.

Generally, corporations as well as other organized communities such as nations or groups of people, seek improved efficiency of communication and operation through a standardized language adopted as its official language (Marschan-Piekkari et al., 1999; Dhir and Savage, 2002). Nevertheless, multinational corporations favour the development of a strong sense of common purpose, managed through soft control processes, that operate through informal communication channels, rather than formal means (Ghoshal and Bartlett, 1995). Personal relationships within an organization define the feasibility and the effectiveness of communication, collaborative learning, and knowledge creation, with direct implications for the corporation's competitive advantage in its strategic environment. Some works draw attention to the relationship between language and power (Foucault, 1978; Bourdieu, 1991; Janks, 2000). Yet, the strategic management literature rarely discusses the impact of language on multinational operations (Gupta and Govindarajan, 1991; Egelhoff, 1993; Ghoshal et al., 1994; Park et al., 1996) beyond acknowledging its importance (Johanson and Vahlne, 1977), even when otherwise focused on the importance of local considerations in effective management of international business (Andersen, 1993; Clegg et al., 1999). The broader communications literature, too, generally ignores the role of language in the development of informal channels of information flow (Nohria and Eccles, 1992; Krackhardt and Hanson, 1993; Macdonald, 1996).

Welch et al., (2001) warn that attempts to impose a common corporate language might hinder or alter information flow, knowledge transfer and communication. Dhir and Goke-Pariola (2002) make a case for language policies in multinational corporations. They, too, argue that the process that constrains a company to a standard language may actually deny it access to critical resources unique to the members' own diverse training and experiences. Diversity of cultures represented and languages spoken by the personnel may offer opportunities to a global organization not available to its competitors. In addition, a number of ongoing changes in the pattern of relationships between nations and societies make it imperative for multinational corporations to take a serious look at developing language policies. With rare exceptions (Marschan *et al.*, 1997; Dhir and Goke-Pariola, 2002), the need for corporate language policies has not been adequately recognized in either the strategic management literature or the communication literature. Dhir and Savage (2002) offer a judgment-analytic approach for corporations to assess the economic value of languages. They posit that different organizations may receive different value from delivered functions of a language. It is imperative that the assessed value account for not only those functional properties and qualities of the language in question, but also the context of the strategic environment in which the organization assessing it exists and operates. For a given corporation, the value of a language may be determined by various factors. Examples of these factors provided by Dhir and Savage (2002) are the degree to which:

1   the language is used in the demographic community defining the organization's strategic environment relative to other available languages;
2   the demographic community defining the organization's internal environment has collectively invested in the language relative to other available languages;
3   the language is demanded as a commodity within the demographic community defining the organization's strategic environment, both external and internal, relative to other available languages;
4   the demographic community defining the multinational business organization's strategic environment, both external and internal, creates knowledge in the language relative to other available languages; and,
5   the language can be developed as the multinational business organization's eco-

nomic means of production within the time frame of its strategic plan relative to other available languages.

With such conception of language, corporations can begin to think in terms of a portfolio of language assets much in the same way as it thinks of a portfolio of financial currency assets. It is noteworthy that the analogy between language and currency holds even in situations where nations (e.g. India) seek improved communication efficiency through adoption of a language not indigenous to them (e.g. English), and improved financial efficiency through replacement of their national currency (e.g. quetzals in Guatemala, colóns in El Salvador, balboas in Panama, and sucres in Ecuador) with a currency of another nation (US dollar) as legal tender. The adoption of both language and currency may be formal or informal, and official or unofficial. For more information on currency replacement, a process usually referred to as *dollarization*, see Calvo (1999), Antinolfi and Keister (2001) and Edwards (2001).

Workforce diversity

Since the 1990s, considerable attention has been paid to the conditions under which cultural diversity enhances or detracts from work group functioning. There is considerable literature recommending that managers should increase workforce diversity to enhance work group effectiveness, both in domestic and global organizations (Thomas, 1991; Jackson and Associates, 1992; Morrison, 1992; Cox, 1993). However, empirical research in support of these recommendations is limited. Studies have been reported on the impact of diversity in (1) identity of group memberships, in terms of race and sex (Cox,

1993; Jackson and Ruderman, 1995); (2) organizational group membership, in terms of hierarchical position or organizational function (Bantel and Jackson, 1989; Ancona and Caldwell, 1992); and (3) individual characteristics, in terms of idiosyncratic attitudes, values and preferences (Meglino et al.,1989; Bochner and Hesketh, 1994). On the one hand, decision scientists have developed sophisticated techniques for seeking optimal solutions to maximum diversity problems (Kuo et al.,1993; Glover et al.,1995; Agca et al., 2000). On the other hand, organizational theorists have generated numerous dimensions for classifying demographic differences. Milliken and Martins (1996) found that very few organizational studies have examined how cultural values affect individuals or groups in organizations. The challenge of defining diversity itself confounds the understanding of the impact of workforce diversity. Yet, diversity management is predicted to be one of the most significant organizational issues of coming decades (White and Nair, 1994).

Diversity is a characteristic of groups of two or more people. It typically refers to demographic differences of one sort or another among group members (McGrath et al.,1995). These differences have often resulted in different kinds of diversity. Consequently, empirical studies have resulted in ambivalent results, depending on the manner in which diversity is characterized. Studies on race and gender, for instance, have demonstrated both positive and negative impacts on work group functioning (Williams and O'Reilly, 1998). In another instance, Pelled (1996) makes one set of predictions about how group work members are affected by racial diversity, and another about how they are affected by functional background diversity based on the visibility of race and the job-relatedness. Different researchers hypothesize different models for the impact of diversity on work group effectiveness. Pelled (1996) expected racial diversity, as a source of visible differences, to impact work group effectiveness negatively. Cox et al., (1991), on the other hand, expected racial diversity, as a source of cultural differences, to have a positive outcome. Ely and Thomas (2001) have reviewed the studies reported in the literature on cultural diversity at work, and categorized them in terms of effects of proportional representation and of group composition. They focused on demographic variables including race, ethnicity, sex, social class, religion, nationality and sexual identity; but not on language.

The merits of diversity are debated widely in a variety of organizations. In the face of admonitions from scholars that neglect of workplace diversity may run the risk of loss of competitive advantage, corporations have undertaken various forms of diversity management initiatives. These initiatives have generally aimed at (1) increasing sensitivity to cultural differences; (2) developing the ability to recognize, accept and value diversity; (3) minimizing patterns of inequality experienced by women and minorities; (4) improving cross-cultural interactions and interpersonal relationships among gender and ethnic groups; and (5) modifying organizational culture and leadership practices (Soni, 2001). Whether the goal of a diversity initiative is achieved depends largely on an organization's diversity climate, which in turn is defined by the organization's culture (Cox, 1993). According to Soni (2001), 'If employees and managers do not accept and value differences and recognize the importance of the employer's diversity management initiatives, these initiatives are likely to have a very low probability of succeeding' (Soni, 2001: 396).

Individuals possess unique personal cultures. Organizations experience the impact of cultural diversity through individuals identifying with different sets of cultural groups, based on some set of shared characteristics. They may identify with more than one cultural group, with different degrees of affinity (Cox, 1993). Language is one of the important factors defining an individual's personal culture. It is a factor contributing to both human capital and ethnicity (Pendakur and Pendakur, 2002). However, none of the studies discussed above included language as a factor contributing to diversity, or explored the role of language in management of diversity. It is noteworthy that workforce diversity studies have mostly focused on personal characteristics that usually cannot be changed, such as age, gender, race, sexual orientation, physical disability and ethnic heritage. Language, on the other hand, *can* be changed to the extent that it can be learned.

The value of the language used by an organization is rooted in its organizational culture. According to Zeddies (2002), 'language is the primary and fundamental medium through which culture, tradition, and custom are transmitted down through history'. Nevertheless, the complexity of managing the language asset of a corporation is apparent in the definition of culture and the nature of workforce diversity. The term culture can have several meanings within the context of social research.

After defining symbol, idea and other necessary terms of the definition, Blumenthal (1940) defines culture as

the world stream of ideas that are communicable by means of symbols from the first of such ideas in the cosmos to the present. Culture includes also the causal relationships between such ideas, all phenomena that are affected by such ideas, and all relationships between ideas and other phenomena that have or have not been identifiably affected by such ideas. The definition is applied to such terms as culture trait, culture complex, culture pattern, etc.

Definitions of culture focus on development of intellectual and moral faculties, often through education; intellectual, artistic, or otherwise creative activity; the process of *acquiring* knowledge of these areas; accumulated and shared beliefs, social forms, attitudes, values, goals, practices and traits of a group, including company and corporation (Dhir and Savage, 2002). Attention to the strategic need for developing the appropriate culture throughout an organization, in turn, brings attention to the choice of language. Language, after all, is the essential skill giving man the capacity for learning and transmitting knowledge. The choice is complicated in the light of workforce diversity. As described by Zeddies (2002):

Language is much more than a mere assemblage of words structured by syntax and grammar; it represents the evolving varieties of human life and living over the vast expanse of time. The values, beliefs, victories, defeats, joys, sorrows, hopes, and visions of generations of human communities are bound up in and preserved by the language of a culture . . . Through language a world is disclosed to us.

(Zeddies, 2002)

According to Gadamer, all aspects of human experience are informed and affected by language (Gadamer, 1975; Zeddies, 2002). Taylor argues that language manifests a way of being in the world (Taylor, 1985). Language links terms or expression to concepts that have content in a specific context. Abrams (1983) describes a term as words or phrases, and concept as the definition of the term. Finegan et al., (1997) describe expression as words or phrases. They describe content as the situations to which the expressions are applied. 'There is no point of view outside the experience of the world in language from which it could itself become an object ... Even to speculate about nonverbal and non-linguistic realms of experience – such as music, dance, or emotions – requires language to describe or articulate the nature and vicissitudes of those experiences' (Zeddies, 2002). In such descriptions, different languages, in different cultural and traditional contexts, succeed to different degrees. Meaning is assigned to expressions through social mediation. As stated by Zeddies (2002), 'the limits in our expressive capacity do not necessarily correspond to a rigid boundary in the expressive power of language. Rather, the meanings that are not available to us in words suggest that our particular cultural and historical moment may not allow for those expressions.' It is important for multinational corporations to recognize this point for effective management of knowledge, globalization and internationalization processes, and workforce diversity. As described by Zeddies (2002), even though we may not be able to use words to describe a feeling, thought, or action, we are nevertheless greatly influenced by that which language presupposes and constitutes.

Corporate vocabulary and language

Corporations, even multinational corporations, often seek to meet their communication needs, and the challenges of knowledge management, globalization and workforce diversity, by adopting a single working language for the entire organization. They may adopt a language that offers the most efficient economic means of management, within the context of the strategic environment in which they exist and operate. Language may be viewed as the means by which an organization communicates its culture to members within the society in which it operates. However, as discussed below, it does more than communicate culture. Through language it produces new concepts to augment its knowledge base, develops vocabulary unique to the organization through which to manage its knowledge base, and exchanges value through the use of its working language that has been enhanced by that vocabulary.

Production of vocabulary and language

Abrams (1983) proposed a hypothesis for individual language behaviour. In the emerging knowledge economy, his hypothesis may be extended to corporate organizational behaviour as well. Abrams views language as a society's most important privately produced public goods. He states:

> The coinage of a phrase or term to formalize a new concept provides positive externalities to other members of society (for example, it facilitates the transmission of verbal and written communication). Based on traditional measures, the language market fits the economist's description of a 'free' market. Over time, countless numbers of individuals ... have contributed to the production process while virtually everyone has functioned as a consumer of language goods.

> (Abrams, 1983)

Abrams (1983) goes on to describe language production in terms of two distinct outputs: terms and definitions. Again, he states:

> Producing a definition involves the combining of already existing terms to describe a new concept or new category for entities. The production – or 'coining' – of a term or word provides a convenient, shorthand means of designating a concept for the purpose of communication . . . The utility maximizing individual would form a new concept whenever the private marginal benefits from that action exceed the attendant private marginal costs.
>
> (Abrams, 1983)

The process of using terms or words that have already been defined to produce a definition of a new concept to which a new term can be assigned, is akin to the process used by knowledge managers who use facts and rules to manage their knowledge base. Facts already known, along with newly acquired facts, are subjected to relationship rules. Language plays an important role in the knowledge creation process. Through those rules that are satisfied by the facts at hand, new facts are inferred, and thus the knowledge base is expanded.

The economics of vocabulary

According to Abrams (1983), assigning a new term, which could be a word or phrase, to a new concept may give to the producer at least two private benefits. One relates to the efficiency of communication. A new term may allow the producer to reduce the verbiage needed to communicate an argument, present a hypothesis or describe a phenomenon or a position. The other relates to psychic benefits accrued to the producer. For instance, if the concept, and the term representing it, is adopted by the larger society of which the producer is a member, then the psychic benefits may come in the form of, say, enhanced recognition of the producer, sometimes even associated with socio-economic rewards. Often, the private costs involved are minimal, and consist of time invested in 'identifying and defining' the concept and in 'pondering and deciding' a term that best describes the concept. Abrams' (1983) hypothesis explains why we see specific vocabularies developed in different corporations. The corporate organization may accrue benefits of enhanced operational efficiency when its members adopt a new term, developed by one or more of its members to describe a new concept, including hypotheses, phenomena, or processes. Further, the individual or persons associating the new concept with a new term may accrue recognition and rewards from the other members of the corporate organization.

The development of vocabulary that is specific to a given organization is a commonly observed phenomenon. Black (1991) provides the following illustrative example of a military briefing that is replete with specialized military vocabulary:

> Between zero-five and zero-seven today allied smart bombs achieved very significant terrain alteration. Because of our belief in the sanctity of human life, we have attrited this main force in a surgical operation that has gone the extra mile to avoid collateral damage, though of course you're always going to break some eggs . . . As for our lead ground forces, they continue to haul ass and bypass, as our Pentagon greensuiters like to say, and they will be kicking some butt preparatory to cutting off the enemy's head.
>
> (Black, 1991)

Corporate examples exist in abundance (Haymes, 1995), both in the United States (Light and Tilsner, 1994; Anonymous, 1998) and outside the United States (Anonymous, 1999; Taylor, 2000). A prevailing example of corporate jargon from the United States is the term 'procrastosnacking', which stands for the negative phenomenon of 'taking endless coffee or snack breaks in the staff canteen' to avoid work (Waller, 2001). Dobrzynski (1993) describes the corporate vocabulary of IBM, which includes words, such as *flatten*, meaning to resolve an issue, as in 'we have to flatten this before tomorrow's meeting'; *non-concur*, to disagree; *pushback*, a non-concurrence, as in 'I took the issue past Mike, but I got a lot of pushback'; *foil*, an overhead slide; and *reswizzle*, to tweak or improve something, as in 'Joe's boss asked him to reswizzle his foils.'

Opportunity in redundancy

Abrams (1983) observes that since the development of new terms to represent new concepts is motivated by private benefits to be had, individuals or groups may coin new terms for concepts that already exist, and ascribe new definitions to terms that already exist. Abrams bemoans the fact that this results in what he refers to as *terminological redundancy*. He cites the example of the economic concept of 'positive externality', for which redundant terms include 'external economy, spill-in, social benefit, beneficial third-party effect, spill-over benefit, beneficial neighbourhood effect, to name just a few' (Abrams, 1983). As an economist, he sees such redundancy to be a problem. However, to a corporate planner or strategist, this possibility of redundancy is attractive, because it offers the possibility to develop the corpora-

tion's unique set of concepts and terms that best suits its unique culture. Corporations seek to use their working language to facilitate the creation of economic value through an exchange of ideas, within the context of their respective corporate culture. Through their language, corporations communicate information, and create knowledge that gives them an edge over their competitors in the marketplace. Thus, the language of an organization may be viewed as the repository of that organization's knowledge base. As such, a language, like currency, is not value in itself, but creates value in its use or exchange (Coulmas, 1991; Dhir and Savage, 2002).

The economics of language

Dhir and Savage (2002) describe two approaches used by economists to empirically measure the value of a language. In the first, language is regarded as a means of exchange and a store of value (Coulmas, 1991; Vaillancourt, 1991: 30). Coulmas (1991) notes that every language has utilitarian value. *Utility value* refers to the sorts of tasks the language is suitable for and the actual opportunities for using a language at a given time and place. Coulmas also notes that in the context of international transactions and global markets, every language acquires an *exchange value*, which is determined by its demand. Both the utility value and the exchange value of language can vary from context to context, and markets to markets. Dhir and Savage (2002) offer an approach to the assessment of the value of a working language in the context of the strategic environment in which the organization assessing it exists and operates. Treating language as human capital (Grenier 1982), Breton (1998) uses the concept of 'network externalities' to describe how a dominant language emerges within historical, socio-cultural conditions, and how learning this language yields benefits.

The second approach looks at language as a characteristic of those who use it (Vaillancourt, 1991). Studies have tried to explain lower earnings of certain groups in terms of discrimination (Raynauld and Marion, 1972; Lang, 1993) and other factors (Migué, 1970; Lavoie, 1983), resulting in contradicting explanations. Language is also seen as acquiring economic value in terms of the knowledge that becomes accessible through it (Dhir and Savage, 2002). Economic studies have examined the spread (Hocevar, 1983) and promotion (Grin, 1990a, 1990b) of languages. Generally, the potential benefit of using economic tools, such as cost–benefit analysis, to assess the benefits to be derived from acquisition of language skills is well recognized (Jernudd and Jo, 1985; Cooper, 1989). For further review of the literature on the economics of language see Grin (1996), Breton (1998), and Dhir and Savage (2002).

Formulating a corporate language policy

At first glance, the problem of adopting a language for corporate communication may seem to be an easy one to solve, especially for organizations operating out of English-speaking countries. In view of widespread use of the English language, one might argue that the English language is the obvious choice, especially for operations in the global markets and dealing with workforce diversity. A standardized language, used both at the home office and in local markets, facilitates efficient communication, and minimizes misunderstanding between the various units of the organizations (Lester, 1994). What is more, a common language adds to the *glue* that keeps

the organization together through soft control mechanisms, such as corporate culture, described by Ferner *et al.*,(1995). However, the adoption of a standardized language is not always the optimal strategy, especially when competitive advantage is to be gained through access to non-English-speaking markets. In finance, it is not uncommon for corporations operating in inter-national markets, to hold a portfolio of currencies. Lester (1994) reports that Nestlé designates both French and English as its official language, but also uses a wider range of languages for inter-subsidiary communications. Siemens, a German multinational corporation, invests heavily in an in-house language training programme, globally available to its employees, through which they may acquire competencies in German, English, French and Spanish (Lester, 1994). In 1994, Lester noted, 'the easiest and cheapest way to approach the language problem is to hire people already possessing the required skills' (Lester, 1994: 43). The problem of language acquisition was seen to be a human resource management (HRM) one. Two years later, Reeves and Wright (1996) suggested that global organizations would benefit from a *language audit*. Soon after that, Marschan *et al.* (1997) called for the issue of language choice and acquisition to be treated as a strategic matter. As they put it:

An important first step might be to include language aspects at the highest level of strategic planning and implementation; thinking through the language consequences of strategic decisions upon global operations; examining their demand on language facility throughout the global entity; and identifying possible barriers to implementation created by the inevitable differences in language proficiency.

(Marschan *et al.*, 1997: 596)

Marschan *et al.* (1997) went on to state, 'language policies, especially when connected with HRM activities, are important in ensuring that language-competent staff are strategically positioned throughout the global organizations'. They also recognized that the language audit suggested by Reeves and Wright (1996) could be made part of the routine strategic assessment of a global organization's strengths and weaknesses. How this was to be accomplished remained unclear.

The analogy drawn in this chapter, not between language and money, but between language and currency, now paves the way for corporate planners to account for the language issues in strategic analyses of global organizations, much in the same manner as they account for the financial issues. Financial assets are managed through their valuation. Corporations that operate internationally to access various markets for factors of production, and intermediate and finished products and services, commonly formulate and implement financial policies for acquiring and holding a portfolio of currencies. Their objective is to maximize the value of their financial assets. Similarly, corporations may now formulate and implement language policies for acquiring competency in a portfolio of languages, so as to maximize the value of their language assets. Dhir and Savage (2002) have developed a judgement-analytic approach for the assessment of the value of a language by a global organization, within the context of the strategic environment in which it operates, facilitating this process. They simulated the situation in which a multinational corporation, with its world headquarters in Switzerland, seeks to develop a language policy for operation within their strategic environment that includes North America, South America, Europe, South and Southeast Asia, Japan, Africa and Australia. The language policy

sought would afford the company the greatest competitive advantage with respect to the strategic environment within which it operates. Ten languages are spoken in Switzerland, including its four national languages: German in one *Schwyzerdütch* dialect or the other, French, Italian and Romansh. In its strategic environment, additional languages are spoken, including various African languages, various Indian languages, French, Japanese, Portuguese, various Scandinavian languages, Spanish, etc.

While seeking a competitive advantage in the marketplace, a multinational corporation would adopt a set of languages for its operations that offers it the most efficient economic means of knowledge creation and management within the context of the strategic environment in which it operates. Different organizations may receive different value from different languages. It is imperative that the assessed value account for not only those functional properties and qualities of the language in question, but also the context of the strategic environment in which the organization assessing it exists and operates. The delivered functions would, after all, be determined by this strategic context. Different managers may perceive the various delivered functions differently. Different managers also may perceive an organization's strategic environment differently. The assessment of value of a language, therefore, is a matter of individual judgement, which may be subjective in nature (Dhir, 2001; Dhir and Savage, 2002).

The simulation study by Dhir and Savage (2002) yielded a language policy for the Swiss multinational corporation in question in terms of the following dimensions:

1   It defined the context of the language policy as the assessment of the economic value of a language, in terms of the

degree to which the language afforded competitive advantage, with respect to the strategic environment within which the multinational corporation operates.

2   It identified and defined the factors pertinent to the determination of the economic value of a language for the purposes of the corporation. These were:

(a) *Demographic range*: the degree to which the language is used in the demographic community defining the multinational business organization's strategic environment relative to other available languages.

(b) *Total investment*: the degree to which the demographic community defining the multinational business organization's internal environment has collectively invested in the language relative to other available languages. The investment refers to the degree to which the community in question learns and prefers the language.

(c) *Demand*: the degree to which the language is demanded as a commodity within the demographic community defining the multinational business organization's strategic environment (both external and internal) relative to other available languages.

(d) *Knowledge creativity*: the degree to which the demographic community defining the multinational business organization's strategic environment (both external and internal) creates knowledge in the language relative to other available languages.

(e) *Functional potential*: the degree to which the language can be developed as the multinational business organization's economic means of production within the time frame of its strategic plan relative to other available languages.

3   It specified the *relative emphasis* to placed on the factors considered.

4   It specified how the information regarding each factor was to be integrated to arrive at an overall judgement about the value of the language. This refers to the underlying principle that governs how the information on the various factors is to be used.

A case study

We now offer a case illustration. Suppose that you have been hired to be a consultant to a corporation engaged in a medium-sized enterprise, based in France. The firm has been using French as its working language since its inception a decade ago. The management of the firm has decided to expand its operations into markets in England, Germany and Spain. Managers feel that they need an additional working language, along with French, to (1) serve as a *medium of communication* to enhance the flexibility of inter-subsidiary communication; (2) provide a *means of identification* so that they may develop appropriate local identity in different markets; and (3) serve as a *medium of development* to create human and intellectual capital in local markets. You are being asked to formulate a language policy for this organization, and to recommend whether the firm should adopt English, German, or Spanish as the additional working language. Answer the following six questions:

1   For what purpose is the policy to be developed? Define the context of the language policy in terms of the criterion variable to be assessed or managed.

For instance, in the context of strategic planning, the criterion may be the degree to which a language affords competitive advantage with respect to the strategic environment within which the multinational corporation operates. Or else, it may be something such as which of alternative languages should be adopted for cross-subsidiary communication that does not involve the home office.

2   What are the key factors that influence the variable to be assessed or managed? Identify the factors for which the policy must account. Ideally, the set of factors identified should be mutually exclusive and collectively exhaustive.

Now suppose the management of this firm has revealed its priorities relative to the functions to be fulfilled by the second working language as follows: The function of the language as a medium of communication is twice as important to the firm as each of the remaining two functions, which in turn are equally important.

3   What relative emphasis or weight is indicated for each of the factors identified in item 2? To indicate this, distribute 100 points among each factor in such a way that the points assigned to each factor indicates the relative importance of that factor in your assessment of the criterion variable. Then normalize the scores to relative weights by dividing the points awarded by 100.
4   On what scale could each of the factors be measured? Factors that are a physical variable may be measurable in terms of physical dimensions such as length, weight, etc. Factors that are not physical may be measurable on a scale ranging from a low of X, to a high of Y, where a measure of X for a factor would indicate that the degree to which that factor is present in the particular language is extremely low, and a

measure of Y would indicate that the degree to which that factor is present in the particular language is extremely high.
5   For each factor, does an increase in the factor change the criterion variable? Is the change an increase or a decrease? In fact, this change also could be linear or non-linear. For the purpose of this illustration, we assume that the change is linear. For treatment of non-linear changes, see Dhir and Savage (2002).

Let us say that the firm's strategy analysts have determined that, in the context of the firm's markets in England, Germany and Spain, the functionalities of the alternative languages, as they affect the firm in question, rate as shown below. Assume that all ratings are on a scale ranging from a low of 1 to a high of 10, where a measure of 1 for a functionality would indicate that the level of that functionality offered by the language in question (Table 25.1) is extremely low, and a value of 10 would indicate that the level of that functionality offered by the language in question is extremely high.

6   What language would you recommend as the additional working language for the firm in question?

Answers

1   The question may be answered variously. For instance, the purpose of the language policy may be said to be to enhance the firm's competitive advantage with respect to the strategic environment within which it operates. Let us say that the criterion variable in the present case is the firm's competitive advantage measured on a scale from 1 to 10, where a measure of 1 indicates an extremely low advantage, and a measure of 10 indicates an extremely high advantage.

Table 25.1 Functionality offered by language

Functionality	Alternative languages		
	English	German	Spanish
Medium of communication	6	8	5
Means of identification	3	7	6
Medium of development	4	5	8

2   The factors are the performance of the language as a (a) medium of communication, (b) means of identification and (c) medium of development.

3   The factor, medium of communication, would carry a relative weight of 50 points; means of identification would carry 25 points; and medium of development also would carry 25 points. The normalized relative weights would be 0.50, 0.25, and 0.25, respectively.

4   Each of the three factors can be measured on a scale ranging from a low of 1 to a high of 10, where a measure of 1 for a factor would indicate that the degree to which that factor is present in the particular language is extremely low, and a value of 10 would indicate that the degree to which that factor is present in the particular language is extremely high.

5   For each factor, an increase in the factor increases the competitive advantage.

6   The following analysis should be performed. For each language, discount the functionality rating by the relative weight of that functionality. Then, add the resulting scores by columns, yielding a cumulative rating of the corresponding language.

In the example shown in Table 25.2, the highest cumulative rating is associated with the German language. German would, therefore, be recommended to the firm as the additional working language of choice.

Summary

In this chapter, the concept of language as a corporate asset was presented. An analogy was drawn between money and message, and between currency and language. This analogy formed the basis of the ideas developed here. The role of language in the evolving trends of emerging knowledge economy, globalization of business, and workforce diversity was examined. The literature on the economics of language was reviewed from the perspective of corporate planners. Finally, an example illustrated how a multinational corporation may formulate and apply its language policy.

Table 25.2 Functionality analysis

Functionality	Alternative languages		
	English	German	Spanish
Medium of communication	$6 \times 0.50 = 3.00$	$8 \times 0.50 = 4.00$	$5 \times 0.50 = 2.50$
Means of identification	$3 \times 0.25 = 0.75$	$7 \times 0.25 = 1.75$	$6 \times 0.25 = 1.50$
Medium of development	$4 \times 0.25 = 1.00$	$5 \times 0.25 = 1.25$	$8 \times 0.25 = 2.00$
Total score	4.75	7.00	6.00

REFERENCES

Abrams, B. A. (1983) 'An economic analysis of the language market', *The Journal of Economic Education*, 14(3), 40–7.

Agca, S., Eksioglu, B. and Ghosh, J. B. (2000) 'Lagrangian solution of maximum dispersion problem', *Naval Research Logistics*, 47, 97–114.

Amidon, D. M. (1997) *Innovation Strategy for the Knowledge Economy: The Ken Awakening*, London: Butterworth-Heinemann.

Ancona, D. G. and Caldwell, D. F. (1992) 'Demography and design: predictors of new product team performance', *Organization Science*, 3, 321–41.

Andersen, O. (1993) 'On the internationalisation process of firms: a critical analysis', *Journal of International Business Studies*, 24(2), 209–21.

Anonymous (1998) 'Fluent jargonspeak', *Management Today*, March, 104.

Anonymous (1999) 'A new corporate vocabulary', *Malaysian Business*, 1 December.

Antinolfi, G. and Keister, T. (2001) 'Dollarization as a monetary arrangement for emerging market economies', *Review* (Federal Reserve Bank of Saint Louis), 83(6), 29–39.

Bantel, K. A. and Jackson, S. E. (1989) 'Top management and innovations in banking: does the composition of the top team make a difference?', *Strategic Management Journal*, 10, 107–24.

Black, G. (1991) 'Briefingspeak', *Nation*, 252(9), 292–3.

Blackler, F. (1995) 'Knowledge, knowledge work and organizations: an overview and interpretation', *Organization Studies*, 16(6), 1021–46.

Blumenthal, A. (1940) 'A new definition of culture', *American Anthropologist*, 42, 571–86.

Bochner, S. and Hesketh, B. (1994) 'Power distance, individualism/collectivism, and job-related attitudes in a culturally diverse work group', *Journal of Cross-Cultural Psychology*, 25, 233–57.

Bourdieu, P. (1991) *Language and Symbolic Power*, Cambridge, MA: Harvard University Press.

Breton, A. (1978) 'Nationalism and language policies', *Canadian Journal of Economics*, 11, 656–68.

Breton, A. (ed.) (1998) *Economic Approaches to Language and to Bilingualism*, Ottawa: Canadian Heritage.

Calvo, G. A. (1999) *On Dollarization*, College Park, MD: Department of Economics, University of Maryland.

Clegg, S. R., Ibarra-Colado, E. and Bueno-Rodriquez, L. (eds) (1999) *Global Management: Universal Theories and Local Realities*, London: Sage Publications.

Coleman, A. and Cree, R. (2002) 'Speaking in tongues', *Director*, 55(11), 21–3.

Cooper, R. (1989) *Language Planning and Social Change*, Cambridge, New York: Cambridge University Press.

Coulmas, F. (1991) 'The language trade in the Asian Pacific', *Journal of Asian Pacific Communication*, 2(1), 1–27.

Coulmas, F. (1992) *Language and Economy*, Oxford: Blackwell Publishers.

Cox, T. H., Jr (1993) *Cultural Diversity in Organizations: Theory, Research, and Practice*, San Francisco: Berrett-Koehler.

Cox, T. H., Jr, Lobel, S. A. and McLeod, P. L. (1991) 'Effects of ethnic group cultural differences on cooperative and competitive behavior on a group task', *Academy of Management Journal*, 34, 827–47.

Dhir, K. S. (2001) 'Assessment of the value of knowledge transferred: a mixed mode approach', in M. G. Nicholls, S. Clarke and B. Lehaney (eds), *Mixed-Mode Modelling: Mixing Methodologies for Organisational Intervention*, Dordrecht: Kluwer Academic Publishers, pp. 137–69.

Dhir, K. S. and Goke-Pariola, A. (2002) 'The case for language policies in multinational corporations', *Corporate Communications: An International Journal*, 7(4), 141–51.

Dhir, K. S. and Harris, J. E. (2001) 'The emerging paradigm for information and knowledge creation in academic organizations', *International Journal of Management Literature*, 1(2, 3, 4), 305–15.

Dhir, K. S. and Savage, T. (2001) 'The value of a language: can decision science and linguistic perspectives converge?,' in V. L. Smith-Daniels and M. Rungtusanatham (eds), *Proceedings of the 2001 National Decision Sciences Institute Conference*, Atlanta, GA: Decision Sciences Institute, Georgia State University, 258–60.

Dhir, K. S. and Savage, T. (2002) 'The value of a working language', *International Journal of the Sociology of Language*, 158, 1–35.

Dobrzynski, J. H. (1993) 'An exclusive account of Lou Gerstner's first six months', *BusinessWeek*, October(4), 96–7.

Edwards, S. (2001) 'Dollarization: myths and realities', *Journal of Policy Modeling*, 23, 249–65.

Egelhoff, W. (1993) 'Information processing theory and the multinational corporation', in S. Ghoshal and E. Westney (eds), *Organization Theory and the Multinational Corporation*, London: Macmillan Press, pp. 182–210.

Ely, R. J. and Thomas, D. A. (2001) 'Cultural diversity at work: the effects of diversity perspectives on work group processes and outcomes', *Administrative Science Quarterly*, 46, 229–73.

Ferner, A., Edwards, P. and Sisson, K. (1995) 'Coming unstuck? In search of the "corporate glue" in an international professional service firm', *Human Resource Management*, 34(3), 343–61.

Finegan, E., Blair, D. and Collins, P. (1997) *Language: Its Structure and Use*, 2nd edn, Sydney, Australia: Harcourt Brace.

Fixman, C. (1990) 'The foreign language needs of US-based corporations', *Annals*, 511(September), 25–46.

Foucault, M. (1978) *The History of Sexuality*, Vol. 1, tr. R. Hurley, London: Penguin.

Fromkin, V., Blair, D. and Collins, P. (1999) *An Introduction to Language*, 4th edn, Marrickville, NSW, Australia: Harcourt Australia Pty Ltd.

Gadamer, H. G. (1975) *Truth and Method*, New York: Crossword.

Ghoshal, S. and Bartlett, C. (1995) 'Changing the role of top management: Beyond structure to process', *Harvard Business Review*, 73(2), 86–96.

Ghoshal, S., Korine, H. and Szulanski, G. (1994) 'Interunit communication in multinational corporations', *Management Science*, 40(1), 96–110.

Glover, F., Kuo, C. C. and Dhir, K. S. (1995) 'A discrete optimization model for preserving biological diversity', *Applied Mathematical Modelling*, 19(11), 696–701.

Grenier, G. J. A. (1982) 'Language as human capital: theoretical framework and application to Spanish-speaking Americans'. Ph.D. dissertation, Princeton, NJ: Princeton University.

Grin, F. (1990a) 'The economic approach to minority languages', *Journal of Multilingual and Multicultural Development*, 11, 153–74.

Grin, F. (1990b). *A Beckerian Approach to Language Use: Guidelines for Minority Language Policy*, Montreal: Cahiers du Centre de recherche et développement en économique.

Grin, F. (1996) 'The economics of language: survey, assessment, and prospects', *International Journal of the Sociology of Language*, 121, 17–44.

Gupta, A. and Govindarajan, V. (1991) 'Knowledge flows and the structure of control within multinational corporations', *Academy of Management Review*, 16(4), 768–92.

Haymes, R. D. (1995) 'Corporate lingo: a new meaning', *ETC: A Review of Semantics*, 52(2), 222–7.

Hocevar, T. (1975) 'Equilibria on linguistic minority markets', *Kyklos*, 28, 337–57.

Hocevar, T. (1983) 'Les aspects économiques de la dynamique fonctionnelle des langues', *Language Problems and Language Planning*, 7, 135–47.

Hood, N. and Truijens, T. (1993) 'European locational decisions of Japanese manufacturers: survey evidence on the case of the UK', *International Business Review*, 2(1), 39–63.

Hume, D. (1964) *A Treatise of Human Nature*. Book 3, 258–73, reprint of the 2nd edn. Aalen: Scientia Verlag.

Ingram, D. E. (1994) 'Language policy in Australia in the 1990s', in R. Lambert (ed.), *Language Planning Around the World: Contexts and Systemic Change*, Washington, DC: The National Foreign Language Center at the Johns Hopkins University, pp. 69–110.

Jackson, S. E. and Associates (1992) *Diversity in the Workplace: Human Resources Initiatives*, New York: Guilford Press.

Jackson, S. E., and Ruderman, M. N. (eds) (1995) *Diversity in Work Teams*, Washington, DC: American Psychological Association.

Janks, H. (2000) 'Domination, access, diversity and design: a synthesis for critical literacy education', *Educational Review*, 52(2), 175–86.

Jernudd, B. and Jo, S. H. (1985) 'Bilingualism as a resource in the United States', *Annual Review of Applied Linguistics*, 6, 10–18.

Johanson, J. and Vahlne, J. (1977) 'The internationalisation process of the firm: a model of knowledge development and increasing foreign market commitments', *Journal of International Business Studies*, 8(1), 23–32.

Kolodny, H., Liu, M., Stymne, B. and Denis, H. (1996) 'New technology and the emerging organizational paradigm', *Human Relations*, 49(12), 1457–87.

Krackhardt, D. and Hanson, J. R. (1993) 'Informal networks: the company behind the chart', *Harvard Business Review*, 71(4), 104–11.

Kuo, C. C., Glover, F. and Dhir, K. S. (1993) 'Analyzing and modeling the maximum diversity problem by zero-one integer programming', *Decision Sciences*, 24(6), 1171–85.

Lang, K. (1986) 'A language theory of discrimination', *Quarterly Journal of Economics*, 101, 363–82.

Lang, K. (1993) 'Language and economists' theories of discrimination', *International Journal of the Sociology of Language*, 103, 165–83.

Lavoie, M. (1983) 'Bilingualisme, langue dominante et réseaux d'information', *L'actualité économique*, 59, 38–62.

Leibniz, G. W. (1983) *Unvorgreifliche Gedanken, betreffend die Ausübung und Verbesserung der deutschen Sprache. Zei Aufsätze*, ed. Uwe Pörksen, Stuttgart: Reclam.

Lester, T. (1994) 'Pulling down the language barrier', *International Management*, July–August, 42–4.

Light, L. and Tilsner, J. (1994) 'A learner's guide to corp-babble', *Business Week*, 7 March (3361), 8.

Locke, J. (1959) *An Essay Concerning Human Understanding*, New York: Dover Books.

Macdonald, S. (1996) 'Informal information flow and strategy in the international firm', *International Journal of Technology Management*, 11(1–2), 219–32.

Marschan, R., Welch, D. and Welch, L. (1997) 'Language: the forgotten factor in multinational management, *European Management Journal*, 15(5), 591–8.

Marschan-Piekkari, R., Welch, D. and Welch, L. (1999) 'Adopting a common corporate language: IHRM implications', *International Journal of Human Resources Management*, 10(3), 377–90.

McGrath, J. E., Berdahl, J. L. and Arrow, H. (1995) 'Traits, expectations, culture, and clout: the dynamics of diversity in work groups', in S. E. Jackson and M. N. Ruderman (eds), *Diversity in Work Teams*, Washington, DC: American Psychological Association, pp. 17–45.

Meglino, B. M., Ravlin, E. C. and Adkins, C. L. (1989) 'A work values approach to corporate culture: a field test of the value congruence process and its relationship to individual outcomes', *Journal of Applied Psychology*, 74, 424–32.

Migué, J. L. (1970) 'Le nationalisme, l'unité nationale et la théorie économique de l'information', *Revue Canadienne d'économique*, 3, 183–98.

Milliken, F. J. and Martins, L. L. (1996) 'Searching for common threads: Understanding the multiple effects of diversity in organizational groups', *Academy of Management Review*, 21, 402–33.

Morrison, A. M. (1992) *The New Leaders: Guidelines on Leadership Diversity in America*, San Francisco: Jossey-Bass.

Nohria, N. and Eccles, R. (1992) 'Face-to-face: making network organizations work', in N. Nohria and R. Eccles (eds), *Networks and Organizations: Structure, Form and Action*, Boston, MA: Harvard Business School Press, pp. 283–308.

Nonaka, I. (1994) 'A dynamic theory of organizational knowledge creation', *Organization Science*, 5(1), 14–37.

Park, H., Sun Dai, H. and Harrison, J. K. (1996) 'Sources and consequences of communication problems in foreign subsidiaries: the case of United States firms in South Korea', *International Business Review*, 5(1), 79–98.

Pasmore, W. A. and Purser, R. E. (1993) 'Designing work systems for knowledge workers', *Journal of Quality and Participation*, July–August, 78–84.

Pelled, L. H. (1996) 'Demographic diversity, conflict and work group outcomes: an intervening process theory', *Organization Science*, 7, 615–31.

Pendakur, K. and Pendakur, R. (2002) 'Language as both human capital and ethnicity', *International Migration Review*, 36(1), 31.

Peters, T. (1992) *Liberation Management*, New York: Alfred Knopf.

Petersen, B. and Pedersen, T. (1997) 'Twenty years after: support and critique of the Uppsala internationalisation model', in I. Bjorkman and M. Forsgren (eds), *The Nature of the International Firm: Nordic Contributions to International Business Research*, Copenhagen: Copenhagen Business School Press.

Peterson, T. (2002) 'The importance of being multilingual', *Business Week Online*, 4 September, Academic Search Premier.

Raynauld, A. and Marion, P. (1972) 'Une analyse économique de la disparité inter-ethnique des revenus', *Revue économique*, 23, 1–19.

Reed, M. I. (1996) 'Expert power and control in late modernity: an empirical review and theoretical synthesis', *Organization Studies*, 17(4), 573–97.

Reeves, N. and Wright, C. (1996) *Linguistic Audit*, Clevedon: Multilingual Matters.

Scarbrough, H. (ed.) (1996) *The Management of Expertise*, London: Macmillan.

Schwandt, T. A. (1999) 'On understanding understanding', *Qualitative Inquiry*, 5(4), 451–65.

Skyrme, D. J. and Amidon, D. M. (1997) *Creating the Knowledge-based Business*, London: Business Intelligence.

Smith, A. (1904) *An Inquiry into the Nature and Causes of the Wealth of Nations*, London: Methuen.

Soni, V. (2001) 'A twenty-first-century reception for diversity in the public sector: a case study', *Public Administration Review*, 60(5), 395–408.

Starbuck, W. H. (1992) 'Learning by knowledge-intensive firms', *Journal of Management Studies*, 29(6), 713–40.

Sveiby, K. E. (1997) *The New Organizational Wealth: Managing and Measuring Knowledge-Based Assets*, San Francisco, CA: Berrett-Koehler Publishers.

Taylor, C. (1985) 'Language and human nature', *Human Agency and Language: Philosophical Papers*, 1, 215–47. Cambridge: Cambridge University Press

Taylor, N. (2000) 'Buzzword bingo', *Australian Personal Computer*', 21(10), 6.

Thomas, R. R., Jr (1991) *Beyond Race and Gender*, New York: American Management Association.

Vaillancourt, F. (1980) *Differences in Earnings by Language Group in Québec*, Québec: Presses de l'Université Laval.

Vaillancourt, F. (1991) 'The economics of language: theory, empiricism and application to the Asian Pacific', *Journal of Asian Pacific Communication*, 2(1), 29–44.

Welch, D. E., Welch, L. S. and Marschan-Piekkari, R. (2001) 'The persistent impact of language on global operations', *Prometheus*, 19(3), 193–210.

Waller, M. (2001) 'Procrastosnacking', *The Times*, 22 August.

White, S. A., and Nair, K. S. (1994) 'Cultural renewal: an operational model for sharing diversity through participatory communication', presented at the 44th Annual Meeting of the International Communication Association, Sydney, New South Wales, Australia, 11–15 July.

Wiedersheim-Paul, F. (1972) *Uncertainty and Economic Distance*. Uppsala: Uppsala University Press.

Williams, K. Y. and O'Reilly, C. A. (1998) 'Demography and diversity in organizations', in B. M. Staw and R. I. Sutton (eds), *Research in Organizational Behavior*, 20, Stamford, CT: JAI Press, pp. 77–140.

Zeddies, T. J. (2002) 'More than just words: a hermeneutic view of language in psychoanalysis', *Psychoanalytic Psychology*', 19(1), 3–23.

CHAPTER 26

Arrival of the global village

Michael Morley

In this chapter the author looks at the premise that the global village predicted by Marshall McLuhan some thirty-five years ago is finally here. With its arrival the author considers how, if any, the impact of technology has influenced both the roles of the corporate communicator and global business practice, and the core skills that a professional communicator will need to possess in this new age. The chapter looks at what those skills might be and why, for an international practitioner, mastering them will be important in dealing with the new business age.

The primeval forces that drive entrepreneurs to establish global empires have combined with those that enable them to achieve their ambitions. The driving forces are the quest for survival, power, peace, pride and profit. Company leaders know they must grow in size if they are not to be swallowed up by a bigger corporation.

Leaders of industry are just as hungry for power as presidents, prime ministers, generals and bishops. Many also believe that an economy in which nations are interdependent is a significant force for peace and that global corporations have a pivotal role to play in bringing that about. For some individuals, the status conferred by being leader of a global corporation is sometimes more important than the power or profit that position brings. National rather than personal pride is a clear driving force for many of the huge corporations that emerged in post-war Japan and more recently in Korea as they sought to reach parity with – and then overtake – companies in the United States and Europe. Profit is the primary reason for the existence of business enterprises. To achieve maximum profits, the corporation must co-operate on a global scale. Technology, privatization, the dismantling of protectionism, swifter, cheaper travel, less restricted movement of capital and labour, standardization and education have been important factors in helping business leaders achieve their global ambitions. All of these factors have contributed to the remarkable growth of public relations. There is every prospect this growth will continue, notwithstanding the bursting of the dot.com bubble, the aftershock sustained by the entire technology sector and the general slowdown in the global economy that started at the turn of the millennium.

The world's ten biggest PR firms in 1990 recorded fee income of $910 million, according to O'Dwyer's Directory of PR Firms. Ten years later the top ten fee income had risen to $2.5 billion, as reported by the Council of PR Firms and published in *PR Week* (Table 26.1).

A massive consolidation of the largest PR agencies took place as the twentieth century came to a close and continued at the beginning of the twenty-first. Larger agencies continued to acquire smaller ones as the principal agency networks sought to flesh out their service to clients geographically and by specialty practice. To this a phenomenon new to the world of public relations – but which had been seen in the world of advertising for many years – was added a series of acquisitions that has created the formation of three global super-groups, each comprising several

Table 26.1 The world's largest PR firms

	Firm name	2001 Worldwide revenue ($)
1	Weber Shandwick Worldwide	426,572,018
2	Fleishman-Hillard Inc.	345,098,241
3	Hill and Knowlton, Inc.	325,119,000
4	INCEPTA (CITIGATE)	266,018,371
5	Burson Marsteller	259,112,000
6	Edelman Public Relations Worldwide	223,708,535
7	Ketchum, Inc.	185,221,000
8	Porter Novelli	179,294,000
9	GCI GROUP/APCO Worldwide	151,081,645
10	Ogilvy Public Relations Worldwide	145,949,285
Total top 10		2,507,174,095

Source: Council of PR Firms/*PR Week* rankings

agency networks or brands. Omnicom agencies combined to record $810 million, Interpublic $708 million and WPP $844 million in fees for the year 2000, in the Council's rankings. These new groupings have made bedfellows of previously fierce competitors such as Hill & Knowlton and Burson-Marsteller, now both owned by WPP, the British-based communications conglomerate.

Media impact

With the premise that the global village has arrived, the PR practitioner should examine closely how this will impact his work. The internet, television, telephone and radio have converged to take us into the age of instant communications, worldwide.

In the length of time it took news to circulate within a village of two hundred people two centuries ago, it is now possible for five billion people to become aware of an environmental disaster, war or the outcome of a major sporting event. The internet alone can disseminate news of a faulty or dangerous product to a worldwide audience in minutes.

The existence and speed of the new media should not be the only subject of concern for the PR practitioner. Its ownership is of equal importance. The period since the 1990s has seen the emergence of powerful international media holding companies – Rupert Murdoch's News Corp, AOL Time Warner, Disney, GE through NBC, Bertelsmann in Germany, and Berlusconi in Italy. They all wield immense power nationally, regionally and, increasingly, internationally.

Languages

Proficiency in more than your native language is a major advantage. It signals both your respect for and interest in people of other nations, in addition to allowing you to work more easily in a variety of environments. You will put interactions with your colleagues and audiences in other nations on a different and stronger footing.

However, a warning: do not imagine that a mere facility to speak foreign languages is sufficient to establish a worthwhile career in international public relations. I have known people with a knack for learning several languages who, sadly, had little of consequence to say in any of them, or were incapable of real communication.

Customs and etiquette

Respect for the customs and etiquette of each distinct society, country, nation or religion is essential. Not only should these customs be learned, they should be practised.

In the learning, you will often find the keys that open the door to improved communication, and that is your business. Without this knowledge, there can be no success, even for someone well qualified in all other respects.

International work experience

At a seminar of the Arthur W. Page Society entitled 'Public relations leadership in 2001: greater importance, greater competition', Frank Vogl pointed out that 'Globalisation will impact every aspect of the PR chief's work.' Stressing that the communication function must reflect the new international approach apparent in so many major corporations, Vogl referred to an article in the *Wall Street Journal* on 29 January 1996, which said that 'the executive suite is going global. With nearly every industry targeting fast-growing

foreign markets, more companies are requiring foreign experience for top management positions.'

Switch places

Even if you plan to make your career in an agency or consultancy, a spell of two or three years working in-house at a corporation, government department or other institution will be valuable experience. It will give you special insight into the minds of your clients and the pressures they face within their own organizations. Some in-house PR executives are sceptical of the advice given by their external counsellors because they suspect it is given without accountability for the outcome. Your advice will be more respected if your client knows that you have at one time stood in his shoes.

Survival of concept

It will be interesting to see if the concept of the global corporation survives. To do so, it will have to overcome some powerful forces of economic nationalism and protectionism, as well as the internal pressure in many corporations, which together work to break up enterprises into smaller pieces – either by geography or by the various lines of business in which they are engaged.

It will not be easy for most corporations, however big they are, to become truly global. This would mean a revolution in thinking which some will argue is against human nature. It means abandoning the enterprise's national identity, origins, centre of gravity and community commitment, at least to a certain extent.

When hard decisions have to be made, say on the matter of selective plant closures in an economic downturn, the global corporation should, in theory, make its choices based on economic imperatives, even to the extent of closing facilities at the heart of its original home office. Sentiment, lobbying, industrial and political unrest can often be powerful factors in changing the best plan on paper into one that stands the highest chance of being implemented.

Trust in institutions 2003

An increasingly important movement dedicated to reversing the tide of globalization and its institutions – the IMF, WTO and the World Bank – first came to general notice at the G7 meeting in Seattle in 1999. This uneasy alliance of anarchists, political activists and established NGOs is becoming a formidable opponent that reflects and focuses widespread public fear about some of the consequences of globalization led by international corporations.

The ascendancy of NGOs as trusted sources is shown in a recent round of research by Edelman. For the first time since tracking began, NGOs became the most trusted institutions in both the United States and Europe,

according to this inquiry among opinion leaders (Figure 26.1).

In Europe the four most trusted brands are NGOs – Amnesty International, World Wildlife Fund, Greenpeace and Oxfam. Meanwhile, Johnson & Johnson, Coca-Cola, Microsoft and Ford still sit atop the trust league table in the USA (Figures 26.2 and 26.3).

The specialization of international public relations

Specialization, globalization and communication technology are currently the three most potent forces affecting the practice of international public relations. Of these, specialization has had the longest history and the greatest impact since the 1970s.

Until the mid-1960s, public relations was a calling for generalists, whether they worked in-house at companies or in consultancies or agencies. As a youthful profession or craft, it also had to draw its recruits from other fields, mostly journalism, which at that time was also much more general than it is today.

It was clear this could not last. The huge horizon of PR activity, which defies easy

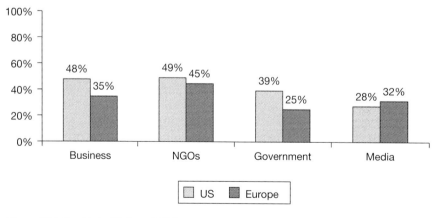

Figure 26.1 Trust in institutions, 2003
Source: Edelman survey, 2003

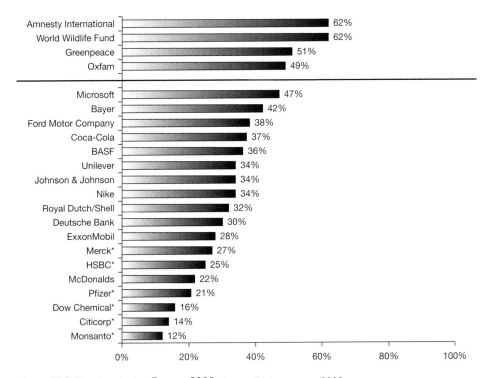

Figure 26.2 Brand evaluator: Europe, 2003 *Source*: Edelman survey, 2003

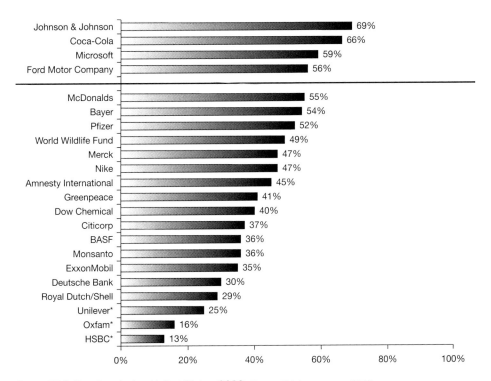

Figure 26.3 Brand evaluator: United States, 2003 *Source*: Edelman survey, 2003

definition, demanded that it be broken down into manageable components. And in the intervening years this has happened with a vengeance.

Why specialization?

Four factors are at work. The first is the increased recognition of the importance of public relations by different industries. This has meant the allocation of increasingly large budgets which, in turn, call for greater numbers of dedicated, qualified personnel.

The second is the accelerating complexity of almost every industry, as the knowledge base of science-driven fields of endeavour increases exponentially each year. The third factor is an increasingly educated and inquisitive consumer public served by a newly aggressive and growing media, which is itself structured on specialist lines.

The fourth force driving specialization has been the emergence of many industries and professions which traditionally had shunned communication. In some cases, as with law and medicine, self-imposed or common-law regulations forbade self-promotion. Many of those taboos have been torn down.

A careful look at the PR league tables shows that the engines of growth in recent years have been the boutique agencies which have offered specialist PR services of some kind. Even the major international full-service agencies mostly owe their successful growth to the performance of their individual specialist divisions.

Categories of specialization

What are these specialties, and how have they reshaped the public relations landscape?

There are three broad categories, and within each many specialties:

- *Industry, business or organization*. There are discrete PR specialties in healthcare and pharmaceutical products, consumer products and services, financial service organizations, technology, defence, professional services and many more.
- *PR practice areas*. No matter what industry, there are PR specialties in investor relations, public affairs, community relations, employee communication, sponsorship and event management.
- *Technical skills*. Within PR structures, there are specialist roles played by dedicated experts in publications, speechwriting, video production, media relations, CD-rom and website development, and a number of other functions.

The movement toward specialization began in the mid-1960s with pharmaceuticals and with the investor relations branch of financial public relations, specialties that are still the most dynamic and global within public relations. Technology began its dramatic growth two decades later.

Pharmaceuticals

No one ever dreamed that the day would arrive when prescription-only drugs would be advertised to the public in general print and TV media, as has been the case since the early 1990s in the United States (albeit under tight control). Pharmaceutical companies turned in increasing numbers to PR practitioners to step in and fill the informational and promotional gap to support what is now known as direct to consumer (DTC) marketing. In 2000 over $2.5 billion was spent on DTC advertising in

America, an increase of 212 per cent over five years, according to IMS (Table 26.2).

Financial

The growth of financial public relations has been powered by a battery of forces combining to create a major practice area.

Increasing individual wealth in many countries has multiplied the number of individual share owners. Unit trusts and mutual funds have attracted huge sums of money from investors, allowing them the chance to participate in baskets of stocks of every kind. The media coverage of the performance of companies makes heroes (or villains) out of those who lead them and has captivated large audiences previously unmoved by the making of money or the movements of markets.

Internationalization of money markets and the world's major stock exchanges and the introduction of 24-hour trading in stock shares and bonds have supercharged the growth of international financial communications.

Although both require a mastery of finance, public relations on behalf of financial institutions that sell products and services (insurance bank, brokers, mutual funds, mortgages, etc.) and investor relations are two quite different practices. Public relations for financial service organizations is usually considered to be a speciality within the category of consumer marketing communication.

Internationally, investor relations (IR) as a general rule does not even report through the PR channel to top management. Most public companies have vice presidents (or directors) of investor relations whose direct reporting line is to the chief financial officer, who in turn reports to the CEO. In only a few companies does the senior IR executive report to a chief communication officer.

Table 26.2 Industry sector: healthcare 2001 revenues

	Firm name	2001 revenue ($)
1	Fleishman-Hillard Inc.	60,050,000
2	Ketchum, Inc	49,265,000
3	Porter Novelli	41,100,000
4	Edelman Public Relations Worldwide	40,427,331
5	Ruder Finn Group	33,268,000
6	Ogilvy Public Relations Worldwide	29,562,958
7	Weber Shandwick Worldwide	28,244,697
8	Manning, Selvage & Lee	28,189,631
9	GCI GROUP/APCO Worldwide	24,542,462
10	Burson Marsteller	20,701,000
	Total top 10	355,351,079

Source: Council of PR Firms/*PR Week* rankings

IR in the United States even has its own professional organization, the National Institute of Investor Relations (NIRI). Similar organizations exist in other countries, operating outside the orbit of PR organizations.

Some of the largest IR/financial PR firms are not included in the rankings of PR firms because they do not reveal their income. The total is impressive. Possibly the largest in the specialty is Kekst & Company, in the United States. And Brunswick, followed by Financial Dynamics is the dominant power in the United Kingdom, where it represents twenty-five companies of the FTSE Index. Through a series of acquisitions and mergers by Citigate, a new global player has been created under the name Incepta. Reporting $266 million in fees for the year 2001, this firm entered the rankings as the fifth largest of all global PR firms.

Technology

Anyone practising public relations in the financial sector today will testify to the importance of technology as possibly the single most critical element in the economies of the developed world.

Technology stocks have, for some investors, even taken over as the barometer of performance of the stock market from the traditional baskets of blue chip shares such as the FTSE in the UK, the Dow Jones Index in the United States, and the Hang Seng in Hong Kong.

The 'bust' in technology stocks that began in 1999 and gathered steam, leading to the bursting of the dot.com bubble, had a ripple effect that was felt throughout the entire global economy. In 2001, every positive report from a major tech sector company was put under the microscope as a possible harbinger of a return to boom conditions for all shares.

This leadership among investments was the result of technology's explosive growth over three decades, with the arrival of Clive Sinclair in Britain and Steve Jobs, Paul Allen and Bill Gates in the United States.

The drivers of this phenomenon have been the internet, the personal computer (PC), the digital revolution and the mobile phone and personal digital assistant (PDA).

If money represents the building blocks of the new global economy, technology is the cement that will hold them together. These are the two most international specialties within the entire field of public relations. And according to the statistics of the Council of PR firms, in 2001 technology was still by far the largest specialty within public relations even though revenues dropped by 20 per cent from their record level in 2000 (Table 26.3).

Table 26.3 Industry sector: technology 2001 revenues

	Firm name	2001 revenue ($)
1	Weber Shandwick Worldwide	90,613,120
2	Fleishman-Hillard	88,020,000
3	Waggener Edstrom, Inc.	56,685,000
4	Hill and Knowlton	47,357,000
5	Porter Novelli	41,862,000
6	Brodeur Worldwide	39,600,000
7	Edelman Public Relations Worldwide	37,646,937
8	Ketchum	31,545,000
9	SCHWARTZ COMMUNICATIONS	30,375,804
10	Ogilvy Public Relations Worldwide	28,678,821
	Total top 10	492,383,682

Source: Council of PR Firms/*PR Week* rankings

Consumer products and services

In the broad consumer and lifestyles field there are PR specialties in food and nutrition, retail, home improvement, household durables, fashion and beauty, luxury goods, the home office, toys, entertainment and the arts, personal finance. Because of the size of the industries they encompass, some consumer sub-specialties deserve special mention.

Trade associations, not for profit organizations and business to business are further broad categories of public relations.

Specialties by practice

Specialization in PR occurs in practice areas as well as by industry category. Important practice areas are public affairs, which includes public policy, governmental relations and legislative affairs; environmental affairs; crisis and issues management; employee communication investor relations; corporate identity and reputation; sponsorship and event management and diversity.

Such practices can span a wide range of industries and organizations but, increasingly, individuals and agencies conduct their practice in a single industry or a small number of related industries.

Specialization by function

The final form of public relations specialization is found in the various functional skills called for in PR departments or agencies. They are the communication techniques and tools used by the international PR practitioner to implement his strategies and concepts. Because they have the capability of delivering messages and information in very targeted forms, the specialties can reach specifically identified audiences as well as the general public. Companies have organized to create and deliver these tools, directly for corporate communication departments or as subcontractors to PR agencies.

Functional specialties in constant use by PR practitioners are:

- publications, print production, graphic design;
- computer graphics;
- interactive communication, website development;
- video and film production and distribution;
- research;
- media tour planning and booking;
- advertisement creation, copywriting, layout, media planning;
- advertorial production;
- conference and event planning and management;
- media training.

Convergence

A phenomenon of the late 1990s is the recognition that the techniques of several specialties can be combined for more powerful marketing PR results that better meet the demands of a more sophisticated consumer. The following description is excerpted from an article by my colleague, Nancy Turett, managing director of Edelman Healthcare Worldwide on how 'convergence' is being applied in the health sector. It can be applied equally in other industry sectors such as technology, consumer or business to business.

Now, consumers are, themselves, the influentials. In many cases, it is the consumer who alerts the clinician to a novel treatment or new use for a medication that he or she has learned about from the media, the internet, or direct marketing. Through advocacy groups, it is often consumers who are deciding where research dollars are spent, and increasingly, how the research should be conducted.

Healthcare marketing today is increasingly calling for a melding of the creativity and mass appeal of traditional consumer marketing with the credibility and professional targeting associated with ethical pharmaceutical marketing. In Convergence Marketing, for example, target publications for a new osteoporosis diagnostic device might include Redbook, for a new fertility drug they might include GQ, and for a cholesterol drug they might include Bon Appetit. A programme venue could be a hotel or hospital health fair, but marketers should also open their eyes to other sites, including sports events, day care and senior centers, shopping malls and airports. The 'professional' audiences that influence consumers now reach far beyond doctors, nurses and pharmacists, and include coaches, hairstylists, mothers-in-law, travel agents, and so on. In addition, consumer advocacy groups have grown in number as well as influence, and building relationships with these opinion leaders now is as important as forging alliances with physician thought leaders'.

Study of 100 companies

A major benchmarking survey, conducted in 1997 by Edelman Public Relations Worldwide, the Medill School of Journalism and Opinion Research Corporation, sheds some light on how companies organize themselves to handle corporate communication. One hundred international companies participated. Here are some of the more interesting findings about reporting lines and infrastructure. These findings are broadly confirmed by late studies involving global corporations.

Of the top communication officials 60 per cent are at the vice president/vice chair level. Nearly 2 in 10 hold the title of director, and 1 in 10 are senior vice presidents. The remaining 13 per cent hold the following titles: manager (8 per cent), corporate vice president (3 per cent) and executive vice president (2 per cent). The senior-most communicators report directly to the CEO at 54 per cent of the companies surveyed. For those communicators who do not report directly to the CEO, 30 per cent report to the vice president, senior vice president or vice chair level of the organization. Regardless of direct lines of reporting, 93 per cent, nearly two-thirds of the most senior communicators, counsel with the CEO at least weekly and 15 per cent counsel with the CEO on a daily basis. Although survey respondents reported a variety of functional communication areas for which senior-most

communicators are primarily responsible, the core public relations functions are much better represented at this senior level than are other areas such as advertising or marketing. Nearly one-third of these senior-most communicators have corporate communication as their primary functional responsibility, followed by public relations (16 per cent) and public affairs (12 per cent).

The range of specific functions which fall under the corporate communication umbrella is becoming more diverse. More than 4 in 10 report that corporate communication maintains final oversight for advertising, marketing and promotional activities. Surprisingly, more than 10 per cent are also directly responsible for customer service at their respective organizations. Nearly 9 in 10 respondents indicate the use of external communication agencies at corporate headquarters, with more than 7 in 10 also using external agencies at the discretion of each business unit. Further, more than 5 in 10 also employ external communication agencies within their various geographic regions. Only 5 per cent do not use outside communication agencies. Overall, the annual operation budget (excluding salaries) for corporate communication activities was reported as follows:

Corporate communication responsibilities

- Media relations: 99 per cent
- Crisis/issues management: 93 per cent
- Employee communication: 88 per cent
- Corporate identity/image: 83 per cent
- Financial communication/investor relations: 75 per cent
- Research and measurement: 75 per cent
- Community relations/corporate philanthropy: 74 per cent

- Advertising, marketing and promotions: 43 per cent
- Government affairs: 35 per cent
- Customer service: 11 per cent

Global corporate communication budget (US$ equivalent):

- Less than $1 million: 25 per cent
- Greater than $1 million, but less than $5 million: 39 per cent
- Greater than $5 million, but less than $10 million: 11 per cent
- Greater than $11 million, but less than $15 million: 4 per cent
- Greater than $20 million: 15 per cent

It is customary for most companies to draw a clear line between communication in the 'home country' of operations and in international operations, with one person assigned to be responsible for management of communication in non-domestic markets.

There are good practical reasons why the separate role of the international PR manager within corporations continues to exist: most companies have a long history in their own communities and know their way around the local and national media, the influential groups important for the business, their political representatives and their customers. They are less certain of themselves in their overseas markets, which vary widely in almost every respect. An international PR manager who makes it his business to be knowledgeable about these markets and can manage a network of widely dispersed PR representatives is worth his weight in gold.

In a more recent survey among corporations in the United States, Europe, Asia and Latin America, conducted for Edelman by Professor Rob Wakefield, the PR activities and procedures of respondents were measured against a list of criteria. These criteria were chosen to determine the degree of sophistication, or development, of the firm's public relations. The results showed that it was not the very largest firms that were 'best in class'. This honour went to medium-to-large organizations with a headquarters in Europe.

The Wakefield evolution model

- *Early evolution*: Few resources, little interaction between HQ and local units.
- *Moderate evolution*: Growing resources, incomplete local staff, little or no HQ authority.
- *Advanced evolution*: Almost complete resources, better trained PR personnel, incomplete HQ – local units co-ordination.
- *Complete evolution*: Full staff, trained PR officers in every unit; interaction for mutual goals (Figure 26.4).

The qualifications of the international PR manager might be quite different from those of an executive who needs only to operate in the home market. Some of these qualities are described in Chapter 1.

Briefly, he will need to be culturally aware, patient, open-minded and inquisitive about alien customs and government procedures, with the ability to work with people from a variety of nations. At the same time, the international executive must never become detached from the 'mother company' and totally concentrate on the non-domestic operations. One vital role is to act as a bridge to the PR staff overseas who need and rely on him to be their link to headquarters, the conduit of policies and news. Never underestimate how most employees who work a

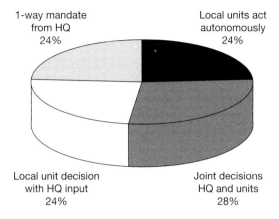

Figure 26.4 Strategic decision making

great distance from headquarters feel starved of information. Finally, he is the coach and inspiration who transmits that most indefinable but, arguably, most important element: the corporate culture.

Qualities of good PR consultants

Over and above the qualities needed by *all* PR practitioners, the following are those required of agency executives:

- Observe the successes and failures of techniques employed for other clients and bring this knowledge and experience to bear for the benefit of clients you are currently serving. Achieve mastery and knowledge of the subcontracting services available to the agency that will benefit clients.

- Use the resources and expertise of other professionals within the agency when faced with a complex problem.

- Sharpen your creative edge by maintaining regular contact with other professionals in the firm.

- Maintain strong powers of analysis, presentation and creativity, because an agency has to sell its services in competition with other agencies. In short, consultants have to win the right to practise public relations.

- Understand budgeting and business management, vital elements for a career in a PR organization.

- Keep abreast of media developments, new communication techniques and the current mood of public opinion on a variety of issues, if your advice is to be valued as smart, objective and reliable.

- Manage your own time expertly, allocating it appropriately among client contact, programme execution, monitoring results, reporting to the client and maintaining direct contact with the media and other publics.

- Though difficult, the right time blend must be achieved because the client pays for a combination of expertise and time.

CHAPTER 27

Ethics and the corporate communicator

Albert S. Atkinson

What is understood by the word ethics? Critically, what contribution does a corporate communicator make to the ethical debate within today's company boardrooms? Here, the author charts the historical role of corporate communicators in 'creating a soul' for the company; and the specific role played by corporate communication officials in the financial reporting of companies. The events of Enron and other high profile scandals have raised the spectre of corporate greed and the lack of corporate governance as primary reasons for the collapse of organizations, with much of the criticism directed at accounting firms and their procedures for monitoring business. Whilst the accounting world is now actively addressing financial issues derived from these scandals, there are nevertheless clear lessons to be learned by corporate communication professionals, both in-house and outsourced.

A consideration of ethics based upon the definitions below requires some consideration of conduct and morality. ('*Ethics*' – 1. the study of standards of conduct and moral judgement; moral philosophy. 2. a treatise on this study; book about morals. 3. *the system or code of morals of a particular philosopher, religion, group profession, etc.*) It is a concept that is difficult to discuss and while there is immediate understanding of when it is lacking, its presence is often viewed as naive or weak. While much of the trust upon which transactional business is based relies upon its existence it does not occupy a significant place in the business school's focus. It would appear that perhaps more attention should be paid to incorporating ethics into our everyday business activity.

The fall of the dot.com industries and such giants as Enron, WorldCom, Global Crossings, Quest Communications International, Inc., Tyco and so many other firms, during the years 2000 and 2001, has brought forth a plethora of disclosures of corporate wrongdoing. Much of this is attributed to the failure of accounting firms and corporate boards to exercise appropriate governance. During this time much discussion has centred on the accounting procedures being used and how the greed of corporate officers has led to the downfall of companies and the subsequent loss of millions of dollars. These millions are represented in jobs cut or lost by business failures, the pension losses affecting thousands of employees and the huge losses in the stock market.

For a time there was some outcry as to who would be punished for these failures and violations of principles. There was castigation of accounting firms and of the investment bankers whose analysts failed to disclose the irregularities and fallacious reporting. The press was on hand to point out the inequities and every politician from local to state to federal was involved in some form of investigation.

A Gallup poll, done in late 2001, showed in its annual gauge of the honesty and ethics of different professions that people placed business executives at a 25 per cent level while firefighters ranked 90 per cent, nurses at 83 per cent, US military at 81 per cent, stockbrokers were at 19 per cent, and advertising practitioners were at 11 per cent (Table 27.1). These percentages were a measure of those who indicated that these professions were very high or high in ethical practices. (Gibson D., 2002) Data Source: Gallup News Service.

Such polls and information can be significantly biased and if individually reviewed can be found wanting; however in view of the need for trust in the capital markets to ensure a stable environment for business growth and development the position of accountants and business executives is disturbing.

Certainly, the accounting profession has reacted to the unfavourable publicity with new guidelines and there have been many articles written about how certain practices have been changed to ensure that proper accounting procedures are followed.

Throughout all the press and business news about the collapse little was said about the corporate communicator and their place in all this. While accountants provide the financials and corporate executives provide the direction, the corporate communicator provides the words – often of late words that have not reflected the true situation of the company. What are the ethical boundaries involved? Is there a place in all of this for ethics and what if any ethics are being taught to the corporate leader today?

The role of corporate communication has its basis in the advertising and public relations attempts of the corporations in the late nineteenth and early twentieth centuries to provide an image for their companies and their

Table 27.1 Ethics by profession

Profession	% saying 'very high' or 'high'
Firefighters	90
Nurses	83
US military	81
Police	68
Pharmacists	68
Medical doctors	66
Clergy	64
Engineers	60
College teachers	58
Dentists	56
Accountants	41
Bankers	34
Journalists	29
Business executives	25
Congressmen	25
Senators	25
Auto mechanics	22
Stockbrokers	19
Lawyers	18
Labor union leaders	17
Insurance salespeople	13
Advertising practitioners	11

Source: Star Ledger, Newark, NJ, 17 February

products. Its purpose to a large degree has been to 'create the soul' of the corporation, as noted by Roland Marchand. Marchand traces the use by many corporations of advertisements that portrayed the corporation has having a high moral value, and often linked small towns and the initial small businesses to their now hugeness in terms of hard work, artisanship, and power. The purpose was to gain the allegiance of the people across the country, and gain a presence in their community.

Throughout this period the large corporations were gaining the position and status of real entities and the messages were designed to support this growth and overcome the fears of the general public that the corporation lacked conscience. The efforts were initially to demonstrate that 'Victorian' values were part of the corporations being paternalistic, linking their business to family and community (Marchand, 1998).

In the year 2002 much was written concerning the lack of accuracy in corporate financial reporting, as well as the attempts to hide unhealthy financial situations. There was a twenty-year period of deregulation of corporations accompanied by almost the same period of continual growth in the economy and in corporate profits. It was a period of great change in business operations and the technology supporting these businesses. The advance of the computer, the internet, telecommunications and globalization of business served to accelerate the rate of change. While the accounting firms may have played a significant part in reporting financial data, the corporate communication professional has certainly had a large part in the activity as well. Some of the creative ways that losses are downplayed and that wordsmithing has been used to cover detrimental news demonstrate how communication professionals have played their part.

As these changes occur and as society adjusts to the changing environment of business several serious complications have arisen. The employee has become increasingly responsible for his own welfare. After some three decades of the government being responsible for the welfare of its people through such programmes as Social Security, Medicare, welfare supports, pension regulation, and various laws affording the right to work to a multitude of people, there has been a shift in power back to the corporation. Many corporations have found that layoffs and labour reductions are greeted by a rise in stock price. The adoption of 'pay for performance' for executive compensation seems appropriate at first glance and works well during a rising business cycle. The link to stock price as being an indicator of that performance has led to executives acting at times only in the short-term interest and can create some ethical dilemmas during a business downturn. There has also been a transfer of the previously corporate responsibility for health insurance, pension benefits and long-term employment to the individual. The employee must now select the health care plan that best serves his or her needs, and in most cases participate financially in it on an increasing scale. The employee must maintain a skill level to maintain employment, often obtaining these skills outside of the work environment. The employee in many situations has been given the responsibility to manage their own retirement funding either through 401(k) programmes offering some degree of selectivity and individual retirement accounts (IRAs) from their own salaries. Gone is the paternalistic approach to employees that was so much a part of the business environment of thirty to fifty years ago. But often these very plans offered by the company are subject to investment in the companies' own stock. This is part of the tragedy of Enron, that 90 per cent of the asset value of their 401(k) was in company stock. Similarly, Lucent Technologies stock, which also lost 90 per cent of its value due in large part to financial misrepresentation, comprised 70 per cent of its employees plan assets.

The deregulation of utilities and other businesses has also brought to the consumer an increasing need to take responsibility for themselves. The choices in services have never been so vast: what telephone service to use? What electric, gas or other power provider should one select? Which bank to chose? What types of savings plans are best? Who to invest with? These are all questions that the everyday employee did not face thirty years ago.

During this time of rapid change there has been a continued acceptance that corporations will do their reporting properly and fully. Such actions are most important to a capital marketplace. Financial reports form the basis of corporate valuation and as such become the basis for investment and stock prices.

It is important to remember that as the responsibility for retirement was transferred from the corporations to the employee the number of individual stock investors has risen to an all-time high. The need for confidence in the capital markets is essential to both employees, and ultimately to the corporations and the governments who depend upon investment (and taxes).

Taking all of the above into consideration demonstrates the importance that financial reporting be beyond reproach. Both those within the corporations and their auditors must treat it as an awesome responsibility. However, with deregulation, increased competition and the increasing pressure for better performance each quarter this has not always been the case.

We have only to witness Enron, Global Crossing and the fall of the various 'dot.com' enterprises to observe that this is not the case. How many other companies are in the same situation or very close to it is an unknown.

The ability to invest with any degree of certainty is dependent upon factual financial information, delivered in a clear and comprehensible format that is uniform and replicable across industries. This is the basis for the stock market and the development of valuation. There now exists an 'investor class' of 100 million Americans. Over half of the adult population of the United States has invested in securities through direct investment in companies, through mutual funds or through their 401(k)'s.

Certainly with the events of Enron and Arthur Andersen much criticism has been directed towards the accounting industry, but much must be directed towards the corporate communicators as well. The annual reports, the quarterly reports, the press releases, and speeches delivered all failed to reveal the problems and in fact may prove to have been presented to cover up the problems. Not that these two entities are alone in taking any bad news and making it good news or failing to bring any attention to it.

Thus the crux of the concern: ethics and the corporate communication professional and the reporting of financial data, and what if anything can be done about it?

To see what was being done in the educational process concerning ethics courses I selected a number of universities offering advanced degrees in both accounting and communication (master's programmes). I found that out of thirteen universities offering advanced accounting degrees only one required an ethics course while of the twelve universities offering advanced communication degrees none made ethics a required course,

Table 27.2 Business ethics courses

University	Programme	Ethics required	Ethics elective	Other
University of Pennsylvania	Wharton	Yes	No	Accounting
University of Pennsylvania	Annenburg	No	No	Communication
University of Chicago	MBA	No	No	Accounting
Stanford University	MBA	Yes	No	Accounting
University of Texas, Austin	MBA	No	No	Accounting and communication
Seton Hall University	MS	No	No	Accounting
Seton Hall University	MA	No	Yes	Communication
Fairleigh Dickinson University	MS	No	No	Accounting
Fairleigh Dickinson University	MA	No	Yes	Communication
NYU Stern	MA		No	MS, accounting
NYU Stern	MA	No	No	Communication
University of Illinois, Urbana	MS	No	No	Accountancy
Pace University	MS	No	Yes	Accountancy
Northwestern University	MBA	No	No	Accounting
Northwestern University	MS	No	No	Communication
University of Southern Calif.	MA	No	No	Communication
University of Southern Calif.	MA	No	No	Accounting
Rutgers University	MBA	No	No	Accounting
Rutgers University	MCIS	No	No	Communication
Monmouth University	MBA	No	No	Accounting
Monmouth University	MA	Yes	No	Communication
Kent State University	MS	No	No	Accounting
Kent State University	MA	No	No	Communication
University of Hartford	MSPA	No	No	Accounting
University of Hartford	MA	No	No	Communication
Baylor University	MAc	No	No	Accounting
Baylor University	MA	No	No	Communication
University of Kansas	MAc	No	No	Accounting
University of Kansas	MA	No	No	Communication

Source: Al Atkinson, personal research © 2002

but two did offer a course as an elective (Table 27.2). When I reviewed the requirements for these same institutions for their MBA programmes I found that approximately 50 per cent had a course in 'business ethics' as a requirement.

Selection of schools was not scientific but based on the 'US News Annual Guide for Graduate Schools (2001)'. I looked to personal knowledge of schools of communication, except where the accounting school also had a communication advanced degree. Additional help was obtained from the National Communication Association and the American Institute of Certified Public Accountants websites.

Does offering an ethics course or making it a requirement have any effect on the actions of the participants at a later point in their life? That is an unknown. But certainly the concept of making it a part of the curriculum for any advanced degree in business would at least expose the student to some thought processes that could prove beneficial to them in the future.

A survey done by Donald Morris and published in *Business Ethics Quarterly*, volume 11, issue 4 entitled 'Business Ethics Assessment Criteria: Business V. Philosophy – Survey Results' discussed several issues concerning differences when the courses were taught by the philosophy professors or by the business professors. This study defined and established assessment criteria and ranked various courses based upon these criteria. What seems clear from this survey is that there is no overwhelming sentiment among those teaching business ethics that what they are doing is attempting to educate people to be more ethical. The primary exception to this relates to those who believe that if students can be educated to be more rational or logical (whatever is intended by those terms) then they will act more ethically (Morris, 2001: 635).

There is very little written about the role of the corporate communicator and ethics and financial reporting. The ethics of financial reporting seems to be directed towards the accountants only, yet much of the public perception of a corporation is based more upon the corporate communicator than the accountant. It is how the information is presented that makes the difference.

Nearly every corporation has corporate creeds, statements from CEOs as to their own convictions, ethics hot lines, codes of conduct, and other programmes in place to establish the ethical standards for the organization. There are many scholarly papers written supporting ethics in business and suggesting how to implement programmes to encourage ethical practices. The reality of practice is however somewhat different.

The very basis for a corporation's existence, corporate law, could be construed as to inhibit executives from being socially responsible or ethical. The law covering the corporation states 'the directors and officers of a corporation shall exercise their powers and discharge their duties with a view to the interests of the corporation and of the shareholders'. The very law that creates the corporate purpose, distilled to its essence, says that the people who run corporations have a legal duty to shareholders, and that duty is to make money. Failing this can leave directors and officers open to being sued by shareholders. (Robert Hinkley, 2002).

MBA programmes often require ethics courses and corporations tend to have 'codes of conduct' to which all employees are subject. The view from the trenches is very different, and it offers little comfort for senior executives who are trying to implement corporate ethics programmes, for academics developing philosophy-based approaches to business ethics, or for those who hope that communitarian values will soon take root in corporate soil.

A study, performed by Badaracco and Webb, which is based principally upon in-depth interviews with thirty recent graduates of the Harvard MBA programme, revealed several disturbing patterns. First, in many cases, young managers received explicit instructions to do things they believed were sleazy, unethical, or sometimes illegal. Second, corporate ethics programmes, codes of conduct, mission statements, hotlines and the like provided little help. Third, many of the young managers believed that their company's executives were out of touch on ethical issues, either because they were too busy or because they sought to avoid responsibility. Fourth, the young managers resolved the dilemmas they faced largely on the basis of personal reflection and individual values, not through reliance on corporate credos, company loyalty, the exhortations of senior executives, philosophical principles, or religious reflection (Badaracco and Webb, 1995).

The National Investor Relations Institute (NIRI) has taken an active role in suggesting methods of improving how financial information should be communicated. This action by NIRI is most welcome as they as an organization have recognized the importance of the ethical reporting of financial data. They have taken the courageous position of making the following recommendations.

Companies should help investors understand how a company makes money and it should be communicated in plain English.

Investors should know what the company's GAAP (generally accepted accounting principles) earnings are before being told that the adjusted earnings are on a pro forma basis. GAAP may not provide investors with a completely accurate picture of a company's performance, but it is the best thing we have until a better system is created.

The SEC has recently called for an expansion of the MD&A (management disclosures and announcements). NIRI agrees with this. Companies should explain in plain English what are the key factors that drive the company's business, what significant trends exist that could impact the company's performance going forward, and other key factors that affect the company's business both on a historical and prospective basis. When companies notice a significant change in one or more or these factors, they should consider, on a current basis, disclosing that information broadly to investors.

The SEC should examine whether the 'Management Responsibility for Financial Reporting' section of the annual report (Form 10-K) should cover all written disclosures. Whether it should be required instead of optional as it currently is, and whether to require management to formally affirm quarterly, instead of annually, that its disclosure is complete and current.

They recommend that companies that have off-balance sheet businesses disclose that information to investors in an aggregated form. Companies should consider broadly disseminating that information, preferably in a company news release and posted on the company's website. The disclosure should include the business purpose of the investment, what current or special charges were recorded to set up the entity, contingent liabilities, if any, and what the impact would be on the earnings if they were consolidated.

As recently proposed by the SEC, companies should report insider transactions on a current basis and there should also be current reporting of material compensation actions, such as annual option grants, instead of waiting for the annual proxy to be published.

Companies should have formal 'window periods' that govern when insiders may buy and sell securities and the dates of those windows should be published so investors know when they are.

Companies should be more aggressive in educating employees regarding the benefits and risks of owning the company's stock (Thompson, 2002).

NIRI is a professional association of corporate officers and investor relations consultants responsible for communication among corporate management, the investing public and the financial community. With over 5,000 members in 35 chapters around the United States, NIRI sets the highest standards in education designed to advance the practice of investor relations and meeting the growing professional development needs of those engaged in the field.

Based upon the material available and the pressures being applied by regulatory processes and the understanding that 'trust' in the capital markets is essential to continued investment and growth I believe some steps will be taken to improve the quality of financial reporting. This offers a unique opportunity to the corporate communicators to utilize their talents: informing their stockholders as to what their companies do and how they make money, as well as the opportunities open to those who invest in those companies. Perhaps too it is time to support the change in the law that creates corporations. A possible addition to the phrase 'the directors and officers of a corporation shall exercise their powers and discharge their duties with a view to the interests of the corporation and of the shareholders' to include 'but not to the expense of the environment, human rights, the public safety, the communities in which the corporation operates or the dignity of its employees' (Hinkley, 2002). While such a step is doubtful, certainly the need to ensure that corporate reporting does not undermine the very foundation of corporate investment upon which the market place relies is essential.

The attempt to control the accounting industry by making it responsible for its actions has led to an increasing number of lawsuits over the past several years, and has also led to a significant increase in political donations from major accounting firms. The links between government enforcing regulations and the amount of monies being spent on the political scene is disturbing. The tendency to move towards influencing legislation to limit exposure from suits brought due to the failure to provide accurate accounting by the very companies being paid to provide this accounting is cause for concern in itself.

From what I have found to date there has not been much study performed in this area. It is most complex and almost confessional in nature. It may be that additional emphasis needs to be placed on this topic during courses. But in reality the corporation needs to reaffirm the importance of honesty and propriety in its dealings with its employees and the public at the highest executive levels to truly make a change in current practice.

The role of the corporate communicator remains challenging. There will continue to be a requirement to 'soften' or 'control' the effect of 'bad' news whether financial or otherwise. There will continue to be pressure to create the perception that all is fine even when it is not. There is a strong probability that the accounting profession will have some degree of regulation that, if enforced, will require more appropriate disclosure of the facts. But I would be most surprised to see any such regulation providing any direction for the corporate communication professional.

REFERENCES

Gibson, D. (2002) 'Object of devotion', Star Ledger, 17 February.

Hinkley, R. (2002) 'How corporate law inhibits ethics', Business Ethics, January–February, 4–5.

Marchand, R. (1998) Creating the Corporate Soul, Berkeley, CA: University of California Press.

Morris, D. (2001) 'Business ethics assessment criteria', Business Ethics Quarterly, 11(4), 623–50.

US News (2001) US News Annual Guide for Graduate Schools, New York: US News.

RECOMMENDED FURTHER READING

Badaracco, J., Jr and Webb, A. (1995) 'Business ethics', *California Management Review*, 37(2), 8–28.

Dugan, I. (2002) 'Before Enron, greed helped sink the respectability of accounting', *Wall Street Journal*, 14 March.

Thompson, L. Jr (2002) 'Statement before the SEC Financial Disclosure and Audit Oversight Round-table', 6 March, Washington, DC.

CHAPTER 28

The new frontier for public relations

Richard R. Dolphin

International public relations (iPR) is recognized as one of the most rapidly growing areas of public relations but perhaps one of the least understood. In this chapter the author looks at the issue of international public relations from the perspective of an empirical study conducted by the author in British organizations focusing on the role of international public relations within a co-ordinated marketing communication strategy. He addresses the management of the relationship between organizations and those audiences overseas who might be considered significant international stakeholders as key variables in iPR.

Pavlik noted some twenty years ago, that international public relations (iPR) was one of the most rapidly growing areas of the profession – and one of the least understood. The chairman of one of the largest PR firms entitled his introduction to the 1999 ICO summit 'Public Relations – truly a global business' (Hehir, 1999). Comor (2001) suggests that a central pillar in this growth is the recent explosion of electronic forms of transnational communications.

Scholars of management *are* hampered by the lack of an established body of knowledge about the fledgeling domain of iPR – and of practice in different parts of the world (Krishnamurthy and Dejan, 2001). But, accord-

ing to Culbertson and Chen (1996), iPR has spread rapidly throughout the world; and Taylor (2001) suggests that for practitioners the desire for competency in the skills necessary for the successful execution of iPR grows yearly. Taylor and Kent (1999) suggest that further knowledge about iPR is important in order to explore the assumptions underlying differing national practices; and to examine differing practices worldwide.

Although Botan reported in 1992 that 130 articles had been published on iPR, the present body of scholarly knowledge makes only cursory reference to the world outside Europe and to the United States in particular (Krishnamurthy and Dejan, 2001). Taylor and

Kent (1999) suggest that detailed introspection may persuade PR practitioners that many of the assumptions guiding western public relations are simply *not applicable* to the growing field of iPR.

It becomes increasingly critical to assess ways in which PR professionals can prepare themselves to meet the growing challenges of communicating with publics of various countries and cultures (Krishnamurthy and Dejan, 2001). Perhaps not surprisingly one of the most interesting trends in recent years has been the growing use of professional PR consultants by national governments (Manheim and Albritton, 1983); Schuybroek noted in 1999 that there were at least fifteen PR networks offering these services worldwide.

Kruckeberg and Starck suggested (1988) that the practice of iPR offers an active attempt to restore and maintain a sense of community in an increasingly global world – a world where communities become by the day ever more disparate and fragmented. PR practitioners have a social responsibility to understand and respect the concerns of the diverse populations with which they communicate (Guzley, 1995): therefore mutual understanding is needed between organizations and international publics (Taylor, 2001).

Public relations only crossed the ocean and became accepted as a management tool in Europe after the Second World War (Vercic et al., 2000). But third world public relations is largely a communication, information generating function; not a management function (van Leuven and Pratt, 1996). However, Kruckeberg (1996) reports that sophisticated public relations is being practised in the Middle East; an emphasis on management function that reflects the original association of iPR with business (Zaharna, 2000). Taylor and Kent (1999) relate that since Independence in 1963 the Malaysian government[1] has used PR for nation building – but is slowly shifting to a new focus on market development.

Grunig et al. (1995) noted that most of the conditions that foster professional PR in the United States may not exist in (and around) organizations in other countries; so, perhaps, professionals practise different models of public relations elsewhere in the world. Al-Enad (1990) suggested that the forces behind the evolution of public relations in western societies were not always found in developing countries. He questioned why, therefore, public relations is needed in such cases and asked if professionals may be employing models that *may or may not* be effective in the countries in which they are used.

Sriramesh (1992) found that most Indian respondents defined public relations as publicity; while Grunig et al. (1995) found that Greek practitioners see public relations as primarily focused on image building. Lyra (1991) reported that many Greek practitioners paid media contacts to place news stories! In other countries, Russia for instance, the PR profession has only recently begun to evolve into a recognizable structure (Guth, 2000); although interest there in public relations does continue to grow.

Global – *or international*?

There is little consensus about whether it is realistic to talk of the existence of a truly international, let alone global, model of PR best practice (Moss, 2001). But, almost all the PR theory building activity centres in the United States or in a few western European countries (Krishnamurthy and Dejan, 2001). Some scholars question whether public relations can be practised in a similar way in different countries or whether localized approaches are necessary (Grunig *et al.*, 1995). For instance Taylor and Kent (1999) report that public relations in Asia is often influenced by Eastern theology and hierarchic relationships.

Some refer to iPR as *globalization* (Zaharna, 2000); referred to by Hill and Knowlton's CEO as one of the most important changes affecting the function of public relations today (Mellow, 1989). Botan (1992) discussed ethnocentrism – which in public relations is the belief that what is known about it in one country is applicable across all countries.

In 1989 Wilcox *et al.* defined iPR as *the planned and organized effort of a company, institution or government[2] to establish mutually beneficial relations with the publics of other nations.* Anderson (1989) used the terms *global* and *international* to distinguish between public relations practised in the same way throughout the world and public relations customized for each culture.

Differentiated does not necessarily mean that messages have to be altered wholesale; they can be adapted to appeal to identified customer needs (Kitchen and Wheeler, 1999). In endorsing a strong version of the *global* approach, Sharp (1992) noted that the principles regarding *what PR is – and can do – remain the same worldwide.* Botan (1992) came to the opposite conclusion. Grunig *et al.* (1995) suggest that emerging from the merits of two extreme positions seems a consensus that the ideal model for iPR lies somewhere in the middle.

Synnott and McKie (1997) suggested that the political system in a country might well influence that country's perception and use of PR; while, Krishnamurthy and Dejan (2001) propose three factors of the relevant country:

1   *infrastructure*: political system, economic development, level of activism, culture and media environment;

2   *environment*;
3   *societal culture*;

that might impact upon iPR practice.

In 1992 Baskin and Aronoff suggested that iPR has three main functions:

1   representing a corporation in its home market;
2   bridging the communication gap between foreign management and home management;
3   facilitating communication in the host country.

Target audiences

The general public is not always the target of public relations (Taylor and Kent, 1999). Overseas government officials may be the focus (Haug and Koppang, 1997); such a relationship will influence the practice of public relations (Taylor and Kent, 1999). Taylor and Kent suggest that in the developing world those who control access to scarce resources may be a key public.

Key management role

Since the 1970s, public relations has matured within the advanced western economies into a modern, sophisticated management function (Moss, 2001). It continues to evolve as a strong discipline (Krishnamurthy and Dejan, 2001) playing a key role in the success of many organizations with a well developed local body of knowledge – in both Europe and Australia in particular (Moss, 2001).

Botan (1992) discussed PR functions, roles and goals and how they vary between countries; while Van Leuven and Pratt (1996) identified variations deriving from:

- communication infrastructure;
- market economy;
- political stability;
- linguistic/cultural integration.

Unchanged role

Moss (2001) suggests that in many parts of the world public relations remains wedded to its publicity origins. But, Krishnamurthy and Dejan (2001) suggest that, in political systems that do not value public opinion, PR tends to be propagandist (although Al-Enad (1990) questions whether government institutions in *authoritative societies* care about public opinion).

However, Krishnamurthy and Dejan note that varying stages of democratization offer different opportunities and challenges to PR professionals. They suggest that the western definition of public relations assumes a democratic political structure where competing groups seek authority and legitimacy through the power of public opinion.

International PR practitioners must understand the extent of media outreach[3] in countries where they operate. But that media may not provide an effective means for wide dissemination of organizational messages in every country.

In developing countries the media reaches a fairly homogenous small segment of the total population; accordingly, in order to reach the largest populace the iPR consultant will have to think of other media that reach out to untapped publics (Krishnamurthy and Dejan, 2001).

IT impact

Among PR practitioners, increasingly complex relationships must be nurtured satisfactorily; and this has, by and large, to be done through unproven means (Kruckeberg, 1996). The computer has become central to PR activity and the global potential of the internet suggests more intercultural activity (Neff, 1998).

Interactive communication technologies are providing groups and individuals with unprecedented capacities to form meaningful transnational networks (Comor, 2001). The rapid expansion of communication technology has increased the dissemination of information (although the level of development of a country's infrastructure vastly influences a practitioner's ability to plan and implement communication programmes). This rapid increase in international communication through emergent IT is putting PR practitioners at the forefront of managing relationships with peoples of varied nations and cultures (Krishnamurthy and Dejan, 2001).

Culture

Taylor and Kent (1999) suggest that detailed introspection may well persuade PR practitioners that many of the assumptions guiding western PR are simply *not applicable* to the growing field of iPR. Taylor (2001) suggests that it is important to remember that iPR is always intercultural PR.

Intuitively, one would posit that different cultures would require different PR theories and practice (Kruckeberg, 1996). In arguing that cultural distinctions among societies must affect the way that PR is practised within those societies Sriramesh and White (1992) lend credence to this assumption.

Kruckeberg (1996) notes that when they practise beyond their borders western PR practitioners face an extreme range of cultures; and that they will be challenged by culture-bound perspectives and assumptions. North American scholars Howard and Mathews (1986) noted that the astute practitioner recognizes that competence in the United States does not necessarily translate to competence in other countries.

For instance, Kruckeberg (1996) reports, Muslim culture heavily influences much Middle Eastern practice; while Gunn (1994) points to the strong influence of Bhuddism in Thai society – an influence that clearly affects the form of PR practice in Thailand. Guth (2000) notes the likelihood that Russian public relations will emerge with a distinct flavour reflecting the unique culture of that nation. Accordingly, Taylor (2001) refers to a real need for *cross-cultural sensitivity* from PR specialists. Scholars can look for parallels between their own culture and the host culture for shared similarities and potential differences. Such cultural knowledge may be used to develop campaigns that creatively incorporate features unique to a particular culture (Zaharna, 2000).

Two fields that appear on the surface to have little in common are *intercultural communication* and *iPR*. While intercultural communication has its roots in the academic field of anthropology iPR is very much a product of a practising profession (Zaharna, 2000). However, beneath the surface both are concerned with how culture influences communication.

Culture was seen as important, guiding three critical variables in communication:

1 verbal communication (Moss *et al.*, 1997 note that one aspect of culture, relevant to its relationship with public relations, is language);
2 non-verbal communication;
3 perception (Zaharna, 2000).

Communication influences, and is influenced by, culture. As Krishnamurthy and Dejan (2001) note, it behoves scholars of iPR to study how the cultures of individual countries affect the choice of PR strategies in those countries. Albert (1992) argues that in today's organizations the term *polycultural* may be more appropriate than multicultural. She proposes that while *multicultural* has been used primarily to designate activities involving minority groups *polycultural* refers better to multiple cultures.

Vasquez and Taylor (2000) propose that Botan (1992) captured the inherent paradox of the struggle to understand culture as a PR variable. His observation was that the very practices that enable western scholars to understand public relations in Japan and western Europe might actually blind us from seeing other enlightening practices.

Media relations

Before they are able to develop strategies for conducting effective media relations in any particular country, iPR practitioners must understand how the media operate – and who controls media content in that particular country (Krishnamurthy and Dejan, 2001). Sriramesh (1992) reported that in India many public information campaigns used folk media (such as dances and skits) *and that* some multinational corporations might want to follow the same strategy to communicate with various publics.

International strategies

Krishnamurthy and Dejan (2001) report a number of academics having proposed the formulation of global PR practices; for international marketing[4] implies that marketing must be co-ordinated across nation states. Kitchen and Wheeler (1999) suggest that Coca-Cola, McDonald's and Levi's are exemplars of the new global philosophy – corporations who operate with resolute constancy as if the world was a single large identical entity. The question is especially important for multinational organizations (Grunig *et al.*, 1995); but Budd (2001) reports that even Coca-Cola, pinup of a global brand, now advises *think local, act local*, versus its old slogan, *think global, act local*.

Issues management

Tixier (2000), in a survey of large Australian corporations, noted a major change facing communication specialists, the growing internationalization of issues identification. Budd (2001) notes that the velocity of events suggests the creation of an internal directorate charged with monitoring, assessing and reporting on trends in those parts of the world pivotal to the company's interests.

Ethics

Taylor (2001) suggests that issues of ethics have growing importance in international situations. Kruckeberg (1996) proposed that (as between a third world country and one in the west) corresponding PR ethics in (say) the Middle East, would be substantially different from those embraced in a first world country. Of course, ethics and legal issues need to be considered in the context of Islamic theory and Arabic law.

The research

Twenty-four organizations were approached through personal contact or by written request. Twenty-one (87.5 per cent) agreed to participate in the research.[5] Of those organizations interviewed only 45 per cent were involved in iPR; so the findings of this initial investigation are indicative. The findings suggest that more research is needed; but are not conclusive. Of those communicators involved with iPR some are not engaged all the time; for example, the bank spokesman commented *I deal with iPR when it touches on corporate reputation.*

However, 100 per cent of those who do practise iPR use the same techniques to communicate with audiences overseas as they use at home; none adopted a specific set of communication techniques for an overseas constituency. The communication executive at the tobacco company noted that *the techniques are the same.*

All respondents – whether they were involved in iPR or not – agreed that globalization is one of the big communication issues today; one likely to impact increasingly on communication practice. The consensus is that the approach (suggested by Anderson, 1989) that iPR involves communication customized for each culture is probably the way ahead. The communicator for the pharmaceutical organization (with satellite organizations worldwide) remarked *we communicate subtly different messages to our companies around the world:* while the rubber company spokesman commented *we have to translate into four languages.*

The recommendation from Grunig *et al.* (1995) that localized approaches are necessary was confirmed by 75 per cent of respondents; a drugs company spokesman noted that he spent *a lot of time ensuring the consistency of the messages – orchestrating them – making sure that they all work together internationally.* This remark was made in the context of responsibility for a wide range of audiences; in addition to communicating *in a wide range of countries.*

The spokesman for Scotland's largest brewer of lager – with responsibility for a brand exported to most corners of the globe – noted *we deal with particular publics in different ways.* This tends to suggest that the approach taken by Kitchen and Wheeler (1999) to adapt messages to appeal to identified customer needs is the one widely adopted. As the Scottish brewer remarked *we adopt a different emphasis where necessary.* He gave his company's launch of canned Tennent's Lager in China (where Bass have a joint venture) as one example where this had been done.

There is some evidence to support the views of Baskin and Aronoff (1992). The organizations interviewed all use public relations to represent their corporations in the home market *and* lead their company's efforts to bridge the communication gap between foreign management and home management. The communication executive at the pharmaceuticals group commented *I provide strategic leadership for the group and would manage serious international issues.* The spokesman for the airline specifically referred to his responsibility for facilitating communication in his host country. Referring to the US market – one of great importance to his company – he told the researcher that his company employed almost fifty staff in their New York office – all of whom were American – and all of whom were journalists. A specific approach, he explained, because his organization wished to convey appropriate messages and themes to audiences in that country.

Overseas *players* spoke to the researcher about the varying challenges facing them abroad. They discussed the differing profiles of international audiences. The rubber company spokesperson talked of communication

with suppliers in countries as diverse as those in continental Europe, Mexico, Portugal, China and India. A high street retailer (one having recently disposed of a subsidiary with offices in United States, Africa and India) commented *until three years ago I was responsible for public relations in those countries*; and referred to cultural differences between suppliers in all of them.

As noted, Krishnamurthy and Dejan (2001) see iPR emerging as a strong discipline with a key role to play in corporate strategies. The rubber company – an organization with developing interests in Mexico, in particular – commented that not only was iPR *difficult*; he elaborated that it was *still developing.*

This spokesperson referred to the growing number of factories opened by his organization around the world. He noted *we now have more factories outside the United Kingdom than within it* (the bulk being in the United States and Mexico) and discussed the challenges presented by this new communication phenomenon. Talking of the need for more local spokespeople he said *we need people on the ground as foot soldiers.*

Even a high street retailer – better known for its roots in Nottingham than in New York – referred to the fact that he gets involved *in international issues from time to time* and spoke of his need to deal with *international groups, politicians and media.*

Ovaitt (1988) suggested that iPR programmes might share strategic elements even if the strategies are implemented in different ways in different countries; and according to differing economic and political infrastructures. Van Leuven and Pratt (1996) argued that economic and political factors might impact on iPR programmes. This is confirmed by this research. Sixty per cent of the organizations interviewed communicated with audiences in third world countries; as well as those in the first world. All referred to the various ways in which differing national infrastructures impact upon iPR programmes.

As noted, Krishnamurthy and Dejan (2001) suggested that in some countries iPR tends to be propagandist. This research does not sustain this suggestion. One hundred per cent of respondents stated categorically that they saw no part of their communication role involved with any sort of propaganda anywhere – either at home or abroad. Neither was the issue of media outreach one of concern to those interviewed. On the other hand, all international interviewees were significant global players communicating either with satellite divisions abroad or with sophisticated publics; so this response might have been expected.

An example of the methods used to reach *sophisticated* audiences overseas was given by the pharmaceutical organization. The spokesperson mentioned the academic publications produced by his organizations and circulated worldwide – *worldwide, internationally driven* he remarked – which, he indicated, were a communication vehicle used to influence important research audiences around the world.

Twenty-five per cent of respondents do business around the world on a daily basis. Each confirmed that the computer has become central to their iPR activity, as Neff (1998) thought probable. Organizations like the rubber company manufacturing tyres in Mexico and the tobacco firm selling its products in India reported that they mainly used technology for communicating with employees. Evidence from the airline was that IT is being used increasingly to address local audiences with marketing PR messages – the US audience being one very obvious example.

The ability to communicate quickly with external consultants used abroad was also given; particularly by the tobacco company who, at the time that the researcher visited it, had engaged consultants to assist them *with a spat in India.* The spokesman referred to how little he used consultants generally; but found them useful in overseas markets; and giving the Indian example said *I have retained a PR consultancy to handle it.* Clearly, increasing use of IT – where the infrastructure has been developed – helps enormously.

All organizations with international operations spoke of the challenges presented by the need to produce iPR programmes in a context of cultural and societal distinctions; and all but two confirmed that these inevitably affect the way that iPR is practised within widely differing societies. As the telco spokesman remarked of the international communicator *he must know his audience.* One point made by the global airline was that these *cultural differences* are as apparent in first world countries like Canada, the United States and Australasia as they are in more remote parts of the globe.

The airline spokesman agreed with the academic who noted that the astute practitioner recognizes that competence in the United States does not necessarily translate into competence in other countries; speaking of his carefully chosen US media team, he explained that this was the reason that he only employed locally trained journalists.

Both the rubber and the pharmaceutical companies – between them having divisions in most parts of the world – spoke of the need for communication programmes that demonstrate a distinct flavour; one honed to reflect the national characteristics of the country in which they are transmitted. The bank spokesman – fronting communication programmes for an organization with long associations in South America – confirmed Taylor's (2001) suggestion of a real need for *cross-cultural sensitivity* from iPR specialists.

All respondents agreed that knowledge of local audiences must be built into iPR campaigns; to reflect a sensitivity of cultural features unique to audiences in the target country. One hundred per cent of respondents agreed that a deep knowledge of how local media works in individual countries is of crucial importance and, indeed, may result in the success or failure of an iPR campaign. The airline's American experience has been noted already. Other organizations (the pharmaceutical company, the international bank, for instance) explained that one reason why they occasionally engaged overseas consultants to deal with iPR was specifically because of their sophisticated knowledge of local markets and their media.

The finding of this chapter is that British organizations trading internationally believe that *think local, act local* is the right approach to adopt when communicating internationally. It was summed up well by a national retailer with operations overseas – *local public relations is handled locally* – he said that this was so in order that a local message could be produced. No evidence was given to the researcher by anyone interviewed that any effort was made to impose a transglobal message.

In sectors as controversial as the tobacco industry, the financial services sector *or* the airline business it is no surprise that the role of the corporate communicator has expanded increasingly – and now embraces international environmental scanning. The telco spokesperson referred to being *the eyes and ears of his organization* – increasingly using modern technologies – observing issues that might impact upon his organization. The rubber company spokesperson spoke of the challenges of spotting future problems in countries as diverse as Mexico and China; the airline spokesperson echoed this, highlighting that *a global airline needed to scan globally.*

Discussion

The findings suggest that those British organizations with significant overseas trading interests do set out to achieve – and to maintain – a sense of community with those stakeholders perceived to be crucial to their organizational success around the world. Initial indications from this research are that British communication executives are aware of their social responsibility to understand and respect the concerns of the diverse populations with which they communicate.

On the other hand, it is noteworthy that only a small cross section of British organizations seek to communicate internationally; and of those *that do so* only a small sample communicate full time; some, like the bank (with very long established interests in markets as diverse as New Zealand and South America) being involved in iPR from time to time.

A debate is noted concerning the use of different techniques for communicating in different cultures; but all those interviewed believed in the value of using the same techniques in whatever area they communicate. The researcher reflected and wondered if this was because all the companies concerned had very large operations overseas – or could it be because they were using a tried and tested set of techniques – and that *if it worked, don't fix it?*

The debate proceeds and concerns *the message*. Should the message be the same (noting one company translating its message four times – might something be lost in translation?)? Should it be a specific message for a specific audience (favoured by an airline for its US audience) or should the message be *subtly different* (favoured by the pharmaceutical company and by the Scottish brewer, who referred to favouring a different emphasis where necessary)? No one seems sure. What does seem certain is that *orchestration* is needed to ensure that nuances and subtle differences are brought together to ensure an internationally integrated communication programme. No easy task, the researcher surmises.

One aspect struck the author of this chapter. Even when an organization is involved in little international communication; even where overseas consultants would normally be brought in to sort out a problem locally; the UK practitioner regards him/herself as *communicator in chief*; and normally becomes involved if the matter is serious. The communicators from the pharmaceutical company, the high street chemist, the tobacco company – all made the same point – and strongly – they would *become involved*. Further, the tobacco spokesman made it plain that no one but the communication executive would *speak for the company*.

The one organization that took the local message really seriously was the global airline. Perhaps the success or failure of a British-based global airline depends heavily on audiences overseas – none more so than that in North America. But the author was impressed by the media organization that this organization had set up in New York and by the number of local staff it employed. The airline, it struck him, was out to send the correct messages: and to communicate them in a way that would be understood by local publics communicating in American rather than English!

Clearly, British communicators regard iPR as a *challenge* – recognizing that messages need to be tailored for the local audience and communicated in a manner that will achieve the desired results. One spokesman emphasized that communicating to countries as diverse as Mexico, India, China and Portugal was a demanding exercise for someone who had started off as a press officer in a west country plant. Perhaps this suggests that company spokespeople require special training for iPR? Maybe this is the case – the company concerned now has more operational plants outside the United Kingdom than within it.

Perhaps the challenge gets bigger when differing socio-economic infrastructures are considered, and when one reflects on the need for international companies to communicate with audiences at macro level; particularly governments. The researcher felt that, however experienced the practitioner, they might find their expertise stretched by having to communicate with such widely diverse audiences sometimes in far-flung places.

There is no disputing the view of some management scholars that in some countries public relations may be viewed as a propaganda exercise. Equally beyond dispute is that not one of the British organizations interviewed considered themselves involved in propaganda – either at home or in any country abroad; all rejected the idea. In fact, on the opposite side of the spectrum, there is the evidence of one global organization – with a huge international communication operation – investing a seven figure sum publishing academic research as a contribution to global debate and scientific advancement. Not propaganda.

In an age when even a one-person business can become an international concern the need to be able to communicate globally accelerates by the day – and with some velocity. The evidence from this research is that e-PR is seen by large British organizations as a useful tool; but the researcher uncovered no evidence that it has yet replaced traditional communication channels. Likewise evidentially external consultants are engaged *when they add value*; helping with cultural issues or because the organization does not have its own PR people in a particular country (witness the rubber company needing more *foot soldiers* in Mexico and elsewhere). Significantly, the typical UK based communication executive regards his or her role very much as hands-on – getting involved overseas if needed.

The underlying theme running through this chapter is that British practitioners are very much aware of cultural sensitivities and language differences. They recognize increasingly that communication across nations does need to take into account the audience to whom it is addressed – as noted, giving a distinct flavour honed to national characteristics; demonstrating a knowledge of local audiences (presumably this is where the local foot soldiers come in); acknowledging that there has to be a choice of PR strategies appropriate to different countries (Krishnamurthy and Dejan, 2001).

One area of the literature that seems fairly thin concerns the use of iPR for global environmental scanning. The finding of this chapter is that in controversial industries (tobacco, financial services, perhaps alcohol?) a primary task of the international communicator in-chief is international issues management. The importance of this role should not be underestimated; note the telco spokesman seeing his role as the *eyes and ears*; a task transglobally that has quite frightening implications. One even questions to what extent it might be feasible?

Conclusion

The importance of this chapter is that currently only a handful of studies exist that help to build a body of knowledge of iPR (Krishnamurthy and Dejan, 2001). Of these, few have been written in the British context. However, because of its small size this research makes no claims to be conclusive. It does, however, seek to add to the body of knowledge concerning international communication grounded in the British experience; and to provide fresh insights.

The first conclusion is that a minority of British organizations are involved in iPR on a regular basis. Those that *are* recognize that *it is* problematical. Apparently they do, by and large, take into account the difficulties presented in communicating across diverse frontiers; and in the context of different cultures, social norms and, sometimes, religious backgrounds.

Kitchen and Wheeler (1999) noted the debate concerning the co-ordination and control of international campaigns – the key issue being whether campaigns should be standardized or adapted locally. Clearly, the British communication executive recognizes that if there is a major problem (s)he becomes involves and – in doing so – uses much the same techniques as would be used at home – albeit adapted to fit local conditions.

For many British communicators the iPR role may be very much a part-time involvement. But, in an age of global markets and instant communication – ones that are accelerating by the day – any communicator in any organization needs to be able to communicate – and to do so fast – and to do so with competence – with any – and diverse – stakeholders anywhere. In today's global economy any spokesperson may find themselves communicating directly with an audience in any corner of the globe – dealing with problematical languages, diverse and puzzling cultures, disconcerting religious influences; the list is endless. This is a new and challenging frontier for today's communication executive – but it is a challenge from which, if the practitioner is successful, great strategic advantage may be gained for the organization; and on an international platform.

APPENDIX

The identities of these organizations

Asda plc
Avon Rubber plc
Avon and Somerset Constabulary
BAT Industries
Boots Group plc
British Airways plc
British Telecommunications plc
GlaxoWellcome plc
Lloyds TSB plc
London Transport
Wm Morrison plc

Northumbria Ambulance NHS Trust
J. Sainsbury plc
W. H. Smith plc
South Western Electricity plc
Storehouse plc
Tennent Caledonian Breweries Ltd
Vaux Group plc
Wessex Water plc
Whitbread plc
Yorkshire Tyne-Tees plc

NOTES

1   Which controls the media.
2   Kruckeberg (1996) notes Al-Enad reporting that PR practice has been sometimes exploited by some third world governments.
3   The extent of media saturation in a society.
4   Not as Anderson (1989) sees it.
5   See appendix.

REFERENCES

Albert, R. D. (1992) 'Polycultural perspectives on organisational communication', *Management Communication Quarterly*, 6, 74–84.

Al-Enad, Abdulrahman (1990) 'Public relations roles in developing countries', *PR Quarterly*, spring, 25–26.

Anderson, G. (1989) 'A global look at public relations', in B. Cantor (ed.), *Experts in Action: Inside PR*, 2nd edn, New York: Longman.

Baskin, O. and Aronoff, C. (1992) *Public Relations: The Profession and the Practice*, Dubuque: Wm. C. Brown.

Botan, C. (1992) 'International public relations; critique and reformulation', *Public Relations Review*, 18, 149–59.

Budd, John F. (2001) 'Opinion . . . foreign policy acumen needed by global CEOs', *Public Relations Review*, 27, 123–34.

Comor, Edward (2001) 'The role of communication in global civil society: forces, processes, prospects', *International Studies Quarterly*, 45, 389–408.

Culbertson, Hugh M. and Chen Ni (1996) *International Public Relations: A Comparative Analysis*, Mahwah, NJ: Lawrence Erlbaum Associates.

Grunig, James E., Grunig, Larissa A., Sriramesh, K., Huang Yi-Hui and Lyra, Anastasia (1995) 'Models of public relations in an international setting', *Journal of Public Relations Research*, 7(3), 163–86.

Gunn, J. (1994) 'Environmental public relations: consultancy practice in Bangkok', unpublished BSc dissertation, Bournemouth University.

Guth, David W. (2000) 'The emergence of public relations in the Russian Federation', *Public Relations Review*, 26(2), 191–207.

Guzley, Ruth M. (1995) Review of Banks, Stephen. P.

(1995) *Multicultural Public Relations: A Social Interpretive Approach*, Thousand Oaks, CA: Sage, source unknown.

Haug, M. and Koppang, H. (1997) 'Lobbying and public relations in a European context', *Public Relations Review*, 23, 233–47.

Hehir, P. (1999) 'Public relations: truly a global business', ICO Summit, 23–5 September, Lucerne, Switzerland, p. 6.

Howard, C. and Mathews W. (1986) 'Global marketing: stop, look and listen', *Public Relations Quarterly*, 32, 10–11.

Kitchen, Philip J. and Wheeler, Colin (1999) 'Issues influencing marketing communications in a global context', *International Public Relations Review*, March, 19–25.

Krishnamurthy, Sriramesh and Dejan, Vercic (2001) 'International public relations: a framework for future research', *Journal of Communication Management*, 6(2), 103–17.

Kruckeberg, Dean (1999) 'A global perspective on public relations ethics: the middle east', *Public Relations Review*, 22(2), 181–9.

Kruckeberg, Dean (1996) 'Answering the mandate for a global presence', *International Public Relations Review*, September, 19–23.

Kruckeberg, Dean and Starck, K. (1988) *Public Relations and Community: A Reconstructed Theory*, New York: Praeger Publishers, p. 21.

Lipschutz, R. D. (1999) 'From local knowledge to global environmental governance', in M. Hewson and T. J. Sinclair (eds), *Approaches to Global Governance Theory*, Albany, State University of New York Press, pp. 259–83.

Lyra, A. (1991) 'Public relations in Greece: models, roles and gender', unpublished master's thesis, University of Maryland, College Park.

Manheim, Jarol B. and Albritton, Robert B. (1983) 'Changing national images: international public relations and media agenda setting', *American Political Science Review*, 78, 641–57.

Mellow, C. (1989) 'Remaking PR's image across the board', *Public Relations Journal*, July–August, 33–9.

Moss, Danny (2001) Editorial, *Journal of Communication Management*, 6(2), 103–17.

Moss, Danny, MacManus, Toby and Vercic, Dejan (1997) *Public Relations Research: An International Perspective*, London: International Thomson Business Press.

Neff, Bonita Dostal (1998) 'Harmonising global relations: a speech act theory analysis of public relations forum', *Public Relations Review*, 24(3), 351–76.

Ovaitt, F., Jr (1988) 'Public relations without boundaries: is globalization an option?', *Public Relations Quarterly*, 33(4), 3–11.

Pavlik, J. V. (1987) *Public Relations: What Research Tells Us*, Newbury Park, CA: Sage.

Schuybroek, Y. L. (1999) 'Sharing knowledge', ICO summit, 23–5 September, Lucerne, pp. 7–8.

Sharp, M. L. (1992) 'The impact of social and cultural conditioning on global public relations', *Public Relations Review*, 18, 103–7.

Signitzer, B. and Coombs, T. (1992) 'Public relations and public diplomacy', *Public Relations Review*, 18, 137–47.

Sriramesh, K. (1992) The impact of societal culture on public relations. An ethnographic study of South Indian organisations, unpublished doctorial dissertation, University of Maryland.

Sriramesh, K. and White, Jon (1992) 'Societal culture and public relations', in James E. Grunig (ed.), *Excellence in Public Relations and Communication Management*, Hillsdale, NJ: Lawrence Erlbaum Associates.

Synnott, Gae and McKie, David (1997) 'International issues in PR, researching research and prioritising priorities', *Journal of Public Relations Research*, 9(4), 259–82.

Taylor, Maureen (2001) 'Internationalising the public relations curriculum', *Public Relations Review*, 27, 73–88.

Taylor, Maureen and Kent, Michael. L. (1999) 'Challenging assumptions of iPR: when government is the most important public', *Public Relations Review*, 25(2), 131–44.

Tixier, Maud (2000) 'Australian public affairs: links to European corporate communication', *Corporate Communications: An International Journal*, 5(3), 152–7.

Van Leuven, J. and Pratt, C. (1996) 'Public Relation's role: realities in Asia and in Africa south of the Sahara', in H. M. Cuthbertson and Ni Chen, *International Public Relations: A Comparative Analysis*, Mahwah, NJ: Lawrence Erlbaum Associates.

Vasquez, Gabriel M. and Taylor, Maureen (2000) 'What cultural values influence American public relations practitioners?', *Public Relations Review*, 25(4), 433–49.

Vercic, Dejan, Razpet, Ales, Dekleva, Samo and Slenc, Mitja (2000) 'International public relations and the internet: diffusion and linkages', *Journal of Communication Management*, 5(2), 125–37.

Wilcox, D., Ault, P. and Agee, W. (1989) *Public Relations: Strategies and Tactics*, Philadelphia: Harper and Row.

Wright, D. K. (1995) 'The role of corporate PR executives in the future of employee relations', *PR Review*, fall, 181–98.

Zaharna, R. S. (2000) 'Intercultural communication and international public relations: exploring parallels', *Communication Quarterly*, 48(1), 85–100.

Zaharna, R. S. (2001) 'In-awareness approach to international public relations', *Public Relations Review*, 27, 135–48.

Index